Petar Bojanić
In-Statuere

GEFÖRDERT VOM

Bundesministerium
für Bildung
und Forschung

Series of the
Käte Hamburger Center for
Advanced Study in the Humanities
»Law as Culture«

Edited by Werner Gephart

Volume 28

Petar Bojanić

In-Statuere

Figures of Institutional Building

English translation by
Edward Djordjevic

VITTORIO KLOSTERMANN
Frankfurt am Main · 2022

recht als kultur
käte hamburger kolleg
law as culture
center for advanced study

Bibliographische Information der Deutschen Nationalbibliothek

Die Deutsche Nationalbibliothek verzeichnet diese Publikation in der Deutschen Nationalbibliographie; detaillierte bibliographische Daten sind im Internet über *http://dnb.dnb.de* abrufbar.

1. Auflage 2022

Gedruckt auf alterungsbeständigem Papier ∞ ISO 9706
Satz: mittelstadt 21, Vogtsburg-Burkheim
Umschlaggestaltung: Jörgen Rumberg, Bonn
Umschlagabbildung: Werner Gephart, Babylonian Production of Normativity in Europe II (with the Help of Pieter Bruegel), (elektronische Collage, 2016/2022).
Druck und Bindung: docupoint GmbH, Barleben
Printed in Germany
ISSN 2193-2964
ISBN 978-3-465-04604-2

Contents

IV. Group and Negative Facts

V. To Live Together

Conclusion

Introduction

0 Propositions

It would be difficult for me to make a list in any given order, but I am certain that preceding any operation or set of actions that could be termed ›institutional acting‹ – acts that produce the institution or refer to it, acts ›conducted‹ by an institution – is a very complex and rather vague set of conditions or unconditional conditions. Considerations of two principal pre-institutional conditions – for several individuals to act together or immediately perform certain similar, simultaneous or pertinent acts and patterns in a directed, precise and disciplined fashion (which is to say, properly) – make this book only a threshold, placing it at the doorstep of the institution: a »book-preamble«, an unending introduction into the institutional. A precondition for a number of individuals to live together (in one another's proximity), in a form that can be arranged, or reconstructed and repeated, is also a cessation of violence, or at least its sporadic, dispersed, and inconsistent use. The conditions for a certain action to be jointly conducted properly, which is to say, the precondition for a group to sustain itself, to survive, indeed to live (without killing or violently dying out altogether), is the immediate suspension of two kinds of violence: arbitrary violence of the individual (spreading fear, terror, terrorism; of the kind that a hundred years ago was done by or ascribed to an »anarchist«), and the *proper* and consistent use of violence *together* (war, even defensive war, war for democracy, and war against terror and terrorism). Despite this second kind of violence being institutional, and despite war itself being an example of an institution – quite possibly implying that »war violence« immediately precedes all forms of »institutional acting« we are here dealing with – I am entirely uncertain whether it is possible to speak reasonably of a »transformation« of violence or victorious war into justice, legality, order, or the institution, or indeed insist on a »conversion«, »transition«,[1] »transformation« of subversive individual violence or war and group use of violence into any kind of joint correct »institutional acting« (Raimo Tuomela uses the phrase *institutional acting*, while Christoph Hubig uses *institutionelle Handlung*). It seems to me that the appearance of diverse institutional acts, practices, or actions (above all those that never eliminate, nor institutionally neglect remaining actors, others) is better described as the interruption or cessation of violence or war. A group of individuals (certainly

[1] In the introduction to *Anger and Forgiveness*, Martha Nussbaum uses these verbs for the operation of replacing cruelty and force with »legal institutions«, »health of the city«, and »procedures of reasoned argument« (pp. 1–13).

two or three at the inception)[2] produces institutional acts if its actors temporarily act in the same direction (properly, directly, directedly), but also at the same time while simultaneously and consciously counting on each other (taking care in counting one another to include belonging to a group and its harmony with others), are *a priori* consciously counting on all those not yet or not necessarily a constituent part of the group or part of some other group (or multiple groups at once) – in a word, the broader community of groups. In that sense, a group of individuals is certainly qualified to successfully conduct certain violent acts, but it does not do so, having acquired the status of a new entity or institution (»institutional« status), and is thus always hospitable to others, never completely or finally formed and constructed. If, on the other hand, the conditions of proper joint acting are fulfilled, the amount of so-called »negative acts«, »negative social acts«, or even simply »bad acts« (personal acts and »asocial« acts; written about by Adolf Reinach, Alfred Ayer, Gilbert Ryle, Huw Price, Bruce Vermazen and others) will be reduced, pushed back, diminished, even entirely eliminated.

In this new context of ways and procedures that might suspend violence, end war, and institutionalize peace,[3] war itself »figures« as one of the most important institutions ensuring the more or less long-term unity of a group, although it comes at the cost of major damage or even destruction of another, rival group; meaning that without war and victory in it, without »victorious war«,[4] the collective identity of a group would remain indiscernible. In addition to my interest in this problem, I am also interested in the position of negation in the great institutional construction, as well as the status and significance of various forms of negative or nullifying acts for a society and its institutions. In the preamble of this book,

2 One of the designations of a group is that it comprises at least three members, which implies »interpersonal relations« (*relations interpersonnelles*, because two are always in a »personal relation«). Walter Ruprecht Bion mentions an interesting proverb: »*Deux, c'est l'intimité, trois, c'est la foule*«. Bion: Recherches sur les petits groups, p. 64. Probably when we speak of »group belief« it means at least three members. Cf. Lackey: What is Justified Group Belief?.

3 I am referring to the books *Nasilje. Figure suverenosti* (Violence. Figures of sovereignty, 2007), *Granica, znanje, žrtvovanje. O poslednjem ratu* (Border, Knowledge, Sacrifice. On Final War, 2009) and *Sila i oblici rata* (2012). The last book has been translated (with a few minor changes) into English as *Violence and Messianism*, and also into Italian, French, Spanish, and Russian.

4 In his doctoral thesis, dedicated to Otto Gierke, one of the first theorists of group acting, Erich Kaufmann thematizes victorious war as the ultimate norm that decides on the existence of a legally ordered state (or group). »The social ideal is not ›the community of free-willed persons‹, but victorious war, as the ultimate means for the highest purpose.« Kaufmann: Das Wesen des Völkerrechts und die clausula rebus sic stantibus, p. 153. ›Victory‹ is a carefully chosen word, since, on the one hand, it belongs to protocols of game and balancing (equilibrium) that constitute the institution (e. g., the institution of the game called tennis, with a given set of rules, but also requiring exchange and equilibrium of action), while, on the other hand, it assumes competition and gamesmanship, profit and gain, but also underhandedness, all of which eliminates poor players from the game and ultimately leads to the cessation of the exchange. A good serve (an ace) brings victory and confirms the institution, while it represents one of the rules of the institution of tennis, can, if it is the victorious point, bring the exchange to a close, breaking the relation between the players (and is a negative action).

in describing the first-known institutional ur-scene of building a monstrous corporation in Babylon, I insist on the traditionally unclear and complex function of negation and negative engagement of *Adonai* (the highest institutional instance) in destroying the tower, dissolving the group and sowing linguistic confusion among its builders. Further, I understand negation in the context of invisible and extreme violence, the possibility of genocidal acts, as well as a way to probe Immanuel Kant and various theories of negative quantities, negative numbers, and the institution of debt, in addition to certain anti-institutional practices, resistance to the institution, as well as the distinction between negative acts and negative social acts. Towards the end of the book, when I thematize »opposition«, and the word »counter« (*contre*), as well as the idea or institute of the »counter-institution«, certainly a pseudo-alternative attempt at institutionalizing and incorporating negation into a general institutional project, which is to say abolishing everything not an institution or that has not as such been institutionalized. Two propositions further complicate my endeavor: that there is nothing which is not institution or is outside the institution, and, in a deontological register, that nothing should or ought to be outside the institution, that is, exist outside the good or just institution. They do so by showing the various forms of institutional coercion and negation of freedom of certain actors to simply ›act‹ non-institutionally (negative social acts, such as inaction, various abstinences, or withdrawing from action). If there is such a thing as non-institutional or extra-institutional acting,[5] my intention would be to reveal in these actions not only resistance to coordinating action and balanced play with others (other actors) or subjection to rules and norms of an institution or community at large, but also some residual traces of pre-institutional violence that sometimes elicits from groups (and often some institutions) very aggressive, even brutal, comportment. The great French revolutionary and institutionalist Louis Antoine de Saint-Just, who understood the revolution as a comprehensive institutionalization of society (as they exist, above all, to protect society from corruption), ascribed asocial acting (although doubtful as acting at all) that denies all *affectio societatis* and thus negates or subverts the institution and institutional responsibility to those who were ›neutral‹ (who did not participate, are neither ›for‹ nor ›against‹, are not ›present‹) – these were the main enemies of the revolution. I differentiate such deformed »acting« and in general the »institute« of neutral

5 This fiction is above all a »French matter«, enduring at some intensity since Madame de Staël to Foucault. Against Hegel's understanding of the institution of objective spirit, for example, Madame de Staël takes existing institutions to be neither »states of affairs« nor »states of the spirit«, which is why it is necessary to emancipate the spirit (meaning philosophy or action) from existing institutions. Cf. Gehlen: Moral und Hypermoral, p. 102. In her famous text, *On Literature Considered in Connection to Social Institutions*, De Staël insists that in a country in which enlightenment cannot penetrate the institutions there really exists or remains a facile philosophy or thinking that does not amend the lives of people. How can there be an extra-institutional field or a quasi-institutional potential not yet fertilized or built into already existing institutions?

or asocial actors (who *de facto* either do nothing or do so »poorly«), from forms of (in)action that are only seemingly opposed to protocols of institutionalization. I would like to produce a classification of negative acts as well as the presence and significance of asocial acts for the constitution of a group; further, I am interested in protocols and strategies of diminishment and neglect of such (in)activities, and the possibility of their elimination. Several problems present themselves: the first refers to the determination of asocial acts (of which negative acts are only a part), which I would define provisionally as acts that actively or passively endanger the relations that exist within a group, or (potential) relations of one group with other groups (i. e., apologies, complaints, justifications, tardiness, sluggishness, neglect, unresponsiveness, irresponsibility, hypocrisy, underhandedness, lying, delays, etc.). To what extent can such acts be ignored and go unheeded? Does the institution as »openness« (two words that should be synonymous) *a priori* diminish the significance and danger of such operations to the survival of the group or institution, that is, does the arrival of new members and increase of social connections perform this task? How can we preserve the right to difference and exception or the »right« to, for example, reject bearing and using fire arms for the sake of defense of one's group (recalling that the stamp *Asozial* and black armbands were infamously used for a particular group of prisoners in Dachau that included homosexuals, emigrants, political prisoners – in a word, those who did not conform to the demands of the Third Reich)?

The book must also give a convincing answer to the question of why violence or certain negative acts still cannot be entirely left outside the doorstep of institutional action. Committing violence together, eliminating the unfit from one's own group or destroying other opposed groups and formations have perfectly bound and united group members, and forcefully shaped its identity, collective consciousness and responsibility. The cessation of destruction and killing would bring an end to an enforced period of group unity. Is it then possible to find another directed common activity (at once, all together) that would have nothing to do with sacrificial rituals of killing or hunting, or rituals of persecution of others? The idea that violence can be transformed, which is to say preserved in a different and acceptable form, appears as a perfect fiction to keep a group, large or small, together. If the community is still active, that is, still acts jointly, with its members in close proximity to one another, sharing language, goods, money, affection, labor, etc. – this is a good sign that force has been, at least seemingly, successfully transformed, bad acts either hidden well or incorporated into a group holding together. What remains of war or readiness for war, killing, and slaughter, is only the group itself, being drawn into the group, memory of (non-)deeds past and successful violent (heroic) acts. Sacrifice, as one of the first institutions of transformed violence, is not efficient because it alters reality, but because it holds us together, giving form to the group through continuous repetition. Similarly religion, that is, the trust in the ordering power of words and voices (like the efficacy of prayer when conducted together or learned communally), or else utterances made jointly (aloud) of forgotten text that recounts the fierce battle for living space of our ancestors, of experience of catharsis in theater, victory in sport, etc. Still, however successful and exemplary these illustrations of collective intentionality or communal focus of group actors towards the group – which also include banalities, such as soldiers marching, mentioned by Sartre, or its transformation into a podium dance, mentioned by Margaret Gilbert – a group stripped of violence as its primary integrative factor is truly forced to carefully and always anew construct the principle bringing and holding its members together in time, moving them in a single direction. Transforming or leaving behind violence for an entirely new and different form of acting or conduct is decisive for the possibility of creating a new institution.

Naturally, this book deals with the sluggishness of institutions in a time of new and future wars, and a time of continuous violent activity disseminating fear across the world and across borders (at airports as borders). In a time when institutions are degraded and lapse back into violent techniques that more easily ensure the unity and survival of a group, I have chosen to begin this book with a *de facto* defense of a »group on the move«, and the difficulties and problems it faces: namely, a group of migrants, coming from somewhere, is forced to pry open the doors of institutions it encounters, and build institutions it does not. And I have chosen to close the book with a vision of Europe as a new counter-institution, a Europe in permanent crisis, yet ever reducing the sovereignty of its constituent states, but open to those who wish to join or return.

Group (Ever) On the Move

What does it take for a group that can count itself »internally« to account for its members and add them up,[6] to become a new entity (have a new name, be an agent or subject) different and above all of its members? What is *institutio*? Is »institution« still a word used all too easily for a field that remains still unknown (Charles Parsons; Raimo Tuomela; John Searle)? I will reduce hundreds of definitions and variations of institutions and the institutional to only a few: the institution is an artefact – pure human invention, something nature cannot produce on its own

6 The thematization and theory of the group appears relatively late in Western thought. It probably first appears in Otto von Gierke's Rector speech at the beginning of the twentieth century. Cf. Gierke: Das Wesen der menschlichen Verbände, pp. 3–32. Later, Tomoo Otaka's book surpasses earlier efforts in the Anglo-American philosophical world with the term ›social group‹. Cf. Otaka: Grundlegung der Lehre vom sozialen Verband.

(Samuel Pufendorf; Antoine Furetière; Étienne Bonnot de Condillac); the institution concerns the structure, investment, and engagement of all interested actors, and not only a few; *institutio* is the beginning of something entirely new, above all with a written document or charter, implying the discovery of the common good or *commons*, and which in turn creates new actors, generations and inheritors; the institution designates the discovery of place, its disposition and occupation.

What is *actus instituendi*? Communal learning for the sake of being together means that institutional act(s) surpass the interjections of a tutor (which generally concern the work of individual members and work with each of them). Therefore, one of the main conditions of the institution is really communal learning and study conducted by the group – discipline. If a group begins to project its own future plan or is planning its future and future activities (Michael Bratman), and in doing so is also thinking about all those who will only join it later – i. e., thinking about other groups, or the community at large – or else if the group is working on the development, expansion and construction of a big city (not merely shelter or fortress, meaning that architecture is one of the key figures of institutional and disciplined acting, and is thus a latent presence throughout this book as the key »institutional thesis«), then the degradation of the institution back into a group will indeed be slowed down. On the one hand, therefore, the institution is an instrument (the words have a tautological connection), which the group uses, through specific protocols, to preserve its unity and its ›groupness‹; on another level, in the face of further uncertainty and violence, in the face of terror from others (foreigners, refugees, minorities, or maniacs), the institution reduces to a group, setting up an opposition and opening up space for the constitution of a rival group and thus conflict. Still, such institutional closing must be temporary, because in reality only the group (of migrants) arriving from somewhere (as in the building of the great Babylonian institution) initiates the new process of institutionalization and gathering of all. Does that mean that the institution or institutionalism is necessarily a cosmopolitan effort and that any institutional act immanently counts on all those who are not present or who ought to be present?

Yet, I remain skeptical that cosmopolitanism is a sufficiently fertile protocol to generate answers to the dramatic set of problems we face today. In the same vein, we should not follow Kant or some passages in Hannah Arendt, nor Jacques Derrida's 1997 fanciful daydreams of a »a new city«, »a different notion of the communal right to the city«, or right to a »free city« [*une ville franche*],[7] nor the Biblical analogy of »city of refugees« he thematizes in detail, and which in fact structures the famous text in which he calls for readiness. Although in writing about cosmopolitanism, Derrida uses the word ›institution‹ several times, and calls for the institutionalization of such refugee cities, I am not sure how applicable these

7 Derrida: On Cosmopolitanism and Forgiveness, p. 9.

cities, or the Hebrew word *miqlat* (from the root *qlt*, meaning to absorb, shelter, stow away), are to the refugees we see today in the squares of our cities, or even to the group of refugees that arrived many centuries ago to the city we will recall as Babylon. *Miqlat* refers to one who has killed unintentionally, and who bears a certain type of responsibility (the accent is always on responsibility). Equally, I am unsure of the applicability of ›temporariness‹ mentioned by Derrida, or the temporariness of the *miqlat* status (which is abolished with the death of the high priest), the temporariness of guest and hospitality. The aporia of hospitality lies in this very temporariness, whence it can be absolute and unreserved; yet does not refer to today's refugee group fleeing violence, whose city is destroyed and can never be rebuilt in the same spot. Does this mean, alternately, that the group must incorporate itself in its new place, along with us all, reconstruct the encountered institutions, and alongside us seek solutions for our great new common city?

I find the conditions for such a perspective in Michael Dummett's 2001 book, *On Immigration and Refugees*, published in the same collection as the English translation of Derrida, as well as in the text that inspired Dummett, Pope John XXIII's *Pacem in Terris*. Far clearer in supplying Dummett with his positions than the endless hesitations and reservations found in Kant, Pope John insists on immigrants being given citizen status, because being a citizen of one state does not strip one of their belonging to the overall human family, that is, citizenship to universal society, humanity overall. There are, nevertheless, three unavoidable difficulties in any thematization of immigration and refugees or a group on the move and its efforts to institutionalize and undertake the great endeavor of total institutionalization.

The first difficulty is the advantage given to things and ownership of things over people. To consistently follow liberalism and capitalism in whatever form is above all an attempt to level and equate humans with things. Michael Dummett explains succinctly: »all borders should be open«,[8] which follows from the principle of the free market: if things and money move freely across the Earth, so should humans. Analogously, there is still no human *right to stay* (Walzer) since *ius situs* or *lex situs* necessarily refers to things (possibly owners of things), and not persons and the possibility and right of their common occupation of a space.

The second difficulty refers to the general impossibility or at the very least near insurmountable obstacle of collective and simultaneous regulating the status of a (big) group of refugees who have crossed one or more borders, seeking the *right to stay* in one or several sovereign states. Today's immigrant context is only a partial novelty in the great population shifts in history. It is not only a matter of endangering the identity of a country or group of people in a given place, required to accept a large group of guests; nor simply the danger of quickly (all too quickly?)

8 Dummett: On Immigration and Refugees, p. 48.

eroding the identity of a culture (as opposed to gradually, as in the case of the population move from Algeria and Tunisia into France in the last century); what is at stake is also the necessity to entirely reform international law and with it the status of refugees in such a way to allow them access to European citizenship.

The third difficulty regards the law, such as the law of asylum and the right to cross borders. It is less a matter of unclear articles and deliberately vague and opaque conventions (about which Dummett writes), rather a more long-term (on very rare occasions, also short-term) processes of institutionalization that have nothing to do with strict legal procedure. In »We Refugees«, when she writes about »so-called Jewish problems«, Arendt confirms that we are indeed a kind of economic »immigrants or newcomers«: we have indeed left our country, but only with the desire to »build our own lives anew«, to which end we must remain »strong and very optimistic«.[9] Possibly, a kind of life energy and pure will to change drive a joint *incorporation* to overcome in time not only the obstacle of borders or laws, but the crucial one of the destruction of the group, the dispersion of its members and dissolution of the first person plural: »we«.

»I« within »We« / I – (A Single) Part of a Group and Institution

The slow and burdened writing and production of this book[10] – which can never really be completed – is perhaps only a sketch of a real book of history of institutional acting and constructing institutions (once upon a time, Avner Greif announced one such systematic book, but then abandoned it) is probably the consequence of the problem or impossibility of joint writing (»How to [*correctly*] write *together*«?) and »accounting for everyone« and the meticulous »taking into account« myriad elements from sundry sides. Apart from great and unfinished projects of entirely diverse theorists, across various languages of the institution and institutional (Helmut Schelsky, Niklas Luhmann, Johann August Schülein, Cornelius Castoriadis, Avner Greif, Mary Douglas, Amartya Sen, Paolo Napoli, Benedetto Croce, Roman Schnur, Jack Knight, Robert Grafstein, Douglass North, Ota Weinberger, etc.), and texts that belong to completely different genres and disciplines – the greatest problem is that the term ›institution‹ and institutional protocols have imperfectly overlapping meanings in different languages, and consequently considerations of joint work, groups, cooperation and institutional act-

9 Arendt: We Refugees, p. 110.

10 A sketch of this book was published in Serbian a few years ago. Cf. Bojanić: O institucionalnom delovanju. Kako je moguće ispravno raditi, pisati, hodati, disati, živeti zajedno?

ing. The result is a field of fractured and incommensurable traditions of thought. This is particularly conspicuous in philosophy and it would be easy to show that »social ontology« (to use Husserlian vocabulary, although he was not the first to use the phrase) and the various theorists who belong to the phenomenological and pseudo-phenomenological tradition, as well as the founders of sociology, practically announce and forecast what has been carefully demonstrated in recent years by Searle, Tuomela, Margaret Gilbert, Tony Lawson, or Geoffrey Hodgson, all the while constructing an entirely new philosophical discipline. I have endeavored to follow these differences without separating so-called analytic and continental philosophies and their respective contributions in the construction of subject and field of »social ontology«. I am certain that without an attempt to thematize the distinction between *institution* and *establishment* (both words introduced by Hume), without elucidation of the first translations – and consequent mistakes and shifts in meaning – of the Latin words *impositio* and *institutio* into European languages, without meticulous differentiation of several quasi-synonyms referring to the notion of institution in German or, for example, elaboration of the Russian word событие (event, but literally with-being, meaning that whether something is an event is determined by the existence of a group, since ›we‹ happened because something happened that constituted the connection among those now ›we‹) – it is not possible to understand the complexity and uncertainty of successful and efficient institutional acting.[11] The first person plural of to be in English, for example, (»we are«) does not reveal the same possibilities as Sartre uncovers in the French with *»nous-objet«* and *»nous-sujet«* because ›We [*nous*] are looking at them‹ does not have the same ontological value as ›us‹, as in ›They are looking at us [*nous*]‹.[12]

I have resolutely collected these elements in the past years (and there are more and they are more complex in the main body of the book), and have done so jointly with colleagues across disciplines and institutions. The diversity and amount of input imply the need for a specific common presentation, even common (group) writing. Therein lies my problem, and the problem of possibly writing as a group about a group or institution. It is at once the reason there are no comprehensive studies (or very few) on the subject of institutional acts. As part of a group or various research groups and institutions, I have consistently endeavored to transmit the »spirit«, or better still, the dilemmas and variables of joint work into this text, thus emulating common writing, and have only partially succeeded in this (after

11 In Russian, to institutionalize is учреждать [*utschrezhdat*]. Only in this language is the institutionalization connected to order, with the line, the sequence comprised of individuals. Чередить [*Tscheredit*] means to gather or undergird, and is close to the French *dispositif.* The institution is an arrangement of a system of objects. In »Norms, Institutions, and Institutional Facts,« Neil MacCormick uses the example of queue formation (for a shop) as a spontaneous construction of a group, that is, an institutional fact. MacCormick: Norms, Institutions, and Institutional Facts, pp. 301–345.

12 Sartre: L'être et le néant, p. 486.

all, I am not a ›We‹). However, I do feel that after this text I remain within those groups (as the author whose signature appears on this book, holding a privileged place over other parts gone into its writing), and that thus this book or sketch of a future real jointly-written book truly falls within the notion of ›group act‹ and not merely a presentation of a common effort that has exhausted itself. In that sense, many parts of this book still remain to be amended and edited.

Portions of this book have in previous years been presented in a number languages and cities. Hence, the tone of certain chapters aims to preserve the style of speaking to colleagues and collaborators. The lectures I have given to PhD candidates in Belgrade, Rijeka, Turin on ›architectural philosophy‹, ›social ontology‹, and ›theory of institutions‹ have helped refine and polish my understanding of these concepts. The numerous conferences I have helped organize with Jean-François Kervégan, Maurizio Ferraris and Tiziana Andina have, of course, given me the opportunity to develop various portions of this book. Discussions with Jonathan Wolff, Étienne Balibar, Axel Honneth, Michael Walzer, John Searle, Margaret Gilbert, Raimo Tuomela, Peter Eisenman, Francesco Guala, Emmanuel Picavet, Hans Bernhard Schmid, Paolo di Lucia, Monika Betzler, Giuseppe Lorini, Markus Gabriel, Jocelyn Benoist, Adriano Fabris, Emmanuel Alloa, Paolo Napoli, Roberto Esposito, Ugo Mattei, Giuseppe Mastruzzo, Dario Gentili, Giusi Strummiello, Elettra Stimilli, Judith Butler, Virgilio Cesarone, Christoph Hubig, Luca Illetterati, Bernard Stiegler – have all continuously advanced my understanding of institutional acting. Finally, I must thank Edward Djordjevic, Miloš Ćipranić and Jure Leko for help with the language and the final preparation of the manuscript. Various foundations and institutions have helped my research and that of my collaborators in joint projects, that is, my colleagues in institutions I have headed and even founded – holding negotiations and reaching agreements was always most inspiring and highly instructive for my comprehension of how institutions work and how work is conducted within them. Without the experience of establishing and collaboratively running institutions, this book would certainly be impossible.

I owe special gratitude to another great institutionalist, Werner Gephart, the *scienziato e artista*: his friendship and invitation to be a fellow of the Käte Hamburger Kolleg, »Rechts als Kultur« in Bonn allowed the time for this book to come into existence. It was his idea for this book to be published in the series of which he is editor.

Preamble

1 Theater of Institutional Design

How do we begin to describe institutional protocols, even in a fragmentary manner, without strict thematization? How to begin a sketch of what I call *In-statuere*? What are the various moments or conditions required for something to subsist in time and space, to maintain its invisible stability of a statue (*statuere*)? Can this be designated by the word ›institution‹? Here are three key protocols:

Institution (*Stiftung, Anstalt*) is a set of acts, factors, and facts, which under the right conditions and following certain rules, are able to endure standing together. The complex and polysemic connection of the figure and the figurative to the institution and its practices (Deleuze) probably has an advantage over other kinds of designations of something that in the first place stands upright and endures in time (*in-statuere*). The institution (or the multiplicity of actions that institutionalize [Parsons]) is above all an architectural and artificial creation: it is created by people, and does not concern either nature or God (the construction of the Tower of Babel is the first scene of institutional creation). It protects joint work from decay and stabilizes ties among people through their joint and engaged acting. Institutional generative and regenerative potential is conditioned by its necessary openness to new engaged members and innovative actors. The ontological incompleteness and institutional deficit due to constant latent absence of new engaged and institutional members and acts, could be represented as a fictional social body (Santi Romano) always lacking a piece of reality. A few established characteristics and paradoxes of the institution are that the institution depends on other institutions and is always connected to them, that its origin includes force and violence (Hume) and that war is one of the first institutions, that the institution is coercive in that it at once satisfies instincts (Hume) and limits desires of the individual (Searle), that it precedes the individual and individuals (Mauss), that the institution of language is crucial and precedes all other institutions, indeed is the institution's a *priori*. To these we should add the projective and documentary substance of the institution and the institutional. As a project, the institution guarantees the survival of the group as a group of diverse actors and elements in time and space, while documentary and archival protocols confirm that the institution exists and endures standing.

Engagement (*Impegno*; *Engagement*; *Compromiso*) is a type of social act crucial to the constitution of a group or institution. An act is engaged above all when it is public or announced (otherwise it is a negative or an unannounced social act performed in silence). It is a provocative act that calls or addresses others, all others (*com-mittere* also means to send), not just members of a given group, and an incitement of those present to draw closer. *To commit* refers to an act that spurs those around into action, or else obligates them to do something by acting as members of a future joint body, *a committee*. According to Margaret Gilbert, »joint commitment obligates the parties one to the other to act in accordance with the commitments.«[13] However, engagement is particular in that it requires a high degree of commitment (»to give one's all«, »complete commitment«), as well as a kind of sacrifice (for others, with others, even towards others and in their stead, sacrifice as binding together), which is also at once acting that calls to others to join, to repeat ›our‹ act, thus constructing future joint work (for more on the difference between *commitment* and *engagement*). In this sacrifice we grow closer to others (the word *engage* comes from the verb *vado*, from the Germanic *wadi*, and the Latin *vas, vadis*, meaning ›advancing towards another‹[14]). We are bound to others in offering a »gage«, in »en-gaging« (*mettre en gage* or *donner en gage*), thus also ›burdening‹ and ›obligating‹ them to follow our action. Two words or two protocols – the French-English-German engagement (*engagement*) and the English-French commitment (*commettre*) – imply that we are speaking of a specific kind of obligation (neither perfect or imperfect) responsible for the constitution of *group agency*, an *engaged group* or institution.

Counter-institution (*contre-institution*; *Gegeninstitution*) is a separate, parallel institution, one even in opposition and resistance to existing institutions and various individual and group acts. It is characterized by the production of myriad critical and engaged acts whose aim is novelty, change, and deconstruction of ossified, authoritarian models. The term *counter-institution* seems to have first been used – without going into detail – by Saint-Simon, referring to England where there are some ›adjacent‹ and ›regulative‹ institutions. Counter-institution ought to be synonymous with, for example, a new institution or Europe. While we could associate old institutions with closed sovereign institutions of sovereign states, Europe would be a counter-institution. Yet, the state too can be a counter-institution if it opposes those institutions that represent individual interests or endanger and neglect others (Derrida). If old institutions encourage ignorance and prejudices of the times in which they were established (Saint-Simon), counter-institutional practices are the condition for the discovery of new, modified rules that then alter the ties among social actors. Counter-institutional practices could reveal the fundamental institutional paradox: institutions shape people, while at the same time people shape institutions; people are shaped in advance or at least primed to take on and produce new forms of institutions. Contemporary sociology deploys the term counter-institution only very rarely, with other terms, such as non-governmental organization, corporation, or civic association in more

13 Gilbert: Commitment, p. 899.

14 Kemp: Théorie de l'engagement, p. 16.

common use. However, in the 1960s, the term counter-institution was used to designate certain civic groups that resembled what Saint-Simon noted existed in early nineteenth-century England.

The operation or operations setting certain elements into relation, connecting them into an order – the word for which is *In-statuere* – is artificial and an architectural action. It is conducted by a group of people, rather than God or occurring in nature. The ›architectural‹ is thus the fourth protocol constructing the existence and subsistence of certain elements in time and space. There can be no institution without the various architectural states and movements: concept, design (*disegno*), project, platform, diagram, border, wall, transparency (of walls taken down), threshold, form, ground.

The first moment of an institution (which is always an architectural construction even when not material; e. g., there can be no institution without design and projection) could be the threshold as set in the ground, as the beginning of something entirely new in time and space. The threshold, then, is the first of an institution, since it is at the beginning of the *new* or new construction, and at once on the boundary from the old to the new. Both philosophy and architecture are essentially institutional practices, that is, practices that institutionalize all that exists and is in our hands, and that part of an institution which is first or comes first – or assumes ›first position‹ – and which I would name threshold. Of course, if we now went into detail and began to reconstruct the issue of whether all institutions have a threshold and under what circumstances they might not (quarantine is sometimes a completely closed institution, without threshold; the house, further, is sometimes entirely open, without threshold, in particular when we are ›online‹; or else the institution of property also deals with various threshold models, and so on), we would reach a parallel option to the position of the threshold: the counter-position of the threshold. If the threshold is the *primum* and beginning of the institution as such, then the fate of a new and always possible counter-institution is also decided ›on the threshold‹.

The threshold is above all a small wall, or the smallest possible wall that can still be stepped or jumped over. Meaning that there is no threshold without step or leap. Not only that: the threshold is a text, a formula, a password, an inscription, or document. In accordance with François Rabelais' idea of a new institution, one opposed to the bishopric or abbey, which brings freedom, education, and help to a large group of people (there is no institution that does not in its program contain various protocols of help), the threshold ought to be ›something impossibly small‹ or ›something possible to the smallest possible degree‹, and which ›leads us into the impossible‹. How is this possible? Across some ten pages of *Gargantua*, Rabelais, inspired by the architect Francesco Colonna, elaborates his crucial idea of how to design and construct Thélème (*thelema* is will in Greek), an institution without walls (and thus without a threshold, without *confine*).[15] Even though Rabelais invents certain filters and conditions about who may and may not be part of this institution, who has the right to enter, and even though there is only *appearance* of an entrance and *appearance* of an entrance inscription (like Plato's Academy)[16] – the institution is still supposed to be available to all. There are no rules, deadlines, schedules; everyone does what they will and wish, but in accordance with the will of all other individual wills. This is possible, says Rabelais, above all if there are no walls: »*où mur y a, et devant, et derrière, y a force murmur, envie et conspiration mutue*« (I, 32).[17]

We have yet to fully grasp and justify this explicit ode to transparency (and condemnation of lies and hypocrisy), as well as democracy (but also to glass – meaning that the twentieth century is a material architectural response to Rabelais). We still lack a good argument in favor of free will, of a transparent and reciprocal exchange of love[18] among actors: we still lack a good argument against rules and norms on which our institutions are founded.

The fifth and last protocol issues not from resistance or antagonism contained in the power and potential of the word ›counter‹ of the counter-institutional protocol. Rather, here is something new: critique, or better, joint critique, a register of provocation and democracy.[19] The institution always implies inclusivity and generativity: the elements not yet part of it are as-if present, already tied within its existence (are its institutional fiction). We are speaking of all possible and impossible elements, since every institution potentially has room for all. It is for this reason justified to claim that *there is nothing outside the institution*. These

15 The »Abbaye de Thélème«, is the first utopia of French literature, constructed by François Rabelais in Book I (Chapters 52 to 57) of *Gargantua and Pantagruel*. René Loureau claims that this is the first example of a counter-institution. Loureau: L'analyse institutionnelle, pp. 29–31.

16 The opening line of Rabelais' manifest is »*Cy n'entrez pas, hypocrites, bigotz* …« On the connection with the inscription at the entrance of Plato's Academy, see Saffrey: »*Cy n'entrez pas, hypocrites* …«.

17 Rabelais: Gargantua, p. 170; »where wall [mur] is, front and rear, there is abundant murmur [mur-mur], envy, and mutual conspiracy.« Rabelais: The Complete Works, p. 116 (transl. D. M. Frame).

18 In the 1860 poem with the opening line »I hear it was charged against me …,« Walt Whitman repeats Rabelais' intention. »I hear it was charged against me that I sought to destroy institutions; / But really I am neither for nor against institutions; / (What indeed have I in common with them? Or what with the destruction of them?) / Only I will establish in the Mannahatta, and in every city of These States, inland and seaboard, / And in the fields and woods, and above every keel little or large, that dents the water, / Without edifices, or rules, or trustees, or any argument, / The institution of the dear love of comrades.« Whitman: Leaves of Grass, p. 136.

19 By which I do not mean democracy as a metainstitutional concept or protocol as it appears in Karl-Otto Apel: »Stellungnahme der Diskursethik zur Hommann'schen Letztbegrundung der Institutionenmoral durch die Demokratie qua politische Metainstitution aller Institutionen«. Cf. Apel: Transzendentale Reflexion und Geschichte, 316 ff. I analyze the famous old democratic institute of *ius provocationis* elsewhere. The right of any citizen to question the decision of a judge and seek its reconsideration before the public and the people. This is probably the first deliberative model in the history of Western thought. Cf. Bojanić: Provocatio.

elements impact, correct, criticize, and amend one another. In this way they alter the forms of their association, anticipating the arrival of new, as yet imaginary members. Affinity, sympathy, friendships, groupings, joint survival – these are the preliminary models of true institutional practice. It seems that just such a theater of operation could explain ›what joint critique is‹ or what is the status of critique – *statut critique* is mentioned by Derrida when speaking of *critique vulgaire* and distinctions in Bourdieu – within a group which meets from time to time. So, a group of elements (imaginary or otherwise) meets in order to constitute itself as a group (the word consortium contains the Latin *consort*, *sort* is the partner sharer). In order for any of this to take place, ›critical engagement‹, or even just ›critique‹ or ›engagement‹, must be immanent to this construction *con-sort*. How does critique happen in a group, or what allows for it, or what is its origin? At issue is the reflection (sometimes it is judgment or disputation or neurosis) upon everything each one of us individually places before the others or before us. A critique implies that we are part of a group body, a *universitas* (which is opposed to the individual, and which Cicero, translating the Greek words *kath'holon* and *ho'lotés*, uses five times), that is ever in crisis because it could at any time dissolve. We, the group, are always reforming anew, and constructing ourselves as *universitas*, we construct some kind of totality of knowledge (*universitas* is necessarily *et universum, et totum, et omne*) or a plurality of various protocols of truth.[20] Critique, then, destroys us, but simultaneously, holds us together, because this ›capacity‹ (to be critical, to critique, to question, to cause crisis) or ›protocol‹ is immanent to joint work and presence.[21] A university or consortium produces certain knowledge or complete knowledge; at the same time, it sometimes produces a complete individual (Cicero would say man) or a group of people, a kind of new university or new institution or *counter-institution*. Of course, joint critique or engagement is an instrument (*instrumentum* and *institution* are synonyms in many texts) that constructs such a complete and well-formed individual. Paradoxically, such an ideal individual is such if and only if he can be a partner or sharer. This is important. This already disqualifies leadership and inequality. We can easily see that the ideal researcher is not usually thought of within the boundaries of such categories (to be a partner, to produce acts easily expanded by others). It seems that this is the very reason we

20 My sentence here stands in opposition to Karl Jaspers' opening line of his *Die Idee der Universität* (1946). »The university is a community of scholars and students engaged in the task of seeking truth.« (*Die Universität hat die Aufgabe, die Wahrheit in der Gemeinschaft von Forschern und Schülern zu suchen.*) Jaspers: The Idea of University, p. 1; Jaspers: Die Idee der Universität, p. 9.

21 In several places in his book *Des Universels*, Étienne Balibar mentions critique or »*un discours critique*« or »*ce genre d'attitude critique*«, still tied to »*les catégories de l'universel, de l'universalité, de l'universalisme*« (he makes no mention of the university). Cf. Balibar: Des Universels, pp. 131, 129. Here is Jean-Claude Milner's definition that explains the universal: »like a road that carries the multiple towards the one by way of the everything« (*comme un chemin qui relie la multiple á l'un par l'intermédiaire du tout*). Milner: L'universel difficile, p. 825.

have trouble constructing a group or a new *universitas*, because critique that is insufficient or not constructive, or is false engagement (hypocrisy), means that each works for themselves and not for others or for all, and results in the impossibility to construct the common, the joint, the university, *universitas*.[22]

Let me give a few examples to describe how elements (individuals) are in a group, and what it means for ›one to be next to another‹, and what it means ›to be together‹, ›to play together‹, what is an orchestra.[23] ›To be next to‹ or ›to be near‹ – at distance, touching, sensuality, connection, presence – assumes a mutual production of acts and addressing one another. Relations and ties, facts as the products of acts, hold the various elements together in a set or sets. Elements originally establish direction towards each other, focus on each other, they have instinct or desire for proximity, for binding, but also for untying. Each element must individually manifest, express itself, and announce themselves to those around them, always taking into consideration those not yet present. All these are acts or actions, not states.[24] To (with)stand (to be *In-statuere*), it is necessary to act towards others, to run alongside them, simultaneously in the direction of each individually. These are always actions, that is, verbs, not nouns; which is why ›institutionalization‹ always has the advantage over ›institution‹, and why some philosophical traditions thematizing the institution display the importance of the subject-object dyad. If the subject is a set of various acts (as in Hegel), and if these acts have their own devilish strength and action,[25] only those acts that construct social facts can be

22 We know that Humboldt sometimes uses *Universität* and sometimes *Anstalt*. It is he who introduces the dilemma that there is something interior and exterior to an organization. A corporation or *incorporatio* is not by definition anything negative, but one of humanity's greatest inventions. It is a necessary reconstruction of one of the main institutes of civil society. The university, however, is a self-managed corporation (*eine Korporation mit Selbstverwaltung*). So goes the second sentence in Jaspers' book on the university. The corporation is here certainly more than a mere technical and juridical notion. According to Jaspers, the university is concerned with the objective spirit. I am referring to chapter 6, »Institution« of the book in which he speaks about the necessity of the institution: »The University exists only to the extent that it is institutionalized. The idea becomes concrete in to institution.« Jaspers: The Idea of University, p. 70.

23 The word orchestra appears once only in John Rawls, in a long footnote, in which he illustrates the social union. Cf. Rawls: A Theory of Justice, p. 524. By contrast, describing the phenomenon of integration in »A Community's Communal Life«, Ronald Dworkin reconstructs the orchestra as ›a unit of agency‹ in which we associate our actions. Cf. Dworkin: Liberal Community, pp. 492–496.

24 This is a distinction found in John Locke, who, however, speaks not of intersubjective or interpersonal acts, but those that bind the Person to the Commonwealth. Cf. Snare: Consent and Conventional Acts in John Locke, pp. 28–29.

25 »The subject is the series of his acts« (Was das Subjekt *ist, ist die Reihe seiner Handlungen*) § 124; »Manifestly more or fewer circumstances may be included in an act. In the case of arson, e. g., the fire may not take effect, or it may spread farther than the agent intended. Yet in neither case is the result due to good or bad fortune, since man in acting must deal with externality. An old proverb rightly enough says, »A stone flung from the hand is the devil's.« In acting I must expose myself to misfortune; that also has a right to me, and is the manifestation of my own will.« § 119. Hegel: Philosophy of Right, pp. 52, 50.

determined as objective, and then as objects based on which further actions can be conducted (social objects). If the principle of reciprocity is satisfied, being adjacent to one another implies the existence of some third (being one adjacent to a third): as long as there is mutual and simultaneous production of many actions (that is to say, social objects) that far surpass the number of those elements producing them. This moment, when the number of acts, or connections and relations, grows ever greater, when social facts or social objects are multiplied among group elements, is of particular importance in the development and construction of a future entity, which we will soon enough designate as the institution.

Whence this increase in number of acts, and what are the consequences to the construction and duration of elements in space and time? Also, what is it that these elements are doing to one another, what is it they exchange? I will describe these communicative activities of elements (Kant thematizes *commertium* or *Wechselwirkung*) in a few ways, attempting to find a decisive moment in the production of a group of elements (a social group) and thus the institution. The elements exchange touches, gazes, symbols, language, small talk, gestures, money, objects, documents, wills, etc. – in a word, anything we can name as »the third« that implicitly introduces yet another instance of another ›third‹, with whom the exchange is currently not taking place. (In the construction of the Tower of Babel, this instance of the third is the figure of the inspector or controller overseeing the joint work of the group.) The number of mutual acts and reciprocal exchange among various elements already allows us to call this a reciprocal or spiral construction that holds the agents of action. Notwithstanding that theories of reciprocity vary between connections established between two or perhaps three members, it would appear that the very exchange of (social) acts allows the foreshadowing of a possible ›expansion‹ (in space and time), as well as the ›holding together‹ and subsistence of the elements. What does it mean to deploy the word ›together‹ here as a kind of new constructive model? In what way does ›together‹ surpass the position of ›being next to one another‹?[26] ›Being together‹ obviously means something more, something extra, such as being with some third, someone not yet present. If we had to describe this novelty in the development of the ›In-statuere‹ construction, let us begin from the number of acts continuously enlarged, increased by the reciprocal activity of multiple actors. There is an urgency in the exchange of acts among various individuals and a haste in producing a chain of acts. The speed of

26 The word ›together‹ in various European languages means being in one body, incorporated (*gaduri*); holding in one, associatively, simultaneously (*insimul*) or being in one or for one in a given place (in Russian, together implies being or living in one place). The Yugoslav Praxis School philosopher, Miladin Životić, a great fighter for peace during the Yugoslav conflict, insisted that not only was the common life of the three ethnicities in Bosnia necessary and more worthwhile than »life merely next to one another – but it was the only solution«. There would be no life if it is not ›together‹, if not lived together.

exchange or the swiftness of interaction among elements (without delay or interruption between acts), but also the long-term intensive and priority exchange of acts, these are the source of the institute of common action or joint resolution of a problem. The models that concern ›urgency‹ and ›priority‹ actually decisively determine the institutional practice as such. A group of individuals gathers together to solve a problem, to transparently publish a project for its resolution, to construct a future general action of providing help and organize a series of future actions that bring about a given social change. An institution is impossible if there are no experiments or discoveries of something new, a universal solution to a general problem, one that affects everybody. There can be no institution without organization of protest, joint resistance and a project of social change. Common or orchestrated action of various individuals that the group both constructs in that moment, but also projects into the future, is proof that the association of various elements has produced power (power is in the *together*). However, power is not acquired at the moment when the group gathers, closes, and then antagonistically directs itself externally. On the contrary: Georg Cantor transformed the ties and relations that circulate among the elements of a gathering or group (the framework of a gathering or group is an abstraction whose borders are always overstepped) into the *ambitus*, expansion and striving out, the *Umfang* of the »gathering« outwards, towards elements who ought to join it. The outward openness or excessiveness of the group or gathering could be termed institutional power (or, as per Cantor, *Potenz* or *Valenz* as *Institutio*).[27]

Still more complicated is a description of common acting in a theater troupe[28] or an orchestra, as they possess immanent institutional capacity. We should look at a few moments in particular, without which there can still be no institutional building. First, temporarily and occasionally, the troupe or orchestra *lives* together. An orchestra of various elements confirms its common life, and *vice versa*, the institution protects the common life of all.[29] For collective action to be ensured, all individual actors must produce enthusiastic and collegial acts, thus reducing asocial, negative social acts, negative or bad acts. Further, the acts produced individually

27 Cantor: La filosofia dell'infinito, 86 p. (»Principien einer Theorie der Ordnungstypen« [1885], § 4.)

28 Edith Stein uses two terms: social group (*soziale Gruppe*) and (theatrical) troupe (*Truppe*) to describe the organization to which she belongs, of which she is a member. She analyzes the structure of experience of grief for the loss of a group member. »I grieve as a member of the troupe, and the troupe grieves through me« (*Ich trauere als Glied der Truppe, und die Truppe trauert in mir*). Stein: Individuum und Gemeinschaft, pp. 119–120.

29 This can be specified further: »The collective acts of a community constitute its communal life. On the metaphysical view of integration, a community is a super-person, and its collective life embodies all the features and dimensions of a human life. But the practice view defines a community's communal life more narrowly: it includes only the acts treated as collective by the practices and attitudes that create the community as a collective agent. The communal life of an orchestra is limited to producing orchestral music: it is *only* a musical life.« Dworkin: Liberal Community, p. 495.

(while producing the multiplicity of common acts), cannot be reduced exclusively to reciprocal or social acts. The orchestra does not contain only reciprocal social acts, that is, the actors are not addressing exclusively each other. Passages of text or musical scores are integrated into a collective action of all that surpasses mere interactive and communicative acts of the individuals (elements, members). They are no longer acts for themselves or towards others in the troupe or orchestra, but a collective action of the group, and they concern all.[30] It seems to me this new kind of act can now be problematized and designated with quite rare and insufficiently thematized phrases such as ›institutional acts‹ or ›official acts‹. Engaged acts are certainly incorporated into these kinds of act, perhaps even crucially determining them, but they also contain a new potential that additionally constitutes institutional practice. What does this mean? What is it that I am doing, when working for an orchestra, a troupe, or an institution? What am I performing when the institution to which I belong performs a very specific action, ascribable to the institution itself? If I in fact do nothing and produce only self-oriented or even acts detrimental to the institution, what protects the institution from me (that is, from any such member)? What is the general or the commons we all produce, and which must on occasion protect us from any one of us individually?[31] Avoiding »a baroque metaphysics«,[32] I will attempt to classify a few possible models that together might explain the institutional of an institution (as such, in general), the communal or the commons of institutional practice as such.

First, the general or the institutional of the institution is dispersed across the individuals who belong and the commitment of the members of the orchestra. If, as a flautist, I obstruct the orchestra by not playing or playing poorly, the collective act of the orchestra is still performed. The orchestra will fall apart if a majority of members cease to play, just as a bank would go bankrupt if a majority of its customers choose to withdraw their money at the same time. The general or common is a depot, stock, an accumulation of individual acts or individual institutional commitments.

Second, what is the institutional act if each member performs their role in spite of my obstruction? Or how does everyone individually produce their institutional

30 »Something is common when it exists not just for me and for you, but for us, acknowledged as such.« Taylor: Irreducible Social Goods, p. 139.

31 »We have created a third thing, and each of us is one of the parts.« Or »love (...) is neither you or him. It is a third thing you must create.« Gilbert: Joint Commitment, pp. 269, 259.

32 »All this may suggest that integration depends on a baroque metaphysics which holds that communities are fundamental entities in the universe and that individual human beings are only abstractions or illusions. But integration can be understood in a different way, as depending not on the ontological primacy of the community, but on ordinary and familiar facts about the social practices that human beings develop.« Dworkin: Liberal Community, p. 494. This is an unproblematic position, although it is debatable how some other positions would function in Dworkin's system: for example, Arthur Eddington's famous claim that human thought is harmonious with set theory.

duty? There are a number of answers that should be considered, separately and together. The first, whether there is some kind of collective intentionality or »co-operative intention«,[33] individual awareness that everyone is part of the orchestra and that all others are also orchestra members or parts. And this awareness ought to be in harmony with the product, with the act performed by the orchestra as such. A small metaphysics of belonging – that I belong or that we all together belong to an orchestra, and that without my contribution, the concerto will not sound the way it should – gives collective intentionality, we possess all individually and at once (hence, commons), a moral character.[34] At least three characteristics of the institutional act will explain the moral institutional obligation. An act is institutional if it has to be performed (I have to keep my promise that I will do my job and play properly), if it is recognized and understood by other members of the institution, and if the institutional act is actually a public act addressed to others who do not necessarily integrate their own action into the commons (such as the audience listening to the concert).[35] The normative character of participation and integration of one's action into the collective orchestral act has been achieved by placing all the elements in the same place and they each fulfilling the obligation they have taken on. The obligation (*officium*) to properly read the score and play the music, to do one's job and that everyone individually is in the service of all and the common, that is, the common good, interest, aim,[36] transforms or renames the ›institutional act‹ into an ›official act‹.[37] Aside from the official act being necessarily public, its most significant characteristic is that it constructs something communal, which we name as ›office‹. It is the act of building a general institution. What does this mean? Above all, the interchangeability of elements, that is, indi-

33 »The orchestra performs a particular concerto only when its members play with a cooperative intention; it would not perform at all if its musicians played exactly the notes assigned to them in the score, at exactly the designated moments, and in the same room, but with no intention of playing together as un orchestra.« Dworkin: Liberal Community, p. 495. Michael Bratman uses the phrase »shared intention«, while Natalie Gold and Robert Sugden, »team reasoning«. Gold / Sugden: Collective Intentions and Team Agency, pp. 116–117. Annette Baier terms this as »mental commons«. Baier: Doing Things with Others.

34 The importance of the institutional act for the institution can be gleaned from two texts by John Cameron (»Ought and institutional Obligation« and »The Nature of Institutional Obligation«). Cf. Lorini: Dimensioni giuridiche dell'istituzionale, pp. 318–319.

35 Cameron: The Nature of Institutional Obligation, p. 320. Cf. Moini: Interpretare l'azione pubblica.

36 Peter von Moos examines the connection between the public and the *summum bonum, commune et totale bonum omnium* or the *vita communis* in the Middle Ages, when the Church (or its interest) »swallowed up« elements or members of the institution. »*Pars extra totum existens non est pars.*« Moos: »Öffentlich« und »privat« im Mittelalter.

37 Parsons mentions the possibility of such institutional practice in a passing comment without further explanation. »Its (bureaucracy's) crucial feature is the institutionalization of the *authority of office*. This means that both individual incumbents and, perhaps even more importantly, the bureaucratic organization itself, may act »officially« for, or »in the name of,« the organization, which could not otherwise exist.« Parsons: On Institutions and Social Evolution, p. 309.

viduals. The institution is an office because it surpasses its parts and individuals. Should one wish not to perform the office of an institution, they can be replaced by one more engaged or simply better. Further, as public, the official act is in the service of the audience (or client) for whom the communal act is performed. The institution is thus in the service of other institutions. Institutional action is primarily testamentary (many meanings of *institutio* connect it with the will and testament): I have to produce such acts as open the possibility for those not yet present to join, that is, those with whom I will only be in the orchestra in the future, who might replace me. The communal or commons of the institution is an act that makes a deposit, opens time and space for a future act, an act of another.[38] An institutional act is one that immediately takes the subsequent act into account. There are sundry examples: the essence of giving a toast is the expectation of others joining it, as I also toast to those not present; I hasten to move when the light turns green, so that as many cars behind me could also pass; when taking a coffee at a local bistro, I pay for another coffee, for one who will drink it without paying (*caffe sospeso*); I pay my *charge*[39] and tax now, while employed, in advance, to help those who are currently out of work; etc.

Third, an orchestra is an institution because we all hold documents that show we are engaged to play and because we fulfill our contracts. The institution is a documentational building capable of producing further documents that confer status on everyone who is engaged by it (thus becoming its part). The document is the communal of the institution, binding every institution to other institutions by way of various official acts.

[38] Cf. Napoli: Il »deposito«. »A foundation (*Stiftung*) (*sanction testamentaria beneficia perpetui*) is an institution (*Anstalt*) that has been voluntarily established, and confirmed by a state, for the benefit of certain members of it who succeed one another until they have all died out. (...) Those institutions (*Anstalt*) for the benefit of the poor, invalid and sick which have been set up at the expense of the state (foundations [*Stifte*] and hospitals) can certainly not be done away with.« Kant: The Metaphysics of Morals, p. 133.

[39] The word office, the title of Chapter Five of Walzer's book *Spheres of Justice*, is translated into French as *charge et emplois réglementés*«. *Charge* is a burden, of the public and general, a deposit that ensures the generative power of the institution. Cf. Walzer: Spheres of Justice, p. 129.

2 The First Scene of Institutional Building. Babylon *Incorporatio*

The painting »Babylonian Production of Normativity in Europe (with the help of Pieter Bruegel), 2016« features twice in the exhibit catalog of Somerset House – King's College, with differing text accompanying the two catalog photographs (one of which has a white passe-partout). In the painting, Werner Gephart adds a few elements to Pieter Bruegel's Babylon fantasy, explaining in the adjacent text what he has done and why. So, let us first consider the connection between the text about the Tower of Babel and the commonly held vision.

Look at – the imperative mood is a most important instance of institutional acting – verse 3, chapter 11 of the first book of the Torah (*Bereshit*). Genesis, chapter 11 describes the first instance of human building and the first great architectural endeavor. Let us recall the various visual fantasies of this great action (Bruegel's is perhaps most famous) and let us remember that this fragment is one of the most repeated and interpreted places in the history of thought, precisely because of the ever-lingering enigma of destruction and failure of this great action or set of actions. Could we say that this endeavor (which follows divine creation of the world), this first ever architectural impulse, fails precisely because of inadequate technology and poor material (it would appear that there was a terrible wind, destroying the edifice)? Does that mean that the technical readiness and equipment of a community or a group determines the strength of its compactness and its duration? Or might there be other reasons for (the lack of) success?

1. Everyone on earth had the same language, and the same words.
2. And as they migrated from the east, they came upon a valley in the land of Shinar and settled there.
3. They said to one another, »Come, let us make bricks, and burn them hard.« Brick served them as stone, and bitumen served them as mortar.
4. And they said, »Come, let us build us a city, and a tower with its top in the sky, to make a name for ourselves; else we shall be scattered all over the world.«
5. The *Adonai* came down to look at the city and tower that man had built.
6. And *Adonai* said, »If, as one people with one language for all, this is how they begin to act, then nothing that they may propose to do will be out of their reach.
7. Let us, then, go down, and confound their speech there, so that they shall not understand one another's speech.
8. Thus *Adonai* scattered them abroad from there over the face of the whole earth: and they stopped building the city.

9. That is why it was called Babel, because there *Adonai* confounded the speech of the whole earth: and from there *Adonai* scattered them over the face of the whole earth.[40]

Is technology *the first* (above and before all others) and decisive condition of any potential joint action? Such a question assumes a few preliminary gestures that ground the idea of primacy. In order to accept the idea that an established practice ought to be continuously altered and amended, that activity generally ought to be reconfigured and transformed, that it is crucial to change conduct, means, and materials – in a word, to accept the imperative of change, it is necessary to show that a) there can be no joint endeavor without simultaneous work on change and amendment of established technological practice (since a group is together not only because its members work together, but also because joint work is possible only if the means, materials, and technology are continuously modified as well). b) Only amendments conducted together in common conditions turn joint work into directed and permanent institutional action. c) Only institutional action, that is, activity in accordance with technological development and achievements, can be named as human action and practice, and only as such can it compete with ideal and imaginary (divine) creation (and then with other competitive actions).

In order for a group to confirm communication among its members, its residence in a single place together, prior to the plan and design (»let us build us a city, and a tower with its top in the sky«), and prior to incorporation and registration (of a department of study or) architectural bureau (»let us make a name for ourselves«), there must be a strong awareness of the group itself and its readiness to experiment (Buber and Rosenzweig translate the Hebrew *havah, havav*, »let us«, into German as *auf*), to uncover something new, to replace previous practice with something entirely different. Even though the mixing of elements (contents, materials, forms) is certainly concomitant with the mixing and overlap of words and space of residence, the (lack of) success described by the Babel narrative lies in the encounter of the group with grounds and its joint manipulation of material. Let us, then, assume immediately that this group first and for the time being discovers a ›new problem‹ or ›is solving an old problem in a new way‹. Either way, we are dealing with invention and new technology, since there is no institutional action without novelty, that is, the novel which also must be renewed and repeated, and then amended again.) This encounter with the ground is preceded by the fact that the group comprises refugees relocating from somewhere, arriving to a new location already formed as a group by a common language and single speech (held in memory, reiterated), all of which keeps the group unified over the course of their arduous journey.

40 Berlin / Brettler (eds.): The Jewish Study Bible, p. 29.

When the refugees finally find themselves in a plain, and rest from an uncertain journey, before verse 5, thereupon unfolds a detailed control of documents (personal ID, building license, community approval certification, geodesic approval, inspection of architectural design, site inspection, company [name] registration into the transcendental registry, etc.). The group has one single goal, and in two moves conducts at least six distinct operations (the author divides and distributes them at random, although the nature of narrative and counting makes them seem temporally sequential): the first three are simultaneous, 1.) speaking and complete mutual comprehension (»they said to one another«), 2.) mutual encouragement through speech, using the imperative (»let us«), mobilization and readiness of the actors to hold (self-)aware membership of a larger whole, 3.) the invention of a new kind of building. The second three simultaneous actions are, in addition to mutual encouragement and imperative to move, 1.) their focus, care, and joint movement (»let us«), 2.) their collective intentionality in creating a grandiose common building design, and 3.) the creation of an institution (documentation, company), named and thus recognized as an independent actor. Of course, it is entirely clear that this group (its attribute is the use of the pronoun »us«, that is, the imperative »let us«) comprises individuals of different genders and ages (a plurality of I's), none of which is in some way distinguished. There is no special member, leader, chief of this group, standing above others in any way, repeating orders more than others. And the only goal of this group is that it remain a group (»else we shall be scattered all over the world«), have its identity, its own »I«. In order for the group of refugees to hold together, for the belonging and trust in the group to be ensured, lest it be scattered, that is, for it to be what it is, it is necessary that they all together, in a disciplined way, conduct the listed activities (in a disciplined way means to learn together, produce science or a segment of science – a discipline[41] – with joint work). Only if they conduct these actions together (plural) does the group remain a group (singular) and they do not become scattered (plural).

The questions of whether the appearance of the institution as such (»and let us make us a name«), is preceded by certain acts or actions or certain cooperative manipulations, games, equilibria, or indeed whether the institution as a normative group is preceded by certain group models and social facts, gatherings, associations – are sophist questions, even if philosophy is of necessity composed of the (again very disciplined) practice of thinking such questions and corresponding answers. There remain still other dilemmas: does the cooperation precede or is it simultaneous to the institution? Is the institution composed of constitutive or

[41] Werner Gephart writes about discipline and its significance (*Geist der Disziplin*) in his text on the Great War, insisting on the importance of Weber's definition of discipline. Cf. Gephart: Bilder der Moderne, p. 95.

regulative rules or are those in fact different? Is the institution a game, and if so what kind? Are the principles of justice separate from the institution, meaning that they should not be confused and mixed with the principles that suit individuals and their actions in special cases (as Rawls would have it in *A Theory of Justice*[42])? Further, in what way does a group become *incorporated* and what kind of documentary and *policy* actions mean that an institution endures and successfully delays its inevitable end and decay (why is there an end and why is it inevitable)? All these dilemmas are already contained in the testimony regarding the grand action in Babylon, where a group, coming from somewhere, is already constituted, since it speaks the same language, and is traveling or relocating.

However, new science or new learning (*discipline*), just like new learning about a group and joint work, at which insight this ancient group arrives, takes time, endurance, and perseverance. If there is no common language at the beginning, no trust and transparent communication, the group cannot survive long enough to work together. Even if it works together and works in an entirely new way together, without a great plan, without its company name, it cannot endure. Imagine now that this group indeed discovers the ingenious invention of lasting and that it has indeed found a way to endure. It is still completely uncertain whether it is successful or unsuccessful: the history of great visual fantasies about these few lines from the *Bereshit* shows us that this work, this plan and institution lasted for centuries before it was interrupted. It is not evident that we, now, as a large group that has come from elsewhere and has occupied the world, have *de facto* the same task and are in the midst of a great endeavor to institutionalize lest we be scattered and perish.

Verses 8 and 9 describe how the group's underlying construction intention tends to become ever bigger, to become a city (leaving aside the potential variations that might result from ambivalences in the Hebrew). The place where this group with the perfect language arrives (from elsewhere) to undertake its common endeavor actually becomes a place of prattle, jabber and babble: hence Babylon. On one hand, in building a city, the group intends to mark this action with its name, thus preserving itself in one place with the act of naming. On the other hand, an action by some higher, more dominant instance (The Lord, *Adonai*) annuls the institutionalized act of the group with its own intervention and its new label (»That is why it was called Babel«). It turns out that the sudden, brutal dissolution of the web of actions holding together the group whose goal was endurance and preservation means that initial group unity (»Everyone on earth had the same language, and the same words.«) is damaged once and for all. Why and how is this possible?

A group of people (refugees) relocates for whatever reason, plans to create a *counter-institution*, seeking to set up something new, contemporaneous, and par-

42 Rawls: A Theory of Justice, pp. 54–55.

allel with the institution of the cosmos and world given by some other, higher instance, (in this case *Yahweh*, *Elohim* or *Adonai*). I am using *counter* here not as *against*, but, as it originally meant, parallel or *ad*jacent (an *ad*-institution) or towards (in the direction of something, advancing toward the institution). The first normative moment, then, in the weakest possible sense of the word (norm before norm itself, hence possibly called *Kulturnorm*, following Max Ernst Mayer who in 1903 made a distinction between cultural and legal norms),[43] or else an institutional moment *par excellence*, can be found in 11:4, when the group decides to grasp itself (to have identity by speaking to itself): »And they said [the members of the group], Come, let us build us a city, and a tower with its top in the sky, to make a name for ourselves; else we shall be scattered all over the world.« It would appear that this new institution (in)tends towards the already existing institution (high up in the sky), towards the sky, from whence (in verse 5) »the *Adonai* came down« (towards the group down below). There is also danger of contest between two institutions, as well as idolatry. These are standard interpretations of the impending or future failure of the group and its grandiose construction. If we make use of this nearly forgotten distinction between cultural and legal norms,[44] it seems that this institutional gesture performed by our group could belong to both culture (since it is a group that becomes a group, develops, is nurtured) and normativity (an act that then obligates all members of the group to remain together in one place). In order for the group to have an identity (name), in order to be big (as big as possible, »whose top *may reach* unto heaven«), it is not necessary that it be essentially different from other groups or an already established instance (such as our group). As a group, soon enough a corporation, company, alliance of states, it is in competition with (measuring, calculating) other groups and cultures (as it is part of a large market of opulence), but not necessarily in conflict, opposition, or war with them. A group does not exclude other groups or cultures of groupings,

43 The term *Kuturnormen* was coined by Max Ernst Mayer in a 1903 book, *Rechtsnormen und Kulturnormen*. This pupil of Ihering is mentioned also by Hasso Hofmann in *Recht und Kultur*, p. 40. The interesting chapter for us is where Hofmann analyzes the history of the *Begriffspaar Recht und Kultur* and the emancipation of the term culture (p. 34 ff) in law and philosophy, which begins with Wilhelm Arnold's book *Cultur und Rechtsleben*, published in 1865. Seeking the ›reality‹ underpinning the norms is a typically ›institutional action‹: »Confronted with the loss of concrete world I went my way looking for reality. I tried to get onto the facts before their normative assimilation.« Schelsky: Auf der Suche nach Wirklichkeit, p. 8.

44 In the words of Max Ernst Mayer, »*Normen* (or *Rechtsnormen*) *sind Regeln* (...) *sie sind also Imperative, entweder positive (Gebote) oder negative (Verbote)*«. *Rechtsnormen* should be harmonized with *Kulturnormen* »(»*daß die Rechtsnormen übereinstimmen mit den Kulturnormen*«).« Mayer's definition is: »*Den Ausdruck ›Kulturnormen‹ gebrauche ich als einen Sammelnamen für die Gesamtheit derjenigen Gebote und Verbote, die als religiöse, moralische, konventionelle, als Forderungen des Verkehrs und des Berufs an das Individuum herantreten.*« Mayer: Rechtsnormen und Kulturnormen, p. 17.

nor does the group as *counter-institution* have to be destroyed, as it happened to that group of masons many centuries ago.

Still, why then was this group or institution or *counter-institution* destroyed? Verses 5–7 describe the descent of the higher instance and his control (in the masculine), his testimony and assessment, description of the ambitious and extraordinarily powerful party, not to be hindered in their unusual intention and action (the description is simultaneously a challenge to this higher instance to prove its greater power). Verse 7 is the *chef d'œuvre* of the author of this story: the higher instance, always presenting itself in the first person plural (power being always presented as plurality in one, the royal we, the sovereign, Leviathan), mobilizes its plurality with the same words with which the group constituted itself (»let us«) and takes away the group's unconditional condition of institution or institutionalization: language (»Let us, then, go down, and confound their speech there, so that they shall not understand one another's speech«).

The result of intervention by this higher instance (a fundamentally genocidal act, given that there is a clear intention to destroy the groupness of a group, the connection among its members and what makes it a group: language, building structure, living space, etc.) is that the individuals are once again dispersed and play the way Pieter Bruegel the Elder painted them in *Children's Games*: as disconnected individuals or tiny groups.

Here are five trivial suppositions. Was this very cooperative and mobile group, in which all worked with one another, jointly endeavoring to execute a grand project, destroyed because still insufficiently institutionalized? (For example, was there, perhaps, a sudden spread of corruption and negligence that prevented an efficient realization of the project, delaying it?) Was it destroyed because it was a *counter-institution*, which would mean that the higher instance does not care for the emergence of any competing institutions (which is the standard interpretation of this passage), even using force against it? Was it destroyed because the group was relocating, changing its dwelling, and began, as refugees on still-foreign territory, building an ill-advised and illegal structure, without license and proper documentation? Was it destroyed because this new institution was itself unjust (poor working conditions with many worker fatalities, too many benefits for the indolent)? (Both Rawls and Scanlon speak of an »unjust institution«, where individuals advertise or protest against the institution, against inequality and hierarchy, seeking balance and equality.) Or was the group perhaps destroyed because the amount of its negative social acts, because cruelty and a lack of engagement acts rendered it fatal?

All these questions, dilemmas, paradoxes stand before Werner Gephart when he has to make a quick description of Europe in the form of Babylon. He swiftly adds a few new elements. First come the main European institutions, the main buildings, skillfully inserted into Bruegel's dilapidated walls. Thus, European institutions or Europe becomes part of this grandiose ruin. Then there are two moments in the upper left. The hot air balloon flying the British flag, as if fleeing, but certainly separating in protest or dissatisfaction with the great ruined European structure. A group of people disengages and is no longer part of the all-together, which is also Gephart's way of confirming that there is certainly something outside the monstrous European institution. Then there is the lower right, the figure of Max Weber, that is, the instance that »critically observes the scene«, as Gephart writes. Both Max Weber (probably the instance of the social and legal theorists as »forming form of society« [Simmel] or perhaps the reader, or indeed the author himself, Werner Gephart), and the Brexiting balloon are, however, a consequence or remnant of the great normative chaos emanating from the heart of the tower in great concentric waves resembling a large target and spreading towards the structure's periphery. At the center, we find the symbol »§«. Thus, the paragraph, §, »paragraphing« is at the center, a chaotic plurality of minuscule paragraphs, stuck to the walls of the tower's façade. Why §? What is Werner Gephart's intention?

It seems that in the course of coordinating common work and the work rules of various groups, that is, in coordinating different characteristics of individual parts of one single group, certain irregularities and abnormalities appear. The paragraph, § represents the norm, that is, normative capacity, and Werner Gephart locates the European problem there. It leads to further uncertainty and eroding the compactness of this large group. Hence, Europe ought to be represented, according to him, as the Tower of Babel in ruins; but ruins that still survive (as ruins), even with insufficient chance of true reconstruction and renewal. Visually, Gephart inserts many paragraphs, »§« into the great body of the European structure, which means many disharmonized and dispersed norms, incoherent and disordered (since their intervals are random). This scattering and excess of norms precedes misunderstandings in language and separation and dispersion of members of the great European family. In the text accompanying Gephart's visual intervention, he speaks about the lack of transparency in the production of laws across so many national legal cultures; his response is to insert an abstract scheme of a process of non-production. Variations of the word production and non-production are certainly more difficult to understand than the visual interventions. It thus seems to me that Werner Gephart's interpretative action belongs to the family of very successful attempts of resolution of the secret destruction of the Tower of Babel (which, after all, is the great common work). His effort, paradoxically, leaves hope that the time of building, the time of institutional design and of correction (of paragraphing) still lies ahead, and that the enemies of Europe will have to wait a while longer for the final failure of the European project. Max Weber, our sage in the bottom right corner of this painting, »critically [observing] the scene«, is the true guarantee that this is still possible.

I. Violence and Institution

1 The Institution of Sovereignty. Fictional Entities and Violence

> »In explaining sovereignty (*Suprematu[s]*), and this is surprising, the difficulty is that I am entering an entirely neglected field. The reason for this is that those who write about it most often write gazing into the past, towards the stunted remains of sovereignty that are barely even there, while completely disregarding what is happening now. I am least astonished by the common lawyers (*jurisperitis vulgaribus*), for whom no wisdom can be found outside of the tomes of Roman Law; I am confused precisely by our illustrious dignitaries (*illustres dignitate*), who, when they encounter a difficulty in writing, reach for authority and erudition rather than experience and ability to think for themselves (*quam experientie atque judicii*) (...).«[45]

A century after Jean Bodin's renowned work, *Les Six Livres de la République* (1576), in which the old word ›sovereignty‹ (*souveraineté*) is used for the first time to refer to a completely new ›figure‹, Leibniz attempts to reorder and rethink a word because it is no longer clear what it indicates, or hides, or neglects. His intervention and his attempt to resolve this great confusion and vexation spread by books and »learned people« are today both current and forgotten. I assume that the basic reason for Leibniz's rehashing of the word sovereign (and sovereignty) does not exclusively concern the nature and complexity of this grandiose fancy that nevertheless beset theorists and rulers, both before and after the famous German philosopher. Perhaps the elements that indubitably make Leibniz our contemporary, and facilitate our own job in finding borders and impropriety in sovereignty in today's age, towards which Leibniz himself nudges us, are the more important: Leibniz is counsel to numerous rulers of his time, founder of various institutions, a realist and pragmatist who for the first time speaks of the person of international law (*persona jure gentium*)[46] and a fraternity among sovereigns (*Fraternité entre les Souverains*) of Christian Europe (*Respublica Christiana*)[47]; Leibniz the mathematician is the forerunner of contemporary science of statistics and the new tax politics; a Protestant and European, he was a great enemy of Islam, an aggressive stoker of hatred and war against Turkey, and the first sophisticated theorist of clashes between civilizations; Leibniz, undoubtedly the creator of the ›Philosophy of Europe‹, is the first thinker who places the security and defense

45 Leibniz: De Jure Suprematus ac Legationis Principum Germaniae, p. 51.
46 Leibniz: Codex Juris Gentium Diplomaticus, p. 33.
47 Leibniz: Entretien de Philarete et d'Eugene, p. 306.

of a regime in the foreground, even prior to any potential patriotism;[48] finally, Leibniz writes his books in several languages, and is, along with Hobbes, the one foremost responsible for the dissemination and thematization of the French word ›sovereignty‹ in Europe of the time.

It is my intention to follow Leibniz's efforts in interpreting and reconstructing the institution of sovereignty and thus show the militaristic character of this theological-political fiction by Jean Bodin. Although the figure of sovereignty and the idea of a group of sovereign rulers represents Bodin's, and consequently Leibniz's, attempt at pacifying a Europe of raging civil and religious warfare, and bringing peace, the struggle for sovereignty at the same time implies »bloody sacrifices of the innocent by ambitious rulers«,[49] constant insecurity, and the production of enemies. The theory, or more precisely the fiction or narrative of sovereignty, could thus represent an unconditional condition for war.

At the outset, let us imagine a small territory[50] and a small Republic. And let us imagine it in the same way in which Leibniz »conceived« of the small imaginary kingdom of *Ivetot*, all those centuries ago.[51] *Ivetot* is simply his example or fantasy that ought to regulate the strength or importance of a word handed down to us from books or self-proclaimed and self-important rulers. The imagining of a small territory, small population, small government, and small ruler, as well as a language spoken by a small number of people, is not completely opposite to the imagining of the greatest, the incomparable, and greater than anything comparable, which can be found in the first gesture of the discovery of the adjective ›sovereign‹ or ›super‹ (*superus*, *supra* are complex Latin words in the root of the French word *souverain[e]*). The small territory that Leibniz is talking about and imagining is not entirely in the register of sovereignty, since it is not any kind of smallest, incomparably small, unimportant, and indiscernible form, which as such would be equally sovereign, and, paradoxically, equally awe-inspiring, and the only true enemy of the ›supra‹, or ›super‹ that is above everything great.[52]

48 In a letter to Falaiseau (Hanover, 8 July 1705), Leibniz uses the Roman (*les Latins*) name for a state for the first time, and defines it as a society whose goal is collective security (*la seureté commune*). Towards the end of the letter, Leibniz says: »Subjects who have been conquered by a new lord ought to be allowed to swear allegiance to the enemy, since their previous lord was not able to provide their security.« Leibniz: Die Werke, 9, pp. 142–143.

49 Leibniz: De Suprematu Principum Germaniae, pp. 111–113.

50 A territory (*territorium*), according to Leibniz, does not only include the status or ruling or distribution of land, but the entirety (the aggregate, *aggregatum*) of established (and valid) legal documents that apply to a portion of land. Cf. Leibniz: De Jure Suprematus ac Legationis Principum Germaniae, p. 54.

51 Ibid., pp. 18, 61.

52 *Babilonian Talmud* (*Shabat* 77b) carries the reading that the greatest monster and true sovereign on Earth, with which only God can come to terms, *Leviathan*, is only afraid of a little worm (*kilbit*, the forerunner of the contemporary terrorist), who enters through the gills of the massive lumbering fish and kills it.

Already in the act of imagining this small territory, certainly not large, but also not minute, Leibniz somewhat tarnishes maximalism and the effort for maximalism, inherent to everything that belongs to the field of sovereignty. The function of the small (small territory, small population, small ruler, etc.) or the not too large, reintroduces the relativism of measurement, counting, comparing, grading; something Jean Bodin wanted to prevent and forever stop with his theories of the number, closed set, and proportion. The existence of the small does presuppose the large, larger, or the largest, but doubtlessly abolishes the incomparable, the serene, the above-all-else. Apart from the acceptance of the existence of the plurality (another sovereign or other sovereigns), and apart from being in relation (and relativization) with others, and in comparison with others, the existence of the other (smaller or larger or different) introduces time (constant repetition of collation and measurement with the other[s]), and destroys the noun (sovereign or sovereignty) to the benefit of the adjective. Leibniz's statement »the territory is small« (*le territoire est petit*) immediately assumes an uncertainty about the level of its sovereignty. If it is small, is it actually sovereign, and to what extent?

But are these questions justified in their abolishment of the possibility of sovereignty of something small? For example, if we imagine something ›small‹ to also be ›closed‹, if a territory is unbreachable, is it not sovereign? Indeed, does an order (*imperium*) valid for this territory not suppose its agent – ruler (or people), and have they not the right to call themselves sovereign?[53] And if someone from the outside wants to break in, does the sovereign (the ruler or the people) not defend the ›sovereignty‹ of this small territory? Is ›sovereignty‹ not defended when a portion of this small territory, a portion smaller still from the principal, announces its secession and independence? How are we to imagine the indivisibility of the small, if division is already manifested in resistance, separation, and defense of sovereignty?

These questions easily show the disappearance of the adjective in the nouns sovereign and sovereignty – this is the foremost way of establishing sovereignty – and reveal at the same time the difficulty of relativizing and Leibnizizing Jean Bodin's

53 Bodin constantly vacillates. »The first prerogative of sovereignty is ordering everyone in general and each individually« (*La premiere marque de Souveraineté est donner loy à tous en general, et à chacun en particulier*). Bodin: Les six livres de la République, 1, p. 306. A few lines prior, on the same page: »(...) that the first prerogative of the sovereign prince is power (*puissance*) to order everyone in general and each individually.« A few pages before that (p. 300) Bodin reveals: »(...) the law (*loy*) is an order of the sovereign which touches (*touchant*) all subjects or things in general.« The law (*lex*) marks the right to an order and this right is held only by the one who has the sovereignty (*qui a la souveraineté*). Three forms are in play: sovereign, sovereignty as a state, and sovereignty as possession. Two more comments: the sovereign neither gives nor passes any laws which he himself is not subject to; this is a mistranslation and improper understanding of the phrase *donner loy*; sovereign orders, dictates, commands etc. Bodin differentiates *lex* as *imperium*, as an order which is effectuated in the domain of legislation, and *lex* as *ius* in the sense of equality and fulfillment. Heller: Die Souveränität, p. 36.

project. In addition to that, to show the limits and paucity of the fiction of Bodin's sovereignty presupposes the reconstruction of all these questions and all the political fantasies of sovereignty before and after, and completely outside of him and his influence. There is no reference to Bodin in Kant (or Hegel for that matter) when he differentiates between internal and external sovereignty, nor does Fichte mention Bodin in his *Closed Commercial State* (1800), but the matrix that Bodin laid down remained intact in all these philosophers. It seems to me, then, that in order to imagine a small territory and hence announce the limit of sovereignty or anything else that calls it into question, it is most important to follow Bodin's omissions, and take an interest in some of the places that hide those. For example, Bodin, a substantialist, constantly compensates for the weakness of his definition of sovereignty using an entire assortment of various (bio-)analogies. These analogies could, following Vaihinger, be called ›analogical fictions, or else ›fictitious analogies, as opposed to ›real analogies‹, which achieve results through induction and based on hypotheses. ›Fictitious analogies‹ – »according to one modern and quite popular fiction, the state is compared to an organism, or the world with an organism or work of art« – is a purely subjective construction and ›mythological‹ creation.[54] In his earliest extant large text about sovereignty, Bodin indicates, all the while criticizing it, the importance of Aristotle's definition of authority, and his and Cicero's absurd insistence on the importance of the size of a territory or the size of the population for constituting and marking of an entity:

Let us note here that our stipulation of the Republic refers equally to towns (*bourgs*), settlements (*villes*), cities (*cités*), kingdoms, regardless of how far they reach, as long as they remain within the same authority (*autorité; modo ejusdem imperio coerceantur*). The state could not be discerned based on its vastness or minuteness of its territory (à *l'ampleur ou à l'exiguité de son territoire*), just as an elephant could no more be called an animal than an ant, as they both have the same force (également *la force*) to sense and move. Thus Dubrovnik or Geneva, whose empires do not surpass the city walls, have no less right (*droit au titre*) to be called Republics from the Tartar Empires whose expanses are measured by the movement of the Sun.[55]

The ritual of naming or the right to title (*droit au titre*) – ›right‹ is never actually mentioned in the Latin original – is truly always the opening gambit and end game of Bodin's strategy. This is the first resistance to Aristotle who uses different names for significantly larger territories. Bodin's conception is that in this context sovereignty or the Republic are an alternative name for authority (a word made from the combining of medieval uses of the words *auctoritas* and *maiestas*)

54 Vaihinger: Die Philosophie des Als Ob, pp. 27–31.

55 Bodin: La Méthode de l'histoire, pp. 143–144; Bodin: Methodus ad Facilem Historiarum Cognitionem, p. 169.

or *imperium* (order). There follows that all these names refer to, and are identical for, any entity, irrespective of its size. This confusion regarding the translation and piling up of words of various origins can be resolved with a quite clear definition found in a short text by Bodin, which is hard to locate in time, although it seems that it precedes the *Method*, even if published much later. *Imperium*, the order (command), says Bodin in *Tableau du droit universel*, can be public or private (*Publicum est, aut Privatum*). If it is conducted outside of public government, an order which regards a university, various social groups, the family, the wife, children, or slaves, it is private. Only the public (general) order is sovereign and is found in the jurisdiction of the ruler, the aristocracy, or the people (*Publicum rursus aliud Summum, velut Principis, Optimatuum, Populi*).[56] Analogy and counter analogy allow Bodin to conclude that two ›organisms‹ (this word will assume importance for the understanding of the whole and will replace aggregate; Bodin usually uses the word body, *corps*), completely different in size, function in equal measure because they are ruled by one single *imperium* (order, law, sovereign), which covers and unites the entirety of their quantity. This makes each of these two entities sovereign.[57] Their strength or their force is equal, analogous or proportional to their mass, giving them both the identical or symmetric capacity, thinks Bodin, to sense and move (*cùm utrique movendi ac sentiendi vis insit*). For these classifications to really work and to crop up throughout the history of political demagoguery, hypocrisy, or pure fantasy, it is necessary to count on the essential incommensurability of the things being compared (ant and Dubrovnik), a prohibition on being literal (which we could call the terror of analogy), on the refusal to draw all the consequences of an analogy (wherein lies its persuasiveness), and a lack of sense of reality (something constantly mentioned by Leibniz). For it is ultimately impossible to break down all the thousands of analogies used by Bodin (and not just Bodin), and to show them meritless. If brought together by way of analogy, an ant and Dubrovnik should, by counter analogy, be shown to possess at least a few more characteristics in common, not only the one – that Dubrovnik, when compared to the Tartar Empire is small in the way that an ant compared to an elephant is small. An ant has many other determinants. One of its properties could manifest itself at the moment when accidentally crushed by that same colossal elephant.

56 Bodin: Tableau du droit universel, p. 94.

57 Bodin later returns to this analogy and adds that a city is not made up of individuals or persons (*personnes*), but of the unity of the people under sovereign power (*l'union d'un peuple sous une seigneurie souveraine*). Two extra points are unusually important. Aside from the ant, Bodin introduces another smaller being – *le ciron*, the flee, louse, nit, ›bacterium‹ (the ant is in La Fontaine's opinion a real colossus for this last creature). Aside from the Tartars, Bodin also speaks of the Turkish Empire. Ten years later, Bodin states his opinion on the sovereign person: »(...) thus a little King (*un petit Roy*) is sovereign as much as the greatest monarch on the Earth« (*le plus grand Monarch de la terre*). Bodin: Les six livres de la République, 1, pp. 41–42.

Let us note a few imprecisions and conditions of this ingenious analogy by Jean Bodin, one neither exceptional nor particular in the context of his writing. At the same time, this will be the condition for the ›revenge of the real‹, which strategies of analogies constantly provoke and announce. Finally, it is a good opportunity to separate the first and most important attributes of sovereignty in the way that they have crystallized in the word's use over the course of several centuries, and then to place them in opposition with the other attributes, the ones Leibniz first thematized.

It is important, I repeat, to constantly hold in the mind's eye a small territory, a small population, a small government, and a small ruler, as well as a language spoken by a small number of people. The right to this simple and unpretentious vision and version of the small ought to function as a regulating factor of this sovereign difference or fundamental sameness between the elephant and the ant, which Bodin speaks about. Contrary to the discrepancy and animosity between the largest and the smallest, between the *Leviathan* and *kilbit*, Bodin presupposes that the largest and smallest are indivisible (hence sovereign, the ant so small, and the elephant so prodigious), that they are incomparable and distant one from another (neither Dubrovnik nor Geneva share a border with the Tartar Empire), but that they still both have complete independence and self-containment which is written into their names. »Sovereign« (the old French word *sovrain*, derived from the medieval Latin use of *superanus*) denotes what is above all else, but for that very reason abolishes all else, and that which is absolute and one. To play with this marker or to be careless in the use of the word ›super‹ – one of the most popular words on the planet – would mean to prejudge the existence of one single global super-sovereign (super sovereign being a redundancy), a *Leviathan*, because it contains within itself all other, and because nothing exists outside of it. Lest we forget, the ›terrorist‹, and the ›enemy‹, the *kilbit*, dwells within the *Leviathan's* body, and it will be perfectly clear that the crossing and change of the understanding of the term sovereignty from Bodin to Hobbes is dictated by fantasies and ›visual strategies‹, and not at all the work on the term itself or a cognitive activity. If either the elephant or the nit are therefore sovereign and self-contained (that is independent, indivisible and one) based on their mark or their title, their war unto annihilation is already announced. This conflict between species or within one species, between the parts or the organs, is a ›struggle for the name‹ and a war for sovereignty (or so-called defense of sovereignty). It is important to note and follow – this could be a definition for the caution on which I insist – that this conflict pulses in the rhythm of the change of the attribute into the superlative (›super‹), into the noun, and in the rhythm of the change of the symbolic and ritual into the ›real‹. Certainly Jean Bodin's ›innocent‹ fantasies about the equal force to ›sense‹ and ›move‹ felt by the ant and elephant could not prevent the conflict. Both the ant and elephant limit space for other members of their species, as well as to one another. If they sense, they should be able to sense each other's presence. Apart from sensing and moving, their force is also expressed in work, in grabbing and gluttony, in killing and devouring, in mating and co-living, in communication, in relation to others and with others.

What remains in that case of the identical name ›Republic‹ or of the identical ›sovereignty‹ of Dubrovnik or Geneva, or the Tartar Empire or Babylon, mentioned both by Bodin and Aristotle, if to this potential meeting between the ant and the elephant we add:

a. that the strength of the large elephant *de facto* greatly surpasses the strength of the tiny ant,
b. that there is not a sufficient reason for something minute in nature to be named in the same way as something grandiose, or to be given a name whose meaning presupposes a superiority in size and mass (sovereignty [*maiestas*] is derived from *magnitudo*),
c. that the order (*imperium*) that rules and is valid within the confines of a single body or entity, cannot always be named as sovereign because not always public or not ›re-publican‹,
d. that the order (*imperium*) that rules and is valid within the confines of an organism tends unerringly towards the overstepping of the border of its own entity and towards occupying the body of another (paradoxically only making it public and sovereign at that point),
e. that force or violence (*vis*) mentioned by Bodin, translates the validity of an order (or norm) into its implementation (principle of efficiency[58]), hence it is possible for an *imperium* not to be efficient and *de facto* not rule over the entire territory of an organism,
f. that the same force and (excessive) violence can be found at the source and principles of every Republic or any sovereign entity,[59]
g. that there are parts of the organism that take precedence over other parts because they produce the orders or decide on special measures[60] or execute them (this is the unconditional condition of difference, opposition, and conflict between the sovereign and sovereignty),

58 The state implements the validity (*Geltung*) of the norm because »the state is power, force, in short, a natural reality, and as such, efficient. The manifestation of this are canons, guns, bombs, fortresses, prisons, gallows, and the guillotine.« Kelsen: Les rapports de système entre le droit interne et le droit international public, p. 237

59 »Reason and clear thinking (natural illumination, *lumière naturelle*) has lead us to the belief that force and violence (*violence extrême*), subduing natural laws (*forçant les lois de nature*), are at the origin of Republics.« Bodin: Les six livres de la République, 1, p. 112.

60 The origin of the connection between the decision, decision of extraordinary measures, and the decision of the sovereign of extraordinary measures which establishes sovereignty (C. Schmitt), can be found in Bodin. Heller: Die Souveränität, pp. 36, 90–92.

h. that there are parts of the whole that can be amputated, mutilated, sacrificed in accordance with the very same extraordinary measures,
i. that there are primitive and undivided entities (organisms) that break up and continue to exist separate and divided?

When it comes to the future of the sovereign ant or Dubrovnik-animal, again Bodin makes his basic analogical maneuver before its paradoxical betrayal and shortening of its action. His ideas of confinement and borders, including his paranoia that the intruder or enemy is always on the inside (the reasons for which are not to be found exclusively in the horrific civil wars which he witnesses), and whose »feminine« face hides a satanic aspect, as well as a completely defensive political perspective. Sovereignty is always already defended and cleared in Bodin, but it is given in advance (and immediately under attack), and the author is completely lacking in developed ideas of conquest, expansion, and ›aggressive warfare‹. The Republic has all the characteristics of a house or home, and the sovereign resembles the head of household. But instead of taking advantage of the ›comparative potential‹ and emancipatory dimension of the proliferation of households and creation of new houses, and then new citizens, thus analogously giving the sovereign of the Republic a representative role and power to spread his own sovereignty outside the borders of the Republic, Bodin's sovereign/head-of-household is not a sojourner, and does not know other sovereigns from Adam. There is no crossing of borders of the Republic, no movement toward the largest possible community of republics. The foreign relations of the sovereign are reduced to hiring the enemy and organizing defensive wars with view to eliminating the internal enemy.

Still, in this case, both the inside and outside enemy are ghosts. The sovereign or subject busy with self-creation or self-limitation has before him no prospect of another in its otherness, such as another state or other states, friend or foe, with whom he could occupy and construct a common European space. We are dealing with an anonymous, absolute other, or absolute shadow of another, whose function is only to limit and negate, thus interfering with the sovereign's independence. Indeed, the sovereign does not recognize the shape of this negation or the face of this enemy from whence come the coerced or self-coerced borders. This is why the »formless« enemy appears throughout »his own« sovereignty (territory) and strikes him as some sort of absolute or sovereign enemy. His function can be twofold: regulative – since the auto-censure or self-limiting of the sovereign (the subject) is only conducted based on this negative and fictitious limiting principle (lest we forget, Bodin's great accomplishment is the secularization of medieval authority and granting the ruler absolute power; the sovereign is sovereign because he determines the borders of his own sovereignty); and terrorist – the sovereign no longer recognizes anything that does not call him into question, negate him, and which does not awaken his panic and terror.

The paradox or contradiction of sovereignty is based on the necessity of the non-existence of another sovereign or other sovereignty, for in that case there would be no sovereignty at all. It excludes anything that it itself is not.[61] Similarly with the enemy. How is it possible for something above everything else, and is, by the by, one and only, to leave room for the existence of something that threatens to destroy it? The announcing and justifying of the danger of war (virtual war, the virtual other, the enemy) is an important form of assistance to the sovereign in order for his rule to tie together and hold all the parts of a Republic into an unbreakable unity. The fame of the geometer and expert for proportions, Jean Bodin, and his unusual engagement, consisted mainly of inciting fear among heads of households and small rulers of his time. His task was to show what is going on behind the backs of rulers and husbands and to prescribe the appropriate remedy for the defense of sovereignty.

Two years after the publication of *Les six livres de la République*, the jurist Bodin chairs the committee in the case against Jehanne Hervillier. Accused of being a witch, she admits everything (»without questioning or torture«, adds Bodin), and is found guilty and subsequently executed on April 30, 1578. Three years later, in the introduction to his book *On the Demon Worship* (*De la démonomanie*), one of the most popular books ever written (and on account of which Bodin will later have problems not only because of the content, but also because of various intrigues and accusations that he is an admirer of Jewishness and that he converted to Judaism), Bodin explains the epilogue of the process, citing various confessions of the fifty-year-old woman, and expounding on why there was no hesitation among the judges to carry out the harshest punishment:

The witch was accused of causing the death of several people and animals (*bestes*). (…) She admitted to being introduced to the devil by her mother when she was twelve years old, that he was disguised as a dark man, unusually tall, and dressed in black. Her mother told her that as soon as she gave birth to her, she promised her to the Devil, who in turn promised that he would treat her well and make her happy. From that moment she forsook God and promised to adore the Devil. At the same time, she had carnal relations with him (*copulation charnellement*) right up to her fiftieth year, which is how old she was when arrested. She stated that the Devil came to her whenever she felt like it, clad always the same and in the same form as when he appeared for the first time, with spurs, boots, a

61 In his Hague lectures, revealing various difficulties with the term sovereignty, Kelsen formulates the so-called rule of singularity (*l'unicité*, *Ausschließlichkeit*), a necessary characteristic of a sovereign regime. »The theory of the sovereignty of a state (…) leads us to the consequence that only one state can have the characteristic of highest judicial entity (*le caractère d'entité juridique suprême*), that the sovereignty of a state is incompatible with the sovereignty of another state and for that reason excludes the existence of the other state as a sovereign regime.« Kelsen: Les Rapports de Système entre le Droit Interne et le Droit International Public, p. 259. Six years prior, Kelsen determines the *Ausschließlichkeit* or *die Einzigkeit* of a sovereign state as pure analogy, i. e., a solipsistic consequence of subjectivism. Kelsen: Das Problem der Souveränität, p. 315.

sword, and on horseback before the door, and that no one saw him, save her. Also, he sometimes had relations with her unnoticed by her husband who slept in same bed next to her.[62]

The confession of this woman, which was changed and denied several times (without any coercion from the court, as he says), serves Bodin as the reckoning with pleasure and a way of controlling naked life. In his book on obsession with demons, he expounds freely on the idea that the Devil can make no one happy and that no one has made their fortune serving him. On the other hand, for the betrayal of the head of household and for intercourse with the Devil, the punishment is death. Reading these lines in the context of the sovereignty of the republic, which is what really interests Bodin, implies taking the stand by the head of household, his voyeurism, his clandestine cognizance, and pleasure. Pleasure could be marked as the key danger for the voluptuous body of sovereignty, or the voluminous sovereign home, but only as a symptom of an already divided and un-unified body. That pleasure could appear or be concealed in any segment of a sovereign (a »sovereign« entity) proves that sovereignty is not produced »in one piece«, that it is living, that it lives through another, that any part can come into independent and (un)authorized contact with another – stranger, enemy, a »high other«. Any portion could have pleasure because it is mortal, could give life, reproduce, spread, and take life of »people and animals«. Being with another in unauthorized ways, or with a falsified authorization (when the mother gives the mandate) or willingly (»the other came to her when she felt like it«), represents the betrayal of sovereignty, breaking of and breaking away from the household.

Bodin describes what is happening »behind the back« of the household sovereign. The house functions poorly because it is complex and divisible (*divisible*) (thus failing yet another criterion for sovereignty), and the head does not possess a monopoly on the use of violence, or monopoly on negotiating with a dangerous enemy. Along with Bodin's claim that the sovereign is the favorite target of Satan (if the sovereign is contaminated, so are the people; »the people are such as is the ruler«), or that the fight against Satan ought to begin with the sovereign, it becomes clear, again by analogy, that the act of »turning over« of mothers (wives) to a secret enemy is no more than a manifestation of the already essentially soiled head and lord of household by the Devil. Mutual friendship (*l'amitié mutuelle envers un chacun*[63]), devotion of women, and fear of the husband are achieved if a common enemy is produced: »The only way to maintain a popular state (*l'estas populaire*) is to conduct war and forge enemies (invent enemies; *forger des ennemis*), even when they are not at all there.«[64]

62 Bodin: Demonomanie contre les sorciers, Preface, s. p.

63 Bodin: Les six livres de la République, 4, p. 206.

64 Enemies ought to be cultivated and never fully destroyed, otherwise friends will begin warring among themselves and killing each other. Bodin Les six livres de la République, 4, pp. 34–35.

The genius of Bodin is in the manipulation of a theological matrix and the finding of a name for a form familiar to all, and which is latent in every home of the Republic and is enemy of all. The names »Devil«, »sorcerer« (»witch«), into which one could write all the potential difficulties of a sovereignty and life, represent the »natural enemies« or »enemies of the human race« or »malefactors«, because they are the great grinch.[65] This is the first cunning of Jean Bodin to prevent civil war. Later, in this same mold, peace or state alliance will be made possible with the discovery of pirates (or anarchists, or terrorists) as the main common enemy of humankind. The second strategy of Jean Bodin is elaborated upon in the fifth of *Les six livres de la République*.

The most beautiful way to preserve a state and safeguard from rebellion, uprising, and civil war, and to keep subjects in good friendship (*en bonne amitié*) is to have an enemy to face off to (*auquel on puisse faire teste*). (...) nor has more beautiful antidote (*antidote*) been found for civil war, nor safer medicine, than opposing the citizenry to the enemy. (...) fear of the enemy holds subjects obedient (*en devoir*). (...) it is useful for subjects to be brought before an enemy often, and not to accept peace except under very favorable conditions (...) and as for rapists, murderers, drones, vagrants, trouble makers, and thieves (...) the best way to clear the Republic of this filth is to send them to war, which is like a purging medicine (*medicine purgative*), and quite needed to clear the stench of the universal body of the Republic.[66]

There are multiple layers to the figure of sovereignty. But perhaps it is now possible to present some of the imbalances and confusions to which Leibniz was referring. First, sovereignty requires a sovereign tone for its secrets and functions to manifest themselves. Bodin, using thousands of examples from old books and legends, suggests a fantastical closing off of the community through its constant readiness for war. In order for the Republic to be sovereign (simple, indivisible, and one), it should be in a state of war, but without war or enemies. It should be continuously exposed to its own fictitious demise and ruin. In a word, whether it be a nit, little Dubrovnik, or Turkey, the Republic has to be in a state of illness and dying away. Its »destructibility«, however, is not to be found in the place from which Bodin wants to prevent and remove it – between parts (subjects). Rather, it is between the ruler and the subjects, between the sovereign and sovereignty, the head of state and the body, between the gaze of the Emperor and the horizon of the territory. In a further step, which perhaps surpasses all efforts both by Bodin and Leibniz, and one which could guarantee and substantiate a, let us provisionally call it, »world government«, the sovereign is closer to this fictitious enemy

65 »(...) *ils sont appellez ennemis de nature, ennemis du genre humain, & malefiques, pour les meschancetez grandes qu'ils font* (...)«. Bodin: Demonomanie contre les sorciers, Preface, s. p.

66 Bodin: Les six livres de la République, 5, pp. 137, 140, 142.

(enemies) than to his own body and his own sovereign government. The place of this »fictitious enemy« will a few centuries later be recognizable and replaced by another sovereign or group of sovereigns of great powers, and only then render visible the alienation of the world, the rift between sovereigns and global sovereignty. Indeed, how else can we explain the power of the sovereign to order an enemy (to determine the proportion of poison in the medicine), to organize his attack, or arrange an enemy bombing or war? Whence comes the power of the government to »shake up through war« an entity that was previously isolated?[67] This homeopathic strategy announced by Bodin, and echoed by Hegel, intuitively envisages a space in which the sovereign, if still sovereign, moves like a ghost even though it does not at all belong to him. Based on this fiction, the sovereign would have the scope and ability to control *the regulation* of its own governance over its own body, by using the power of another sovereignty and the force of the enemy.

Two characteristics of this fictitious theory of correcting sovereignty always imply pain and bloodshed in the name of the superlative. For the house to be a house, the whole whole, and the subject subject, it is essential to move and tilt the condition of the tautology, and take a portion of the whole and destroy it. The sovereign really does only worry about his own power (about the whole, and the connection between the parts, but not about every individual part), and the attribute sovereign refers only to that which is compact and stable. That which falls away, which is excluded, or which excludes itself (unfaithful wife, a rogue scientist, a bandit, even an unskillful sovereign, etc.) is completely worthless and rejected. The other characteristic is analogous to the first and refers to the calculation that a portion of the whole ought to fall off (be punished, sacrificed, or destroyed) and forever thrown away for the whole to remain unified. This second property concerns a hidden division and the controversy surrounding the territory (space, land), and a population currently living on a given territory. Bodin's stance that »the city is not made up of individuals or persons (*personnes*), but of the unity of the people living under a single sovereign rule« (*l'union d'un peuple sous une seigneurie souveraine*) could be upset and complemented by the claim that the space or the land of the city also complements or immortalizes the sovereign power. Then, the Republic or the city is made up of »the unity of the people living under a single sovereign rule« on a single territory. Sovereignty exists up to the point where the order is effective, to the point where there are those who obey and those who respond. Bodin (but not only him) becomes sensitive when, for one reason or another, the order ceases to be ›in effect‹ (acting or efficient) in some part of the house or territory of the Republic. Using strictly theological arguments, the sovereign then decides, as we have seen, to give priority to the integrity of the house or the territory at the expense of the lives of other household members or citizens.

[67] Hegel: Phänomenologie des Geistes, pp. 334–335.

The sovereign then ›appropriates‹ the territory and abolishes the key difference between »having sovereignty« over a territory and »ownership« of that same territory.[68] This reversal, a consequence of the ›materialization‹ of sovereignty (the sovereign is never satisfied with a divided or ›partial‹ sovereignty), always implies force and the use of violence.

To follow Leibniz, and yet to still imagine a small territory as it is described in old books, from erudition and from Jean Bodin, ought to have as its goal the reconstruction one of the greatest fantasies of the West and the submitting of the institution of sovereignty to a new and different name and form. Perhaps not to »gaze into the past« and not to »neglect what is happening presently«, as implored by Leibniz, would mean not only finding a new criterion to measure and discover a new entity – until now it was enough to measure according to others, and move toward or before them – but also accepting certain dicta from the past. Despite sovereignty itself, are not today Bodin's tiny Dubrovnik or the minute Republic of Geneva the exemplary forms of survival from the other side of sovereignty? Do these two ants not have, and have they not always had, a considerably safer future from the lumbering, bulky mammoths? Are not Corsica or Bavaria, Catalonia or Kosovo, Kurdistan or Andalusia already *names* that promise so much?

Imagining »the small«, emulating Bodin's two ants, ever between sovereignty and non-sovereignty, immediately announces a paradox. How can we imagine something small, how to envision and have measured thoughts, with borders, about something that is not already in danger from something large (or larger), and something not already divided or reduced for another yet smaller small? If we imagine the small, the first thing that we are abandoning is the sovereignty of the fiction. »To imagine«, or the »imagining« is already absolute and sovereign, based on its two characteristics: for a fiction to be declared a fiction, no one is ever allowed to deny its »fictitious content«. Something that would have to modify its potential existence with something else – larger or smaller than itself or smaller within itself – cannot be imagined. More precisely, that something, »the small«, can be conjured up and even exist, but it then abandons its »fictitious order«. This »small« is no longer a figment because it abolishes its highest (sovereign) property: that it is unthinkable and impossible. The other direction, which only emphasizes the circular moment of the first, is characterized by the necessity that the imagined can never be accomplished, but that it represents the only measure of everything, while remaining incomparable to everything that exists. Thus, to imagine the small at once limits (prevents) the small to be larger and incomparable, which in turn denies the function of the highest fiction to encourage the real to strive for the unimaginably large. If we imagine the small, »the small«

68 Vaughan Lowe writes about the difference between »having sovereignty« and »owning (that) territory«. Lowe: International Law, p. 138.

immediately defies the imagination and sovereign fantasies precisely because it is »small« and is discrepant to the size of the author of the fiction. Without the fantasy of the large and monstrous, there is no sovereign.

For the great »confusion regarding sovereignty« and the fantasy about the sovereign to finally be interrupted, Leibniz says, it would be good to deconstruct the fantasies, to read and heed authors and authority less (»erudition and role models«, »legal acts and articles«). What there ought to be more of is reasoning based on what has been experienced and lived, thinking in the interests of life. To side with Leibniz against Bodin at this moment means to be current, leading to being against both Bodin and Leibniz. The function of Leibniz would be to correct perhaps the last great indication of »superlatives« taking precedence over the »comparative«, and forgetting life force and victims. But not only that: Leibniz's interjection in the field of the »sovereign« and »sovereignty«, his reduction of these figures, precisely reveals them to have a warring nature, and shows that sovereignty follows special rights to wage war. Before I cite a few forgotten conditions for any future writing and »laying« claim to the word sovereignty, according to Leibniz, let me reiterate once again the little fiction about the »small« that has to survive and evidently come through the other side of sovereignty. This is the only goal.

Let us imagine the »small« which inexorably flows into something »larger« such as Europe with the contours of *Republica Christiana*, with the same outlines of Leibniz's dreary resistance towards Turkey. And let us imagine this small territory which in turn is torn apart because it contains another »small« (and another, and another ...). The smaller small is not annexed by something else, but it does necessarily enter and belong to the aforementioned larger, to Europe, even the world.

Leibniz's imaginary interjection into one such fiction anesthetized with Bodin and with a right to balance and equality of all territories in general, erasing the differences between the small and large, carries complete disorder and confusion. From the off, Leibniz's vision resolves the »hypocritical« moments in the relations between the small and the large (the rest). The small stops simulating the large, and the large no longer presents itself equal to the small. Peace and self-confidence are no longer sufficient conditions for sovereignty (»Sir, if you are sovereign for yourself, you are not such for others.«[69])

There follows a series of corrections and cautions by Leibniz, at one time meant to encourage rulers in efforts to be strong and large, but that could today only give hope to the small that only the small »free cities« will survive:

69 *Monsieur, si vous estes Souverain pour vous, vous ne l'estes pas pour les autres.* (Leibniz: Entretien de Philarete et d'Eugene, p. 306). »I am forced to admit that all the rulers of Kingdoms are equally free, but it does not seem to me that they are equally sovereign.« Ibid., p. 304.

a) In international law, personhood is held (*Personam juris Gentium habet*) by the one representing public freedom (*libertas publica*), and in such a way that he is not subject to tutelage or the rule of another, but has the right to wage war (*jus armorum*) and enter alliances; although (he can be) tied with a strong duty to a higher (than himself) and pay him tribute, faith, and obedience. If his authority is sufficiently large (*Quod si magna satis ejus sit autoritas*), let us call him *Potentatus*, and let us call the one holding the authority *souverain* and *potentat*; here is the moment of birth of right (*inter Potentatus*) which the Gauls call *souverainété*, in Latin *suprematus* (...) The one who has sufficient freedom and power to effect a certain influence (*cum autoritate intervenire posit*) in international transactions, by way of military or treaty – has his place among the powerful (*inter Potentatus*) and is granted sovereignty (*suprematum habere creditum*).[70]

Leibniz eats away or relativizes Bodin's theory of sovereignty in several ways. The position by which »he may be forced by a strong duty towards one stronger« (*quanquam forte obligationum vinculis superiori sit astrictus*) is a novelty that removes the absolute of any sovereign power. Competition and comparison with others, the ability to make coalitions and pacts, to influence other sovereigns (the community of sovereigns) had never been so explicitly stated. Further, Leibniz believes that »sovereignty« is proportional and prone to gradations, because he talks about the amount and comparability of influence or strength of one's »sovereign rule« (he uses the word *satis*, enough, twice). Leibniz renames Bodin's connection between the Latin *maiestas* and *souverainété*, because he finds the origin and translation of sovereignty in the Latin word *suprematus*.

b) An able man (*un habil homme*) explained to me the difference between Majesty (*la Majesté*) and sovereignty (*la souveraineté*). He says that *Majesté* (the highest right to order or highest legislative right) is the right to order and not to execute someone's orders; sovereignty, on the other hand, is legitimate power (*pouvoir legitime*) to subdue subjects into obedience while at the same time remaining unforced oneself, unless one is at war. Majesty is the highest and simple executive right (*le droit supreme et ordinaire d'execution*). For it is one thing to hold the right to order, and quite another to enforce the accepted law without difficulty. Hence the one who is sovereign, who alone holds power or shares it with a few others, should have the undisputed accepted right to maintain military forces and be capable to control them, gaining him recognition even from abroad (*et mémes de se rendre considerable par dehors*).[71]

Leibniz conducts a reformulation and transfer of the meaning of the word sovereignty, in several steps and on several levels. Sovereignty is less concerned with the order and more with efficiency and execution. More precisely, the *imperium*

70 Leibniz: Codex Juris Gentium Diplomaticus, pp. 74–75.

71 Leibniz: Entretien de Philarete et d'Eugene, pp. 308–309, 360.

already represents for Leibniz a certain power to force others and subdue them into obedience. Leibniz's »addition« is the introduction that allows the main characteristic of »sovereignty« to be found on the other side of »lawgiving« and simple »use of force«. The subtlety is in that sovereignty represents the right to military power (*jus manus miliratis*) by which an entire unit or territory is governed. The Lord of a region can have the right to legislate or to use various violent measures (e. g., the death penalty), but the Lord of a territory is only one who maintains a military on a large territory, by way of which he subjects the entire community (and not just individuals) to his rule (*sed totam aliquam communitatem expedienda vis erit, Dominum territorii implorabit*).[72] In addition, sovereignty is complemented and executed based on an acceptance (recognition) that always comes from without and from the other.

c) (...) and only those who have (hold) a large territory and who can amass an army (*qui territorium majus habent, exercitumque educere possunt*) can be called *Souverains* or *Potentats*. This is precisely what I call *Suprematum*. And when the Gauls reason about things regarding international law (*jus gentium*), here I am thinking of peace, war, or alliances, and when they name certain *Souverains*, they are not thinking of free cities (*urbibus liberis*) or about rulers of smallish territories that a rich merchant (*Mercator*) could easily acquire for himself, but about the great powers which could conduct war, sustain it (*bellum sustinere*), survive and remain, make an alliance, and are able to intervene in the affairs of other peoples with authority (*rebus aliarum gentium cum auctoritate intervenire possunt*).[73]

In explaining the difference between sovereignty and majesty of a territory (*la Superiorité territoriale*), Leibniz insists that there are degrees of Lordship or degrees of sovereign rule. The first is the legislative ruler (*Seigneur de Jurisdiction*), whose influence is quite limited for he holds no right to lead people into war, nor holds a military force that could act on the entire territory. Only the one who holds the highest position, the majesty, on a territory is capable of this. Then follows Leibniz's key differentiation: if the territory is small, an ordinary garrison can prevent any kind of disorder and rebellion, but the Lord of this territory has no influence outside the borders of his rule, when it comes to peace, war, foreign alliances or general affairs of Europe (*affaires generales de l'Europe*).

The latter is reserved for those who are Lords of especially important territories, and they can be called Sovereigns or Potentates. For it is indeed one thing to call oneself Sovereign, and quite another, speaking in the absolute (*absolument parlant*), to be sovereign of a certain place (*estre souverain d'un certain lieu*), i. e., to be the head of a certain territory.

72 Leibniz: De Jure Suprematus ac Legationis Principum Germaniae, p. 54.
73 Ibid., p. 56.

Leibniz renames Bodin's (Gaul) uses of the words »sovereign« and »sovereignty«, searching for the »absolute meaning« of the word »sovereign«, and at the same time searching for a sovereign who absolutely deserves this name. Leibniz insists on using power and real balance of forces as criteria when comparing various rulers on various territories. Leibniz's originality is precisely in comparing rulers or pseudo-sovereigns (the deconstruction of the superlative and introduction of the comparative), a method that reveals the military origin of these figures. If Bodin imagined, but never thematized peace in Europe by equating disproportional territories and powers through his use of the name of sovereign for both large and small rulers (a principle still valid in the Charter of the United Nations), it seems that it was Leibniz's insistence on the differences between various sovereigns that announces the true community of unequal rulers and a peace whose very foundation contains interventionism and interference in the affairs of other peoples. Leibniz's idea that others – not only the sovereigns of large territories and armies, but the community of all rulers and sovereigns – decide on space, power, and identity of a group of people that live together, remains current in international law to this very day. Leibniz's engagement announces the disappearance of the figure of the sovereign and the production of a great world governance, which is, paradoxically, one of the conditions of the existence of small-large cities without territories, and then without borders between them.

2 »*L'institution révolutionnaire*« (The Revolutionary Institution)

»Formons la cité«![74]
(Let Us Build the City!)

For Deleuze, the institution and/or the figure of the ›institution‹ are, without doubt, that which is positive. He is careless from the outset in differentiating the singular and plural of ›institution‹ and ›figure‹, allowing for the emergence of another problem with »*L'institution, (...) est un système préfiguré*«; »*L'institution, c'est le figure*«.[75] Nevertheless, there is not a single place where Deleuze treats the institution as an obstacle, as something ›petrified‹ and ›dead‹, nor where he calls for reconstruction, resistance, struggle, and tearing down of institutions. Even in *Anti-Oedipus* (1972), in which he develops detailed models of thinking the institution and institutional analysis, completely transforming the ›theory‹ of the institution from his first texts (fragments, really), Deleuze says that the great socialist utopias of the nineteenth century function as *»désinvestissement ou une »désinstitution« du champ social actuel*«, precisely to the advantage of a revolutionary institution of desire (*au profit d'une institution révolutionnaire du désir lui-même*).[76] Even twenty years earlier, while analyzing Hume and *›l'institution du gouvernement*‹, and really speaking about the correction of sovereignty, the right to resistance, and the legitimacy of revolution (*légitimité de la révolution*),[77] the goal is still the new and ideal institution. Institutions that ›deinstitutionalize‹ are not really institutions because they are determined by order and law (*les institutions légales et légalisés*).[78] That which is institutional ought likely to be that which is revolutionary. Conversely, it seems that the revolutionary should not be found anywhere outside the institution, or the revolution is, in one way or another, »the institutional revolution« (*la révolution institutionnelle*).

First, I am interested in the preference Deleuze has for the phrase *l'institution révolutionnaire* (revolutionary institution), as opposed to the less original

74 Saint-Just: Institutions républicaines, p. 1138.

75 Deleuze: Empirisme et subjectivité, p. 37, 39. This *›figuré‹* is translated into English as ›the figure‹ (»The institution is the figure«). Cf. Deleuze: Empiricism and Subjectivity, p. 49. The institution is figurative, not literal, or the institution marks the figurative (that which makes exist figures in a different place and becomes something else, something transformed). This figuring elsewhere represents institutionalization, while the institution is the completion of this process.

76 Deleuze: L'anti-Œdipe, p. 38.

77 Deleuze: Empirisme et subjectivité, p. 42.

78 Ibid., p. 74.

la révolution institutionnelle (institutional revolution).[79] Deleuze uses *l'institution révolutionnaire* in his texts, certainly completely aware that this phrase has a rather chaotic and vague history during post-revolutionary periods, but also that it is perfectly in the spirit of Saint-Just. We should investigate whether this phrase best describes Deleuze's imaginary theory of the institution,[80] as well as his engagement with the theory more generally. A much more serious task would consist of comparing Deleuze's theory of the institution, which emerges in the context of various influences of French phenomenology and philosophy of law, with Searle's and recent Anglo-American theories of the institution and the new institutionalism. The preliminary difficulty, which immediately questions and devalues my commentary, is Deleuze's own refusal to thematize the institution, thus refusing to answer his own questions from the 1950s: what is it that explains the institution (*ce qui explique l'institution*[81]) and »*quelles doivent* être *les institutions parfaites, c'est-à-dire celles qui s'opposent à tout contrat, et qui ne supposent qu'un minimum de lois?*« (what are perfect institutions like? That is, those that oppose all contracts and assume the bare minimum of laws?)[82] Deleuze's responses are inspired and suggestive, but rudimentary. For example, »*Les lois lient les actions; elles les immobilisent, et les moralisent. De pures institutions sans lois seraient par nature des modèles d'actions libres, anarchiques, en mouvement perpétuel, en révolution permanente, en état d'immoralité constante.*« (Laws tie down actions; they immobilize and moralize them. Pure institutions, free of laws, would be the very model of free action: anarchic, in perpetual motion, permanent revolution, in a constant state of immorality.)[83] But he writes too quickly and carelessly, without differentiating among influences and fragments copied or taken over from Hume, Saint-Just, de Sade, Renard, Hauriou, Durkheim, Malinowski, and others. In the end, he succeeds in relegating to oblivion his ingenious project from 1953, *Instincts et institutions.* Of course, the consequences of such writing and theoretical work call into question the status of theory within the framework of institutions and within the actions of revolutionary changes to institutions. (Who changes institutions, who purifies and who sullies them, and who, at all, is the subject of institutionalization or deinstitutionalization?) Also – and this is precisely our problem – Deleuze's carelessness and (effectively) abandonment of his own early attempt at thinking the institution could possibly imply that his intuition and recognition that the thematization of the institution remains an impossible task. After all, did John Searle also not show that a

79 Deleuze: Présentation de Sacher-Masoch, p. 80.
80 A theory of the institution is certainly impossible. Cf. Castoriadis: Figures du pensable, p. 115.
81 Deleuze: Empirisme et subjectivité, p. 38.
82 Deleuze: Présentation de Sacher-Masoch, p. 80.
83 Ibid., p. 79.

theory of institutions has not yet been constructed and that its development is still in its infancy?[84]

Still, despite ›institutional‹ or perhaps even ›un-/ extra-/ anti-institutional‹ resistance, let us attempt to explain this impossibility, that is, let us attempt to think the systematic integration of the institution into the framework of the great and pioneering work of Saint-Just, Hume, Deleuze, Gehlen, and Searle. Let us assume, with Saint-Just, that neglecting to systematically think about institutions means, first, an obstacle in founding a republic and building revolutionary institutions. If we sought Gilles Deleuze's main contribution to a future imaginary theory of the institution – built on his forceful use of the phrase *l'institution révolutionnaire* that incorporates the efforts of Hume, Saint-Just, or de Sade – it is his insistence that a kind of reversal and sudden turn, the perversion of *something*, is carried out by the institution, within the institution or within institutionalization. Let us call this revolutionary. The pure institution or a permanently revolutionary institution – new concepts left to us by Deleuze – abolish, for example, corruption in the republic[85] or they re-appropriate non-institutionalized spaces into the republic. They transform or force the transformation of anything that is *limited* or in some way *particular*.[86] By contrast, the impotence of systematic thinking or the impotence of institutionalization (since this is a process that ›institutionalizes‹ everything, including that which confronts or opposes it), paradoxically, shows that we are still in a truly pre-institutional, pre-revolutionary, time; we are in Saint-Just's time. Our eternal contemporary, Saint-Just detects two phenomena or two entities outside of institutions, which only the (revolutionary) institution can incorporate and resolve: terror and corruption. We can confirm that these two forms of violence – treading carefully regarding the as of yet completely uncharted relation between corruption and violence – continue to oppose the institution, representing perhaps its main challenges. Already in Hume, Deleuze uncovers – although he fails to fully thematize it – the great beginning of the story of violence as the source and origin of the institution and order. Well before Hegel and Engels, and

84 Searle: What is an institution?, p. 22. Hugh Heclo showed this problem analyzing twenty-one definitions of the institutions (in fact there are many more) which are currently used. Cf. Heclo: On Thinking Institutionally, pp. 48–51.

85 »*La terreur peut nous débarrasser de la monarchie et de l'aristocratie; mais qui nous délivrera de la corruption? Des institutions. On ne s'en doute pas; on croit avoir tout fait quand on a une machine à gouvernement* (...)« (Terror can rid us of the monarchy and the aristocracy; but who will save us from corruption? Institutions, surely. It would appear that all is done when we have governance machine ...). Saint-Just: Institutions républicaines, p. 1135. Cf. Deleuze (ed.): Instincts et institutions, p. 35.

86 Deleuze's engagement is different from Merleau-Ponty's, as is his reconstruction of Husserl's *Stiftung* and re-institutionalization. For Merleau-Ponty the revolution is something already set in the *foundation*, in the first violence. The revolution is »*réinstitution, aboutissant à renversement d'institution précédente*« (the re-institutionalization, the accomplishment of overturning the previous institution. Cf. Merleau-Ponty: L'institution, p. 42.

much before Benjamin and then Balibar,[87] Hume discovers that violence always goes before the contract in establishing and giving institutions their dynamic.

Deleuze's Hume, Deleuze's Saint-Just

It is entirely possible to reconstruct Deleuze's effort and his difficulties regarding the institution based on the sixty-six fragments from his collection *Instincts et institutions*.[88] The Introduction[89] and a few pages and fragments he wrote allow only the recognition of the advantage Deleuze gives certain authors. He includes two passages from Hume, which he will later analyze elsewhere, and the famous paragraphs by Saint-Just about *»institutions, mœurs et loi«* (institutions, customs, and law). Further, a few fragments on institutions and organization from Buytendijk and Halbwachs. From Hauriou, Deleuze takes the differentiation between institution and personification, from Renard the difference between contract and institution (which he then wrongly attributes to Hume), from Lévi-Strauss and Frazer the relationship between instinct and propensity (*tendance*) on the one hand, and institution on the other. From Durkheim he learns that enforcement is the main characteristic of the institution, from Malinowski the link between the institution and the means, and between charter (*charte*) and institution.[90] It is also possible to show oversights and hesitations, what he did not do and what

87 A long text on violence that explains the process of ›conversion‹ (and reversal) of violence into an institution. Balibar: Violence et civilité, p. 48, 66, etc.

88 Deleuze collected portions of various texts about institution and intuition. The book contains writings by Malinowski, Alain, Hume, Levi-Strauss, Kant, Frazer, Freud, Eliade, Plekhanov, Bergson, Goldstein, Saint-Just, Renard, Bachofen, Comte, Marx and many others. It appears that Deleuze translated only four fragments from English (for example Malinowski and Frazer), while most fragments are taken from already existing French translations. Deleuze's early texts and intentions were discussed inspiringly by Guillaume Sibertin-Blanc in his doctoral thesis *Politique et clinique* (Political and Clinical), defended in 2006 (pp. 48–74, etc.). Cf. Esposito: Pensiero istituente, pp. 75–155.

89 The short »Introduction« (p. viii–xi) was republished in the magazine *Philosophie* (no. 65, 2000) and in the book *L'île déserte.*

90 Cf. Deleuze (ed.): *Instincts et institutions*, p. 4–5. The sentence from the Introduction, *»L'institution se présente toujours comme un système organisé de moyens«* is in fact a sentence from Malinowski, *»The institution as the organized means of realizing the values* (...)«, not translated by Deleuze (Cf. Malinowski: Freedom and Civilization, p. 157). The two Malinowski passages found at the very beginning explain the socio-psychological moment in Deleuze's explanations of the institution. Social institutions exist to ›answer‹ or ›meet‹ psychological needs, and every institution possesses *personnel, a charter, a set of norms, activities, apparatus, functions*, etc. Deleuze later uses the term ›charter‹ (which he could have also encountered in Renard's 1939 book *La philosophie de l'institution*), which gives universality of structure to an institution, in a book dedicated to Foucault: »An institution includes its own utterances, such as a constitution, a charter, agreements, inscriptions, and records« (*Une institution comporte elle-même des énoncés, par exemple une constitution, une charte, des contrats, des inscriptions et enregistrements*). Deleuze: Foucault, p. 19.

remains to be done. For example, it is necessary to come back to that place in the *Introduction* where Deleuze asks about the institution of the state, towards which there is no propensity (*auxquelles ne correspond nulle tendance*). What does the state as an institution satisfy in the first place? Or what is the position of the state in the order of institutions (for Searle, as well as Carl Schmitt, the state is the *ultimate institutional structure*, while Renard recognizes a federal state which he calls the institution of institutions)? We ought to read again and anew Deleuze's sudden conclusion of *Empirisme et subjectivité*, specifically the page that contains the line »what explains the institution is not propensity, but the reflection of propensity in the imagination« (*ce qui explique l'institution, ce n'est pas la tendance, mais la réflection de la tendance dans l'imagination*).[91] Whence all of a sudden imagination? Still, to explain his discovery or sketch of a ›new‹ interpretation of the institution, we need to formulate a theory about Deleuze's ›interruption‹, that is, abandonment of work. This ›interruption‹ means that Deleuze, without huge complications, is able to make use of his early research in his later ›theories of institutional analysis‹, and that he is able to somehow grasp ›the essence‹ of the institution, while at the same time showing the difficulties and limits of its thematization. The results of research from the fifties can ›in effect‹ be found later, primarily in his work in the eighties: in his model of constructing his arguments, or the movement of thought and sequence of terms, and we could call it ›institutionalization‹ or ›reversal‹ (*renversement*). Deleuze might have found the origin of this method in those sixty-six fragments about the institution, a mixed influence of Hume and Saint-Just, but also in conscious or unconscious opposition to all classical forms of dialectical and Hobbesian understandings of the institution. The lack of Hobbes among Deleuze's passages means the rejection of a specific use of the verb ›to institute‹, which Hume himself ignores and relegates in importance. In Hobbes, ›to institute‹ means to decide, to begin something with determination.[92] It is the decisive subjective act of starting something (out of nothing), which is actually opposite (but analogous) to the creation of nature and an act committed by Hobbes' active subject.[93] The uncertainty of the subject, but also the sudden appearance of the object of institutionalization (*institué*)[94] is achieved through at least three simultaneous and complementary operations. Ignoring the sovereign

91 Deleuze: Empirisme et subjectivité, p. 38.

92 Cf. Rangeon: Approche de l'institution dans la pensée de Hobbes, pp. 92–93.

93 Hobbes' use of *›to institute‹* harkens back to the Medieval meaning of the term *›institutio‹* (an order or command). It is interesting that Pufendorf in *De iure naturali et gentium* uses the word *impositionis* (imposition) in this sense, which the French translator, Barbeyrac translates as *l'institution*. Since he cannot find an equivalent in French for *impositionis*, he is forced to defend his solution. »(...) we use institution most often for that which is invented and established, as opposed to coming from nature. (...) our author (Pufendorf) wants to say when he posits that in fact moral things are such by imposition, and not in themselves or by nature.« Cf. Orestano: »Institution«, pp. 175–176.

94 Cf. Deleuze: Trois problèmes de groupe, p. 274.

act of founding the social form by presenting it as a contract: because the latter is between some two sides coming to agreement, as opposed to a sovereign decision. Then, by introducing multiple subjects or a group (a collective), whose members together ›accomplish‹ the process of institutionalization or ›legalization‹ of, say, property. And finally, the discovery that the decision or institutionalization is neither perfect nor complete. Why institutionalization (or institution) is not perfect and hence not sovereign, is shown by Hume explicitly in two places, which Deleuze knows very well, but never analyzes. Whatever else they show, they also highlight the significance of translation: the reversal of ›institution‹ from Latin to English and back into French:

Time and custom give authority to all forms of government, and all successions of princes; and that power, which at first was founded only on injustice and violence, becomes in time legal and obligatory.[95]

Time, by degrees, removes all these difficulties, and accustoms the nation to regard, as their lawful or native princes, that family, which, at first, they considered as usurpers or foreign conquerors. In order to found this opinion, they have no recourse to any notion of voluntary consent or promise, which, they know, never was, in this case, either expected or demanded. The original establishment was formed by violence, and submitted to from necessity. The subsequent administration is also supported by power, and acquiesced in by the people, not as a matter of choice, but of obligation.[96]

Probably no one prior to Hume says and reiterates as clearly as this that ›violence and injustice‹ are at the beginning, that is, that Hobbes' *to institute* or his own *to establish* are completely infused with violence. However trivial this demystification of the ›sovereign‹ and ›institutional act‹ may seem today, Hume will forever change the accent from the institution as such or the sovereign who founds the institution, to the process of institutionalization (a verb) and the object (that which is being institutionalized, *institué*, as well as that which can be institutionalized). Hume's intervention will be a preamble of any future, no less important, finesse and nuance in thinking the institution, including various theories of ›counter-institutions‹, which can be followed from Saint-Simon to Durkheim and Derrida, complex theories dealing with institutions (and customs) not established by norms, or indeed those in which the origin of social institutions lies in conditions in which there is no common will for their establishment (for example, the institutions of money, language, the market, law, etc.).

What does Hume do? How was the perspective or the accent changed from ›the institution‹ to ›the institutionalized‹ (*institué*)? Further, how does Deleuze read Hume, and then how does he combine this question with, above all, Saint-Just?

95 Hume: A Treatise of Human Nature, p. 566.
96 Hume: Of the Original Contract, pp. 474–475.

The answer to these questions should justify my insistence that Deleuze uses and transforms Hume's intervention or discovery of the drama of ›institutionalization‹ (whereby something *forcibly* changes from one thing to another), into the main mode of execution of his argument and his analysis. In other words, in the Introduction, institutions »transform propensity itself by introducing them into a new context« (*transforment la tendance elle-mêmes en introduisant dans un milieu nouveau*),[97] at once forcing, oppressing,[98] and satisfying a desire. The gerund turns into the passive voice with »space instituted by the state apparatus« (*l'espace institué par l'appareil d'Etat*),[99] and then into practice, into the discovery of a noun – institutionalization, stratification – derived from the verb to institute. Deleuze formulates all this in the following way:

Institutions are not sources or essences, and they do not have essences or interiorities. They are practices, operational mechanisms that do not explain power: having merely a reproductive (and not productive) function, they assume and merely stabilize power relations. There is no State, only stratification, which also goes for all other cases.

(*Les institutions ne sont pas des sources ou des essences, et elles n'ont ni essence ni intériorité. Ce sont des pratiques, des mécanismes opératoires qui n'expliquent pas le pouvoir, puisqu'elles en supposent les rapports et se contentent de les »fixer«, sous une fonction reproductrice et non productrice. Il n'y a pas d'Etat, mais seulement une étatisation, et de même pour les autres cas.*)[100]

Even though Deleuze's and Foucault's common insights into institutions incorporate Saint-Just's and de Sade's visions of new, future institutions[101] dominated by »a dynamic model of action, power, and force« (*un modèle dynamique d'action, de pouvoir et de puissance*),[102] they would not exist without those of Hume. Both Hume and Saint-Just construct the institution as a big, common action that unfolds in unfinished time. And time is precisely the key difference between the institution and a contract. Deleuze writes about this inspiringly, without mentioning Hume:

We are aware of the legal difference between the contract and the institution: the former, in principle, supposes the will of the parties involved and defines a system of mutual rights and responsibilities, does not refer to some third and has a period of validity. The latter, on

97 Deleuze (ed.): Instincts et institutions, p. 24.

98 Cf. Deleuze: Empirisme et subjectivité, p. 37.

99 Deleuze: Mille plateaux, p. 592.

100 Deleuze: Foucault, p. 82.

101 Cf. Deleuze: Pensée nomade, pp. 353–354. »Three principal means of coding: law, coding, and the institution. (...) And then there is the third kind of book, the political, preferably revolutionary, which presents itself as a book of institutions, either those extant or to come.« (*Trois principaux moyens de codage: la loi, le codage et l'institution. (...) Et puis il y a une troisième sorte de livres, le livre politique, de préférence révolutionnaire, qui se présente comme un livre d'institutions, soit d'institutions présentes, soit d'institutions à venir*).

102 Deleuze: Présentation de Sacher-Masoch, p. 78.

the other hand, defines an open-ended status, involuntary and unbreakable, constitutive of power, force, and results in opposition to some third.

(*On connâit la distinction juridique entre le contrat et l'institution: celui-là en principe suppose la volonté des contractants, définit entre eux un système de droits et de devoirs, n'est pas opposable aux tiers et vaut pour une durée limitée; celle-ci tend à définir un statut de longue durée, involontaire et incessible, constitutif d'un pouvoir, d'une puissance, dont l'effet est opposable aux tiers.*)[103]

A multitude makes institutions or the people makes an institution (*l'institution des peuples*[104]), and this work happens before everyone's eyes, in public, it concerns everyone, like the republic. In both fragments quoted above, Hume points out that time, before the eyes of a multitude, gradually hides (or reveals) what is at the root of power and establishments. Over time, again gradually, the process of institutionalization happens, and the reversal of violence and injustice into stable forms takes place; forms which bind not only those who participate in the original violence and injustice, but also all those who will in due course become members of a given community (›other parties‹, those third [*tiers*]). Hume thus recognizes two processes: the silhouette of violence and injustice within the power of institutions, *underneath* institutions, which is the process of ›founding‹ (»was founded only on injustice and violence«), and the process of ›forming‹ (»was formed by violence«), claiming that several factors will contribute to the fading of this silhouette, and its eventual ›institutionalization‹. And although it seems that the key factors in the realization of this second process are time (its passage) and the common engagement of the multitude – there is no institution without the pressed, controlled, obligated, forced, bound,[105] etc. – it is necessary to add that the process of ›institutionalization‹ is *a priori* expansive, and never partial. Everyone must be engaged, and every form of violence abolished. There is nothing that is *outside* the institution. To prevent or stop violence that destroys parts of the community and forcibly occupies objects and territory, violence that comes from simple egotism and personal limitation, Hume thinks that it is necessary to stabilize the given establishment together, and that the result of this process will be power, i. e., the *institution* as manifestation of power. Hume differentiates between *establishment* and *institution*, a difference Deleuze or French translators do not detect, but which could, paradoxically, explain everything we owe

103 Ibid., pp. 77–78. This slightly changed interpretation of Renard's difference between the institution and the contract is ›pressed‹ by Deleuze's both early and later attempts to construct an implicitly Humean differentiation between contract and institution. Cf. Deleuze: Empirisme et subjectivité, pp. 35–37; Deleuze: Hume, p. 232.

104 Saint-Just: Institutions républicaines, p. 1091.

105 »He who has no friends is banished.« »He who has no faith in friendship is banished.« »If he commits a crime, his friends are banished.« (*Si un homme n'a point d'amis, il est banni. Celui qui dit qu'il ne croit pas à l'amitié est banni. Si un homme commet un crime, ses amis sont bannis*). Ibid., pp. 1102–1103.

Saint-Just.[106] Terror and corruption, the two ›forms‹ of violence that are outside the institution, or have yet to be institutionalized, according to Saint-Just, are in the exact place of Hume's analyses: in places of prepositions *under (establishment)* and *outside (institution)*. When institutions become damaged or perverted (*perverti*),[107] when people and human nature sully them, when they become occupied by perversion (another word Hume uses) and corruption, it is then possible to recognize that at the origin of these *establishments* lies that same terror or violence (killing, robbing, etc.). Violence and terror become visible *elements* of order and the institution (for example, the institution of property, which greatly interests Hume, and which Deleuze, along with obedience, analyzes carefully in reading *A Treatise of Human Nature* and *An Enquiry Concerning the Principles of Morals*) when they seem insufficient to prevent the opposition to the process of institutionalization: their reversal or revolution.

Of Reversal (*Renversement*)

Let us assume that the ›deformation‹ or ›perversion‹ that Hume writes about, and which is caused by people and their corruptible human nature, is what marks the failure of reversal and a misguided revolution. There ends up being no revolutionary institution because not everyone is engaged in a process of grouping or cooperation, there are still those who are passive, who are in the way, to whom Saint-Just often refers and earnestly explains the importance of their engagement. The idea that someone is missing, and is beyond the control and pressure of the group, the idea that there is no group or collective (institutional) responsibility, is truly an important condition for violence to forever be institutionalized, meaning erased and transformed. This dynamic process presumes no exception, no special case (no state of emergency): everyone working together and engaged *in toto* in the creation and formation of the city – a conception that suits Hume's and Saint-Just's use of the word *institution*. When Hume uses two other words, *institution* and *establishment*, which imply that the violence has stopped, his intention may have been to construct two different moments or steps in the undertaking of legalization of ownership acquired by way of violence. The first step, Hume calls it *establishment*, implies the building of power (the change of force or violence into

106 In the most important place where he thematizes the institution in *Empirisme et subjectivité*, Deleuze first drops an important portion of the section from Hume's *An Enquiry Concerning the Principles of Morals*, and then quotes Hume from *The Treatise of Human Nature* (page 620 in the French translation): »*Bien que l'institution de la règle sur la stabilité de la possession soit non seulement utile* (…)« (p. 37), while the original reads: »*Tho' the establishment of the rule* (…)«.

107 Hume: A Treatise of Human Nature, pp. 549–553.

power) through stabilizing the given state immediately after the various crimes took place. This step is simultaneously the birth of the institution of property (this is Hume's term, although elsewhere he uses the institution of social property) and becomes binding for all social actors. He particularly emphasizes the factor of time, which refers to the gradual expansion of institutionalization to all, their inclusion and binding. Here is how Saint-Just and Deleuze understand this process:

Institutions ought to substitute force and the inflexible justice of laws that are subject to personal influence. Only then is the revolution consolidated: there are no more jealousies or factions, no more pretensions or libel.
The aim of institutions is to establish all the social and individual guarantees that would guard against dissent and violence; to substitute ascendancy of traditions with the ascendancy of man.

(*Il faut substituer, par les institutions, la force et la justice inflexible des lois à l'influence personnelle. Alors la révolution est affermie: il n'y a plus de jalousies, ni de factions: il n'y a plus de prétentions ni de calomnies.*
Les institutions ont pour objet d'établir de fait toutes les garanties sociales et individuelles, pour éviter les dissensions et les violences; de substituer l'ascendant des mœurs à l'ascendant des hommes.[108]

Institutions ought to stand in for, replace something that precedes them (violence, force, or whatever else divides people), and only after is the revolution actualized and fully executed. The complete prevention of violence and force through institutions both caps the revolution and is revolutionary. At the same time, institutions prevent conflict and violence, which are the result of an insufficiently actualized ›replacement‹. Saint-Just obviously thinks that this process of replacement of violence with institutions occurs within a certain timeframe, within which the dynamics and activity within institutions can be explained. Deleuze uses the same verb as Saint-Just:

A moral world affirms its reality when the contradiction is effectively resolved, when it is possible to substitute a conversation for violence, when property replaces greed (...) To be in society is above all substituting violence with potential conversation.

(*Le monde moral affirme sa réalité quand la contradiction se dissipe effectivement, quand la conversation est possible et se substitue à la violence, quand la propriété se substitue à l'avidité (...) Etre en société, c'est d'abord substituer la conversation possible à la violence.*)[109]

Writing about Hume, Deleuze is channeling Saint-Just. Thanks to his mixture of two different registers and two different commentaries, it is clear that Deleuze announces yet again (although neither explicitly nor without reserve) ›the subject‹ of institutionalization. It is, however, completely different from Hobbes' subject.

108 Saint-Just: Institutions républicaines, p. 1091.
109 Deleuze: Empirisme et subjectivité, pp. 27, 29.

To be part of society or to be together presupposes ›the substitution‹ of revolutionary institutions for violence. All I could add is to perhaps tentatively list the conditions and give the framework of this task that remains untouched from Saint-Just to Deleuze. It seems that this sketch of turning violence into institutions can only be successful if it carefully positions different forms of violence within this revolutionary theater:

a. the substitution is violent or the institutionalization is violent if it does not only consist of one act that births or founds a new order or *establishment*, but rather comprises many permanent actions and acts that become more complicated over time. Institutionalization reveals the violence that precedes it and which it has interrupted (raw violence or terror), as well as violence which is opposed to it (corruption).
b. three types of violence, different in form and strength, determine the number of actors who perform it. Violence is minimized in the process of institutionalization because it is performed by all or by the largest possible number of actors.
c. violence of institutionalization is violence undergoing conversion.[110] Violence of founding (*fondation*) and violence of terror are transformed (translated, transposed, reversed, substituted) into the coercion of rules, into symbolic or institutional pressure.
d. the revolutionary institution supposes that there is no violence which has not been turned into the ›body‹ of the institution, leaving no remainder, and therefore nothing outside the institution.

Annex I: *La violence extrême, la violence institutionnelle* (Balibar)

I would like to consider a few problems and questions regarding violence and the institution, that is, extreme violence. First, I would like to mention some problems Etienne Balibar speaks about in his Wellek Library Lectures (held May 6–9, 1996) and writes about in the Introduction of *Violence and Civility*, and which he says he was able to resolve in the book itself. Namely, in several seminars at Nanterre in 1998, 1999, even 2000, he analyzes in detail Hegel's interpretation of violence. In a personal letter sent to me in November 2000, written in a tone of his customary kindness and abiding trust, Balibar is attempting to answer a question posed earlier in his seminar. Where, then, is this fragment in Hegel about the *conversion* of violence? (This was, in a certain way, the topic of my dissertation.) Balibar writes:

110 Cf. Balibar: Violence et civilité, p. 48.

I've looked for the passage in the Introduction to the Lectures on the Philosophy of History from which I took the idea of »conversion of violence«, or rather, confirmation that Hegel himself used this phrase: I must say that the results are rather meager, because not only is it not a single phrase, but also the original German term translated into French loses some of the connotations (although it is itself interesting – *verkehrt* becomes *Verkehrung*, that is, conversion or inversion, a term that will later in Marx play an important role in the theory of political-religious alienation, but that is by the by); in French, the passage is on page 201 of the Papaioannou edition (vol. 10/18): »Ceux qui ont résisté, par conviction éthique, et donc par noblesse morale, à ce que le progrès de l'Idée de l'Esprit rendait nécessaire, se situent, du point de vue de la valeur morale, plus haut que ceux dont les crimes sont convertis, dans un ordre supérieur, en moyens d'exécution de la volonté de cet ordre supérieur etc.« In German (in the Hoffmeister edition, Felix Meiner Verlag, Hamburg 1955), it reads: »deren Verbrechen in einer höhern Ordnung zu Mitteln verkehrt worden wären, den Willen dieser Ordnung ins Werk zu setzen«.[111]

That we find no place in Hegel where violence is explicitly »converted« into something else (Gadamer, who wrote a text on *Verkehrung* would have surely otherwise found it in Hegel) does not, in my opinion, call into question Balibar's project of reconstructing violence that cannot be converted. Nor does either mention of the term in Hegel endanger the project, such that it would deserve particular attention. In *Aesthetics*, Hegel speaks of bad negation, which serves nothing but the negative.[112] He reveals that something does indeed unfold entirely outside of history, yet that it also makes no sense. Be that as it may, Hegel nevertheless forecasts violence that cannot be converted and encompassed institutionally.

The elegance of Balibar's argument (which could not be clearer, even if I am at the same time certain that his argument is less clearly laid out compared to Anglo-American reconstructions of institutions and institutionalisms, including Axel Honneth's position), as well as perhaps the limits of the argument, are both to be found in the fact that Balibar's thinking could indeed satisfy two or all three great traditions of working on the relation of force and violence on the one hand, and justice, law, order, and the institution, on the other. Does this mean that this

111 J'ai recherché le passage de la »Raison dans l'Histoire« dont j'avais tiré l'idée de »conversion de la violence«, ou plus exactement l'affirmation que Hegel lui-même employait cette formule: je suis obligé de reconnaître que le résultat est assez mince, car non seulement il s'agit d'une seule phrase, mais encore le terme allemand qui a été ainsi traduit en français ne comporte pas exactement les mêmes connotations, même s'il est aussi intéressant (verkehrt donne Verkehrung, donc renversement ou inversion, un terme qui par exemple chez Marx joue un grand rôle dans la théorie de l'aliénation politico-religieuse, mais ceci est une autre affaire); en français, le passage est p. 201 de l'édition Papaioannou (collection 10/18): »Ceux qui ont résisté, par conviction éthique, et donc par noblesse morale, à ce que le progrès de l'Idée de l'Esprit rendait nécessaire, se situent, du point de vue de la valeur morale, plus haut que ceux dont les crimes sont convertis, dans un ordre supérieur, en moyens d'exécution de la volonté de cet ordre supérieur etc.« en allemand (j'utilise l'édition Hoffmeister, Felix Meiner Verlag, Hamburg 1955), on lit p. 171: »deren Verbrechen in einer höhern Ordnung zu Mitteln verkehrt worden wären, den Willen dieser Ordnung ins Werk zu setzen«.

112 Hegel: Vorlesungen über die Ästhetik, p. 288.

problem is entirely artificial?[113] Jean Bodin already used the phrase ›force and violence‹ systematically, as if aware of the insufficiency of the French word *violence*, that is, the advantage of the German *Gewalt*, which Balibar constantly invokes. Says Bodin: »the state is founded in history and is based on *force and violence*« (*L'État est de fondation historique et repose sur* la force et la violence), and again »reason and natural intelligence show us that force and violence are at the origin of republics« (*La raison et lumière naturelle nous conduit à cela, de croire que la force et violence a donné source et origine aux Républiques*).[114]

Regardless of the fact that I am certain of the impossibility of reconstruction of this great fantasy that violence and (/or) force produce justice, or that it inverts or converts and institutionalizes, it seems to me possible to claim that in addition to those who think that violence transforms into something else and those who think that it absolutely does not transform into anything else (such as Rousseau or Jacobi) – there is a third option: the revolutionary position of Saint-Just or Lenin's dictatorship of the proletariat. Both assume destructive violence; yet, while Saint-Just carefully separates the terror that destroys enemies and institutions that eradicate corruption (humanize relations among people, civilize them) – that is, terror or extreme violence do not mix with institutions in the narrow sense of the word – for Lenin, the dictatorship of the proletariat excises and fiercely destroys the enemies of the revolution. In other words, aside from the distinction made by Machiavelli between violence that amends and changes something (I do not know how we can understand »conversion« in a minimal form) and violence that destroys, I would like to oppose two fantasies to each other: one is that there is some kind of systematic conversion of violence (with or without remainder). The other is equally phantasmagoric: that violence never changes shape and does not transfer into anything else, nor can be hidden in law, order, or justice (such as Jacobi's insistence that *Gewalt* has never produced any truth nor brought anything good to people anywhere[115]).

113 Walter Benjamin's text, for which Balibar says that it contains »stunning, but obscure statements« (*formulations frappantes mais obscures*), is an example of discord between what Balibar calls »semi-axiomatic semi-argumentation« (*mi-axiomatique mi-argumentation*). In Benjamin's text, absolute violence that destroys (extreme violence) is the one God deploys to destroy Korah and his group (the first leftist and first real rebellion in history).

114 Bodin also writes about »extreme violence«, which for him is violence that accomplishes truly grand feats. In a few places, Bodin says that it is indeed the means, the last means, to subdue natural laws (*les lois de nature*). In another place in his book on the republic, he says that »we have seen the Kingdoms of Sweden, Scotland, Denmark, England, the Confederation of Switzerland, and the German Empire change religion, yet maintaining their states, whether republic or monarchy; yet, in truth this was done but only with extreme violence and much letting of blood in many places.« Bodin: Six livres de la République, p. 399.

115 Jacobi: Über Recht und Gewalt, pp. 259–290.

Annex II: Politics, Political Institutions, and (Sartre's) *»univers de violence«*

Two problems: the first is ›politics and violence‹, and the other is ›cosmopolitanism and violence‹. In both cases, the problems concern the copula ›and‹. The first problem is the connection between politics and violence. I do not think politics and violence are separate, and even less that politics stands in opposition to violence, or that it ought to replace violence. My second problem is the connection and the nature of the connection between cosmopolitanism and violence. I find problematic the idea that only politics ought and should oppose violence, that politics is the ›antidote‹ to violence, that it is necessary to revive politics in order to restore institutions, and that we all have to send a strong appeal to one another, to build a new *polis*, a new city, and new politics. What is needed for an idea like this to be constructed is for all around us to be reduced to violence (for all to see violence all around us, we all confirm that all is force and violence), while at the same time recognize the terrifying danger from violence. In an early text on violence, from the fifties, speaking of a Fichtean comment about »legitimate violence« and the right to violence in the state (which justifies the very existence of the state) or the right to legitimate violence in politics (*la violence legitime dans la sphere politique*), Paul Ricœur writes: »I would then like to show how the political life provokes an escalation of violence under the guise of legitimacy (war, revolution), splitting morality in two: the commandment to love and the painful birthing of history through legitimate violence.«[116]

In my doctoral thesis, as well as in books that followed it, I was not only interested in these provocations and transformations of politics and rights into violence and back – the conversion of violence and force into right or justice, the ›erasure‹ and ›obscuring‹ of violence through law – but also two other moments. I was, first, interested in the manipulation, or chemistry, of the kind and amount of violence: how much violence is needed to create the first Messianic peace? How much more force is needed to eradicate violence and force? Is violence one form of messianic action? Second, a particularly important question for me is whether there is virtue in violence, or put otherwise, whether violence is necessarily morally wrong (which would mean that it is not only justified to defend oneself, but also inflict

116 »*Je voudrais ensuite montrer comment la vie politique, provoque un éclatement de la violence sous les bornes de la légitimité (guerre, révolution) et casse la morale en deux, entre le commandement d'amour et l'enfantement douloureux de l'histoire par la violence illégitime.*« Ricœur: Le problème de la violence, p. 7.

harm and physical injury on another person or persons). As you can see, at first glance, all such protocols contradict the idea of separating politics and violence.

What, then, are we doing when we make a strong appeal for politics? Above all, we are announcing and engaging with a new politics, beyond violence (or announcing a peaceable Messiah beyond war). If we were to imagine a new city, a new *polis*, and the politics we are dreaming (politics as the glue that keeps us, the community together) ought to shape that new city, new *agora* – to be a *polis* beyond *stasis* (as the opposite of *polemos*, *stasis* is latent conflict, whereas *disputatio* or a kind of violence that is the basic characteristic of an ancient people, a violence that holds the city in potential danger that could tear it apart, such as corruption, inequality, sexism, etc.). What does it mean to strongly (which is a force) and jointly appeal for that which will once again bring us together or reconstitute us as a polis or group? Can a group or institution ever really be just or is it by definition immoral, thus quick to violent intervention and war (*polemos*)?

If we leave aside choral singing, then appealing in unison, in one voice, at the top of our lungs, indeed puts us together in a way. I assume that when we insist on a new and different collective intention and intentionality, we require a social ontology that distances us from violence more than heretofore. An appeal for politics (all the while holding on to our reservations about the concept) would mean: much more serious and additionally careful discussions about the notion of damage and injury, and further about group or individual use of violence;[117] very precise distinctions of social and non-social acts, and an incessant attempt to render all violence transparent and visible; an appeal for a reconstruction of the city and the group, which necessarily implies adding new members to the city and expansion of the group (violence exists because someone is latently missing), and not the exclusion and elimination of parts of the *polis* (exclusion of minorities is a major heritage of democracies and politics of violence).

Three moments seem to me the preamble of such a new politics: a) awareness in all members of the group or city that violence always precedes a new future politics (*appeal* is birthed of violence, on the ruins of a social group or city);[118] b) the necessary introduction of ever new elements and a new complication of the life-world that renders a decision on violent acts impossible (Clausewitz speaks of frictions, new sudden facts and problems that make it more difficult for a military commander to make a decision about battle action; the more complex the relations

[117] Perhaps the most exact definition of violence comes from John Harris' *Violence and Responsibility*: »An act of violence occurs when injury or suffering is inflicted upon a person or persons by an agent who knows (or ought reasonably to have known) that his actions would result in the harm in question.« Harris: Violence and Responsibility, p. 19.

[118] More precise than Hume, in his *Vorlesungen über Moralphilosophie*, notes taken by Vigilantius, Kant says that »without might no right can be instituted, then might must precede right« (*daß ohne Gewalt kein Recht gestiftet werden kann, so muß dem Recht die Gewalt vorausgehen*) (p. 515).

between members of a group, the more difficult they are to reduce and the less room for non-social acts); c) finally, the success of such a ›strong appeal‹ above all depends on the good hearing of all in the choir, as well as very specific attention and vigilance of the extremely strong voices, or those not singing at all, or those simulating singing, or those simply singing off key. This is the unconditional condition for the prevention of extreme violence, heretofore continually produced by politics and the greatest problem of our age.

Analogously, or better counter-analogously, cosmopolitanism is, by definition, supposed to be precisely this new form of politics and a big new city. Although cities and states can enter alliances, their unity cannot be based on violence because they do not hold a unified monopoly on violence, nor do they have a common enemy. The prohibition of aggressive war, although one of Kant's greatest and most exact ideas, remained but a sketch, was never really fully developed, due above all to his theory of international relations referring only to a few countries of the West; the world as such remained *de facto* excluded through this lack of awareness. The world or cosmos exist neither for Kant nor for us. There are, however, a few other decisive normative or pseudo-normative principles that Kant also elegantly formulated (although he was, as Carl Schmitt will later be, a total compiler and plagiarist in international right and law), but never seriously developed and elaborated. These principles not only never became part of the mandatory portion of an ideal ontology of international law, but have, in one way or another, resulted in incessant and indelible violence among states. Why is it today more difficult than ever to send a strong appeal for the establishment of a new institution or international of cities? Is the reason to be found in the fatal amount of extreme violence in the world, in the cosmos? Has the »*univers de violence*« contaminated any possible sketch of a new *cosmo*-politics? Sketch is Kant's word – a sketch of a peace project, while »*l'univers de violence*« is Jean-Paul Sartre's phrase, which he comes up with in notes on violence, written immediately upon the end of World War II and later published as *Cahiers pour une morale*. When the presidents of certain states join in a struggle against extreme violence, when they beget strong violence against extreme violence, they are all invoking the principle necessary for all to unify against one international actor producing violence. This principle is explicitly and implicitly justified in various manuals of international law, such as the UN Charter, but has never been accepted by all cities, nor applied to all. A second principle, the existence of a so-called unjust enemy or enemy of humanity (enemy of all), which Kant also reiterates, and Schmitt, for example, will later criticize in the context of his own political efforts, could also today mobilize and unify disparate cities of the world against dangerous violence. Paradoxically, each of these principles, in addition to its normative dimension, contains within itself a strong appeal for the mobilization of all. The very unity of all cities in resisting violence would not only represent a foundation of a new cosmopolitics, but would *ad hoc* reduce violence and put aside violent defense or preemptive attack. Instead of a scenario like this, the recent decades have seen the constitution and theoretical formulation of a third principle of violent military emergency intervention, allegedly in order for violence not to become extreme and uncontrollable. If we take into account that a cessation of violence has never meant the elimination of the problems leading to violence (*de facto* and *de jure* failure of the state-building theory, the collision of principles of unchangeability of borders [*uti possidetis juris*] and right to cessation, etc.), then it is possible to assume that the current potential for great violence is larger than ever before. It seems that all these elements along with the amount of destructive weaponry combines to give extreme violence an entirely new meaning, adding new complexities to spontaneous cosmopolitical engagement. Extreme violence today is not the means, but the end. In his note on violence, written in the immediate aftermath of World War II, Jean-Paul Sartre writes: »That means a negation of legality, a destruction of the world that confronts you with an end conceived as the absolute. The end does not justify the means, but the means justify the end, conferring upon it, through violence (finally, this is a sacrifice of the entire world), an absolute value. In this sense, violence has as its end the revealing of a universe of violence.«[119]

In the very next sentence, Sartre says something he will go on to explain in detail, as it is the essence of existentialism and his philosophy. »The universe of violence is certainly a specific genre of affirmation of man« (*L'univers de violence est certainement un certain genre d'affirmation de l'homme*). This reversal and happy ending to the confrontation of man and world through violent play, nevertheless, does not refer to the affirmation of man (singular), but the affirmation of us all. Only in this way can *cosmo*-politics be affirmed in relation to *l'univers de violence.*

Annex III: Analysis of Violence or *Gewalt* (Engels)

There are a number of passages in Engels explaining what is *Gewalt* and even more ambitiously, what is *Gewaltstheorie*, criticizing the (at the time) renowned and influential philosopher, Eugen Dühring.[120] Why Engels? First, Engels' deconstruction of force and violence has been entirely unjustly forgotten in the context

119 *»C'est-à-dire la négation de la légalité, la destruction du monde qui vous laisse en face de la fin conçue comme absolue. Ce n'est pas la fin qui justifie les moyens, c'est le moyen qui justifie la fin en lui conférant par la violence (sacrifice du monde entier à la fin) une valeur absolue. En ce cas la violence a pour fin de faire apparaître l'univers de violence.«* Sartre: Cahiers pour une morale, p. 181.

120 All we have left of Dühring in the history of thought is precisely Engels' »Anti-Dühring,« which may not itself be all that little. Dühring criticizes Marx, ›from the left‹ even, considering his

of other texts about violence, the connection between violence and law, violence and justice, and the various conversions and transformations of violence into order. Second, since Engels, like Marx, does not make use of the literature about violence (force) and law and order (Hume, Rousseau, Spinoza, Fichte, Jacobi, Hegel, etc.), this carries certain novelties, tensions, difficulties, and incongruities that could be very useful in better understanding the always current, paradoxical value and influence of violence. Third, the word *Gewalt* (or *Kraft*) sets off an adventure and discovery of Engels' ambitious endeavor to find the best meaning. Namely, the German *Gewalt* contains both violence and force in meaning (as a ›third‹ solution, in English one could simply deploy the German word[121]), a theory of *Gewalt* is crucial in determining the scope and strength of Marx and Engels' engagement, the meaning of revolution, and fate of the weak and oppressed, but potentially organizable as a collective agent into a forceful instrument of struggle.

Let me begin at the end. The background of the position Engels reaches in his construction, at the end of Chapter IV, »*Gewaltstheorie (Schluß)*«,[122] is a famous line from Marx's *Capital*. It functions as the cornerstone of Engels' account of violence, and we should always keep it in mind. Speaking of the process of accumu-

theory reactionary, thus trying to substantially reform socialism. Engels was initially urged to write a defense of Marx by Liebknecht (in a letter of 1 February 1875), but later also by Marx himself, who actually edited the entire manuscript and read it together with Engels. Hence, Engels opens the introduction of the book (Lenin's favorite, published several times) by saying: »The following work is by no means the fruit of any »inner urge« (*Inner Dranges*). On the contrary.« Engels: Anti-Dühring, p. 5; Engels: Herrn Eugen Dührings Umwälzung der Wissenschaft, p. 5. He compiles several texts into the book, publishing it in 1878 under the title *Herrn Eugen Dührings Umwalzung der Wissenschaft* (the *Umwälzung* was rendered in the English as ›revolution‹, but should be ›overthrow‹). The book parts are often re-combined and published together with »Gewalt und Ökonomie bei der Herstellung der neuen Deutschen Reichs«, written ten years later and published posthumously, as *Die Rolle der Gewalt in der Geschichte*.

121 Although the French edition of Engels' book renders *Gewalt* as ›*violence*‹ (certainly a minor mistake and problem), in English (and some other languages), the translation should be ›force‹. The problem for English then is that it lacks an appropriate solution for the German *Kraft* (which is also translated as ›force‹), and which Engels thematizes in »Grundformen der Bewegung,« a chapter in *Dialektik der Natur*. Engels: Dialectics of Nature, p. 362; Engels, Dialektik der Natur, p. 359. It seems to me impossible to understand *Gewalt* unless we can understand how Engels manipulates the word *Kraft*, deploying various quotations from Hegel and Helmholz. We could even say that for Engels, force (*Kraft*) is foremost abstract, all too subjective, but also imprecise. Engels constantly discovers weaknesses of the word force: »Just because we are not yet clear about the »rather complicated conditions« of these phenomena, we often take refuge here in the word force. We express thereby not our knowledge, but our lack of knowledge of the nature of the law and its mode of actions.« Engels: Dialectics of Nature, p. 373; Engels: Dialektik der Natur, pp. 365–366. The same thing he does to Dühring regarding *Gewalt*, he does to Hemlholz regarding *Kraft* in *Dialektik der Natur* (claiming he has an imprecise understanding of the word). For example, he mocks the following line from an 1854 lecture: »*Vorrat von Arbeitkraft*« (work force stock): some kind of repository of force capable of producing work or action. This has nothing to do with nature and the objective world, says Engels. Engels: Dialectics of Nature, p. 374; Engels: Dialektik der Natur, p. 367.

122 Engels' *Gewaltstheorie* is laid out in Chapters 2–4 of Vol. 2, »Political Economy«, of the book on Dühring, as well as in several passages in the preparatory notes.

lation of capital and colonialism, Marx names these methods *brutaliste Gewalt* (brute force / violence):

But they (methods) all employ the power of the State (*Staatsmacht*), the concentrated and organized force of society (*Gewalt der Gesellschaft*), to hasten, hothouse fashion, the process of transformation of the feudal mode of production into the capitalist mode, and to shorten the transition. Force (violence) is the midwife of every old society pregnant with a new one. It is itself an economic power (*Die Gewalt ist der Geburtshelfer jeder alten Gesellschaft, die mit einer neuen schwanger geht. Sie selbst ist eine ökonomische Potenz*).[123]

There are, then, certain methods, meaning various uses of violence, which transform one order into another, or transform something old into something new. This method or methods (plural) are violence as such. Marx equates them with economic power or *potentia*, and with midwifery. It is not easy to follow Marx's pilling up of words. A new society, already extant in the old, is ›manifested‹ (led or pushed out) by some kind of violence (spontaneous or very nearly so), after which the new society takes the place of the old. If we remove the figures of speech, and ignore the uncertainty of subject or agent conducting the violence, Marx still makes a leap from colonial violence of plunder and killing to violence of an economic nature. Is it the same violence in different periods and forms, but with nearly the same consequences? In the book on Eugen Dühring, Engels introduces another shift, or another form of violence, still grounding himself in the same passage: revolutionary violence. Interestingly, even though throughout the text, Engels has been proving that violence and force are not important for the transformation of society and play an entirely secondary role, he comes to the finale of his theory of violence only to accuse Dühring that he does not recognize the importance of violence yet to take place:

To Herr Dűhring force is the absolute evil; the first act of force (*der erste Gewaltsakt*) is to him original sin; his whole exposition is a jeremiad on the contamination of all subsequent history consummated by this original sin; a jeremiad on the shameful perversion of all natural and social laws by this diabolical power, force (*Teufelsmacht, die Gewalt*). That force, however, plays yet another role in history, a revolutionary role; that, in the words of Marx, it is the midwife of every old society pregnant with a new one, that it is the instrument with the aid of which social movement forces its way through and shatters the dead, fossilised political forms – of this there is not a word in Herr Dühring.[124]

It seems to me that Engels treats Dühring a tad hastily and unjustly. Dühring stands accused of insufficiently mentioning something (the revolutionary use

123 Marx: Capital, p. 739; Marx: Das Kapital, p. 779.

124 Engels: Anti-Dühring, p. 171; Engels: Herrn Eugen Dührings Umwälzung der Wissenschaft, p. 171.

of force) that implicitly belongs more to Dühring's position than to Engels, the Dühring-critic. It is almost as if Engels, in criticizing Dühring, is building his own position without considering the consistence of his own criticism of Dühring. If we simply ignore Dühring's position and the question of consistency of Engels' critique – it still remains unclear what *Gewalt* can or cannot do. Prior to the finale about violence, Engels claims its insufficiency and inefficiency, relativizing it at every step. Yet at the end, it turns out that violence can be efficient; but even then, it is not clear what exactly it changes or what it can shift in this future Marx and Engels announce: political order, economic relations, or social relations?[125]

The originality of Engels' critique of Dühring actually lies in the systematic degradation of the protocol of *Gewalt* (power, force, or violence) as a phantasmagoria that hides various economic causes and forms of dependence.[126] In no more than a few pages, Engels shows that *Gewalt* does not sit at the base of all social relations, nor that it could explain the transformation of human into slave. Indeed, *Gewalt* is nothing historically fundamental, but rather a means. Further, he shows that property precedes force or arms that could be utilized to enslave (Engels demolishes Dühring's interpretative theater between Robinson Crusoe and Friday: Robinson must have something more than a sword and greater force to turn Friday into his slave), etc.[127]

In a word, says Engels, until the present day or until very recently, there was such a thing as *Gewalt*. But as of now it is *Sozialität* (*bisher Gewalt – von jetzt an Sozialität*). This is certainly an erasure of violence – leaving entirely open whether the transition of *Gewalt* is forever interrupted »with revolutionary effect«.

125 Preparatory Writings: »It is recognised that force also operates with revolutionary effect, namely, in all »critical« epochs of decisive importance, such as the transition to sociality, but even then only in self-defence against reactionary enemies abroad.« (*Daß die Gewalt auch revolutionär wirkt, und zwar in allen entscheidenden« »kritischen« Epochen wie beim Übergang zur Sozialität und da auch nur als Notwehr gegen reaktionäre auswärtige Feinde, anerkannt*). Engels: From the Preparatory Materials, p. 610; Engels: Materialien zum »Anti-Dühring«, p. 587.

126 Preparatory Writings: »In Dühring's reprehensible history *force* holds sway. In the real, progressive historical movement, however, what dominates are the *material gains* which are *retained*.« Engels: From the Preparatory Materials, p. 609; Engels: Materialien zum »Anti-Dühring«, p. 586.

127 Here is how Engels examines the protocol of *Gewalt*: »If force is the cause of social and political conditions, what is the cause of force (*Ursache der Gewalt*)? The appropriation of *products* of the labour of others and of labour-*power* of others. Force was able to change the consumption of products but not the mode of production itself; it could not transform bond labour into wage-labour unless the requisite conditions existed and bond labour had become a fetter on production.« Engels: From the Preparatory Materials, p. 611; Engels: Materialien zum »Anti-Dühring«, p. 588.

3 *L'esprit de l'institution*. Origin and Theory of the Institution in Rousseau

I would like to oppose Rousseau to Hume. More precisely, based on the relationship between justice and violence (force), I would like to reconstruct and open the difference in the use of the term ›institution‹ in Hume and Rousseau. I am guided in my reading of Rousseau by Leo Löwenthal's 1926 Staatsexamensarbeit »Gewalt und Recht in der Staats- und Rechtsphilosophie Rousseaus und der deutschen idealistischen Philosophie«.[128] Although Löwenthal's text had almost no influence at the time of its writing, the critique it contains of Walter Benjamin's »Zur Kritik der Gewalt« could certainly be current today.[129] Furthermore, Löwenthal's use of Rousseau to oppose Benjamin, mirrors my own opposition to Hume.

According to Löwenthal, one result (of four) of Rousseau's theory are the notion that violence founds right is nonsense (*Gewalt begründet nie Recht; rechsbegründende Gewalt ist eine* contradictio in adiecto); indeed, only right can found violence (*Recht allein kann Gewalt begründen*).[130] Rousseau does not use the word ›found‹ (for him *»la force ne fait pas droit«*), but we ought to consider a few questions about Rousseau's potential theory of the institution. Why and whence the institution in Rousseau? Which institutionalists precede him? Why is the word institution in the title of his life project, which ultimately surpasses his abilities?[131] In what way does Saint-Just adopt Rousseau's connection between the institutions and corruption in the theory of revolutionary institutions? What is the difference between contract and institution, or custom and law on the one hand, and institution on the other? Finally, what is Rousseau's importance in building an imaginary theory of the institution? Can we say that we owe Rousseau a positive and concrete theory of the institution, given that, like Deleuze, he never treats it as an obstacle, as ›petrified‹, ›dead‹, or inauthentic, nor does he call for it to be reconstructed, resisted, struggled against, torn down? At the beginning of *Emile*, he says »I do not consider these ridiculous establishments we call schools to be public institu-

128 Löwenthal: Philosophische Frühschriften, pp. 169–206.

129 Löwenthal mentions Benjamin's text on page 174.

130 Ibid., p. 189. *»Auf Gewalt gegründetes Recht ist für Rousseau ein logischer Unsinn«. »Convenons donc que la force ne fait pas droit, et qu'on n'est pas obligé d'obéir qu'aux puissances légitimes«. »La folie ne fais pas droit«.* Rousseau: Du contrat social ou principes du droit politique, pp. 354–356.

131 Letter to Moultou, 18 January 1762. *»Je dois vous dire que je fais imprimer en Holland un petit ouvrage qui a pour titre* Du Contract social, *ou* Principes du droit politique, *lequel est extrait d'un plus grand ouvrage, intitulé* Institutions politiques, *entrepris il y a dix ans, et abandonné en quittant la plume, entreprise qui, d'ailleurs, étoit certainement au-dessus de mes forces.«* Cf. Rousseau: A M. Moultou, p. 504.

tions.«[132] For an institution to truly be an institution, and be properly called that, it is necessary, *de facto*, that it be institutionalized once again. Hence Rousseau's use of the phrase ›*l'esprit de l'institution*‹. This ›positive‹ institutional engagement is identical for Hume, Saint-Just, Gilles Deleuze, and indeed John Rawls.

Let us consider some possible origins of the word institution in Rousseau, since he never thematized the word, nor wrote more than a sentence at a time to explicitly explain its meaning. The first possibility could be Samuel Pufendorf, or more precisely, the French translator of *The Law of Nature and of Nations*, Jean Barbeyrac. In the first section of book I, entitled »De l'origine des Etres Moraux, et de leurs differentes sortes en general«, Barbeyrac translates Pufendorf's paragraph IV in the following way (*Porro uti modus originarius producendi entia physica est creatio; ita modum, quo entia moralia producuntur, vix melius possis exprimere, quam per vocabulum* impositionis):

Like physical beings, originally produced by Creation, we know no better way to express how moral beings are formed than the term *institution*.
(*Comme les Etres Physiques, sont originairement produits par la Création; on ne sauroit mieux exprimer la manière dont les Etres Moraux se forment, que par le terme d'*Institution.)[133]

Using Riccardo Orestano's analysis of the term »institution«, Mario Ricciardi describes how the translation of Samuel Pufendorf's *De iure naturae et genitium* into French changed the meaning and use of this word. Barbeyrac could not find an adequate word for *impositio*, and his proposed solution is very interesting:

I have not found a more appropriate term to express *impositio*. (...) *institution* is used most often for anything invented and established, in contrast to what issues from nature. (...) our author (Pufendorf) wants to say when he says that moral things are such by *impositio*, and not *in themselves or by nature*.
Yet recalling these principles, developed in the following notes, it would be prudent to alter the ordinary meaning of the term *institution*, taking care not to add anything our Author had in mind. I will always give the word in italics, as in the meaning here it is closer to the Latin term *impositio*, which follows for all its further uses.
(*... institution se dit le plus souvent de tout ce qui est inventé et établi, par opposition à ce qui vient de nature. (...) notre Auteur veut dire lorsqu'il pose en fait que les choses Morales sont telles par* impositio, *et non pas d'elle-même ou par leur nature.*
*Mais pourvû qu'on se souvienne bien de ses principes, que je développerai distinctement dans les deux Notes suivantes, il sera aisé de changer quelque chose à l'idée reçuë du terme d'*in-

132 Rousseau: Émile, p. 40.
133 The new translation of this passage into French (by Bruno Gnassounou) is different: »*En outre, de même que le mode originaire de production des entités physiques est la création, de même le mode par lequel les entités morales sont produites ne peut mieux s'exprimer que par le terme d'imposition* (*impositionis*).« Pufendorf: De l'origine et de la variété des entités morales, p. 190.

stitution, *et de n'y attacher précisement que ce que nôtre Auteur a eu dans l'esprit. J'écrirai toujours ce mot en caractere Italique, lorsqu'il répondra au Latin* impositio, *dans le sens dont il s'agit ; ce que soit dit une fois pour toutes.)*[134]

Barbeyrac thinks that when Pufendorf says »*vocabulum impositionis*«, he really has in mind ›institution‹, that is, the word ›*institution*‹ in French is in the spirit of the Latin ›*impositio*‹. Barbeyrac's translations was certainly a novelty at the time, since the medieval uses of the word institution in Old French, just as in English, refer either to education and instruction (formation, college, school), or to a ›command‹. If we now follow Rousseau's project and the ›spirit‹ of his incomplete and insufficiently supported lines about institution, it is clear that he substitutes this first meaning of institution as instruction and education (»*l'instruction publique*« or »*l'éducation publique*«) with Barbeyrac's translation. Is there a collision here? And if so, how does Rousseau resolve it? To institutionalize or, in Rousseau's words »*instituer un peuple*« (»*Du peuple à instituer*«[135]), means to change the nature of each individually and all together, regenerate the degenerated, and recreate what is already created. The contradiction between nature and the institution, mentioned by Pufendorf, the danger of which Rousseau is keenly aware[136] – lest we forget his insistence to preserve the innocence of the first creative act of nature and human nature as such (»*originairement produits par la Création*«) – could be resolved by invoking the regulative attribute ›good institution‹ (*bonne institution*), one in spirit of ancient institutions and what is more, one which returns the true, ›first‹, and ›original‹ human nature corrupted by bad institutions. To institutionalize then is always to ›re-institutionalize‹, that is, regenerate anew, not only political institutions as such (for example, schools, the state, or the opera[137]), but human nature itself. »Anything that ruptures social unity is bad: all institutions that place man at odds with himself are no good« (*Tout ce qui rompt l'unité sociale ne vaut rien: Toutes les institutions qui mettent l'homme en contradiction avec lui-même ne valent rien*[138]):

Natural man is entirely for himself. He is numerical unity, the absolute whole which is relative only to itself or its kind. Civil man is only a fractional unity dependent on the denominator, his value is determined by his relations to the whole, which is the social body. Good social institutions are those that best know how to denature man, to take his absolute existence from him in order to give him a relative one and transport the *I* into the

[134] Cf. Ricciardi: Diritto naturale e ontologia sociale, p. 169; Orestano: ›Institution‹, p. 175.

[135] Rousseau: Du contrat social ou essai sur la forme de la république, p. 318. In the first version of the manuscript of *Du contrat social* Rousseau says »former un Peuple« (ibid., p. 313).

[136] Cf. Rousseau: Fragments politiques, p. 510.

[137] »L'opera de Paris pourroit être une fort belle institution politique, qu'il n'en plairoit pas davantage aux gens de goût.« Rousseau: Julie ou la nouvelle Héloïse, p. 417.

[138] Rousseau: Du contrat social ou principes du droit politique, p. 464.

common unity, with the result that each individual believes himself no longer one but a part of the unity and no longer feels except within the whole.[139]

After nearly three hundred years of various fragments such as these, and after the discovery of tools to aid us in that reading, acquired through distance from such texts, it is today considerably easier to reconstruct Rousseau's idea of the contract. More specifically, for example, it now seems easier to find Rousseau's own trappings and difficulties in formulating a collective intentionality (»*transporter le* moi *dans l'unité commune*«; »*plus sensible que dans le tout*«). It is not only a question of his inclination towards nature, which is always more positive and concrete than the institution, and this certainly degrades his institutionalism. (A few decades later, for example, Kant will insist, squarely within the spirit of his own time, that war is something ever-present and quotidian, here and among us, for which any added effort would be redundant, whereas it is peace that needs to be institutionalized (*der Friedenszustand muß also gestiftet werden*).[140] There is also the issue of Rousseau's miraculous and sometimes monstrous warping of mathematics and causality, hesitation and ambiguity of terminology (*pacte, contrat, convention*: words often synonymous in the manuscript of *Du contrat social*), his paradoxical Swiss nationalism (I would call it his nostalgic Alpine sensibility),[141]

139 Rousseau: Emile, p. 164. Two fragments, analogous to the one quoted here, can be found in *Du contrat social*: »Il faut, en un mot, qu'il ôte à l'homme ses forces propres pour lui en donner qui lui soient étrangeres et dont il ne puisse faire usage sans le secours d'autrui. Plus ces forces naturelles sont mortes et anéanties, plus les acquises sont grandes et durables, plus aussi l'institution est solide et parfaite«... and »Cependant pour que le corps du Gouvernement ait une existence, une vie réelle qui le distingue du corps de l'Etat, pour que tous ses membres puissent agir de concert et répondre à la fin pour laquelle il est institué, il lui faut un *moi* particulier, une sensibilité commune à ses membres, une force une volonté propre qui tende à sa conservation.« Rousseau: Du contrat social ou principes du droit politique, pp. 382–383, 399.

140 Kant: Zum ewigen Frieden, p. 349. Kant, a philosopher and not a jurist, devalues the great efforts before and after him, made by theorists of natural law and rights of peoples, who succeeded in reducing the hidden presence of war around us precisely with their attempts at institutionalizing it. Apart from the verb *stiften* and *urstiften*, Husserl uses the German nouns *Stiftung*, *Urstiftung*, *Nachstiftung* and *Endstiftung*. Husserl's early influence in France, along with the work of various philosophers in his archives and the dilemma regarding the translation of *Stiftung* as *institution*, make Husserl a purely ›French matter‹. Merleau-Ponty translates the word *Stiftung* – »the beautiful word *Stiftung* (*le beau mot de* Stiftung), which Husserl used to signify the infinite fecundity of every moment in time« – as institution.

141 Here I am thinking not only of some of Rousseau's famously ill-measured statements about cosmopolitans and cosmopolitanism, about Europe (»*Il n'y a plus aujourd'hui de François, d'Allemand, d'Espagnols, d'Anglois même, quoiqu'on en dise, il n'y a que des Européens*«, Rousseau: Considérations sur le gouvernement de Pologne, p. 960), but also about his strong conviction that institutions are essentially national and that it is precisely that »national institutions form the genius, the character, the tastes of a people, that make it as it is and not as another, and inspire that ardent love of country based in habits impossible to uproot (...)« (*les institutions nationales forment le génie, le caractère, les gouts, et les mœurs d'un people, qui le font être lui et non pas un autre, qui lui inspirent cet ardent amour de la patrie fondé sur des habitudes impossible à déraciner* (...) (ibid.). Cf. Rousseau: Du contrat social ou principes du droit politique, p. 392.

his various complications in differentiating between man and citizen, and above all, his resistance to accept language as the basic institution of the process of institutionalization. Is then the word ›institution‹ or the phrase ›good institution‹ an addition to the word ›contract‹, or a more particular rendering of the word or his theory of ›contract‹? Institutions, political institutions, hold a society together and allow the social contract to constantly draw our attention to the signature, documents, signed contracts, identification, declarations, birth and death certificates, documents, charters – in a word: written and verbal obligations.

The second meaning of the word ›institution‹ (command) harkens back to Hobbes and leads us to the second possible origin, equally imaginary since there is no sign that Rousseau actually read Hume's main work when organizing his own lists of the uses of the word ›institution‹. Nevertheless, Hume's well-known resistance to Rousseau, his rejection of the theory of social contract, allows me to reconstruct a potential fictitious opposite resistance: Rousseau's to Hume. Rousseau's rejection of the founding sovereign act of a social form is conducted through the appearance of a contract (between some two, or two sides that come to an agreement, as opposed to a single, sovereign decision); further, by the introduction of multiple subjects or a group (a collective), whose members ›accomplish‹ together the process of institutionalization, such as the legalization of their property; and finally, the discovery that the decision or institutionalization is neither perfect nor complete.

What is it that Hume does? How was the accent shifted from the ›institution‹ to that which is ›instituted‹ (*institué*)? Hume tells us that time, before the very eyes of the multitude, gradually covers (or uncovers) what is at the root of power and establishment or administration. The process of institutionalization, the conversion of violence and injustice into stable forms unfolds gradually, over time. These stable forms then do not only bind and obligate only those who participate in the original acts of violence and injustice, but all those who arrive over the course of that given time, that is, who subsequently become members of a community.

In Rousseau, violence is always on the other side of the political body, meaning that the institution is essentially opposed or defends itself from present or future potential violence. In *Du contrat social*, he shows several times that he is completely aware that the institution or political body can degenerate and become prey to the very violence for whose prevention it was created *(à la violence contre laquelle il fut institué)*.[142] However, in opposition to Hume or Saint-Just (at least as I read them), Rousseau is a pessimist and not an alchemist: he does not turn violence into something it is not. »It should be said«, he says in *Lettres écrites de la montagne*, »the institutions you are building are good for the moment, but bad for the future; they are good for establishing public liberty, but bad at preserving it, and what you do now will undoubtedly and very soon be the very links of your

[142] Cf. ibid., p. 432.

shackles« (*Il auroit dit, l'Institution que vous formez est bonne pour le présent, et mauvaise pour l'avenir; elle est bonne pour établir la liberté publique, mauvaise pour la conserver, et ce qui fait maintenant votre sûreté sera dans peu la matiere de vos chaines*).[143]

There are further ambiguities in Rousseau's potential theory of the institution. Namely, Rousseau's position resists Amartya Sen's classification of institutions as comparative and transcendental, belonging to both at once. Rousseau is indeed always interested in the ideal institution, but he is also an absolute and perhaps the first real ›comparativist‹ (an example of this are his texts, his case studies of Poland and Corsica). And Deleuze's differentiation between institution and contract, written in the Humean spirit, never calls into question Rousseau's project and contract theory: for Rousseau, the institution and contract do not exclude, but rather complement one another.

Montesquieu is the third moment in the development of Rousseau's institutional theater, and there is more than mere variation on the title of his famous book. Rousseau repeats the phrase ›*l'esprit de l'institution*‹ several times in his attempt to find traces of the ideal institution in the past and on the other side of existing institutions. Montesquieu is the one who values institutions and examines cases and conditions when an institution can be good or admirable in the first place (*les admirables institutions* of the past, or *les admirables institutions* of olden times, are a favorite obsession of Montesquieu's).[144] Perhaps Rousseau's very idea to create a big book represents a homage or attempt to revitalize Montesquieu's endeavor. Even the title of this ill-fated book was probably taken from Montesquieu. In chapter IX »Que les choses qui doivent être réglées par les principes du droit civil peuvent rarement l'être par les principes des lois de la religion«, Montesquieu writes:

The Romans made rules to protect female practices in the republic; these were political institutions. Upon the establishment of the monarchy, they based civil laws on them, and then civil government principles.

Les Romains firent des règlements pour conserver dans la république les mœurs des femmes: c'étaient des institutions politiques. Lorsque la monarchie s'établit, ils firent là-dessus des lois civiles; et ils les firent sur les principes du gouvernement civil.

›Conservation‹ or ›preservation‹ (*conserver*) is the first function or task of the political institution. Rousseau's entire project could probably be explained with this term from Montesquieu. However, for it to preserve that for which it was created,

143 Rousseau: Lettres écrites de la montagne, p. 816.

144 The first version of *Du contrat social* (this fragment was erased in the original edition), chapter III, *Du Legislateur*, ends with a similar and pathetic ode to the state, whose institution is »celestial and indestructible« (celeste et indestructible). Cf. Rousseau: Du contrat social ou essai sur la forme de la république, p. 318.

an institution must remain stable and endure in time, it cannot fall apart in the future. (This is extremely important, since the institution has to persevere, resist time and corruption by way of certain rules and procedures, as in Montesquieu's example of Roman women.) To this end, Rousseau speaks often of the way how and when the institution was ›created‹ or institutionalized. When is the right moment for an institution? When and how is it begun and decreed that something ought to last and be preserved from time and in time? It seems to me that Montesquieu could help in determining what Rousseau elsewhere calls »*le moment de l'institution*«.[145] It concerns the beginning and founding of the institution, and Rousseau thinks that precisely one entry in Montesquieu's book, *Considérations sur les causes de la grandeur des Romains et de leur décadance* ought to be the paradigm that the beginning of every institution should satisfy.[146]

I would leave aside sovereigns who make the institution (here in the singular). I am interested in the way Rousseau tried to transform this already shifted causality in Montesquieu's sentence. The sovereign makes something that will concern and limit him. Rules form the one who declares them and who produces them. So, the institution is an institution only if it satisfies the condition that it form the ones who can create it. This only when the institution itself is created; otherwise, it is not an institution, nor are we dealing with institutional creation. Here is how Rousseau makes another turn and definitely disrupts the linear causality using something that I can only describe as unclear scholastic computation. In the fragment that follows, the sovereign is the people, but this time the effect or influence of the law and institution on the people ought to precede the institutional act itself. Meaning that the people should already be formed before the creation of the law or institution. The reason for such a construction is that Rousseau is still trying to remove any violence from the institutional or sovereign creation:

For a nascent people to taste the healthy maxims of politics and follow the fundamental rules of state policy, the effect must become the cause: the social spirit, otherwise the result of the institution, needs to conduct the institution itself, and men must become what the laws are supposed to later turn them into. Thus, the Legislator neither reasons nor uses force, but must avail himself of an authority of a different order, must sway without use of violence and persuade without convincing.

Pour qu'un peuple naissant put goûter les saines maximes de la politique et suivre les regles fondamentales de la raison d'Etat, il faudroit que l'effet put devenir la cause, que l'esprit social qui doit être l'ouvrage de l'institution présidât à l'institution même, et que les

145 Rousseau: Discours sur l'origine et les fondements de l'inégalité parmi les hommes, p. 186.

146 In *Du contrat social*, Rousseau is paraphrasing the following statement: »At the birth of societies, it is the heads of the republic who create the institution; after that, it is the institution that forms the heads of the republic« (*Dans la naissance des sociétés, ce sont les chefs des républiques qui font l'institution, et c'est ensuite l'institution qui forme les chefs des républiques*). Rousseau: Du contrat social ou principes du droit politique, p. 380.

hommes fussent avant les loix ce qu'ils doivent devenir par elles. Ainsi donc le Législateur ne pouvant employer ni la force ni le raisonnement, c'est une nécessité qu'il recoure à une autorité d'un autre ordre, qui puisse entraîner sans violence et persuader sans convaincre.[147]

The city of Sparta and its political institutions are my last, fourth assumption about the origin of Rousseau's institutional reflections. Rousseau's evocation of Sparta and ancient institutions shows the difference between laws and customs in relation to the institution, but also the importance of the heart[148] and spirit as part of the process of institutionalization. In a letter to D'Alembert, Rousseau writes:

Another observation, no less important, is that issues of customs and universal justice cannot be regulated, like those of particular justice and rigorous rights, with edicts and laws; or if sometimes laws do influence customs, it is when they draw their strength from them. In that case they return the same strength back to them in a kind of reaction, well known by actual politicians. The first function of the Ephors in ancient Sparta, upon taking power, was a public proclamation in which they joined the citizens, not to oversee the laws, but to love them, so that their oversight would not be hard on them. This proclamation, which was not at all *pro forma*, shows perfectly the spirit of the institution in Sparta, according to which laws and customs, intimately united in the hearts of the citizens, made up one single body. But we should not flatter ourselves that we should see Sparta reborn from the heart of commerce and the love of monetary gain. If we had the same principles, we could set up a similar spectacle in Geneva, but then never a citizen nor bourgeois would set foot in it.

(Une autre observation, non moins importante, est que les choses de mœurs et de justice universelle ne se règlent pas, comme celles de justice particulière et de droit rigoureux, par des édits et par des loix; ou si quelquefois les loix influent sur les mœurs, c'est quand elles en tirent leur force. Alors elles leur rendent cette même force par une sorte de réactions bien connue des vrais politiques. La première fonction des Ephores de Sparte, en entrant en charge, étoit *une proclamation publique par laquelle ils enjoignoient aux citoyens, non pas d'observer les loix, mais de les aimer, afin que l'observation ne leur en fut point dure. Cette proclamation, qui n'etoit pas en vain formulaire, montre parfaitement l'esprit de l'institution de Sparte, par laquelle les loix et les mœurs, intimement unies dans les cœurs des citoyens, n'y faisoient, pour ainsi dire, qu'un même corps. Mais ne nous flattons pas de voir Sparte renaître au sein de commerce et de l'amour du gain. Si nous avions les mêmes maximes, on pourroit établir à Geneve un Spectacle sans aucun risque: car jamais citoyen ni bourgeois n'y mettroit le pied.)*[149]

147 Rousseau: Du contrat social ou principes du droit politique, p. 383.

148 The heart is the most important body part of a state. It is the »legislative power, while the brain is the executive power, making the various parts move. But the brain can fail, paralyzing the individual, yet they still live. A man remains an imbecile, but alive; but if the heart ceases to beat, the animal is dead« (*la puissance legislative, la puissance executive en est le cerveau, qui donne le mouvement à toutes les parties. Le cerveau peut tomber en paralysie et l'individu vivre encore. Un home reste imbécille et vit: mais sitôt que le cœur a cessé ses fonctions, l'animal est mort*). Ibid., p. 424.

149 Rousseau: Lettre à M. D'Alembert, pp. 507–508.

All the conditions and all the problems of institutional building are here in one place: in Sparta and in future capitalist Geneva, an empty city without citizens. To love the law and to love the principle does not mean individually repeating and analyzing and then incorporating the text of the law into the heart. Rather, it means declaring the community publicly (proclamation), being together and staying together in the city. The heart is never in the singular; the heart is together, which is why it is the emblem of the institution for Rousseau. Although he at first separates laws from customs (it is an open question how and when Rousseau gives more weight to customs over laws[150]), at the very end he shows that the (political) body – made up of the hearts of citizens, laws and customs – is united by way of the spirit of the institutions, that is, by way of the presence and declarations (proclamations) of the overseer of laws (the Ephors). Rousseau explains that the overseers or city policemen do not oversee in order to punish, they do not act strictly according to the letter of the law, but rather with their proclamations transform individuals into a group, a community.[151] In *Lettres écrites de la montagne*, Rousseau uses a different point of view to explain the breakdown of the institution. »Any body that works consistently against the spirit of its institution is poorly instituted« (*Or tout Corps qui agit constamment contre l'esprit de son Institution est mal institué*).[152] The responsibility for the restless and resistant Corps towards political institutions, *de facto* towards the Ephores, Rousseau locates exclusively in poor institutionalization. This reversal is surprising indeed! And whenever it crops up in histories of ›the formation of institutions‹, it confirms that Rousseau still remains in our hearts.

150 »Si les politiques étoient moins aveuglés par leur ambitions, ils verroient combien il est impossible qu'aucun établissement quel qu'il soit, puisse marcher selon l'esprit de son institution, s'il n'est dirigé selon la loi du devoir; ils sentiroient que le plus grand ressort de l'autorité publique est dans le cœur des citoyens, et que rien ne peut supple aux mœurs pour la maintien du gouvernement.« Rousseau: Discours sur l'économie politique, p. 252.

151 Cf. Rousseau: Discours sur l'origine et les fondements de l'inégalité parmi les hommes, pp. 187–188; Rousseau: Du contrat social ou principes du droit politique, p. 394.

152 Rousseau, Lettres écrites de la montagne, p. 834.

4 Just Institution. How (and When) to End War(s)?

I believe that it was Jean-Jacques Rousseau who first used the phrase ›just institution‹ a few times. I connect the time of peace or the time of institutional founding with a certain collective action which I call termination of war or end of war. (›Just institution‹, in the singular, is a paradigm or regulative principle of myriad institutions that would have to have elements of justice within them in order for peace to exist at all; justice is a small and important attribute of peace, although there is also such a thing as a »just war«, which is not peace, but whose goal is definitely peace.[153]) Peace, or the minimum requirement for peace, or the minimum requirement for a just institution in time, begins if and only if we terminate war or the extreme conflict taking place. This is a question of collective intentionality, the coordinated and cooperative act of a group of people, that one person alone (a single entity or instance) cannot perform, because war is extreme violence. The subtitle of this chapter contains the dilemma regarding the possibility and time of termination of war. This termination would imply or would be the condition of existence of the just institution. In that sense, peace could really »have its own time« (*»hat seine Zeit«*), just like everything else that exists (*»Alles hat seine Zeit«*). So, I am interested exclusively in the cessation of hostilities and end of war. I further insist (not alone, of course[154]) that this termination be differentiated from war as such or the duration of war. Indeed, the termination of war does not belong to the period after war, or else belongs to *jus post bellum* only partially, since with its termination begins a new period. *Jus terminatio* separates and simultaneously connects the duration of war and the time after war, as well as referring back to the very beginning or reason for war.[155] If there truly is a time aspect or period in which the termination of war is decided, if there are certain difficulties and procedures (since we are speaking of a process of limited duration, but not a moment),

153 Aside from justice as attribute or unconditional condition of peace, I would add Grotius' »good faith« or »the preservation of good faith« that holds states together. Grotius: De Jure Belli ac Pacis, p. 860.

154 There was a colloquium dedicated to the theory of war termination or *jus ex bello* held at Oxford, organized by ELAC (Oxford Institute for Ethics, Law and Armed Conflict). A few texts that deal with this issue: Rodin: Two emerging issues of *jus post bellum*; Rodin: Ending War; Mollendorf: Jus ex Bello; Lazar: Endings and Aftermath in the Ethics of War.

155 »*Terminatio* law stands in the same relationship to *jus post bellum* as *jus ad bellum* stands to *jus in bello*. Whereas *jus post bellum* is most naturally interpreted as governing the rights and obligations of actors once they have transitioned from a state of war into a state of peace, *terminatio* law governs the transition itself.« Rodin: Ending War, p. 54.

and if there are norms based on which it is possible to end any war, and finally if this termination of war directly implies the beginning of peace, then it should be possible to name and reconstruct theoretically this dimension of termination of war or period of extraction from war (*jus terminatio* or *jus ex bello*).[156]

If there is no single instance (some messianic figure) that can terminate war, then there is also no specific time that transcends and dictates peace, or indeed a time horizon of peace absolutely uncontaminated with war and violence. This construction essentially remains faithful to Kant. If the starting point is that we are in war, and that there is then a termination of war, or put more precisely, that »*jus ex bello* and *jus in bello* are not separated by an arbitrary timeline, but by the practices that they regulate.«[157] Further, we are speaking not of peace and time, but of war segmented by time. This is war, in a certain way regulated and then pacified as well, by various practices (set in motion during various periods of its duration). Namely, the very fact that war is reconstructed in time, as having periods before war, a beginning, a duration, a termination, and an end or the period after war (*jus ad, in, post*) – shows an attempt across the centuries (one still insufficiently successful) not only to regulate war and make it less cruel and more just, but in its ultimate instance, an attempt to prevent and eradicate war. If acts of war are recognized and distinguished from one another, and in so doing regulated (and ethically conditioned; the phrase *jus* ›civilizes‹ war) and recognized in a certain time order, there will be substantially modified reasons for fighting, which will »help to justify the standards governing how we initiate and prosecute wars.«[158]

Termination of war, or emerging from war – that first period of transition from war to peace, and not the period after war, not *jus post bellum*[159] – also concerns

156 Here are two designations of this phrase, from two texts published simultaneously in 2008: »I call *jus ex bello* the set of considerations that govern whether a war, once begun, should be brought to an end, and if so, how. For those who believe that war is just if and only if it satisfies certain conditions, matters of *jus ex bello* are of central importance.« Mollendorf: Jus ex Bello, p. 123. »Whereas jus post bellum is most naturally interpreted as governing the rights and obligations of actors once they have transitioned from a state of war into a state of peace, termination law governs the transition itself.« Rodin: Two emerging issues of *jus post bellum*, p. 54. *Jus ad terminationem belli* or *bellum terminatio* concerns, according to Rodin, »victory, defeat, stalemate, or intervention by a third party.« If we follow a distinction made by Brian Orend, the doctrine of *jus ex bello* is the middle phase doctrine. »Conceptually, war has three phases: beginning, middle and end. So if we want a complete just war theory – or comprehensive international law – we simply must discuss justice during the termination phase of the war. After all, there is no guarantee that if you fought justly, for the sake of a just cause, that you will automatically impose a just set of peace terms upon your vanquished enemy.« Orend: The Morality of War, p. 160.

157 Lazar: Endings and Aftermath in the Ethics of War, p. 13.

158 Ibid., p. 21.

159 In his five books published in recent years by Cambridge University Press, Larry May discusses in detail all the problems concerning the period after war's end. May mentions *bellum terminatio* at the very beginning of *After War Ends* (4), but does not dwell on the problem. Michael Walzer of course does not mention *jus terminatio* in the 1977 classic *Just and Unjust Wars*. In the chapter »Jus post bellum« (pp. 315–316) Walzer writes: »Look, justice after war consists in achieving

the birth of the institution. Specifically, the birth of the institution out of violence and war. Because war termination (termination of ›taking up arms‹) means that a group of people or completely different groups of people stop killing and in one way or another begin cooperating, thus institutionalizing peace. To institutionalize peace means to be able to (or at least try) to live together, live side by side, or more specifically, work together. Institutionalizing peace means the self-institutionalization of a group or various groups. Kant's idea that war is given (extant, present, immanent), and that, conversely, it is peace that requires effort, building, and institutionalizing (Kant uses words derived from the verb *stiften*), refers to a collective effort, common work, and in a way, common time.

At this point we are in a position to imagine a change in the intention of a group of people no longer killing, but organizing and preparing to intervene in reality using peaceful means, leaving war activities behind. There are three preliminary difficulties. First, although we live in a period of wars of occupation that seem very difficult to terminate, it is impossible to imagine a war that cannot be terminated and that lasts eternally; it is also, however, possible to imagine a war which, once terminated, does not bring peace. (The last portion of this chapter enumerates more explicitly various problems arising from the termination of war in different practices of times after war [*jus post bellum*].) Let us assume that the wars led in Afghanistan and Iraq, along with some on the horizon, are wars for democracy and peace, and that they ought to be taking place. The more war, the greater and more stable future safety and peace. Second, the horizon of peace, that future peace that has its time is stained with violence and force. (I am not sure that we ought to read something like Kant's text on peace in order to anesthetize ourselves against texts by Benjamin, Hume, Levinas, or even Kant's various lectures for that matter.) The just institution is contaminated with remains of un-terminated violence or violence not transformed into new justice, right, or laws. By the same token, the community is dominated by an un-egalitarian model where the victors systematically terrorize the newly vanquished or the new minority. The Kosovo intervention is an excellent example of a successful termination of violence that left the majority and minority in opposition, and peace on the horizon. Is this a premature peace, or an ill-timed peace, or is this the only possible peace? And the third preliminary difficulty regards our common unshakable faith in force – despite its history of crimes, problems, and various difficulties – that is, our perfect faith that violence is capable of terminating a certain unjustifiably poor situation, and then that this same violence is capable of self-termination, leaving peace in its wake.

the just cause which justified the start of the war to begin with. For example, if the just cause was self-defense from aggression, *jus post bellum* consists in defeating and repulsing the aggressor, successfully defending one's community.«

How and when to end war, and how to recognize the right moment to begin a period of reconstruction of the institution? When has the time for peace arrived, and what are the first obstacles to the termination of any possible war? Several fragments that I am about to quote, extracted from so-called marginal, pseudo-texts (archives, correspondences, interviews, etc.), could show, above all, that peace or termination of war is always decided upon by the other (the adversary or enemy; again, the singular appears in these quotes). The difficulty with peace and pacifism, really with the termination of war, is always about the fiction of the ultimate enemy and our total destruction at his hand.[160]

Enemy

The change in meaning of the term ›victory‹ and the evolution of various protocols referring to victory have to do above all with the changes in the relation towards the enemy. If Thucydides considered victory the complete annihilation of the enemy and the enemy city (*Peloponnesian Wars*),[161] later, after the Crusades of the thirteenth century, the victor was limited not only to not being allowed to kill, but also from destroying the holy sites of the defeated. After the Peace of Westphalia in 1648, the victor's authority was significantly limited: his right (*ius victoriae*) reaches only to the extent of correcting the damage inflicted upon him before the conflict or war began.[162] This means that the right of the victor is not limited by his power and strength to do whatever he can to the defeated, but exclusively by the right to remedy the reason the war began in the first place. Still, the idea of the destruction of the enemy (their property, remains, body – Clausewitz mentions something he calls a destroying battle, *Vernichungsschlacht*) is deeply set in the histories of Judeo-Christianity.[163] Two arguments regarding limits and the sig-

160 »Enmity is the total negation of another being in its complete life action.« (*Feindschaft ist die totale Negation des anderen Seins in allen seinen Lebensbetätigungen*), Husserl: Kosmologische Weltbesinnung, p. 12.

161 »The object taken violently by means of conquest become the property (*oikeia kekteisthai*) of the victorious party.« Chaniotis: »Victory« Verdict, p. 456.

162 Cf. Whitman: The Verdict of Battle, pp. 1–24.

163 »What is our aim? (...) Victory, victory at all costs, victory in spite of all terror; victory, however long and hard the road may be; for without victory, there is no survival.« Churchill: Blood, Toil, Tears and Sweat, p. 149. (»An Address to the House of Commons« [13 May 1940]) We encounter this same passion for victory in General Alexander Suvorov: »When you are preparing to beat the enemy, enlarge your troops, vacate the guard posts, remove communication. Once you have won, you can fix as needed, but make sure to chase the enemy down to annihilation. Pursue him day and night, until he is completely routed (...). A forest that has not been uprooted will grow again. Even if you are peripatetic in your philosophy, you must never be so in your military endeavors (...). Victory covers everything« (Идешь бить неприятеля, умножай войска, опорожняй

nificance of the idea of destruction of the enemy are mentioned at the beginning of the last century. In »Ethics of War«, and specifically in »Wars of Colonization«, Bertrand Russell speaks of English fantasies of the destruction of Germany:

When the present war began, many people in England imagined that if the Allies were victorious Germany would cease to exist: Germany was to be »destroyed« or »smashed«, and since these phrases sounded vigorous and cheering, people failed to see that they were totally devoid of meaning. There are some seventy million Germans; with great good fortune, we might, in a successful war, succeed in killing two millions of them. There would then still be sixty-eight million Germans, and in a few years the loss of population due to the war would be made good. Germany is not merely a State, but a nation, bound together by a common language, common traditions, and common ideals. Whatever the outcome of the war, this nation will still exist at the end of it, and its strength cannot be permanently impaired. But imagination is what pertains to war is still dominated by Homer and the Old Testament.[164]

Since destruction is impossible, it is problematic to see what Georg Simmel is thinking when he thematizes »complete or utter victory« (*der vollständige Sieg*). Complete victory or destruction of the enemy can call into question the existence of freedom, as well as the existence and cohesion of the victorious group:

Consequently complete victory over its foe is not always, in a sociological sense, a fortunate event for a group, because the energy that guarantees its cohesiveness thereby declines, and the disintegrative forces that are always at work gain ground. The collapse of the Roman-Latin Federation in the fifth century BCE has been accounted for by the fact that the common foe was then overcome.[165]

In 1965, Julien Freund, friend, student, and translator of Carl Schmitt, was defending his doctoral thesis, *L'Essence du politique* (*The Essence of the Political*), before

посты, снимай коммуникации. Победивши, обновляй по обстоятельствам, но гони его до сокрушения. Преследуй денно и нощно, пока истреблен не будет (...) Недорубленный лес вновь вырастает. Коли быть перипатетиком, то лучше не быть солдатом (...) Победа все покрывает). Суворов: Наука побеждать генералиссимуса Суворова, p. 253. A famous passage from a sermon by St. Philaret of Moscow (»Слова в неделю 19 по Пятидесятнице«) is often cited in a various versions: »Despise the enemy of God, defeat the enemy of the homeland, love thy enemies« (Гнушайтесь убо врагами Божиими, поражайте врагов отечества, любите враги ваша) Филарет: Сочинения Филарета, p. 264. However, the sentence has been bastardized in later citations and interpretations into »Love thy enemies, crush the enemies of the homeland, despise enemies of God« (Люби врагов своих, сокрушай врагов отечества, гнушайся врагами Божиими). The imperative »defeat the enemies of the homeland« (поражайте врагов отечества) would seem to be synonymous with »beat the enemies of the homeland«, but is weaker in intensity, turning ›defeating‹ the enemy into cut off, exclude, strike off, marginalize.

164 Russell: The Ethics of War, p. 135.

165 »*Darum ist der vollständige Sieg einer Gruppe über ihre Feinde nicht immer ein Glück im soziologischen Sinne; denn damit sinkt die Energie, die ihren Zusammenhalt garantiert, und die auflösenden Kräfte, die immer an der Arbeit sind, gewinnen an Boden.*« Simmel: Conflict, p. 287; Simmer: Der Streit, p. 315.

a committee comprising Raymond Aron, his mentor, as well as Raymond Polin, Paul Ricœur, and Jean Hyppolite. Freund writes about the debate with Hyppolite in his 1991 book of interviews:

Then arrives the moment of Hyppolite's intervention. He had acknowledged my work by adopting Aron's arms; he found me too severe against Kelsen but then settled on our fundamental difference, the source of his refusal. »There remains the category of friend-foe, politically defined. If you are truly correct, he said, nothing is left for me but to go gardening.« To which I said: »Listen, Mr. Hyppolite, you have said two or three times recently that you were wrong about Kelsen. I believe you are about to make another mistake, because, like all pacifists, you think that it is up to you to designate the enemy. You reason that the moment we no longer wish to have enemies, we no longer have them. But it is the enemy who designates you as such. And if he wishes to be your enemy, you can treat him as friendly as you like. From the moment he wishes you to be his enemy, you indeed are such. And he will prevent you even from gardening.« To terrible effect, because Hyppolite retorted: »In which case, there is nothing for me to do but commit suicide.

(*Reste la catégorie de l'ami-ennemi définissant la politique. Si vous avez vraiment raison, a-t-il affirmé, il ne me reste plus qu'à cultiver mon jardin. Car vous penser que c'est vous qui désignez l'ennemi, comme tous les pacifistes. Du moment que nous ne voulons pas d'ennemis, nous n'en aurons pas, raisonnez-vous. Or c'est l'ennemi qui vous désigne. Et s'il veut que vous soyez son ennemi, vous pouvez lui faire les plus belles protestations d'amitié. Du moment qu'il veut que vous soyez l'ennemi, vous l'êtes. Et il vous empêchera même de cultiver votre jardin. Tragique même, « Résultat : il ne me reste plus qu'à me suicider ».*)[166]

Franz Rosenzweig's original contribution to histories of war and pacifism, but also win-win ethics, can be found at the end of a letter to his parents from January 6, 1917. Right after the official offer of peace by Wilhelm II (on December 12, 1916), Rosenzweig writes that only then was it clear to him what pacifism was:

Pacifism is in fact – this has become clear to me in the past days, since the 12th – necessary equipment of war (*notwendiges Zubehör des Krieges*). So, war is not lead in order to *force* (*zwingen*) the enemy (*Gegner*) – it would be impossible for that to last long – but to *subjugate* (*unterwerfen*), to impose (*aufzuzwingen*) on him one's own will, to *replace* (*ersetzen*) his will with mine. The victor does not wish to make a *tool* (*Werkzeug*) of the vanquished (because he *cannot* persevere in it), but rather his slave. The goal of the victor is not the *destruction* of the enemy (*Vernichtung des Feindes*), but the basing of a new *contract*. But this supposes that in the enemy there is a shred of a »desire for peace«, (*Friedenssehnsucht*) which has fallen asleep, and the mission of the war is to awaken this desire. If this desire for »peace at all cost« (*Frieden um jeden Preis*) becomes stronger than the ability to suffer (Heroism), then the hour of peace has struck. All this of course applies to two victors as it does to one. Therefore pacifism is »as old as« war (namely, *human*, slave-directed war (*auf*

166 Freund: L'aventure du politique, p. 45.

Versklavung gerichteter Krieg); animals only know a war of destruction (*Vernichtungskrieg*), and hence have no pacifism).[167]

The third fragment comes from Heidegger's *Schwarze Hefte* (1939–1941), and was probably written in 1939, at the time of Germany's initial war victories. Usually, the defeat needs to be accounted for, with the defeated producing sundry justification for his failure. In this text, Heidegger justifies the power of the victor. In contrast to Alberto Gentili and other founders of international law, Heidegger subordinates law to life and victory, substantively binding the two, seeking to find a place for victory outside law. Victory thus becomes everything and to the victor belongs all:

Victory over an enemy (*der Sieg über den Feind*) still does not prove that the victor is in the right (*im Recht ist*). However, this »truth« is no longer relevant, if law is interpreted as that which is not only confirmed and substantiated (*bestätigt und bekräftigt*) by victory, but above all and primarily established and made (*gesetzt und gemacht*): right is the power of the victor (*Recht ist dann die Macht des Siegers*), the power of overlordship (*die Macht der Übermacht*). Such law resists »codification« (*kodifizieren*), since due to its character of power and position of victory, it presents new legal reach, interpreted as the »right« to the very »life« of the victor.[168]

Although rather diverse, the three fragments are also typical in histories of enmity and constituting the figure of the enemy in the West. The determination of the enemy is substantively theological, since his intention is to destroy or disrupt the existing order (C. Schmitt, J. Freund). The response to the enemy's enmity is theologically oriented: he must be destroyed or else a truce must be made if the enemy abandons his destructive intentions (F. Rosenzweig). Of course, peace with a former enemy is always asymmetrical, unfolding within the victor's right of power over the enemy (F. Rosenzweig), power of domination (M. Heidegger) that celebrates life. However, how to win in the first place, and what means does the victor use to reduce the destructive power of the enemy?

167 Rosenzweig: Briefe und Tagebücher, 1/1, pp. 327–328 (An die Eltern, 6. January 1917). Cf. Bojanić: Pacifism, pp. 1038–1040.

168 Heidegger: Überlegungen XII–XV, pp. 15–16.

»Coda: Can the Good Guys Win?« Revision of a Question or Two

Borrowing the title of a text by Michael Walzer from a few years ago: »Coda: Can the Good Guys Win?«,[169] I would like to briefly problematize two close, but sufficiently different questions, and then attempt to sketch a potentially justified answer. How does the victor achieve victory? And, can a man or soldier in war, who acts and evaluates his own actions, remain good (a good man), despite all the evil (the inhumanity) that surrounds him? As it stands, the question is not clear because it begs the issue why anyone would remain good in war or after it? Is there sufficient reason to refer to an individual man or all men individually in war, which is foremost a group or institutional activity? Walzer's question is more precise: coda is used in music to indicate an ending of a section or movement, it can be a final dilemma or addition to a piece. Thus, Walzer's ›coda‹ is the consideration whether a group of men (›guys‹) can win by remaining good? What does it mean ›to be good‹? This difference in number – man, singular, who must remain good (imperative) and a team, a crew, a group of people who together must remain good – determines the different ethical stance of the Orthodox and Western understandings of the ethics of just war.[170] In case of the former, some man or any man must survive the war and preserve his humanity despite the situation around him; in the latter case, a group of people ought to first of all win, and the only question is whether this will be done by breaking the rules of just war or not.

The word ›win‹ (or ›victory‹) is an entirely vague protocol (or procedure) that determines the substantive difference between the two questions I am considering. There is indeed no doubt that Walzer's dilemma is entirely rooted in a tradition of Western thought where winning is one form of resolution of conflict, entirely opposite to compromise (Simmel) and that »victorious war is a social ideal« (Kaufmann). Yet, even if the concept is not fully clear, it is certain that victory more or less aggressively destroys, perhaps subdues, excludes or entirely marginalizes the opponent or the other. On the other hand, it is very complicated to speak of victory in the context of an Orthodox ethics of war for many different reasons.[171] One of the most basic would be that, paradoxically, defeat in war could better preserve the faith and religious being of a people. (For example, the »Kosovo Covenant« is the very substance of Serbian statehood potential, emerging from a military defeat of the medieval Serbian army by the Ottomans; to the Serbs in that battle,

169 Walzer: Coda: Can the Good Guys Win?.

170 The word ›Western‹ is imprecise, but provisionally covers very different concepts of war ethics, above all the Jewish and western Christian.

171 The etymology and origin of the Slavic word ›*pobeda*‹ (victory) is certainly the first problem. In Max Fassmer's etymological dictionary, ›*pobeda*‹ is also defeat, disaster, containing the word ›*beda*‹ (misery).

so the myth goes, admittance into the kingdom of heaven was of far greater importance than victory in war and holding earthly power.) Further, it is the Lord who determines the victor, not the strength of people or arms. God is also often a direct participant in the war, just as a war is lost because the actors are unbelievers (St. John of Kronstadt).[172] This *de facto* absence of thematization of victory in war and various techniques that construct it carries two crucial consequences for the use of violence and the handling of amount of violence. In his »The Science of Victory«, Alexander Suvorov is explicit in prohibiting unjustified killing, since a soldier is simply not a criminal (»God does not aid criminals«). Interestingly, Russian and then Soviet military leaders principally repeat a fairly univocal repertoire of an Orthodox understanding of justified violence. At this point, there is no difference between Michael Walzer's attempt to secure the conditions for the good guys to truly have a chance at ultimate victory. In the conclusion of his text, Walzer writes:

> Soldiers have to be trained to fight justly, and their officers have to be taught the best ways of doing that. It is incompetence, above all, that breeds brutality. There is plenty of spontaneous brutality in war, especially ›in the heat of the battle‹; I do not mean to ignore that. But well-trained and well-disciplined armies are less brutal – and their officers and soldiers are less likely to think that brutality is necessary for victory.[173]

It seems to me that the phrase or institution of so-called »defensive killing«, in use in the last ten years across various texts having to do with just war theory, is a good explanation how to regulate brutality of violent acts. Still, the problem does not only lie with violence done in affect (›in the heat of the battle‹), whether individual or group, but the level-headed and strategic production of brutal violence and the violation of the rules of war to some end (or to achieve victory).[174]

172 In Missionary Letter 277, Nikolaj Velimirović addresses a writer from Zagreb on war: »You ask: if God allows such misery to happen to people, where is the soothing wisdom of the Savior? On paper. On paper of those who in their peacetime wicked deeds cause war. Were the soothing wisdom of the Savior in human hearts, people would live in perpetual peace« (*Vi pitate: Kad Bog dopušta takvu nesreću na ljude, gde je onda blaga nauka Spasiteljeva? Na hartiji. Na hartiji kod onih koji nedelima svojim u miru izazivaju rat. A kad bi ta blaga nauka Spasiteljeva bila u srcima ljudskim, ljudi bi živeli u trajnome miru*). Velimirović: 277. pismo, p. 283.

173 Walzer: Coda: Can the Good Guys Win?, p. 442.

174 Walzer's dilemma originates in a 1973 text, »Political Action: The Problem of Dirty Hands«. The problem is actually quotidian. Walzer writes: »He wants to win the election, someone says, but he doesn't want to get his hands dirty.« Walzer: Political Action, p. 165 Walzer is evoking Machiavelli's famous conclusion that the ruler or commander must learn »how not to be good,« since the world contains »so many who are not good.« This is the first condition of victory and social success. »Any man who tries to be good all the time is bound to come to ruin among the great number who are not good. Hence a prince who wants to keep his authority must learn how not to be good (*potere essere non buono*), and use that knowledge, or refrain from using it, as necessity requires.« (XV, 57) Machiavelli: Il Principe, p. 115.

The second consequence of introducing or not introducing the institution of victory refers to the distinction between individual and group violence. War is not an individual matter, and individuals mostly do not determine the outcome of war. A clear beginning and aim of conflict, as well as ritual of victory at the end of war can protect from exclusion those individuals who ›successfully‹ and ›efficiently‹ use brutal violence.[175] Not only this: victory implies legitimizing the joint breaking of just war rules or an individual's ›inhuman acts‹, indeed *incorporating* them as necessary for the survival of the group as such. If it is victorious, which means if it still exists, a group is never built on unjust principles. Victory is then a condition for a group not to dissolve and vice versa: only a group still in existence after certain collective acts by its members or by the group as a whole (can a group be an agent?) has fulfilled the social ideal of victory.

The significance of Walzer's dilemma regarding dirty hands is later transformed into much more complicated protocols of supreme emergency and asymmetric warfare.[176] What is important for us is to affirm the difficulty, even impossibility of strictly following the rules in unpredictable conflicts and contexts. Yet, they are our only reality today. I suggest a sketch of a few variations of answers to the earlier questions: it is not possible to remain human while participating in (or being responsible for) situations below the humane threshold; victory conceals the brutality of individuals, while at the same time necessarily implying the existence of a certain amount of »bad acts« it accumulates and archives; good guys can win because the bad acts of individuals actually sometimes have a crucial role in victory and the existence of a group.

In light of this changed perspective, it becomes clear that the termination of war will above all determine the relationship toward the enemy, the victor or vanquished, because peace depends on trust. Trust depends on good faith. To betray this trust is perfidious, a sign of bad faith, and a sin against peace. Nearly all main characteristics of the *jus post bellum* space (before *jus victoriae*) are concerned with the erasure of the space of the enemy's principle. The enemy and the relationship to the enemy are to be found in all these questions: what are the obligations of occupying forces? What rights do victors have to change the domestic political and

175 In the 1973 text, Walzer quotes Basil the Great: »Killing in war was differentiated by our fathers from murder (…) nevertheless, perhaps it would be well that those whose hands are unclean abstain from communion for three years.« Walzer: Political Action, p. 167.

176 Walzer is disturbed by real problems faced by soldiers and citizens. For example, The New York Times in 2010 reports of a soldier complaining about the rules of engagement in Afghanistan, specifically the difficulties in winning the war. Cf. Walzer: Coda, p. 433. In a 2015 interview, Walzer explicitly talks about the problem of asymmetric warfare and victory: »It is possible to win asymmetric wars, as the Sri Lankans proved against the Tamil Tiger rebels, but only if you are prepared to kill high numbers of civilians and the world isn't watching. But you can't win if you are trying to fight according to the moral rules of engagement. That is the general problem of asymmetric warfare.« Walzer: Interview, p. 61.

institutional arrangements of vanquished, or indeed engage in regime change? Do victors have an obligation to assist in economic reconstruction? Do vanquished aggressors have an obligation to compensate the victims of aggression? To what extent ought the perpetrators of an unjust war be tried and punished?

But what does *jus terminatio* have to do with these complicated institutes or the timing of termination and extraction from war? A preamble of a possible answer to this question could begin with a hypothetical consideration of prevention and preventive action as one of the conditions of peace or non-initiation of war. Meaning, war cannot be initiated if there is no clear strategy of exiting war, which is to say, if war cannot be ended under certain conditions, acceptable to all or most. The question of terminating war is thus implicitly present at the start of war, one depends on the other, but the two operations are essentially different.[177] Here, I draw on Hilary Putnam's argument that, as opposed to its beginning, the termination of war is not subject to any epistemological assumptions that it has not already inherited. For something to be a »just war« it necessarily has to satisfy certain epistemological criteria (i. e., clear evidence or knowledge of existence of weapons of mass destruction);[178] if a war ought never have been initiated due to various poor considerations, making it therefore an unjust war, it is impossible to expect that *terminatio* law ignore these facts.

If war is then wrongly initiated (and the most recent ones certainly have been), the nature of these wars is further brought into question, and the damage to international relations is incalculable. Such wars are difficult to end or win, not least because the occupied population has an increasing interest in keeping the occupying forces from leaving the country. Thus, the basic institution of *jus post bellum* (respect of sovereignty), which even Kant advocated in his time, will be irretrievably lost. Making the form of new institutions, new *political institutions* something completely different. As will the form of peace.

177 »But ending wars is clearly different from starting them. *Ad bellum* principles regulate the decision to start killing people, many of whom are innocent. *Ex bello* principles regulate the return to normality, and the end of lethal violence. The constraints on ending wars should be weaker than those on starting them.« Lazar: Endings and Aftermath in the Ethics of War, p. 18.

178 »If we don't know, then what we are doing is immoral.« Here is how Putnam's presentation of his colleague Roderick Firth: *»Both of Firth's principles employ the notion of »knowledge«. According to the principles, justification of war requires that we know that the Bad Things will not happen if we resort to war (resort to maiming and killing) and that we know that the Bad Things will not continue (or be replaced by even worse Bad Things) if we do resort to war«* Putnam: The Epistemology of Unjust War, pp. 318–319.

II. »We« and Document

1 The Possibility of *We* (*Wir*; *Wirsein*). On the Conditions of Institutional Action in Heidegger

Jetzt sei Wir-Zeit.[179]

I will attempt to follow and reconstruct the argument put forward by Heidegger in four paragraphs (§ 10–13) from the spring 1934 lectures. In them, he returns to his *Logic*, that is, to the *logos* and the nature of language, twenty years after completing his doctoral thesis. Above all, I would like to show the importance of a completely new thematization of the first-person plural pronoun (*Wir*), occurring in the context of other suggestions and solutions. At the same time, I would like to insist that Heidegger offers two different and mutually opposed interpretations of the status of *We*, and would like to point out a problematic transition from § 12 to § 13, where he all too quickly and unconvincingly introduces the word people (*Volk*) to designate our self and to answer the question »Who are we ourselves – the questioners?« (*Wer sind wir selbst – die Fragenden?*) The organization of these four paragraphs of the seminar *Logik als die Frage nach dem Wesen der Sprache* could be read as a possible portrayal of an institutionalization of a group (in this case made up of a teacher and several students) who have to live and work together, fulfilling certain tasks and ends through their common action (common responsibility, education, research, etc.). (It is certain that Heidegger completed his arguments regarding the *We* shortly before the end of his one year appointment as rector on April 23, 1934, in the middle of the spring semester.)[180] The institution and *téhne* are explained by at least three common characteristics that Hei-

179 Heidegger: Logik als die Frage nach dem Wesen der Sprache, pp. 50–51. »At the same time, we have, in addition, the advantage that the question of who *we* ourselves (*wir selbst*) are is timely (*zeitgemäß*), as distinguished from the time of liberalism, the I-time (*Ich-Zeit*). Now is We-time (*Jetzt sei Wir-Zeit*).« Heidegger: Logic as the Question Concerning the Essence of Language, p. 45.

180 In his lectures in the fall semester 1933–34, »On the Essence and Concept of Nature, History, and the State« (Über Wesen und Begriff von Natur, Geschichte und Staat), directly preceding the seminar on logic, Heidegger shows the importance of *téhne* in politics and for the constituting a group. I offer here Theodore Kisiel's English translation (since the German original of the seminar and Übung has only recently been published) from his text »In the Middle of Heidegger's Three concepts of the Political«: »Politics for Bismarck is the capacity to see what has to arise essentially from a historical situation accompanied by the skill (*téhne*) to bring about what one at first merely envisions«. (p. 146) »Action can be practically technical, directed toward the realization of a thing, or practically moral, directed toward the actualization of the will of another or of an entire group, a community of will« (p. 150).

degger implicitly presupposes:[181] they are both man-made and supplement what nature is not capable of executing; both are means for the attainment of certain ends (institutional action belongs to instrumental rationality determined by the transformation of the possible into the concrete: that which acquires bodily form through human will); finally, Heidegger repeats several times, equating *téhne* and the institution: *téhne »selber ist eine Einrichtung, lateinisch gesagt: ein instrumentum«.*[182] This last point allows me to link the institution and institutionality through documenting and the theory of a written trace (*documentum* is a synonym for *instrumentum*).

What are the elements of this construction by Heidegger, and how then is a group constituted? Some of the aspects of this portrayal of institutionalization, as a preamble to any potential theory of the institution, include: a) Heidegger asking questions, but not offering his own position; rather, the group constitutes itself fictitiously and through the process of thematization conducted by Heidegger (the question »Who is he himself – the questioner?« is immediately replaced with the question »Who are we ourselves – the questioners?«[183]; b) Heidegger is indeed the subject of the *We* and the auditorium lectures are given exclusively in the first-person plural[184] (in the entire seminar, Heidegger uses the first-person singular only once, and even that only when he is speaking about the priority of each individual individually over the group);[185] c) in his speaking, the leader always adopts the first-person plural, thus suspending not only his own potential first-person singular speech, but also the potential appearance of any other singular and singleness; d) the speaker questions and examines the *We* (and with it ourselves, our own *we*),

181 Cf. Heidegger: Die Frage nach der Technik, pp. 7–8; Fischer: Philosophie der Technik, pp. 59–79; Hubig: Die Modellierung institutionellen Handelns im ökonomischen Bereich.

182 Heidegger: Die Frage nach der Technik, p. 8; *»Institute oder sogar – Instrumente«*, Heidegger: Einleitung in die Philosophie, p. 42; *»Institute (sind) nicht die Wissenschaft sondern eine zu ihr gehörige Einrichtung«, »Institut – Apparate«.* Heidegger: Leitgedanken zur Entstehung der Metaphysik, der neuzeitlichen Wissenschaft und der modernen Technik, p. 168.

183 Heidegger: Logik als die Frage nach dem Wesen der Sprache, p. 39; M. Heidegger: Logic as the Question Concerning the Essence of Language, p. 36.

184 Heidegger's use of the first-person plural far surpasses the usual use in academic writing. For example, in »Über Wesen und Begriff von Natur, Geschichte und Staat. Übung aus dem Wintersemester 1933/34«, the word we is the main bearer and signifier of Heidegger's text, and is repeated many times: »Since at the very least (*wir*) we now do not know what we mean by space – precisely this measurable surrounding of the extended – (*wir*) can pose further questions. Now, (*wir*) do not wish to simply enumerate and list what (*wir*) confidently know regarding people and space, but rather (*wir*) wish that our observation be continued in the direction where (*wir*) compare man's and the people's connection with space, and equally the connection with space of dead matter, plants and animals.« Heidegger und der Nazionalsozialismus. Dokumente, p. 80.

185 »No individual person among you can in any manner ascertain about any individual person how he has decided. You, as well, cannot say how I myself have held my lecture (*wie ich selbst meinen Vortrag gehalten habe*), whether after the manner of decision or only in the manner of reporting or as phrase.« Heidegger: Logik als die Frage nach dem Wesen der Sprache, p. 58; Heidegger: Logic as the Question Concerning the Essence of Language, p. 51.

and through these questions initiates several new operations (the passages here in question, of course, are part of Heidegger's attempts to thematize the political, that is, the state, the fighting group[186]). These operations are, first, that the leader is examining the nature of language through its use (speaking/writing). Second, by examining language, the teacher is really questioning his own self or the human as such[187] (ultimately the examination of *We* will lead to the »historicity of we« (*»Sind wir geschichtlich?«*) or the generative or generational strength of *We*). Third, when questioning, the teacher is constructing two fictional or impossible acts – he names himself and the auditorium a *We* (in the nominative), and attempts to mobilize all with a call or a challenge to all (these passages ought to be read as Heidegger's attempt to utter the unutterable – the vocative of the pronoun we). Fourth, the teacher who shows that reflection (individual or collective, it remains to be seen how he differentiates between the two!) is the essence of *We* (the self or *selbst*) rarely conducts a declension of the noun *We* (placing it in the genitive, dative, accusative, etc.). Fifth, the leader has a mandate to shift and twist the form of questioning,[188] and in the process to declare certain *we entities* inauthentic and ultimately false,[189] as it is in the jurisdiction of the speaker or writer to decide which moment (the ultimate moment, the *now* [*jetzt*]) finally transcends the group,[190] as well as the final version of documents (the synopses and proofs of lectures written and delivered, the various injunctions Heidegger signs during his term as rector, etc.) that also constitute and hold together a group.

In contrast to Heidegger, I would like to pose differently the questions about the possibility and conditions of *We*, by introducing the first person and an imaginary community of Heidegger readers. At the same time, my questions will partially repeat Heidegger's dilemma or hesitation regarding the individual reflection that precedes the existence of the group (*We*), and, on the other hand, the collective

186 In his seminar on nature, history and the state of 12 January 1934, Heidegger clearly shows the relation of the thematization of the state and *We*: *»Wenn wir jetzt nach dem Staat fragen, dann fragen wir nach uns.«* Heidegger: Über Wesen und Begriff von Natur, Geschichte und Staat, p. 69.

187 »Wenn wir jetzt die Frage nach dem Wesen der Sprache fragen, fragen wir nach dem Wesen des Menschen.« Heidegger: Logik als die Frage nach dem Wesen der Sprache, p. 27.

188 Ibid., p. 48.

189 Ibid, p. 51; Heidegger: Logic as the Question Concerning the Essence of Language, p. 45.

190 »What happened? We submitted ourselves to the moment (*Wir fügten uns in den Augenblick*). With the phrase »We are here«, involved in a happening of education, something is carried out. (…) We have carried out no description. This »We are here« does not mean plurality of human beings is present-at-hand, but »We are here! We are ready! Let it happen! (…) »We are here, we are involved (*eingelassen*)« actually out of and from within ourselves and in the manner of engaging ourselves in the moment (*und uns einlassend in den Augenblick*).« Heidegger: Logik als die Frage nach dem Wesen der Sprache, pp. 57–58; Heidegger: Logic as the Question Concerning the Essence of Language, pp. 50–51. »Our task in this historically decisive moment (*kairos*) (*in diesem entscheidenden geschichtlichen Augenblick*) includes the cultivation of, and reduction in, the thought of the state.« Kisiel: In the Middle of Heidegger's Three Concepts of the Political, p. 147; Heidegger: Über Wesen und Begriff von Natur, p. 77.

reflection or reflection of the group that precedes any individual's self-thematization. At the very outset, the problem regards the present conditions of my belonging to this imaginary group of Heidegger readers (what is it »to be one of you«? or what is it to be »one of them«?), and the transformation of the phrase »to be one of you« or »to be one of them« into »being one of us«, that is, the phrase »being a We«. Here are a few questions that interest me: »who is or what is We«? (or how is the *We* constituted, what status does it have?); further, is the thematization of the *We* a condition for any theory of the institution? And finally, does a potential theory of the institution, which I am trying to formulate, necessarily include the work of Martin Heidegger?

In order to answer these questions, I would like to clarify as much as possible what my task is, and then as explicitly as possible justify my position, along with the role Heidegger's passages thematizing the *We* (as well as his university duties at the time) play in a potential theory of the institution. At the same time, it seems to me that this approach could possibly describe and implicitly reconstruct Heidegger's understanding of the institution and institutional action. Thus, my basic intention is to *use* Heidegger's attempts at thinking a *We* and the institution, and possibly compare them with ways of thinking the institution that are entirely different from other traditions. Here I am primarily thinking of Anglo-American philosophy and theories of collective intentionality, as well as the theory of the institution in John Searle, Margaret Gilbert, Raimo Toumela, or institutionalism in economics or law.[191]

Let me then offer two explanations or interjections, as well as refer back to the primal scene of the institution or institutionalization, The Tower of Babel (a scene complementary to Heidegger's thematization of *We* in the seminar on *Logic*). The two interjections and the sketch could possibly serve as a good description of Heidegger's intention and his institutionalism, predicated upon his understanding of *téhne*. Also, both interjections concern the conditions for the constituting our *We* – the *We* that needs to exist in the here and now, in other words, the cooperation in reading Heidegger.

The first interjection is that I do not consider the institution to be essentially constituted of the so-called *inauthentic* and *performative* uses of the word we.[192] These uses appear when I (the one now writing or speaking) *de facto* include you or count you in (institutionalizing you or them) into an institutional framework completely novel to you or to them. I do so by using the pronoun we (e. g., we have all been occupied these last few months with the texts of Martin Heidegger), in others' stead or in your name, thus excluding your own individual discourse about

191 Probably the most complete thematization of the use of the first-person plural can be found in the text »Who are We?«, by Richard Valée, pp. 211–230.

192 Cf. Hart: I, We and God, pp. 127–131.

yourself.[193] Regardless of the fact that within the confines of logical and grammatical modality, it is always an I uttering the pronoun we, and that only an I can utter the pronoun we (»*c'est toujours moi qui dit ›nous‹, c'est toujours un ›je‹ qui énonce ›nous‹*«[194]), these kinds of assertions are completely lacking in performative power, and we could call them performative simulacra. Think of an imaginary conference, »We, Institution and Heidegger«, with an organizer who says, »We are together in Vallendar today, discussing Heidegger«. But this would be, in the first place, only a description or remark, and secondly, we are not together today only because the organizer said or ordered so, but rather, because each one of us was invited, and promised to come, and actually came. The traces of performative actions are in the past. Further, the one who says we (»we are here today (...)«) adds oneself to others, suspending the first person (the I). Franz Rosenzweig (a great forerunner of Heidegger and a philosopher of the *We*) says that from the point of view of grammar, when I utter we, the I is at once both inside and outside it.

It seems to me that linguistic acts that have an advantage over the mentioned assertions are those whose aim is to include or count my own I into the we or *among* you.[195] If I, using the first-person singular, thank you for your hospitality or affirm that it is very important to me that I am here with you, or suggest a new meeting and colloquium on Heidegger – these would be linguistic acts that would certainly imply that I am one of you (but not yet *one of us*). The existence of the group (*you*) would imply your acceptance and acknowledgment of my linguistic acts, and your potential refusal to hear me out and react to what I have said (in a group consultation you could decide, for example, not to accept my excuse). In both cases, the construction of a *We* entity could be satisfied. At the outset, it was no more than an institutional fiction, in the minds of the organizers and friends of the imaginary conference »We, Institution and Heidegger«.[196] But then it was

193 The use of the colloquial and academic we (e. g., »Our opinion of the institution is different from Heidegger's«) really is constitutive for the academic engagement of teachers and disciplines within the institutionalization of knowledge. This formulation fits very well with Heidegger's most often used formulation of the institution as instruction and incorporation of knowledge or science. (»*Aber wissen wir denn, wer wir selbst sind, diese Körperschaft von Lehrern und Schülern der höchsten Schule des deutschen Volkes.*«) Heidegger: *Die Selbstbehauptung der deutschen Universität*, p. 107. It would be interesting to follow Heidegger's (and not only his) uses of the word we in various periods of his writing or during his lectures, especially in phrases such as *Wir fragen* (commonly used as *Wir fragen nach dem Wesen der Wahrheit*) or *Wir müssen*, as well as various strategies of hiding the first person singular.

194 Derrida: Résistances de la psychanalyse, p. 61. Cf. Benvéniste: Structures des relations de personnes dans le verbe, p. 233. »*(...) dans ›nous‹, c'est toujours ›je‹ qui prédomine puisqu'il n'y a de ›nous‹ qu'à partir de ›je‹, et ce ›je‹ s'assujettis l'élément ›non-je‹ de par sa qualité transcendante.*« (»(...) it is always ›I‹ which dominates in ›we‹, for there is no ›we‹ except ›I‹. And this ›I‹ subjects the ›non-I‹ element through its transcending element.«)

195 Cf. Depraz: Une phénoménologie du »nous.«, pp. 104–105.

196 In § 13 Heidegger sort of equates the existence of the community and friendship – both forms of conjoining are preceded by loneliness and the individual's own decision to join others. Cf. Hei-

followed by the organizers' decisions, their invitation to me and others, which was the true beginning of the institution. Each one of us who was invited to participate and be part of this conference is attempting to temporarily incorporate his own action with a preliminary head count of all the others before him. Thus, becoming a participant in the imaginary conference is part of the protocol of *belonging*, and is also designated with personal pronouns. In other words, to institutionalize, for example, one's own work on Heidegger, means being part of you, or being with you, with all of you, or with these others. The personal pronoun our (of ourselves; further implying the pronoun us) is prior to the pronoun *We*,[197] that is, it implies the *We*. It seems to me that this is the place of Heidegger's institutionalism, or better yet, his contribution to the theory of the institution.[198] Self (*selbst*), as the mark of the reflexive potential of the human, precedes, according to Heidegger, all pronouns (this being the first operation that equates and differentiates the human from the animal). Further, Heidegger equates the *We* with ›*selbst*‹ (*ein Selbst*) (meaning that *We* precedes all persons and all pronouns), thus clearly showing that the collective is *reflexively* structured, or better still, that reflection as such is necessarily collective. I am (my)self or I am *We* because as a human being, together with many others, I belong to the collective of human beings, that is, the group as such.[199] I am *We*, really, before I am *I*. Heidegger continues:

degger: Logik als die Frage nach dem Wesen der Sprache, p. 59; Heidegger: Logic as the Question Concerning the Essence of Language, p. 51.

197 In his book Духовные основы общества. Введение в социальную философию (p. 24) – a book that would later be translated into German as *Die geistigen Grundlagen der Gesellschaft* – Semyon Lyudvigovich Frank explains the origin of the »we« in the chapter »I and we«, in the following way: »Truly, at first sight, I exist for myself, ›I‹ is, and in that sense the use of the plural instead of ›myself‹ or ›I‹ is simply meaningless. For that reason, ›we‹ is not the first person plural, nor a ›plurality of I‹, but the plural as the unity of the first and second persons, as a unity of ›I‹ and ›thou‹ (›you‹). (Поэтому ›мы‹ есть не множественное число первого лица, не ›многие я‹, а множественное число как единство первого и второго лица, как единство ›я‹ и ›ты‹ [»вы«].) Herein is an important designation of the category of ›we‹. The eternal opposition of ›I‹ and ›you‹, in which each is independent and for itself, make it impossible for ›I‹ and ›you‹ to change place or negate one another (...) – this opposition and contraposition (противопоставленность и противоположность) is overcome in the unity ›we‹, which is actually a categorial unity of one's own ›I‹ and ›you‹.«

198 Perhaps a cursory and broad view of Heidegger's »institutionalism« ought to be recognized with his discovery of the »self« (*Selbst*) and the thematization of this word. The fragment from § 10 – previously Heidegger equates the human with self (*Der Mensch is ein Selbst*) – is a good example of Heidegger's interjection (which, as we shall see, goes in two directions) – *»Wer ist der Mensch? – Ein Selbst. »Wer ist ein Selbst?« Wir! »Wir sind wir also, wer sind wir, wir, die Fragenden?«* Heidegger: Logik als die Frage nach dem Wesen der Sprache, p. 36. This passage is really a transformation and development of Heidegger's question from his 1929/30 seminar, »We Ourselves?« (*»Wir sind Wir Selbst?«*).

199 § 11 (b) »The fact that the human being is he himself (*daß der Mensch er selbst ist*) entails a manifold belongingness (*mannigfaltige Zusammengehörigkeit*) of the human beings among one another as You (*Du*) and I. Here too, we have no subsequent crowd of several, many, individualized I, just as little as the You (*Ihr*) is a crowd, a mass of our you. We cannot even add ourselves up to isolated I to a sum total, to a We.« Heidegger: Logik als die Frage nach dem Wesen der Sprache, p. 40; Heidegger: Logic as the Question Concerning the Essence of Language, pp. 36–37.

Nor is this You (*Ihr*), in return, the sum total of individual Yous (*die Summe der einzelnen Du*). It is not the number of many You (*Du*) that amounts to the You (*Ihr*), such as one and one and one and one amount to four. It is rather conversely: The belongingness to the lecture (*Zusammengehörigkeit zur Vorlesung*) is that which is essential; it is grounded in the listening-together (*Mithören*), in the inclusiveness (*Einbezogenheit*) of the individuals in the audience. This You (*Ihr*) of the listener is divided in the You (*Du*), which as such, from such relationship, are addressed (*aus solchem Verhältnis heraus, angesprochen warden*).[200]

Indicating that the importance of number and the numerical is not crucial for the constitution of the group, Heidegger insists above all that the self, mediated through (living) language (*lebendige Sprache*) that historically grounds the community, is equated with »I« and with »We«:

We infer positively from this that in the You (*Ihr*) and We what is decisive is not number-like (*Zahlhafte*), but the self-character (*Selbstcharacter*). The character of the self is peculiar neither to the I nor to the You (*Du*), neither to the We nor to the You (*Ihr*) in a predominant sense. The character of the self lies in a certain way *beyond* and *before* (über *und vor*) all I, You (*Du*), We, You (*Ihr*). In which way, that remains the question. (…) But the problem with this kind of thinking can be now recognized in the fact that precisely, if I mean myself (*wenn ich mich selbst meine*), I do not necessarily have to say »I«, but can and must also say »we«. I can take myself in an essential belongingness (*Zugehörigkeit*) to the others.[201]

In constructing the institution as such, personal pronouns carry a reflexive element. The transformation of *you* into *us* (»to be one of you,« into »being ours« or »being one of us« or being an »us«[202]) concerns time, the final division of labor, as well as a partial and (again) temporary *closing* of the institution or institute. I especially emphasize the word *temporary* here. On the one hand, the word *We* is one of the key components of the institution and implies a certain *closing* in relation to others (in relation to all, to you, to them, or to him; *We* as a people in Heidegger[203] or *We* as the chosen people in Rosenzweig, »*Wir selbst*« in Heidegger and »*Wir allein*« in Rosenzweig – all of which could exclude other people).

200 Heidegger: Logik als die Frage nach dem Wesen der Sprache, pp. 41; Heidegger: Logic as the Question Concerning the Essence of Language, p. 37.

201 Heidegger: Logik als die Frage nach dem Wesen der Sprache, p. 40; Heidegger, Logic as the Question Concerning the Essence of Language, p. 39.

202 Cf. »A Simmelian account of social groups«, Gilbert: On Social Facts, pp. 152–153.

203 When speaking of the insufficiency of number and plurality in the constituting of *We*, Heidegger mentions a people already by the middle of § 11, using a colloquial expression: »We can say: ›You (*Ihr*), my fellow Germans‹, and the ›You‹ (*Ihr*) transforms itself immediately into a: ›You (*Du*), my *Volk*.‹ It has a peculiar relationship with the change of the singular into the plural.« Heidegger: Logik als die Frage nach dem Wesen der Sprache, p. 42; Heidegger: Logic as the Question Concerning the Essence of Language, p. 38. At the very end of § 13, Heidegger ensures the horizon on which lies the multiplicity of peoples, the multitude of peoples. »*Wir sind ein Volk, nicht das Volk.*« Heidegger: Logik als die Frage nach dem Wesen der Sprache, p. 60; Heidegger: Logic as the Question Concerning the Essence of Language, p. 52.

But to the extent to which it implies this *closing*, the institution has as its main characteristic a horizon of the future and a permanent openness for the absolutely other, for the new, foreign and completely surprising member and collaborator.[204]

The second interjection regards documents, or more precisely, writing and written acts. *Documental work* is what holds the institution, is the *in statuere* of the institution, and precedes (and also structures) the *We* and the community. It also structures I-intentionality and We-intentionality (that is, collective intentionality),[205] and certain I-reflexivity (or reflection) and We-reflexivity (collective reflexivity). In our imaginary conference, *documental work* appears from the very start of an institutional fiction of this small group. Aside from working on Heidegger's lectures and texts, our group could not be formed without written invitations to the conference, written decisions and requirements, passports, visas, a great number of e-mails, letters, money, airline tickets, various archives, registers, receipts, credit cards, etc.[206] I would call this strategy *Miteinanderschreiben*, paraphrasing (along with Agostino Cera[207]) Karl Löwith's 1928 expression *Miteinandersprechen*. In *Das Individuum in der Rolle des Mitmenschen*, Löwith relies primarily on Fichte's understanding of the writer and reader, criticizes the status of writing (and consequently the text) between any two. Aside from overlooking the advantage of the written exchange and the text as a trace that could ensure responsibility and the carrying out of obligations by members of a community (co-respondence),[208] Löwith insists that the written exchange is lacking and on a lower

204 Writing in an introduction dated 16 February 1928 of Karl Löwith's book *Das Individuum in der Rolle des Mitmenschen* – a book that can be called the first systematic reading of *Sein und Zeit*, and possibly still the most encompassing and critical – in footnote 3, Martin Heidegger insists that to be WITH the other (the condition of *We*) implies the absolute otherness of the other on *that* side of the source of reciprocity, and which would thus block the idealism of intentionality constituted unilaterally. Once again Semion Frank: »This is in direct connection with the second characteristic of we: as opposed to all other forms of personal being (личного бытия), we is in principle limitless (принципиально безгранично). True, the empirical we is always limited: every we, whether a family, a group, nation, state, religion, has something not incorporated within it and opposed to it – some other you and them. But together with these, we in a different, higher unity can encompass and incorporate into itself all other yous and thems – in principle all existing (in a higher, absolute sense, not only all people, but anything that exists is predisposed (предназначено) to be a member or participant of the all-encompassing we, and thus it is potentially part of *We*).« Frank: *Duhovnie osnovi obsestva*, p. 46.

205 Searle: The Construction of Social Reality, p. 26.

206 Cf. Bojanic: Fenomenologia dell'istituzionale, pp. 37–52.

207 The author of the introduction to the translation of Löwith's book into Italian. Cf. Cera: Introduzione, p. 23.

208 Thematizing the *We* and the community in the same decade, Franz Rosenzweig suggests that only the text and its reading can ensure unity and the ear of the entire community. »The sermon, like the text read aloud, is itself there to produce mutual silence of the gathered community. Its essence is not that it is a speech, but exegesis; the reading out of the written word is crucial for the creation of the listening community and the strong bonds of togetherness of those present« (*Die Predigt wie der verlesene Text selber ist dazu da, das gemeinsame Schweigen der versammelten Gemeinde zu schaffen. Und ihr Wesen ist also nicht, dass sie Rede, sondern dass sie Exegese ist; die Verlesung des Schriftworts*

level than discussion and oral conversation (*Gespräch*): writing does not imply a discussion at one time, rather an exchange one *after* the other (*ein abwechselndes* nach-*einander Reden*), *Im Gespräch spricht der eine unmittelbar mit dem andern, sie sprechen mit-einander*; further, »I« and »You« cannot write WITH one another, but only to one another (*nur noch an-einander schreiben*); the autonomy of the text leads to the separation of the two, since its writing and reading do not overlap in time, therefore the writer is not responsible before his reader at once and personally (*Demgemäß »verantwortet« sich der Autor von seinem Leser nicht unmittelbar persönlich, sondern nur denjenigen Anspruch, der in dem beschlossen ist, was er geschrieben hat*).[209] Obviously, the appearance and development of institutes (*Institute*) or instruments (*Instrumente*) such as e-mail and SMS has rendered Karl Löwith's arguments obsolete. Still, this passage by Löwith could allow for a soft analogical construction of Heidegger's understanding of self (*selbst*) and *We* from § 11, in which Heidegger very clearly shows that »the belongingness to the lecture« (*Zusammengehörigkeit zur Vorlesung*) in a way precedes »individual acts« of members of the auditorium (*Hörerschaft*) – their listening, potential questions, discussions before and after the lecture, discussions in nearby parks and restaurants, even their correspondences. Also, this is a good opportunity to sketch out Heidegger's correction of questions (or questionings) of *We* and the shifting of his understanding of self and *We*, which he conducts in § 12, »The self and self-forlornness« (*Das Selbst und die Selbsverlorenheit*). Initially, »*selbst*« as *belonging* to a group or as common belonging to a group that listens to a lecture or presentation at a conference is structured as a document. It is truly possible (as Löwith does) to claim and prove the problematic nature of a text completely autonomous from Heidegger's lecture's listeners and Heidegger himself; but it is, for example, the *charter* of a group that allows, with its existence, for the institutionalization of the individuals of that group; the charter is the condition for those same individuals to mutually discuss or write to one another. The difference between a written and oral exchange is secondary in importance, in the same sense that discussion or correspondence of group members affirms that the group (or institution) exists, but can neither in principle terminate it nor found it (the ever-»institutionalization« of an institution is certainly subsequent to the act of the registering for the Heidegger seminar or our imaginary conference). The written document or charter or simply a list of students[210] (or a list of obligations of the audience and

ist die Hauptsache; denn in ihr allein wird die Gemeinschaft des Hörens und damit der feste Grund aller Gemeinsamkeit der Versammelten geschaffen). Rosenzweig: Der Stern der Erlösung (1921), p. 344.

209 Löwith: Das Individuum in der Rolle des Mitmenschen, § 31. »Die Verabsolutierung des Besprochenen in der schriftlichen Rede«, pp. 119–121.

210 The list of students attending the seminar includes Helene Weiss, who did not turn over her notes from the seminar *Logik als die Frage nach dem Wesen der Sprache* to Heidegger after the war. These notes were published in 1991, edited by V. Farías. Cf. Lógica. Lecciones de M. Heidegger. This

participants of a conference, including that of being at a given place and time, as well as of the support staff to ensure the work of a group, making them part of it) constitutes a group and a *We* as one of the first protocols of conjoining. In § 12, Heidegger shifts the emphasis from the importance of the collective or belonging to a collective (*We* precedes *I*) to the importance of the individual decision of the individual and their commitment to, for example, attend the seminar on *Logic* (the registration for which is conducted with a signature and a written statement). Heidegger writes:

> With the cry (*Ausruf*) »We!« we can miss our self in the same way as in a glorification of the I. Conversely, we can, however, also just as properly find our self-being (*Selbstsein*) by way of the I as by way of the You (*Ihr*) and We; for all that, it is a matter of the self-being, of the determination of the self. That means: The We, at which we now stop with the question »Who are we ourselves?« (*Wir sind wir Selbst?*) the We, also in the sense of genuine community (*echten Gemeinschaft*), does not have the preeminence (*Vorrang*) simply and unconditionally, and that also in relation (*bezug*) to the community. There are things that are essential and decisive for a community, and precisely these things do not arise in the community, but in the disciplined strength and solitude of an individual (*in der beherrschten Kraft und Einsamkeit eines einzelnen*). One believes that the community is responsible for it (*Man meint, die Gemeinschaft macht es*); one believes that if ten or thirty unprepared and ignorant people squat together and babble day after day, then a community or a genuine relation results. This camp delusion is the counter-appearance of any camp.[211]

What is essential, says Heidegger, is not born in the group or *with* the group, but rather long before. Regardless of Heidegger's efforts to declare certain groups or communities much more important or authentic than others, that is, to declare certain decisions more important and complex than others, it seems that only an abiding and concerted decision-making on one's own can be proof of advantage of the collective and collective reflexivity (responsibility before the collective or collective responsibility) over the quick and spontaneous decision of the individual.

Let us return to the construction of the Tower of Babel. This is the key prospect (model), entirely analogous to Heidegger's paragraphs supposed to show the importance of drawing together technology and the institution, technical and institutional action, but also untangle the difficulty in their differentiating and

edition of the seminar is different from the official one published in 1998, also the result of reconstruction of notes of students present at the lectures.

211 Heidegger: Logik als die Frage nach dem Wesen der Sprache, p. 51; Heidegger: Logic as the Question Concerning the Essence of Language, p. 45. In »Recapitulation« for § 12 Heidegger is even clearer: »Even where a genuine community entirely determines the self-being, this is not in every respect that which is decisive, that which is essential for the community. In many regards, that which is decisive is never attained in and out (*in und aus*) of the community, but out of the disciplined strength of an individual in his solitude, who evidently must have in himself the impetus that entitles him to the solitude.« Heidegger: Logik als die Frage nach dem Wesen der Sprache, p. 56; Heidegger: Logic as the Question Concerning the Essence of Language, p. 49.

naming.[212] A single language and a shared set of words (translatability and communicability), as a condition of institutional acting of a group of people who find a place, settle there, and live together, is complemented by a collective mobilization and readiness (decision) to communally acquire new technologies and materials for construction;[213] the group builds a city, and are a carrier of the idea of a grandiose and impossible project (to the sky); the group has to be institutionalized (to be named, self-named, to become an entity, a corporation) in order to be broken up and disseminated; in the end, the last element of institutionalization implies transcendental optics, and the self-supervision of the group (God comes down to see the city, and supervise and control the work), which turns into auto-sabotage of their own project. God, in fact, is the name of the discovery of corruption within the institution. But at the same time, the name »God« is the discovery of the sovereign instance containing the power to always speak in the first-person plural (*We*).[214] Thus God's *arrival* and *descent* are an invitation for *more We*, for more *us*, for »more institution«, since someone is missing. The great failure of the project of institutionalization, or inappropriate action (*Machenschaft*, *machination*, manipulation) within the constitution of the community, all by way of various instruments (something Heidegger constantly writes about, and which ultimately marks his effort in reconstructing technology and the technical) could probably be explained with an insufficiently stable *We*-construction and the secondary importance of thinking politics and the city within the field of Husserlian (and Heideggerian) philosophy.[215]

212 Heidegger uses several words for the institution: rarely *Institution* and *Institute*; much more often *Einrichtung* and *Stiftung*; he uses *Korporation* only in the seminar »Hegel's Rechtsphilosophie« 1934–35, etc. Their intertwinement is most tight in the text »Die Zeit des Welbildes«. In his *Introduction to Metaphysics*, Heidegger uses the old German word for the institution *Satzung*, even though this word is more correctly translated as legal act. I am calling attention here to the difference between *Gesetz* and *Satzung* that Otto von Gierke makes. The state or sovereign creates law (*Gesetz*), but Gierke emphasizes that any collective which is not a state but is autonomous (*Autonomie*) can create a legal act (*Satzung*).

213 In the »Kaizo« essays, written from 1922 to 1923, Husserl speaks of the »primal We«, and differentiates two types of unity of the community: imperial – from above, and communist unity. »There is thus a universal bond of wills present which creates a unity of will. And this happens without an imperialist organization of will, a central will in which all single wills are centered and to which all must subordinate themselves voluntarily and whose functionaries each must acknowledge himself to be. (Note: We can here speak of a communist unity of wills in contrast to an imperialist unity). Here is the consciousness of the communal goal to be pursued, of an encompassing will of which all know themselves to be functionaries, but as free – and not even a freedom which must practice renunciation – and not subordinated functionaries.« Husserl: Aufsätze und Vorträge, pp. 52–53.

214 *»Wohlan, laßt uns hinabfahren, und daselbst ihre Sprache verwirren* (…)« (*Gen.* 11.7).

215 Neither Husserl nor Heidegger follow their students Edith Stein, Gerda Walther, Karl Löwith in thinking the phenomenon of the community.

2 Originary Institutionalization (Husserl's *stiften, urstiften*)

Apart from the verb *stiften* and *urstiften*, Husserl uses the German nouns *Stiftung*, *Urstiftung*, or *Endstiftung*. Even today, despite the fact that there is still a great deal of time before we can expect all of Husserl's manuscripts to be published, it is relatively easy to defend the importance of Husserl's idea and the importance that these, still strange, words have for Husserl's work in general. When the newly built archive opened its doors to its first visitors in Leuven, before the Second World War (one of the first visitors was Merleau-Ponty[216]) or right after the war (the first one certainly was Paul Ricœur), it was impossible to imagine the strength of Husserl's investment and insistence on the pair *Stiftung / Urstiftung*. The responsibility for concealing the uniqueness of these words falls on Emmanuel Lévinas, who translates the word *Urstiftung* in *Cartesian Meditations* (1929) in two ways.[217] Lévinas, who never worked in the archive, could be a very good example of several possible suppositions: 1.) that the importance of Husserl's ›unknown‹ strategies can only be found in unpublished manuscripts; 2.) that completely different generations of users of Husserl's archives (in Leuven or Paris) witness an identical belief in the importance of Husserl's discovery (Derrida or Lyotard or Richir); 3.) that Merleau-Ponty's translation (*Stiftung* is *institution*) dominates and has a bigger influence on the latter interpretations of Husserl than, for example, Ricœur's first solutions of the translation;[218] 4.) that precisely the translation of *Stiftung* as

216 Merleau-Ponty visited Leuven for the first time on 1 April 1939 (he returned in 1946). Of the many texts, he consulted *Die Krisis*, followed by a series of manuscripts marked D (*primordiale Konstitution, Urkonstitution*) which still remain unpublished, etc. Cf. Van Breda: Maurice Merleau-Ponty et les Archives-Husserl à Louvain, pp. 410–430.

217 In § 38, Lévinas and Gabrielle Pfeiffer (Alexandre Koyré examined this translation) translate *Urstiftung* as *formation première*, and in the famous § 50 as *création première*. Husserl: Méditations cartésiennes, pp. 135, 181. Dorion Cairns always translates *Urstiftung* as »primal instituting«. Husserl: Cartesian Meditations, pp. 80, 111. When translating the word *Stiftung*, Cairns gives advantage to the word institution or instituting over the word foundation. Cf. Cairns: Guide for Translating Husserl, p. 108.

218 Ricœur, immediately upon his arrival from Leuven with the first translation of Husserl's 1935 »Vienna Conference«, in his first text concerning Husserl »The Sense of History«, from 1949, speaks of history as a most important moment in the understanding of ourselves and cites § 15 of the book *Crisis* whose title is »Reflections on the Method of our Historical Considerations«:

»That sort of elucidation of history by which we return to ourselves in order to question the original foundation (*die Urstiftung*; *la fondation originelle* in French original) of the goals which connect the chain of the generations to come (...), this elucidation, I say, is only the authentic coming to awareness by the philosopher of the true end of his willing, of what is willing in him, comes from willing, and is willing as such from his spiritual ancestors«.

institution, makes Husserl a purely »French matter« not only because it comes directly from the archives without any influence of German reception or German scholars, incorporates Husserl into the juridical and political milieu of France, and enables it to be interpreted from leftist and Marxist positions) and finally, 5.) (*Ur*) *Stiftung* as a (proto)institution, brings phenomenology into completely varying texts of important French philosophers who have not read Husserl in the archive, but who nevertheless think the institution as such »with him«.[219] This final point is supposed to introduce the idea that the reading, translating and influence of Husserl, which began in his Belgian archive and continued in Paris, can institute what we can tentatively call »Continental Philosophy«. This means that Husserl's strategy with *Stiftung / Urstiftung* can be the source of this syntagma »Continental Philosophy« because the thinking of the institution of philosophy (the question »What is the institution of philosophy?« hides the fundamental question »What is philosophy?«) is structured as the thinking of Europe, as the thinking of humanity (*Menschheit*)[220] and as the thinking of an encounter with the other (intersubjectivity, community).

Merleau-Ponty translates the word *Stiftung* – »the beautiful word of *Stiftung* (*le beau mot de Stiftung*) which Husserl used to signify the infinite fecundity of every moment in time« – as institution.[221] What is therefore institution, and does this Latin syntagma – *in statuere* – truly carry over Husserl's intention to find one operation or one form that differs from all previous ones he used? It is about a creative act which begins something, which provides stability to something, and which should differ from the words *Begründung*, *Letztbegründung*, *Konstitution*, *Setzung*, *Fundierung* etc.

I will, preliminarily and without taking too long, list several meanings of the word institution, which should be compared to Edmund Husserl's intentions: Beyond giving a beginning to something (to originate, to initiate; in French *instituer* means an act through which something is inaugurated) and beyond building (establishing) something on the land of the master (institution is always connected to architecture, to an object), to institute shares the same semantic line as the Latin word *status*. *In statuere* is something that stands (without help, without being held, by itself) or holds itself vertically.[222] The institution secures its status through

»I can know who I am, continues Ricœur, through uncovering an origin (*Ursprung*), a primal institution (*Urstiftung*; *une proto-fondation*, in French), which is also a project toward the future horizon, a final institution (*Endstiftung*; *une fondation finale*)«. Ricœur: Husserl, p. 155; Ricœur: Le sens de l'histoire, pp. 293–294.

219 I am referring to Michel Foucault's project. Cf. Foucault: L'ordre du discours, pp. 9–15.

220 »Philosophy is the »innate entelechy« of Europe, the »proto-phenomenon« of its culture«. Ricœur: Husserl, p. 152.

221 Merleau-Ponty: La Prose du monde, p. 95.

222 Therefore, in contrast to the word »foundation«, which assumes sitting and the stability that sitting affords one (*fundamentum* is the back side, anus). Fund means money. The colloquial mean-

statutes, that is, through internal rules (*institutes*). The second, equally important corpus of the meaning and use of the verb to institute, refers to the openness of an institution to: 1.) signify or create a successor (a deal between generations); 2.) to institute means to give instruction, educate (in this instance the institution and documentation overlap) and 3.) to institute presumes the creation of a reserve or the creation of a place for something that has yet to come, is forthcoming, and is still absent or invisible.

As I pointed out earlier, the phrase *in statuere* into which Husserl's idea is supposed to be translated and transformed, already has a rich and fertile political-law tradition in France. This tradition follows Kant foremost, for whom peace is something necessarily established (*Frieden stiften*).[223] Only in the last decade of his life does Kant frequently use the words *stiften* or *gestiften*. *Stiften*, without a doubt, implies violence or force. Kant believes, and in many places clearly manifests (several times in the notes on his manuscripts) this belief, that something can be established, or rather institutionalized, through violence or force. That is to say, that the act of violence is the inaugural act of any establishing, including the establishing of peace. For example, § 55 *Metaphysics of Moral* begins with Kant's hope that it is possible to establish a condition that comes close to right, through war (*um etwa einen dem rechtlichen sich annähernden Zustand zu stiften*). In the lectures from the winter semester of 1793/94, which were prepared for publication by Johann Friedrich Vigilantius (*Metaphysik der Sitten Vigilantius*), Kant is quite clear: »(...) because without violence right cannot be established, therefore violence must precede right, instead of rule based on rights founding force (strength/power). Take people *in statu naturali*, they are *ex leges*, apart from legal status, without any law, only some outside force, keeping them asleep«.[224]

But let us return to France. Merleau-Ponty, in his notes on the course »L'Institution dans l'histoire personnelle et publique« (1954–1955), points out that it is precisely Husserl who, using his pair *Stiftung / Urstiftung*, manages to find the meaning of permanent revolution: »Revolution and institution: revolution is re-institution which has as its goal the overthrow (*renversement*) of the preceding institution (...) Revolution is a return to the source, the awakening of something that derails the founding idealizations, their context, the future which is the past, the future which is a much deeper comprehension of the past, which is *gestiftet*

ing of *Stifter* is Founder; *Anstifter* is Initiator, while *Stiftung* means a Foundation which provides stipends or grants for projects.

223 Kant: Zum ewigen Frieden, p. 349.

224 »(...) *daß ohne Gewalt kein Recht gestiftet werden kann, so muß dem Recht die Gewalt vorausgehen, statt dessen der Regel nach das Recht die Gewalt begründet muß. An nehme Menschen in statu naturali, sie sind ex leges, in keinem rechtlichen Zustande, sie haben keine Gesetze, noch äußerliche Gewalt, die sie aufrecht erhält*«. Kant: Vorlesungen über Moralphilosophie, p. 515.

(*institute*) instituted thought this past in a dual way. The double aspect of institution: it is itself and it is on the other side of itself, restriction and openness.«[225]

But these sentences do not contain only Merleau-Ponty polemics with Sartre, another French phenomenologist, nor does he just evoke old questions in connection with Marxism or Trotsky. During a course in which he meticulously analyses Marx, Proust, and Freud, Merleau-Ponty strives to show the advantage of the word ›institution‹ (»An institution is not the position of a concept, but of a being, the openness of a field«[226]) in relation to law, contract or constitution.[227] This is mere repetition of tradition: 1.) reading Merleau-Ponty, we hear Saint-Just's celebrated calls for the introduction of institutions into the Republic because they are its soul;[228] 2.) when Merleau-Ponty speaks of a double aspect of institution, he is in fact repeating Saint-Simon (the creator of the expression *contre-institution*, counter-institution); 3.) the relation of restriction and openness of the institution represents the *de facto* convertible and incorporative power of the institution (within the institution of consciousness [Bergson], custom, *habitus*, energy, instinct are converted). In order to presently examine and explain the institution of *(Ur) Stiftung* into this complicated field covered by the words *in statuere* and *institution*, in order to discover the strength of Husserl's intention and how far his opinion exceeds this context – in a word, does the introduction of Husserl into French philosophy mean to institute a new (absolute) *Urstifter*,[229] a new Edmund Husserl, who then institutes not just continental or analytic, but also pure philosophy[230] or the institution of philosophy as such? – I therefore propose three different visions or versions of Husserl's intervention. Only the third one, which was provoked by one of Ricœur's fragments, written more than 30 years ago, could possibly justify my humble endeavor.

225 Merleau-Ponty: L'institution, pp. 42–43.

226 Ibid., p. 101.

227 This is Emile Durkheim's position, but also that of French institutionalists (Maruice Hauriou, Georges Renard, Joseph T. Delos), important jurists and political scientists between the two wars.

228 »Les institutions, qui sont l'âme de la République, nous manquent.« Saint-Just: Rapport sur les personnes incarcérées, p. 191.

229 The Frenchman Descartes is *Urstifter* (»the primal founder, not only of the modern idea of objectivistic rationalism but also of the transcendental motif which explodes it«). Cf. Husserl: The Crisis of European Sciences and Transcendental Phenomenology, p. 73. At the very end of his life, Husserl differentiates between the absolute and relative proto-institution (Document 33 »Die Unterscheidung zwischen absoluter und relativer Urstiftung«, *Sommer* 1937). Cartesian's intention is radical and absolute, just as proto-institution of Greek philosophy. Husserl: Die Krisis der europaischen Wissenschaften und die transzendentale Phänomenologie, pp. 421–423.

230 In a document numbered 32 »Teleologie in der Philosophiegeschichte« written in 1936 and during June and July of 1937, Husserl says: »*Die Methode, sie, die überrelativen Wahrheiten, zu finden, setzt mit voraus die Methode der Reinhaltung des streng theoretischen Interesses, auf das philosophische Wahrheit bezogen ist. Die Erfordernisse dieser doppelten Methode sind die Bedingungen der Möglichkeit einer Philosophie – einer reinen Philosophie.*« Husserl: Die Krisis der europäischen Wissenschaften und die transzendentale Phänomenologie, p. 393.

a) In his 1967 Oslo lectures[231], Ingarden insists that the gradual transformation of the word *Setzung* (position; *setzen*, to set up) into *Stiftung*, signifies Husserl's path towards idealism. Husserl substitutes the word *Setzung* (which can easily be found in Kant and Neokantians) starting with *Meditations* and *Formal and Transcendental Logic*, in order to reinforce the active strength of intentionality. Idealism is not to find one thing, or to accept and confirm its existence; idealism is to create that one thing, to enable the revelation of its being, the revelation of the thing itself. Ingarden points out that this is true in some cases, for example when a university is instituted, when through an act (*stiften*) the being of a university is uncovered. But what if a thing is in question? Ingarden is pretty certain that, after 1929, Husserl changes the form of every act of comprehension and introduces into it a possibility to institute (*stiften*) something (in this way the transcendental and intentional overlap as the area able to create).

b) Another perspective weakens Husserl's idealism if it accepts his insistence of the importance of history. Namely, there exists no order of the ideal (geometry is Husserl's celebrated example) which through language (written and spoken) does not simultaneously secure its own objectivity and its own non-temporality. Language is what constantly re-actualizes and once more completes (*Nachstiftung*; re-institution) what has already been originally instituted. However, this is precisely the fundamental paradox of every *Stiftung* which Husserl insists upon: how come something which is at the beginning, which is potential, which is not present in this actual act, how come this first and potential implicit something is in every work and in the actual (Husserl calls this *leistend* in act)? Three questions: »how does every *Stiftung* renew and repeat *Urstiftung*?«, »how is it that *Urstiftung* is in every *Stiftung*?« and »how is it that the future is anticipated within the *telos* of a proto-act (*Endstiftung* is already in *Urstiftung*[232])«? These questions open the door to a series of famous questions: how is potential, reserve, delay, surplus etc., possible? One more thing: during the reoccurrence of the proto-institution (*Urstiftung*) by every forthcoming *Stiftung*, language simultaneously opens a possible communal world in which I and another, the past and the present, cross paths.

c) The third interpretation of Husserl's pair *Stiftung / Urstiftung* is provoked by a short excerpt, found on page 181 of the text »The problem of the foundation of moral philosophy«, authored by the long-time director of Husserl's archive in Paris, Paul Ricœur[233]. Despite not quoting Husserl, Ricœur implicitly writes in Husserl's hand, using a newly published manuscript.[234] Not only does the exist-

231 Lecture IV (6 October 1967), Ingarden: Einführung in die Phänomenologie Edmund Husserls, p. 124.

232 Merleau-Ponty: L'institution, p. 92; Derrida: Edmund Husserl's Origin of Geometry, p. 138, 141.

233 This text, which has still not been published in French, was first released in Italian in 1975. Ricœur: The problem of the foundation of moral philosophy, pp. 175–192.

234 In question is a manuscript numbered 28 »Problem: Transfer (Tradition) and *Urstiftung*«

ence of this text refute Ingarden's statement (and not only his) – Husserl wrote about the primal institution much earlier than 1929 – this text clearly confirms that Husserl's thoughts about the community are at the beginning of this adventure concerning the *Stiftung*. Ricœur writes:

With institutions a new factor of passivity appears which is compounded with the passivity of the self-actualization of each person by himself and with the other passivity which corresponds to the initial intersubjective situation of inequality which we never stop correcting. (...) I mean that we can only act through structures of interaction which are already there and which tend to unfold their own history which consists of inertias and innovations which themselves are sedimented in their turn. (...) I introduced the word institution here because it seemed to me to respond to a double criterion: On the one hand, every institution leads back to an *Urstftung* – a primordial mythical founding – so that institution signifies that I am already within the instituted. (...) I am never before the beginning of every institution, I am always in an after-the-fact situation. A second indication is furnished by the failure of every effort, phenomenological or otherwise, to draw the social and the political from the immediate I-you relation and, as a consequence, to do without the middle term. This dream of immediacy, of face to face relations without the intermediary of a middle term is well-known. It is the dream that dialogue should be the measure for every human relation. But we also know that even the most intimate dialogical relation is possible only on the basis of institution (...).[235]

Apart from Emanuel Lévinas's implicit critiques (now, it is completely transparent why Lévinas does not mention Husserl's *(Ur)Stiftung* anywhere), it seems to me that, already at this point, the task of philosophy to institute, to generate and to regenerate the community, is revealed. This is the beginning which ends with Husserl's final texts concerning the absolute and relative primal institution of the institution of philosophy (or pure philosophy). The first task of philosophy is not just, as Derrida wrote in 1954, »the genesis of all outside philosophy« (*la réactivation de la genèse*«), but also within it (*la réactivation de SA genèse*).[236] This task of institutionalization is one and the same.

(Übernahme und Urstiftung. Gedanken kollidieren nicht in der Intersubjektivität, aber Zwecke kollidieren eventuell), Husserl: Zur Phänomenologie der Intersubjektivität, 2, pp. 222–225. Ricœur might not have recognized this manuscript before it was published, probably because it was seen as not-classified. Iso Kern found that it belonged to manuscripts concerning the community, that it was written between 1921 and 1922.

235 Ricœur: The Problem of the Foundation of Moral Philosophy, p. 181.

236 Derrida: Le problème de la genèse dans la philosophie de Husserl, p. 259. »La première tâche de la philosophie : la réactivation de la genèse.« Despite being taken by the strength and beauty of Ricœur's first texts concerning Husserl, Derrida translates the word *Stiftung* in a different way: »*fondement originaire*«.

3 Institution of We and Community in Rosenzweig

Much as in the rest of Franz Rosenzweig's *Star of Redemption*, there are a few differences between editions of book I, part 3, »The Fire or the Eternal Life«. The first edition was published in 1921, during Rosenzweig's lifetime, whereas the Nahum D. Galtzer edition (allegedly in accordance with Rosenzweig's instructions) came out shortly after his death in 1930, complete with appendices and chapter titles. How should we read this complicated book? Its entire construction and meaning could really be an answer to two questions at the beginning of the third unit: »But what does that mean – rooting in ourselves (*Verwurzelung im eigenen Selbst*)? What does it mean that here an individual or a people seeks the guarantee of its subsistence (*seines Bestehens*) in nothing external, and precisely here, precisely in its absence of relationship (*Beziehungslosigkeit*), wants to be what is eternal«?[237]

How, then, is an entity constructed or self-constructed? By what means and deploying which strategy, can it be made to be beyond all connection with anything else, yet still last forever and surpass all else? Rosenzweig is here trying to constitute an entirely new »social ontology«, in opposition to Hegel's institutionalism and his state-grounding project in general.[238] Simultaneously working on *Stern*, on his doctoral thesis on Hegel, and participating in one of the most terrible wars in history, it is unsurprising that Hegel (philosophy), Judaism, and war are the first three elements of Rosenzweig's project, and that they intertwine, sometimes entirely chaotically, in the book. His intention is to systematize a few concepts that could explain the eternal life of a community. Yet, before that, is it possible to quickly formulate the nature of Rosenzweig's institutionalism and its novelty? What is it that he does? I think that the first premise could be that Rosenzweig opposes the institution and state[239] (Hegel's state, but not only his) to the

237 Rosenzweig: Der Stern der Erlösung [1921], p. 384; Rosenzweig: Der Stern der Erlösung [1930], p. 339; Rosenzweig: The Star of Redemption, p. 324

238 Later, in a letter to Martin Buber of 3 July 1925, Rosenzweig pens a complicated sentence that describes the terrible travails against institutions, in which he condenses his efforts to remain consistent and uncover all the dangers of institutionalism contained in the Jewish heritage. »The struggle against institutions takes all too breath-taking long for the tempestuous breath of the prophet« (*Kampf gegen Institutionen ist eine viel zu langatmige Sache für den Sturmatem des Profeten*; Rosenzweig: Briefe und Tagebücher, 1/2, p. 1050).

239 In his 1920 lecture, »Der Jude im Staat«, complete with his reservations towards Zionism, Rosenzweig insists that the state in or for Jews was *»nicht lebendig«*. *»Der Jude muß im Staat sein, weil der Staat nicht im Juden sein kann.«* (Rosenzweig: Zweistromland, p. 554).

house. »The chamber of the Jewish heart is at home«[240], and it is in the home that begins and ends »the struggle against death« (in the previous section he speaks about marriage and sexual difference).[241]

Franz Rosenzweig speaks of institutions in which there is no life. In two different places in his texts (from the second half of 1919), he presents the confrontation between life and the institution, the house and the institution, all the while (pro)claiming a new institution that is to be an alternative to the university. (He founded his *counter-institution*, »Lehrhaus Forschungsinstitut« in Frankfurt in 1920.) What, then, is a house for Rosenzweig? It ought to protect life and be separated from the city, just as dwelling ought to be separated from other city activities:

We can no longer wish to remain naked people. We look ›backward‹, but not in a way for us to sacrifice our living life to the image of the holy institution that destroys life. No, the institution may only be the house, we must know and make true that we are more than an institution, a living Jewish people. (*Wir können heute nicht mehr nackte Menschen bleiben wollen. Wir sehen »zurück« aber nicht so, dass wir unser lebendiges Leben wieder dem lebenzerstörenden Bild einer heiligen Institution opfern würden. Nein, die Institution darf uns nur Haus sein, wir müssen es wissen und wahrmachen, dass wir mehr sind als die Institution, lebendige jüdische Menschen.*)[242]

The following passage – from a lecture note – appears as the reconstruction of a fragment from a letter to Rudolf Ehrenberg (of 17 August 1919). In both the letter and the lecture, Rosenzweig goes back and forth. In the letter, he writes:

I do not understand how someone can persist in petrifying people into institutions. We are otherwise happy when able to revive the institution. Here too is real, living, true life good enough to be built into the cornerstone of the institution, yet for which no one knows when or even whether it will be built. (*Ich begreife nicht wie man daran hängen kann, Menschen zu Institutionen zu versteinern. Sonst ist man froh, wenn man Institutionen menschlich beleben kann. Und hier ist ein wirkliches, lebendiges, tatsächliches Leben grade gut genug dazu, in den Grundstein einer Institution eingemauert zu werden, von der keiner weiß, ob überhaupt und wenn, wie sie gebaut werden wird.*)[243]

The institution stands in opposition to life (Rosenzweig first separates them, speaking of the *naked* Institution and naked man), turns life to stone; yet this simultaneously announces the possibility of life not only capable of reviving the

240 Rosenzweig: Der Stern der Erlösung [1921), p. 410; Rosenzweig: Der Stern der Erlösung [1930], p. 362; Rosenzweig: The Star of Redemption, p. 346.

241 In the following, third, book of *Stern*, »Die Strahlen oder der ewiger Weg«, Rosenzweig is even more precise: »*Das ewige Volk ruht schon im Hause des Lebens; die Völker der Welt bleiben auf dem Weg*« (Rosenzweig: Der Stern der Erlösung [1921], p. 471; Rosenzweig: Der Stern der Erlösung [1930], p. 397; Rosenzweig: The Star of Redemption, p. 346).

242 This is a note for the lecture »Lessings Nathan« Rosenzweig held at the end of December 1919 (Rosenzweig: Zweistromland, p. 450).

243 Rosenzweig: Briefe und Tagebücher, 1/2, p. 640.

institution, but also able to *a priori* be in the background and in the foundation of some institutions that do not yet exist, which are yet to come, which we await. »We are otherwise happy when able to revive the institution« (*Sonst ist man froh, wenn man Institutionen menschlich beleben kann*). The institution is not only capable of preserving life (not only ought it protect life), but the reverse is also true: we are the ones capable of preserving the life of the institution, to announce its new life and revive it, to expect it entirely new and alive.[244]

It seems to me that the idea that *we alone* (*Wir allein*), our very own common life can constitute a home or an entirely new institution that has all the characteristics of a new and living house (one that does not petrify us, nor that we petrify and move away from). This is the beginning of Rosenzweig's engagement in whose service are all the concepts he uses.[245] At the very beginning of this book, Rosenzweig anticipates the first-person plural, we, and this is the introduction into the construction of a community or reconstruction of an eternal community. Indeed, this is the basic theme of his book. Rosenzweig needs to show what it is that holds this community together or what binds us all into one entity, which as such is *a priori* outside time. The pronoun ›*Wir*‹ appears at the beginning of the book in quotation marks, as part of the phrase ›*Wir sind ewig*‹, referring to generational transmission, from grandparent to grandson. *We* thus refers to a blood community, to eternity, common language, and a future that affirms the present. Later in the text, Rosenzweig uses ›*Wir allein*‹ several times. In unit six, in which he writes about sin, *Wir* transforms into a very compact community equated with

244 The same hesitation and vacillation appear later in Emmanuel Levinas. In his paradigmatic text from 1953 in which he promotes this ›counter-institutionalism‹ (mirroring John Rawls at this point), he writes: »*Ce qui reste cependant libre, c'est le pouvoir de prévoir sa propre déchéance et de se prémunir contre elle. La liberté consiste à instituer hors de soi un ordre de raison ; à confier le raisonnable à l'écrit, à recourir à une institution. La liberté, dans sa crainte de la tyrannie, aboutit à l'institution, à un engagement de la liberté au nom de la liberté, à un Etat. (...) Concevoir et réaliser l'ordre humain, c'est instituer un Etat juste, qui est, par conséquent, la possibilité de surmonter les obstacles qui menacent la liberté.*« Levinas: Liberté et commandement, p. 266. Further along, on the same page, Levinas explains the contra institutional turn thus: »*Mais le commandement de la loi écrite, la raison impersonnelle de l'institution, malgré son origine dans la volonté libre, prend à l'égard de la volonté, à tous les instants renouvelée, une certaine étrangeté. L'institution obéit à un ordre rationnel où la liberté ne se reconnait plus.*« The effort or engagement that Levinas needs to perform at this point (his entire project can be read in this manifesto-text) refers to the examination of a sort of pre-institutional space (»*cette idée de rapport de particulier à particulier avant l'institution de la loi rationnelle*« Ibid., 267). in which there ought to be no violence. Thus, Levinas' examination of violence and war serves to potentially uncover a new (contra-institutional) space in which freedom will not be forgotten. Put differently, to ensure the space of the institution is free from »*une certaine étrangeté*«.

245 Life is actually the unconditional condition of all that exists, the first concept and the concept that holds all other concepts in order as it constructs it. There is no better sentence about life than the one Rosenzweig writes in the conclusion of the third unit dedicated to »Jewish Essence«: »*Aber das lebendige Leben fragt ja nicht nach dem Wesen. Es lebt. Und indem es lebt, beantwortet es sich selbst alle Fragen, noch ehe es sie stellen kann*« (Rosenzweig: Der Stern der Erlösung [1921], p. 387; Rosenzweig: Der Stern der Erlösung [1930], p. 342; Rosenzweig: The Star of Redemption, p. 327).

humanity or mankind (*Menschheit*), that is, Israel.[246] This shift from a speech act to sin, which strongly binds the individuals of a community into Israel is entirely new and surprising.

Constructing ›*Wir*‹ or the phrase »*Wir sind ewig*« is the axis that holds all other concepts together, giving place to all concepts in a stable order. The various concepts could be divided into a few groups. The first set would include the already mentioned first and crucial articles that determine the difference between Judaism and Christianity. They determine what is Judaism: it is a ›people‹ (›chosen‹, ›holy‹, ›first‹ – these attributes have complementary function), it is ›blood‹, always opposed to ›will‹ and ›spirit‹, it is (holy) ›language‹ and writing, it is (holy) ›law‹, and finally, ›land‹ or ›territory‹, which implies ›Israel‹. Everything Rosenzweig wrote at the time with regard to land and territory would today certainly demand complete revision, in the context of the actually existing state of Israel. Nevertheless, however much the contemporary reader finds Rosenzweig's anti-Zionism hard to understand and perhaps too aggressive and decadent, seventy years since the founding of Israel, his conclusions and arguments remain inspiring.

The following group of terms simultaneously directs and revises all the terms, and in a particular way confirms the self-construction of the ›We-axis‹ or pure flame: this is time or the uses of time and understanding of time always in harmony with eternity. (Rosenzweig insists on an annual cycle that ensures Judaism its eternity; he then further processes all the crucial holy days that regenerate and hold the people together; finally, he constantly mentions the present and the now, which reflect eternity by excluding the temporality of time.) The group further includes the term border, thematized ingeniously in only one place in the book, but further developed in his geopolitical texts from the last period of the war. (A sort of theory of the border in Rosenzweig is a combination of three different sources: Hegel, whose variations on *Schranke* and *Grenze* are crucial for understanding his logic and his system in general; Rosenzweig's experience as a soldier studying maps and thinking borders in the context of crossing, shifting, fluidity; and Rosenzweig the Talmudist, translator and reader of the world text, always distinguishing and separating significance and meaning.) Finally, the last term in this unit is Messiah (»the future of the Messiah, which is surely drawing near«[247]) and messianism, named in the second to last unit of this book as »*messianische Politik*«, implying the existence of something we might call messianic action.

246 In his 1922 lectures, published as »*Die Wissenschaft vom Menschen*«, Rosenzweig returns to the *Wir*. »*Mein Ich wird Wir. Im Wir sehe ich mich gleichzeitig von außen und von innen*« (Rosenzweig: Zweistromland, p. 650).

247 »*Und die Gesänge des ›dritten Mahls‹, zu dem sich im Dämmer des versinkenden Tages Greise und Kinder am langen gedeckten Tische vereinen, sind ganz trunken von dem Rausch der gewißlich nahenden Zukunft des Messias*« (Rosenzweig: Der Stern der Erlösung [1921], p. 393; Rosenzweig: Der Stern der Erlösung [1930], p. 347; Rosenzweig: The Star of Redemption, p. 332).

At the beginning of this unit, Rosenzweig attempts to explain the messianic protocol as such, through an important explanation about the Jewish people, finally »at its goal« (*am Ziel*): »In the cycle of its year the future is the motive power; the circular movement does not give birth as it were by push (*durch Stoß*), but by tug (*sondern durch Zug*); the present elapses, not because the past shoves it ahead, but because the future drags it forward.«[248] Rosenzweig additionally explains the difference between the words *Stoß* and *Zug*, both carrying multiple meanings, in the second part of the sentence: the present elapses primarily because the future drags it along (*die Zukunft sie [die Gegenwart] heranreißt*). The future, being strength (the future does not contain strength, but is strength, says Rosenzweig), *pulls forward* the present. The construction of this sentence, in which the messianic topology, and in general messianic action or messianic movement, is most clearly described, can perhaps be part of an ideal introduction into the theory of messianic time. Rosenzweig's contribution and decisive turn is not achieved by simply opposing the strength of the future to that of the past, nor by the substitution of two forms of movement (›pushing‹ with ›pulling‹), but by the use of the word *Zug* (*sondern durch Zug*). Rosenzweig's *durch Zug* assumes a sudden and surprising pulling out of something hidden, as if from a hole. The messianic is double: it is always present as hidden in the now (»today is not yet the true ›Today‹«), and it appears suddenly and from a spasm.

The third and fourth groups of concepts are particularly interesting. Rosenzweig incorporates them into the ›We-axis‹ as two dimensions that are new and crucial for the ontology of the eternal flame that constitutes itself. The third group refers to the community, and comprises three passages subsequently entitled »Sociology«, wherein the community is elaborated in detail. (Three other sections of the second book of the third part of *Stern* are entitled »Sociology«.) The fourth group of terms could be reduced to the name state or potentially ›of the world‹, rather than politics or messianic politics.

Three chapters of the second edition carry titles containing the word sociology: »Soziologie der Menge: das Hören« (Sociology of The Crowd: Listening – not capitalized in the original edition), »Soziologie der Gemeinschaft: das Mahl« (Sociology of The Community), and finally »Soziologie des Ganzen: der Gruss« (Sociology of The Whole: The Greeting). These last two have a reduced status in comparison to the other six units of the book. With these three, Rosenzweig is attempting to reconstruct the (Jewish) community by way of a few sub-concepts. These are ›silence‹, ›listening‹, ›meal‹, ›greeting‹, ›rest‹, and ›discipline‹. (I believe

248 *»In dem Kreislauf seines Jahres ist die Zukunft die bewegende Kraft; die kreisende Bewegung entsteht gewissermaßen nicht durch Stoß, sondern durch Zug; die Gegenwart verstreicht, nicht weil die Vergangenheit sie weiterschiebt, sondern weil die Zukunft sie heranreißt«* (Rosenzweig: Der Stern der Erlösung [1921], p. 412; Rosenzweig: Der Stern der Erlösung [1930], p. 364; Rosenzweig: The Star of Redemption, p. 348).

these terms to be more significant over all the others that occur more than once.) All these protocols produce a network that constitutes a community, connecting individuals into a *We*. Rosenzweig's originality in this respect is to introduce into social ontology something entirely new and surprising, which he has drawn from living Jewish tradition, its laws and mandates.

›*Silence*‹. Even when speaking of holy language, Rosenzweig insists on »the power of silence« (*Macht des Schweigens*). »With his brother he therefore cannot speak at all; with him the glance informs him better than the word, and there is nothing more deeply Jewish than a final suspicion of the power of the word and a heart-felt confidence in the power of silence«.[249] What is the function of the word or of dialogue, and what is the role of »mutual silence« (*das gemeinsame Schweigen*)? At the beginning of unit 5, he writes: »Because in eternity the word ceases to exist in the silence of the harmonious gathering (*im Schweigen des einträchtigen Beisammenseins*) – for we are united only in silence; the word unites, but those who are united grow silent (*denn nur im Schweigen ist man vereint, das Wort vereinigt, aber die Vereinigten schweigen*) – therefore the burning mirror that collects the sunbeams of eternity in the tiny cycle of the year, the liturgy, must introduce man into this silence«.[250]

›*Listening*‹. The brief chapter »Soziologie der Menge: das Hören« sketches a theory of listening that leads to the community of all who listen to a written text. Rosenzweig presents his own experience of lecturing: »The sermon, like the text read aloud, is there to produce mutual silence of the gathered community (*Die Predigt wie der verlesene Text selber ist dazu da, das gemeinsame Schweigen der versammelten Gemeinde zu schaffen*). Its essence is not that it is a speech, but exegesis; the reading out of the written word is crucial (*die Verlesung des Schriftworts ist die Hauptsache*) for the creation of the listening community (*die Gemeinsamkeit des Hörens*) and the strong bonds of togetherness of those present (*die Gemeinsamkeit der Versammelten*).«[251] Learning how to listen means learning in a way that does not stimulate speaking or the speech of one speaking; rather, listening such that the answer is relinquished while simultaneously encouraging all to listen (to each other). »The silent listening (*das schweigende Hören*) was only the beginning of the mutual participation.«[252]

249 Rosenzweig: Der Stern der Erlösung [1921], p. 380; Rosenzweig: Der Stern der Erlösung [1930], p. 335; Rosenzweig: The Star of Redemption, p. 321.

250 Rosenzweig: Der Stern der Erlösung [1921], p. 388; Rosenzweig: Der Stern der Erlösung [1930], p. 343; Rosenzweig: The Star of Redemption, p. 327.

251 Rosenzweig: Der Stern der Erlösung [1921], p. 389; Rosenzweig: Der Stern der Erlösung [1930], p. 344; Rosenzweig: The Star of Redemption, p. 329.

252 Rosenzweig: Der Stern der Erlösung [1921], p. 395; Rosenzweig: Der Stern der Erlösung [1930], p. 349; Rosenzweig: The Star of Redemption, p. 334.

›*Rest*‹. The chapter that speaks of rest (*Ruhe*) is specific in that three times Rosenzweig uses the word ›*Einsetzung*‹ to mean Sabbath (the word is usually translated as ›institution‹), and only on the fourth occasion insisting that in the house »the day of rest instituted« (*sei der Ruhetag eingesetzt*).[253] Rest means to reacquaint oneself once again with silence and listening, eschewing idle chatter.

›*Meal*‹. Each of these terms align and gather into a community of all. In the unit entitled »Sociology of the Community: The Meal« (*Soziologie der Gemeinschaft: das Mahl*) all these terms finally combine to participate equally in the order of the house:

»The mutual life (*Das gemeinsame Leben*) that is thus born is to be a silent life (*ein schweigendes Leben*), living silence (*lebendiges Schweigen*); so we can only wait to find it in bodily life (*im leiblichen Leben*). The creation in another way, the exchanging of the out-dated material takes place in the meal. For the individual, eating and drinking are already the new birth of the bodily man (*leiblichen Menschen*). For the community, the meal together (*gemeinsame Mahl*) is also the treatment in which it is born again to conscious life (*bewußten Leben*). The silent mutuality of listening and obeying already founds the smallest of communities, that of the home« (*Die schweigende Gemeinsamkeit des Hörens und Gehorchens stiftet schon die kleinste Gemeinschaft, die des Hauses*).

This addition and new term appearing in the home simultaneously with the appearance of the meal and common feast – ›obeying‹ – is immediately deconstructed, with Rosenzweig insisting that all are equal at the table, that »the mutual life of the home does not live in the mutual obeying.«

Most importantly, however, at the table, there is no conversation:

Speaking can be done in the street and marketplace with chance meetings; in comparison, a meal together always means a real, realized and active community (*eine wirkliche, bewirkte und wirkende Gemeinschaft*). This wordless mutuality in itself of the meal is taken together, the mutuality presented as a real mutual participation animated in life (*ist die Gemeinschaft als eine wirkliche im Leben lebendige dargestellt*). Where a meal is taken together, such mutual participation exists. It is so in the home, but so too in monasteries, lodges, casinos, associations. And where mutual participation is lacking, as in classrooms or even in just university lectures, or even seminar practices, it does not exist, although the foundation of mutual participation (*das wirkliche Gemeinschaftsleben*), the mutual listening is indeed by all means here.[254]

›*Greeting*‹. In the conclusion of the fifth unit, in which he states that during holidays the community celebrates itself at mealtime, Rosenzweig also warns that »man has as little stopped at the inn of the mutuality of the last silence as in

253 Rosenzweig: Der Stern der Erlösung [1921], p. 395; Rosenzweig: Der Stern der Erlösung [1930], p. 348; Rosenzweig: The Star of Redemption, p. 333.

254 Rosenzweig: Der Stern der Erlösung [1921], p. 396; Rosenzweig: Der Stern der Erlösung [1930], p. 349–350; Rosenzweig: The Star of Redemption, p. 334.

the holidays of the mutual listening« (*ist der Mensch schon in die Gemeinsamkeit des letzten Schweigens eingekehrt*). There is something higher, he adds, »and this higher may even be located at the outermost border of the mutual participation and be mutuality beyond the mutual life« (*und sei dies Höhere auch an der äußersten Grenze der Gemeinschaft gelegen und eine Gemeinsamkeit jenseits des gemeinsamen Lebens*).[255] What is this ›higher‹, and what is at the border of the community? Rosenzweig differentiates the silence of listeners to lectures, which is the silence of each individual separately, from the silence during mealtime, in which others cease to be others. »One is greeted when encountered (*Man grüßt sich, wenn man sich begegnet*). The greeting is the supreme sign of silence (*das höchste Zeichen des Schweigens*): they are silent because they know each other (*man schweigt, weil man einander kennt*). (...) Only if everything were silent would the silence be perfect and the mutual participation all-inclusive (*die Gemeinschaft all-gemein*). The greeting from all to all (*Aller an Alle*), wherein this fully mutual silence would show itself, would, like every greeting, have at least one's announcement and the exchange of a few words, the mutual listening and the mutual meal as the supposition. But how is this greeting from all to all supposed to happen« (*Wie aber soll dieser Gruß Aller an Alle geschehen*)?[256]

›*Discipline*‹. Rosenzweig's example of a higher order, disciplined community, one containing »the greeting from all to all« (*Aller an Alle*) is the military. Soldiers or *comrades* ought to achieve the greatest unity in discipline. This is Rosenzweig's introduction »into the universal mutual participation (*Allgemeinschaft*) where everyone knows everyone and greets them without words – face to face« (*von Angesicht zu Angesicht*) (Rosenzweig: Der Stern der Erlösung [1921], p. 406; Rosenzweig: Der Stern der Erlösung [1930], p. 359; Rosenzweig: The Star of Redemption, p. 406). ›Discipline‹ is here a new and auxiliary term that first appears at the moment where Rosenzweig needs to explain what is obedience, mentioning the discipline of mutual obeying (›»*die Zucht des gemeinsamen Gehorchens geben*«).[257] »But what it does not give is the feeling of freedom that only a mutual life conjures up before the never dwindling background of this mutual discipline (*ist das vor dem nie schwindenden Hintergrunde jener gemeinsamen Zucht erst ein gemeinsames Leben hervorzaubert*). Such a mutual life as it is presented in the meal together is also not yet that which is last, as little as is the listening together (*das gemeinsame Hören*). But on the road of education toward this last, the mutual silence (*dem gemeinsamen Schweigen*), this is the second halting-place (*die*

255 Rosenzweig: Der Stern der Erlösung [1921], p. 403; Rosenzweig: Der Stern der Erlösung [1930], p. 357; Rosenzweig: The Star of Redemption, p. 340–341.

256 Rosenzweig: Der Stern der Erlösung [1921], p. 403; Rosenzweig: Der Stern der Erlösung [1930], p. 357–358; Rosenzweig: The Star of Redemption, p. 341.

257 I have modified the English translation here, replacing the word ›cultivation‹ with ›discipline‹.

zweite Station), while the listening is the first one«[258]. Discipline or a disciplined military, as a new and higher constitution of a people, as an armed group or a people, as an army – is conditioned upon Rosenzweig's remark that a meal together determines the freedom of a people, but it also instantly opens up the danger of being destroyed. The community achieved in common mealtime as a symbol of freedom and independence necessarily implies danger. »Not only today have there been rebellions against us to annihilate us, but in each generation back to that first one that migrated from Egypt – and in each generation God has saved us«[259].

The fourth group of terms appears in the finale of this book, unit seven, »Die Völker der Welt: Messianische Politik« (The Peoples of The World: Messianic Politics). These are: ›(holy) war‹, ›pacifist‹ or ›pacifism‹, ›people‹, ›peace‹, ›world‹, ›state‹, ›right‹, ›violence‹. Rosenzweig's great project on war is here condensed and abandoned for good in favor of a form of pacifism or a ›messianic dilemma‹ with regard to pacifism that decisively orients the holy people. The war project – let us call it ›war‹ and accept that it was nothing but an ingenious project – was given different code names by Rosenzweig: *»Kriegsopera«*, *»Putzianum«*, *»Hansiaca«*, *»Kriegsausgang«*, and *»Kriegsgrund«*, as well as *»Theatrum Europaeum. Ein Versuch über den Schauplatz der Weltgeschichte«*.[260] After many twists and turns, and many attempts – lest we forget, as early as August and September 1916, Rosenzweig is convinced that pacifism ought to be abandoned because »ultimate peace« (*Endfrieden*) is not man's work (*Menschenwerk*) but a direct act of God (*Einwirkung Gottes*)[261], and as late as December 1922 he still mentions the inade-

258 Rosenzweig: Der Stern der Erlösung [1921], p. 397; Rosenzweig: Der Stern der Erlösung [1930], p. 351; Rosenzweig: The Star of Redemption, p. 335.

259 Rosenzweig: Der Stern der Erlösung [1921], p. 400; Rosenzweig: Der Stern der Erlösung [1930], p. 353; Rosenzweig: The Star of Redemption, p. 337.

260 In the three letters sent to three different addresses in the first half of 1917, Rosenzweig explains in detail the origin of his idea for a big book on the war and says he has begun writing, aware that he would be unable to finish the whole project during his time on the front. For us it is certainly important to notice that »Globus«, conspicuously longer than the other ten, is the basic part of the first projected book, and that the other texts are miniature pieces and portions of that same big book. He tells us that in 1910 or 1911, while writing his thesis on Hegel and the state, he intended to write the history of grounds for war (*Kriegsgrund*). He hastens to finish his doctorate so as to dedicate himself to this task, since on 25 November 1910, Carnegie established a foundation financing projects that deal with the causes and origins of war. In the three letters of January, March and May of 1917 (Rosenzweig: Briefe und Tagebücher, 1/2, pp. 334–335, 375, 395), Rosenzweig offers a few more details: that he wished to analyze wars from 1494 until today, that he is particularly interested in the relationship between the grounds for war (*Kriegsgründen*) and beginning of war (*Kriegsanfängen*). He adds that he writes primarily about what is currently taking place, that previously he wished to work in diplomatic archives and examine all the grounds for war, that is, the reasoning that would lead to the beginning of wars. Yet, he also says that he could never write such a book at present, that if he were to write it now, it would be part of some larger book, which demands even more time. Ultimately, this is why he must ›abort‹ the book …

261 Rosenzweig: Briefe und Tagebücher, 1/1, p. 204.

quacy of believing in pacifism and the power of »spiritual arms«[262] – perhaps it is now possible to insist on two of Rosenzweig's suggestions. Both suggestions about the role of pacifism in war (»messianic and world war«) are based in his acceptance of violence, and the belief that violent means can indeed achieve something that nonviolent cannot (based on his theory of two types of peace and two kinds of pacifism). Hence, Rosenzweig is completely certain, as is Walter Benjamin for example, that violence can make something (that violence makes a new right or justice, or that by way of violence an old justice becomes some new justice).[263] Also, the geopolitical construction helps Rosenzweig claim that only by means of war could the transition of national states and Europe be completed into the planet and the world (war as transition). It also allows him to claim war as a sort of subject (God), deciding on its own beginning, duration and end (*»Der Krieg ist der große Entscheider«*).[264] In an unusually important and detailed letter to his parents from 1 September 1916,[265] he writes about peace before (on the brink) of a possible war, that is, of peace that exists in paradise (*der paradiesische Friede*) and of the peace after the war (or wars) that exists in the time of the Messiah and the thousand year reign. The first peace (the natural state or natural peace), taken care of by the so-called materialist pacifism, is a peace between creations and things that have no connection among themselves, where the frictions and tears are brought to a minimum, and identities and entities are completely separated one from another. In international relations, such a peace is founded on a tolerance of all peoples. The second peace, or the second world peace, the idealistic, messianic (*idealistisch, messianisch*), around which idealistic pacifism is organized, arrives after the last war. (And he notes that it is advocated by German thinkers.) Such peace means a close connection of people and peoples, it questions the reasons behind wars, and tries to transform them into reasons for peace and a new life of togetherness. The condition of this new peace and the stake of idealistic pacifism, according to Rosenzweig, is the last war.

This also shows, continues Rosenzweig, that the national and liberal states are in their beginnings (*in ihren Anfängen*) *einen pazifistischen Zug*. Both of these formulations, the pessimistic – that pacifism does not achieve true world peace and

262 Ibid., 1/1, p. 874.

263 Rosenzweig: Der Stern der Erlösung [1921], p. 418; Rosenzweig: Der Stern der Erlösung [1930], p. 370; Rosenzweig: The Star of Redemption, pp. 352–353.

264 Cf. Rosenzweig often speaks of war that decides and judges, mostly in the texts »Globus« and »Vox Dei,« »Die Gewissensfrage der Demokratie«. (Rosenzweig: Zweistromland, p. 279) *»Der Krieg ist ein »göttliches Gericht«, aber kein einfaches Strafgericht, sondern »Krisis,« Scheidung, Böcke und Schafe«* (Rosenzweig: Briefe und Tagebücher, p. 350). In *Stern* he writes: *»Der Krieg allein, der über das Bewußtsein der Einzelnen hinwegrast, entscheidet.«* Rosenzweig: Der Stern der Erlösung [1921], p. 416; Rosenzweig: Der Stern der Erlösung [1930], pp. 367–368; Rosenzweig: The Star of Redemption, p. 351.

265 Rosenzweig: Briefe und Tagebücher, 1/1, pp. 210–214.

freedom, but only imperial peace determined by borders and governments, and the optimistic, whereby (»idealistic«) pacifism is the part of the war machine that tears down state borders – alter the meaning of the phrase *»pazifistischer Zug«*. The idea (of the national or liberal state) does not contain the *Zug*, but is the *Zug*. And it is the *Zug* at its very beginning, at the moment of its constituting. However, that which is at the beginning of its constitution is also really the beginning of its future end. To be or to have *»pazifistischer Zug«* means at the end to cease to be or cease having sovereignty – not being a national state. Thus, in a different register, Rosenzweig finds within (the main characteristics of) the state – violence, war, and revolution – precisely those elements that will completely destroy the state. *»Pazifistischer Zug«*, as a deconstructive or affirmative element found within the construction and foundation of the national state itself, is foreshadowed in several places in »The Peoples of the World: Messianic Politics«. Rosenzweig writes this at the same time as speaking, with surprising inspiration, of the state and of the Jewish people's resistance to having their own state, as well of the Jews (potentially) belonging to the peoples of the world due to this state. He reveals that there is something that contradicts the Jewish people within the state, something alternative, which, paradoxically, has the power to take away eternity from the eternal people. And he confirms the potential of the state to achieve something new and alternative (»if the State could get what it is reaching for«), and as a result »the people have become master over its enemy«[266]. Is a possible *»pazifistischer Zug«* of the state of Israel not indicated by this?

But who reveals world peace and who is the ideal subject of pacifism? Who should be the agent of this process, according to Rosenzweig?

Opposite this constant life in the war of faith (*Glaubenskrieg*), the Jewish people has its war of faith behind it in a mythic past. Therefore, all wars that it still experiences are purely political wars (*rein politische Kriege*) for it. And since it does possess the concept of the war of faith, it therefore cannot take political wars seriously, like the ancient peoples for whom this concept was foreign (*fremd*). Of course, the Jew is really the only man in the Cristian world who cannot take war seriously, and therefore is the only genuine »pacifist«. (…) by living the eternal peace, the Jewish people stands outside of a warlike temporality (*außerhalb einer kriegerischen Zeitlichkeit*); by resting at the goal that it anticipates in hope, it is separated from the march of those who draw near to it in the toil of centuries.[267]

»Der Jude ist der einzige echte ›Pazifist‹.« »Ja der Jude ist eigentlich der einzige Mensch in der christlichen Welt, der den Krieg nicht ernst nehmen kann, und so

266 Rosenzweig: Der Stern der Erlösung [1921], p. 420; Rosenzweig: Der Stern der Erlösung [1930], p. 371; Rosenzweig: The Star of Redemption, p. 354.

267 Rosenzweig: Der Stern der Erlösung [1921], p. 416; Rosenzweig: Der Stern der Erlösung [1930], p. 368; Rosenzweig: The Star of Redemption, p. 351.

ist er der einzige echte ›Pazifist‹.« The Jew is the real or the authentic *pacifist*, because he cannot take seriously the wars Christian states lead one against another. Twice Rosenzweig underscores that the Jew *cannot* accept or give meaning to these political wars. They are foreign to him because they do not belong to the register or notion (*Begriff*) of religious wars. Regardless of the fact that in the chapter »War of Faith«, which precedes this fragment, he says that as opposed to Christians, the Jewish people knows both types of war, and is the guardian of the knowledge of difference between them, and regardless of the fact that Rosenzweig unveils the possibility of existence of a another, *third* type of war (in which the religious and political are mixed) – the Jewish people remains completely outside the world, and outside »war temporality« (*außerhalb einer kriegerischen Zeitlichkeit*). There are wars between states and peoples (in which, peoples risk being annihilated). This is the main characteristic of so-called »political« wars: they are decided in a miraculous, completely mysterious way, by »God's will« or »war alone«, and are beyond the consciousness of individuals. Is it really possible that such wars are completely without relevance for Rosenzweig, for a Jew? Did Rosenzweig's entire effort not precisely consist of the attempt to bridge the strict distinction between two kinds of wars within the Jewish political tradition, and to construct or renew the idea of last, messianic wars? If we leave aside his doubts, the dissatisfaction with the end of World War I and his abandonment of the *Kriegsgrund* project, what does it even mean to disregard political wars and to be the only genuine »pacifist«?

It seems to me that the correct answers to these difficult questions could justify not only the relevance of Rosenzweig's argumentations in favor of war (they are rather argument sketches, intuitions, suggestions), but could also explain another epoch in the history of the Jewish people, which Rosenzweig did not have in mind – the Holocaust, forming of the state of Israel, its wars, new (preventive, asymmetrical) wars for world governance, etc. Although his political manifesto »The Peoples of the World: Messianic Politics« places the Jewish people beyond any state or conflict among states of the world, perhaps it may be possible to defend the consistency and logic of his project by »inscribing« the existence of the state of Israel into it. In the same vein, it seems important to espouse the paradoxical harmony of his project with the changes in the world that happened after his death.

The defense of Rosenzweig's engagement within a complex Jewish political tradition could move in three steps. Step one looks at the statement »*Der Jude ist der einzige echte ›Pazifist‹.*« Purified of Rosenzweig's ambiguous use of quotation marks over the word pacifist and the controversial proximity of the words genuine and pacifist – is the Jew the only true and authentic pacifist or the only true and authentic »pacifist« (in the latter case, he is the only true pseudo-pacifist, or the real pacifist who is not a pacifist, a »militant pacifist«)? – brings us back to the key word *der einzige*. Only the Jew is the true idealistic pacifist. In that context, the Jew is not interested in purely political wars, but what follows: true »peace at all cost« which interrupts them. God (war) decides on its end, that is, the Messiah turns political wars into last wars, finally bringing about eternal peace.

Step two: Rosenzweig *de facto* guards the difference between religious war and ordinary war (*der gewöhnliche Krieg*).[268] Nevertheless, he very carefully opens up an uncertain field where this difference could be reduced. The existence of a large world war allows Rosenzweig to construct the idea of a political war or wars that cannot be interrupted before they become last and messianic wars. Only the last war can ever stop, and only when God's will brings it to an end or when the enemy unconditionally accepts peace. This is a novelty in the history of thought and justification of war.

Step three: A new world war, and the existence of the state of Israel and its wars, does not necessarily have to degrade Rosenzweig's project, nor the greatness of a people that was once »its goal«. The issue is neither the closing nor the expansion of a particular state, but primarily a new speeding up of world history … the renewal of what Rosenzweig once, a long time ago, called *pazifistischer Zug*.

268 Rosenzweig: Der Stern der Erlösung [1921], p. 416; Rosenzweig: Der Stern der Erlösung [1930], p. 367; Rosenzweig: The Star of Redemption, p. 350.

4 Does to Institutionalize Mean to Document?

In section 5.1.1, ›Documents‹, of *Documentalità,* Maurizio Ferraris writes:

Continuing with a detailed examination of the phenomenology of the institutional and of social differences seems to me a less substantive operation than (the more important) task of noting the importance given to documents in social reality and to a large extent in institutional reality as well. In this way, the theory of social objects and their particularities in institutional objects develops naturally into a theory of the document.[269]

Ferraris uses the phrase »*fenomenologia dell'instituzionale*«, or phenomenology of the institutional (institutionality or institution), only once in his texts. Nevertheless, it gives me the opportunity to consider some difficulties with the figure of the institution. My intent is twofold: to claim, against Ferraris and with John Searle, that the theory or phenomenology of the institution is always the most important task in the construction of social ontology (Searle mentions the »ontology of the institution« or the ontology of the creation of the institution,[270] »institutional phenomenon« and »institutional phenomena«[271]), even though the theory of the institution is »still in progress«, or »still in its infancy«.[272] Along the way, I would like to try to point to the importance of violence (and power) and violent strategies in the creation and maintaining of institutions, as well as describe (using an example from Husserl and Kant) the translation and reception of the term institution in French philosophy of the 20th century – another problem and confusion regarding the institution. It is interesting that both Husserl's and Searle's project is marked with a common resistance towards the written word and the written down, even though we find in both of them a sketch of a very timid »*documentalità*«: with Searle it is the idea of »official documentation« and in Husserl »*der Ausweiss*« (certification). Not only that: two short appendices authored by Husserl

269 »*Proseguire nel dettaglio la fenomenologia dell'istituzionale e della differenza rispetto al sociale mi sembra una operazione relativamente secondaria rispetto a un punto di maggiore sostanza, ossia mettere in evidenza il ruolo che, nella realtà sociale e a maggior ragione nella realtà istituzionale, viene assolto dai documenti. Così, una teoria degli oggetti sociali, e della loro specializzazione in oggetti istituzionali, evolve naturalmente in una teoria del documento.*« Ferraris: Documentalità, p. 298.

270 »*I have not ventured far on the subject of imitation in* The Construction of Social Reality *because it did not have a central place: I was not looking to show how new institutions are born by imitating old ones, but rather to determine the ontology of the creation and sustaining of these institutions.*« Searle: Les Institutions sont-elles dans la tête?, p. 252.

271 Searle: Social Ontology, p. 23.

272 Searle: What Is an Institution?, p. 22.

a hundred years ago and dedicated to social ontology and to the community and norms are incredibly convergent with Searle's intentions. We can say without reservation that these appendices are a precise sketch of Searle's long-term effort to construct a new social and political ontology.[273]

On the other hand, I am interested in the importance of Ferraris' theory of documents or documentation for the making of institutions or the institution, for making a good institution,[274] but also for the construction of a new theory of the institution, which is our main goal. Thus, by asking whether to institutionalize means to document, my intention is to understand Ferraris' project, first as a necessary addition to the ontology of John Searle (or Barry Smith[275]), on multiple levels (the most important being that the document intensifies the normative effect of the use of language because it contains explicitness and stability – that it is given once and for all).[276] But also, I would like to argue that in the future, such a project could *incorporate* these famous theoretical attempts that precede it. In particular, I would like to argue that the future of this project is in political and legal theory, in understanding the great or ›ultimate institutional structures‹. Ferraris, as the inheritor and contributor to the great project of Paul Otlet (*Mundaneum*), surpasses »the government as ultimate institutional structure«,[277] and substitutes the state with Europe and *la Cité mondiale*.[278]

273 Husserl: Zur Phänomenologie der Intersubjektivität, 1, pp. 98–107. The titles of appendices XVIII and XIX in the original are: »Die Gegebenheit konkreter sozialer Gegenständlichkeiten und Gebilde und fie Klärung auf sie bezüglicher Begriffe. Sozialer Ontologie und deskriptive Soziologie« and »Gemeinschaft und Norm«.

274 Jaeggi: Was ist eine (gute) Institution?, p. 528.

275 Smith admits Ferraris' engagement, even if he does not fully understand him and asks for additional explanations (Smith: How to Do Things with Documents). Searle mentions the document or »official documentation« only a few times, although in his last book for the first time he thematizes the importance of writing in social ontology (Searle: What is an institution?, p. 15; Searle: Making the Social Word, pp. 115–116). The resistance to the importance of documents is likely the result of decades-long antagonism of Anglo-American philosophers towards a theory of the text and writing by French philosophers, that is, towards Jacques Derrida (or intellectual nonsense à la Derrida; ibid.), one of Ferraris' main inspirations. Derrida himself rarely mentions the document or the difference in reading the text and the document (Derrida: De la grammatologie, p. 214).

276 Ferraris: Documentalità, p. 183.

277 Searle: Social Ontology and Political Power, p. 96; Searle: Making the Social World, p. 161.

278 Otlet: Traité de documentation, p. 419. »The institution, says Paul Otlet, is a free grouping of forces of the will, a federation of organisms, a union of national and international associations.« Ibid.: 417. Ferraris' book is structured in the same way and the chapters are marked like in Paul Otlet's book. Both books begin with quotations from poems: Ferraris' book opens with Mallarmé, while the verses in Otlet's book are Verhaeren's.

On the Forwarded Object

Does to institutionalize in fact mean to document, that is, to distribute and contribute documents, or forward and transfer them? More precisely, is the document or »*documentalità*« a particular protocol that can bridge and secure (ease) social objects into institutional objects? Is the institution made in this way? If we say that something (a fact, for example) is very well documented, are we already within the space of the institution or institutional facts? It seems to me that questions constructed in this way could, to a great extent, suit the context and rhythm of Searle's expositions and his regime of use of arguments. Only in the case of the institution does Searle have no intention of analyzing the ordinary use of the word »institution«. He does not even find it important whether the institution has anything to do with institutional reality. Regardless of Searle being most interested »in getting at the underlying glue that holds human societies together«,[279] even to begin to think the institution, according to Searle, it is necessary to understand that the institution does not »constrain people as such«, but produces new power relations: institutions *enable* because they create (deontic) powers or human power, and »that institutional structures create desire-independent reasons for action«,[280] that »the creation of an institutional fact is, thus, the collective assignment of a status function«,[281] that the institution of language is at the same time the foundation of all other institutions,[282] etc.

Let me offer two remarks: the position according to which institutional structures create desire-independent reasons for action does not have to be correct; and it essentially does not respond to, for example, the first famous attempts at thematization of the institution in Hume, nor to the relationship between instinct and institution. Can sexuality not be satisfied within marriage, or greed within the institution of private property?

The second remark, following from the first, could also be supported by some considerations in Hume. In his thinking about power, Searle develops and continuously modifies his view of the relation of institutions to brute force. The origin of what we can now begin to call a problem can be found in Searle's discovery of the so-called *extra-linguistic* institution (even if he has, in the course of endless explanation and amendment, complicated it to the hilt). Thinking about performatives as declarations, Searle differentiates *extra-linguistic* declarations »such as adjourning the meeting, pronouncing somebody man and wife, declaring war, and so on – and *linguistic* declarations – such as promising, ordering and stating

279 Searle: What is an institution?, p. 18; Searle: Social Ontology, p. 27–28.
280 Searle: What is an institution?, p. 10–11; Searle: Les institutions son-elles dans la tête?, p. 48.
281 Searle: What is an institution?, p. 22.
282 Searle: Making the Social World, p. 110.

by way of declaration.«[283] For Searle, these non-linguistic cases are prototypical declarations, and their main characteristic is that they are not derived from semantics. In a well-known example, Searle quotes several times in different places and ways, in Islam, a man can divorce his wife by uttering the sentence »I divorce you« three times. In certain Muslim countries, the divorce will actually take place, says Searle, because speech acts in these cases are derived from legal or theological powers.[284] Power or powers is a word which is used here perhaps for the first time in this way, whereas previously, many of Searle's texts were organized around the words force, violence, or constraint. For us it is important that what Searle names power or *extra-linguistic* declaration, could also be named a document. War has been declared because the decision was reached and the declaration dispatched to the other side, the meeting was adjourned because someone holds a warrant, a piece of paper, and exercises their authority, while the procedure of repetition of the sentence »I divorce you«, is in fact a quote found in codices and religious rules of some Muslim minorities and tribes. For war to be declared and of course begin, it necessarily needs to be written down somewhere. A *homo documentator* is necessary.[285] A written declaration is needed, which is nothing other than a *documentum* or its prototype – *instrumentum* (a statement made publicly, or in the presence of a few witnesses). So, what Searle in this place names power(s), in fact comes from the document and the consent that precedes the *linguistic* declaration, and in a sense even institutions in general. What will be a new problem, which here ought to remain aside, is that even so-called speech acts, which are derived from semantics (promising, ordering, stating, etc.), could also follow from various collections of rules and laws, and have a documentary origin.

Searle's reconstruction of the term power, which is initially set in a sort of *extra-linguistic* or pre-linguistic sphere – meaning that there is something that has a non-linguistic power to institutionalize – contains two simultaneous processes. Searle first introduces several new concepts (background, authority, political power, political ontology), which ought to soften and set aside the considerations of the origin of social facts and institutions. Force or violence found in the foundations of authority and institutions, which Hume talks about (»Time and custom give authority to all forms of government, and all successions of princes; and that power, which at first was founded only on injustice and violence, becomes in time

283 Searle: Consciousness and Language, p. 170.

284 Ibid., p. 171.

285 Briet: Qu'est-ce que la documentation?, p. 19. At the very beginning of the book, Suzanne Briet speaks of the antelope (an »*animal vivant*« which is not a document) and of the »*antilope cataloguée*« (which has been put in a cage in a zoo and has thus become a document). While this example only seemingly calls into question the life and freedom of the »*animal vivant*«, it shows ***a priori*** at once the proximity of the institution and documentation, as well as the difficulty of their differentiation.

legal and obligatory«[286]), are displaced elsewhere – in order to protect institutional power. As if brute force (or different coercive mechanisms and coercive powers which characterize the institution itself) protected the institution from itself. It seems to be Searle's view – this being the second simultaneous operation – that the process of institutionalization of social facts or the process of turning social facts into institutional ones, can be secured if and only if the institution protects itself from some of its own disloyal parts (»many people lie, steal, and cheat«). The function of the police and the military, who »presuppose the deontology rather than being inconsistent with it«,[287] meaning that the function of the threat of force or a monopoly on organized violence is *de facto* to break the resistance of counter-institutional actions, or actions that in themselves have desire-dependent reasons. On this second level, or from this second perspective, what would constitute the source of police or military power?

I am not sure that all the uses and wanderings of the term »power« in the construction of Searle's argument can be explained precisely. However, I am convinced that the introduction of the document, Ferraris' »*documentalità*« could strengthen this argument, and perhaps better define Searle's real intention. It should be noted, although not crucial at this juncture, that Searle's thinking about power recalls Hume, but also Benjamin's differentiation between violence that creates right and violence that protects it, as well as certain positions taken by Maurice Hauriou in the theory of the foundation of the institution.[288] In that vein, although he analyzes certain texts by Michel Foucault (unfortunately not the ones that explicitly analyze the institution),[289] Searle's position is entirely opposed to Foucault's. Searle is foremost interested in the power of the institution or the power that founds it, and which the institution then distributes preventing and abolishing any counter-institutional elements. In contrast, Foucault, in order to analyze institutions, insists on starting from power relations that precede the field of the institutional, and on resisting the institution (»*Soyons très anti-institutionnaliste*«):

Far from negating the significance of institutions in relations of power; rather, we seek to suggest that they should be analyzed from the standpoint of power, and not the other way round. These relations are to be found prior to institutions, even when they take hold and crystallize within them.[290]

286 Hume: A Treatise of Human Nature, p. 310.

287 Searle: Making the Social World, pp. 141–142.

288 Cf. Benjamin: Toward the Critique of Violence, pp. 54–55; Hauriou: La théorie de l'institution et de la fondation, p. 89.

289 Searle: Making the Social World, pp. 152–155.

290 »*Il ne s'agit pas de nier l'importance des institutions dans les relations de pouvoir. Mais de suggérer qu'il faut plutôt analyser les institutions à partir des relations de pouvoir et non l'inverse; et que le point d'ancrage fondamental de celles-ci, même si elles prennent corps et se cristallisent dans une institution, est à chercher en deçà.*« Foucault: Le sujet et le pouvoir, p. 1058.

As opposed to Searle, with Foucault there is no »ultimate institutional structure«, no special or last instance that protects and regulates the process of institutionalization. For Foucault, the analysis of power as resistance to the institution or institutions is really the only process by which the institution is institutionalized. Institutions do not simply exist, but rather are ever in the process of institutionalization and endless codification. It seems to me a good idea to define the state – that which has a monopoly on violence, is according to Searle the »ultimate institutional structure«,[291] and absolute paradigm of power – as a collection of documents. Let us say with Ferraris that the document, in the *strong* sense of the word (the constitution being the first and last in a series of such documents), is found in a place of power and is power. In which case we succeed in demystifying the secret reason for authority and the origin of power that cause certain difficulties in Searle's argument, even if that leaves us with a new and complicated task of reconstructing the system and order of documents. The threat of violence and violence are possible because there is a document which limits that violence; at the same time, a document can be reconstructed, changed and weakened with another document. The right of a state to secession, or the accession, for example, of the Ukrainian state into the European Union, or perhaps the integration of the USA into a world state, is a game of documents. In »What is an institution?«, Searle mentions the document as an addition to, but not as a condition or background of any deontology. This precisely is the problem:

> But the deontic powers stop at the point where the larger society requires some official documentation, they lack full deontic powers. Collective recognition is not enough. There has to be official recognition by some agency, itself supported by collective recognition, and there have to be status indicators issued by the official agency.[292]

The third comment could perhaps be the reconstruction or reformulation of the previous reconstruction of power, beyond linguistic and semantic fields or backgrounds. My intention here is to affirm the existence of a paradox – one rejected by Searle, but I think unconvincingly – regarding the institution (or its institutionalization), using Ferraris' theory of the document. In order to do that, it seems to me that I am forced to slightly disturb both Searle's and Ferraris' conception, in

291 For Husserl too, the state has a special place and represents an entity different from everything else. The state can keep its identity for its duration, remains unchanging and unique through time, despite the transformations, changes, death of its officials and changes in government. Cf. Husserl: Zur Phänomenologie der Intersubjektivität, 1, p. 101–102. »For the institutional mode of thinking (*institutionalistische Denkweise*), the state itself is no longer a norm or a system of norms, nor a pure sovereign decision, but the institution of institutions (*Institution der Institutionen*), in whose order numerous other, in themselves autonomous, institutions find their protection and their order.« Schmitt: On the Three Types of Juristic Thought, p. 88; Schmitt: Über die drei Arten des rechtswissenschaftlichen Denkens, p. 47.

292 Searle: What is an Institution?, p. 15.

attempting to offer my own contribution to a new future theory of the institution. Thoroughly simplified, this paradox can be formulated like this: »The creation of institutional facts by declaration presupposes the creation of other institutional facts. In order to avoid an infinite regress, there must be a way of creating institutional facts which does not require any special authority«[293] – which seems impossible. Clearly I would like to remove both the words ›seems‹ and ›impossible‹, since I am not satisfied with the perspective offered by Searle's response.[294] My point, however, is not to claim that there is necessarily something outside the institution (something extra-linguistic) or some necessary authority (special or not), power or violence (about which I will speak more later); rather, it is that an institutional fact is immediately preceded by the document, in the broadest sense of the term. That is, a document is a special kind of institutional fact. And if I had to ›document‹ this paradoxical moment now in Searlean language, I would take a sentence he writes about the corporation in *Making the Social World*: »So the Law is a Declaration that authorizes other Declarations.«[295] In this case, ›Law‹ is the document, and it is not at all surprising that it is precisely when we arrive at »A Complex Case: Creating a Corporation« that the »special role of writing« is problematized and that phrases like »writing language«, »written speech act«, »written constitutive rules«, or »written record« appear.[296] Let me now assume that in between so-called ›brute‹ and ›social‹ facts, and then in between ›social‹ and ›institutional‹ facts, there is some sort of documental reality. And let me tangentially say a few words about the material (the paper, the ink, the body of the text, or if you will, the sound, the phoneme, the materiality of the symbol, the body of one making it – an insight for which we do not need Saussure or Derrida,

293 Prien/Skudlarek/Stolte: The Role of Declarations in the Construction of Social Reality, p. 167.

294 Searle's response to this problem is that it is not a problem. »A further point of disagreement between me and them is that they think you need a special authority to create institutional reality by (representations that have the same logical form as) Declarations. This is a mistake as several of my examples illustrate. You do not need special authority to create every type of institutional fact, otherwise it would not be possible for the system of institutional fact to ever get started. You have to begin somewhere, simply by creating and getting other people to accept institutional reality.« Searle: Reply to »The Role of Declarations in the Construction of Social Reality«, p. 229. I think it was sentences like this, in which someone who creates institutional reality ought to get others to accept it, that sparked Raimo Tuomela's criticism about individualistic collective acceptance of what has been declared and of speech act theory as essentially an individualistic theory. Cf. Tuomela: Searle's New Construction of Social Reality, p. 708. In the book *Making the Social Word*, the word ›making‹ serves Searle to explain the beginning of the institution or institutionalization. »God can create light by saying ›Let there be light!‹ Well, we cannot create light but we have a similar remarkable capacity. We can create boundaries, kings, and corporations by saying something equivalent to ›Let this be a boundary!‹ ›Let the oldest son be the king!‹ ›Let there be a corporation!‹« Searle: Making the Social Word, p. 100.

295 Ibid. The corporation is the novelty in Searle's later work, which he mentions for the first time in 2004 at a conference at the University of Hertfordshire and then in the text »What is an Institution?, p. 15.

296 Searle: Making the Social World, pp. 115, 98–100.

rather any Stoic is enough, for example Vitruvius). Namely, between, on the one hand, the virtual reality of the law or certain rules (a space in which a usually small group of people, certainly empowered or protected by some authority [or more precisely protected by weapons], imposes an institutional reality to others [or to all] by constructing [formulating, designing] the text of the law or rules) and, on the other hand, various statements often read (or uttered) by a rabbi, priest, lawyer, officer or stewardess, or else a money bill, property, marriage, or a declaration of the type ›This is my house‹ – between these two ›realities‹ there is a (so-called) »written record«. This is the charter which creates a legal person or corporation, a decision of the governor to issue bills of this specific design, a record, a birth certificate, marriage license, lease, contract, proof of ownership, etc. I do not have to declare »This is my house,« nor say »I am married to Rachel«, to only then create the right to the house »because the right only exists by collective acceptance.« The possibility to document what I say when I say that »This is my house«, to show my papers, my ID, driver's license, to demand that the lawyer show me the article in the law that allows the creation of a corporation, or demand my employer show the decision based on which I am being let go – is paramount for the creation of institutional reality. But not sufficient. The sentence ›our marriage exists only on paper‹ (in German it would be *Wir sind nur noch auf dem Papier verheiratet*) marks that our relationship is not confirmed by the contract we signed, and that our marriage is not worth the paper it is written on. One of the main characteristics of the institution, which Hume differentiates from and opposes to the contract (law) – apart from that the institution, unlike the contract, supposes the existence of a third party (that is, the possibility that someone else join, a sense in which the institution implicitly counts everyone in, excludes no one, and ultimately assumes that there is nothing outside the institution), and that the institution is coercive because formed by various transformations of violence and force – is its artificial nature, as well as the possibility of incorporating law into a group or tying a collective together. The fact that the paper (the marriage certificate), as a document, is not a strong enough glue to keep a couple in love – after all, neither is the ceremony performed once upon a time, in which we promised to have and to hold one another – does not exclude the institutional fact that our marriage still exists. Do we have a real[297] (or factual) marriage because we are not divorced, or is the document the source of reality and then the institution? In other words, does the document institutionalize, or are we in fact, really separated, we could say organically separated, and together on paper only?[298] This is

297 Cf. Austin: Sense and Sensibilia, pp. 62–78.

298 Hodgson's »organicist ontology« (Cf. Hodgson: Evolution and Institutions, p. 89 ff) thematized the organic and biological analogies throughout the Western world. It seems to me that the introduction of the concept of ›organization‹, as well as the differentiating between an organization and institution in the last century, is analogous to contemporary differentiation between the real

a tough and complicated question, and I immediately have two associations: first, that only something that exists in time[299] (this being one of the characteristics of the institution, something man-made, on the other side of nature or God) and declines in time (marriages decline in time, do they not?) is real. And second is a quote from *Economics and Reality* by Tony Lawson (slightly modified): »No reality, please. We're philosophers!«[300] To defend the first option, that an institution is real if and only if it can be documented, that is, to institutionalize (I choose the verb), means in fact to publish or further attach documents (a synonym for *documentum* is *instrumentum*; in a different context, documentation is nothing other than argumentation), that the institution becomes an institution if it is constantly in the process of institutionalizing or documenting, it seems necessary to me to show that a greater transfer or distribution of paper (documents) between partners, certainly makes the marriage not only on paper. The more invoices, bills, receipts, tax declarations, etc., the more documents, the more love.

A hundred years ago, Husserl had the same problem with mutual recognition or collective recognition. Here is his suggestion:

> How did this being a Master / Servant (*Herr-und-Diener sein*) at all happen? I notice Johann, my servant. In this way, I do not notice him yet as a servant, if we can use the word »notice« at all. It is more a registration (*Ausweisung*), a *fulfilling* (*Erfüllung*). However, the registration (certification, *Ausweis*) is given in the certificate B, according to which he is ready to follow my will in regards this or that action, ready to execute a certain task to which he is committed, such that this certificate is based simply in that Johann, in executing my order, is subject to me.[301]

The insufficiency of which Searle says in the difficult transformation or transfer of a social fact into an institutional one. To reinforce or stabilize collective recognition (institutionalization is precisely this process), it is necessary to *de facto draw* or *extract* (or activate) the document from some, in this case, third place. This pulling out of the document or its transfer from place to place, could be explained by specifying the social. Ferraris compares this relation between the social and the institutional to the relation between »*archiscrittura*« and »*scrittura*«.[302] The prototype of this distinction is certainly Husserl's pair *Urstiftung / Stiftung*.

and the institutional. Organization refers to subjects, to collective actors, whereas institutions to the relations between actors, to the objective (Cf. Knight: Institution and Social Conflict, p. 3); the institution refers to the rules of the game, the organization to the players.

299 This determination of the »real« is constructed by Nicolai Hartmann, and still used by Otta Weinberger and Neil MacCormick, or today Massimo La Torre. Namely, 80 years ago, in the city of Halle, Hartmann holds his famous plenary lecture in *Kant-Gesellschaft* »Zum Problem der Realitätsgegebenheit« (28–29 May 1931).

300 Lawson: Economics and Reality, p. xii. The original quote is »No reality, please. We're economists!« and is taken from *The Times Higher Education*, from 25 March, 1994.

301 Husserl: Zur Phänomenologie der Intersubjektivität, 1, p. 104.

302 Ferraris: Documentalità, pp. 296–297.

5 Obligation and Institution. The Document and Engaged Acts

In the brief final chapter, 12.2, Prospect, of *A Theory of Political Obligation*, Margaret Gilbert constructs over fifty questions before finally concluding: »The theory is essentially an analytic theory. Its primary purpose is to explain that and how there can be political obligations in the sense of this book. In setting out this theory, I have not tried to settle all of the many questions it raises, empirical, moral, or indeed, conceptual. Rather, my ambition has been to set such questions in motion.«[303]

I will try to put together a few questions, aware of the challenge that only good questions announce a change in bad or antiquated laws. Here then is the first question: can a change in the law (in the general sense, change of rights, contracts, constitutions, charters, edicts, documents, institutions, etc.) also be one of the most important purposes of theory or philosophy? This question can be constructed as a good addition to a sentence once uttered by Gilbert (at a conference in Milan): »Perhaps the constitution in question is not written down at all, but simply envisaged by its author.«[304] It seems to me that this very trivial possibility that a law can be written and erased (or amended), envisaged or questioned, forgotten or broken, can explain the connection or the conditions of an imaginary or factual relationship between the work of Margaret Gilbert and that which Ferraris calls *Documentalità*.

My basic question, which I will try to further explain and refine with other questions, is whether *above all* very different protocols of documenting and inscribing, declaring, registering and writing (we are dealing with institutional protocols) can now be a good answer to the question »What keeps society together?« (This question is certainly a form of Searle's project of »getting at the underlying glue that holds human societies together.«[305]) Searle himself uses the plural: societies. Paradoxically, it also seems that the word ›institution‹ first appeared as a substantive in the plural, and only later in the singular.

Right away, I will point to a few problems. First of all, the difference between the law and ›institutional protocols and procedures‹ is uncertain; second, it is always complicated to explain resistance towards the institution (consider Saint-Simon's concept of *contre-institution*) and justify the construction of a subversive

303 Gilbert: A Theory of Political Obligation, p. 297.
304 Gilbert: Rights Without Laws, p. 3.
305 Searle: What Is an Institution?, pp. 27–28.

group or alternative institution or society, or even the subversive individual. In law, as in casual usage of the word, one is responsible when something has to be done, regardless of not wanting to, or no longer wanting to. In other words, so as not to betray my temporary membership in an institution, not to act subversively (anti-socially), not to rupture my relationship with the other members of a group or question the relationships among them (so as not to betray ›joint commitment‹) – I ought to act in accordance with the agreement and promises given to the group. For example, if I promised in an email that I would write about the importance of documents that keep society together (invoices, *lettre de facture*, receipt, tax declaration etc.), I have to do so, and I have to stay on topic. But my responsibilities are not simply professional and do not only relate to this one group. One member of the group is a friend of mine, and another is someone close to me as well. A whole slew of direct and indirect responsibilities (correct and incorrect) today prevent me from analyzing in detail something that could possibly even better explain the problem with the document and the difference between the document and a promise, a letter and a word, written and verbal obligations.

I held a seminar on *jus post bellum* in Austria with Justice Renate Winter of the Special Court for Sierra Leone. A one point, she asked a participating officer of the Austrian military: »In case that in front of you there is a child soldier of some ten years of age, ready to raise its weapon and kill you, what would you do? Where will you find the answer to this question? What document would you consult?« The officer referred to various rule books, codices, and conventions. Thus, the soldier is a documenting machine: the document immanently precedes every single one of his acts. The oath of this officer and his sworn word, his public promise to recognize civilians and differentiate them from soldiers is only possible after detailed training and instruction. Of course, the instruction and institutionalization continue even after the soldier signed his contract in the presence of others or given his word out loud. Hence it would be very easy to document the potential lapses of this soldier in action, as indeed it would be to discover papers that show all of my own oversights here.

Although these two examples look different, it seems more important to me to describe their similarity, which far outstrips the difference in sanction (exclusion from the group, from society) certainly awaiting me or this soldier. If I agree to give a talk at a conference, my signing of letters in which I promise to attend, acceptance (of the gift) of airfare,[306] signature at the hotel front desk, collection

306 »To give« the airfare does not necessarily mean to gift it for free, it is not a grant. *Dare* means the transfer of ownership, a transaction, and not a gift, *donare*. A gift, or for example a ›gifting contract‹ in the French legal system, signifies that the one receiving the gift has agreed to accept it or is obligated to accept it. The existence of such unilateral contracts, where only one side is under obligation calls into question reciprocity or exchange as the key to every obligation. Is it then possible to speak at all consistently about moral or political obligation, if the differences between continental

of receipts for reimbursement, etc. – belong to institutional protocols and codifications, the function of which is twofold: these protocols that we usually call transactions (the institution is more a collection of transactions than interactions) actualize and realize the collective or the group (e. g., when we are together at a conference, working together, building a city together, reading, walking, fighting to survive together, even sometimes trying to die together). Further, these protocols constantly evoke the existence of laws and legal obligations.[307] Thanks to the institution, or more generally, thanks to these tedious documenting games, the law is alive and vocal, or the letter (the paper) »has a voice«.[308] Hence the law and legal obligation is present and constantly evoked in the shadow of a host of responsibilities that determine membership in a group. If I fall short of my responsibilities to the organizers (to the group or institution), aside from institutional responsibilities (*obligatio, Hafnung* in German), the question of compensation for the damage and payment (*obligatio, Schuld* in German, debt) is inevitably brought up. Can we say that the chain of documents points to the law or strengthens the ›voice‹ of the law? Or do various documents often replace the law? What happens if these institutional protocols go missing? Protocols of documentation have to help this process along since to ›incorporate the law or paper into the group‹, or to ›realize the collective‹ really means that the soldiers should constantly recite the articles of the Geneva Convention, the Commandments, etc. And not only soldiers.

Such actions would certainly help sometimes – after all, most of the world religions are continuously grounded in documentary games (reading, reminding, interpreting basic commandments, stories and testimonies about the group and behavior within the group). It is above all a question of solving new problems and

and Anglo-Saxon law are enormous? For example, in the continental tradition a contract is defined as a free agreement between two or more persons, which has as its end and consequence the creation of obligation. As opposed to that, in Anglo-Saxon law a contract is understood as a bargain, as a job, an exchange of payment. This idea of a contract introduces the theory of ›efficient breach of contract,‹ completely inconceivable in the European understanding of obligation: one side in the contract, after having entered into it, can, upon finding a better engagement and better contract, break the first contract with minimal compensation. Cf. Fabre-Magnan: De l'obligation en droit, pp. 23–56.

307 The first uses of the word ›obligation‹ in English are always in regard to address, contracts, or oaths, and often imply the existence of written documents. Cf. Brandt: The Concepts of Obligation and Duty, p. 386.

308 Jewish political theory and Jewish Legal Theory recognize a clear distinction between verbal and written obligation. A written obligation entitles the creditor to recover payment out of the debtor's encumbered assets which are in the hands of a third party, a right unavailable in the case of a mere verbal obligation, since the obligation or debt has no *kol* (»voice«) and does not provide notice that will put prospective purchasers on their guard. In the case of a written obligation, a plea by the debtor that he has repaid the debt is not accepted without proof, as in the case of a verbal obligation. Thus, for example, an undertaking even in the debtor's own handwriting but not signed by witnesses will be treated as a verbal obligation, since only properly written, witnessed, and signed obligation carries a »voice and constitutes notice«. *Bava Batra* 175b. Cf. Elon: The Principles of Jewish Law, p. 244.

producing new documents that evoke old ones and connect them to new ones. A bouquet of flowers presented, a meal together, travel together, new encounters, even the development of new technologies that better protect the lives of civilians and soldiers, development of procedures that preventively reduce the possibility of sudden attack and ›bad actions‹, etc. – all such acts are always followed by documents, issue from and produce new documents.

What is a document? Using two paradoxes or two models in which ›documentality‹ appears – document acts refer exclusively to institutions, that is, corporations, meaning that there is no institution or corporation without documents, or else that the institution (or the corporation, as a specific form of the institution) is real thanks to document acts, and not speech acts – my intention is to explain how to incorporate (with) documents. I would like to transform the three best definitions of the document we currently have (two are Smith's and the third is Ferraris') into three essential characteristics that define the relation between the institution (corporation) and documentational protocols: a) the document is something that is able to endure self-identically through time, b) that through documents things are done and the world is changed »by bringing into being new types of ownership relations, of legal accountability, of business organizations, and other creatures of modern economies, including mortgages, stocks, shares, insurance protection, and financial derivatives«,[309] and c) that the document is at once a representation of some fact and the inscription of an act.[310] The first characteristic that protects documents from change and decay in time, and gives them an always distinct concreteness, is the plurality or series of documents tightly bound together, forming a chain and referring to one another. Documentality always supposes a series of documents, a multitude of permanent acts that refer to and succeed one another, complement and reaffirm each other. A marriage, for example, is composed neither of the marriage ceremony, nor the contract of the two sides, the promises and speech acts of the main actors, the signatures in registrars – their own or that of their witnesses – but rather the hundreds and hundreds of future documents (sometimes even documents that precede the marriage ceremony), which reassert again and again and supplement the identity of the marriage covenant between two persons and its beginning in time. In that sense, a series of documents that are in no way ›accidentally‹ linked and cannot be ›accidentally‹ linked represents and affirms an institution. Without the series of document acts, there is no institution of marriage, nor the memory that the marriage ever existed. The written record cannot be preserved »accidentally«, but rather only in connection with in-

309 »(...) by bringing into being new types of ownership relations, of legal accountability, of business organizations, and other creatures of modern economies, including mortgages, stocks, shares, insurance protection, and financial derivatives.« Smith: How to Do Things with Documents, p. 180.

310 Ferraris: Documentality, p. 250.

stitutions.[311] The second characteristic of the document or documentation process refers to the documents' authors, who are always plural (despite the fact that there is, for example, the corporation *sole*, comprising only one person). The procedure that we designate with the words ›to incorporate‹ or ›to institutionalize‹ ought to be twofold or operate in two directions. The document is the product of a collective process, and at the same time, that same group is constituting itself ›with‹ those same documents. This always double process of the same procedure represents the institution (or corporation). The third characteristic refers to the power produced by institutions or corporations, and which is essentially documental. The size, and then the power of a group producing documents, and produced with those same documents, ought to be proportional to the ›documental power‹ to further commit all the actors of the institutionalization or incorporation.

Let us return once again to marriage or, better, to the document whose letters say nothing, but still testify to its existence. Ignoring the possible, albeit rare option when such letters are revived by the couple making new documents and renew their vows, or else the final divorce document that confirms their separation such that they have no mutual obligations. How is it possible for a marriage to exist on paper only? Or conversely, when is a marriage, a group, ›simply bad‹?[312] Is the idea of a subversive individual or a subversive group (faction) only a regulative idea that only preserves and further integrates already existing social groups excluding any subversion?

I suggest three elementary answers to the hidden danger and uncertainty that issues from this fantasy of the individual or group that is excluded from institutions without founding any new institutions itself. Since we are dealing with individuals who do not participate (*munus*) in the community and do not contribute taxes, they exist on the community's margin, but do not declare their existence, the first clear answer is given by Jean Bodin in hailing the role of the censor. The censor, a pseudo-sovereign, ought to count all the people and all the property of a republic in order to »banish loiterers, layabouts, thieves (...) they should be seen, marked, recognized everywhere« (*bannir les vagabonds, faineans, voleurs* (...) *on les verroit, les marqueroit, les cognoistroit partout*).[313] Two variations on this answer can be recognized in Saint-Just and in John Searle. The former insists that the passive and indifferent are the real enemies of the revolution, as well as groups of people who band together to work against and oppose the revolution (*faction*). Saint-Just also predicts the banishment of all who are outside institutions, for institutions ought to cover the entire space of the republic (anything outside the

311 Gröbner: Der Schein der Person, p. 124.

312 »Some groups are simply bad, and would be better if they changed completely, or ceased to exist.« Gilbert: On Social Facts, p. 438.

313 Bodin: Les six Livres de la République, 6, p. 14.

institution is the enemy of the revolution). In »Institutions and Brute Force«, a chapter in *Making the Social World*, Searle speaks of the monopoly of violence and coercive powers of the institutions towards those who have »strong motivations to break the rules«, because »Many people lie, steal, cheat in various ways.«[314]

The second attempt at an answer (in the form of a chain of very precise questions) can also be found at the end of *A Theory of Political Obligation*. Gilbert here uses her favorite metaphor of the island (let us recall a certain Rose, from the book *On Social Facts*, who has been shipwrecked and is now alone on an island[315]). Gilbert finds a very precise name for this set of people: »hold-outs«. She tries to announce a future integration of ›residents‹ and ›hold-outs‹ into new political institutions:

> Suppose, in any case, that the population of those living on a certain island – the ›residents‹ – contains some individuals who are self-styled anarchists – the ›hold-outs‹. The residents who are not hold-outs are party to a joint commitment to support certain political institutions. The hold-outs refuse to become parties to the joint commitment. Perhaps each lives reclusively in a particular part of the island, and each has explicitly rejected the residents' invitation to join them in their joint commitment. This is not because there is anything especially immoral about these institutions in particular. The hold-outs simply do not wish to be bound to uphold them.[316]

It seems to me that the third response could, paradoxically, emerge from that famous definition of obligation (legal obligation) found in Justinian's collection *Institutes*, which accurately shows the economic and ›transactional‹ nature of obligation. This is precisely the main reason I previously referred to a complicated task: invoice, *lettre de facture*, receipt, tax declaration, to which we could add some other institutions that keep society together, like the balance sheet, credit card, bill of exchange, ledger book, etc. Starting from the theory of social facts (Durkheim, Mauss, Gilbert) and the differences among social and institutional facts, I intend to present a different status of such documents in the constitution of a group or institution. Further, I would like to include the origin of the idea of counting, accounting, inventorying (administrative statistics), as well as the idea of egalitarianism and ›proportionality‹ of tax as the condition of social peace. For example, the concept of the invoice (*facture*, *factura*) and its derivatives, always refer to a group that works together and forms its identity through interaction and production (*facere*, *factor*). All these papers absolutely do not belong to the same family of documents, but their common thematization could not only revise the term obligation, modifying it and bringing it back to the field of economy (this

314 Searle: Making the Social World, p. 141.
315 Gilbert: On Social Facts, p. 35.
316 Gilbert: A Theory of Political Obligation, p. 296.

supposes a completely new reading of Aristotle, as well as the resurfacing of certain positions by Bodin), but could also reconstruct the existing theories of the institution. »Obligation is the bond of law that forces us towards payment (benefit, prestation, indemnity) to someone, based on the laws of our city« (*Obligatio est iuris vinculum, quo necessitate adstringimur alicuius solvendae rei secundum nostrae civitatis iura*).[317]

Vinculum iuris. Vincula are the shackles or the iron used to hold a prisoner. The law binds – in the republic, island or city – but payment or debt also necessarily crosses borders. When Cicero's friend Atticus pays his son's allowance while he is at university in Athens, or when on March 28, 1210, a certain Rubeus de Campo agrees to pay 100 Marks Sterling in London to the count Vivianus Jordanus de Lucques, these transactions certainly hold human societies together.

317 Justinian, *Institutes* (3, 13).

6 Charter and Institution

Here are two reasons why charter, or charter and institution (the problem, of course, is in the copula ›and‹), or two or more reasons why it is constantly necessary to justify the status of writing or the document in the context of social or institutional facts.

1. I dare claim that Ferraris' detailed explanation of Derrida's famous position that there is nothing outside the text or outside the letter needs to be complemented with the argument for or against the claim that there is nothing outside the paper (in Greek *hartis*, in Serbo-Croatian *hartija*, in other languages charter, *die Urkunde*, *charte*, *carta*, *cartula*). The unease felt when uttering the phrase *the ontological status of the charter*, *the ontological status of the document*, or when thinking that paper can be »*the underlying glue that holds human societies together*«,[318] is truly a consequence of oblivion, but also the mistrust in the importance of various ›paper trails‹. Let me once again take as an example an imaginary academic conference. Upon arrival at the conference, no one asks to see ›the papers‹ that confirm the registration of your home institution, of your function there, invoices, bank statements, or even the decision allowing the conference to be held in the first place. It is much more important to the participants, for example, that everyone has arrived, that everyone fulfilled their obligation to write a paper, that the space is adequate and will be filled – in a word, that the conference is in fact happening. The fact that socializing over a two-day conference could be ›covered‹ with papers of some kind does not increase the importance of the charter for »*Ontologie der sozialen Gemeinschaften*«,[319] but nor does it sideline its triviality. The value of the charter is found in the origin of this word, and the charter is as great as the size of the diminutive ›paperette‹, ›piece of paper‹ (*cartula* is the diminutive of *carta*).

2. The ›and‹ between charter and institution or the ›conjoining‹ of charter with institution needs to do two things. The institution needs to be structured and incorporated as a charter (and vice versa, the charter is the institution embodied, which above all ought to be explained in the context of the moment of the institution's falling apart – the appearance of corruption in Saint-Just, a dead letter, as in ›our marriage exists on paper only‹, or ›we are married only on paper‹). In

318 Searle: What Is an Institution?, pp. 27–28.

319 I borrow here the title of the famous text by Gerda Walther, »Zur Ontologie der sozialen Gemeinschaften,« published in 1923 in Husserl's *Jahrbuch für Philosophie und phänomenologische Forschung*, pp. 1–158.

this sense, can the institute of the charter be the beginning of a possible theory of the institution? On the other hand, the charter (and not law, contract or norm, neither Searle's *declaration* nor Husserl's *Ausweiss*[320]) could improve the theory of documentation and its connection with institutionalism.[321]

What, then, is the charter? At the end of chapter XXVI of *Leviathan* (»Of Civil Laws«), Hobbes writes:

Likewise laws and charters are taken promiscuously for the same thing. Yet charters are donations of the sovereign; and not laws, but exemptions from law. The phrase of a law is *jubeo*, *injungo*; I command and enjoin: the phrase of a charter is *dedi*, *concessi*; I have given, I have granted: but what is given or granted to a man is not forced upon him by a law. A law may be made to bind all the subjects of a Commonwealth: a liberty or charter is only to one man or some one part of the people. For to say all the people of a Commonwealth have liberty in any case whatsoever is to say that, in such case, there hath been no law made; or else, having been made, is now abrogated.[322]

Hobbes wants to cut through the ambiguity regarding the difference between charter and law. If we look at Hobbes' understanding of the institution and his use of the verb ›to institute‹ – the decisive act of creation, act of establishment or an order – it seems that charter can have nothing to do with the institution. In order to truly first examine and then defend the connection between institution and charter, and to truly construct the origin of the institution from privilege, as a gift of the sovereign, and to show that the institution ensures freedom, several steps are necessary. More than fifty years ago, in his first book, *Instincts et institutions*, consisting of a short introduction and sixty-six fragments about the institution, Gilles Deleuze showed a certain number of key commentaries in the interpretation of the institution. One of which is Hume's differentiation of law and contract (on the one hand), from the institution (on the other), which Deleuze, using certain opinions of Georges Renard, formulates as follows:

We are aware of the legal difference between a contract and the institution: the first in principle assumes the willing participation of the parties, defined between them as a system of rights and obligations, it does not refer to a third, and it lasts a definite duration; the latter tends to define a long-term status, it is involuntary and uninterrupted, constitutive of power, possessing force, and is open to third parties.[323]

320 Husserl: Zur Phänomenologie der Intersubjektivität, 1, p. 104.

321 Can charter ever figure as an ›intentional object‹ in any community (for example, for the German community during World War I, the intentional object was *Sieg Deutschlands*). Cf. Walther: Zur Ontologie der sozialen Gemeinschaften, pp. 27–28.

322 Hobbes: Leviathan, p. 200.

323 *»On connaît la distinction juridique entre le contrat et l'institution: celui-là en principe suppose la volonté des contractants, définit entre eux un système de droits et de devoirs, n'est pas opposable aux tiers et vaut pour une durée limitée; celle-ci tend à définir un statut de longue durée, involontaire*

Along with Saint-Just's engagement (we know he says that the Republic has too many laws and too few institutions) and his insistence that institutions are something positive and the soul of the Republic, as well as Maurice Hauriou's ideas about the foundation of institutions, about corporation and personification being the basic characteristics of an institution, Deleuze mentions two other moments that essentially determine his future analysis of the institution: the analyses of Georges Renard in *La philosophie de l'institution* (1939), and Bronislaw Malinowski in *Freedom and Civilization* (1947):

Every institution has its charter, which gives it being while determining its manner of being and consequently of behaving: this is its constitution, written on parchment or immanent, like customary law, in its structure, its internal development, and its external activity – it matters little! This institutional charter does not merely provide for a system of mutual obligations among its members; it effects a mutual integration.[324]

The theory of the institution was a reaction against the voluntarist and subjectivist theory that base all law upon contract; a reaction against the theory of fictitious personality; a reaction against the theory of fictitious personality; a reaction against a too static conception of law.[325] Above all, it is the concept of ›freedom‹ – which Hobbes mentions in the quotation above or Shylock in *The Merchant of Venice*[326] – that Malinowski finds to be the goal and purpose of the institution:

(...) no man ever achieves anything, new or old, fundamental or peripheral, sound or fantastic, through his own unaided efforts. It is clear that the freedom of his personal purpose and its pragmatic success is always a by-product of the freedom of institutionalized activities.[327]

Every institution, continues Malinowski, has its charter or ›collective purpose.‹ The theory of the institution is based on the term ›charter‹ or the charter is ›the universal structure of an institution‹. Regardless of the fact that Malinowski's effort is almost entirely an attempt to determine the origin of ›the charter of an institution‹ (of a mythology, religion, moral principles, emotions, etc.), it is precisely to him that we owe the discovery that the charter ensures the organization in which a group of people agrees to cooperate, to work together and construct a city:

et incessible, constitutif d'un pouvoir, d'une puissance, dont l'effet est opposable aux tiers.« Deleuze: Présentation de Sacher-Masoch, pp. 77–78.

324 Broderick (ed.): The French Institutionalists, p. 290.

325 Ibid., p. 292.

326 »If you deny it (previous verse: And by our holly Sabbath have I sworn/ To have the due and forfeit of my bond), let the danger light upon your charter and your Citties freedome«. *Merchant of Venice*, IV. I. 38.

327 Malinowski: Freedom and Civilization, p. 157.

From our definition of charter as collective purpose it results that such a purpose has to be translated into activities. Structurally this means that at a primitive level, such activities as hunting, fishing and herding are carried out by a group, with the aid of its tools or implements and the rules necessary to the carrying out of the activity. (…) In a modern community the charter would be found in the codified or customary laws as well as in the religious and moral values.[328]

The brings us back immediately to Hobbes' differentiation. In a register completely different than Hobbes, Malinowski concludes that the »charter obviously contains the fundamental rules« and does not at all contain the norms or laws that regulate the behavior of social actors. Is it, though, possible to compare the charter as a set of »fundamental rules« with Hobbes' sovereign act which gives a certain privilege (the charter) only to one man or part of the people? Further, does the institution begin with an extraordinary measure of the sovereign, which itself does not, however, suspend norms or laws, as Hobbes claims, but rather simply transforms their function – instead of obligating and binding, the norms integrate and at the same time bring freedom?

A law may be made to bind all the subjects of a Commonwealth: a liberty or charter is only to one man or some one part of the people. For to say all the people of a Commonwealth have liberty in any case whatsoever is to say that, in such case, there hath been no law made; or else, having been made, is now abrogated.

Two Hobbes' maximalistic suggestions: first, the phrase »a liberty or charter« – meaning that the charter certainly brings freedom, which obviously depends on the decision of the sovereign; and the second, »all the people of a Commonwealth have liberty« – the vision that all can be free under the condition that there are no laws or that laws be abolished. If by any chance all the parts of the state are included, encompassed or freed by a charter of the sovereign, the coercion of law will be diminished and erased. Perhaps we ought to leave aside for now Hobbes' resistance to the charter and the justification of the danger that he foresees in the sovereign systematically conceding or granting parts of the state (neighborhoods, cities) to the people who live in it. Much more interesting is that Hobbes notices the importance of this act of the sovereign, and its awesome power to erase the force of (its own) laws by way of a single public act, and find a completely new social order, which paradoxically does not yet threaten the sovereign. However, the institution or institutionalization is expansive: »one man«, »one part of the people«, »all the people of a Commonwealth«. The institution frees from laws, according to Hobbes, but also from the absolutism of the sovereign. »After a debate of a few days, the king (John, 1215), with a facility somewhat suspicious, signed and sealed the charter which was required of him. This famous deed, commonly

328 Ibid., pp. 161–162.

called the »Great charter«, either granted or secured very important liberties and privileges to every order of men in the kingdom.«[329]

It is hard to explain Hume's phrase »every order of men in the kingdom«. His description of the making of a big decision can serve as the protocol for commencing something extraordinary and new, which mobilizes or groups in a completely new way, or, if you like, constructs social reality. The paper or the charter interrupts something, which it also, at the same time, continues to uphold. When a document like this appears – or, if we were to put it differently, when the institution is initiated – its validity is not automatically achieved. The charter counts on all, for it is directed at each and every one, individually. We are speaking of a call or proclamation to join, for all those who have not yet done so. Therefore, the charter is really a challenge or provocation.

The protocol and staging of how a document gains this appellation and becomes a charter (all of which is straightforwardly described by Hume) shows that the ritual of signing and stamping a small piece of paper is neither the beginning nor the end. Prior to the time of its writing and signing, there is a debate, difficulties that are overcome, and the writing and signing are followed by its distribution and a call to reading and potential corrections. Sovereign acts (signing and stamping) that truly do something extraordinary and that truly announce a change (greater freedom, privileges, new relationships, new friendships, higher income, more justice, greater security, etc.) are not sovereign because done by King John (the sovereign), but rather because they are completely new within an already existing »order of men in the kingdom«. Here are a few unconditional conditions (there are five and they are in charter form) of existence of the connection between the institution and the charter. I will assume that this connection is *in-corporating* and mutually dependent: the charter incorporates the institution, the city, the corporation, while at the same time the charter is incorporated in the institution, the city, or corporation:

1. *Dédoublement* (doubling). The institution begins within a broader legal field, to which it belongs (*le milieu juridique plus vaste auquel elle appartient*) and which it occupies, or more precisely, in which the institution achieves its internal law that then organizes it.[330]

2. The sovereign is the one capable of producing the paper, the charter; or the sovereign is sovereign if he has the competence (*die Befugnis*) to produce the institution.[331] Only one who can produce the charter possesses institutional

[329] Hume: The History of England, 1, p. 152.
[330] Renard: La philosophie de l'institution, p. 269.
[331] I am calling attention here to the difference between *Gesetz* and *Satzung* that Otto von

competence. We speak of the institution only if the sovereign or a group of people can adopt a common document (charter), publicly, after a (complicated) debate, and if the charter ensures the freedom of anyone to leave the group and the possibility that a third (currently absent) person join the group. The mafia is not an institution, even though its running is under constant codification. Pirates, terrorists or Kant's gang ruled by an evil principle, are not institutions.

3. Public donation (charter) is a proclamation, making something known (*die Urkunde*; *Althochdeutsch*: *urcundo* is *Zeuge*, *Zeugnis*, *urchundi* is *Erkenntnis*). This act is authentic because others testify to its authenticity.[332]

4. *Great Charter*: The charter of a city shows the autonomy of a city or of an institution in relation to the sovereign. The conflict between the law of the state and the charter of a city, between sovereignty and municipality, is a theme of the debate that happens prior to the signature and stamp. To found an institution by way of charter is to register and record it. Foundation is registration.

5. The charter integrates rather than obligates. There is no violence of tautology or tautological violence (*Gesetz ist Gesetz*; law is law). There is no »charter is charter«.

Gierke makes (Deutsches Privatrecht, p. 142). According to him, different organized communities have the capability to create right (*Rechtserzeugung*), and although the sovereign state leads in this regard, it has no exclusive right to create right. The state or sovereign creates law (*Gesetz*), but Gierke emphasizes that any collective which is not a state but is autonomous (*Autonomie*) can create a legal act (*Satzung*).

332 The charter is different from *notitia*, *diploma* or a letter.

7 What Is an Act of Engagement? Between the Social, Collegial and Institutional Protocols

I would like to describe a special kind of social acts and attempt to determine the function they have in relation between various agents and most importantly define their significance in the transformation of a group or social group into an institution or higher order entity. My premise is that there are acts whose aim is to engage others or all others, since they refer to all of us together, and in so doing reduce negative (social) »acts« as well as various asocial behaviors within a group or institution. In this sense, engaged acts could alternatively also belong to a kind of institutional acts, since they introduce certain adjustments to the institution, changing or modifying its rules, increasing its consistency and efficiency.

Engagement is not synonymous with commitment, even though the two words are used in translation between English, French, and German.[333] However, engagement is also not some supplementary phenomenon or a technical term that the phrase social acts already includes in itself or that the concepts of ›commitment‹ or ›joint commitment‹ somehow necessarily imply. Let me begin by sketching the nature of neglect and diminishment of importance of the verb ›to engage‹ (or ›engagement‹ or ›act of engagement‹). Here is a list of a few basic characteristics of this specific protocol in relation to others, such as the social, collegial, and committed acts:

a) Both engagement and commitment refer to the will (»commitment of the will«[334]), but engagement explicitly assumes the transfer or import of certain burden or amount of burden that can then be compared to other similar engaged acts. Engagement is never the same as some other engagement, and the quantity of the burden (*gage*, pledge) always determines its efficiency and success, as well as strength of bond to some future actions that the engagement could initiate. This quantitative characteristic (e. g., amount of enthusiasm and will to perform some

[333] Although ›commitment‹ is now often not translated at all into European languages, Howard S. Becker's text or Margaret Gilbert's ›commitment‹ are translated as ›*engagement*‹. While in the opposite direction, Sartre's or Adorno's ›*engagement*‹ is translated into (American) English as ›commitment‹. Cf. Becker: Notes on the Concept of Commitment, pp. 32–40; Notes sur le concept d'engagement, pp. 177–192; Gilbert: Marche ensemble, p. 15. ›Joint commitment‹ is translated into French as ›*engagement conjoint*‹ and not as, for example, *co-engagement*, which would be much more straightforward. Ibid., p. 152.

[334] Gilbert: Commitment, p. 899.

task or introduce or change a rule) has resulted in the verb ›to engage‹ becoming the condition for an action or simply preceding some following action (»The engagement of the agent is already needed before acting«[335], »(...) they had indeed engaged in some acts«[336]). If person P is engaged to be a manager of a company (to conduct certain business acts and make decisions), then the same person P could be very *engaged* at their new job. They would, in that case, produce many, rather than few, various acts, which could be described as engaged and be called acts of engagement. Engagement of person P at their new job could then incite other agents-coworkers to also engage and follow the engagement of person P in their own activities. In that sense, person P would not produce acts that ›engage no one‹ (the French equivalent of this would be ›*n'engage à rien*‹), that is to say, acts that leave others indifferent; yet, we could not say that these acts necessarily bind all other agents to follow the enthusiasm of person P. The act of engagement would therefore be one to which another act is joined, which it follows without obligation or coercion.[337]

b) If the term ›engagement‹ describes several or more »acts of engagement« then these acts should be frequent and directed at the same goal (»consistent line of activity«[338]). Both engagement and commitment share this characteristic because both protocols allow acts to issue and follow one another. Person P, engaged or committed to the new position of management, for example, produces acts that we can describe as strongly dedicated to the goal or task before them. It would appear as if person P no longer has a choice »and must continue the line of action, whether she is personally committed to it or not.«[339] If after a period of time the commitment of person P is relegated because the promises, agreements, contracts or duties of person P surpass their personal preferences and enthusiasm (»she must continue the line of action«), I assume that the characteristic of engagement of person P on the contrary, still surpasses the obligations it has accepted and tasks to which they have agreed.

335 Tuomela: *Social Ontology*, p. 121.

336 Johnson: Commitment, p. 403.

337 Let me offer two comments regarding the act. In »On Promises«, Georg Henrik von Wright insists, in an entirely Aristotelian manner, that »the act cannot be performed solo. It requires two parties, (for example) promise-giver and promise-receiver. They are human beings. (...) When a promise is given collectively or jointly by several agents, or when a promise has more than one receiver, it seems that these cases are essentially similar to the simpler case« (p. 287). In his »L'Acte symbolique«, Émile Bréhier defines the efficiency of an act with the possibility of it being interchangeable with another act or whether its author can be another subject: »*l'acte est impersonnel*« (p. 350). In *Theory of Constitutional Rights*, Robert Alexy defines acts as something that cannot be performed merely on the basis of natural abilities, but which presuppose constitutive rules (p. 152).

338 Both Becker (Notes on the Concept of Commitment, p. 33) and Johnson (Commitment, p. 395) underscore this basic characteristic of commitment.

339 Johnson (Commitment, p. 395) differentiates personal and behavioral commitment.

c) Commitment and engagement could be separated in the following manner: as a matter of fact, person P has been committed by the board or some committee to perform the job of the manager, much as person P has the capacity or authorization to commit or delegate various coworkers in the job at hand. Thus, person P has been committed to do something, and in turn this person has the »right to demand of someone a certain action«,[340] to give command and thus obligate others. In that sense commitment is chain operation that puts together multiple actors (*committere*; *zusammentun* or *zusamensetzen*)[341] in several ways: by each individually, through an act, places themselves under an obligation, by one who has a mandate to obligate others by command fulfilling in that way an obligation given to them or ordered by someone else. Person P could be committed to performing act A (or person P could commit person S to performing act A), but also person P could engage such that their actions are not at all obligating and are not in accordance with ›commitment‹. For example, person P attempts to improve the system as they found it in the new company and thus begins a quality improvement project that is outside their task description. This action has resonated and intrigued person S and they have decided to join. Regardless that with person S's act of ›joining‹ person P has certainly created a certain normative order and an obligation between them (joining is also the condition for their joint action that Gilbert names as joint commitment), I nevertheless insist that this pseudo-obligation is purely temporary and can always be broken by either side (which is why I call it engagement and not [joint] commitment).[342] It is the reciprocal response and answered call on behalf of person S (their engagement) to the action of person P that determines whether person P is indeed conducting engaged acts or not. Some conditions for person S to ›be moved‹ and then potentially join the common

340 It is ›commitment‹ (and not ›joint commitment‹) in its medieval uses that explicitly assumes of someone to do something. For Margaret Gilbert, however, ›joint commitment‹ is ground of ›right‹ to demand of one to do something or »a right against another person has the standing to demand a particular action from that person.« (Gilbert: Rights and Demands, p. 11).

341 Wartburg (ed.): Französisches etymologisches Wörterbuch, p. 955.

342 Gilbert's interventions over the years have rendered the phrase ›joint commitment‹ rather vague. It seems to me that the reconstruction and introduction of the term engagement (along with related terms such as ›act of engagement‹) could in one way or another correct and pin down the meaning of joint commitment. Joint commitment would first of all be a semi-pleonasm as it only emphasizes one of the meanings commitment already carries within itself. Nearly twenty years ago, Gilbert introduced the phrase ›relevant joint commitment‹ that implies successful joint commitment if the actors, paradoxically, are more engaged or if they act in a specific way. »(...) people who can engage in joint activity;« or »(...) acting together as stemming from a prior agreement to engage in the relevant joint action;« or again »only if a certain condition is satisfied will he or Lily be committed through the relevant joint commitment.« (Gilbert: Joint Commitment, pp. 24, 26, 47) The problems only multiply in her book *Rights and Demands: A Foundation Inquiry*, in the chapter »The Ubiquity of Joint Commitment« (pp. 218–232) where the meaning of joint commitment is expanded and surpasses promises, agreements and contracts (although it still retains normative power; it is unclear how this is possible?) and where all intersubjective relations are reduced to joint commitment.

action (and not be ›joined‹ to it, that is, that there is no entity that decides) would be that person P publicly and transparently manifests their own goals, that they are of general interest or in the interest of all (all members of the company, but also of the public at large). And when these acts are conducted jointly, when the reciprocal responses are joined (P+S+…), there is necessarily a change in the institution (company, organization, city, etc.).

Let us now consider a few more uses of the word ›engagement‹, to which we usually pay no attention or consider unimportant enough to specifically thematize. In a few places in »Valuing [the] Interpersonal. Relationships and Acting Together« (which mostly follows the 2007 German version »Interpersonelle Bezeihungen und gemeinsame Handlungen«), Betzler renders the French or French-German word *Engagement* into English as ›engagement‹. She also adds it (›engagement‹ and not ›commitment‹) in a few places to the English in comparison to the German. For example:

> A friendship or a band's jazz improvisation can become a valuable engagement only if the participating persons relate to each other reciprocally (*wenn sich die daran beteiligten Personen in besonderer und noch näher zu charakterisierender Weise wechselseitig aufeinander beziehen*).[343]

Engagement then is, or engagement (as a condition, evidently) exists, when several persons are in question (not only one) and they »relate to each other reciprocally«. In the forthcoming manuscript »Collegial Relationships« (which Betzler has graciously allowed me to consult), Betzler and Löschke mention this word nine times, e. g., »person who engages in the same business« or »kind of engagement for a common purpose«, etc. On page 13, we find the following formulation:

> Work relation*ship* between colleagues is characterized by ongoing interactions that two colleagues engage in because of the relation that holds between them. These interactions are limited to the context of those features that constitute the status of colleagues, but they are enduring, orientated towards the other as colleague, rooted in a shared history and marked by shared expectations for future thoughts and actions. Two colleagues thus establish a relationship by actualizing interconnected but temporal chains of behavior.

In addition to a common goal (›business‹ or ›common purpose‹), and individual action that is also simultaneous or reciprocal to those of others, a chain sequence

343 Betzler: Valuing the Interpersonal, p. 259; Betzler: Interpersonelle Beziehungen und gemeinsame Handlungen, p. 445 In the English version, Betzler mentions several times, »the valuable engagement« and connects it with »reciprocal interpersonal reference.« On page 261 of the English edition, Betzler writes: »In order to realize such engagements at all, the act of referring to others has to be valued for its own sake. But what turns valuable engagements of the kind mentioned into interrelational values is the fact that, in order to be realized, the participating persons must refer to each other reciprocally and for the sake of their relationship's own value.«

of actions in a time to come, the first sentence of this passage indicates that in engagement / commitment, some kind of relation exists among colleagues (a kind of ›primordial we‹), which in this case precedes their engagements. Or else, these colleagues are ›engaged‹ by the interaction because it holds them together, which is termed ›relation‹ (»relation of collegiality«). If the first text presents engagement through simultaneous, above all reciprocal, actions, the other text makes engagement a consequence of something already given in advance through a »relation of collegiality«. And the guarantor or source of the latter is, for example, the institution (such as the university). Even if this second were the case, it seems to me there is no collision if we conclude that »valuable engagement« between colleagues will be one in which they »relate to each other reciprocally« and which simultaneously conducts the process of institutionalization (e. g., confirms the institution of the university and the rule of collegial communication). If colleagues conduct themselves institutionally or with collegiality or if they produce engagement acts, then this means that they »relate to each other reciprocally«. Based on observations found in texts here cited, it is still uncertain whether ›engagement‹ is an act or condition, and what kind of ›reciprocity‹ we are speaking of, given that engagement always begins with a certain asymmetry and stimulative activity or increased attention in relation to other actors. (»She, Martina is more engaged in the association to fight cancer from Martin«, or with the reciprocal response, »Martin has changed and become much more active and dynamic, working much more – Martina and Martin are now a real team or tandem«.)[344] Further, it is uncertain whether engagement is part of what Adolf Reinach or Edmund Husserl call a »social act« (in the sense of a step or degree a social act can but does not necessarily have to contain – at issue is the rule of reciprocity) or wether it is actually an entirely special case of social acts whose function would be to institutionalize a group, to convert a group into an institution.[345]

344 Explaining in 1711 who Hercules was, the Earl of Shaftsbury says (in »A Notion of the Tablature, or Judgment of Hercules«): »He admires, he contemplates; but is not yet ingag'd or interested.« Cf. Berger: Attention, Deficit, Democracy, p. 36. In an English-German dictionary of 1763, the word ›ingagement‹ is translated as *verbinden* or *anreizend*.

345 Long before Husserl and Adolf Reinach, Mauss is practically the first to thematize *»l'acte sociale«*. »Ultimately, without being obligatory, magic rites are nevertheless social. Obligation properly speaking is not for us the distinctive characteristic of things, of social acts and sentiments. We still regard the illicit magic act as social, without contradiction. This act is social because it retains the social form, which would not have meaning without it« (*Enfin, sans être obligatoires, les rites de la magie sont néanmoins sociaux. L'obligation proprement dite n'est pas pour nous le caractère distinctif des choses, des actes et des sentiments sociaux. L'acte magique illicite reste pour nous social, sans qu'il y ait là contradiction. L'acte est social parce qu'il tient sa forme de la société et qu'il n'a de raison d'être que par rapport à elle*). Hubert / Mauss: Introduction a l'analyse de quelques phénomènes religieux, p. 186. In his 1930 *Autobiographie*, Marcel Mauss says that he is above all interested in common work, being part of a team (group), and in following the belief that collaboration with others brings much more than pretentious solitary and isolated search for originality. If we reconstructed all of Mauss efforts and projects, from the various ritual, collective acting or institutions to the grandiose

What then is a social act? In the brief sketch »Nichtsoziale und soziale Akte«,[346] Reinach offers a very deft definition of social acts, and summarily rejects and excludes everything not in the definition by calling it *»nichtsoziale Akte«* (which then functions as irrelevant refuse, that is to say, anything not a social act is not a social act – there should be no new special entity entitled *nichtsoziale Akte*).[347] But right on the heels of this definition, he suddenly calls into question his own distinction with the example of prayer:

The appearance form exists only because among us people things are such that we can only know our inner acts (*unsere inneren Akte*) by way of their appearance forms (*Erscheinungsformen*). Prayer (*das Gebet*), for example, *is* a social act (ist *ein sozialer Akt*). The first [therein] exists, while the second not (it has no apparent form). The religious man assumes that the addressee hears the prayer without the apparent form (*ohne Erscheinungsform vernimmt*). Thus, a silent prayer is also possible (*Darum ist also ein stilles Gebet möglich*).

Prayer *is* (the *ist* in the original is italicized)[348] a social act because regardless of the uncertainty of existence of one who hears the prayer (here I follow Reinach's

project of overcoming capitalism and competition through engagement for cooperatives (commons), we would see that his interest is always connected with the »act of a collective nature« (*acte de nature collective*). Mauss: Discussion a L'Institut français de sociologie (intervention), p. 61. Which is further to say, his interest is always for the largest form of collective activity, »the nation or the very meaning of the social« (*la nation ou le sens du social*). Cf. Mauss: L'œuvre de Mauss par lui-même, pp. 209–210.

346 *Nichtsoziale Akte* is Reinach's phrase, which he mentions only in passing, in a short 1911 text (really a reconstruction of his lecture notes from Göttingen). The text was only published for the first time as part of his collected works (Reinach: Nichtsoziale und soziale Akte, pp. 355–360). Reinach never explicitly explains what are *nichtsoziale Akte* (in the notes they are mentioned two or three times as opposite from social acts), nor indeed do almost any of his commentators.

347 In a few steps, entirely in rhythm with Reinach's chapter on social acts, we can classify their difference from negative social acts: a social act is spontaneous (a negative is not). Spontaneity designates inner actions of the subject (*inneres Tun des Subjektes*). A social act is not at peace in itself; it demands to be externalized (a negative not). A social act penetrates another (*er dringt in den anderen ein*), while the negative does not. A social act can be perceived, a negative cannot. A social act has an inner and external (phenomenal) aspect; negative acts only the inner. The expression of a social act is not accidental or inadvertent, while the negative one is. A social act can have many addressers and addressees (*Soziale Akte können eine Mehrheit von Adressanten und eine Mehrheit von Adressaten haben*), the negative cannot. (Reinach: Die apriorischen Grundlagen des bürgerlichen Rechtes, pp. 158–161)

348 Reinach makes generous use of italics, while Husserl, around the same time (1910), in constituting social ontology and descriptive sociology in *Zur Phänomenologie der Intersubjektivität*, insists on the use of the quotation marks. All the themes we have today in social ontology are already present in Husserl, but in an unsystematic way, in contrast with a few developed texts by Reinach. I would like to insist, regardless of the hesitations they have in common, that a) there is an obvious influence of Husserl on Reinach, but also a contemporaneity – Husserl himself quite early discusses acts of address or communicative acts, and also »acts,« orders, acts of love, the unity of social life based on mutual and unilateral exchange (*auf der Einheit eines sozialen Lebens, mit aktiver und reaktiver Wechseleinigung oder einseitiger Bezogenheit*), and further conduct of a higher unity by way of acts that produce mutual consciousness of the actors (Husserl: Zur Phänomenologie der Intersubjektivität, 1, p. 98). b) I would also like to insist on Reinach's resistance to Husserl's empathy

realism) and with whom there is really no connection, there is, nevertheless, an inner act or experience, as well as an addressee of whom one who prays (the religious man) assumes not only the existence but acceptance of what is being sent (even if the believer sends nothing, that is, a series of unuttered words from a familiar protocol). In his book, however, Reinach reworks and enhances this »prayer« scene:

Let us imagine a community that comprises beings capable of directly and immediately perceiving their mutual experiences. We would be forced to admit that in such a community, there very well could appear social acts that possess only soul, but no body. If we assume that a being to which we address ourselves in our social acts is capable of directly grasping our experience, we humans would in that way truly renounce the outward appearance of our social acts. Remember that silent prayer addresses God and seeks to manifest itself to him. It thus must be seen as a purely spiritual social act.[349]

The sentence »Let us imagine a community that comprises beings (*Wesen*) capable of directly and immediately perceiving their mutual relations,« as perhaps one of the crucial places of Reinach's chapter on social acts, demands certain entirely different and more complicated examples from that of a religious person addressing an invisible addressee through prayer. And not only examples, but also, analogously, collectively engaged activity that would indeed turn non-social into social acts, or else entirely eliminate them.[350] If we imagine a community in which negative social acts are eliminated in mutual interaction,[351] then this would call

and affection. c) Husserl explicitly speaks of linguistic acts and a linguistic community, but in an entirely different and insufficiently focused way compared to Reinach. Later, Husserl opens the possibility of the existence of consciousness or cogito of a superpersonal unity. d) Husserl is probably one of the first social ontologists who is aware of the importance of the document, of the ID (*Ausweisung*). Ibid., p. 104. e) Husserl neglects Reinach in his notes after the war (around 1920) when he speaks in detail of social acts.

349 »*Denken wir uns eine Gemeinschaft von Wesen, die imstande sind, ihre gegenseitigen Erlebnisse direkt und unmittelbar wahrzunehmen, so werden wir anerkennen müssen, daß in einer solchen Gemeinschaft soziale Akte, welche nur eine Seele und keinen Leib besitzen, sehr wohl vorkommen können. So verzichten wir Menschen in der Tat darauf, unsere sozialen Akte in äussere Erscheinung treten zu lassen, sobald wir annehmen, daß das Wesen, an welches wir sie richten, unser Erleben direkt zu erfassen vermag. Man denke an das stumme Gebet, welches sich an Gott wendet und sich ihm kundzugeben tendiert, welches demnach als ein rein seelicher sozialer Akt betrachtet werden muß.*« (Reinach: Die apriorischen Grundlagen des bürgerlichen Rechtes, p. 161.)

350 One of the foremost characteristics of engaged acts is the elimination of the negative, unengaged, non-social, anti-social acts (if they are acts at all). In »Negative ›Actions‹« Gilbert Ryle calls into question these acts as acts (»if they *are* acts«). Namely, negative actions (refraining, abstaining, postponing, shirking, neglecting, disobeying, overlooking, condoning, etc.) »is the class of acts which consist in the agent's intentional *non*-performance of some specifiable actions.« (Ryle: Negative »Actions«, pp. 81–93).

351 In St. Märgen, in 1921 Husserl develops »communal acts« or »acts in a social community« (*Gemeinschaftsakte, Handlungen in der sozialen Gemeinschaft*). Cf. Husserl: Zur Phänomenologie der Intersubjektivität, 2, pp. 192–205. In April of 1932, Husserl speaks of various forms of linguistic expression and the expectation that the one to whom we have addressed a message answers, and of the disappointment if the answer goes missing. In order to receive an answer, it is necessary to give

into question one of the most important distinctions between social and non-social acts Reinach produced: a social act can have many addressers and addressees (*Soziale Akte können eine Mehrheit von Adressanten und eine Mehrheit von Adressaten haben*); a negative one, on the other hand, cannot.

In contrast with his student, Husserl neither recognizes nor accepts any forms of asymmetry or non-reciprocity between social actors. Even when experimenting several times in notes taken later in life with the possibility for empathy to also be truly reciprocal and active, Husserl still rejects such an idea because I cannot see whether the other notices me simultaneously, whether they are observing themselves, that is, whether they are at all interested in me when I am directed at them. In order for true *communicatio* to take place (Husserl uses the Latin[352]), my activity needs to be explicitly declared and reciprocated (actively oriented towards me).[353] Husserl insists on the words activity (*Aktivität*), directedness and project (*Vorhabe*), and insists on the will for something to be explicitly declared (*Wille der Kundgebung*) to the other (or others) as the main conditions for the social and communicative unity to take place (*soziale, kommunikative Einigung*).

Husserl first insists (very early, around 1910) that intersubjective relations are in themselves real and that the individuals who conduct them are real (*reale Individuen*).[354] Further, acts, communicative acts (*kommunikative Akte*), »acts addressed to others« (*die sich an den Anderen wenden*) imply that the other is aware that they are being addressed (*in denen der Andere bewusst ist als der, an den ich mich wende*). The other needs to understand the address from which certain acts have been sent and respond with an act of the same kind (*zurückwenden wird in einem gleichartigen Akte*). »These are acts that produce a higher unity of consciousness of person to person (…)« (*Das sind die Akte, die zwischen Person und Person eine höhere Bewußtseinseinheit herstellen*).[355] The third characteristic of social acts I would like to point out here, and which Husserl ingeniously develops, refers to the norm of the community (*Gemeinschaftsnorm*) or joint norm. Husserl finds that social acts are actually not norms that force, but rather that they are pseudo-norms or pseudo-obligations:[356] »it is a common willing regulation (*eine Einheit der Wil-*

silence to one or those of whom we expect a response, which in a way is also a negative act. Cf. Husserl: Zur Phänomenologie der Intersubjektivität, 3, pp. 474–475.

352 In saying so, Husserl is really saying that »communication creates unity« (*Kommunikation schafft Einheit*, Husserl: Zur Phänomenologie der Intersubjektivität, 2, p. 199).

353 »*Ein Besonderes ist es nun, daß ich ihn verstehe als* vice versa *auf mich aktiv und explizit auf meine Bekundugen, auf meine darin bekundete Aktivität gerichtet.*« (Husserl: Zur Phänomenologie der Intersubjektivität, 3, p. 472).

354 Husserl: Zur Phänomenologie der Intersubjektivität, 1, pp. 96–97.

355 Ibid., p. 98.

356 This would be another decisive characteristic of engaged acts that is never biding while possessing the capacity of initiating or moving along the linking activity in another or others. In »Commissives«, a chapter in his most important book, John Austin explains the protocols (›engage‹ and ›pledge‹ are some of them) that are not binding – such as ›promise‹ – yet could still »commit you to

lensregelung), acknowledged by individuals and is a super-individual (überindividuell). (...) One who does not respond to a salutation, who does »not thank« is a lout (*Flegel*). (...) if I address someone politely, I have the right (*Ich habe ein Recht*) to expect a polite response from them, that is thanks as response to the polite salutation, etc.«[357]

In Freiburg in 1921, Husserl attempts one more perspective: he negates or eliminates social acts which are not social acts or not yet social acts. First, love, my love or admiration is not yet a social act of any kind. If I love, this is not yet an act of social love (*Akte der sozialen Liebe*). If I do something deliberately for another to notice and behave in a way that I am myself displaying – none of this is yet a social act. It is a social act if I do something hoping that the other, noticing my intention, will respond in their way.[358] In the same year, Husserl discovers something else new by analyzing the family. He demonstrates how a temporary unit (*vorübergehende Gemeinschaft*) turns into an orderly institution (*geregelte Institution*) if its members routinely eat together. Having meals together (social acts) are the basic elements for the institution (*Stiftung*) of the family as a social institution (*soziale Institution*). For a family to be a family (for a ›We‹ to become an institution) it is insufficient to be side by side, to live next to or near another. »Much more than that, it is a matter of the way of being together, way to be in relation to another, mutually exchanging within living situations (*wechselseitige Aufeinander-Bezogenheiten des strebenden Lebens*), in acting, in reciprocal influence of one another, in relations that function reciprocally, and based on which the action of one penetrates into the action of the other.«[359]

The final characteristic of social acts, as imagined and defined by Husserl, quite probably his greatest discovery, appears suddenly in January 1931, when Husserl names this other (one close to him, with whom he is exchanging acts) as ›the third‹ (*dritte*). It seems to me that formulated like this, ›the third‹ is the premise for the discovery of ›We‹, that is, of the institutional act. »My neighbor (one close

doing something, but include also declarations or announcements of intentions.« A statement that commits the speaker to some future action simultaneously performs two functions: on the one hand, it prevents ›omissions‹ and negative acts, and on the other, engages the audience who are supposed to respond to the speaker in one way or another (Austin: How to do things with Words, pp. 152, 156–158).

357 Husserl: Zur Phänomenologie der Intersubjektivität, 1, pp. 105–106. A toast could be a still better example that would shed light on what I call an engaged act. It is not a matter of my right to expect anyone to respond, nor is it a matter of right of the person not to respond. It is, rather, a gage or a pledge that engages (burdens) another when I salute them with a toast, one I always feel as unease: I invite someone to do something they otherwise (perhaps) would not do and the unease since they might not respond in equal measure to my invitation.

358 Husserl: Zur Phänomenologie der Intersubjektivität, 2, p. 166. For a social act to be an act there needs to be a chain process, not mimesis. Each next person, each person following an act by someone else confirms that the act is social. If my act engages another whose act in turn engages me or someone third – then my act is social. The sociality of an act is decided by each following act. Cf. ibid., p. 193.

359 Ibid., p. 179.

to me), who I now perceive (*ansehe*), is now already the third (...) who helps in the continuous formation of the world from the initial world-state »for us two,« to a world for us three.«[360]

This last moment that for Husserl determines the social act opens the question of the nature of reciprocity. If two persons »relate to each other reciprocally,« and if we have previously defined this situation as (their) engagement, does their developing and increasing interaction imply the appearance of the third or the group, and then the institution?

Let us return once more to collegial engagement and the institution (the university). An interesting scene (a possible analogy) appears in the introduction of the recently published book by Francesco Guala, *Understanding Institutions*:

> If I look to the right, I see my colleague Antonio reviewing a paper for a scientific journal. On the left, a map of China hangs on the wall. In front of me, past the door of my office, two students are walking in the corridor of the Department of Economics. Out of the window, I can see the second floor of the Faculty of Social Science of the University of Milan. (...) Antonio, for example, is a colleague of mine because we are both employees of the same university, and the University of Milan is an institution.[361]

Gilbert Ryle describes a foreigner (that is what he calls him) visiting Oxford or Cambridge, hopelessly seeking the institution of the university. Finally, he asks, »But where is the University?« (Frank Hindriks also has a text, from 2012, with this same title). I am interested in Antonio, the colleague (»Antonio, for example, is a colleague of mine because we are both employees of the same University«) who is performing an institutional activity (»reviewing a paper for a scientific journal«). It only seems that Francesco Guala is merely describing Antonio (it does not look like they are really doing something together); the fact is that Antonio produces institutional or academic acts *par excellence* because, as an employee of the university, he is performing an action the university as a group agent has formulated as its goal.[362] Since Antonio is certainly not only a member of this group-institution (Antonio has, for example, a rather large family, renowned for its production of wine, meaning that Antonio holds shares, he goes bowling at a club called »Inter Sempre«, and in his free time is a serious poker player – in fact, he is the president of the Italian association; Milton Friedman insists that we must never forget that we are never members of only one group, which fact has various theoretical and

360 Husserl: Zur Phänomenologie der Intersubjektivität, 3, p. 134.

361 Guala: Understanding Institutions, p. xii.

362 This too could be a basic paraphrasing of the »we-mode« of Raimo Toumela's protocol. »An individual member derives the reasons from which she/he acts from the intentions that the group agent forms. (...) Given that members derive their participatory intentions from the intention of the group agent, the level of the group agent is in an important sense primary and prior to that of an individual member.« (Hindriks: Group Agents and Social Institutions, p. 198).

practical consequences).[363] And since Antonio is a very busy man, Antonio, for example, does not have time to be very engaged as the Vice Dean for International Cooperation of the University of Milan.

Now, my problem, or our problem, begins with a certain Frederique who works at another university, who has not published a text in an academic publication in thirty years, is a few years from retirement, is late with her submission, neglects her lectures, has had some reported incidents with students, in fact she is currently under investigation for harassment, and has poor relations with her fellow colleagues (Bernhard Schmid named all these acts »bad acts« or »evil actions«).[364] To make matters interesting, the recently elected president of the university, Etienne, a vainglorious jurist and ambitious administrator, has coauthored a paper with Frederique, the theme of which is harassment, and which has received positive feedback for publication. Before we attempt to classify some of these acts – and of course there is always the question what is an act and whether some negative actions are actions at all – it seems important to me to insist right away that the institutional or collegial acts performed by Etienne (such as those towards or in relation to Frederique) are not necessarily the consequence of Etienne's having an institutional mandate or the function of University President. Nor due to Frederique and Etienne's simultaneous belonging to the same entity in which they share potential institutional responsibility. I will call these acts »engaging,« above all because they change the institution (alter it but simultaneously create it) by introducing new rules – even if it is sometimes very difficult to develop or differentiate an action or event, an engaged act is one that decidedly creates something new, such as a real event. Thus, a new institutional fact is that now Frederique is »reviewing a paper for a scientific journal.« Of course, this new situation could produce a certain form of obligation in all members of a group (and in those who have yet to become so; meaning, it is imperative to engage all), that is, that they oblige the group as such (»group agent«) to form new kinds of obligation.[365] To

363 In a certain way, this »freedom of association« (Kimberley Brownlee) and simultaneous membership in multiple groups always implies disharmony and so-called »moral messiness«. Postponing the execution of an obligation undertaken by membership in a group in order to execute a task implied by membership in another group always manifests in »negative actions« or »negative social acts«.

364 Cf. »Where have all those negligent, sloppy, unfocused, forgetful and weak-willed people gone whom we know from real life, all those who for some reason or another fail to do (or even fail to intend to do) their part in their collective projects?« (Schmid: On not Doing One's Part, p. 47) Although »the power of the negative is an important power, and our dissidents and our cultural subversives provide that power« (Annette Baier), we ought certainly to differentiate non-participation in a group and not performing certain tasks from negative activities that directly call into question the group or institution. There are other problems too. Tuomela employs the example of a car that has broken down, with one of those now having to push the vehicle to the side of the road an invalid. All this must not be conflated with so-called »non-cooperative game theory«.

365 Likely, this is »*une obligation librement consentie*« [a freely-agreed obligation]. Von Ihering

be engaged means to count on all others and work so as to produce a great stake or burden (*gage*, pledge)[366] that ought to reiterate obligation and institutional responsibility even in those we have labeled hold-outs, subversive or simply ›Frederique(s)‹.

Therefore, I insist on there being an entirely imprecise or uncertain number of different unclassified activities that have the capacity to: a) not only encourage or activate another (or others) into identical or similar action or reciprocal reaction, but also to produce a pseudo-obligation that implies a joint, group action (»to do something as a group«), and b) not only to, so to speak, obligate members of a group to do something together, but to exceed the borders of joint commitment of the group, *a priori* ›obligating‹ non-members or all potential and future participants towards joint and coordinated action.

What are these actions like, then, the ones that engage others (all others) or that have the capacity to commit (to bring together, collect and bind even those who are not present in one place simultaneously)? Engaged action would then be one that is above all public or announced (for it cannot be a kind of negative social act or a secret, an undisclosed action performed in silence). Further, it is provocative in nature, really a call or message to all, to others (*com-mittere* can mean to send), a prompting of all to come closer, to join (not only members of a group, but also those outside and beyond the group), because »to commit« precisely means an action that encourages or obligates others to do something together by doing so as members of a future committee. However, engaged action is specific in that it supposes this type of great or grand work, adherence (»giving one's all« »committed to the end«) and abandon (a kind of sacrifice for others or with other or towards others, or in their stead, sacrifice for the sake of bringing closer, but also as work that calls others to join, to repeat our action and thus construct future joint work) – all with the goal of bringing us closer to others.[367] We advance towards

uses a potentially analogous term in 1886, *die active Solidarobligation*. Cf. Ihering: Die aktive Solidarobligation.

366 Or hostage (*hostage*). This is one of the most important meanings of the word pledge. More interesting still is the word *toast* that holds in itself both the call and response to call, as well as the community beyond all obligation. It seems to me that Sartre is wrong when he writes that the group or institution always changes with the introduction of a new member, just as there is no abstract member »without baggage« (sans baggage): »*Si vous avez un bagage, vous pouvez vous engager parce que vous-même, vous négocierez (…) Mais si vous n'en avez pas, vous entrez inconditionnellement dans un groupe, donc pour vous engager il faut que vous acceptiez toutes ses théories.*« (If you have baggage, you can still be engaged because you yourself negotiate (…) But if you have none, you join the group conditionally, that is to say, to be engaged, you must accept all its theories). (Astruc: Sartre, p. 46)

367 The word *engager* comes from the verb *vado*, with the German word *wadi*, Latin *vas, vadis* meaning »*je m'avance vers quelqu'un*«, »I am advancing towards another.« (Kemp: Théorie de l'engagement, p. 16) Kemp fails to mention a much more interesting meaning of »engagement« that draws this protocol fatally close to the words *institutere* and *instituo* (institution). *Instituetere* (*einsetzen*) is continuation, the production of heir (Französisch Etymologisches Wörterbuch, p. 724), while Gaffiot says this same thing by insisting on some uses in Cicero that refer to »*se créer des amis*«, and

or are brought closer to others, either when we become bound to them or bind them to us, when we »invest« or »place something« into or before others, when we »*mettre en gage*« / »pledge« or »*donner en gage*« / »give a pledge.«

What does this mean? What does it mean to place a pledge or burden (guarantee, bail, *hypothéque*; »*engager, c'est hypothéquer*«) before another or before all (the whole community), and to what extent is that a form of modest violence and forcing others (or all) to choose whether they would join this specific action or not? What kind of action does not principally have to be strictly in direct relation with another (»if I am doing something, then you or he must do likewise«), but that certainly binds me to another (and the other to me) such that it jointly obligates us to conduct it (»if I act, then we all act,« »if you act, then all act«)? If my public activities involve collecting money for caring for gravely ill children, organizing temporary shelter for war refugees from a neighboring state, or if I often visit slaughterhouses to protest against the (way of) killing animals, would not all these activities be called engaged (and »activist«)? Each could represent »personal commitment,« and at the same time, none could be performed individually, but would always require smaller or larger groups of people. However, this transformation of individual into group agency need not necessarily be the most significant characteristic of these actions. The beginning of the explanation of this transformation was long ago constructed by Kant, where he speaks of duties to oneself as such (*Pflicht gegen sich selbst*), of debt or obligation to oneself that always precedes and underpins any possible obligation to others (which he will call external duty).

Far more complicated, but also perhaps more crucial, is the set of actions that could be located in that place in English where two complementary words or strategies overlap and at the same time diverge: engagement and commitment. Personal committed action (crucially perhaps in contradistinction to the French *engagement*) remains personal, such as me being engaged in my career or caring for the ill. Only a handful of people, in my more or less immediate circle, will recognize this commitment, and in recognizing it might feel that it is »a thing of public importance,« and thus an obligation to join in. Commitment or joint commitment, for it is always in the plural, calls for a different kind of obligation. Namely, when I call a lunch meeting of our poker players group, or what have you, to a nearby restaurant, and promise to attend the beginning of the meeting, then I am truly committed and all those who answer the meeting call will confirm my action, thus also becoming committed. But the engagement of our group occurs only when the actions of the group produce sufficient reason or some form of ob-

to »continuing« in the sense of »chain-linking« not »repetition« (»*continue comme tu as commencée*«). (Dictionnaire Gaffiot, p. 833) If several Turin families band together of their own accord to remove trash (as a group), they are calling others to join them (›friends‹), to do as they do (›repetition‹ is really linking and creating a chain of institutional gestures), which further implies the possibility of creation of an alternative counter-institution whose many and diverse actions produce a cleaner city.

ligation for those who do not initially belong to our group, or those who are still not at the scheduled meetings, to necessarily join. If our group truly acts together, if it is jointly engaged (such action always referring to the vital connections and relationships that hold the community or the group together), then it would seem I am obligated to join it, to become engaged (»if all act, then I act«). This, let us call it new, so-called obligation is different from a non-perfect obligation, because the person that gives charity or uses polite protocols or helps the poor in no way produces the identical obligation in me. By contrast, engagement of a group could never leave me indifferent.

These acts obligate and connect above all those who are not yet part of the group or institution, who have yet to become so, yet are nevertheless always present. This is decidedly not the same kind of obligation as exists within an agreement (a result of a promise, money-lending or various other kinds of transactions), nor the obligation of the actor in joint commitment. The cry »help,« paradoxically, ›obligates‹ those who are definitely not present, refers to anyone who hears it, even who has never heard it before. Nor is its imperative force and its »*ad hominem* capacity« certainly any weaker if it is an individual call or cry or plea: ›help me‹. Joint commitment assumes above all an act that implies belonging to a group, such as those who could help (I act, therefore I am an agent, a part of a whole, of all together). Only if I do something publicly, potentially addressing everyone and affirming the existence of all, only then do I prove the existence of a large group and my belonging to it.

This very act is institutional. Why? Because my help to a migrant or a small group of migrants actually represents a small committed act that necessarily implies a multiplicity of new (engaged) acts that could then further construct systemic institutional help to all migrants (and all future migrants). An institutional act is not necessarily normative[368] – that I ›have to‹ help one who is endangered because I so confirm that I belong to an institution whose task it is to provide first aid to ones who need it. An institutional act is also an engaged act that calls for the engagement of all, for the sake of transforming occasional, one-off acts of help into consistent institutional actions, that is, institutional agency.

368 J. R. Cameron (»Ought« and Institutional Obligation, pp. 309–323; The Nature of Institutional Obligation, pp. 318–332) proves that ›has to‹ and not ›ought to‹ is substantial for institutional obligations.

III. Institutional Realism

1 Realism and Institution. What is (in)*corporatio*?

I am interested in money and profit (or more precisely, ›amount‹ of money or profit, or even better, ›amount‹ as such) as the integrative element or factor of a community, as well as one of the main attributes of realism. Here is an entirely trivial case: a few years ago, in Milan, a professor from the University of California was out to dinner with a couple of other participants of the conference they were attending. Just before the food was ordered, hesitating over the menu, the American professor discreetly asked one of the other persons at the table who was paying for dinner. It was important to establish, before the food is ordered, the fact that neither they, nor any other individual person was paying (out of their own pocket) for dinner in Milan. A simple question, then: why do we eat more freely and with considerably less pressure at someone else's cost? Why the occasional excess? And why is the awkwardness lessened if the food is shared, if all eat together, but at someone else's cost, and further still, dining in Milan and having, let us say, the University of Torino pay?! Imagine that the University of Torino, which is indeed paying for this expensive dinner in Milan, is a corporation – and not just an institution, but a corporation (one of the simpler definitions of a corporation could be »a collection of many individuals united into one body, under special denomination and authorized by law to act as a unit«[362]). If we accept further that the intentions of the diners quickly harmonize around the fact that they should order, eat, and drink more than normal, since it is ultimately free, as it is paid for by someone seeming insufficiently existent, someone without soul and body (»*universitas non habet corpus nec animam, est res inanimata*«, Innocent IV), someone fictional etc.[363] Along with that, the professor in question at one point marvels

[362] Karl Olivecrona's text »Corporations as *universitates*« opens with the following words: »One of the outstanding contributions of the Roman jurist to legal thought is the idea that rights and duties can be ascribed to an organization as an entity distinct from its members.« Olivecrona: Three Essays in Roman Law, p. 5.

[363] It seems to me that an interesting differentiation could be made between two schemes or two forms implied by the institution – a differentiation which is always thematized within canonical law. As such it could help in the disagreement between the fictive or anti-real and realist in law (in the ontology of law). Sinibaldo de' Fieschi (Sinibaldus de Flisco or Pope Innocent IV), the great canonist, is the first to recognize the institution of the Church as *d'un nouvo tipo di persona guiridica* (for him it is a *persona ficta*). Later, however, the Church as an institution will separate: on the one hand it becomes *corporazione, persona guiridica che ha il suo substrato nell'elemento personale del collegium*, and whose goal is the unification of common powers; on the other hand, *fondazione*, which occurs based on a creative act coming from outside or above (meaning authority, *voluntas Superioris*). »*La corporazione agisce secondo la volontà dei propri soci, mentre la seconda agisce conforma alla volontà*

that the University of Torino has a significant budget or funding. Yet, who at all is the University in Torino, what is the status of the ›institutional person‹ (Pettit) or ›corporative person‹ of the university? We very nearly have all the elements of a concrete and living, ›real‹, theater. These four ›kings of reality‹ truly eat, together and in great quantities – destroying something (food) and incorporating something (the body grows, bellies bloat, and in time, expand; they concretize and grow along with [*con crescere*, grow and develop together is the etymology of the word ›concrete‹]). All this being simple proof that something real is happening in the restaurant in Milan. And then, someone is paying for dinner (the restaurant will send the University a bill or one of the hosts will pay and be reimbursed at a later date by the University) – without money it would be truly impossible to spend two and a half hours in a restaurant in Milan or organize a philosophy conference in that city about realism. Finally, the restaurant in Milan (an establishment registered as a partnership, for example), the University of Torino (an institution or corporation or ›company‹, the continental name for a corporation), registered or incorporated Italian banks through which one pays, etc., are, for instance, three sites among which certain documents, receipts, copies, contracts, and charters flow. These documents, then, issued and controlled by certain departments or agencies of the state, ensure the reality and duration of these organizations. It seems to me that it is above all the number of people, money, documents, institutions, food, enjoyment, as well as the level of responsibility for the expenditure or crisis or bankruptcy, that determines the power or degree of realism here in play.

I am suggesting that the concept of ›amount‹ and number regulate the status of the ›real‹. This is one of two reasons why I placed the word corporation in the title: it is a specific kind of institution that immediately represents business, earnings, profit, and expansion.[364] For something to be ›real‹ (»real is, like good, a dimension word«[365]), it must exist in time and be in a process of realization. The most important characteristics and themes initiated by the corporation (certainly one of the more significant human inventions) are the protection of the rights of the individual, limited liability and corporate responsibility (the sentence ›I didn't do

autoritativa che ha presieduto al suo nascere, e della quale gli organi di essa istituzione (fondazione) continuano ad essere gli esecutori.« Later this difference can be found between Hobbes and Hume in their interpreting *»institutio«*, but remains to this day obscured by the later concept of *»corpus mysticum«* or *»corpus Christi.«* Cf. Caron: Il concetto di »institutio« nel diritto della chiesa, pp. 330–335.

364 In his thesis on institutionalism, *L'institution, le droit objectif et la technique positive* (1933) André Desqueyrat speaks about »institution corporative« which has three characteristics: the idea of a goal that ought to be realized in a social group; organizational power for the purpose of realizing that idea; and the manifestation of a community emerging from the social group for the sake of the idea and its realization.

365 Cf. Austin: Sense and Sensibilia, p. 71. Let me offer a reminder that in his 1959 lectures, Austin designates the »little word real« first as a »normal word,« and then claims that »real is not a normal word at all.« Ibid., p. 64.

it; the company did‹ belongs to this protocol), the relation between corporate and canonical law, the partnership and corporation, and not least, the decades-long resistance and critical and hypocritical stances toward the corporation as a foundation of capitalism. Nevertheless, the second reason why I have introduced the corporation is of course the status of the real (or the status of realism) – immediately called into question when this ›judicial hallucination‹ is mentioned. In other words, could the corporation or the company be a good instrument for the reconstruction of our concept of reality, and then all the alternative terms that have always stood side by side with the term ›real‹: effective, actual, concrete, evident, objective, material, physical, factual, etc.? How do we harmonize the ›corporation‹ (the institution) with the first portion of Russel's famous phrase from the title of the lecture held in French on March 23, 1911 at the Association of Philosophers of France: »Le réalisme analytique?«[366]

Before I mention a few details from Searle's analysis of the corporation from 2010, I would like to construct a connection between realism and the institution using a phrase by Robert Grafstein, »institutional realism«.[367] It is this link between the institution and realism,[368] and the triad in the title, Realism, Institution, and Corporation, that ought to affirm three circular moments that I intend to defend, and which are key to a small theory of the institution that I am trying to formulate. First, to register or to be incorporated (by way of charter or document) means to be ›real‹ or, more generally, to ›exists‹. Second, even before the incorporation that assumes making a new person or new body (public and official) along with others (transforming oneself into something else along with others), there

366 Russell explains first what is ›analytical‹ and what is ›realist‹: »The philosophy to which I belong is analytical only in second place, because it believes that we ought to search for simple elements that make up the more complex ones, and that complex things presuppose simple ones, while simple things do not presuppose complex ones.« (*La philosophie dont je suis partisan est, en second lieu, analytique, parce qu'elle soutient qu'il faut chercher les elements simples dont se composent les complexes, et que les choses complexes presupposent les choses simples, tandis que les choses simples ne presupposent pas les choses complexes*). Russell: Le réalisme analytique, p. 5.

367 »Institutions represent – in a sense, are – our connectedness (…) Institutions are physical wholes composed of human parts.« Grafstein: Institutional Realism, pp. 13, 22. Institutional realism is supposed to oppose new institutionalism, as yet another extreme form of conventionalism, as well as anti-realist philosophy of social science. »Realism assures us that those reciprocal influences which we are then in a position to attribute to institutions and participants are physically realised in ways that, in principle, are comprehensible to science. As aggregates of human beings, institutions are, unproblematically, entities determined by their participants. As distinct physical entities, institutions can be distinct social forces.«

368 Santi Romano writes: »The institution is some kind of being or social body that holds a stable and permanent order, and gives form to its own body and life« (*Istituzione è qualsiasi ente o corpo sociale che abbia un assetto stabile e permanente e formi un corpo a sè, con una vita propria*). Cf. La Torre: Norme, istituzioni, valori, p. 125. Further: »The institution is not some order or demand of the mind, an abstract principle, an ideal *quid*, but a real and effective being« (*L'istituzione non è un'esigenza della ragione, un principio astratto, un quid ideale, è invece un ente reale, effettivo*). Romano: Ordinamento giuridico, p. 96.

is a multitude of relations and they are social facts (which is why the corporation or institution will be real).[369] Third, that a ›written document‹ or a ›written act‹ (written Declaration or Charter) constitutes or institutionalizes a group or collective (and protects their existence in time). Thus, the institution is always preceded by certain, less developed, institutional elements. (Cautiously, we could here use Searle's term ›institutional background‹.)[370] And although the three steps cannot be discretely pulled apart, just as it is impossible to ›begin somewhere‹ or ›take the first step‹ (there is no first, there is only the next step), the circularity cannot hide the importance of the multitude of documents (of writing, of letters, of paper). Nor can it hide the fact that several individuals or several groups of individuals coordinate their goal together, and are in the process of cooperation, always complicated and problematic, that these individuals intend to register together, and temporarily become real (realized) in a new and unique form. This new form is above all simpler, less expensive, and safer. On the other hand, the circularity protects me from certain other elements which, in Searle's theory of institution and corporation, for example, play a role: the advantage of speech over writing, and the absence or hesitation in the introduction of the document (and a document is not an object);[371] the importance of power and its ultimate example – the state (the institution above all institutions), which always has the first and last word in

369 In a sense, this is a reformulation of the so-called Reality Theory defended by Otto von Gierke. »Reality Theory recognizes corporations to be pre-legal existing sociological persons. (...) Law cannot create its subjects, it only determines which societal facts are in conformity with its requirements.« French: The Corporation as a Moral Person, p. 209. The Law only recognizes the corporation; it did not create it. Regardless of the fact that von Gierke differentiates the corporation from the institution (*Anstalt*), collective personality is, according to him, not a fictitious person, but rather a real existence (*eine reale Existenz*).

370 For a critique of Searle and norms and normativity as the essence of the institution, as well as debates whether such a »social construction« precedes the institution as such (as well as Searle's response), a few texts are useful: Hindriks: Reconstructing Searle's *Making the Social World*, pp. 1–17; Hinrdiks: Deconstructing Searle's *Making the Social World*, pp. 363–369; Guala: The Normativity of Institutions, pp. 118–128; Searle: Status functions and institutional facts: reply to Hindriks and Guala, pp. 507–514; Guala: Understanding Institutions.

371 Searle thanks Barry Smith for the topic of corporation in the 2005 text »What is an Institution?«. It is in this text that Searle mentions »official documentation« for the first time, and connects the corporation with written language. In the book *Making the Social World*, Searle speaks considerably more about »special role of writing«, »written speech act«, or »written constitutive rules«, but not in the chapter that deals with the corporation. He talks about the corporation in the chapter dedicated to »Creating institutional acts,« whereas »Creating a Corporation« is a so-called »complex case«. Searle: *Making the Social World*, p. 97. Double Declaration is here mentioned for the first time. In »Declarations d'independence« from 1976, Jacques Derrida mentions something he had not problematized prior: a »theory of performative writing« (*une theorie de l'ecriture »performative«*), and mentions »a declarative act or act of declaration« and »foundational act of an institution (*l'acte fondateur d'une institution*). Derrida: Otobiographies, pp. 15–17. Paradoxically, his adversary from the 1980s, John Searle developed a theory of the declaration and »declarative acts«, and then also thematized the connection between human rights and the institution, and institutional facts. Chapter 8, »Human Rights«, Searle: Making the Social World, pp. 174–199.

registering a corporation; the collective is secondary, and Searle displays carelessness that acceptance of others is a necessary condition of creating deontic powers (thus Searle does not exclude the possibility of a one-man corporation [›*corporatio sole*‹]; and finally, Searle's understanding of the physical object is too obscure and points latently to his anti-realism.

What is ›the first step‹ and what precedes the first document (along with the registration and all the myriad documents that follow, thus confirming the existence of the corporation)? »If you are planning to start your own business, you should know how to incorporate«.

Does the second part, »how to incorporate«, have anything to do with the institution? More interesting, I think, than enumerating all the differences between the institution and corporation (or company), and the usual disdain towards the corporation as an emblem and essence of capitalism, would be to insist on a set of various operations or co-operations that come along with the claim made by person X about the necessity of possessing a certain kind of knowledge as the basis of, ultimately, producing profit and sustaining that profit or company. A company, a firm, a partnership, a *société anonyme*, a corporation, has to be registered (to be set in the register, to be incorporated) according to rules that are set by the state, generally simple, and that should be familiar (»you should know«).[372] X is first a person (an »institutional person«, not just a subject or agent[373]). X has certain interests and is surrounded by others with whom they wish to work and who share that interest (right away we encounter the representative of this group, which will quickly lead us to Hegel and the problem of interest representation or identity representation; in that case, the unit or group will be incorporated in the action of a certain portion of the whole that represents – because considers itself identical to – that whole). Further, this is neither a group of thieves, nor criminals, nor undocumented workers, since the group is ready to publicly declare its work (through declarations; of course, it still remains to be seen whether the institutional structure allows the group to make certain public declarations, or the other way round, the public declarations institutionally design the group). X can also be single, in which case we are speaking of a »*corporatio sole*; a legal entity consisting of a single (»sole«) incorporated office, occupied by a single man or woman (however, in that case, what has been abandoned is, in Searle's words, one of the main discoveries of contemporary capitalism, that is, limited liability: thus, *corporatio sole* is characterized by unlimited liability, meaning that if you have business debts,

[372] »In America, for example, there are 6 million companies, employing 120 million people, which is two fifths of the entire American population. Around 3 million new companies are registered world-wide every year.« Mayer: Firm Commitment, p. 22.

[373] This is my paraphrase of Pettit, that the personal point of view is the condition for institutional design: »The personal point of view must have this indexical, first-personal character.« Pettit: Groups with Minds of Their Own, p. 260.

personal assets would be used to pay them off). Further still, »plan to start your own business« implies constituting a new, dynamic entity, capable of competing with other entities, fighting for profit, expanding and developing; finally, »to incorporate« (with all the theological and above all Christian connotations of the term) *de facto* represents a certain documentation procedure, or writing act or acts. In these last two operations certain real, living people,[374] exist and »transform«, through a given procedure (which is objective because made up of documents), into a completely new entity or new form in order to more simply, quickly, or safely achieve certain goals (gather new people, money, property, reserves, funds, only to redistribute them again, since »to have« always also means to distribute, to (ex)change that which is). It is precisely these last two operations that introduce the word reality or realism.[375] Paradoxically, the question of the real existence of this new, incorporated entity (or corporation) cannot be separated from the real existence of a group that has just been constituted and united by incorporating and is now together »on paper«.

The document amount, various transactions and contracts within the corporation and institution, truly surpasses the importance of the act of the founding of the corporation (»executing and filing articles of incorporation« or »filling a legislation document with a state officer«), and places less importance on the function of the state, and in general the medieval institution of creating a corporation (*fiat doctrine*), something that especially interests John Searle. If we plot the role of the state in founding corporations (or institutions in general) through history, we can notice that only in certain very rare periods (of colonialism, for example) does the state found and control, meaning gives the privilege to incorporate to certain powerful groups. For that reason, it seems to me that even a moderate

374 »Corporations are at least as real as people.« »Corporation is real because it is an artifact whose constituents typically include real people as well as real assets, as well as intangibles such as credit and goodwill.« Dejnozka: Corporate Entity, manuscript, pp. 71, 102.

375 A hundred years ago, a group of American realists (or new realists) appeared, and could be considered the forerunners of today's attempts at reevaluating realism in thought. »The Program and First Platform of Six Realists« was written in 1910 (*Journal of Philosophy*, No. 21), and the book *The New Realism* in 1912. It was authored by Edwin Holt, Walter Marvin, William Pepperrell Montague, Ralph Barton Perry, Walter Pitkin, and Edward Gleason Spaulding. »This dawning spirit of fellowship (…), accompanied by a desire for a better understanding and a more effective cooperation, has prompted the present undertaking.« The six insist on a few moments: although necessarily »polemical«, »new realism must be a complete philosophy, or must at least show promise of completeness.« (…) »The authors of the present book thus entertain the hope that they may have succeeded not only in amplifying, clarifying, and fortifying the realistic critique, but also in exhibiting that critique as a basis for the solution of special philosophical problems, and for the procedure of the special sciences.« Holt et al.: The New Realism, p. 1. »The new realism is not an accident, nor a *tour de force*, nor an isolated and curious speculative eruption«; New Realism implies »the separation of philosophical research from the study of the history of philosophy«, »realism is a constructive philosophy« and a »rejection of all mystical philosophies« (ibid., pp. 30, 32).

institutional realism necessarily assumes an »ontological egalitarianism«, completely lacking in Searle.[376]

Let us return to the hunt for physical objects as a latent anti-realism:

He (Barry Smith) pointed out that there are some institutions that have what he calls ›free-standing Y terms‹, where you can have a status function, but without any physical object on which the status function is imposed. A fascinating case is corporations. The laws of incorporation in a state such as California enable a status function to be constructed, so to speak, out of thin air. Thus, by a kind of performative declaration, the corporation comes into existence, but there need be no physical object which is the corporation. The corporation has to have a mailing address and a list of officers and stock holders and so on, but it does not have to be a physical object. This is a case where following the appropriate procedures counts as the creation of a corporation and where the corporation, once created, continues to exist, but there is no person or physical object which becomes the corporation. New status functions are created among people – as officers of the corporation, stockholders, and so on. There is indeed a corporation as Y, but there is no person or physical object X that counts as Y.[377]

»(...) but there is no person or physical object which becomes the corporation.« It seems to me unnecessary, easy and complicated at once, to show the shift in understanding of the phrase ›physical object‹ in our day and age – is it necessary to prove the physical existence of an SMS, deposit, bank account, electronic signature, the displayed plaque of a company (which even if it did not exist at the address of the building where company X is registered, would still be paid for by company X, lest a fine be levied against them), the existence of telephone calls among the signatories of the charter, etc.? The physical object is never singular, as in Searle. On the contrary. When it is in fact singular, the object cannot be found, making Searle and Jacques Lacan perfectly compatible.

376 »Relational descriptions tying objects together – son of, slave of, president of, votes for, interrogates – are not, according to ontological egalitarianism, ontological superior to other collections of objects.« Grafstein: Institutional Realism, p. 24. It seems to me now, that if we took all these various types of old and new ›realism‹, and fit them into the little sketch of a theory about three worlds that Karl Popper constructed in 1974, perhaps the origin of the relationship between realism and the institution would become clearer, as would the origin of the resistance towards realism, and the locus of the dispute. Popper: Replies to my critics, pp. 949–1180. »Remember that between world 1 (the material, the world of objects, of physical force) and world 3 (objective knowledge, institutions, true and false theories, art), there lies world 2 made up of experiences, subjective representation, mental states, etc. For something to ›pass‹ from world 3 to world 1 (becoming objective, real in the broadest possible sense of the term), it has to necessarily pass through world 2.« Cf. Bessis: L'institution comme réalisation du collectif, pp. 75–76. So for example, for institutions of world 3 (which are ontologically subjective because they are both dependent on and independent from world 2) to become objective and part of world 1, simply put, for rules to become embodied and material (manifested), the engagement of the collective, a common effort, is necessary. I think it is always complicated to show how individuals cooperate, what is the experience of the other and of the community, how a collective is made, etc. but New Realism's destiny will precisely be determined at this juncture.

377 Searle: What Is an Institution?, pp. 15–16.

Allow me to sketch another scenario, this one even more ›real‹ than the diners in Milan. I am one of the founders of the Institute for Advanced Studies in Rijeka. It has become a rather large institution with an annual budget of a few million euros. But there was a moment, when the institution was not yet registered, yet it was there, it existed in the heads of some people, who were engaged in writing its charter and working on its incorporation (including the president of a country). At that point, the institution is there and yet not there. Various power dynamics precede the institution soon to be incorporated. Money is needed (*Stiftung*, and not *Anstalt* or *Einrichtung* is the correct translation of the word *institutio* into German[378]), and the head of a foundation who constantly insists on visibility and had been promising money (a grant, naturally, on condition that the institution be a ›physical object‹, that is, visible even before it becomes an institution), toasted with me over dinner, wishing the new Institute become a reality as soon as possible. He wished it to pass from, he said, words into action, from paper onto money, and then from money onto words, documents, and then further onto lunches together (like the one we were having during his toast), with food menus ...

378 »For us Germans, the word »institution« has all the disadvantages and few of the advantages of a foreign word. It can be translated neither as *Einrichtung* (establishment), nor as *Anstalt* (institution), nor as »organism«, although it embodies something from each of these concepts. The word *Einrichtung* is too general and only permits the factual-external organizational side to protrude. *Anstalt* has become unusable because in the nineteenth century it had acquired a political-polemical meaning as a counter-concept against *Genossenschaft*, which binds it to the situation of the domestic political struggles of the nineteenth century.« Schmitt: On the Three Types of Juristic Thought, p. 89; Schmitt: Über die drei Arten des rechtswissenschaftlichen Denkens, p. 47. Cf. Croce/Salvatore: Come si fa ordine.

2 Deontic Power of Institutions. »Background« as »Ultimate Institutional Structure«

»Deontic Power of Institutions«[379] is a phrase constructed by John Searle. I will here attempt to briefly explain what is institutional reality,[380] and what are its characteristics. In a word, »what makes something count institutionally«.[381] Does this institutional scene I am trying to understand have anything to do with the norm or with a pseudo or *»neo-normative Paradigma«*, as mentioned by Werner Gephart?[382] More precisely, do the verbs I use stand in a certain relation to the order that could explain or institutionalize the group? Does the process of institutionalization (the *de facto* function of the norm is to institutionalize) produce what we usually call »power«? How do we create power and is a ›we‹ really power?

379 Searle actually formulates it differently: »Deontic Powers of Institution«. He determines deontic powers in various texts in an almost identical manner. »Deontic powers are rights, duties, obligations, authorizations, permissions, privileges, authority and the like.« J. Searle: Freedom and Neurobiology, p. 98. Titus Stahl has already written quite inspiringly in German about Searle in two texts from 2011: »Institutional Power, Collective Acceptance and Recognition«, and »Soziale Gerechtigkeit und institutionelle Macht«. It seems to me that the origin of all the main ideas today in circulation within so-called »social ontology« are to be found in Austrian and German philosophy. For the existence of the noun »Deontik« we can thank two students of Alexius Meinong, both born on the territory of today's Slovenia: Ernst Mally, the author of *Grundgesetze des Sollens: Elemente der Logik des Willens* (1926) and France Veber who defended his doctorate on the topic *Die Natur des Gegenstandes Sollens.* Mally writes: to the »*Logik des Denkens* (the logic of thought, logic of judgement) we ought to add a discipline called *Logik des Willens* (the logic of the will). However, it would not be a branch of logic in the sense of the *Logik des Begriffs* (the logic of the term) and *Logik des Urteils* (the logic of judgement), but rather a part of logic with an analogous name, which we could call *Deontik.*« Mally: Grundgesetze des Sollens, p. 232. Georg Henrik von Wright (his book *Deontik Logik* appeared in 1951) says that he adopted the word *Deontik* (for example in the phrase ›deontic statements‹, *deontische Aussageformen*) from Dunbar Broad (who uses it in a 1950 book *Imperatives, Categorical and Hypothetical*). In Broad, deontic refers to all terms associated with duty, which is not the case in von Wright who takes into consideration promises, prohibitions, etc. Cf. Di Lucia: Normatività, pp. 69–70.

380 Michael Tomasello uses this phrase in »Institutional Reality«. Tomasello: A Natural History of Human Thinking, pp. 90–92.

381 Cf. MacCormick: Norms, Institutions, and Institutional Facts, p. 332.

382 Gephart mentioned George Herbert Mead that war surpasses national and cultural boundaries, and probably forms a completely new collective identity. Gephart writes about the Great War (*Images de la Grande Guerre: la »culture de guerre«*) in the book *Voyages sociologiques France-Allemagne*, pp. 161–183. Cf. Gilbert: Culture as collective construction, pp. 383–393. Searle mentions the norm and normativism very rarely, almost never. In his answer to Raimo Tuomela, Searle insists that Toumela cannot use »norms«, the origin and function of which he cannot explain. Searle: Replies, p. 735.

What things determine the social or institutional fact of a ›we‹, of becoming a ›we‹, and of collective intentionality?[383]

Imagine that I said I particularly *desired* to meet my friends at an imaginary conference, that this is among the reasons I signed up to participate in it. When I insist on a social and entirely para- or pseudo-legal phenomenon (the word »politeness« in Slavic languages contains the word »love«, while the word for »friendship« has the word for »comfort« – a friend is one with whom I am comfortable), then I am opening for myself the possibility not only to show the importance of norms as desires,[384] but conduct two operations that would most succinctly allow me to explain my present project.

First, I would like to prioritize and reevaluate the difference between »*Die Norm as Gedanke und (die Norm) als Realität*«, with respect to contemporary divisions of norms into formal and informal, or legal, moral, and social norms. Second, I would like to suggest that we consider the theory of »deontic powers of institution« in the shadow of its four secret normativist gestures (for which I have compared some ten texts by Searle from 1995 to 2012), which are the unconditional conditions of its »theoretical actions«: a) Searle translates von Wright's »deontic status« and »normative relationship«, and builds them into his own theory of the institution: namely, the reduction of norms to commands and reduction of the »normative relationship« to an asymmetrical relation of power between two (one who binds and one who is bound), completely disregards the nature of a group and different kinds of statements that exist within it; a group is not a collection of »normative relationships« between each two of its individual members; b) Searle transfers his own resistance to David Hume's and Bernard Williams' internalist position that desires constitute the basis or at least a necessary component of the reason for action into his theory of the institution and the powers of the institution. »Desire independent reason for actions«, as one of the conditions for institutional action is in conflict with the fact that, for example, sexuality can

383 I have used the same verbs as Thomas Reid in *A Brief Account of Aristotle's Logic* from 1774: »Aristotle observes justly, that, besides that kind of speech called a proposition, which is always either true or false, there are other kinds which are neither true nor false, such as a prayer or wish; to which we may add, a question, a command, a promise, a contract, and many others.« Reid: Philosophical Works, p. 692. However, Searle practically reduces all verbs that construct institutional reality to commands, and adopts from von Wright the definitions that will come to determine his understanding of positive and negative deontic powers. Searle's status function is von Wright's »deontic status« or »normative relationship«. I am paraphrasing von Wright: when the uttering of a command statement constitutes command act, from that moment, lasting some time, there will be a relation between the one who ordered and the one who took the order. These relations are necessarily called normative. Von Wright: Norm and Action, p. 117.

384 »Norms as Desires« is a new idea at the origin of which are Kelsen's theory of norms and the vision of Ernst Mally. In chapter 2.2 of *Explaining Norms*, »Norms as Desires« (pp. 22–28), Brennan, Eriksson, Goodin and Southwood analyze in detail, above all Cristina Bicchieri and her book *The Grammar of Society*.

be satisfied within marriage or greed within the institution of private property; c) Searle privileges speech over writing, which shows that, paradoxically, norms for him represent neither linguistic acts and entities (a linguistic phenomenon), nor social facts, but rather a world of pure objects that need not at all be realized (it is important that this world be harmonized with human rationality). He follows Kelsen entirely and thinks that a norm remains a norm even if entirely ineffective (*Auch die wirkungslose Norm bleibt Norm*). d) Searle smuggles legal, and not social, norms into the foundations of the institution, which implies that institutions are not an alternative to the state and laws, nor really counter-institutions (as per Saint-Simon's *contre-institution*), but are rather, essentially tied to the state. If legal norms are supported by a coercive State, institutions are always dependent on this institution of institutions (*die Institution der Institution*[385]) or on the »ultimate institutional structure«.[386]

Which leads to the question, how does the norm function within institutional reality or institutional realism? It seems to me that an old antagonism between Benedetto Croce's *»irrealtà della legge«* and Santi Romano's *»realtà giuridica«* (in one way or another, Larenz and Schmitt also belong to realism in law) could finally be formulated with much more accuracy. Law, from the perspective of institutional realism, that is, empirical ontology of law, is not a set of abstract entities (norms, values, duties), but rather a set of social facts. (I think that ›social facts‹ correspond, for example, to Theodor Geiger's ›*subsistente Norm*‹, Alf Ross' ›social state of affairs‹, Adolf Reinach or Herbert Spiegelberg's ›*Sollenssachverhalt*‹, or Gerhart Husserl's ›*Rechtssachverhalt*‹.) Indeed, legal norms are above all linguistic acts and entities, created necessarily by the lawgiver: norms are never ›pure‹ and independent, nor do they exist without interpretation.[387] In »Die Norm als Gedanke und Realität«, Ota Weinberger writes:

> My reflections refer to (...) the ontological status of the norm. I would actually like to show that my concept of the two aspects of the norm (the first being its ideality [*Idealität*] as thought, as an ideal construction [*Gedankengebilde*], and the second its social reality [*gesellschaftliche Realität*]) is precisely relevant because it concerns the nature and problem of the legal science.[388]

385 Santi Romano uses the identical formulation of Carl Schmitt in paragraph 12 of *L'ordinamento giuridico*. Searle's use of Schmitt in his book from 2010, as well as that of Max Weber in the »Human Social Reality and Language« from 2012 (p. 35), are both entirely unwarranted.

386 Searle: Making the Social World, p. 161. In addition to using it only very rarely, Searle only introduces this formulation in his work in 2003, in »Social Ontology and Political Power«.

387 When he writes about Thomas P. Wilson and his differentiating between a normative and interpretative paradigm, Gephart says that the norm is rendered concrete through interpretation (»Die Norm als symbolisches Gebilde«). Gephart: Gesellschaftstheorie und Recht, p. 79.

388 Weinberger: Die Norm als Gedanke und Realität, pp. 203–216. Cf. Conte et al. (eds.): Filosofia del diritto, p. 401.

And then a little further on:

Ideality and reality can be conceptually opposed to one another in such a way that one could fundamentally lose the sense that it is the reality of a thought that is being spoken about, and also the reality of the norm (»ought to«). This happens, for example, when reality is supposed to coincide with material things, when the only thing defined as the real is what can be perceived with the senses or identified as extant by way of physics instruments.

Thus, the real can be defined as everything that exists in time, as ›the place‹ where the power of cognition is entirely separate from the sphere of reality and the criterion of existence. The real existence of norms is thus in close relationship with the existence of social institutions (i. e., with the existence of the group) whose functioning is above all observable. Thus, the group is the group, and we are a we, when we are visible and when the connections among us are visible.

Still, using Searle's (although not only his) language, what gives reality or actuality to norms within an institution? Or, what is it that turns it into power?[389] Is it enough to say that social norms constitute institutional reality? Also, is it necessary to differentiate among social norms?[390] It seems to me that the claim, trivial,[391] unimportant, and all too simplified, that this group (the institution), which is identified as a group, which works as a group and is affirmed as such through the constituting of various projects (which means it survives to exist another day), is efficient (together we are certainly capable of more than in isolation), and always considerate towards new members (in contrast to law or the contract, the institution counts on the third, one who has still not arrived and become its member) – all of which is associated with power, has power, is power, or is constantly augmenting its own power. Even if it is now necessary to show the origin of this

389 Maurice Hauriou tangentially points out the connection between power and the institution in »La Thèorie de l'institution et de la fondation«: »*Les grandes lignes de cette nouvelle thèorie son les suivantes: une institution est une idée d'œuvre ou d'entreprise qui se réalise et dure juridiquement dans un milieu social; pour la réalisation de cette idée, un pouvoir s'organise qui lui procure des organes.*« Hauriou: Aux sources du droit, p. 96.

390 As far back as 1995, Toumela developed a notion of collective intentionality similar to Searle's and made a distinction (albeit possibly suspect) between rules and norms. Collective intentionality arises when an individual attributes an intention to the group in which he or she belongs while holding that intention and believing that other group members hold it too. We act thus because we believe that others have a similar aim. Clearly, many behavioral regularities develop in society because of such reciprocating intentions and expectation. Tuomela described regularities as norms. They involve a network of mutual beliefs rather than actual agreements between individuals. Norms involve approval or disapproval. In contrast, rules are the product of explicit agreement brought about by some authority, and they imply sanctions. Cf. Hodgson: What are Institutions?, p. 5.

391 »I think that Searle's account in terms of deontic powers is too strict and one-sided, although it does capture the most central idea involved in social institutions. Yet it does not comply with, e. g., ordinary dictionary accounts and common sense understanding of social institutions.« Tuomela: Searle's New Construction of Social Reality, p. 713.

power, and then locate this power with the utmost precision, I am unconvinced that Searle's positions can be of any use.

John Searle's mantra regarding deontic powers remained unchanged for twenty years, and it unfolds in several steps: power is carried, increased (»status forms are the vehicles of powers«); deontic power or deontology is the key thing that distinguishes us from animals; the formulation that deontic powers are the glue and the thing that binds and holds us together appears for the first time in 2010 and 2012; language (by which are meant exclusively spoken acts) is the institution that institutionalizes all other institutions, and deontic powers do not exist without language; institutional facts never constrain[392] (as Durkheim or Foucault would have it) institutions, never limit us or take away our freedom (Searle wonders in numerous places, »why do people accept institutions and institutional facts«, and answers, »for our benefit by increasing our powers«).

Finally, here are three criticisms or difficulties with the concept of deontic powers, which could possibly explain the subtitle, »Background« as »Ultimate Institutional Structure«. »The Basic concept of Background power is that there is a set of background presuppositions, attitudes, dispositions, capacities, and practices of any community that set *normative* constraints on the members of that community in such way that violations of those constraints are subject to the negative imposition of sanctions by any member of the community.«[393]

The first difficulty refers to the definition or the determinations of power that Searle uses. The basic manifestation of power is one that forces people to do what they would rather not. If the institution is the alternative name for power, if these two words are somehow synonymous, then Searle's basic motto, »desire independent reason for actions«, becomes clear. Institution is power, because it is making me do what I do not wish to (or as Searle puts it, »force without using force«). Thus, to act institutionally really means to be rational and follow norms (norms in the sense of orders and norms in the sense of that which Toumela calls rules). What is problematic here is that the institution, according to Searle, does not in principle coerce (the police, about which Searle speaks often when writing about deontic powers, holds monopoly on force). In addition, the problem, and this immediately leads us into the second and third difficulties, is that deontic powers are »not powerful enough«:

> But the deontic powers stop at the point where the larger society requires some official documentation, they lack full deontic powers. Collective recognition is not enough. There

392 Searle: Making the Social World, p. 105; Searle: What is an Institution?.
393 Searle: Making the Social World, p. 160.

has to be official recognition by some agency, itself supported by collective recognition, and there have to be status indicators issued by the official agency.[394]

In order to preserve the secret guarantor of normative power (»ultimate institutional structure«), Searle, who is particularly interested in *»l'ontologie de la creation«* of the institution, performs two moves or gestures I would like to mention. The first, in essence Kantian, is that we ought not rack our brains too much about the origin of that most important of institutions, the state, or how it functions, or about the violence or power necessary for its creation. How does Searle answer this paradox regarding authorization, that each institution implies the authorization of some other institution? The paradox states: »The creation of institutional facts by declaration presupposes the creation of other institutional facts. In order to avoid an infinite regress, there must be a way of creating institutional facts which does not require any special authority«, – which seems to be impossible.

The second move is the mystification of the first one. Searle first clears up and protects the state from Foucault's anti-institutionalism (*»Soyons très anti-institutionnaliste«*) and his understanding of power and the state as a machine exclusively for coercion.[395] Thus was invented a new fictitious instance (»background«) to which Searle now assigns regulative power and coercive techniques usually practiced by the state. I think this strategy is not correct and that it serves no purpose.

394 Searle: What is an Institution?, p. 15. Searle also writes about documents and the corporation in a text from 2006, »Social Ontology: Some Basic Principles« (p. 20).

395 In 1973, in the seminar »Le pouvoir psychiatrique«, Foucault insists: *»Soyons très anti-institutionaliste!«* (Le pouvoir psychiatrique, p. 34). In 1971, in a discussion with Chomsky, when speaking of the family and state, Foucault says: »It seems to me that in a society such as ours, the real political task is to criticize the ruse that institutions are apparently neutral and independent; they should be criticized and attacked such that the political violence surreptitiously performed by them is unmasked and can be struggled against« (*Il me semble que, dans une société comme la nôtre, la vraie tâche politique est de critiquer le jeu des institutions apparemment neutres et indépendantes; de les critiquer et de les attaquer de telle manière que la violence politique qui s'exerçait obscurément en elles soient démasquée et qu'on puisse lutter contre elles*). Chomsky / Foucault: De la nature humaine, p. 69.

3 Institution and Life as Institution. Uterus: Mother's Body, Father's Right

I would like to draw on a mixture of lesser and better known texts to evoke (this being perhaps a better word than reconstruct) not only the scene of birth, but also the first encounter of law and life. (I use the phrase mere life [*blosse Leben*] with considerable trepidation and hesitation.) More specifically, I would like to begin with the question, what is »life as such«, even if the actual answer is secondary to me. I will also consider the question of when life begins and when its crucial characteristic first crystallizes, and even the legal status of (the beginning of) life and the various actors involved in ›creating‹ life; and my intention is to evoke pregnancy. I use the word uterus (belly, cavity, viscera, *viscus*) as a legal fiction in order to make a clear distinction between the institution and the norm. I would like to draw a line of thought against Foucault, but in harmony with French (and other schools of) institutionalism that affirms, with no restriction or reservation, the institution (the stomach, the uterine lining, the uterus, the body, a woman's body, a mother's body) as that which protects life. This line of thought assumes a more complicated addition than the institution »includes within its scope the establishment (the protection) of the norm as well«,[396] or even the general possibility of the norm, that is, the limits of normativity itself.[397]

Let me offer two disclaimers. The first refers to my intention to thematize the rather complicated relationship between life and the institution. There are myriad questions. Does life oppose the institution[398] (is the power of life precisely that it always resists all power)? Does biopolitics (biopoetics, bioethics) *a priori* imply an anti-institutionalism? Recall that Foucault writes relentlessly about institutions that cause subjection (*assujettissement*).[399] Is life stronger than the norm? Is phil-

396 Romano: L'ordinamento giuridico, p. 52

397 In two brief texts from 1996, »La norme et son suspens« and »La norme doit manquer«, Derrida explains the paradox in which the condition of the existence of freedom and responsibility is the inexistence or absence of norm. The institution or *contre-institution* (parallel institution) ought to ensure that space of the *prenormative* (Derrida: Le génome et son double, pp. 143–146).

398 Mauss and Fauconnet insist in multiple places that the institution is not a »living thing« [*une chose vivante*], but rather a »static thing« [*chose fixe*] (Mauss/Fauconnet: Sociologie, p. 168).

399 Biopolitics even appears within the institution as such, in the *La volonté de savoir*. The decisive moment of opposition to institutions is in Foucault's lectures from 1974 (Foucault: Le sujet et le pouvoir, p. 1058). He describes several functions of subjection done by institution: »The second function of institutional subjection is not to control individuals' temporality, but to simply control the body« (*La deuxième fonction des institutions d'assujettissement est non plus celle de controler le temps des individus, mais celle de controler simplement leur corps*).

osophical thinking normative, and does philosophy then call life into question?[400] Should life on occasion, or necessarily, be sacrificed in order to preserve the common good? All these questions lead us to once again examine both the status of life or the concept of life. However, I would like to emphasize that the term »life«, the way I am using it here, does not appear until the late nineteenth century, as part of the always »ambivalent *Lebensphilosophie*«.[401]

Here is a passage, quoted by Georges Renard, that illustrates the »biopoetic moment« or »biopathetic moment«, implicitly present in his texts years prior. It reveals that life is always present in the figure (or the construct) we call »the institution«. Indeed, aside from it assuming a process of constant institutionalization (*Institutionalisierung* is Axel Honneth's term),[402] that is, a certain systemic and ethical acting (as there can be no institution without what Christoph Hubig calls *Ethik institutionellen Handelns*),[403] the institution protects or conserves life (individual life, but also the life of all, life as such). Moreover, the institution protects precisely that which undermines and resists it.

If we imagine the first institutional acts or gestures (acts are institutional because they constitute the group that works together or is in some cooperative), it seems clear that the life of the individual or the lives of individuals are incorporated or surpassed in some new legal or pseudo-legal entity (fictitious or real). Not only does such a legal entity or identity not possess or produce greater power, it is supposed to protect and generate or regenerate life itself. An institution is always generative. Here are Renard's words, that is to say, allegedly the words of an anonymous Chinese philosopher:

I love life, but I also love those close to me; those whose blood courses through my veins, those whose soul awakens when they smell the same native ground, those who carry in the lines of their face the same pride of memories and the same hopes, those who are nothing other than the same spiritual body as me. *I am one of them*, and there is something of me in them as well. I love life, but my life is interwoven in the lives of those close to me, for we are of a feather ... I love life, but I also love my family, my homeland, the civilization

400 In a 1966 unpublished seminar entitled »Les normes et le normal«, specifically in the chapter »Judgement, value and life« (*Jugement, valeur et vie*), Canguilhem writes about philosophy that introduces a negative element into life, that is, negates it. Canguilhem continues: »Philosophy can only come second, compared to life. This secondary characteristic of philosophy directly introduces the notion of the norm« (*La philosophie ne peut être que seconde par rapport à la vie. Le caractère second de la philosophie introduit directement la notion de norme*). Quoted in Le Blanc: Canguilhem et les norms, p. 18.

401 Cf. G. Canguilhem: Vie, p. 527. Cf. § 5.1; »Ambivalenzen der Philosophie«, Gehring: Theorien des Todes, pp. 142–154; tekst iz 1966, Canguilhem: La nouvelle connaissance de la vie, pp. 335–364.

402 I draw entirely on Honneth's protocol of social institutionalization (*soziale Instituzionalisierung*) when he speaks of protocols of intermingling of friendship and the institution. Cf. Honneth: Das Recht der Freiheit, p. 238. Cf. Boltanski / Honneth / Celikates: Sociology of Critique or Critical Theory?.

403 Lipp / Hofmann / Hubig: Institution, pp. 99–109.

to which I belong, the Church that holds the best of my soul; and should I be unable to keep both, I should sacrifice my life, and keep the *common Good*, being greater in value of the two.[404]

The structure of this passage, whose origin Renard does not specify (with a translation theologized to the hilt, given the mention of the Church), gives rather good indication of the latent problem between life and the common good, which, for Renard, is synonymous with the institution. Although it would be easy to explain that the word ›life‹, as it appears here, is beyond the biopolitical register[405] (it is sufficient to note that the narrator or subject is manipulating and instrumentalizing their own life, separating it from the group, and not protecting it sufficiently), it seems to me in fact that the thematization of the relation and tie between the institution and life could reveal the limits of biopolitics.

The second disclaimer refers to the second part of the title, a paraphrase of the late French jurist Yan Thomas' »Le ›ventre‹. Corps maternel, droit paternel«.[406] I have added my suggestion that assumes that the institution ought to correspond to the maternal, while the norm corresponds to the paternal intervention in life. Thomas, an expert on Roman Law and close to Foucault, was the man in France who promoted the development of one other legal scholar, Giorgio Agamben. In this text about the Roman tradition, he explains the act of giving birth as a juridical ritual (*l'accouchement est un rituel juridique*).[407] The stomach (*venter*) is a legal fiction (or a metonymy that reduces the woman or the pregnant woman to the stomach), or a legal person who belongs to the man or the father. For example, if the father dies in war, the pregnant woman finds herself in a strange situation. Her uterus holds the male lineage (*un lignage masculine*). The uterus is the incarnation of the absence of the father. The woman carries what is no longer even there. Paradoxically, in this protocol, the woman becomes a whole (a unit) only together with the ›stomach‹ (the Latin word for embryo is *partus*, that is, part),

404 In the original French: »*J'aime la vie, mais j'aime aussi les miens; les miens dont le sang coule dans mes veines, les miens dont l'âme s'est dilatée au parfum de la même terre natale, les miens qui portent sur le front la fierté des mêmes souvenirs et des mêmes espérances, les miens qui ne sont avec moi qu'un même corps spirituel. Je suis l'un d'eux, et il y a en eux quelque chose de moi-même. J'aime la vie, mais ma vie est engagée dans la vie des miens, car nous sommes embarqués* (…) *J'aime la vie, mais j'aime aussi ma famille, ma patrie, la civilisation dont je suis tributaire, l'Eglise qui tient le meilleur de mon âme; et si je ne puis garder les deux à la fois, je sacrifierai ma vie, et je garderai le Bien commun qui vaut plus que ma vie.*« Renard: La théorie de l'institution, pp. 31–32.

405 Complicated places like this should be used to probe the distinction between *zoê* and *bios* (which was current in both Agamben and Foucault). Indeed, it would be interesting to examine whether some Scheler's work, or Simmel's »Metaphysik des Lebens« or Plessner's »metaphysics of the living« and »biophilosophy« (*Die Stufen des Organischen und der Mensch*, from 1928) imply a politics within the frame of biopolitics. For example, in Rickert's 1920 *Die Philosophie des Lebens*, we find the following formulation: »*So muß das biologisch-politische Ideal demokratisch sein*« (p. 82).

406 Thomas: Le »ventre«.

407 Ibid., p. 221.

which is at the same time designated as something not at all her, since the cause of it is the father, while the mother is matter.[408] In law, the woman is determined as a subject incapable of carrying itself over (*se transmettre*). Hence Ulpianus' aphorism: »She is the beginning and end of her own family.«[409] Complete transfer is exclusively in the male domain, since the father *transfers himself* into the son. It is the father who gives birth to the child. First, thanks to this fiction, the son is »born of a father«. Further, custom dictates that the father unburdens or releases the child (really, the son) from the land. At birth, the child is first lowered to the land from which it must be raised by the father (*tollere liberos*), thus giving it the status of human.[410] I leave aside for the time being all the various problems within this context that emerge throughout the numerous sources mentioned by Yan Thomas: the birth of a daughter, the question of abortion, the detailed elaboration of the argumentation in the chapter »Feeding the Stomach«, according to which it is really the father (the city, state), and not the mother, who feeds the embryo …

Drawing on the early texts of Roman law and the conclusions of Yan Thomas, I would like to explain two obscure words, »life« and »law« (and I have broken down the word »law« into two different words, »norm« and »institution«), by way of three models. Two models are within the register of fiction, while the third is potentially defined as institutional realism. I begin from the third. The third model ought to refer to several registers that affirm the reality of the institution, that is, the reality of the mother's or the woman's body. It is this body that feeds the embryo. No external force, e. g., work or money by a father, not even the past work of the mother, feeds the stomach of the future mother. An abortion impacts or injures this same body. In this body, life develops and exists before its first breath or cry. It is statistically more likely that this female body will give birth to the same, female sex than the male. This body exists, and therefore it can be publicly shown or displayed. The pregnant body is still a woman's body that is living. It experiences pleasure and is attractive to others (maiesiophilia is the term for the fetishization of pregnant women).

The first model opposes Canguilhem's opinion by positioning life as secondary and consequent in relation to norm or philosophy. Norm is not only that which precedes life, and which surpasses life in every sense, but norm ›births‹ new life (produces nature). Simultaneously, for norm to exist, there is no necessity for a biological basis (*support biologique*). »As a body, the embryo is foreign to law. (…) When they needed to invent the father's child (*l'enfant du père*), an heir and the male tree, jurists institutionalized the fiction of *venter*, as a subject of law.«[411]

408 Ibid., pp. 212–213. Ulpianus comments that »*partus* is an integral part of the woman, of her stomach. Yet it is also entirely separate from her (*plane post editum*)«.

409 *Digest* 50.16.195.5.

410 Thomas: Le »ventre«, pp. 226–227.

411 Ibid., pp. 215–217.

The explanation of the second model consists of the »voguish« attempt at determining yet another fiction, entirely opposed to life ruled by norm. The model suggests a fiction of mere or bare life (*blosse Leben*), that is, a life that seems to precede everything not itself (and thus also law, i.e., norm). What is this bare life (*blosse Leben*)?[412] What is life? More precisely, what is the life of one living (*la vie d'un vivant*)?[413] We have only one famous sufficiently convincing definition from the beginning of the nineteenth century. »Life is a set of functions that resists death« (*La vie est l'ensemble des fonctions qui résistent à la mort*).[414] Incorporating a negation, the definition also implies a concept of organization or plurality of functions that life ought to possess in order to resist and withstand its own end. Thus, this definition that implies that life is a complex and complicated order still defies the fiction of ›mere or bare life‹ (*das blosse Leben*).[415] It seems to me that this

412 The phrase »*bloße Leben*,« which Benjamin uses four times in *Zur Kritik der Gewalt*, Agamben unjustifiably turns into »bare life« (*nuda vita*), *nachtes Leben* (in *Homo sacer*). Agamben: Homo sacer, p. 75. Similarly, in *Nudità*, the phrase *nuda corporeità* makes an appearance. Agamben: Nudità, p. 89. Benjamin uses this phrase in order to oppose Kurt Hiller and his position that existence as such is more important than happiness and a just existence or life (*Falsch und niedrig ist der Satz, daß Dasein höher als gerechtes Dasein stehe, wenn Dasein nichts als bloßes Leben bedeuten soll – und in dieser Bedeutung steht er in der genannten Überlegung*). Benjamin: Zur Kritik der Gewalt, p. 62. Hiller, a great activist in the pacifist movement (Benjamin is in constant opposition to his pacifism), as well as the homosexual movement of his time, defends his doctorate in 1908, entitled »*Das Recht über sich selbst*«, in which the encounter of norm and life is constructed in an entirely different way. Cf. the difference between über sich selbst and *an sich selbst* is explained in the Introduction. Hiller: *Das Recht über sich selbst*, p. 65. It does not seem plausible to me that Benjamin could have followed Rickert's analysis of Max Scheller's 1915 book on the war in real time. Nevertheless, there is a remark by Rickert he finds very insightful and shows Rickert's position on violence and war. »Therefore, war must be valid as a permanent institution of all truly living life (*alles wahrhaft lebendigen Lebens*). Pacifism is the enemy of life and the state (*Der Pazifismus ist lebensfeindlich und staatsfeindlich*).« Rickert: Philosophie des Lebens, p. 102. Benjamin's texts on the life of students, aside from being the first to mention critique and radical critique, insist on life forms and institutions (*Lebensinstitutionen*) that surpass life as such. Creativity, spirituality, science, and academic study all determine life and continuously contribute to its ›reconstruction‹ (*Neuaufbau*). Cf. Bojanić: »Leben und Gewalt« or »Gewalt und Leben«, p. 327.

413 Canguilhem: Vie, p. 764. At the beginning of his lecture »La nouvelle connaissance de la vie« of 1966, Canguilhem is more precise, I think: »By live, we mean the present participle or the past participle of the verb to live, the living and the lived.« Canguilhem: Études d'histoire et de philosophie des sciences, p. 335.

414 Bichat: Recherches physiologiques sur la vie et la mort, p. 57. A variation of this position is also put forward by Claude Bernard in »Définition de la vie«, published in 1875 in *La Revue des deux mondes*. »A surgeon at the school in Paris, Pelletan, teaches that life is the resistance offered by organized matter to causes that seek ceaselessly to destroy it« (*Un chirurgien de l'école de Paris, Pelletan, enseigne que la vie est la résistance opposée par la matière organisée aux causes qui tendent sans cesse á la détruire*). Bernard: Définition de la vie, p. 23.

415 In 1930, Georg Misch used the phrase *bloss menschliches Leben*. Misch: *Lebensphilosophie und Phänomenologie*, p. 24. The origin of the phrase is in various repertoires of »right to life« as well as theories of life worth living. Hegel mentions the right to life or the right to live (*Das Recht des Lebens*) in § 118 of his 1817/18 Heidelberg lectures on *Philosophy of Law* (Hegel: Vorlesungen über Naturrecht und Staatswissenschaft, pp. 221–222). The commandment ›Thou shalt not kill‹ implies the existence of some such right to live or right to live freely.

fiction could potentially be thematized anew, but that would require a preliminary evocation of yet another great attempt at critique of various forms of ›biologizing‹, which Heinrich Rickert looks at in his 1920 book *Die Philosophie des Lebens* (Benjamin attended his lectures, could not stand him, but nevertheless consistently deployed the phrase *bloße Leben*).[416] The subtitle of the book is *Darstellung und Kritik der philosophischen Modeströmungen unserer Zeit*, which is why I insist on the fashion and trendiness of various contemporary narratives about life.[417] The idea that life can be determined without the help of other terms, that life can be directly experienced (in *Die Philosophie des Lebens*, Rickert assigns this fantasy to intuitive vitalism) – is indeed empty banter. *Das bloße Leben halte ich für sinnlos*, Rickert says, because it is of no value[418] and because it is naught but vegetating.[419] Explaining over the course of a hundred places that *die Philosophie des bloßen Lebens* has no future whatsoever, Rickert is adamant to reveal the limit of this model, more current in our times than any other.

Paradoxically, these two fictitious models complement one another. I oppose both, and suggest a more realistic (corporative) institutionalism that would equally affirm both the primacy of the norm and primacy of life simultaneously. Precisely as with the woman's body and its capacity for *in-corporatio.*

In one way or another, this third model will have to be cleared of negation, and certainly of the influence of Rickert's theory of value.[420]

416 Rickert: *Philosophie des Lebens.*

417 Part I of Rickert's book is entitled »Das Leben als Modebegriff« (pp. 3–16).

418 Rickert: Philosophie des Lebens, p. 129. Bruno Bauch repeats this argument seven years later in *Philosophie des Lebens und Philosophie der Werte.* In the foreword of the second edition, Rickert writes: »I consider bare life meaningless. Only a philosophy of a meaningful life, which is always more than mere life, would seem to me to be a goal worthy of striving, and only based on the theory of non-living valid values that give meaning to life can promise that a goal will be achieved« (*Das bloße Leben halte ich für sinnlos. Erst eine Philosophie des sinnvollen Lebens, das stets mehr als bloßes Leben ist, scheint mir ein erstrebenswertes Ziel, und nur auf Grund einer Theorie der unlebendigen, geltenden Werte, die dem Leben Sinn verleihen, wird das Ziel sich erreichen lassen*). Rickert: Philosophie des Lebens, p. XI.

419 Rickert: Philosophie des Lebens, p. 129. Rickert varies the term »vegetating« several times, even using the phrase »*vegetative Dasein*« in one place.

420 For example, in *Die Tyrannei der Werte* from 1960, Carl Schmitt, a major inspiration for Agamben, reveals his debt to Rickert and his theory of negation (*System der Philosophie*, p. 117). This model, or secret member of Schmitt's realism, his theory of the enemy (as Schmitt was always criticized that there is an essential asymmetry between friend and enemy in his understanding of the political, that the enemy has a greater significance and that negation dominates this distinction), although trivial, improves the theoretical value of Schmitt's endeavor. Namely, there is no negative existence, only negative value. »The relation to the negative«, says Schmitt in this text, »is the criterion according to which something belongs to the sphere of value (while something else is excluded).« Schmitt: Die Tyrannei der Werte, p. 25.

Annex IV: Marcel Mauss with Madame de Stael; The Institution as a ›Living Thing‹ in Constant Change

Marcel Mauss' thematization or reconstruction of the ›institution‹ is philosophical-anthropological and of course precedes Malinowski's and that of Mary Douglas,[421] whose writings on the institution are also inspired. It implicitly contains all these mentioned steps,[422] but also carries several important (and probably first) models for understanding the institution today. It is, in other words, entirely current. I will list the models as well:[423]

Institutions depend on one another. (*Les institutions dépendent les unes des autres*).

Comparative history of law and religion has revealed the idea that certain institutions in combination with institutions comprise a system, and that none can be transformed without the others also transforming.[424]

It is clear that the connections among the wills of individuals rule over individuals:

Such interdependence of phenomena would be inexplicable as the product of particular, more or less capricious, wills; the interdependence is explained, on the contrary, as the product of impersonal forces that dominate the individuals.[425]

The institution is always connected to coercion:

A rule to which an individual is considered submitted cannot be the work of that individual: for all obligation implies a higher authority to the obligated subject, which inspires respect in him, an essential element of the feeling of obligation. Excluding interventions by supernatural beings, it is impossible to find, outside and below the individual, any source of obligation other than society, or rather the totality of societies to which he belongs (*Une règle à laquelle l'individu se considère comme soumis ne peut être l'œuvre de cet individu:*

421 Mary Douglas is the author of one of the most important texts in the thematization history of this concept or protocol, first published in Italian as the entry »Institution« in *Enciclopedia delle Scienze Sociali.* In English, it was published as »Institutions: Problems of Theory«. The chapter »Perverse and Benign Institutions« is particularly inspiring and belongs to the long tradition of texts that thematize poor institutions. Cf Certeau: L'institution de la pourriture.

422 In »La magie«, Mauss continues: »We seek first of all to understand the institutions, that is, the rules of public conduct and thought. In sacrifice – the public face of the institution – the collective nature of the act and its representations is quite clear [*Nous nous proposions au début de nos études, surtout de comprendre des institutions, c'est-à-dire des règles publiques d'action et de pensée. Dans le sacrifice, le caractère public de l'institution, collectif de l'acte et des représentations est bien clair*]« (Hubert / Mauss: Introduction a l'analyse de quelques phénomènes religieux p. 187).

423 They are in an early text authored with Paul Fauconnet (Fauconnet / Mauss: La sociologie).

424 »*L'histoire comparée du droit, des religions, a rendu commune l'idée que certaines institutions forment avec certaines autres un système, que les premières ne peuvent se transformer sans que les secondes se transforment également.*« Ibid., p. 167.

425 »*Cette interdépendance des phénomènes serait inexplicable s'ils étaient les produits de volontés particulières et plus ou moins capricieuses; elle s'explique au contraire s'ils sont les produits de forces impersonnelles qui dominent les individus eux-mêmes.*« Ibid., p. 168.

car toute obligation implique une autorité supérieure au sujet obligé, et qui lui inspire le respect, élément essentiel du sentiment d'obligation. Si donc on exclut l'intervention d'êtres surnaturels, on ne saurait trouver, en dehors et au-dessus de l'individu, qu'une seule source d'obligation, c'est la société ou plutôt l'ensemble des sociétés dont il est membre).[426]

The institutional precedes the individual or individuals:

(...) all forms of acting and thinking the individual finds pre-established and whose transmission is conducted most often by way of education are social (*sont sociales toutes les manières d'agir et de penser que l'individu trouve préétablies et dont la transmission se fait le plus généralement par la voie de l'éducation*).[427]

The name for social facts is institution:

It would be good if a particular word designated these special facts, and it seems that the word institutions would be most appropriate. After all, what is an institution if not the totality of acts or ideas, all presenting themselves to, and imposing themselves more or less on individuals? There is no reason to exclusively reserve, as it is customarily done, this expression to fundamental social arrangements (*Il serait bon qu'un mot spécial désignât ces faits spéciaux, et il semble que le mot institutions serait le mieux approprié. Qu'est-ce en effet qu'une institution sinon un ensemble d'actes ou d'idées tout institué que les individus trouvent devant eux et qui s'impose plus ou moins à eux? Il n'y a aucune raison pour réserver exclusivement, comme on le fait d'ordinaire, cette expression aux arrangements sociaux fondamentaux*).[428]

The institution, however, is not the past; it lives. Institutions transform. »Nothing comes from nothing« (*Rien ne vient de rien*):[429]

But, one might say, the institution is in the past; it is, by definition, a fixed entity, not a living one. (...) Nothing comes from nothing: new institutions cannot be made but from older ones, for those are the only extant. (...) True institutions live, which is to say, change incessantly.

(*Mais, dira-t-on, l'institution est le passé; c'est, par définition, la chose fixée, non la chose vivante.* (...) *Rien ne vient de rien : les institutions nouvelles ne peuvent être faites qu'avec les anciennes, puisque celles-ci sont les seules qui existent.* (...) *Les institutions véritables vivent, c'est-à-dire changent sans cesse*).[430]

There is nothing outside institutions:

The only facts one might without reason consider social, yet which would nevertheless be difficult to place within the definition of institutions, are those produced in societies with-

426 Ibid.
427 Ibid.
428 Ibid.
429 Ibid., p. 169.
430 Ibid., pp. 168–169.

out institutions. Yet the only societies without institutions are social aggregates, unstable and ephemeral (such as a mob of people), or else those undergoing formation. In neither case do we have societies properly speaking, but only societies in becoming. (*Les seuls faits que l'on pourrait non sans raison regarder comme sociaux et qui, cependant, rentreraient difficilement dans la définition des institutions, sont ceux qui se produisent dans les sociétés sans institutions. Mais les seules sociétés sans institutions sont des agrégats sociaux ou bien instables et éphémères comme les foules, ou bien en cours de formation. Or des unes et des autres on peut dire qu'elles ne sont pas encore des sociétés proprement dites, mais seulement des sociétés en voie de devenir.*[431]

We find these basic designations of the institution in the classic text co-authored by Mauss and Fauconnet. They could once again be classified and reduced to a few directions. Institutions are under constant change, and change is their first characteristic (they transform, they are dynamic and living; as such, they represent a collection of acts or actions, etc.); institutions possess and produce strength and power, yet are resistant to violent protocols that stand at their origin (it is probably possible to easily justify this hypothesis from Hume).

I would like to briefly show how this paradox (using Rousseau's phrase »*le moment de l'institution*«,[432] of change or restauration of the institution(s) has been thematized or problematized in the history of European thought or philosophy (along the axis of French institutionalism: Montesquieu, Rousseau, Madame de Staël, Saint-Simon, Mauss). These thinkers, each in their own way, have confirmed this condition of all conditions, which today (or especially today) is neither obvious nor straightforward. In it resides the chief contrast between Hume and Hobbes, but also among the various German, Italian or French philosophers in history and today. This axiom could be formulated as follows: violence or force produces nothing or is not transformed into anything (does not produce right, justice, freedom, order or institutions). In contrast to Hume, this is clear to Montesquieu, Rousseau and Mauss. Thus, for them, any potential notion of protest or amending institutions or of restauration[433] of institutions refers to the elimination of conflict, violence, and aggressive strategies that always already reside in institutions. In *De la littérature considérée dans ses rapports avec les institutions sociales*, M. Germaine de Staël writes:

431 Ibid., p. 169.

432 Rousseau: Discours sur l'origine et les fondements de l'inégalité parmi les hommes, p. 186.

433 The 18th century, already the century of revolution is also always the century of institutionalization and restauration. What is ›restaurant‹? Originally, food, »meat-based consommés intended to ›restore‹ a person's strength.« Such strength or institutional capacity is, as we know, ultimately very limited. Institutions die. The mortality of those who feed is trivial. However, not trivial is that »a person's strength« is restored by eating together or in others' presence. We should always return to the group which implies restitution and vice versa.

Military spirit runs equally through all ages and countries. It is not particular to any nation, nor binds a people to some given institution: it ought to defend them all equally. Rhetoric, love of literature and art, of philosophy can make a homeland of a territory by giving to that nation similar tastes, habits and sentiments. But force speeds past time and bypasses the will. Yet, by this very manner, it can establish nothing among men. It was often repeated during the French revolution, that tyranny was needed to establish liberty. Words of opposite meaning were thus put together into a mere phrase, which changed not one bit the truth of things. Institutions established through violence might imitate liberty in every way except in its natural course. It is thus like a doll that might scare you with its resemblance: you will see in it everything but life.

(*L'esprit militaire est le même dans tous les siècles et dans tous les pays; il ne caractérise point la nation, il ne lie point le peuple à telle ou telle institution: il est également propre à les défendre toutes. L'éloquence, l'amour des lettres et des beaux-arts, la philosophie, peuvent seul faire d'un territoire une patrie, en donnant à la nation qui l'habite les mêmes gouts, les mêmes habitudes et les mêmes sentiments. La force se passe du temps et brise la volonté; mais par cela même elle ne peut rien fonder parmi les hommes. L'on a souvent répété, dans la révolution de France, qu'il fallait du despotisme pour établir la liberté. On a lié par des mots un contre-sens dont on a fait une phrase; mais cette phrase ne change rien à la vérité des choses. Les institutions établies par la force imiteraient tout la liberté, excepte son mouvement naturel; les formes seraient comme ces modelés qui vous effrayent par leur ressemblance: vous y retrouves tout, hors la vie.*[434]

In addition to life, since it is already incorporated within institutions, and is not (as the anti-institutionalist mantra goes) opposed to them, Madame de Staël insists on time: force speeds it up, introducing a false and uncertain short-term process. And she insists on will (elsewhere in her writing, the appearance of new institutions implies a new spirit of freedom and desire [*désir*]).[435] She repeats, modifies and affirms as crucial, four models of ›French institutionalism‹. First, entirely original, that above all literature, new linguistic forms and new expressions could disrupt the asymmetry between thought and institutions (writing, putting pen to paper brings forth something new, and thus new institutions). Second, also never before formulated as succinctly as this, that it is possible »to judge institutions philosophically« (à juger *philosophiquement les institutions*).[436] Otherwise, »philosophy is but a frivolous pastime of countries in which no enlightenment pierces

434 De Staël: De la littérature considérée dans ses rapports avec les institutions sociales, p. 29.

435 Ibid., p. 24.

436 Ibid, p. 148. »Recall yet again the meaning I have given to the word philosophy throughout this work. Philosophy for me is inquiry into the principle of all political and religious institutions, analysis of characteristics and historical events, and finally, study of the human heart and natural rights of man. Such philosophy takes liberty as its guiding goal« (*Il faut rappeler ici de nouveau le sens que j'ai constamment attaché au mot philosophie dans le cours de cet ouvrage. J'appelle philosophie, l'investigation du principe de toutes les institutions politiques et religieuses, l'analyse des caractères et des évènements historiques, enfin l'étude du cœur humain et des droits naturels de l'homme. Une telle philosophie suppose la liberté ou doit y conduire*; ibid., p. 144).

the institutions« (*la philosophie elle-même n'est qu'une occupation frivole dans un pays où les lumières ne peuvent pénétrer dans les institutions*)[437]; the third model is inherited from Montesquieu and Rousseau (Saint-Simon also adopts it later): that it is necessary and certainly possible to compare institutions across cities and states. A comparative model of study presents differences among institutions and can advance them. Finally, the last idea Madame de Staël thematizes refers to observing institutions in time, their transformation, transience, obsolescence, and death. Here is how she writes of *chevalerie*:

Any institution that is good at a given moment, but not for eternal reason, becomes incorrigibly onerous, having corrected previous wrongs. Thus, *chevalerie* was necessary to palliate military savagery through femininity and religious spirit. However, the order or rank of *chevalerie*, just like anything that divides instead of reuniting men, had to come to be seen as dreary as soon as it ceased to provide necessary remedy (*Toute institution bonne relativement à tel danger du moment, et non à la raison éternelle, devient un abus insupportable, après avoir corrigé des abus plus grands. La chevalerie était nécessaire pour adoucir la férocité militaire par le culte des femmes et l'esprit religieux; mais la chevalerie, comme un ordre, comme une secte, comme tout ce qui sépare les hommes au lieu de les réunir, dut être considérée comme un mal funeste, dès qu'elle cessa d'être un remède indispensable*).[438]

This construction shows rather well how a given convention is initially established and regulated, enabling and ensuring transactions among members of a community and reducing militarism; and it shows how it degrades over time. If an ›institution‹ (is it now perhaps a little clearer what this noun designates or hides?) ceases to be a conduit and becomes an obstacle »that divides instead of uniting men« (*qui sépare les hommes au lieu de les réunir*), then urgent change is necessary. And indeed, there is something urgent in this diagnosis of the institution that has suddenly become dreary (*un mal funeste*). Yet, it is also entirely implicit that Madame de Staël indicates where the problem lies or where knowledge of the problem begins, and how to solve it. The diagnosis is simultaneously an urgent call to cooperation and action sent out to all members of the community.[439] If we say that an institution must ceaselessly institutionalize itself (so as not to become pacified), what that means, in my opinion, is that a group of individuals ought to produce an entirely different kind of act (individual and group social act) that might renew the unity of the group and ensure its transition into an institution

437 Ibid., p. 262.
438 Ibid., p. 131.
439 I think that the significance of cooperation for the institution could be Eloi Laurent's important distinction between collaboration that embodies association of usefulness and aims at efficiency. Cooperation, by contrast, is a sharing process of employing »communal knowledge« (*connaissance communes*). Cf. Laurent: L'impasse collaborative.

(some new institution or counter institution). These I call engaged acts.[440] My premise is that a novel reconstruction of engagement (and related terms)[441] could introduce or advance or ease the shift into »social freedom« (a term of A. Honneth). Furthermore, as in the case of Madame de Staël's chevalier, this is another negative example that confirms the necessity of certain conditions, or strictly speaking norms (even if they alone are insufficient), for something to be labeled a ›European Value‹. For example, ›European values‹ does not refer to characteristics specific to Europeans, such as their willingness to urgently mobilize into a group and, for example, help one who is in harm's way or simply resolve some problem. European values would be twofold and concern something else: 1) normativity, since individuals *must* be together in order to be able to *have to* help one (or ones) in trouble; 2) although engagement precedes the norm, it nevertheless constitutes it if and only if there is ›communal engagement‹, which is to say if the engagement is free or willed (this is a specific aspect of obligation). Absent these acts of communal engagement, there can be no shift from group to institution, and thus no norm. If I say, for example, that the institution is actually a *repertorium* (*répertoire* is a relatively recent French word that means a set or list of elements), this assumes that the institution comprises diverse content and that it is potentially defined as a collection of acts – institutional acts.

When is the right moment for an institution? When and how begins, and when and how is it decreed that something ought to last and be preserved from time and in time? It seems to me that Montesquieu could help in determining what Rousseau calls »*le moment de l'institution*«, concerning the beginning and founding of the institution. Rousseau thinks that an entry in Montesquieu's *Considérations sur les causes de grandeur des Romain et de leur décadance* is the paradigm the beginning of every institution should satisfy. In *Du contrat social*, Rousseau is paraphrasing the following statement: »At the birth of societies, it is the heads of republics who found institutions; from then on it is institutions that form heads of republics« (*Dans la naissance des sociétés, ce sont les chefs des républiques qui font l'institution, et c'est ensuite l'institution qui forme les chefs des républiques*).[442]

I would leave aside the heads who found the institution (here in the singular). I am interested in the way Rousseau tries to transform this already shifted causal-

440 Cf. Bojanić: Che cos'è un atto d'impegno?. Also, the completely reconstructed version of this topic is Bojanić: What Is an Act of Engagement?, p. 157.

441 A few years ago, *La Stampa* published a lecture by Norberto Bobbio from 1997 about the relation of the intellectual and power. Interestingly, Bobbio makes simultaneous use of the words ›impegno‹ and ›l'engagement‹. »*Il termine ›impegno‹ può sembrare inadatto a designare il rapporto tra l'esperto e il potere, giacché fa pensare a un'azione volontaria del soggetto che la compie, mentre il contributo che il tecnico dà al politico è quasi sempre richiesto da chi se ne serve*«. Bobbio: Filosofi e tecnici, meglio tenerli separati.

442 Rousseau: Du contrat social ou principes du droit politique, p. 380.

ity in Montesquieu's sentence. The head makes something that will constrain and limit him. Norms form the one who declares or establishes them. An institution is an institution only if it satisfies the following condition: it must form those who have the capacity to establish it, and this only after it itself has been established. Otherwise, it is not an institution and no institutional establishing has taken place.

4 How to Be Together *beyond* Corporations and Firms? Hegel at the ›End of Capitalism‹

At the beginning of »Briefe aus dem Wuppertal«[443] (March 1839) Friedrich Engels is ruthless in speaking about the bitterness of leaving the Rhine. Before him are the fog and soot enveloped factories and the Wupper filled with bright red sludge, yet the color having nothing to do with a bloody battle (*aber seine hochrote Farbe rührt nicht von einer blutigen Schlacht her*).[444] »The only battle here in Wuppertal«, continues Engels, »is between theological pens and verbose old women, usually over trifles« (*denn hier streiten nur theologische Federn und wortreiche alte Weiber gewöhnlich um des Kaisers Bart*). The phrase used by the nineteen year old Engels, »*Streit um des Kaisers Bart*«, is immediately contradicted by his detailed and brilliant analysis of various curates, cheats, preachers and mystics (undoubtedly an analysis of several forms of corporations, their members and leaders, the church, of course, being a corporation) – all of whom hide something much more serious, which Engels mentions only in passing: the back-breaking work in factories, the people, the flock who breathe carbon dust instead of oxygen, children who work in factories instead of going to school, etc. The factories here also represent clear examples of pseudo-companies or firms.

The young Engels' dramatic line – »this red color has nothing to do with a bloody battle« (*aber seine hochrote Farbe rührt nicht von einer blutigen Schlacht her*; this timid announcement of a new violence that could potentially destroy the lie of pietism, the injustice and inequality of capitalism also functions as nothing other than a trifle) – could potentially be replaced with the pronoun »We«, and thus set the premise of a specific and precise regulative instance of communal life and work »beyond corporations and firms«.

It would seem that what is possible, or as if possible, *beyond* corporations is an entirely uncertain, indefinite »together«, and a quasi-we (*»wir«*). Paradoxically, in order to precisely describe this possibility of being together in the (near)[445] future at all, to function and subsist within a new »we«, it is perhaps necessary to recon-

443 Engels: Schriften der Frühzeit, pp. 20–24. This letter in the form of a brief travelogue was penned in March 1839.

444 Ibid., p. 20.

445 It is more a process than event. »Conceiving of the end of capitalism as a process rather than an event (…).« Streeck: How will Capitalism end?, p. 47.

struct, as concretely as possible,[446] these »artificial persons called bodies politic, bodies corporate (*corpora corporata*) or corporations«,[447] and then announce a potential discovery of an entirely new corporativity and common life.[448] If corporations as we know them today – a »nexus of contracts« with limited liability – have been treated as a privilege and one of the greatest human (or at least capitalist[449]) inventions, and if capitalism was able to discover forms of associative work and life that brought great pleasure and a good life to (many, if not all) its members – and in the hopes and under the condition that the latest invention of capitalism is also its last: the turning of fellows (the original form of corporation) into followers on Facebook or Instagram – then the discovery of something new in the near future would mean that some capitalist protocols will be partially continued, albeit perhaps under a different name and substantially reformed.[450]

Therefore, my intention is really to sketch a supposition about the new discovery of associative work and the community, analyzing or conceptualizing some consequences of Hegel's interpretation of the idea of the corporation or ideal corporation (with all the terminological confusion he encountered that still remains).[451] I am thus interested, since the end of capitalism has been identified as process and not event, in those »institutional channels« or »modes« that would be most successful in changing or replacing or supplementing the familiar and insufficiently func-

446 In the commentary of paragraph 190 of *The Philosophy of Right*, when speaking of a system of needs, within a bourgeois society, Hegel uses the word *concretum* (to designate what is named human), which then Marx, in the *Introduction* from 1857, transforms into *Gedankenconcretum*. Thinking concretely or »Concrete Thinking« suits the man citizen who works along with others. Hegel: Elements of the Philosophy of Right, p. 228.

447 Blackstone: Commentaries on the Law of England, p. 455. (Chapter 18 »Of Corporations«.)

448 The four-page chapter »The Capitalist Corporation and Beyond« at the very end of Geoffrey Hodgson's book *Conceptualizing Capitalism. Institutions, Evolution, Future* (pp. 376–380), can function as a sketch for a future program and project of corporate reforms and transformation of corporations into »numerous smaller cooperatives«.

449 Cf. Barry: »The Theory of the Corporation«, pp. 22–26.

450 »It is in this sense that Geoffrey Hodgson has argued that capitalism can survive only as long as it is not completely capitalist (...)«. Streeck: How will Capitalism End?, p. 50.

451 In a significantly limited context, this portion of my project could serve as a complement to Hodgson's project in conceptualizing capitalism, since Hegel is mentioned in his book only twice and in passing. To be more specific, Hegel's reconstruction of the corporation could be confirmation that the corporation implies cooperatives (associations) and that it completes Hodgson's vision. Incidentally, many contemporary authors who write about the institution, such as Tony Lawson, Philip Pettit, or John Searle, never mention Hegel. But this is not in the least surprising. Two of the leading theorists of the corporation and community at the turn of the twentieth century, Frederic William Maitland and Otto von Gierke, also entirely ignored Hegel's understanding of the corporation. An exception (albeit partial) is Roger Scruton and John Finnis' 1989 text »Corporate Persons«. Speaking of Hegel, who was anticipated by Burke, and also Rousseau and Fichte, Scruton says: »whatever the virtues of those writers, none of them had that instinct for valid argument which would recommend them to an analytical philosopher, and everything they said must be rewritten, in the language which they would have abhorred« (Scruton / Finnis: Corporate Persons, pp. 254–255).

tional protocols that belong to capitalism.[452] There are other reasons why it seems to me that it would be important to, yet again, identify the corporation (or company) as the »crucial agent or actor in capitalist economy«,[453] and then once again thematize some of Hegel's intuitions from many years ago about the corporation. I think that, much as in the case of the company, economists (although not only they) are not in agreement about what is a corporation, nor do we have a sketch of a definition that could be partially accepted in different states or traditions.[454] This last fact is worrisome and is a consequence of a very complicated framework that constructs the field within which the corporation functions. The corporation is at once a legal phenomenon (it is always in some relation to the state and laws of a country); it is an institution (meaning that a kind of institutional legalism would best suit a potential reconstruction of corporation as such); also, the corporation is a social, as well as moral phenomenon, and the key element of bourgeois society; finally (or above all), the corporation is an economic institute (or »the economic bond which ties individuals together, such as transactions, debts, property rights, etc.«[455]), and is probably essentially indistinct from the market.

My goal is to show that it is vital to read Hegel (in the current case, that it is necessary to analyze this excerpt from *Philosophy of Right*, concerning the corporation) and that every thematization of the corporation depends on Hegel's insights and his understanding of civil society. However, my intention is certainly not to reinterpret the status of the theory of the corporation in Hegel's system (which, it seems to me, has already been done and any addition would be superfluous[456]). Nor is to rummage around Hegel's system, insisting, for example, that protocols of ›the corporation‹ in some way precede the institution of marriage and family,

452 Here I am reiterating Joseph Schumpeter's idea or strategy from his 1928 »The Instability of Capitalism«: »The new processes do not, and generally cannot, evolve out the old firms, but place themselves side by side with them and attack them. Furthermore, for a firm of comparatively small size, which is no power on the money market and cannot afford scientific departments or experimental production and so on, innovation in commercial or technical practice is an extremely risky and difficult thing, requiring supernormal energy and courage to embark upon. But as soon as the success is before everyone's eyes, everything is made very much easier by this very fact.« Schumpeter: Essays, p. 70.

453 Cf. Hancké (ed.): Debating Varieties of Capitalism.

454 »A problem is that economist cannot agree what a firm is.« Hodgson: Conceptualizing Capitalism, p. 204.

455 Commons: Institutional Economics, p. 734.

456 Cf. Ellmers/Hermann (eds.): Korporation und Sittlichkeit. I should also mention Yoshihiro Niji's text »Hegels Lehre von der *Korporation*«. The innovation in this text was the attempt to examine the extent to which Hegel was familiar with the articles referring to the corporation in the »Allgemeinen Landrecht fur die Preussischen Staaten« of 1794. Cf. Niji: Hegels Lehre von der *Korporation*, pp. 288–295 The author ends up following the suggestion of Friedrich Müller, from the well-known *Korporation und Assoziation*, p. 16. Wolfgang Kersting writes about the corporation in »Polizei und Korporation in Hegels Darstellung der bürgerlichen Gesellschaft«, pp. 373–382, along with Rolf-Peter Horstmann in »Hegels Theorie der bürgerlichen Gesellschaft«, pp. 193–216, as well as Stefan Mertens in *Die juridische Vermittlung des Sozialen*.

which in turn precede the state, meaning that the state is not, nor can be in any case »prior«, as Hegel says.[457] To be exact, it is not my intention to question the criterion and form of anteriority of the state – the state can be prior because, for example, we must begin somewhere, or because »the state« can be a name of a collection of documents, for a book, a register, a text altered and deconstructed by the addition of each newly founded corporation and institution. In short, all that I would like to attempt is to select a few of Hegel's innovations in interpreting the corporation, without which an ideal theory of the corporation is absolutely impossible (and according to which, the main strength of a latent reconstruction of corporation would be in the hands of the poor, those continuously excluded by bourgeois society). I would also like to possibly submit the idea that could put aside a largely trivial construction regarding Hegel's institutionalism. Finally, the third reason is implicitly already in the »primacy« of the state and that which is actually performed when a group of people wants to »incorporate«. I am interested in how the *de facto* and *de jure* corporation becomes a corporation (is there harmony between social and legal acts?), how it acquires legitimacy, whether all the so-called »writing speech acts« are the unconditional conditions for the existence of a corporation. In *Politica* (chapter IV, »Collegiate Association«, Article 8), Althusius writes:

Collegiate intercourse (*communicatio*) is indeed support between colleagues and the performing of life favors, according to agreed pacts. These pacts and laws of the colleagues are registered in the collegial books (*in libris collegiorum*), which in German we call *guild books* (*quos Zunftbücher vocamus*).

Continuing in article 17:

The communal right of the faculty and the colleagues is usually written in collegial books (in *guild books, in den Zunftbüchern*). Such right is accepted and introduced among colleagues based on their common consensus, or is granted and awarded to colleagues based on the special privilege of the highest *magister* (*superioris magistratus*).[458]

457 »In actuality, therefore, the state in general is in fact the primary factor (*in der Wirklichkeit ist darum der Staat überhaupt vielmehr das Erste*); only within the state does the family first develop into civil society, and it is the idea of the state itself which divides into these two moments«. Hegel: Elements of the Philosophy of Right, p. 274. Further, marriage or family imply a status for women in this construction by Hegel: women as a marriage partner, but also as citizen, a member of a collegium or »sisterhood«, that is, member of a corporation. For example, my marriage or my family only came about after I »incorporated« with my future wife, her sister and my sister, which I did in a company together with her (or them) and because we belong to the same guild (because our profession is the same; the word »company« is currently the word in Europe for »corporation« more commonly used in the Anglo-American world).

458 Althusius: La Politica, pp. 306–307.

The third quote is a portion of Hegel's amendment § 253:

If the individual (*der Einzelne*) is not a member of a legally recognized (*berechtigten*) corporation (and it is only through legal recognition that a community becomes a corporation) (*Ohne Mitglied einer berechtigten Korporation zu sein* [*und nur als Berechtigtes ist ein Gemeinsames eine Korporation*]), he is without the *honour of belonging to an estate* (*Standesehre*), his isolation reduces him to the selfish aspect of his trade, and his livelihood and satisfaction lack *stability* (*seine Subsistenz und Genuss nichts Stehendes*).[459]

This third reason I would like to insist on the corporation, along with these three quotes regarding a particular institutional instance in the background, the register (official agency or special authority), the book, and legitimation, these three help me to formulate my idea of the corporation as institution or institutionalization and the connection, on the one hand, between the written record and the state (as the keeper of the book or state as book), and a group of people (a community) on the other. Of course, the individual, in the Hegelian sense of the word, is in one way or another limited and powerless in relation to already existing institutions (hence the problematic dilemma about strong and weak Hegelian institutionalism[460]). And of course, »ontological priority« belongs to institutions that already exist and that the individual encounters in the world in which they live.[461] However, the institutional subject is always plural (a group, »We«, never »*Das Ich im Wir*«, or possibly »*Wir im Ich*«) and has the potential to change and transform the existing institutions. Which is why the police[462] and the corporation (an institution in the contemporary meaning would probably contain within itself a combination of these two basic Hegelian institutes of civil society) constitute the most important institutional scene, one that greatly surpasses both the family and the state. When we speak of the institution or problem of institutionalization in

459 Hegel: Elements of the Philosophy of Right, p. 272.

460 Institutionalism could be the position according to which socially accepted types of action have »ontological priority« or absolute primacy in comparison with the thinking and acting of the individual. Dieter Henrich evokes Hegelian institutionalism in the strong sense of the word (Hegel: Philosophie des Rechts. Die Vorlesung von 1819/20 in einer Nachschrift, p. 31), in opposition to Jean-François Kervégan with a weak or moderate institutionalism (*institutionnalisme faible*). Cf. Kervégan in Hegel: Principes de la philosophie du droit, p. 329; Kervégan: L'effectif et le rationnel, pp. 311–314, 367–373.

461 »Ontological Priorities« or »ontologically prior« are Roger Scruton's phrases. For him, in a completely different context, individual persons (plural) are »ontologically prior« to corporations. Scruton: Corporate Persons, p. 254.

462 The police appear in this place in Hegel's system as early as the Jena lectures of 1805–1806 (*Jeneser Realphilosophie*), while the corporation or »*der zweite intitutionelle Kanal*« appears only later. This is Wolfgang Kersting's formulation in »Polizei und Korporation in Hegels Darstellung der bürgerlichen Gesellschaft«, p. 379.

Hegel, this certainly refers exclusively to the »institution of corporation«[463] that appears within the group (civil society).[464]

Hegel's and Althusius' first problem, above all, is the terminological confusion that follows the instrument or institution of »corporation«, but also the crisis of capital and political upheavals occurring in various countries, to which they are witness. What is a corporation and from where does Hegel adopt the term *Korporation*? The first, probably most accurate answer would be from English newspapers Hegel reads, as well as some books by an English economist. For Hegel, *Korporation* ought first be understood as an English thing. At the same time, Hegel's ambition is to reconstruct the English ban on corporations, as well as its prohibition in Italy and France (in France corporations were banned in 1791 only to become legal again under Napoleon).[465] He is also seeking to »improve theoretically« the recently badly deteriorated position of the poor in England (there are authors who thought of corporations as a union). In all the versions of his lectures on law, from beginning to end, he speaks of corporations as on the wane, in crisis, of uncertain future, all the while imploring on their behalf.[466] It seems to me that the concept of *Korporation* was chosen because it best suited all these various languages Hegel reads. Still, the problem of meaning of the word »corporation« remains unresolved. Just as at the beginning of the seventeenth century, Althusius combines Latin with German (*Describuntur haec pacta et leges collegarum in libris collegiorum, quos Zunftbücher vocamus*),[467] as well as the Roman and German understanding of the community, Hegel uses the word *Korporation*, at the time completely non-existent in colloquial use.[468] In the beginning, during

463 *»Die Institution der Korporation«*, says Hegel in § 253.

464 Hegel does not use the word »group« or the theory of a group (*Verbandstheorie*).

465 Cf. Fritzsimmons: From Artisan to Worker.

466 Just as in Hegel, the latent crisis of the status of corporation or the institution as such can be found in John Dewey (who publishes »The Historic Background of Corporate Legal Personality« in 1926) and in Robert Hessen (*In Defence of the Corporation*, 1979).

467 In his book on Althusius, Von Gierke translates *»consociatio collegarum«* as *Korporation*. Cf. Gierke: Johannes Althusius und die Entwiklung der naturrehtlichen Staatstheorien, p. 22. Althusius's *»consociatio collegarum«* ought to correspond to Henning Boehrer's *collegia Iusti*, which he opposes to *universitas* and divides into *private* and *publica* (*Ius publicum universal*, p. 442). In several of his books, Gierke attempts, drawing from Latin sources, to translate a multitude of various names for various associations into German. Sometimes his solutions are quite successful, but at other times, they are entirely obscure and inconsistent. When writing about the corporation in his great work *Das deutsche Genossenschaftrecht*, Gierke, a realist much like Maitland, initiates a host of currently relevant problems completely missing from Hegel: the nature of the personhood of a corporative group, the possibility of corporation owning property, entity status (whether it is a voluntary or privileged association), capacity of corporation to act independently, whether the *universitas* of a body (*corpus*) changes with a change or removal of members, etc.

468 In contemporary German, this refers to a student association of the neo-feudal period. The German equivalent of the English, French and Italian word »corporation« are *Zunft* or *Innung*. Obviously, Hegel opposes the old-German institution *Zunft* (in amendment § 255: *Korporation ist keine geschlossene Zunft*; incidentally, for Hegel, the family is »closed« unlike the corporation) because

the winter seminar 1818–1819, Hegel still vacillates between the words *Zünfte* and the English word *corporation.*[469] Still, a few months prior, in Heidelberg (when giving the natural law course of 1817–1818), Hegel shows clearly that his task is to find harmony between corporations and the state, keeping in mind what is going on in other countries and what has taken place »here« during feudalism: small states developed out of corporations when rulers of these states were not able to quash resistance and movements of popular struggle (§ 125). Even as early as that, Hegel, imagining a future state (singular), wary of the danger of private rights of individuals being carried out through association,[470] takes several things under consideration. First, that the state does not create or ought not itself create privileged corporation as had been the case in England. Second, that the state in no way be shaped or formed by these associations and that corporations are necessary because they guard from the ongoing atomization and dissolution of individuals (starting in 1816, hunger and poverty that swept across southern Germany forced many people to emigrate to America and other countries, § 121). Third, that civil society form through corporation and that enjoyment lies in what is common, that is for people to find entertainment only communally, never alone (§ 121).[471] Fourth, that any future state certainly ought to oversee corporations and find instruments that ensure their coexistence (»danger« is the word Hegel associates with corporations throughout his lectures on the philosophy of right[472]).

his intention is to distinguish between a civil from a feudal corporation. In the 1817 *Ständeschrift*, Hegel differentiates old corporation (*Zünfte*) or (*Zunftgeist*) from the professional, modern corporation. Still, Hegel's contrasting of words *Zunft* and the like (in § 289 he speaks of *Korporationsgeist*) still does not mean that he, strictly speaking, is renewing the Roman legal tradition and its theory of community, precisely because at the same time he is Germanizing the Latin word *corpus*. Still, regardless of Rosenzweig's exaggeration regarding the corporation as a reactionary or most reactionary element of Hegel's *Philosophy of Right*, his diagnosis of Hegel's intention still remains unsurpassed: »*Theorie der Korporation entwickelt und einer Erneuerung des alten Zunftwesens das Wort redet, die aber Arbeiter und Kapitalisten in gemeinsamen Körperschaften zusammenfassen muß.*« Rosenzweig: Hegel und der Staat, p. 124.

469 »§ 113. *Zünfte – In neuern Zeiten ist man den Corporationen abhold geworden [(Bemer)] des besondern Gemeinwesen in dem Allgemeinen.*« Hegel: Naturrecht und Staatswissenschaft, p. 323. It is interesting that after Hegel's death, Gans, in his lectures on natural law, still uses the same word, »*Corporation*« (with a capital C).

470 In § 125 Hegel quotes Johann Jacob Moser, *Neues teutsches Staatsrecht* (1766–1782).

471 § 121 »*da war der Genuss im Gemeinsamen, und der Einzelne vergnügte sich nicht für sich, sondern im Allgemeinen.*« Hegel: Vorlesungen uber Naturrecht und Staatswissenschaft, p. 169. Or in the same paragraph: »*Das Vernünftige der Korporation ist, dass das gemeinsame Interesse, dieses Allgemeine, in bestimmter Form wirklich existire.*« Hegel: Die Philosophie des Rechts: Die Mitschriften Wannenmann (Heidelberg 1817/18) und Homeyer (Berlin 1818/19), p. 143. Although the Church is also a corporation, Hegel clearly distinguishes the association of people in a corporation or community (*Gemeinde*) from »*religiöse Gemeinschaftlichkeit von Individuen*«.

472 Cf. »*Die Corporation kann auch gefährlich werden, für den ganzen Staat, wie in der älteren Geschichte Frankreichs und Deutschland diess vorkommt, dass sich ganze Corporationen frei gemacht haben.*« Hegel: Philosophie des Rechts, K. G. v. Griesheims 1824/25, p. 628.

Of all these points, which seem crucial for Hegel's endeavors regarding the creation of corporations (certainly »corporations are easier to create than to understand«, Robert Hessen), three seem to me to have a historical or technical importance. Only the third point, I think, which refers to the relation of the communal, and thus the moral and corporate, has the potential to be further developed. In addition, for two sets of problems of crucial importance for today's understanding of the concept of corporation, Hegel is of no use to us. The first refers to the differentiation of the entity of corporation from other similar forms of association, still relevant as we can see from Pettit or Lawson.[473] In that sense, corporation is more easily defined than differentiated from related concepts of different historical and linguistic origin.[474] The other set of problems refers to what is usually called »corporation as a judicial hallucination«. Being a realist, there is no doubt that for Hegel (as for Marx, lest we forget[475]) the corporation indeed exists (in contrast with Searle, for Hegel people exist, work, produce, experience pleasure, etc.) and that the corporation is a »*moralische Person*«.[476]

In § 252 Hegel writes:

> In keeping with this view, the corporation, under the oversight of the public authority (*öffentliche Macht*), has the right to look after its own clearly-defined interests, according

[473] Cf. Pettit: Two Fallacies about Corporations, and Lawson: The Nature of the Firm and Peculiarities of the Corporation.

[474] Here is a definition both contemporary and interesting. I cite it freely, with no precise reference: a corporation is a group of individuals authorized by law to act as a unit. The corporation assumes corporative responsibility, limited liability (widely considered one of the greatest inventions of the previous century: »I did not do it, the company did«). Pettit's French translator renders the English word »corporation« as *entreprise, compagnie*, as well as *corporation*, and the word »corporatization«, as *privatisation*. Petit attempts to solve the complete terminological chaos that always follows the corporation and related terms by drawing on Patrick W. Duff's book, *Personality in Roman Private Law*. Duff defines *corpus* as »any set of men who are for any purpose regarded as a group«. Every *collegium* is a *corpus* (p. 26; p. 28). There are two key books that deal with the genesis of concepts related to corporation, but as detailed as they are, they are of little help to carefully delineate the semiotic field of terminology for the corporation. The first of these is from 1933, by Schnoer von Carolsfeld, *Geschichte der juristichen Person*, of which only the first volume has been published, dealing with the terms *universitas, corpus* and *collegium in* classical Roman law. The author insists that the *Körperschaft* always refers to three words: *Gemeinde, Zunft* and *Verein* (p. 59). The other is from 1970, by Pierre Michaud-Quantin: Universitas. On page 64, the author presents the difficulty with the word *corpus*, which, discounting legal texts, very rarely refers to a collective, although there are uses that concern associations of painters and other trades: »*Quant aux documents officiels, il semble que le mot aie eu un sens trop imprécis ou trop abstrait pour y figurer.*«

[475] In many places in *Kritik des Hegelschen Staatsrechts*, Marx emphasizes the reality and materiality of corporations.

[476] »*Eine Corporation stellt »eine moralische Person«* (§ 13, 50, 81, 88; *Allgemeinen Landrecht für die Preussischen Staaten*). *Eine moralische Person ist in diesem Zusammenhang als gesellschaftliche und juristische Person zu verstehen.*« Niji: Hegels Lehre von der *Korporation*, p. 291. *Eine moralische Person* is also a reappropriation of Pufendorf's phrase *persona moralis composita*.

to the objective qualifications of skill and rectitude to adopt members, whose number is determined by the general system, to make provision for its adherents against fortuitous occurrences, and to foster the capacity necessary in any one desiring to become a member. In general it must stand to its members as a second family (*zweite Familie*), a position which remains more indefinite than the family relation, because the general civic community is at a farther remove from individuals and their special needs.[477]

Nowhere does Hegel present the problem of such a right, nor the success of such »action« of the corporation in the name of the moral personality of their members.

Hegel's focus, however, is not primarily on the transformation of one's personhood into a new entity that has the right to protect and perform certain actions in that person's name. Nor is it on the production of a new instance, one more powerful than the individual person or a number of individual persons together. When Hegel says in amendment § 207 of the *Philosophy of Right* that *»Ein Mensch ohne Stand ist eine bloße Privatperson und steht nicht in wirklicher Allgemeinheit«*, then the belonging to a group of people that works together and functions on the market and has a proper name (an entity, a legal person) would only ever be fulfilled or completed with the help of another similar entity and in collective action for profit and recognition.[478] This collective and common action, much like the police that guards the rules of the game, are a guarantee of morality or what Hegel calls *»Die Korporation als sittliche Institution.«*[479] The corporation or *Stand* implies the existence of others and competition with others, which would then lessen the importance or set aside the plan for the fiction and the ›mereness‹ (*blosse*) of individuality (an individual *Stand* or corporation is equally fictitious as a private person or individuality taken on its own). Hegel's intention, which could still be central in thematizing the corporation, and certainly a subject not yet exhausted, refers to the necessity of working with others and for others, of conducting a general and communal activity (to discover and create a common cause), of participating in public affairs, as well as public property (as commons). The generalization of connections that exist between people (*die Verallgemeinerung des Zusammenhangs der Menschen*, § 243) is Hegel's great socio-ontological endeavor, one that is more relevant, and certainly more comprehensible, than before. It seems to me that this *»Verallgemeinerung«* or *»öffentliche Macht«* is a forerunner of Marx's phrase, appearing only once in *The Grundrisse* and rendered in English as »general intellect«[480] or even Rawls' »public reason«. These moments

477 Hegel: Elements of the Philosophy of Right, p. 271. Cf. Vieweg: Zur logischen Grundlegung des Begriffs der Korporation in Hegels *Rechtsphilosophie*, pp. 34–41; Schülein: Die Korporation als zweite Familie in Hegels Theorie der bürgerlichen Gesellschaft, pp. 101–116.

478 § 253 *Die Korporation als Basis sozialer Anerkennung.* Hegel: Philosophie des Rechts, Hotho 1822/23, 3, p. 709. Certainly, Axel Honneth's project finds inspiration and direction in this moment.

479 Hegel: Philosophie des Rechts, p. 688.

480 »Nature does not construct machines, locomotives, railways, electric telegraphs, self acting

too could be the unconditional condition for the transformation of the corporation into a cooperative. After all, if we were to make a careful comparison today of all the variations, finesses, and shades of Hegel's lectures on the corporation from the beginning of the nineteenth century with a chapter of Adam Smith's *The Wealth of Nations*, »Of the Public Works and Institutions which are necessary for facilitating particular Branches of Commerce«, not only would it be clear that Hegel is in a way copying and reiterating Adam Smith's project,[481] but corporations as imagined by Smith, years prior to Hegel, really do seem like cooperatives, as alternative institutions, or better still, as »counter-institutions«.

mules, etc. They are products of human industry; natural material transformed into organs of man's will over Nature, or of man's activity in Nature. They are *organs of the human mind which are created by the human hand*, the objectified power of knowledge (vergegenständlichte Wissenskraft). The development of fixed capital shows the degree to which society's general science (*allgemeine gesellschaftliche Wissen*), knowledge has become an *immediate productive force*, and hence the degree to which the conditIons of the social life process (*des gesellschaftlichen Lebensprozesses*) itself have been brought under the control of the general intellect and remoulded according to it (*unter die Kontrolle des general intellect gekommen, und ihm gemäß umgeschaffen sind*). It shows the degree to which the social productive forces are produced not merely in the form of knowledge but as immediate organs of social praxis, of the actual life process (*als unmittelbare Organe der gesellschaftlichen Praxis; des realen Lebensprozesses*).« Marx: Outlines of the Critique of Political Economy, p. 92; Marx: Grundrisse der Kritik der politischen Ökonomie, p. 602. Paolo Virno's great project of thematizing the institution in the context of the »general intellect« continues and its finalization is still anticipated. Cf. Virno, Dell'impotenza, pp. 107–131.

481 Perhaps Hegel did not really have »in mind any concrete historical institution that existed in his time«, as Schmidt am Busch and Lisa Herzog claim (Herzog: Two Ways of »Taming« the Market«, p. 152), but the project of Adam Smith is deeply incorporated into his intentions. »Corporation spirit«, for example, is Smith's phrase and it certainly orients Hegel's fragments, as well as Marx's reading of Hegel.

5 Institution of Poverty. The Status of House in Institutional Building

What is poverty and how could we design housing for the poor today? What, further, is the relation of the house and the institution? The institution and poverty? Are the Roma, the *sans-papier* or migrants poor because they have no permanent dwelling place? Is it possible to design housing for those who travel or those who do not wish to dwell in one place or those who dwell together only temporarily? Who are we, the ones who dwell without the poor? If someone *has* an apartment (what would »having« an apartment mean, and does »having« have anything to do with dwelling?), does this mean that their poverty has ceased to be? All these question show, perhaps, that poverty no longer resides among those all too rarely mentioned as the poor – workers, who usually have unstable and temporary jobs but reside in a given place. It is as if the category of worker with temporary residence, those who work »under the table« which for a long time functioned as a pseudo ›stand-in‹ for the poor worker of the 19th century, has been replaced with new figures of the precarious poor. What kinds of apartments – and what kind of institutions – do the precarious need and how should they dwell?

Reading various texts in various languages regarding poverty and the poor, it is becoming clearer to me that war and violence above all create and consistently maintain a ›poor group‹ that is supposed to somewhere, somehow build something (such as a group of migrants working together, attempting, a long time ago, in Babylon, to incorporate). Or else they constitute a group that ought to be pushed out to the periphery of a city, placed outside a city (how can a million migrants build apartments for themselves in Germany? Where? Will this work be what turns them into German citizens?), or a group that becomes either dispersed or is compressed into a ghetto or a ›city of refuge‹, etc.[482] If this is indeed our main problem today, and if we put aside that what is going on with workers in China corresponds with the terrible conditions of life and work in the West in the 18th and 19th century, then these issues would belong to a single family designated by phrases such as ›social equality‹, ›poverty (relative or absolute)‹ or ›marginalized

482 2016 Venice Biennale, the German pavilion carried an exhibit entitled »Making *Heimat*« with the explanation that Germany hosted some 12 to 15 million Germans expelled immediately after World War II from other European countries where they lived before 1945. Urban settlement models from the fifties were offered as examples of solutions for current problems of resettling refugees in Germany. There is nothing cynical in today's refugees building their *Heimat* in Germany, given that this country has a shrinking population. The problem lies in demography still being strictly tied to sovereign states and not with Europe.

group‹. The thematization of these problems at present, which Jonathan Wolff designates as *the* task of »real world political philosophy«[483] corresponds to what Marx in the *Grundrisse* (1858), entirely in the spirit of Rawls, calls »general intellect« (even in the German original the phrase is in English), that is, »social practice« or »real life process«.

Before I return to Wolff and then Engels (and his large text »Zur Wohnungsfrage« from 1872), I should mention two, almost complementary pseudo-projects from different epochs that add to the problem of poverty something that is in our day and age always latently present.[484] The first is *Draft of a Representation, Containing a Scheme of Methods for the Employment of the Poor* (or *The Report on the Poor*) by John Locke from 1697,[485] in which he seeks a profound reform of social life. The second is Hegel's consideration of poverty in the context of civil society that necessarily produces it (from his lectures on the philosophy of right).[486] Locke is excited by the statistical analysis published by Gregory King in 1696, which showed a 25 % rise in the number of poor, and that despite the *Act of Settlement* from 1662, 50 % of the population was poor. In brief, Locke is looking for a way to put to work vagrants and saboteurs, whose number, despite stricter penalties, is ever greater – because only those who work can eat, drink, be clothed and sheltered (the age at which both boys and girls begin their working lives at this time is fourteen).[487] Locke is *de facto* inventing punishments and strategies for the successful functioning of workhouses, opening all over England at the time.

Just like Locke, Hegel will construct a kind of group identity for the poor (although not only for them), ascribing to them a dangerous, generally unknown and inexplicable role. What is significant is that Hegel recognizes that a) civil society excludes many others (not only women, for example), which is entirely unjusti-

483 Wolff. Political Philosophy and the Real World of the Welfare State.

484 Ostensibly, there is really nothing problematic about poverty in Adam Smith's or David Ricardo's liberal theory. In *Theory of Moral Sentiments*, for example, Smith reiterates the analysis of Mandeville (*Fable des abeilles* [Fable of the Bees], 1714), regarding the necessity of great spending by the rich to ensure work for the poor. Ricardo, meanwhile, offers a few arguments against poor laws and insists that they be entirely abolished.

485 It is now possible to deliberately connect the report Locke writes in his capacity as Commissioner on the Board of Trade, with something entirely different, but nevertheless concerns England: »A Philosophical Review of Poverty« (J. Wolff, along with Lamb and Zur-Szpiro, 2015), which appeared as part of anti-poverty strategy of the UK, financed by the Joseph Rowntree Foundation (Joseph is the father of Seebohm Rowntree, the author of the famous *Poverty. A Study of Town Life*. Both father and son were Quakers.)

486 John Rawls noted this passage in his *Lectures On the History of Moral Philosophy* (345ff). He concludes that Hegel does not have a solution for the problem of poverty or that it does not fit into his system (which, when it comes to Hegel, is in itself impossible and entirely paradoxical). Rawls there refers to a few pages from Allen Wood's book *Hegel's Ethical Thought*.

487 »He who does not work – does not eat« is a cliché repeated by apostle Paul, the utopians, the Quaker John Bellers, Locke's contemporary, who reminds his readers that in China literally everyone works (the feebleminded, the blind), etc.

fied and inexplicable: »The emergence of poverty is in general a consequence of civil society and on the whole arises necessarily out of it.«[488] Further, he insists that b) charity is no solution to the problem of poverty, opposing to it the solution in place in Scotland, where they sought »to leave the poor to their fate and direct them to beg from the public« (§ 245). c) Probably under the influence of Adam Smith, Hegel becomes a »real world political philosopher«, preferring social analyses he reads (mostly) in English books and newspapers, to his own speculative constructions. d) Hegel is perhaps the first to recognize that the poor are excluded »from the spiritual benefits of modern society, from education, even from the consolation of religion.« Finally, e) Hegel concludes, introducing the moral degradation of the poor, that no entity, not even the state can resolve this problem (Hegel takes it as axiomatic that the state is immanently present in civil society). Here is Hegel: »The poor man feels himself excluded and mocked by everyone, and this necessarily gives rise to an inner indignation. He is conscious of himself as an infinite, free being, and thus arises the demand that his external existence should correspond to this consciousness.«[489] Poverty in itself does not reduce people to a rabble (*Pöbel*) (this is the passage quoted by Rawls); a rabble is created only by the disposition associated with poverty, by inward rebellion against the rich, against society, against the government, etc. (§ 244)

The »rabble« is characterized by »envy and hatred against all those who have something«, as well as laziness and the right to live by the work of others. »The rabble is a dangerous [social] ill, because they have neither rights nor duties.«[490] Finally, Hegel reverses himself and relativizes the link of poverty and the rabble, insisting on an entirely new point: the »rabble [is] distinct from poverty; usually it is poor, but there are also rich rabble.«[491] This last point of turning the rich into the rabble (for example, a kind of *nouveau riche* who has all the characteristics of a poor person »who hates all those who have something or have more than him«) could be an example of the transformation of absolute into relative poverty, which often depends only on context and comparison with others.[492]

488 Hegel: Philosophie des Rechts. Die Vorlesungen von 1819/1820 in einer Nachschrift, p. 193; »When there is great poverty, the capitalist finds many people who work for small wages, which increases his earnings; and this has the further consequences that smaller capitalists fall into poverty.« Hegel: Philosophie des Rechts, K. G. v. Griesheims 1824/25, p. 610.

489 Hegel: Philosophie des Rechts. Die Vorlesungen von 1819/1820 in einer Nachschrift, p. 195.

490 Hegel: Naturrecht und Staatswissenschaft, p. 322.

491 Ibid., 4, p. 608. Many of the lines quoted here have already been translated into English by Allen Wood.

492 It is comparison with others that turns the poor into rabble, allowing them to be recognized or connect with those similar, and then potentially be categorized as part of a group whose constitution is never completed (for the rabble is never a group, but a mass of people that lives in pre-corporate or pre-institutional space). There is a passage in »Leviticus Rabbah«, where the English translator, Jacob Neusner, attempts to differentiate a few characteristics of the poor: »Seven names were given to him [the poor]: poor (*ani*), impoverished, despised, dispossessed, denuded, crushed, and

Hegel's conceptual theater (although he is not alone, I have only used him as an example) carries at least three quasi-opuses of problems always present in the case of ›poverty‹ and the poor. The first concerns the general problem of description and evidence of the existence of the poor and poverty, sometimes even testimony and experience of one's own indigence or poverty of others (as if poverty must be felt; or that, for example, the smell of a French or Russian vagrant is not the same; and the question of how to detect, explain, and produce motives for the construction of action or productive social action).[493] The second refers to differences, levels and gradations of poverty (a problem probably unwittingly opened by Seebohm Rowntree at the turn of the 20th century). The third refers to the group or pseudo-group of the poor. And only at this point does the issue of housing appear – the poor are such because of lack of dwelling or permanent residence (the politically correct acronym for the homeless in France is SDF, »*sans domicile fixe*« [without permanent residence]); but at the same time, the poor dwell huddled, in groups, together, in blocs.

The study produced by Seebohm Rowntree and his associates in 1901[494] includes two thirds of the population of York, or some 46,000 people. They excluded »those individuals who were able to afford to employ a domestic servant« (such criteria make matters more complicated, since the proportion of the population of the Italian city of Udine, for example, in the same year who can employ a domestic servant is certainly much smaller than in York, which does not necessarily speak of poverty in Udine, but of culture of dwelling in York; and let me be upfront that I do not know what a »culture of dwelling« would be). Rowntree's book, *Poverty. A Study of Town Life* shows that 20,000 people in York live in poverty, while 28 % live in »most serious poverty«. In the introduction, obviously written when the book was already finished, presenting the research results, the author explains:

lowly. »Impoverished« because he desires everything. »Despised« because he is held in contempt by everybody (...) »Dispossessed« because he is disposed of all his property. »Denuded« because he is denuded of all his property. »Crushed« because he is crushed. He sees something to eat but does not eat it, sees something to drink but does not drink it. »Lowly« because he is lower than anyone, like the lowest threshold.« Neusner: The Components of the Rabbinic Documents, pp. 226–227. Cf. Ben Shalom: Poverty, pp. 43–44.

493 Martha Nussbaum speaks of the significance of narration (mentioning Dickens, Thomas Hardy and others) in the course of presenting data, specifically in order to be »inclined to think of the lives of the poor (especially, perhaps, the distant or foreign poor).« Nussbaum: How to write about poverty?. For example, in »Social Equality, Relative Poverty and Marginalized Groups«, when Wolff talks about his visit to the city of Katatura, »a township built 5 miles outside Windhoek, the capital of Namibia«, the information that »Katatura« translates as »the place we don't want to go« is more significant to the readership than any statistic (pp. 3–23).

494 In the introduction opening, Rowntree writes: »My object in undertaking the investigation detailed in this volume was, if possible, to throw some light upon the conditions which govern the life of the wage-earning classes in provincial towns, and especially upon the problem of poverty?« Rowntree: Poverty, p. vii.

As a primary object of my inquiry has been to ascertain not only the proportion of the population living in poverty, but the nature of that poverty, I have divided the population so living into two classes: a) Families whose total earnings are insufficient to obtain the minimum necessaries for the maintenance of merely physical efficiency. Poverty falling under this head I have described as »primary« poverty; b) Families whose total earnings would be sufficient for the maintenance of merely physical efficiency were it not that some portion of them is absorbed by other expenditure, either useful or wasteful. Poverty falling under this head is described as »secondary« poverty.[495]

This pair, »primary«/»secondary« poverty, which might have seemed entirely arbitrary a hundred years ago and refers to families and not individuals, has been transformed into the pair absolute/relative or extreme/intermediate, and then further into subsistence/status poverty, etc. Two further sources are usually quoted to complicate matters regarding »secondary« poverty, serving to reconstruct or provide »a radical redescription«[496] of poverty: Peter Townsend's 1979 definition of relative poverty;[497] and more importantly for us, a famous sentence from *The Wealth of Nations*, probably first referred to in this context by Amartya Sen (in 1983), in which Adam Smith is discussing the concept of necessaries:

By necessaries I understand not only commodities which are indispensably necessary for the support of life, but whatever the custom of the country renders it indecent for creditable people, even the lowest order, to be without (…) Custom has rendered leather shoes a necessary of life in England. The poorest creditable person of either sex would be ashamed to appear in public without them.[498]

These examples are not always exactly aligned with the concept of poverty, nor do they correspond well with the intentions of Seebohm Rowntree (»leather shoes« in public are not dissimilar to the institution of »employ[ing] a domestic servant«). Still, they help in considering poverty as a certain impossibility of participation in

495 Ibid., p. x.

496 Shaw: Poverty, p. 27.

497 It is often quoted by Wolff, as well as others: »Individuals, families and groups in the population can be said to be in poverty when they lack the resources to obtain the types of diet, participate in the activities and have the living conditions and amenities which are customary, or at least widely encouraged or approved, in the societies in which they belong. Their resources are so seriously below those commanded by the average individual or family that they are, in effect, excluded from ordinary living patterns, customs and activities.« Townsend: Poverty in the United Kingdom, p. 31. Shaw comments that »The abolition of relative poverty seems, in principle, incapable of achievement. For as Townsend has argued, even if societies become wealthier and living standards rise accordingly, the relative poor will always be with us. Rising living standards will increase the proportion of the relative poor whose income does not permit access to all the goodies an affluent society can provide for its citizenry«, Shaw: Poverty, p. 33.

498 Smith: The Wealth of Nations, pp. 351–352. Cf. Sen: Poor, Relatively Speaking, p. 159. Commenting on this passage, Jo Wolff says: »Relative poverty is a matter of not having the resources that will allow you to fit in.« Wolff: Social Equality, Relative Poverty and Marginalized Groups, p. 9.

the work of a group (a corporation) or simply being part of a group (status, custom). Here we reach the social exclusion of which Townsend speaks. Even if a poor man or woman, for example, participates or thinks he/she is participating in society or in a group, sub-group (Jo Wolff gives an example analogous to that of Smith, citing that citizens of Katutura, on the verge of hunger, nevertheless all have mobile phones), it still does not mean that this whole group is not socially excluded or marginalized.[499] What is far more important, and this is certainly Jo Wolff's effort, is to defend an elementary definition of poverty as low income compared to capability deprivation.[500] I think that it is not only that poverty is more easily measured this way, but that income already implies the existence of membership and belonging to various groups – in other words, inclusion, connection with society and ties to others. It is not sufficient to have a mobile phone, hold it in hand, play games, and treat it as »equivalent to Adam Smith's linen shirt« (Jo Wolff). It is necessary to communicate, to speak, to write. Of course, a mobile phone in the hands of someone on the streets of Katatura, or in destroyed cities of Afghanistan, is certainly an opportunity and a great chance for them to soon be on the border or a ship, on their way to Munich. If their action is not careful enough, and speech acts are not precise enough (producing and accepting responsibilities »with those who matter to him or to her«), the poor become migrants who could perhaps join the conglomeration of poor on the peripheries of large Western cities.[501]

499 In Pierre Bourdieu's famous book *La misère du monde*, whose great novelty consists in the poor speaking, in being interviewed by Bourdieu and his assistants (Wolff and Shalit also speak in detail of an interview with an anti-poverty officer in *Disadvantage*, pp. 54–55), there are testimonies of a certain married couple Demoura (of Portuguese origin) who have lived a very long time in a small apartment in Paris, without any furniture or drapes, under »*conditions défavorises*« (the French translation of »disadvantage«), with the state's help. They are happy in France and they consider themselves well integrated in society. However, when they fall victim to quite rare and complicated illnesses, they suffer great injustices, and realize that it would be much better to have the French name Dupont, rather than Demoura.

500 In chapter 3 (pp. 9–16) of »Philosophical Review of Poverty,« Wolff (along with Lamb and Zur-Szpiro) present a detailed review of Amartya Sen's position, while chapter 5, »Is poverty ›capability deprivation‹?« (pp. 25–27) is ultimately a critique of Sen's position. It seems to me that this redefinition of poverty is complementary to the strong efforts of Claudia Card for reconsideration and relativization of genocide, previously having to do with a great number of victims, now proclaimed to be acts that generally speaking destroy the entity of a group (for example, rape of women in civil war).

501 Thirty or forty years ago, it was possible to apply, and with a few strings pulled, receive (provided one had regular employment, on the books – which on the other hand one could not get without proof of residence, basic traps immigrants find themselves in) an HLM (*habitation à loyer modéré*) apartment on the periphery of Paris. The phrase exists since 1945, having taken over from the so-called HBM (*habitation bon marché*), established in 1889 by contemporary hygienists and paternalists of the modern bourgeoisie of the Second Empire to prevent revolutionary outbreaks. Today it is very difficult to acquire such an apartment, with rent for a three-piece apartment some 600 euros (or a small one-piece apartment, 500 euros). Minimum guaranteed pay in France is set at 900 euros. Such apartments in France are not only for (active) workers, but also retired workers, disabled workers receiving payments from the state, in a word, they are social housing.

Even though in this search for a better life, it is possible to see some elements of the first groupings and joint dwelling with members of one's extended family for the sake of common work (which are the first forms of incorporating),[502] it is certain that two hundred years after the identification of the problem of poor conditions of life in poor and working-class neighborhoods, such pseudo-joint dwelling still exists, and such neighborhoods are still erected.[503]

A hundred and fifty years ago, Engels, a master of description of cities and terrible life conditions (his descriptions of Manchester or Wuppertal are unforgettable), held before him a multitude of books and texts from various hygienists and so-called bourgeois urbanists, a few manifests and appeals to the bourgeoisie,[504] as well as books and texts of socialists such as Proudhon – all of whom he criticizes sharply for their ignorance and counter-revolutionary positions that workers dwelling could be radically improved.[505] I will end here by listing a few problems, agreed upon and registered by all (without any major differences), and with a few suggestions that have of course never been fulfilled. In 1872 Engels finds (the reform by Haussmann [or, as he calls himself in his memoirs, *»artiste démolisseur«*] is already complete and known to all) that the workers have already been pushed out to the periphery, that smaller apartments are rare and expensive because the construction industry produces large apartments more profitably. Further, Engels (in what is at the time perhaps a unique position for a European intellectual, familiar with the conditions of social justice in countries across Europe) identifies the better position of the English worker (he speaks of England and the continent), all of which is insufficient since the capitalists are lying when promising to build

502 Perhaps the best description of the medieval origin of the Joint Economic Household of the Family, that is, Household Communities Outside the Family come from Max Weber in his thesis »The History of Commercial Partnerships in the Middle Ages«, (1889).

503 The only alternative I would mention here, of which there certainly has not been enough written in English, which could potentially satisfy the social parameters of equality and productive social action, refers to the incredible engagement of Otto Neurath, in Vienna, immediately upon WWI. Neurath attempted to build settler communities, to unify urbanism with an organization of work and life. Two passages from his writing are as follows. »The similarity of the apartment, the similarity of the building's parts (norms) is an expression of modesty, but also an expression of the sense for equality, which roots in both, fraternity and envy alike. Not one singular building is like the brick within a house. A new community is created from the class solidarity of the labor-forces.« and »A complex of low rise buildings with small gardens, which has not been born out of a collaborative cooperative companionship's organization, is of similar lifelessness as a large Kamienica tenement (...) Only via a life based on cooperative association will a new common life style emerge.« Cf. Hochhäusle: Otto Neurath, p. 146.

504 Perhaps the most famous appeal to the bourgeoisie comes from Georges Picot in *Un devoir sociale et les logements d'ouvriers* (Paris, 1885), in which he calls for a struggle against socialism in order to achieve something better still than socialism and to restore the family, custom and life of workers in a healthy and moral household.

505 Proudhon (for Engels this is probably a forerunner of Rawls) is one who seeks »eternal justice«, who speaks only of justice ... *Fiat justitita, pereat mundus!*, writes Engels – may there be justice, even if the world perishes. Cf. Engels: Zur Wohnungsfrage.

new apartments, leaving aside the question of hygiene in workers' neighborhoods. Rather, they simply displace out of the city center the cesspools of disease, i. e., workers. (This, in any case, is how Engels defines Haussmann's strategy.) The extraodrinary speed and development of nineteenth-century capitalism resulted in there no longer being twenty to thirty families living in a single house (something that will appear in the Soviet Union after the revolution), nor any more talk of fatigued workers deprived of sleep, working thirteen hours a day, or child labor and dying.[506] Similarly, there are no more projects (some of which are indeed ingenious) of monstrously large social houses or blocks in which several thousand workers live and eat in common kitchens.

There are not many optimistic protocols in 1872, but the difference from 30 years prior, it seems to me, far greater, than in the last 150 years. In 1872 there is still an almost unnatural enthusiasm that the mobilization of a large group of people that would destroy the few who rule was possible, just as it is possible – which is perhaps for us more interesting – to pass from one class (those who have nothing but their labor) into another. One great idea certainly speaks to this (although Engels calls it minimally positive, he allows himself to fantasize about it): that the solution to the housing question consists in each renter becoming the owner of his apartment, transferring the value difference between the initial cost of a house and its current market value to society.

From the point of view of population shifts taking place the last few years, due to war, poverty, and precariousness, with completely uncertain places of residence or ownership over real estate, the concept of dwelling, apartment, or group living has completely changed. And the new concept of design certainly depends on these changes.

506 Only twenty years prior, in *Des classes ouvrières en France pendant l'année 1848* (Paris 1849), Jérome-Antoine Blanqui describes workers' housing in Rouen and Lille and carries a report by a famous doctor from Lille, Gosselet, saying that 21,000 children are stillborn in France each year, and another 20,700 die by the age of five.

IV. Group and Negative Facts

1 *Social Gestures* as the Condition of Efficiency and (Existence) of Social Acts

My intention is to argue, drawing on entirely marginal suggestions of several authors who belong to different genres of philosophy and sociology, that there are indeed acts that are justifiably called »social gestures«. Their role in the construction of a group or institution may be significant. Not only would they not be a parasite or addition to social acts (which usually refers to linguistic acts), but they would directly participate in the construction of social acts and enable their efficient conduct. In addition, the role of social gestures, whose main characteristics are corporeality, visibility, and vivacity (»living gesture« is Aby Warburg's expression[506]), could be a kind of *a priori* to the existence of the social group as such.

There are only a few places in which Adolf Reinach writes about the form of appearance of our inner acts (*unsere innere Akte*). And when thematizing social acts, he mentions the possibility that they can be known in ways other than through language or words. Namely, the form of appearance (*Erscheinungsform*), necessary to be certain of the existence of an act, is the condition for people to be able to connect with one another. But this form seems to come in different forms itself:

Social acts are those that do not rest in themselves (*die nicht in sich selbst ruhen*). The essential assumption for social acts is (the existence of) another subject, to whom they wish to reveal themselves. This person to whom they are directed ought to acquire familiarity in this way. However, direct connection among people is not possible; what is necessary are expressions: thus, social acts must find an expression to reveal themselves to another. They have, to that end, various forms at their disposal: words, gestures, etc. (*Worte, Gesten* [*usw.*]). The addressee is thus clearly necessary for social acts, and therefore also the form of appearance (*Erscheinungform*) of such acts. Their directedness to the addressee (*die Richtung auf den Adressaten*) is the very heart of these acts, this is their soul. Second, their form of appearance is not in their essence, but is rather their body (*die Erscheinungform, liegt nicht in ihrem Wesen und ist ihr Leib*). It exists merely because we humans are incapable of knowing each other's inner acts other than through forms of appearance (*daß wir unsere inneren Akte nur an ihren Erscheinungsformen erkennen können*).[507]

Two years later we find two further similar passages in Chapter 3, »The Social Acts«, of *The Apriori Foundations of the Civil Law*:

The act of deciding is an internal act. It can be performed (*vollzogen*) without being announced (*verlautbart*) or needing to be announced. Of course the decision can express it-

506 *»Die lebhafte Geste: die Antike hat's erlaubt«.* Gombrich: Aby Warburg, p. 158.
507 Reinach: Nichtsoziale und soziale Akte, p. 357.

self in facial expressions and gestures (*in Mienen oder Gesten ausprägen*). I can express it (*kundgeben*), communicate it to others if I want. But this is not necessary for the act as such. It can unfold entirely within, it can rest in itself and not receive an expression in any sense (*er kann beruhigt in sich selbst bleiben, ohne in irgendeinem Sinne eine Äusserung zu erfahren*). One sees right away that it is otherwise with certain other spontaneous acts. Commanding or requesting, for instance, clearly cannot be performed entirely within.[508]

And then a few pages later:

But the social acts have an inner and an outer side, as it were, a soul and a body. The body of social acts can widely vary while the soul remains the same. A command can be expressed in mien, gestures, words (*in Mienen, in Gesten, in Worten in Erscheinung treten*). One should not confuse the utterance (*Äusserung*) of social acts with the involuntary way in which all kinds of inner experience, such as shame, anger, or love can be externally reflected. This utterance is rather completely subject to our voluntariness and can be chosen with the greatest deliberation and circumspection, according to the ability of the addressee to understand it.[509]

These fragments fit together and complement each other very well (even if Reinach never makes a precise distinction between acts, social acts, and negative social acts), and they could be lucidly interpreted if we introduce a new repertoire of actions that actually precede acts, but which also hold them together and allows their existence and efficiency. Let us look at how Reinach's theater of functions and naming of these acts plays out. It is immediately clear that the form of appearance or »body« of the social act has been degraded in relation to experience, to the interior or the »directedness (*Richtung*) towards the other« of the social act. The soul of the social act always has two moments: the experience, which is inner, and direction, or path of transmission of the experience to the addressee. In that sense, the other or addressee is for Reinach also in the background, and their answer, also realized in the »form of appearance«, does not determine the success of the social act.[510] Since for Reinach the ideal acting would be telepathic (without any exterior instruments or »material« connections between the actors), and since an ideally constructed community would be one *a priori* established by a common inner ex-

508 Reinach: Die apriorischen Grundlagen des bürgerlichen Rechtes, pp. 158–159; The Apriori Foundations of the Civil Law, p. 18.

509 Ibid., p. 20. The concluding lines of this passage in German are as follows: »*Man darf die Äußerung sozialer Akte nicht verwechseln mit der unwillkürlichen Weise, in der allerlei innere Erlebnisse, Scham oder Zorn oder Liebe, sich nach außen hin spiegeln können. Sie ist vielmehr durchaus willkürlicher Natur und kann, je nach den Verständnisfähigkeiten des Adressaten, mit größter Überlegung und Umsicht ausgewählt werden.*« Reinach: Die apriorischen Grundlagen des bürgerlichen Rechtes, p. 160.

510 In contrast to Reinach, Husserl estimates that the social act is realized only at the arrival of the other's response. The social act is social only if there is a reciprocal response to the initial address. Cf. Bojanić: Che cos'è un atto d'impegno?.

perience (we see here hints of »collective intentionality«) making it unified prior to any factual unity, the significance of the manifestation and the »visibility of acts« and explicit connections between actors is entirely secondary. Two paradoxical consequences follow from here: the first is the construction of the »interior« or the »myth of the interior«, a fantasy about the existence of »acts« or experiences that supposedly exist and supposedly arrive at the addressee, but would never have to become expressed or manifest or indeed even concern those others; and second, the very vague description of the form of appearance essential for a coherent transfer of an individual's inner experiences to others. Reinach thinks that there are some kind of, let us provisionally call them »personal acts«, which lie completely still within the interior of a person and do not concern others in the least. An example he provides is the »decision«. Further, the implicit assumption would be that such acts (among which certainly making a »decision«) can thus be completely hidden from others. However, the very existence of such acts would then imply a domain of the interior or some kind of an »individual's inner«, which would be *a priori* antisocial or negatively social, and can never or under any circumstances be manifested. If our inner acts (*unsere innere Akte*), as he calls them – which include the experience of »shame«, »wrath«, or »love« – are unjustifiably stripped (by Reinach) of their status as »social acts«, Reinach thinks that they would have to be included in a new class of »social gestures«. All three of these protocols imply the existence of some other or others, even depend on those others, and are secretly directed at them, although the protocols in no way obligate these other persons to either reciprocate or respond. Thus, they do not belong to the class of social acts, but are still more than mere »inner gestures« or »inner (social) gestures«, and allow for the existence of social gestures or social acts without possibility of themselves being manifested as such. The fact that wrath, shame, or love can be experienced without being externalized or manifested to others because they do not necessarily bind us to those others when they are manifested, does not abolish their capacity to represent social value or socially integrate a group. Not only that: perhaps only when I manifest my wrath will the necessary conditions be met for my ensuing command to be uttered thus fulfilling its function of social act. The function of a social gesture would thus be to prepare and ensure the appearance of social acts.

Let us now attempt, in a few preliminary steps, to combine Reinach's formulations with some complementary, kindred ideas and thus potentially reconstruct the relation between social acts and social gestures (or acts and gestures more broadly). To begin with, let us assume that in one way or another, inner life or inner experience concerns others and refers to others (those external), and that the distinction between inner and outer is weak, albeit at the origin of the gestural protocol. Let us also assume that experiences or »inner« could in one way or another be expressed or exposed, which is to say that nothing can remain hidden such that it is impossible to be revealed.

Form of Appearance (*Erscheinungsform*)

In this regard, Reinach privileges the linguistic expression. Indeed, the social act is necessarily a linguistic act. Regardless of the fact that not all linguistic acts are necessarily social, Reinach (who is not alone on this point in the histories of social ontology and social epistemology) defines social acts primarily normatively. Social acts are actions that create connections between actors that can be broken or modified only through a new mutual agreement. By contrast, gestures imply non-normativity since they would appear not to be obligatory for others.[511] If I laugh, another may not necessarily, even if something is truly funny and everyone else in the group is laughing; if I am toasting something, someone else does not have to respond to my toast; if I produce a mocking gesture, there is no obligation for the addressee of the gesture to return in kind. Similarly, my outstretched hand obligates no one to respond to my gesture by shaking it. Gestures ought to be filled with meaning, but not necessarily be repeated, followed, or remembered. In several places, Reinach mentions various forms of appearance: *Worte*, *Gesten*, *usw.* (although we do not know what is included in the *usw.* or etc.). *Mienen* is a complicated word that functions well in German, English, and French, referring to facial expressions (grimaces),[512] while *Geste* is generally ascribed to hands and less often to body parts or the whole body). *Gebärde* and *Geste* (the former is difficult to translate, but would possibly be gesticulation, a movement more sudden and aggressive than mere gesture, and would not necessarily refer to hand motions).[513] In 1911, Reinach writes the following:

> The form of appearance (*Erscheinungsform*) exists only because the way things stand among us humans is that we can only know our inner acts through their forms of appearance (*dass wir unsere inneren Akte nur an ihren Erscheinungsformen erkennen können*).

But in *Introduction to Philosophy* from 1913, we encounter a new formulation and a new question:

511 »(...) *la pensée »antinormative« a toujours eu pour la gestualité.*« Kristeva: Le geste, pratique ou communication?, p. 48. For this reason gestures are usually banal or irrelevant (*gesto banale*, *gesto irillevante*). Cf. Loddo: Manifestare gli atti sociali, p. 72.

512 In Italian this word is rendered as »*espressioni del volto*«. Reinach: I fondamenti a priori del diritto civile, pp. 27, 30. The designation *la mine* is perhaps best constructed by Montaigne: »*signes qu'un muet fait pour faire comprendre ce qu'il ne peut pas dire.*« Montaigne: Essais, p. 169.

513 Perhaps the difference between these two words can be elaborated better. However, the definition for *Geste* indicates that it is »either a spontaneous or intentional« gesture (primarily with the hands or head) conveying an inner state, and can either accompany or replace words, or an action that communicates something indirectly. *Gebärde*, on the other hand, is primarily with hands and arms and *intended* to convey a message, though the secondary definition indicates it can also be a behavior or demeanor to indicate something specific. *Gebärde* is more direct and intentional, while *Geste* could be involuntary and simply indicative of inner feelings or attitudes that a person may not have intended to communicate, yet are nonetheless apparent.

We do not (in this way) participate in another's experience (*Fremderlebnis*). The only thing that can be noted from another's experience are the gestures (*die Gesten*): I understand another's experiences first in the gesticulations (*zuerst erfasse ich in den Gebärden des Anderen seine Erlebnisse*). What then compels one to say that they only notice their own acts (*Was drängt dann dazu zu sagen, ich kann nur meine eigenen Akte wahrnehmen*)?[514]

The last question seems to come out of nowhere; sloppily constructed, it brings with it an odd dilemma. Regardless of this throwing around of the pronouns (»we«, »our«, »I«), what is clear is that forms of appearance, such as *Geste* and *Gebärde* are opposed to *Akt*, in this case inner acts (*innere Akte*). Inner acts can only be known if they are manifested – I can only know what I have in me if I manifest it in some way.[515] Three years later, Reinach wonders about the possibility that one can note (but probably not really know) only one's own inner acts. My power to notice my own decision or wrath or shame is not only trivial, but also does not abolish the capacity of another to also notice them in my gestures or movements that I manifest either simultaneously or occasionally. This new perspective muddies Reinach's order of concepts: the »soul of act« suddenly appears not only in words as the decisive form of appearance, but also in gestures.

The expression of promise is not exhausted in words. The soul of the promise can in different bodies be manifested through gesture, facial expression, etc.[516]

How can we understand this sudden consolidation of body (form of appearance) and soul of an act in the gesture? What does it mean that the soul of the act is manifested or expressed in the gesture? Is this a consequence of Reinach's reading of Bergson? Be that as it may, the gesture has a soul if and only if it can construct a group by holding (temporarily) multiple bodies in one location. All of a sudden, this becomes the condition of production and efficiency of social gestures.

514 Reinach: Einleitung in die Philosophie, p. 391.

515 »Only in the gestures of others do I see how I appear in this case (*Ich weiß nur aus anderer Leute Gebärden, wie ich in dem Falle auch aussehe*): only their wrathful looks indicate the ugliness of my affect.« Ibid., p. 390.

516 »*(Der) Ausdruck des Versprechens erschöpft sich nicht in Worten. Auch in Gesten, Mienen etc. kann (die) Seele des Versprechens sich in verschiedenen Leibern kundgeben.*« Ibid., pp. 449–450.

What Is a Gesture? On the Corporeal or Material of a Gesture

There is a famous definition of a gesture from the twelfth century by Hugh of St. Victor, which could provide us a bridge from the complex meaning the word had in Cicero, to the present. In Chapter 12 of *De institutione novitarium*, dedicated to gestures,[517] he writes:

Gestus est motus et figuratio membrorum corporis, ad omnem agendi et habendi modum.

I would like to follow Clemens Grün's insight of a potential double translation of this sentence.[518] »A gesture is a motion and figure of body parts, such that they are adapted to any mode of acting or being«; or otherwise: »a gesture is a motion and figure of body parts befitting the mode of any acting and being.« When the body emits a gesture, it is already in the figure that allows for that gesture, that is, the body is figured to manifest it. The gesture, then, ensures its own manifestation by figuring the body, how it is held, and how it carries out or »bears« the gesture. It would appear that the gesture is an agent that produces its own manifestation or action, adapting the body to itself; while the body ought to »carry« it out, to carry itself specifically to be able to manifest that gesture. Although written down at the heart of Scholastic thinking, the definition releases us brilliantly from Scholasticism, a hefty heritage according to which God usually acts or produces his acts through human gestures (*gestus*). It contains a novelty that returns us to Cicero and the first original uses of this word. Gesture as agent (as alternative name for desire; in many Medieval protocols, the words »gesture« and »desire« are synonymous) represents an introduction into a »relative autonomy of human action«, and thus a completely new situation wherein the human is capable of acting alone and manifest their own acts through gestures (*gestus*).[519] Moreover, the word »gesture« does not limit itself to a motion of the hand, but rather the entire body is engaged in its production, liberating it as a whole to open and present in space, as both a physical and social fact.[520] Perhaps, however, it is possible to closer still reconstruct the consequences of Hugh of St. Victor's determination of the gesture,

517 Hugo de S. Victore: De institutione novitarium, col. 935.

518 Cf. Grün: Gestus, gesta, gesticulatio, p. 23. Cf. Jean-Claude Schmitt: »Gestus« – »Gesticulatio«, pp. 383–385.

519 The distinction between *gesta* and *gestus* belongs to Jean-Claude Schmitt. Cf. Schmitt: La morale des gestes, pp. 35–36.

520 The reconstruction of the history of gestures by the archeologist Salomon Reinach is evidently guided by Hugh of St. Victor's definition. »*Le geste est un movement du corps ou d'un membre du corps qui exprime une pensée ou une émotion.« Reinach pays particular attention to the relation between gesture, attitude, and movement.*« Reinach: L'histoire des gestes, p. 64. This formulation, a variation on Cicero, in which gesture »refers to a movement of the body or of any part of it that is expressive of thought or feeling« today stands in myriad dictionaries. Cf. Kendon: Gesture, p. 109.

in an even more systematic way, or at least in a way that would ensure a potential future epistemology of the gestural and its clear position in the structure of actions that ultimately constitute a group and its joint acting. Several moments can be presented without hesitation: a) a gesture produces the body or a body is bodily only if it produces gestures that in turn, paradoxically both confirm and surpass the body as such. *Gestation* is pregnancy, an interior state or interval of time from conception to (giving) birth. *Gestation* is also the maturing of an idea or a project or *affection anima*,[521] becoming a mother or creator, which has as its result (or expression, since the result is an expression) what we call a gesture or gestures. b) The gesture carries or brings (*gerere*) an expression of the former and what originally forms the body itself, while simultaneously being cultivated in the body and in the interior from where it is then manifested.[522] c) A gesture designates (*disegno*; drawing or sketch) the development of the concept or conception, first by hand and then in an effort of the whole body. Through such a gesture (first of the hand, and then the rest of the body), the body is placed in a social space. d) The appearance of tools attached to the hand – a pen, brush, or conductor's baton – leads us swiftly to the thematization of the body itself as an instrument, one constituted by gestures in order to then be manifested by it.[523] e) Marcel Mauss designates the »ensemble of techniques of the body« (*l'ensemble des techniques du corps*) as humanity's most natural instrument and prior to the »techniques of instruments« (*les techniques à instruments*).[524] Even though Mauss alternates in the use of acts and gestures, insufficiently differentiating between them, it is clear that »techniques of the body« or patterns of distribution of bodies in society always refer to classifications of a plurality of uniform social gestures. People imitate and transmit them among each other, thus producing the social space that

521 In *Idee zu einer Mimik* (letter 6) Johann Jakob Engel thematizes expressive gestures which in German resemble what Cicero designates with the word gesture (*gestus*): »*Gestus nur von den äußern Zeichen des Gemuthszustandes, der affectionum animi, erklärt.*« Engel: Idee zu einer Mimik, p. 60. *Significatio* Engel designates using the word *Ausdruck* and is different to *demonstratio*, a protocol reserved for painting.

522 This protocol is usually tied to a famous lecture by Aby Warburg in February 1927: »Urworte leidenschaftlicher Gebärdensprache« (Ur-Words of the Affective Language of Gestures). Gestures are not mere movements expressive of emotions in man or animal, originally having a stimulus-reaction model (Darwin). The function of gestures is symbolic. They are expressions of inner affect (pre-shaped forms, original forms, primordial words). »Original significant visual elements as gestures are presented in concepts and in cultural artefacts.« Cf. Woldt: Ur-Words of the Affective Language of Gestures, pp. 133–157.

523 Cf. Flusser: Gesture, pp. 1–9. A number of times over the course of his career, Agamben writes about the gesture as »the exhibition of a mediality: it is the process of making a means visible as such« (*Il gesto è l'esibizione di una medialità, il render visible un mezzo come tale*). Agamben: Mezzi senza fine, p. 52. The problem is that the body is not erased by the gesture, but amended to it and inextricable from it. Yet, the body cannot be reduced to the gesture or a means, since it can also be immobile even before its complete demise.

524 Mauss: Les techniques du corps, p. 278.

allows for more complex human relations to even take place. These inter-human ties would certainly be the products of social acts that bring people together, further organizing their time and change of location. For example, if walking down the street requires (greater than normal) distance between bodies, if touching or handshakes are discouraged, or conversation must be held at a »controlled physical proximity« – the production of social relations will be disturbed. The order of various gestures will thus alter the efficiency of social acts and their power.

Inner Gesture, Pressure, and Expression

»Waiting«, »listening«, and »silence« (a kind of manifestation of the first two, which also usually follows them) are three different operations that refer to the »interior«, the »inner«. Can the »inner« be given order? What would that mean? It can be said that the function of the gesture in Wittgenstein – both architect and philosopher – serves to organize the great confusion in the »inner«?[525] Thus, waiting for the bus or for a friend to arrive at the cinema in time, or perhaps waiting for urgently-needed help to arrive, could all be termed negative actions. If I utter »hello« to a newsagent (expecting a response) but am greeted only with »silence«, is this a negative social act? Is silence not a constitutive part of every social act, and is the exchange of such negative acts not the condition of the social act's efficiency? In preparatory notes for two paragraphs (671 and 672) of *Philosophical Investigations*, Wittgenstein introduces and problematizes the »inner gesture«:

> How can the inner gesture belong to the sentence? to the language game? It ›accompanies it‹ not in the sense in which a gesture accompanies it; it is simply no gesture. A receptive attitude (listening e. g.) to be sure can be a gesture and function as a pointing, but the sensory impression (hearing e. g.) that we get by means of it does not correspond to the object which was pointed to. By the gesture of listening I do not point to what one calls ›my auditory impression‹.[526]

[525] In a wealth of places across myriad fragments, Wittgenstein deploys a dizzying array of variations that refer to the inner or the »concept of the ›inner‹«, as he calls it at one point: »inner eye«, »inner move«, »inner object«, »inner seeing«, or inner evidence, voice, life, picture, experience, life, process, etc.

[526] Cf. Hark: Beyond the Inner and the Outer, p. 37. Paragraphs 671 and 672 are as follows: 671. »And what do I point to by the inner activity of listening? To the sound that comes to my ears, and to the silence when I hear *nothing*? Listening as it were *looks for* an auditory impression and hence can't point to it, but only to the *place* where it is looking for it.« 672. If a receptive attitude is called a kind of »pointing« to something – then that something is not the sensation which we get by means of it. Cf. Wittgenstein: Philosophical Investigations, p. 169.

Let us put aside the numerous dilemmas regarding meaning and logical form of gestures, which are ever on Wittgenstein's mind and ultimately animate this fragment too.[527] Even though there seems to be no gesture when listening since nothing is performed publicly, undoubtedly present is the act of listening or a motion with intent or an action connected to the will of the one listening.[528] A receptive attitude (*»rezeptive Einstellung«* in German) or an »attitude of vigilant expectation« is stripped of an object and in that sense appears lacking. It leaves no trace and therefore appears as no gesture at all. However, were we to, entirely arbitrarily, adopt a never fully elaborated idea by Husserl, that there is such a thing as empty intention or intention whose object is not present but might appear in, say, the future, it would be possible to develop the »realization« of careful listening in what has yet to be heard (which, unless it were »allowed« to be heard, would not even appear). It seems that an entirely incomplete social gesture can still be designated as an inner gesture precisely because it gives the location of appearance of a public gesture or act, which has the form of appearance and can be heard or granted. If my careful observation is grounded in the expectation that someone will emerge from a nearby building, such action is not simply without gestural force; although, of course, the gesture will be a failure if no one appears.

The thematization of the »inner« and the topic of the uncertain interior gesture leads us into several topics the architect and philosopher Wittgenstein is continuously attempting to develop. Two remain mere hints: the connection of expression and gesture (the theory of pressure is understood to belong to protocols of the gestural because pressure is achieved by way of gesture to arrive at expression or new gesture); and the idea of translation of words into gestures and vice versa.[529] The third topic has, due to the abundance of fragments in which it is found, become very important for architects, since the gesture is determined in different ways that are supposed to explain Wittgenstein's statement that architecture (real or good architecture) is a gesture.[530] In defining architecture as gesture, Wittgenstein notes that the purposive motion of the human body is not a gesture, nor is

527 The anecdote about a Neapolitan gesture Wittgenstein discusses with Pierro Sraffa, which was written about by Norman Malcolm and Amartya Sen, recalls vividly Napoli as the birthplace of the gesture's thematization. I mean Andrea de Jorio's 1832 book, *La mimica degli antichi investigata nel gestire napoletano*, only recently translated into English.

528 »Pointing« is probably not the happiest translation of the German *Hinweisen*, but does also cover, apart from the hand gesture indicating direction, the masonry act of laying brick and mortar.

529 »How curious: we should like to explain our understanding of gesture by means of a translation into words, and the understanding of words by translating them into a gesture. (Thus we are tossed to and for when we find out where understanding properly resides.) And we really shall be explaining words by a gesture, and a gesture by words.« Wittgenstein: Zettel, § 227.

530 »Architecture is a gesture. Not every purposive movement of the human body is a gesture. Just as little as every functional building is architecture.« Wittgenstein: Culture and Value, p. 42. The gesture and architecture in Wittgenstein are scattered across many texts. Daniele Pisani wrote a book that remains the best systematic overview of this problem. Cf. Pisani: L'architettura è un gesto.

any constructed edifice executed through appropriate purpose or intention. There are five characteristics of the gesture, making a gesture a gesture.

First, a gesture is a miracle, something miraculous that above all interrupts or disrupts the routine.[531] A divine gesture, according to Wittgenstein, can be called a miracle. An architectural gesture, if it is to be one, should have a miraculous quality. Second, a gesture is an event. For something to happen, it must of necessity be sudden, significantly pleasurable or rather unpleasant – it forces us to cease, stop, take a stand towards what has befallen or overcome us, determining at once what has appeared and taken place. For something to be a gesture, or for an event to be an event, it must excite and provoke self-thematization of those who perceive and accept it. Third, the gestural is not sudden or original or auto-mobile (automatic) production. »You design a door and look at it and say: ›Higher, higher, higher (...) oh, all right‹. (Gesture). What is this? Is it an expression of content?«[532] Wittgenstein is thus using the word gesture for a set of operations or work adjusting and amending the visible to the invisible, proportion with measure, leading to an expression of pleasure or satisfaction. For a »gesture« to take place, there must be shifting and amending. Fourth, a gesture is architectural and marks good architecture if the architect has managed to express a thought or emotion well (»Remember the impression made by good architecture, that it expresses a thought. One would like to respond to it too with a gesture«).[533] A gesture is to be found in the interval between thought and expression; the expression, in turn, is adequate if and only if the gesture is correct and fitting. The fifth characteristic of the gesture assumes that what is »gestural« cannot be recognized through rules. If we lack the rules and means with which to grasp the observed or anticipated expression filled with soulfulness (*der seelenvolle Ausdruck*) – we are before or in the presence of a gesture.[534]

531 »A miracle is, as it were, a gesture which God makes. (...) A so-called »miracle must be (...) as it were sacred gesture.« Wittgenstein, *MS* 131 221: 08.09.1946.

532 Wittgenstein: Lectures and Conversations on Aesthetics, Psychology and Religious Beliefs, p. 13.

533 Wittgenstein: Culture and Value, p. 26.

534 *»Der seelenvolle Ausdruck in der Musik. Er ist nicht nach Graden der Stärke und des Tempos zu beschreiben. Sowenig wie der seelenvolle Gesichtsausdruck durch räumliche Masse.«* Wittgenstein: *MS* 138: 29a.

The Social Gesture

What then is the relation between acts and gestures, and is it possible to determine a stable conceptual distance (or proximity) of these two crucial protocols in the construction of a group of people working together? Only the distinction between *agere* and *gerere* could indicate that gesture reorganizes space and time,[535] amending both; while the function of acts is to hold and maintain what they encounter in space and time, when bodies are already distributed and fixed. Still, what is it that changes? Or how does the gesture (as a kind of act) prepare a future exchange of acts and social acts?

In an old text (from 1976) about Cy Twombly, Roland Barthes compares gesture and action: »What is a gesture? Something like the surplus of an action. The action is transitive, it seeks only to provoke an object, a result; the gesture is the indeterminate and inexhaustible total of reasons, pulsions, indolences which surround the action with an *atmosphere* (in the astronomical sense of the word).«[536]

Actions or acts imply communication between actors, while the object of the gesture is actually the future or the project (the object that has yet to be constructed), or even the preliminary, nearly mechanical construction of social reality.[537] What is the meaning of this pseudo-Searlean phrase pre-construction of social reality? It would probably be best to recall how at the dawn of the twentieth century, Bergson twice terms laughter a »social gesture« whose function is to maintain the reciprocity of the basic activities of society (or the »*corps social*«).[538] Even better, »the attitudes, gestures and movements of the human body are laughable in exact proportion as the body reminds us of a mere machine«.[539] Here is Bergson's contribution to the thematization of the gesture, still very relevant today:

> Instead of concentrating our attention on actions, comedy directs it rather to gestures. By gestures we here mean the attitudes, the movements and even the language by which a mental state expresses itself outwardly without any aim or profit, from no other cause than a kind of inner itching. Gesture, thus defined, is profoundly different from action. Action is intentional or, at any rate, conscious; gesture slips out unawares, it is automatic. In action, the entire person is engaged; in gesture, an isolated part of the person is expressed,

535 Cf. Lyotard: Gesture and Commentary, p. 40.

536 Barthes: Cy Twombly, p. 160.

537 »Under the term *gestus* we need to understand a group of gestures, facial play and (more often) statements made by one or several people to one or several others. A person selling fish shows, among other things, the *gestus* of selling. A man drawing up his will, a woman who seduces a man, a policeman who beats up a man, a man who gives his wages to ten others – there we always find a social *gestus* (*sozialer Gestus*). Following this definition the prayer a man offers up to God only becomes a *gestus* if the man prays while thinking of other people or in a context that includes relations of men to men (the king's prayer, Hamlet).« Cf. Hecht (ed.): Brechts Theorie des Theaters, p. 347.

538 Bergson: Le rire, pp. 20, 89; *Laughter*, pp. 20, 87.

539 Ibid., p. 30 (transl. p. 29).

unknown to, or at least apart from, the whole of the personality. Lastly – and here is the essential point – action is in exact proportion to the feeling that inspires it: the one gradually passes into the other, so that we may allow our sympathy or our aversion to glide along the line running from feeling to action and become increasingly interested. About gesture, however, there is something explosive, which awakes our sensibility when on the point of being lulled to sleep and, by thus rousing us up, prevents our taking matters seriously. Thus, as soon as our attention is fixed on gesture and not on action, we are in the realm of comedy.[540]

Bergson does not systematically differentiate action from act, but it does not crucially change his argument. Clearly gestures and acts are coordinated and complement one another, rather than exclude or alternate in function. Still, certain actions, such as laughter or comedy, as a repertoire of spontaneous gestures and gesticulations, outside any kind of normative framework, mobilize different groups of people. It seems possible to me to find many such actions that improve the social capacity of common life.

540 Ibid., pp. 146–147 (transl. pp. 143–144).

2 Social Acts, Negative Social Acts, Negative and A-Social Actions

Colloquially we would say that violent acts are those that exclude and impede common living. Be that as it may, violence is present in common living or in ›public space‹, and my question is how is it present, how does it manifest, and how can it be controlled or diminished? What is its origin? Is negation the origin of violence? On the other hand, although violence is present, strong connections, social connections among those living, certainly minimize violence. In a word, there is always an excess of violence because someone is missing, some new entity, some third (who is not present), who should be included and invited, and because there is insufficient common living or social acts. Let me bring up an institution of Roman Law, often mentioned in daily life and an important part of common living and acting: provocation.

What does Horatius mean when he says, according to Livy, »I challenge.[541] And the challenge was investigated by the people« (*Provoco. Ita provocatione certatum ad populum est*)[542]? *Ius provocatio* is a *provocatio* with the *ius* added (pressed or added). We could translate this phrase as law named or called as a challenge. *Ius provocationis* is the right to challenge. Meaning that this is a right confirmed or conducted through a call or challenge. The right of a Roman citizen to address the people or call to the people for help, thus opposing the decision of the magistrate or judge (above all when concerning violence, torture, death or high treason[543]), refers to two laws: »Lex Valeria« from 300 BCE (passed by the consul Marcus Valerius) and »Lex Sempronia« from 123 BCE. There are three

541 What does Đoković (or Federer or Nadal) mean when he utters the word ›challenge‹, calling on that institute?

542 Horatius is found guilty of treason, and one of the two judges exclaims: »*Publius Horati*, I find you guilty of treason (*tibi perduellionem iudico*). Go, lictor, bind his hands« (*I, lictor, colliga manus*). Livy tells us that the lictor approaches him and even manages to wrap the cord around his hands, when Horatius, acting upon advice of the king Tullus Hostilius, mild mannered reader of laws (*clemente legis interprete*), says: *Provoco. Ita provocatione certatum ad populum est.* The people are then convinced by Horatius' and his sister's father's long and moving speech. His tears make the people soften the heavy punishment and Horatius' life is spared. The Latin call ›*appello*‹ belongs to later times and refers to the institution *appellatio*. It designates an appeal against a lower level judgment and a call for the decision to be considered at a higher level. P. Bojanić, *Provocatio*, p. 23 ff.

543 Elsewhere, Livy says: »if and when the accused challenges against the *duoviri*, he *gains* a provocation [a debate before the people]« (S*i a duoviris provocarit, provocatione certato*). The *provoco* is in the present tense, ensuring performativity, and then ›fulfilling‹ the provocative action. There can be neither provocation nor the performative in the past tense. For this reason, the translation of this word requires one pronoun at the beginning and one at the end: *I* provoke (call to/challenge) *thou, you, them* (those not present). Ibid., p. 22.

further, unofficial, laws that implicitly contain one of the versions of *provocatio ad populum*: »Lex Valeria« from 509 BCE, »Lex Publicola«, the law adopted after the plebeian rebellion from 493 (or 473) and »Lex Duilia de provocatione« from 449 CE. The last three (I would call them pseudo-laws) are all mentioned by Livy in his history. I would leave aside here the consideration of the (perhaps even crucial) fact that the institution of *provocatio* practically vanishes with the fall of the Roman Republic:

a. The exclamation *PROVOCO* is addressed to the people who are supposed to come out, gather, and appear in order to assist in the reinvestigation and reconsideration of the verdict. The exclamation is directed at all those who are not there, who are not present at the place of dispute (conflict) and arrest.
b. The exclamation *PROVOCO* is addressed to the magistrate (that is, the »adversary«) as a challenge to a new match that should be played in an entirely new setting (before the people), because the magistrate has a legal duty (or an order from the sovereign) to indulge the desire of the accused if the accused expresses it publicly and out loud.

»Provoco« – to call, challenge, invoke a third entity (using the vocative case) is a good example of a social act *par excellence*. Here are some reasons for this, and some characteristics of a social act as an act of provocation. Certainly *»provoco«* and the institute *»ius provocatio«* are directly tied to what we today designate as »provocative«. If a person produces or issues what we call a »provocation« or a »provocative act«, their intention is to gather those not present or to make their call reach those still not there. This call, voice, exclamation to others (to some third) is the basic characteristic of a social act. When Horatius challenges with *»provoco!«*, aside from a social act, a performative act has taken place (with which Horatius triggers a public institute), because the police that come to arrest and beat him, is obligated to stop (to stop the violence and introduce an inquiry, discussion and therefore more justice), just as those who hear Horatius' call have an obligation to answer and approach him.

Since this law lasted a relatively brief time in the Roman Republic (some think it was never even established), it is clear that if in a different time someone cried and implored, nothing out of the ordinary would happen as there was no legal obligation. It is similar with the performative statement »I do« (most often an answer to the question posed to partners during a wedding ceremony), given its performative strength by the law.[544] However, a call, such as a scream or howl of

544 An alternative to law giving performative power to a social act, it is possible to imagine plethora social acts in a public space that simultaneously and often at once go into effect and imply an obligation. If partners (one or more) promise one to another while also, let us say, looking at the starry night, that they will be faithful to one another and that they will struggle for each other until the end, then their oath, their promise, is, above all because it is collective, a set of performative

a migrant resisting arrest (because, for example, his freedom of movement is being taken away) or else, a declaration of love and the »I do« with which we confirm living with someone having lunch – mobilizes and draws people towards each other (»the public« as a democratic institution is an example of a remnant of the institute »*ius provocatio*«). These are all social acts, just like ›a promise‹, ›an order‹, ›a question‹, or ›a request‹. They all have as their goal the bringing closer of the members of a group, they are all direct and directed *ad hominem* (another, always provoking another – a question is a provocation, just as an order or promise can be a burden to both sides), and they are all, in one way or another, ›violent‹ or ›disturbing‹ (*dérangeant*, as there is force in calling for help, and an awful inconvenience in a plea, request, promise).

Let us now imagine that Horatius is mute (unable to speak) or that he simply does not wish to call to others out of shame of his own mistake, or else because he wishes to suffer his own, entirely unjust, punishment in solitude, suffer arrest all alone – what would such acts be? What is Horatius doing when he does nothing? Can we call the intentional absence of doing anything a ›negative act‹?[545] Or conversely, is the action of the police officer or executor (*lictor*) negative? Is their act precisely a social act that rejoins and returns to the community one accused of treason? Is a thrashing or resistance to thrashing negative or not? Can we say at all that thrashing denies or rejects something (*rejicere* means to »throw back«)? This very simple example witnessed by Livy (the arrest of Horatius, probably made famous by Corneille and others), brings us to negative social acts or non-social acts, and my fundamental question of the origin and position, significance and justification of violence (or a certain kind of violence) in public space or when living together. Why violence when living together? And before I attempt to briefly explain the difference between social acts and negative social acts, it would be good to complicate Horatius' position (as the one suffering violence) a little further. Is it possible to imagine a situation in which Horatius does not call for help because

acts or »group speech acts«. These social acts are not only social acts but also performative. Not only that, but the number of these acts and the various intentional rituals will result in the formation of another group, which, depending on the content of its acts, has its identity and exists temporarily (in time). Such an idea could immediately bring into play a forgotten text by Justin Hughes, »Group Speech Acts«. Let us imagine now that the content of these group oaths is quite odd. The partners, or perhaps the members of this group, have vowed to meticulously destroy all persons in white shirts. Are these social acts still only social or is there something that could define them as negative social acts or as »real negative facts« (a phrase from Gilbert Ryle, p. 80). Mabbott / Ryle / Price: Symposium: Negation, pp. 67–111. Ryle insists that negative facts are always »facts about« and never »facts of« (p. 96), and thus it would be impossible to connect »negation in terms of our acts of excluding, rejecting or eliminating«, which Mabbott constantly does (p. 81).

545 If Horatius does not do anything (intentionally does nothing), such as not calling for help or crying out, or not performing some action X (not-do X), then this is a negative act. Bruce Vermazen explicitly shows this in a text that attempts to complement Davidson's theory of actions and events. Vermazen: Negative Acts, pp. 93–104. Davidson's answer is in the same volume, pp. 217–221.

there is no one in the vicinity, meaning that no one can hear him? If we establish that this position is impossible, that is, that violence is only possible where people live together and where by definition they can help each other (and interrupt, delay, diminish violence), we encounter a new problem that refers to violence in the home (violence completely hidden from the public) or the sovereignty of the house as such (as right to privacy of the home and the right for the home to be excluded and protected from public space, the right to common living within a home where a third or the public is excluded). We have a situation where it is very difficult to reconstruct the connection or the opposition of common living in houses and apartments to living in a city, in public.

A long time before Adolf Reinach[546] (but note that already Aristotle recognized that »besides the kind of speech called a proposition, which is always either true or false, there are other kinds which are neither true or false, such as a prayer or a wish«[547]), in *Essays on the Active Powers of the Human Mind*, Thomas Reid writes:

> Between the operations of the mind, which, for want of a proper name, I have called solitary, and those I have called social, there is this very remarkable distinction, that, in the solitary, the expression of them by words, or any other sensible sign, is accidental. They may exist, and be complete, without being expressed, without being to any other person. But, in the social operations, the expression is essential. They cannot exist without being expressed by words or signs, and known to the other party.[548]

»Solitary operations« would then be a kind of asocial act that is no act at all. Such non-acts are not necessarily negative, although they *de facto* negate social acts and could therefore be called negative social acts. It seems that such ›acts‹ (»solitary operations«) do not necessarily exclude and are not in disjunction or collision with social acts. This is particularly important for me, because I am interested in the way in which asocial ›acts‹ (or negative acts) could remain to some extent an integral part of institutions and public space. I differentiate such deformed ›acting‹ and in general, the ›institute‹ of the neutral or asocial actors (those who *de facto* do nothing), from some other forms of (in)action, only seemingly opposed to protocols of institutionalization.

546 Lest we forget, Reinach is entirely convinced that he alone introduced a completely new concept to which nothing else should be ascribed, for that would be wrong.

547 Reid: Brief Account of Aristotle's Logic, p. 692. There is one other use of »social acts« that appeared after both Reid and Reinach. In *The Philosophy of the Present*, G. H. Mead tells us: »A social act may be defined as one in which the occasion of stimulus which sets free an impulse is found in the character or conduct of a living form that belongs to the proper environment of the living form whose impulse it is. I wish, however, to restrict the social act to the class of acts which involve the cooperation of more than one individual, and whose object as defined by the act, in the sense of Bergson, is a social object.« (p. 180). Schuhmann / Smith: Elements of Speech Act Theory in the Work of Thomas Reid, pp. 47–66.

548 Reid: Essays on the Active Powers of the Human Mind, p. 438.

I would like to briefly describe negative social acts and affirm their difference from both »negation« and »social acts.« Following this, I would also like to explain the importance of these acts for acting together and for group agency. My intention above all is to take the designation *»nichtsoziale Akte«* (Negative Social Acts or Non-Social Acts), which Adolf Reinach mentions but does not thematize, in his brief 1911 text, »Nichtsoziale und soziale Akte«, and compare this phrase to Gilbert Ryle's distinction between »negative ›actions‹« and »nullifying acts«. My claim is that there are acts or actions that are negative and are at the same time social because practiced repeatedly by multiple actors, thus confirming or establishing the identity of a group (likely a temporary identity, that is, a group of temporary duration), but foremost in competition and through exclusion, in one way or another, of other groups.

It is not straightforward to classify the differences, first between facts and acts, and then between brute facts (Anscombe) and social facts (Gilbert) (and there are also *subjective facts*, Crane), that is, between negative facts and acts (negative legal acts, Ruiter), and negation.[549]

First, I am interested in whether there are certain acts, which in recurring constitute identity (even if temporary) of a group to such an extent that we could say that the group's existence is due to them, that they make the group itself exist (temporarily). Let us say a group of children is collecting money in public, across various towns of a region, all in a given day (for example, a big Red Cross charity drive for the benefit of developmentally challenged children).[550] If children in town A collect more money than children in town B, we could say that there is a group of kids in town B (members of this group) who are responsible for the group collecting less money than the town A group. Naturally, some of the members of group B are aware right away why there is less money (which is hearsay and rumor at first, but soon, a few of the boys and girls publicly admit as much to the rest of the group): a few of the collection purses have been partially picked and not all the collected money has been turned in at the end of the day, leaving the total short, compared to the town A group. Instead of the common purse, part of the money from town B ends up in the particular pockets of different boys and girls who acted with all the children on that day.

The example is at once good and bad. It gives me pleasure to make the main actors of this construction those who are not at all subjects (not individuals, group

549 Negative acts, in the broadest sense, are unequivocally those acts or actions committed by one (an individual or group) intending to negate, deny, erase or abolish something; or else, they are acts that tolerate or allow the existence of something negative. Such acts are not necessarily linguistic (or necessarily pejorative), but themselves represent gestures (certainly gestures of force, aggression, violence) in the broadest sense of the term.

550 My Red Cross example is not an allusion to the Red Cross example that Kurt Lewin uses in his famous text »Group Decision and Social Change«, p. 342.

or collective) – children. Children are, of course, not magically innocent, and they, of course, steal. As great consumers, they are probably the main engine of liquidity of capital and thus stability to capitalism as such. (By capitalism here I mean inequality, that is, the production of inequality.) This example is bad because this scene, this theatrical moment, with a whole host of anonymous actors (those who collect money and those donating it), is *a priori* great social theater in which money as a social factor *par excellence* connects all. The goal of money collecting is to strengthen social integration by helping those children who are unable to be part of the group, who are in a state of precarity.

On the other hand, the example is good because we can assume several other kinds of act (and myriad groups):[551] there are children who refused to participate in this gesture of good will because they actively train football and their team is playing the team from town A on that day. Or else some children are helping their parents pick apples, some children are lazy, or cannot stand other children, or are simply more interested in video games. Further, one of the boys spent all the money he took from his collection purse to buy chewing gum for the entire group (meaning that the children were asking for donations while chewing stolen gum). One girl skimmed her collection purse, abandoned the charity drive and went to the movies. Still another girl who took money from the purse, took it home and turned it over to her parents and sister who suffers from polio.

I am interested in how we can differentiate and classify all of these, shall we call them, corruptive or pernicious (bad, malevolent, deleterious) acts, which are either a constitutive part of the functioning of a group and any given ›acting together‹, or else are ›in the vicinity‹, are ›near‹, form part of the context (space and time) of acting together. Further, I am interested in differentiating (although certainly not exhaustively) whether such actions or acts are negative, or whether they are simultaneously negative and social acts. Furthermore, I am interested in whether negative actions are actions at all. Finally, my main preliminary aim is to recognize which social acts are the unconditional conditions of the existence of a social group and its identity.

To begin with, recall the three grand and perhaps most important visual fantasies of groups in the history of the West: one of the versions of the motif of the Tower of Babel, a drawing of Hobbes' Leviathan, and Bruegel the Elder's 1560 »Children's Games.« It seems to me that any other image we might imagine – the day of prayer at Mecca, cars on a bridge, the supporters of Bayern München on the stadium terrace, or else the student strike at the University of Belgrade, ISIS fighters in the back of a truck somewhere in Syria, etc. – any of these would be but

551 Actors or members are at once temporary »members« or »actors« of several more or less fully constituted and stable groups. Cf. Friedman: The Social Responsibility of Business is to Increase its Profits.

a variation of one of the three mentioned constructions of the identity of the group. I ought to explain that the construction of identity (what does it mean to name ›us‹, or belong to ›us‹, or how ought we utter or write ›we are‹, ›let us‹?). Further, what is a group or ›social group‹? (It is a question of number, the existence necessarily of two or more than two persons or things, mutually connected while in the same place. The origin of the word group is Italo-German: *gruppo* or *groppo* is a knot (a set, a clutch), while *kruppa* in Old Germanic is a fully formed whole, where the idea of circle is important, the form being closed and fully framed. I also have to re-evaluate the phrase »*Nichtsoziale Akte*« (the English non-social or anti-social acts does not quite capture the meaning) and show that negative acts are directly connected to the group, or better still, the identity of a group.

Here are a few difficulties right away. The first of such difficulties could be entirely trivial, but it would appear that in the course of building an argument about the difference in conduct between a group and a collection of individuals, it turns out that the shift from singular to plural (the transformation of a large and total group into multiple groups) implies a confrontation and presence of negative acts. All three (institutional) fictions about the group simultaneously depict *universitas* (the word Cicero uses to translate the Greek word ›all‹, ›whole‹, *to pan*), a total and a universally all-encompassing group (Babylon, Leviathan-sovereign and this city, an assortment of children's games, filled with children playing). They also immediately imply the existence of other towers, other sovereigns and cities. If something is *universitas* then it is at once a representation of the whole universe and all of human kind (we are all at once in the body of the Leviathan, because the sovereign is by definition singular) – *universitas* means that a collective activity and the common goal transform a plurality of elements into an organized collective – and alternately, I repeat, *universitas* or an organized group (*corpus*, *societas*, *collegium* are three forms of group we find in Roman law) does not preclude the existence of other groups, absent and often in opposition.[552] On the contrary.

The second difficulty is the designation »*Nichtsoziale Akte*«. Reinach's text has never been translated into English, despite the intention of Karl Schumann and Barry Smith to, by publishing his collected works in 1989, present Reinach (along with the rest of Austrian philosophy) as the forerunner and actual source of the theory of language games and subsequent distinction by Austin between performatives and constatives. If »social relations are constituted by way of social acts« (*Soziale Verhältnisse konstituieren sich durch soziale Akte*), negative acts would be those acts that break the knot (knots) or connections between the elements (of the group or groups). It goes without saying that these are violent acts,

552 Cf. Schnorr von Carolsfeld, Geschichte der juristischen Person; Michaud-Quantin: Universitas.

but also private acts, such as hatred.[553] On the contrary, a lie could potentially be a social act (although »private lies« could be non-social, a private lie would be nonsense).[554] For example, if the mayor of a city constantly displays to his constituents what their city will soon look like, and puts up a bunch of billboards to that end, the citizens' trust could be increased for the next elections, and the connection between citizens enriched by the idea of common belonging to said future city. Further, what status would we give to telepathic or empathic acts? Are they acts at all? Is reciprocity another feature of the social act, giving mutual hatred or mutual envy a place in the space of social relations?

The third difficulty concerns the destruction and perishing of a group, which is part of the aforementioned visual strategies. The Tower collapses, the sovereign is dismembered, and the city in which most are playing alone is in jeopardy and would be difficult to defend. Apart from the basic question about the transience of the group, and the »contingent identity« of a group (lest we forget the very beginning of Saul Kripke's text »Identity and Necessity«: »how are contingent identity statements possible?«, and similar questions that can be found in Derek Parfit), the problem of necessity remains: each group must be swiftly dismantled and transformed into a different form or construction. My premise is that if negative acts are necessary for the existence of a group (or group identity), or if they are impossible to exclude, making the group unjust by definition, then the duration of a group is measured, or can only be understood through negative acts. It seems that at this point, I truly cannot establish a clear connection between the identity of a group, its duration and »*Nichtsoziale Akte*« (or non-grouping acts), but I am certainly interested in what it is that devastates a group that also makes it possible in the first place.

But how a group executes such actions (not how they are done by the individuals, but individuals together with other individuals, individuals that possess a collective identity)? »Collective individual« (*individu collectif*) is a term by Vincent Descombes from 1992, with which he tries to thematize the possibility that what is individual is also at once collective. I would like to answer the question

553 »This leads us into an entirely new class of acts which are particularly important for civil law. They have a social aspect (*soziales Moment*) and a direction (*Richtung*) towards another subject. This direction is not intentionality in relation to some subject. (...) These acts here ought to be differentiated from hatred, envy or the like. They have a direction toward someone through something (*Sie haben eine Richtung an jemanden über etwas*). Envy is not spoken to another subject, does not refer to the other subject. The question, in contrast, is essentially directed at another, penetrates into that other (*eindringen in ihn*), calling him to reveal himself.« Reinach: Nichtsoziale und soziale Akte, p. 356. These are the preparatory notes and outline of paragraph 3, »Die soziale Akte,« of the book, published two years later, *The Apriori Foundations of the Civil Law* (»Apriorische Rechtslehre«), pp. 158–170.

554 Charles Travis is preparing a text entitled »Private Lies,« although I do not know what will come of it. Is a private lie the one that is uttered to someone close (wife, brother, parent, child, psychoanalyst, confessor), but not in the family circle (the family being the primary group)?

whether such acts impact all the members or parts of a group, and whether they impact another group. Does the survival of a group require breaking the rules and a lack of morality (the subsistence or survival of a group could be defined as a victory – calling into question that old adage that the ›good guys cannot win‹, in war or any other competition)? And does the existence of a group (the ›We‹ of the institution, being part of the public space) necessarily contain a negative part, always contaminated and ›outside the law‹? One of the most important assumptions of inhumanity or immorality of a group ought to refer to its identity (I am operating on the premise that one of the main criteria of identity is naming, giving a designation). I would like to defend the thesis that the construction of identity or the name of a group is the condition or the beginning of the process of opposing another group or another identity. Such a group or such groups can then issue negative acts with the goal of exclusion, not to mention destruction of the other group or parts of it.[555] In the original scenes of the first institutional action within the Babylonian corporation, to which we must always return, it seems that the constitution of the identity of a group (the name that connects and binds the group together) is directly connected with its future dissolution.

Once again, how can we determine negative social acts as precisely as possible?[556] Are they acts that negate social acts – in which case they are not ordinary negative acts, but are negative and at the same time social acts – or are they all acts that are simply not social. When Reinach defines hatred or envy, he says:

They are directed towards someone through something (*Sie haben eine Richtung an jemanden* über *etwas*). Envy (*Neid*) is not spoken to the other subject, does not refer to (*wendet sich nicht*) the other subject. The question, in contrast, is essentially directed at another, penetrates into that other (*eindringen in ihn*), calling him to reveal himself (*kundgeben*).[557]

But what about self-hatred? What is the status of acts that manifest (publicly, before others) hatred for oneself? If social acts (*soziale Akte*) are spontaneous acts (*spontane Akte*) (something Reinach is attempting to explain in detail), if they

555 Sometimes parts of a group perform negative social acts or asocial acts in the name of the group itself or the survival of the group itself. For example, it is possible for multiple members of a given group to immorally or negatively act, in order to, paradoxically, ensure the morality of a group as such, or to make the group morally better and make its actions more transparent. In a text which he spent years revising, Scanlon thematizes the difference between the morality of the individual and the morality of the group or the institution. Scanlon, Individual Morality and the Morality of Institutions, pp. 3–19.

556 In »Negative ›Actions‹«, Gilbert Ryle call these acts as acts into question (»if they *are* acts«). Paolo Virno, in *Saggio sulla negazione* follows Ryle's determination with the phrase *azioni negative* (hesitation, delay, secrecy, tolerance, expectation, abstinence, askesis, holding back, etc.). Ryle differentiates these negative ›acts‹ from ›nullifying acts‹ such as obstructing, resisting, hindering, refusing, demurring, dissuading, repudiating, rescinding, canceling, forbidding, hiding, disguising, erasing, purging, scrubbing, correcting, recanting, unfastening etc. (p. 81).

557 Reinach: Nichtsoziale und soziale Akte, p. 357.

manifest exclusively through a physical medium (*durch Physisches hindurch*), if an act is not »only related to another subject, it also addresses the other« (*er hat nicht nur eine notwendige Beziehung auf ein fremdes Subjekt, sondern er wendet sich auch an es*), if the act penetrates into the other (*er dringt in den anderen ein*), if it is necessary that acts are in need of being understood and heard[558] – then negative acts are the exact opposite. However, it does not follow that hatred or envy have no social effect, that they do not produce certain social facts and that they do not bind the group while at the same time reconstructing the relations between its parts. Although it is possible to openly show hatred or envy, plainly express it, and address it to another, the role of envy or, for example, jealousy within a group could bring additional cohesion within members of a group. Reinach speaks implicitly about the group (when writing about the multitude of social acts or when attempting to explain the criminal law concept of complicity [*Mittäterschaft*]), as well as about acting together, about performing the act »together with the other« (*zusammen mit dem anderen*), and about a very distinctive kind of »togetherness« (*Zusammenhang*), but social acts themselves are never capable of achieving a consistency of common social action thus bringing about the identity of the group. What is »a very special ›togetherness‹ (*eine sehr eigenartigen »Zusammenhang«*)?

It should not be reduced to identity of content or of addressee (*Inhalts- und Adressatenidentität*), and even less to the deliberate simultaneous performance of the act; in these cases we would always have several distinct acts. We have rather to do here with the case where each of the persons performs the act »in union« (*im Verein*) with the others, where each knows of the participation of the others, lets the other participate, and participates himself: we have *one single* act (*einziger Akt*) which is performed by two or more persons together (*zusammen vollzogen wird*), one act with several subjects (*einen Akt mit mehreren Trägern*).[559]

But what is necessary in the first place for an act to be imputed to a group, and not to a multitude of subjects? Reinach foresees a very special unique act of a group as such. Remember that Reinach is here speaking of complicity of several actors who acted as a group and clearly inflicted damage to some other party. Are negative acts, in one way or another, as an addition to social acts, the unconditional conditions for the existence of a group agent? In other words, it would appear to

558 »*Wir bezeichnen die spontanen und vernehmungsbedurftigen Akte als soziale Akte.*« Reinach: Die Idee der apriorischen Rechtslehre, pp. 158–160.

559 »*Wir haben hier einen sehr eigenartigen ›Zusammenhang‹. Er darf nicht reduziert werden auf Inhalts und Adressatenidentität oder gar auf bewußte Gleichzeitigkeit des Vollzugs; in diesen Fällen hätten wir stets mehrere selbständige Akte. Hier aber haben wir den Fall. wo jeder der Adressanten den Akt ›im Verein‹ mit dem anderen vollzieht, wo er von der Teilnahme des anderen weiß, den anderen teilnehmen läßt und selber teilnimmt: wir haben einen einzigen Akt. der von zwei oder mehr Personen zusammen vollzogen wird, einen Akt mit mehreren Trägern.*« Ibid., p. 164.

be possible, in an organized or collective (social) way, while connected (*Zusammenhang*) and mutually bound, to execute negative social acts.

Still, Bruegel's canvas »Children's Games« is a little different to the other two images, and perhaps does not correspond to the idea of the group as much as the other two. What is the attention, focus, concentration, intention of the gaggle of children playing in a town (each on its own)? Or, what is the intention when each child in our previous hypothetical example collects contributions? Are they »separately tied«? Are they in a group? Does their collecting assume the existence of a group?

»We are looking at the Bruegel painting«

However, each one of us can not only say ›we are looking‹ or ›let us look‹ – Sartre thought that ›We‹ is constituted by collective attention, when we all look in the direction of a situation of excess; his example was of a road accident happening suddenly and drawing attention – but can also utter the words ›I am looking at the Bruegel painting‹. The significant difference between these two possibilities occurs if we ask who is excluded when uttering the statements ›I am looking‹/›we are looking‹: in the former, I exclude all who are not myself, whereas in the latter I am excluding only myself. In the sentence ›we are looking‹, the fact that I too am looking at the painting while uttering this is only implicitly taken into consideration. Regardless of the fact that within the confines of logical and grammatical modality, it is always an ›I‹, and that only an ›I‹ can utter the pronoun ›We‹, these kinds of assertions are completely lacking in performative power, and we could call them performative simulacra. Either way, although many are not even looking at the painting when I utter the statement ›We are looking at the painting‹, and although this ›We‹ is really a highly fantastical fiction, it seems that the power of this constative is far greater than, for example, the performative protocols of a group of soldiers who repeat out loud, all together, in the first person, the words to an oath, or a choir in which all sing and recite a single text.

What is it that Bruegel has done here? Bruegel placed before us a collection of all kinds of children's games he knew, many of which are known to us today. We find dozens of different games. Some are indeed collective, many more are individual games played by little painted people of differing or indeterminate gender. As you can see, all these games take place in a city, publicly, in a city square, in one place, at once, but they appear to be each onto themselves. Is this a group and is this ensemble of activities sufficient to recognize this as a group of children playing in this city? Does the content of the painting meet the sufficient conditions for these individuals to construct a collective (»*Wir-Identität*« or »*Wir-Ich*

Balance«)?[560] Can this situation be at all described by the sentence ›we are playing‹ or ›a group of children is playing‹,[561] if the majority of the children is having a terrific time individually? Can entertainment or play, collective or individual, at all refer to a group?

It seems that this situation is a really good example of how for the existence of a group, it is not at all decisive that each of the actors be entranced and entirely engrossed (in the game) while simultaneously still aware that the rest are also at the same time entirely absorbed (anesthetized) in playing, and that they all be aware, also simultaneously, that they are all playing together. The argument about the very complicated phrase »collective intentionality«[562] is today developed and elaborated through various examples (›walking together‹, praying together, collective cheering for Bayern München, soldiers marching in unison at a parade, the queue formed at the cinema box office, etc.), and it seems to be pulsating in this balancing and equilibration of the consciousness of all the individuals. If several persons conjure spirits together (*evocano spiriti riuniti*; »the mental state« of the group,[563] or masturbate or are enjoying sex) and if each individually is in a trance, and if they are all together entirely dedicated to a form of expectation (anticipation) – it would still be insufficient for the constitution of a group or a we (Elias also uses the terms *Wir-Gruppe* or *Wir-Gefühle*). Of course, despite looking like joint conjuring of spirits could be more efficient than doing so individually or that individual pleasure can be greater if the pleasure-deriving act is committed simultaneously with others or before others, it is quite clear that in either of

560 Elias: Die Gesellschaft der Individuums.

561 There is a difference between British and American English in the use of the word group. Namely, where British English would use the plural, e.g., Chelsea *are* currently the best team in the Premiership, or the BBC *are* being completely irresponsible in their reporting, American English would render this in the singular: this team *is* currently in terrific form, or Fox News *is* sensationalist. Thus, the phrase ›a group of children is playing‹ can also be rendered as ›a group of children are playing‹.

562 This phrase or term does not appear in Gerde Walther, but she is likely the creator of the problem and described it best: »Take, for instance, an old simpleminded peasant woman (*ungebildetes Bauernmütterschen*) who has never left her far flung village. She has heard that Germany is at war and that it must win, and she therefore knits socks for soldiers to contribute in *her own way* to »German victory.« This German victory is the intentional object that directs her intentional activity. On the other hand, take the German Emperor as the high commander of the imperial army and his activity directed at the victorious advent of German troops. For him too German victory is the motivating intentional object. Clearly, there is an unbridgeable gap between the idea of German victory held by the Emperor and his efforts for the cause, and those of the old peasant woman. Still, both the Emperor and the peasant woman are bound to the same object (German victory) and the activities motivated by this object, which despite all their differences, can be bound up in the same meaningfulness, i. e. the common activity (*Gesamthandeln*) equipped with a unique motivational construct, even if mediated by multiple elements.« Walther: Ein Beitrag zur Ontologie der sozialen Gemeinschaft, p. 27.

563 Cf. Tollefsen: Groups as Agents, in various places in the book, mostly in the Introduction and conclusion, pp. 137–138.

these cases there is no communal action of all or common benefit (excepting the potentially greater individual benefit).

Were we to now imagine an attack on Bruegel's city of games and play, the interruption of this children's play (or games), and imagine that the children are in peril; worried, they begin, together, to build stone walls around the city for protection from invasion or migrants (like the ones who, once upon a time, came and tried to start a big company in Babylon), the scene changes suddenly. If it is possible to separate and segregate the children from one another, then it is certainly possible to bring them back together, giving them an entirely new identity (children warriors and defenders of the city; children builders, managers, and renewers of a besieged city). It would seem that only »this special kind of bond« (*Zusammenhang*), closeness, common work, and implicity of the identity of city defenders, that is, the continuous danger that their unity will dissipate – only this ensures the possibility of negative, annihilating, perhaps even inhuman acts that the group might potentially perform together, simultaneously and as its main or incidental activity. Or *vice versa*: that the negative social act not present in Bruegel's painting (or only latently present as individual acts – which is insufficient), are proof that the group is still not constituted, but are also at the same time the condition that the group might exist.

In both cases, negative social acts decide on the identity of the group and strength of its ties, about the forms of its constitution; and also its demise. If, due to a general danger from migrants, mobilization occurs in the city of games and play, along with a general bond among players (members) – such as protests of those who oppose militarization or human rights violations or closing of borders, as well as a growing number of those indifferent about the destiny of the city – this will correspond to what we call negative social action.[564]

564 What is the connection between negative social acts and documents? To what extent is, for example, the history of human rights (assuming these are social acts) necessarily documentary (we brake human rights when we do not follow certain documents, or we break them because we are in fact acting in accordance with existing documents, which, we follow in turn because we have promised to do so)? Despite the innumerable pacts and international conventions established after World War II (the Universal Declaration of Human Rights was adopted in 1948, whereas the Convention on the Right of the Child was adopted in 1989), the slew of obligations to which states have agreed in the last few decades, the establishment of rights to secession or humanitarian intervention (it is possible today to intervene forcefully in order to protect the human rights of certain ethnic groups – paradoxically, it is possible to kill people in the name of a free life of other people, entirely in harmony with various protocols and pacts followed by »signatories«) – it is as if the classification of basic human rights and their universality are far from being constituted. Why is this so? For two reasons. The answer to the question, why do people have human rights and what are they, one of the correct answers could be that people actually have their rights or human rights because a multitude of states has agreed on the Universal Declaration. However, not all states have signed and agreed to the international conventions (immediately taking away from the universality of the Declaration, as well as from human rights, which thus become instantly subjective normative evaluations not establishing any universal obligation). Not only that, but the Declaration has created space for a differentiation

In terms of defending the institution of the city, such acts may sometimes be entirely negligible for the group that defends the city, or else they could be pacified and corrected, meaning that the city can be further institutionalized (an open city will certainly be the final consequence of the process of institutionalization). However, if we imagine that the city of games (just like the Babylonian corporation or the sovereign ›Leviathan-state‹ of Dubrovnik) was destroyed because the amount of negative social acts of this group, its brutality and inhumanity, was insufficient for its survival. This assumption can be reformulated in an even more precise and provocative way if two premises are respected: that in accordance with the attack on Bruegel's city of games and playing children, they are suddenly forced to indeed work and play together, to build defensive ramparts together, but then also kill together those trying to enter and occupy the city – that the institutionality and ›institutional amount‹ of an institution does not only depend on the cooperation of the actors (on social acts, work, technological invention, etc. that tie them all together), but also on non-social acts (exclusion of layabouts, migrants, anarchists, terrorists, and the destruction of another group or groups). A group is insufficiently institutionalized not only if it does not lead a defensive war, but also if it does not break the rules of defensive war and war in general, to lead a victorious war – thus surviving. The second premise calls into question the first premise and the general possibility for a group to simultaneously produce both social and non-social acts – to produce its own ontological stability, while at the same time destroying another group or the ›groupness‹ of a group.

between democratic and non-democratic states (Rawls, Christiano), or between more or less democratic states. And perhaps most importantly, the Declaration as such (as a document) establishes neither procedures nor bodies or institutions for the protection of human rights.

3 The Institution of Group(s) and Genocidal Acts

I will attempt to problematize a small theory of the constitution of a group through the simultaneous exclusion of some other group. Is it possible, then, to produce social and non-social acts at the same time? Or is it possible to construct a group that acts »genocidally«, meaning that it destroys another group or »the groupness« of a group (that which makes the group a group), and at the same time affirm its own unity and its ontological stability (I have used the word »institution« in the chapter title, since we are dealing with a group that is lasting and not temporary)? Finally, does this thematization of the group through inter-group antagonism have anything to do with Lemkin's word »genocide«, a completely new word, which came to stand for what was until then defined, for example, by the British Prime Minister Winston Churchill, as »*a crime without name*«,[565] or in international law as *scelus infandum*?

If the figure of ›deconstruction‹ has any meaning at all, and if the most significant strategies of deconstruction ought to be defended (pseudo-method or method which is not method), it seems that the great efforts of the jurist Raphael Lemkin[566] and everything that occurred around the »institute« of »genocide« or »the Convention on Genocide«,[567] in the last fifty years, would be the perfect example of the affirmation of deconstruction. Regardless of the terribly problematic use and conceptualization of this word, the various methodological difficulties and reductions (the »pushing« of genocide on occasion),[568] it seems to me that the future of the Convention is safe – meaning that its text will not be significantly

565 Cf. Kuper: Genocide, p. 12.

566 Upon emigrating to the US, Lemkin dedicated his life to lobbying for »genocide« to be acknowledged and accepted in various political circles and jurisprudence of various countries. For example, in an attempt to convince Ernest Gross, the American delegate to the Paris Assembly (ultimately held on 28 November 1948), that America accept the Convention, Lemkin writes: »Genocide has taken the lives of my dear ones; the fight against genocide takes my health. I am ready to give my life for this cause.« Cf. Cooper: Raphael Lemkin and the Struggle for the Genocide Convention, p. 169.

567 »Convention on the Prevention and Punishment of Genocide«, adopted December 9, 1948; entered into force January 12, 1951, 78 U. N. T. S. 277.

568 An author spoke about »genocidalism«, genocidal uses of the word »genocide«, the irresponsible and incorrect uses of this word for crimes that have nothing to do with the Convention. »The fact that genocide is a coined technical term implies that anyone using it must either use it to mean this technical concept or must explicitly supply an alternative definition. One cannot use the word »genocide« without supplying some definition or other, because one cannot rely, as one might with a word of ordinary language, on some common understanding that we all have of that word, whether or not we are able to define it.« Boghossian: The Concept of Genocide, p. 3.

modified, while the corrections will certainly be reconciled with the intentions and previous suggestions by Lemkin, on which the Convention's critics often insist. At the outset, I would like to put forward a double claim: (i) that the three big and probably most important projects of the thematization of genocide in the last ten years (I am thinking here of the work of William A. Schabas, Larry May, and Claudia Card) still draw their inspiration from Lemkin's endeavors seeking to reconcile the Convention with the terrible crimes that have occurred in the meantime (Rwanda, Yugoslavia),[569] and (ii) that the two most ambitious reconstructions announced, which are still in the process of being defined and crystallized, remain in the spirit of Lemkin's outlines and intentions.[570] It is interesting that all these projects, with the exception of Schabas' books and texts, reconstruct the concept of genocide exclusively through philosophical reflection,[571] insisting on the need for many more serious philosophical debates. Why? It seems to me that aside from the fact that genocide certainly presents a task for the philosopher (the philosopher who complements the jurist and judge, or historian) and a philosophical problem (and a »philosophical focus«, as well[572]), the various processes that took place, above all, at the International Criminal Tribunal for the Former Yugoslavia (ICTY), and the first convictions of genocide, the various media and political reductions and simplifications regarding these wars and crimes, could be particularly inspiring for philosophers.

I will attempt to briefly sketch[573] some of these complications (and there are many), and show or enumerate certain important philosophical critiques that

569 Yugoslavia was one of the first countries to ratify the Convention, as early as 1949, and incorporate it into its own legislature.

570 The first attempt refers to Chandran Kukathas' text »Genocide and Group Rights«, in which he insists that the definition of genocide present in the Convention is simultaneously too broad and too narrow. Kukathas thinks that the essence of genocide is not in the destruction of the group itself (he develops a difference between the collective and corporative concept of a group, and he insists that the introduction of the group into the Convention has pushed aside the importance of the crime against a population), but rather that the killing of a large number of individuals ought to be the main characteristic of genocide. Lemkin translates the word »genocide« from his book, *Axis Rule in Occupied Europe*, as *ludobojstwo* (*lude*, meaning people, and *zabojstwo* murder). This book was published in Polish at the same time it appeared in English in 1944. In contrast to this, Claudia Card tries to defend the importance of the group (along with the destruction of a group without killing) within the definition of genocide, citing various testimonies, which confirm that this was Lemkin's true intention. In the explication of genocide, thus, social death has the advantage over killing or killings.

571 Cf. Card: Confronting Evils.

572 Here I repeat and follow, along with Virginia Held, Annette Bayer's words, chairing the plenary meeting of »*The Eighty-Seventh Annual Eastern Division Meeting of the APA*« in Boston on 29 December 1990, in a text entitled »*A Naturalists View of Persons*:« »(…) when we are in any kind of war we are prepared to switch from individual to collective responsibility. (…) Our *philosophical focus ought* to be as much on collective as on individual responsibility, when we seek to understand ourselves as persons.« (*APA Proceedings*, vol. 65, n. 3, 6. Cf. Held: Group Responsibility for Ethnic Conflict, pp. 157–178.)

573 The ›presence of philosophy‹ or the ›presence‹ of complicated and heaped together arguments

could truly allow for a possibility to more easily tie the Convention with the criminals, but also, to ensure distance and prevent deformations to the Convention. The philosopher's engagement certainly has as its goal to change and restore norms, to make new norms and create and modify new concepts. However, it seems to me that the philosopher's task is also the protection from excess of theory (of philosophy), from fictitious consistency of theory and the violent deformation of facts or norms.

A crime without name. The importance of the new, so-called ›secular‹ thematization of evil (great or grandiose evil) and the construction of the theory of atrocities is an invaluable contribution of the philosopher Claudia Card, and has allowed for the possibility and necessity of the processing of great crimes.[574] Card follows Lemkin's perspective since she does not focus »on the group character of the perpetrators but the group character of the victims.«[575] The idea that a great crime can be recognized by the size of the harm (severe harm), which is then impossible to forgive (»intolerable harms produced by inexcusable wrongs«[576]), implies a standpoint from which genocide, as opposed to murder, cannot be justified.[577] But then, how is one to process and punish it? The sources of this difficulty can be explained by the fact that in the histories of crimes and punishments, no justification of great violence against a group, small or large, has ever been demanded, nor was this violence considered harm. Let me give you three examples: (i) the violence of the holy people against neighboring tribes and the destruction of all that breathes (Joshua 10:40: »Destroyed all that breathed, as the Lord God of Israel commanded«) can be renamed into ›holy total war‹ for living space and survival;[578] (ii) piracy was the only recognized Universal Criminal Jurisdiction crime, which allowed for a group (one certainly neither national, ethnic, racial or religious, even less so political or accidental) to be declared as enemy of humanity and be freely destroyed (institutions of excommunication, *herem* and *sacer*, are the threatening figures of pirates, it was possible to kill with impunity those who were declared *sacer*); and finally (iii), Kant's unjust enemy (*der ungerechte Feind*[579], of course, not only Kant's, since this construction can be found in Vattel

is easy to recognize by the way texts on genocide are put forward. Such books and texts are full of classifications, meta-language, hesitations and modifications. The positions of the authors writing about genocide are full of reservations, are constantly corrected or promise future corrections – in a word, these texts are never finished.

574 Cf. The difficulty in construction such a theory on evil is shown on the example of the endless insistence of Card that she is guided by a secular approach to the understanding of evil. Card: The Atrocity Paradigm; Card: Confronting Evils.

575 Cf. Luban: Fairness to Rightness, p. 574.

576 Card: Confronting Evils, p. 18.

577 Ibid., p. 254.

578 Cf. Walzer: The Idea of Holy War in Ancient Israel, pp. 215–228.

579 The first to write on Kant's unjust enemy in the fifties was Carl Schmitt, and later S. M. Shell, H. Müller, H. G. Schmitz and M. Frank.

and Achenwall), who appears in *The Metaphysics of Morals* and in his various lectures, and who, since he does not follow basic moral principles, ought to be destroyed (for Kant, an unjust enemy at the time was Poland, which, similarly to Turkey for Leibniz, was a group of people bellow the civilizational minimum, incapable of creating a good constitution, and which therefore ought not to exist). »*A crime without name*« is really the name for evil or evil in itself (*mala in se* or, in the singular, *malum in se*[580]), a fictitious evil for which we do not have legal instruments and which therefore cannot be punished.

Actus reus and *mens rea.* Genocidal Acts or the Acts of Genocide, that is, their ›physical element‹ and, on the other hand, the ›mental element‹, *dolus specialis* (special intent) are the basic characteristics of genocide. This latter characteristic is usually emphasized as the key, the one that distinguishes genocide from all other crimes and which is described as special intent.[581] The perpetrator's intent must be to destroy the group and Shabas claims that the *mens rea* really consists of two components, knowledge and intent.[582] Amending or further clarifying Card's definition of endangered social vitality,[583] I insist that genocidal acts (negative acts or acts of negative violence) are acts that destroy everything that makes a group exist (the connections between the members of the group, or in Searlian language, the »glue« or the »it« that holds the members of a community together; the »social ontology« of the group). One committing genocidal acts does so at the same time according to a pre-existing plan (developed with others), of which there is knowledge and is trying to be implemented. The individual (I am still using the singular) has the intent of implementing the idea of the destruction (found in the plan or project, or else, is the plan itself). However, how are social acts alternated with non-social or negative or genocidal acts? Simultaneously, while one group is being constituted, another group ought to be falling apart because its

580 The idioms *mala in se* or *scelus infandum*, wrongs in themselves, or unspeakable crimes (a crime greater than any possible crime), are used by Carl Schmitt in a footnote from 24 August 1945 in Berlin. Schmitt: Note as Conclusion of the Opinion of prof. Dr. Carl Schmitt on ›Das internationalrechtliche Verbrechen des Angriffskrieges‹ (August 1945), pp. 80–81. Schmitt's s phrase that »*scelus infandum* must necessarily be a precedent«, as well as his insistence that »Hitler's *scelus infandum* and especially the monstrous horrors committed by the SS and *Gestapo* cannot be subject or covered in their particularity by the rules and categories of positive law, set the conditions of a constant reconstruction of international law and the procedures (judgments) of a »Tribunal«. For example, in an indictment signed by Richard Goldstone on 13 February 1995, one defendant at the Hague is accused of 140 heinous crimes (»The Tadić Case«). In a later text by Schmitt, *malum in se* is committed by the so-called »world criminal« (*Weltverbrecher*), for whom to this day there is no international criminal court to be found. Schmitt: Völkerrecht, pp. 766, 823. Cf. Bojanić: Will the Judgment in the Hague Trial Constitute a Precedent in International Law?.

581 Shabas: An Introduction to the International Criminal Court, p. 102.

582 Shabas: Genocide in International Law, p. 242. With regards to the aspect of knowledge, the usual example cited is that of Eichmann who was »convicted of genocide only for acts committed after June 1941, that is, when he was aware of the plan for a »Final Solution«.« Ibid., p. 247.

583 Card: Confronting Evils, pp. 237–241; 278.

parts or members have ceased to be held together. How is this possible? It is now certain that genocidal acts (or acts that break down a group) can be committed only collectively (of course, regardless of the fact that in the above example, Kant does not at all consider collective action), that is, that the implementation of the ›plan‹ is always collective (»capacities for agency are enhanced when agents join together to do things none of them could have done alone«[584]). The plan, always a collective plan, is between members of a group and represents the apparent form of social acts (*Erscheinungsform*). This is the documenting work that unifies a group, of which members of the group are aware, because it really represents the network of various acts that are yet to come to fruition (responsibilities, promises, oaths, threats, etc.). Intent is thus always collective intent.

The lone genocidal maniac.[585] The first judgment of the International Criminal Tribunal for the Former Yugoslavia in a genocide case was issued in October 1999. Goran Jelisić, nicknamed Adolf, was found guilty of the murder of dozens of Muslims in an (improvised, this is my addition) concentration camp of his own construction (along with some ten similarly genocidal, anonymous maniacs; this too is my addition) in a part of a town (my addition) where he lived. (Recently, his wife, wanted for years by the authorities, was also captured. Adolf committed almost all the crimes of which he is accused together with her.) Since the court (finally accusing a couple of Serbs for genocide in the nineties) could not prove that genocide was committed in Bosnia and Herzegovina, in order for Krstić, Tadić and Jelisić to be charged with complicity, The Trial Chamber chose a strategy Schabas calls the »Lee Harvey Oswald theory of genocide«, that is, that Adolf could have »committed genocide acting alone, as the principal perpetrator, rather than as an accomplice.«[586] In order to ensure such a construction, The Trial Chamber adopted »the proposition that genocide may be committed without any requirement of an organized plan or policy of a state or similar entity.«[587] Here is paragraph 100:

584 Ibid., p. 38.

585 *Jelisić* (IT-95-10-T): para. 100. Shabas: An Introduction to the International Criminal Court, p. 103.

586 Schabas: Was Genocide Committed in Bosnia and Herzegovina?, p. 31.

587 The asymmetric assumption put forth by The Trial Chamber is that a certain legal construction, fiction or institution, such as »a state or similar entity« can usually have »an organized plan or policy«, while, at the same time, such a similar entity or institution (the state) cannot be the recipient of the violence of genocide. This asymmetry always questions »the entity« against which the genocidal acts are being carried out, since it is always a group of individuals only in the making (for example, a minority). In the case concerning the Application of the Convention on the Prevention and Punishment of the Crime of Genocide (Bosnia and Herzegovina v. Serbia and Montenegro) from February 2006, a newly formed state (B&H) is trying to, in the words of one of its representatives, Maître Pellet, »to establish the responsibility of a state in a genocide which translated into over a hundred thousand deaths, including women and children, simply because they were not Serbian« (*d'établir la responsabilité d'un Etat* (referring to Serbia and Montenegro, a state which no longer exists) *dans un génocide qui s'est traduit par la mort de plus de cent mille personnes, des femmes, des enfants, simplement parce qu'ils n'étaient pas nés serbes*). This means that the state, Bosnia and

Such a case is theoretically possible. The murders committed by the accused are sufficient to establish the material element of the crime of genocide and it is *a priori* possible to conceive that the accused harboured the plan to exterminate an entire group without this intent having been supported by any organization in which other individuals participated. In this respect, the preparatory work of the Convention of 1948 brings out that premeditation was not selected as a legal ingredient of the crime of genocide, after having been mentioned by the *ad hoc* committee at the draft stage, on the grounds that it seemed superfluous given the special intention already required by the text and that such precision would only make the burden of proof even greater. It ensues from this omission that the drafters of the Convention did not deem the existence of an organization or a system serving a genocidal objective as a legal ingredient of the crime. In so doing, they did not discount the possibility of a lone individual seeking to destroy a group as such.[588]

Regardless of the fact that The Appeals Chamber held up this decision of The Trial Chamber, it could be interesting for us that in this case individual responsibility for genocide and the existence of a plan to exterminate an entire group, are mutually exclusive. The crimes and murders committed by Jelisić prove not only that there was no plan or collective intent, but that there was only his own »plan« (or »sketch« of a plan), which need not at all be published, have phenomenal form (*Erscheinungsform*), be shared or told to others. »(...)it is *a priori* possible to conceive that the accused harboured the plan to exterminate an entire group without this intent having been supported by any organization in which other individuals participated«. This *genocidal maniac* (hundreds of similar men on all three sides in these wars massacred civilians) is first imputed to have committed crimes he could not have in any way committed alone (although it is »theoretically possible« that he committed them – the word possible appears three times in this paragraph), and is then further imputed with *dolus specialis*. The »theoretically possible« case is that this entirely accidentally formed group of people (Jelisić is the only one, if perhaps the most ambitious, in the production of ›non-social acts‹) answers individually for committing genocide. In other words, that some thirty people who, over the course of several months, terrorize, rape, and murder their neighbors and acquaintances from the part of town where they lived together, be individually convicted of genocide, similarly to the one who is currently serving his sentence in the Hague. Let me identify three possibilities that could determine the attribute »genocidal« in Lemkin's sense of the word: number of killings or number of those killed (if the essence of genocide is killing and destruction of individuals); the size of the group (a substantial group or a substantial part of a

Herzegovina, *de facto* in the name of non-Serbian populations of which it is made up (even though its constitution includes the Serbian population as well, which it does not represent at this time), is seeking responsibility of another state, which also does not exist at this time, that it supplied the Serbian population or a group of Serbs in Bosnia and Herzegovina with »an organized plan or policy«.

588 Prosecutor v. Jelisic, Case no. IT-95-10-T, Judgment, para. 100 (Dec. 14, 1999).

group) destroyed by the murders (for example, in Brčko, one group attempted to destroy another group of people – some were killed, some were forcibly relocated, leaving no Muslim »minority«[589]); and finally, the third possibility: if all thirty maniacs are convicted of genocide through individual charges, did genocide take place in the town of Brčko, on the territory of the state Bosnia and Herzegovina? Is the accumulation of individual responsibilities (individual acts) and their transformation into collective responsibility, in the spirit of genocide and the Convention?

Male and female fantasies. Serb rapist. It is »theoretically possible« for individual genocidal acts to carry terrible consequences (they almost certainly carry them for a certain time and a certain location). However, only a combination of individual and collective genocidal acts, as well as individual and collective responsibility for genocide, could potentially lead to a lasting end to violence.[590] The testimony of another group of genocidal maniacs and other fantasists, on the other hand, has been very useful not only in constructing an argumentatively compact fiction regarding the so-called »genocide by forced impregnation« (rape is certainly built into the convictions for genocide of some criminals, but had no particular »genocidal« force), but also, and much more importantly, it seems to me, to prevent the genocidal acts by Bosnian Serbs on a greater scale, since the international community succeeded in detecting the existence of a few centers (usually called camps) in which non-Serbian civilians were gathered.[591] Concurrently with the appearance of these stations, completely improvised and unorganized, begins the great campaign about rape committed by maniacs or bands of maniacs who declare themselves as Serbs.[592] The so-called »Brana Plan«[593] is

589 The possibility that genocide not be geographically located (in a limited zone) appears for the first time in Prosecutor v. Krstic, Case no. IT-98-33-T, Judgment, para. 590 (Aug. 2, 2001). »Indeed, the physical destruction may target only a part of the geographically limited part of the larger group because the perpetrators of the genocide regard the intended destruction as sufficient to annihilate the group as a distinct entity in the geographic area at issue. In this regard, it is important to bear in mind the total context in which the physical destruction is carried out.«

590 The city of Brčko, in which there were many more Muslims than Serbs in 1991, is a town in the Serbian part of Bosnia and Herzegovina (meaning that these very crimes of genocidal maniacs, their killings and cleansing, have ensured the ›sovereignty‹ of Brčko as a Serbian town). The Muslim community still exists in this town and is very active. This last fact, I repeat, lessens the importance of another fact: that it is certainly not the same group or the same Muslim community from twenty years prior, that this group does not have a damaged identity or »the loss of significant aspects of its identity« (which would according to Card be the main characteristic of »the harm of genocide«). As opposed to Larry May, similarly to Claudia Card, I am interested in the identity of the group, not the identity of the individual belonging to a group. Cf. May: Genocide, pp. 84–85.

591 The worldwide campaign against the so-called death camps and the so-called genocidal acts of Bosnian Serbs, of course, was a media war against Serbs, leading to the end of the war and their defeat.

592 Which is exactly what Card simply calls them: Serbs.

593 »Brana Plan« is appended to the so-called »RAM Plan«, itself much more famous and also entirely uncertain. Card cites both of these plans. In the case concerning the Application of the Convention on the Prevention and Punishment of the Crime of Genocide (Bosnia and Herzegovina v. Serbia and Montenegro) of 28 February 2006, one of the members of the Serbia and Montenegro

written about by an Italian journalist, citing a report from a meeting of officers »in a Belgrade suburb« in 1991. The text is in the form of a charter or plan, and Card carries the quote from a book of a certain Beverly Allen, whose book, in turn, was the result of her former student, a Croatian woman, »(showing) her translations of testimonies of dozens of Bosnian and Croatian women who had survived two things: ›rape/death camps and what we later came to recognize as genocidal rape‹«.[594] Here is the quotation in question:

> Our analysis of the behavior of the Muslim communities demonstrates that the moral, will, and bellicose nature of their groups can be undermined only if we aim our action at the point where the religious and social structure is most fragile. We refer to the women, especially adolescents, and to the children. Decisive intervention on these social figures would spread confusion among the communities, thus causing first of all fear and then panic, leading to a probable (Muslim; Allen's addition, says Card) retreat from the territories involved in war activity.[595]

Theoretically it is indeed possible for a true and crafty ›social ontologist‹ to write a clear and precise text such as this, the function of which would be to not only explain and connect completely incomprehensible crimes committed haphazardly by a multitude of maniacs and criminals over a large territory (it is the plan that gives the criminals their meaning and makes them genocidal), but also, to inspire us, the philosophers (particularly Claudia Card) to make the argument regarding the social death of a group or community (»social structure« or »social figure« are truly bewildering expressions appearing in this fragment). The author of the analytical strategic plan (the group, officers, ›our analysis‹, ›we‹, ›we-intention‹) finds the most fragile »points« (thus satisfying Nagel's definition of the condition for massacre), a »decisive intervention« (in the singular; a softened paraphrasing of ›final solution‹), implying only a »probable« destruction of these »communities« (in the plural) and their vanishing from the territories on which they (the communities) are not united and compact (in the singular) even now. The figure

team, Ian Brownlie writes: »Madam President, what is remarkable is the absence in these passages of evidence of a plan. In any event the purported RAM plan consists of suppositions based upon the insufficiently legible part of the transcript of a telephone conversation between Milošević and Karadžić of 29 May 1991. Not a single ICTY indictment contains details about the existence of a plan entitled RAM. The controverted evidence of the RAM plan has been examined at some length in the Rejoinder (pp. 590–598).«

594 In the same passage, Card continues to recount what she read in this book: »One of the Serbian policies was to enforce pregnancies resulting from the rape of Muslim women by Serb soldiers. Women were raped until they became pregnant, held prisoner until abortion was no longer safe, and then released.« Card: Confronting Evils, p. 268. On page 283 Card speaks about »systematic rape of women and girls of all ages and all conditions (...)«.

595 Ibid., p. 269.

of »points« here is really the integrative factor of these communities, whereas the three social figures mentioned can be reduced to one: the »woman-mother«.[596]

I would assume, at the very end, that this ›scene‹, which will by definition or according to the Convention (*a priori*) produce successful ›Genocidal Acts‹, is made up of two components or agencies. (And I suggest we completely ignore the question of the author of this perfect construction, as well as the true connection of the institutional, social and brute facts at the beginning of the nineties on the territory of Bosnia and Herzegovina). Further, both of these agencies are fictional. The first is already pseudo-constituted by the text of this ›charter‹ and is completely in harmony with Reinach's theory of the addressee. (The direction the expression takes towards the addressee (*Adressat*) is at the heart of these acts, and is their very soul (*liegt im Wesen dieser Akte, ist ihre Seele*). Their apparent form, however, is not their essence, but rather their body (*ist nicht in ihrem Wesen und ist ihr Leib*). The unified group presents itself as if its unity and existence depended exclusively on this traffic and communication between members of the group and their incorporation (*Leib*) into ›the apparent form‹ (document, analysis or directive, the plan we are presently all reading together), and not on the negative acts (»decisive intervention«) or above all on negative acts as such. The second agency is multiple, fictitiously dispersed and disseminated even before it truly starts to suffer genocidal action, and would, paradoxically (for here is the paradox of the group harmed through great evil or atrocity), first have to constitute itself with the help of ›Genocidal Acts‹ only to expire immediately following.

The fictitiousness of both of these two entities is almost certainly still conditioned by the difficulty of determining ›non-social acts‹ (for example, in his text, Reinach does not speak about them at all) or ›genocidal acts‹. However, regardless of how certain it is that genocidal acts are committed in wars past, present, or those to come, it is probable that there is no genocide since groups usually do not disappear, nor retreat from the territories involved in war activity.

596 Cf. Mother as a »sexual container« or »biological box«. Card: Confronting Evils.

4 *With* – The Group as Event and Origin of Event. On Empathy (Compassion) as the Constitutive Element of the Group (Institution)

To begin with, in order to show the importance of compassion for the transformation of a group into an institution, it seems to me possibly prudent to simplify the understanding of the constitution of a group by introducing the notion of ›event‹. But in an unusual way. What is gained when using the Russian version of this word and its meaning? For example, when Sartre mentions grammar or when Ryle concludes that »negative action« is based on colloquial use of various verbs, it is clear that the language (in why they speak and write, their mother tongue) is incorporated or ›tattooed‹ onto what we call their ›philosophy‹ or ›thought‹.

The word order of the title and subtitle of this chapter could be altered or complemented. The copula »with« could seamlessly become »for« or »with/in«. If we empathize with others (»with« always implies the existence of others and relation with them), then we are jointly advocating a single feeling (a feeling of oneness) or a common memory to be shared and be only ours. Or else, we are (»within«) one single protocol, within which we can be counted, to which a new participant or witness can be added and counted-in (*sobitčik* in Russian means one who is with, who exists-with). Two quite basic words, »group« and »event«, can be arranged entirely differently in the title.

The word »event«, however, functions entirely differently in different languages: in Russian, which I am here privileging, it is со-бытие, which translates as ›with-being‹; ›*Mit-Sein*‹. When speaking of something ›taking place‹, Slavic languages use (variants of) ›*udesiti*‹, ›*dogoditi*‹, ›*zgoditi*‹, which refers to a group of people constituting itself, living, and undergoing change together, in the now no less (in the continuous present tense, the *perfect nominans*), despite the event concerning the past and what has already ›emerged‹. The group creates ›the event‹ (which also in turn creates the group or the groupness of the group), or the group is happening, such that the parts or members of the group are brought closer together, more tightly, truly together (with-being, со-бытие).

The complementarity or correlativity of the words ›group‹ and ›event‹ have unfortunately not been properly achieved in the title »Group as Event and (Group) as Origin of Event«. This vagueness is the very initiator of work on this description, that is, in this chapter. My intention is to describe precisely this relation (it varies between interaction and equivalence) that occurs at the intersection of group and event, and which could therefore represent a preamble to a theory of the institution or even an introduction into institutional action. In order to show that without a group there can be no event, and that the group is the condition for something to be named as an event, that is, that the event implies the existence of a group and with-being (addition) – I would like to draw on the meaning of the Russian word for event, со-бытие, and its difference compared to *event*, *evento*, événement, or *Ereignis*. Further, it is my intention to thematize ›empathy‹ (*saosećanje, socustvie, compassion, Einfühlung*), as the fundamental field of constituting a group and therefore event – event by way of group and group by way of event – as well as the ›initiation‹ or ›beginning of institution‹ or as ›institutional condition‹ and ›minimum‹.

My premise – in the way I draw it in Russian, at once counting on and claiming advantage to the understanding of the event in Russian and in some other Slavic languages and its difference from other languages – is that the event is created and prepared (regulated), that it is predictable and always expected and possible, rather than impossible and suddenly, necessarily surprising. ›Event‹ is a name for a change or continuous process of change and sequence of changes[597] happening in accordance with place and time, always with an author – the group (because the event necessarily refers to all and concerns all), and not the individual. This premise would require additional explanation regarding connections (relations) of individuals which imply a new situation or change, or in general the existence of a group, that is, event or ›event of group‹. Here are a few short remarks and comments that could further clarify my premise:

a) First, this premise directly opposes the theological and messianic protocol that presupposes a few characteristics and different variations inscribed in the Latin word *eventus*, and further built into the vocabulary of the big Western European languages. *Eventus* refers to the arrival, a happening that implies some kind of a new coming from the future (*a-venir*), to expectation, which is to say we expect something from somewhere. And that which is to come, the event, really has nothing to do with our expectation and awaiting; what is to come or will happen takes place ›despite‹ this readiness of ›acceptance‹ of event. What is to come and what should come actually comes from nowhere, unplanned, unpredictable and is completely outside the register of the possible.[598]

597 An understanding of event as change falls within the register of Davidson's consideration. Here is one of the new definitions by Kirk Ludwig: »Events are changes. If something shrinks or expands, rotates or grows warmer, moves a foot or a mile. A change has occurred – of size, orientation, temperature or position. Something's shrinking, or rotating, or growing warmer, or moving is in turn an event.« Ludwig: From Individual to Plural Agency, p. 17.

598 With smaller or greater differences, this conception is present in all great thematizations of the term »event« of the last few decades, in particular in French philosophy (H. Bergson, G. Deleuze, A. Badiou, M. Zarader, C. Romano, etc.). In one way or another both Jacques Derrida and Jean-Luc Marion consider the event always opposite to the object or fact, always surprising, eliminating the

b) The event concerns the group – the group produces it, anticipates it, accepts it. In that sense, we anticipate or prepare the event (there is a change in the situation), while it also forms and determines us as well (our status has changed).[599] The surprise (the surprising act that is not implied by some preceding act) cannot be the main characteristic of the event because it is a mere consequence of general ignorance, cognitive incapability and deficiency of a group to predict what some other group is already turning into reality or ›conducting towards the event‹. One group knows what some other group does not; the ›event‹ the first group is preparing has the status of complete surprise for the second group.[600] This is still not the event, as it has not yet happened and has not simultaneously surprised all the actors and various groups (including those who have been preparing it meticulously). The intensity of the ›sudden‹ event is produced, above all, by the common focus of all actors (collective intentionality; the actors are simultaneously concentrated on each other), those who prepared it, as well as those who only accept it as fact (noting its happening as it becomes obvious to them). Both sets of actors accept it as their own; but only as property of the joint and constituted group does the event acquire its status of having taken place.[601]

c) An event was unsuccessful to the extent to which it refers (or does not refer) to the community of all, that is, the communal life of all. This regulative principle eliminates accidental incidents and differentiates local and temporary changes that refer to small groups, a small group of people, or else the individual.

d) Force or violence, as well as the various ensuing phenomena (damage, vulnerability, injury, pain, death, etc.) are probably the most intense movers and carriers of disquiet and change that could potentially belong to the term ›event‹. If one who is ill or if a group in trouble express their problem and call for help, simultaneously with my response to their call, with my compassion and empathy towards their suffering, I repeat together with them their call for help, announc-

horizon of all expectation, making it radical and impossible to anticipate (*inanticipable*), catastrophic and in some way traumatic, always referring to the experience of the impossible (what is possible is predictable, and either arrives or not). In a recent interview given to *Philosophie*, Jean-Luc Marion gives a few new and indeed surprising characteristics of the event. Apart from being impossible to organize, that it is unrepeatable and never identical to the event that precedes it, the event also opposes the politics of prediction and the metaphysical tradition in which everything has its cause and where within time there can be no sudden interruptions and unrecurrable shocks. Marion: L'événement, c'est l'impossible qui se réalise, p. 66.

599 In contradistinction to Marion (and not only him) who writes: »*Ce n'est pas moi qui fais l'événement (...) c'est l'événement qui me fait*«. Ibid.

600 Again, in contradistinction to Marion who thinks that surprise, which we show only sometimes, such as on »September 11th 2001« uttering »*C'est impossible*«, is sufficient evidence that the event has taken place. For a different group of people, one that had been preparing this surprise for others, there was nothing impossible about it.

601 One of the German words that designates the event, *Ereignis*, carries the operation of appropriation, property, ownership, but also self-evidence.

ing it further, amplifying it, and calling (all) others to become engaged to help. When I offer or give help, I am simultaneously calling to a group, thus confirming that my help is entirely inadequate for the problem of an individual or group to be resolved. Such awareness and need for association or for the group or for the institution, my cognizance that only in association can we all reduce or entirely abolish the problem ›before me‹, ›before us‹ – this is the beginning of the construction of the event that unites us all before a problem. (The problem is now ›before us‹.) My obligation to make my problem now our problem, our common problem, implies common acting by a group, that is, the constituting of identity of the group based on the initial compassion and empathy. Thus, engaged acts transform a social group into an institution.

Yet, what is the fundamental, first or perhaps preliminary compassion, and in what way is it a constitutive element of a group? Does the chapter subtitle present a new and nearly impossible task? A constitutive element implies that without compassion (or empathy, commiseration – words that are not synonymous, but have historically been difficult to differentiate) a group can neither form nor last. When we say that compassion is a constitutive element of a group it means that necessarily among the rules of the group is the element of compassion. Certainly, we can imagine the existence of one such association that »acts in compassion«,[602] but it seems to me that there are some other groups, such as a small group of Köln FC supporters, on their way to a game (visiting another group), whose actions seem not to (now or ever) be in accordance with ›compassion‹ and ›commiseration‹. However, if the members of this group have recently paid a visit in a hospital to a couple of their members beaten up in Dortmund by another group of fans, if some of these Köln fans are collecting money to help their convalescent mates' families (since help provided by social institutions is not sufficient), can we speak of an act by a group or only some of its members? The paradoxical possibility that a group can be formed at the very same time it destroys a different group (as we have seen in a previous chapter, genocidal intentions and acts are often convincingly proven this way), allows us to leave entirely aside the group that ›acts in a compassionate way‹ only towards its own members or parts. Still, if a group or portion of a group possesses the capability of ›acting in a compassionate manner‹ towards its own members, does it not then possess equal capability to do the same towards a foreigner or other group, such as a large group of refugees? Is this potential capacity

602 »Acting with compassion, thinking (together) common care« (*Agir avec compassion, penser un soin (en) commun*) is the title of the seminar led by two young female philosophers, Pauline Bégué and Zona Zarić, held in 2016–2107 at the »Hotel-Dieu« in Paris. The construction of this phrase »acting with compassion« (*agir avec compassion*) assumes that compassion is an addition to acting and that there is no acting (through words or gestures) that is authentically »fulfilled« exclusively with »compassion«, as well as that there is no such action that would exclude anything that is not »compassion«.

or potential for ›good acts‹ the group possesses as such not a sufficient reason to imagine that it can act in the same fashion ›outwardly‹?[603]

In order for compassion to truly be ›a constitutive element of a group‹, it is necessary that a group not be able to constitute itself as an *agent* without compassion. (In English, this problem could be reduced to the problem of collective agency.) Further, the group has an obligation to ›act compassionately‹ (meaning, always and necessarily in accordance with this obligation, not only occasionally). The obligation to act so is implied precisely by this protocol we all too vaguely call ›compassion‹, ›commitment‹ or ›empathy‹.

Aside from the problem of finding a precise characteristic of ›acting compassionately‹ (what is at question is that compassion or empathy be not only additions to action [›acting with‹], but always recognizable forms of acting), our most important task could possibly consist in finding a protocol that obligates both ourselves and others, indeed ›all others‹ (the We) to ›act compassionately‹. My assumption is that we are all individually obligated to ›act compassionately‹, but also that the ›strength/intensity of obligation‹ implies that our acting constitutes a new entity or group, which then ›acts compassionately‹. Is this possible, or why would it not be possible?[604]

Given the context of social ontology and the framework of theories of institutional acting (or in the classification of the repertoire of various social acts), I think that protocols such as ›compassion‹ or ›empathy‹ would be more justified (they would have a much more precise determination) if they were expressed as being at the threshold between the individual and collective (in one way or another opposite to Husserl and Edith Stein, thus probably falling into the context of some rather undeveloped and insufficiently thematized ideas of Theodor Lipps

603 ›Compassion‹ or ›empathy‹ (or sympathy) are secondary acts (I hesitate to call them emotions, but I also hesitate to call them acts; Edith Stein calls *Einfühlung* in a few places *Akte*) and represent a kind of ›response‹ to action or someone else's expression (»*La primauté de l'autre*«, N. Depraz). Husserl and Stein, at the beginning of the twentieth century, call this other the foreigner (*Fremde*), precisely due to the impossibility of creating a more stable relation with them. A friend, also mentioned by Stein in one place, also has an ontological status of foreigner. In paragraph 2 of the first part of »Deskription der Einfühlung im Vergleich zu anderen Akten« of *Zum Problem der Einfühlung*, Stein writes: »A friend approached me and told me he lost his friend; I noticed (*gewahre*) his pain (*seinen Schmerz*). What kind of understanding took place (*Was ist das für ein Gewahren*)?« Stein: Zum Problem der Einfühlung, p. 4.

604 In the following passage of »Compassion: The Basic Social Emotion«, Martha Nussbaum explains what is at issue with the status of compassion or commiseration: »Both compassion's defenders and its opponents in legal theory seem to grant that this emotion is ›irrational‹. Some would exclude it from legal reasoning on that account; some, by contrast, wish to let it in as irrational and yet valuable in addition to reason – a week position, and one that opponents eagerly assail. (…) it also seems true that the construction of these institutions influences the development of compassion in individuals. Because compassion requires fellow-feeling, its birth is very much aided by institutions that place people in similar circumstances, weakening or removing hierarchies of wealth, gender, and class.« Nussbaum: Compassion, pp. 29, 57. Also Nussbaum: Upheavals of Thought.

and Max Scheler).[605] Even Husserl's sketch of a project about empathy, which he thematizes in his intersubjective writings, as well as Edith Stein's actual project (she defended her thesis, »Zum Problem der Einfühlung« in 1916),[606] are both grounded in a strict antagonism and critique of a new protocol that Lipps, and later Scheler, call *Einsfühlung* (spelled with an »s«, »feeling of oneness«).[607] Namely, the possibility to ›empathize‹, to have ›compassion‹, that is, to jointly feel and live through something with someone (*Mitfühlen*; *mitfülender Akt* or *Akt des Mitgefühl*; the English translation of *Mitfühlen* is Fellow Feeling, »*sentire-con*«), leads to the ›I‹ and the ›you‹ together constructing or executing an act. This ensures the condition for a potential creation of a new subject: We. For Lipps, *Einsfühlung*, the feeling of oneness or simply oneness, identification, represented true, accomplished empathy.[608] Edith Stein, entirely following her teacher, denies the possibility of this transition from the »psychophysical constitution of an individual« to a higher unity, that is, the constitution of »a new subject of higher order«. However, around 1910, in his manuscripts (published long after), Husserl describes this moment of ambiguity and transition in the following way:

It is therefore necessary to consider the following issue: marriage, friendship, these are all collective entities (*kollektive Einheiten*) developing (*erwachsen*) in »psychic« relations of people and these mutual connections ascend to the highest unit (*sich zu einer höheren Einheit verbinden*). Persons are connected with one another; this connection between them

605 I am faithfully following Nussbaum. Ibid., p. 28. I think that such social or institutional dimension of ›compassion‹ or ›empathy‹ ought to complement the political or solidary or cosmopolitan or medical dimension developed by Zona Zarić and Pauline Bégué. In the chapter »E. Public institutions«, Nussbaum writes: »(…) it also seems true that the construction of these institutions influences the development of compassion in individuals. Because compassion requires fellow-feeling, its birth is very much aided by institutions that place people in similar circumstances, weakening or removing hierarchies of wealth, gender and class.« Nussbaum: Compassion, p. 57.

606 Cf. »Dass Einfühlung ein falscher Ausdruck ist« (1914–15), in Husserl: Zur Phänomenologie der Intersubjektivität, 1, pp. 335–339.

607 In the first part of *Zum Problem der Einfühlung* (chapter »Einfühlung und Einsfühlung«), Stein offers no justification for the rejection of Lipps' idea and possibility of the production of a »We« and »a new subject of higher order«. »During his course »Nature and Spirit,« Husserl said that the external, objective world can be understood exclusively intersubjectively, that is, by way of a multitude of individual possessive cognition, communicating with one another. The experience of the individual is thus, already acquired. Husserl called such experience *Einfühlung* (empathy) and connected it with the work of Theodor Lipps, although he did not explain it in detail. It is therefore necessary to overcome this absence: I sought to examine what is *Einfühlung*. The teacher did not like this. Still, at the very moment when I was supposed to swallow another pill, he directed me to conduct my work in direct opposition to Theodor Lipps.« Stein: Vie d'une famille juive, p. 351.

608 Later, Scheler uses the phrase *Einfühlung qua Einsfühlung*, which Depraz translates into French as »*empathie émotionnelle*«. Depraz: Empathie et compassion, p. 195. In *Wesen und Formen der Sympathie* (1923), Scheler finds that this *Einsgefühl* is, for example, fulfilled in war. Cf. Depraz: Lipps et Husserl. References to war are also to be found in Stein when thematizing the phenomenology of camaradery at the front (*Kameradschaft der Frontsoldaten*). Stein: Individuum und Gemeinschaft.

can »consist« (*besteht*) of different forms (can manifest differently) and of ensuing (belonging) acts (*in Dispositionen und zugehörigen Akten*). This takes place when person A relates to person B through some act, when their connection is in some relation to other corresponding acts (*entsprechenden Akte*), and in such a way that they both truly become aware of their mutual reciprocity, or potential reciprocity, in their relationship.[609]

It would appear that the different versions of closeness of person A to person B, and their exchanges of acts (feeling [as] one [together] with another [*sich Eins fühlen mit*] or ›feeling as one‹, as well as ›being in common‹ or ›being one‹ or ›being unified‹), of which Husserl speaks in this passage, along with the few and brief excerpts from Lipps and Scheler have all been neglected in the histories of understanding a group through empathy or compassion.

Let me offer two examples of this: at the beginning of »Individuum und Gemeinschaft« of 1922 (published in Husserl's *Jahrbuch*), Edith Stein returns once again to the »streaming experience of community« and »structure of common experience« (*Der Erlebnisstrom der Gemeinschaft. Die Struktur des Gemeinschaftserlebnisses*). She writes, yet again steadfastly refusing to deal with what I find most significant:

It is entirely wondrous (*wunderbar*) how this I (*Ich*), independently from its unity and solitariness (*Einzigkeit und Einsamkeit*), could enter into a living community (*Lebensgemeinschaft*) with other subjects, that is, how the individual subject becomes member of a supraindividual subject, and how in the real life of such a community of subjects (*Subjektgemeinschaft*) or joint subject (*Gemeinschaftssubjekt*), a supraindividual streaming experience (*Erlebnisstrom*) is constructed. How is it that other subjects are given for one subject, and to what extent does such givenness represent the assumption of communal life – that is what we wish to examine here.

She continues:

(...) [The theater] troupe to which I belong is in mourning (*Trauer*) for loss of director (*Führer*). Let us compare that to the mourning I feel at the loss of a personal friend (*die ich beim Verlust eines persönlichen Freundes fühle*). 1) the subject of experience is different, 2) the structure of *experience* is different, 3) the *streaming* of experience to which the given feelings belong takes a different form. (...)

The individual that is me is certainly filled with sadness. (...) We who feel sadness do so in the name of the whole group and all those who belong to it. Sadness is the subject of common experience living in us, individual subjects who belong to it. If we participate in a common experience, we feel our subjectivity affected. I mourn as member of a troupe,

609 Husserl: Zur Phänomenologie der Intersubjektivität, 2, p. 101. Husserl later substitutes the word collective or collectives with the phrase »new objectivities of higher order« (*neue Objektitäten höherer Stufe*). »These objectivities of higher order are no longer simply grounded in one more way in natural objects having embodied consciousness, but rather, man, as would be expected from an egotistical being such as myself, disposed as I am to natural sciences, himself becomes the object of his environment«. Cf. ibid.

and the troupe mourns in me (*Dieses Subjekt fühlen wir in uns getroffen, wenn wir ein Gemeinschaftserlebnis haben. Ich trauere als Glied der Truppe, und die Truppe trauert in mir*). (...) The common subject (*Gemeinschafssubjekt*) of which I speak, if seen as a »pure I« (*reines Ich*) ought not be understood as something individual. The experience of the community does not emerge from the common subject in the same way that the individual experience does from the individual I. (...) The experience of the community, just like individual experience, ultimately emerge from individual I's that belong to the community. But the impossibility of emergence of a »pure community-I« (*reines Gemeinschafts-Ich*) is not in contradiction with our deductions about the common subject. The expressions »I« and »subject« are polysemous. (...) A common subject does not exist as an analogue to the pure I.[610]

All of Stein's hesitations display an incredible resistance to the construction of a group or community. Several of her fatal operations ›ground‹ the impossibility and unjustifiability of the identity of a group or group as agent (in our contemporary parlance) that has the ability to produce group acts or be truly in mourning: a) individual experiences take precedence over some kind of pseudo-experience of the community as such; b) individual experiences are reduced to imaginary understandings or personal contemplation of what is happening to another – mostly pain; c) individual experiences are not added up, mixed up, never exchange place, nor are amassed and counted together, but are, rather, entirely abstractly ›gathered‹ in something that does not really exist: the community or group – in a word, they all remain discrete; d) individual experience is personal, hidden from others, never public or manifested; e) an encounter with another, affection, sympathy has no expression or manifestation of its own, and therefore belongs to so-called negative social acts.

A second example appeared in 1943, in Part III of *L'Etre et le néant*. The young phenomenologist, Sartre spends a few pages in the chapter »L' ›être-avec‹ (*Mitsein*) et le ›nous‹« attempting to constitute a »We«. French grammar (and not only grammar as such, as he alleges) allows him originality and ease to execute this construction using »Le ›nous‹-objet« and »Le nous-sujet« (the we-object and we-subject). Sartre is quite convincing in revealing the meaning and distinction of a We conducting an action (seeing others) and others who see and objectivize us.[611] Here is his example, which is supposed to ensure the existence of a group and collective intentionality:

610 Stein: Individuum und Gemeinschaft, pp. 119–120.

611 »Furthermore, the philosopher who wants to study the »we« (*Le philosophe qui veut étudier*) must take precautions and know of what he speaks. There is not only a We-as-subject (*un nous-sujet*); grammar teaches (*la grammaire nous apprend*) us that there is also a We-as-complement – i. e., a We-as-object (*un nous-complément, c'est-à-dire un nous-objet*). Now from all which has been said up till now it is easy to understand that the »we« in »We are looking at them« (*le nous de »Nous les regardons«*) cannot be on the same ontological plane as the »us« in »They are looking at us« (*le nous*

I am on the pavement in front of a café; I observe the other consumers and I know myself to be observed. We remain here in the most ordinary case of conflict with others (the Other's being-as-object for me, my being-as-object for the Other) *(l'être-objet de l'autre pour moi, mon être-objet pour l'autre)*. But suddenly (*tout à coup*) some incident occurs in the street; for example, a slight collision between jeep and a taxi. Immediately at the very instant when I become a spectator of the incident, I experience myself non-thetically as engaged in »we« (*je m'éprouve non-thétiquement comme engagé dans un nous*). The earlier rivalries, the slight conflicts have disappeared, and the consciousnesses which furnished the matter of the »we« (*la matière du nous*) are precisely those of all the consumers: »we« look at the event, »we« take part (*nous regardons l'événement, nous prenons parti*). [...] The »we« is experienced by a particular consciousness, it is not necessary that *all* the patrons at the café should be conscious of being »we« in order for me to experience myself as being engaged in a »we« with them. (*Le nous est éprouvé par une conscience particulière; il n'est pas nécessaire que tous les consommateurs de la terrasse soient conscients d'être nous pour que je m'éprouve comme étant engagé dans un nous avec eux*).[612]

The biggest mistake in this scene lies in Sartre's conclusion: for a group to be truly compact and well constituted, it is insufficient for someone (anyone, Sartre, for example) to be the only one aware that they are its part, that they belong to it. What is necessary for a group to be at all is collective awareness of all individually that they all belong to it, and collective attention and intentionality of all individually and simultaneously (Gilbert), something which is not achieved in Sartre's example. The group dissolves at the moment it is constituted because Sartre does not mention true engagement in solving the issue that arose due to the incident, and potential help for the injured. Sartre's diminishment of the importance of the incident that takes place (he calls it a »fender bender« [*collision légère*;]), *de facto* prevents the constitution of a group through a joint mobilization of all who would thus have an obligation to help those in peril. Since the incident is insignificant and since the damage is quite small, since there is no change, the group simply has no time to self-thematize (which would otherwise be an association that attempts exclusively to bind and repair connections between group members). Even though Sartre uses the word event – there is actually no event.

In contrast, let us imagine the incident that took place as terrifying, that the damage is great, and yet that the passers-by and »*les consommateurs*« still do not *urgently* (this word is crucial) constitute a single group that can act and conduct

de »ils nous regardent«). (...) In the sentence, »They are looking at *me*, (*Ils me regardent*) I want to indicate that I experience myself as an object for others, as an alienated Me, as a transcendence-transcended (*comme Moi aliéné, comme transcendance-transcendée*). If the sentence, »They are looking at us,« (Ils nous regardent) is to indicate a real experience, it is necessary that in this experience I make proof of the fact that I am engaged (*je suis engagé*) with others in a community of transcendences-transcended, of alienated »Me's.« (*une communauté de transcendances-transcendées de »Moi« aliénés*).« Sartre: Being and Nothingness, pp. 414–415; Sartre: L'être et le néant, p. 486.

612 Sartre: Being and Nothingness, pp. 413–414; Sartre: L'être et le néant, p. 485.

itself ›with compassion‹. Help was thus late and the violence was ultimately not prevented or not mitigated quickly enough. Why is that so, and would such a scene even be possible? Is the ›weight of the event‹ or ›intensity of the event‹ asymmetrical to the constitution of the group?

Let us look at Article 223–6 of the French Penal Code, specifically its first part, passed a few years ago. In question is »the notion of non-assistance to a person in danger and omission to help a person in peril« (*la notion de non assistance à personne en danger et l'omission de porte secours à personne en peril*):

> The same punishment will be given to anyone not helping a person in danger while their own life or that of a third person is not put in jeopardy by so doing, having the opportunity to help either by themselves acting or calling others to help.
>
> (*Sera puni des mêmes peines quiconque s'abstient volontairement de porter à une personne en péril l'assistance que, sans risque pour lui ou pour les tiers, il pouvait lui prêter soit par son action personnelle, soit en provoquant un secours*).

Although the author of the code used language in this Article to refer exclusively to an individual in danger and the individual who abstains from help (such »infractions by abstention« [*infractions d'abstention*] are quite rare in penal codes; that a person X, despite having the intention to do something, in fact does nothing – the very definition of a negative act), their intention is to punish all individuals who are not capable of unifying and constituting as a group. Only the constituting of a group (unification increases power and strength) can remove fear, thus preventing even greater danger. In order for this to be possible, it seems to me necessary first to abandon – as quickly as possible, at that – old romantic notions about empathy (or compassion) as a drive or capability to ›take the place‹ of the victim, or ›put one in the place‹ of the damaged party or one who is in pain and who suffers. We are dealing with something else entirely. I think that the group, that is to say, social and disciplined action, a multitude of engaged acts, can bring individuals closer together (such acting is *a priori* empathic and compassionate), thus reducing violence and pain. It is at this point that we can begin to speak of the institution.

5 Collective Responsibility. On Imputing and Imputability of a Group

At the outset I would like to explain why, instead of responsibility, I use a word very close to it – Imputation or *die Zurechnung*. At first glance, the word ›condition‹ could successfully tie together collective responsibility and peace; but the same word could just as well tie together collective responsibility and war. Collective responsibility is not the only condition, but it is one of the conditions (it is another condition, although I sometimes think that it is the last and unconditional condition) that brings peace. If there is collective responsibility, then there is peace. Or, more precisely, if to the already existing conditions that lead to peace, and the existing forms of responsibility (individual responsibility is without doubt the first and foremost) one adds collective responsibility, then we are witness to a process that appeases and brings peace. How does the condition and conditioning ›work‹ between these two domains? It appears that it is much more problematic to show, and if you will, classify, all the difficulties in establishing both collective responsibility and peace. Besides that, there is a key asymmetry in use and investment: while the theories of possibility or impossibility of collective responsibility have been expanded and developed after every big or small war in the last century – ›peace‹ always remained in the shadow of grand and interesting discussions of just or unjust wars and the ethics of war.[613] Leaving now aside the very complicated history of the construction and deconstruction of »collective responsibility«,[614] I would like to introduce a few preliminary observations. My intention is to try to

613 I am not sure that it is possible any more to follow Kelsen's dilemma of »peace through force or through law«, or the following definition: »Peace is a state characterized by the absence of force.« In the UN charter, peace is not at all explicitly defined. Instead, it is implicitly a negative definition of peace (the lack of war or the lack of interstate war) and not a positive definition. The problem with saying that peace is broken when two countries go to war with one another is that the definition does not cover civil wars, for example. The only new attempt of thinking peace is the sketch of »grand theory of peace« of the Japanese thinker Shin Chibo, commented upon by Richard Falk.

614 It seems to me very difficult to construct research that could encompass entirely disparate attempts to define the collective and (collective) responsibility through the history of thought and action. Such an adventure would have to take into account different thematization of self-responsibility (from Husserl's »Meditation über die Idee eines individuellen und Gemeinschaftslebens in absoluter Selbsverantwortung«, and Weber's famous lines on responsibility to Weischedel, Ingarden, Jonas or Lévinas) or the works of Arendt (above all the text »Collective Responsibility« from 1968, in which she wonders about the origin of this idea and distinguishes it from collective guilt; Margaret Gilbert, however, quite easily implicitly called into question Arendt's conclusions. Cf. Gilbert: Group Wrongs and Guilt Feelings, pp. 65–84). Still, I am sure that today's moral arguments are stronger than the arguments from the philosophy of language or metaphysics. It is very hard anymore to declare meaningless statements such as »nation X attacked«, »the team scored«, »the board dismissed Peter«, or

explain the connection between responsible members of a »responsible« collective or group – which connection immediately assumes peace; being ›at peace‹ happens during peace, just as it announces peace between groups and institutions, a new global peace (Martha Nussbaum prefers the phrase »global responsibility«) – by evoking Kant's interpretation of the alternative term for responsibility or accountability – the term *die Zurechnung* (imputation).[615] My intention is also to try to »impute« to Kant an idea, or show that his fiction about the existence of some higher instance (humanity, God, the world) before which we are all responsible (to which we *de facto* and not *de jure* ›impute‹ ourselves), represents the preamble for any future being counted in a group or collective. A self-responsible acceptance of the collective responsibility of everyone could institutionalize a group, which is then imputable (ascribable, attributable; *Zurechnungsfähig*), and this operation could take place during peace. The institutionalization of peace (I am here trying to avoid Kant's phrasing that peace *muss also gestiftet werden*) presumes first that the process of imputation is carried out on all levels of society (to be responsible means to be an author, an agent, one who accepts all acts as one's own and common at the same time). The damage from *unzurechnungsfähig* or the unimputable individual – who is not only the person who refuses to accept what he has done, but, paradoxically, the one who refuses to accept *a priori* what he has not done[616] – could only be reduced if there preventively existed the acceptance of all that they are part of humanity (and then a part of an institution, corporation, group, nation, state, etc.).[617] If we named the act of one who refuses to accept as one's own that which one has not done as primitive or barbarian (to paraphrase H. D. Lewis' well-known characterization of collective responsibility[618]), it seems to me that only then could we execute the true reconstruction of our concept of collective,[619] as well as the identity theory of a group, i. e., sovereignty of state and world governance. Institutions are unimputable (or ›substantially‹ irresponsible – if you will allow me to carelessly and analogously use Scanlon's famous phrase) because they

»film X was produced«. That is why the area of »collective responsibility« seems to me very receptive to a meaningful meeting between continental and Anglo-American traditions of philosophizing.

615 Kelsen and Joackim Hruschka wrote important papers on this subject, and the same family of terms includes attribution, shift, inculpation etc.

616 *A priori*, means together with others, all together. *A priori* assumes a community.

617 In a different context, collective responsibility can as a preventive institution significantly reduce damages in a society. Thus, Virginia Held: »(…) ones I have suggested as central: a practice in which people see themselves as sharing responsibility will decrease the enormous harms that groups bring about«. Held: Group Responsibility for Ethnic Conflict, p. 166.

618 Lewis: Collective Responsibility, p. 17.

619 I would like to draw attention to a few new and very successful attempts at redefining the collective: McKenna: Collective Responsibility and the Agent Meaning Theory, p. 17; Gilbert: Who's to Blame? Collective Moral Responsibility and its Implications for Group Members, pp. 95–96 (this text was translated into German in Gerber / Zanetti (eds.): Kollektive Verantwortung und internationale Beziehungen, pp. 31–66).

are organized hierarchically. Irresponsible individuals in power ›guard‹ the identity (sovereignty) of their institutions either by a) sacrificing their parts (insisting that individuals are responsible) or b) preventing the resistance and distrust of individuals who would share and accept the responsibility of all.

Allow me to use the negative form in the word »distrust« and approach Kant from a different perspective. Here is a first scene of responsibility or irresponsibility.

›It wasn't me‹. ›It wasn't me‹, ›we didn't do this‹, ›I am not, or we are not the author‹, ›I am not in front of the computer‹ (*com+putare*), ›do not count us as accountable‹, ›do not burden us‹, ›we are not responsible‹...

The primordial form and the beginning secret of an (ir)responsibility and every response is the rejection and shifting of the burden of response and responsibility to some other or someone other who cannot call back, respond, be responsible or *bear* responsibility. The breach of responsibility and search for the responsible author of an act is described by Ambrose Bierce in his *Devil's Dictionary* as the first and key entry of the noun »responsibility«:

RESPONSIBILITY, n: A detachable burden easily shifted to the shoulders of God, Fate, Fortune, Luck or one's neighbor. In the days of astrology it was customary to unload it upon a star.

My first question is whether we could here also add the uncertain entities such as group, state, institution, corporation, etc.? If a group exists and from there stems the responsibility divided among its members[620] (each remains responsible for their individual share in the group), in what way can such a group present itself, to announce its own responsibility and itself as the author of an act? Or how does a group deny its authorship, or co-authorship (who at all can be the ›individual‹ to utter, in the plural, ›It was not us‹)? How to assign or impute an event to a group? How does a group sign its authorship and how does it accept responsibility, maintaining at the same time the responsibility of each separate part of the group? How to be both *individually* and *collectively* responsible (at the same time)?

Hence this ›Devil's way‹ always begins with the disavowal of the child (the madman, the weakling, the impaired (*imbecillus*) to be near and to *remember*,[621] to *accept*, to *accept its own* act or the event it caused (›I did not do this‹, ›he or she

[620] Ingarden calls this *geteilte Mitverantwortung*. Ingarden: Über die Verantwortung, p. 23.

[621] Of »Unterbrechung des Gedächtnisses«, Ingarden writes: »Die Identität des Leibes eines Menschen bzw. einer Person scheint für die Identität dieser Person zwar unentbehrlich, aber nicht hinreichend zu sein, ihre Erhaltung ist aber für das Tragen der Verantwortung und auch für das Zur-Verantwortung-Ziehen notwendig. Es gibt aber gewisse pathologische Tatsachen, die sogenannten »Spaltungen des Bewusstseins«, bzw. des Ichs, die, wie es scheint, beides gefährden können«. Ibid., pp. 56–57.

did that‹, ›I do not know who did that‹, etc.) and is continued with the acquisition of consciousness and freedom, and »the extraordinary privilege of freedom« (*ausserordentliches Privilegium der Verantwortlichkeit*).[622] At the end of the road, during which the identity or the sovereignty of the group, community, nation, people, state, the world and their responsibility is further captured and formed, one probably ought to incessantly maintain and affirm the power (strength?) of the conjunction »and« – »individual *AND* collective responsibility«.[623]

Is it possible to find the conditions and a framework within which collective responsibility can have, not a simple advantage, but precisely symmetry in relation to individual responsibility? First, group or collective responsibility should not replace but complement individual responsibility. Group responsibility without individual hides the authors of events and acts, limits knowledge and history, and *de facto* destroys all responsibility. Individual responsibility without group responsibility excludes and sacrifices portions of a community in the name of its forever deficient integrity and unity. »To share responsibility« assumes that each is individually responsible, and all are together responsible as one.

Second, ›share‹ introduces a number, amount, calculus, degree and measure of responsibility (or, for example, measure and countability, ›percentage‹ of responsibility or ›percentage‹ of sovereignty[624]). The reconstruction of the figure of ›responsibility‹ is therefore multiple: a) ›responsibility‹ is derived from the procedure of ›imputing‹ (calculating, counting and adding) of an action or an event to a sum of laws and some subject as actor; b) the subject need not be single or singular (individual);[625] c) the relationship of part or parts of a whole (grouping) is the basic characteristic of ›responsibility‹; d) the word ›responsibility‹ is complex and derived, and so assumes several relations, terms or criteria which explain it more closely: subjectivization, quantification, adherence, causality, commitment, sanctions and reparations, prevention and representation, etc.

622 Nietzsche: Zur Genealogie der Moral, § 2.

623 Ingarden describes a situation in which multiple ones take part like this: »*Und eben damit ist auch die Verantwortung der Gemeinschaft in gewißem Sinne geteilt und verteilt auf ihre einzelnen Mitglieder, die in ihrem eigenen Bereich nur ›mitverantwortlich‹ sind, aber eben deswegen doch verantwortlich auf die besondere Weise der beschränkten, bedingten, geteilten Mitverantwortung. Im vollen Sinne ist aber die Gemeinschaft als Ganzes, als ein neues Subjekt, verantwortlich.*« Ingarden: Über die Verantwortung, pp. 23–24.

624 In the first real instances of resistance towards horrifying punishments and ›collective‹ responsibility, by Abraham (Gen. 18:20) or Moses (Num. 16) it is always a question of ›number‹. For example, in the case of Sodom and Gomorrah, how many good people does a city need to have to prevent its total destruction? Held writes: »Moral responsibility does have degrees. While we may be required in cases of legal responsibility to conclude that persons are either legally responsible, or not, we should resist such rigidity in moral contexts. It is more appropriate to assess degrees of responsibility and degrees of sharing responsibility for the wrongs for which our groups are to blame.« Held: Group Responsibility for Ethnic Conflict, p. 168.

625 Jan Narveson stands in opposition to Ingarden. Narveson: Collective Responsibility, p. 179.

Third, a crime, monstrous and incontrovertible, and always difficult to imagine (*mala in se* or *scelus infandum*), a crime that *surpasses* crime, and then a potential adequate punishment, obligation and responsibility, brings in group, collective, state, national and global (international) responsibility. The trace of this *malum in se* still exists today in international law in the phrase »internationally wrongful act«, used for a breach of an international legal obligation by a state. Namely, an »internationally wrongful act« is an act that should not have happened in the first place, and if it did happen, imposes reparative and not punitive damages on a state.[626] In this uncertain and complicated transition between individual and collective responsibility (or shared responsibility), we find the task of the philosopher (the philosopher who complements the jurist and judge) and a philosophical problem. And a »philosophical focus«, as well.[627]

These three complex ›moments‹, which in turn have many other tangential consequences, will always be difficult to prudently formulate and ›translate‹ into a precise argument in support of a symmetry between individual and collective responsibility. Questions can start at the end, with philosophy. Why with philosophy and why is the philosopher's task above all directed at the apprehension of group or collective responsibility? Is it necessary that there be war and an unspeakable crime, a crime one individual could not commit without coordinating an entire community, for responsibility to be a common thing? Or conversely, are wars the result of the predominance of individual responsibility, or the result of fateful asymmetry between individual responsibility and that of groups or nations? In what way is the mathematical or accounting »basis« of the phenomenon or term ›responsibility‹, during the long history of confessing to God, processing guilt, questionings and interrogations, ripped out from under it? How was the economy ›ritualized‹ and ›theologized‹, and why does the community take precedence over the individual? (Although indictments were issued against all the leaders and the military elite of the countries involved in the conflict in former Yugoslavia, and although there was a search for culprits of great crimes committed by all sides, why was the sovereignty of the newly-formed states never brought into question?)

626 »In the event that a state breaches an international obligation and commits an »internationally wrongful act,« it incurs an obligation (i) to cease that wrongful act, if it is still continuing, and (ii) to make full reparation for any material or moral damage caused. (…) An internationally wrongful act is not a permissible act for which a price is charged or an act which a state is entitled to perform so long as it provides adequate reparation for any resulting harms; it is an act which should not be done; if done and the performance is ongoing (as when one state is unlawfully occupying the territory of another), it should cease.« Crawford / Watkins: International Responsibility, pp. 285, 286.

627 As mentioned in footnote 572, I am here following Annette Bayer's words from the APA meeting: »(…) when we are in any kind of war we are prepared to switch from individual to collective responsibility. (…) Our *philosophical focus ought* to be as much on collective as on individual responsibility, when we seek to understand ourselves as persons.« *APA Proceedings*, p. 6. Cf. Held: Group Responsibility for Ethnic Conflict, pp. 157–178.

Finally, can a group or a collective, and how can a group or a collective be a person, for only a »person (can be that) subject whose actions are appropriate for accounting« (*dessen Handlungen einer Zurechnung fähig sind*)?[628]

In the chapter where he defines ›preconditioned‹ terms (*Vorbegriffe*) of morals, Kant says that as opposed to the moral personality (*Persönlichkeit*) or Person, which is nothing other than the freedom of a thinking being subject to moral laws,[629] the thing (*Sache*) is not capable of accounting and does not have freedom (*Sache ist ein Ding, was keiner Zurechnung fähig ist*). A person, continues Kant, based on all of this, follows laws or is subject to self-proscribed laws – »to itself, or at least together with others« (*entweder allein, oder wenigstens zugleich mit anderen*). Only a few pages later, Kant gives his own definition of imputation, or more precisely, Kant is trying to specify or combine different stipulations of a legal category with a rich history of usage, from the end of the seventeenth century, in Pufendorf, Baumgarten and other theorists of right and morals:

Imputation (*imputatio*) in moral sense is the judgment by which someone is regarded as the author (*causa libera*) of an action, which is then called a deed (*factum*) and stands under laws. If the judgment also carries with it the rightful consequences of this deed, it is an imputation having rightful force (*imputatio iudiciaria s. valida*); otherwise it is merely an imputation appraising the deed (*imputatio diiudicatoria*) – The (natural or moral) person that is authorized to impute with rightful force is called a judge or a court (*iudex s. Forum*).[630]

It need not be a particularly daring or hasty assumption that in this text, written at the very end of the eighteenth century, Kant deftly sketches out a three-dimensional figure, today marked by the word responsibility or *Verantwortung* (in the feminine). Without straying too far into other texts and fragments by Kant, and without a strict thematizing of a more complicated difference between Kant's *Zurechnung* and *Verantwortung*, I dare indicate that *Die Metaphysik der Sitten* reveals or sums up three faces or three moments of responsibility. It reveals three

628 »*Person ist dasjenige Subject, dessen Handlungen einer Zurechnung fähig sind.*« Kant: Die Metaphysik der Sitten, p. 223. The English translation is as follows. »A person is a subject whose actions can be imputed to him.« Kant: The Metaphysics of Morals, p. 16.

629 »*Die moralische Persönlichkeit ist also nichts anders, als die Freiheit eines vernünftigen Wesens unter moralischen Gesetzen (die psychologische aber bloß das Vermögen, sich der Identität seiner selbst in den verschiedenen Zuständen seines Daseins bewußt zu werden), woraus dann folgt, daß eine Person keinen anderen Gesetzen als denen, die sie (entweder allein, oder wenigstens zugleich mit anderen) sich selbst giebt, unterworfen ist.*« Kant: Die Metaphysik der Sitten, p. 223.

630 »*Zurechnung (imputatio) in moralischer Bedeutung ist das Urtheil, wodurch jemand als Urheber (causa libera) einer Handlung, die alsdann That (factum) heißt und unter Gesetzen steht, angesehen wird; welches, wenn es zugleich die rechtlichen Folgen aus dieser That bei sich führt, eine rechtskräftige (imputatio iudiciaria s. valida), sonst aber nur eine beurtheilende Zurechnung (imputatio diiudicatoria) sein würde. – Diejenige (physische oder moralische) Person, welche rechtskräftig zuzurechnen die Befugniß hat, heißt der Richter oder auch der Gerichtshof (iudex s. Forum).*« Kant: Die Metaphysik der Sitten, p. 227; Kant: The Metaphysics of Morals, p. 19.

and at the same time, hides one. The first two moments are mentioned in that fragment and both regard the word *Zurechnung*. Namely, Kant distorts the familiar distinction (from before him, but also his own) between *imputatio facti* and *imputatio iuris*. Let us say right away that the word *imputatio* presupposes a certain amount of ›force‹ to find and determine the author, person, face, entity or the like, behind an action or an event (Kant's word *Handlung* covers both). To impute means first of all to ›re-trace‹ an action back into the auspice and near the one or in the vicinity of the one who is ›responsible‹ for it. For the author of an act to be an author, they need to accept (to accept explicitly, to sign), to commit, or not to disavow this same action. This is a ›causal action‹ because it presupposes that the act fell from its maker, that it was amputated, removed and forgotten (in both time and space). This is why imputing comes into play, as a reattaching and suturing of that which was amputated and neglected. When I mentioned the ›forcing‹ of this re-tracing of an act to its causer, this conversion of an anonymous action to an act that has its own signatory, I am not yet at the doorstep of right (the police, interrogation, torture, inquisition, trial etc.) and in *imputio iuris*, but rather I follow the negative connotation or the negative accent that follows this Latin word and its possible uses and etymologies.[631] Except for a completely cognitive operation, which in itself need not be devoid of the use of force – simply, the author has moved, time has passed, and we no longer know who can be ›questioned‹ or who is ›responsible‹; the disquiet of not knowing urges one to search and hurry to find the one to whom this act or this event can be ascribed – the institution of the imputatio refers primarily to such acts that create some kind of debt obligation. These are such actions and events that are possible to sum up or count, for which it is possible to calculate and account someone's obligation and debt. To impute something to someone means to make them remember, for the action committed be appended to them, and constantly ›present in them‹. Being subject to account-

631 The Etymology of the verb *putare* is quite uncertain. The meaning of the word *imputatio* could be glimpsed if we first take into account the phrase ›to take into account‹ (accounting, accounting for someone, making them count, but also bringing them to account, holding them before one's eyes, inspecting their action). *Putus*, the adjective, refers to a cleaning, cleaning of silver, clearing up and settling. Further, the word *putatius* can refer to an assumption and a ›fact‹ that is not certain. Let us say that putative verbs and obligating verbs (in English *may, can, should*) indicate something not at all certain, and their use introduces the search for what has yet to become evident. Still, words such as *imputationis, imputator, imputo* and so on, refer exclusively to the calculating of someone's debts, burdening with money, credit, taking into account someone's expenditure and debt, or the counting (ac-counting) and ›marking down‹ someone's financial acts and transactions. Words such as *Zurechnung* (*rechnen* is to calculate, arrange) or *accountability* are quite literal translation of the Latin *imputatio*. Cicero uses the words *assignare* and *ascribere*, writing-in or ascribing (Kant also uses the word *Zuschreiben*), which hints at the double movement of the initial *imputatio*: that which is counted is at the same time written down (remembered through the written, set into the account), and can therefore be presented on paper; and that which is counted (and remembered) to someone can be written in, to be subject to, to be part of the law or rules in written form.

ing, of course, is marked by the word ›accountability‹. The coercion on which I am insisting, the coercion of conversion of one act or event into a fact (*factum, That*), as Kant says, obligates the accountable subject to pay his debts and not to behave as if he were not the progenitor of an act, that is to say, as if the act had never happened. The reformulation of the institution of *imputatio facti* and Kant's originality is certainly based on a reduction, but also on a transformation of these two moments (the cognitive ›Who did this?‹ and the accounting ›Who ought pay?‹), but in two completely different ways.

The first question, ›Who did this?‹ (which is the silent question to which I replied in my first line, ›It wasn't me‹), and the first moment leading to ›responsibility‹ – which Kant hid from us since it appears nowhere in *The Metaphysics of Morals* (and it is precisely this moment that is a condition for the other three that I am trying to formulate) – represents at the same time the usual definition of *imputatio facti*. Twenty years prior, in a few fragments on moral philosophy (later catalogued and published in the nineteenth volume of his works), Kant is working out the difference between assigning or ascribing (*Zuschreiben*) and accounting (*Zurechnung*). *Imputatio practica*, says Kant, is »*Zuschreiben nach regeln der freyheit*«. As opposed to *imputatio legis* (or *imputatio iuris*), »which brings an action under the purview of moral law«, *imputatio facti* (or assigning) brings an action into the purview of law in general, based on rules of freedom. »Accounting (*Zurechnung*) always concerns an action that has a legal basis« (...) »so that someone's death can be assigned or ascribed (*Zuschreiben*) to a man, without being imputed to him (*ohne ihn ihm zuzurechnen*)«.

Kant's example that follows opens up the second question (›Who ought to pay for this?‹), which regards accounts and accounting, and the fatal putting aside the *mathema*: and the ›economy‹ of responsibility: »If it were the death of a bull, not a man, there would be no place for accounting.«[632] The killing of a bull belongs to the vocabulary of assigning and *imputatio facti*, and not the vocabulary of accounting, i. e., *imputatio moralis*, which Kant had already by then equated almost completely with *imputatio legis*. The reason is that »imputation is done on the basis of the law of morality« (*Zurechnung nach Gesetzen der Sittlichkeit*), and these rules regard only humans and not animals. In other words, the assigning does not obligate, and the »process of assigning« ends with the »recognition« of an author of an action. To kill a bull – Kant of course is not talking about a bull that is the property of someone else (but perhaps that is even more important, does a bull exist, or has one ever existed, that was not someone's property?) – means

632 »*Die Zurechnung betrifft immer die Wirkung, welche eine legale Folge hat. Man kann dem Menschen den Tod eines andern Zuschreiben, ohne ihn ihm zuzurechnen. Wenn es ein Ochs und kein Mensch wäre, so würde keine Zurechnung statt finden. Wenn es ein Ochs und kein Mensch wäre, so würde keine Zurechnung statt finden.*« Kant: Reflexionen, § 7298.

not being obligated to pay for anything (or answer for anything). The killing of a bull is evidenced and assigned, but does not count, is not accounted and does not matter (Yes, I killed it, so what!). The very possibility that there are actions or events that do not belong to the law (which are not facts; which happened, but are not remembered, do not belong to history because we never go back to them, nor does anyone force us to return to them), reveals the important consequences for the forms and distortions of the figure of ›responsibility‹ from Kant to our days. First, there are damages that do not have to be remembered, because they are not part of anyone's or any kind of account – there is no ›register‹ which tallies them up (responsibility and acting thus definitely lose their common basis, which I would mark with the word ›calculation‹); second, animals, and not only animals, are excluded from the world of morality; third, the animal state (*der Zustand des Tiers*, Hegel's Eden or zoo (*Tiergarten*) are stripped of knowledge of good and evil) or the consciousnessless state (*Bewusstlosigkeit*) is still present within the state of humanity. Thus, Hegel's famous position that »the state of humanity is a state of accounting, that is, the ability of accounting (*Der Zustand des Menschen ist der Zustand der Zurechnung, der Zurechnungsfähigkeit*) or the capability to be guilty« (*Schuld heißt im allgemeinen Zurechnung*).[633]

Kant's last change (a few years prior to death), begins with the neglecting and putting aside these first ›contents‹ of the figure of »*imputatio*«, on which I am constantly insisting. I quote Kant again: »Accounting (*Zurechnung*, *imputatio*), in the moral sense (*moralische Bedeutung*) (…)« – thus begins his definition, and the accent is on this sense – is a judgment (*das Urteil*). Accounting or responsibility regards a judgment or a position; in other words, accounting is judgment (judging) which as its result has a sentence or a group of phrases that obligate to some degree. The degree of obligation or lack thereof is threefold – these are the three moments that I have intimated and on which I *count* to exhaust today's ›concept‹ of responsibility – and it depends on the way in which the judgment is reached, that is, how the ›carrier‹ (subject) of the judging, does this. Let us not forget that the accounting itself is an action that ›treats‹ and ›values‹ other actions, that is an »action, the object of which is action«.

Three moments of responsibility are three conditions for responsibility to extend into and form a community of peace. More precisely, the community, as a network of obligations and commitments, exists if and only if accounting is carried out ceaselessly and simultaneously in all three forms. If any one is missing, Kant's subject (person) is not fully appropriate for accounting and cannot be counted. We ought not underestimate too easily Kant's intention and consider his subject not to be the same as the community, and that the importance of the presence of others is lessened or callously weakened (lest we forget Kant's

633 Hegel: Vorlesungen über die Philosophie der Religion, 2, p. 263.

phrase »at least« [*wenigstens*] when speaking about a person that gives laws to itself, to itself or at least with others [*entweder allein, oder wenigstens zugleich mit anderen*][634]), and that Kant finds the process of »accounting as judging« more important than »accounting as accountability«, as acceptance and »taking of responsibility«, etc.

When I used the word ›community‹ and imputed it to Kant (a word that exists only in quotes and implicitly in Kant's fragments on imputation), I attempted to use it to mark or foreshadow the existence of a group of people who is not ›accountable‹ and whose accounts are, in one way or another, not accounted for (*putus*). On the one hand, we have an ideal state of accounting and accountability, a state of peace, where the three conditions that I will presently flesh out, are met. In this state, collective and individual responsibility are inseparable and indivisible, and *a priori* present and symmetrical. On the other hand, we have an entity, a group or a community,[635] in which more is disavowed than is affirmed or signed for, and where killing, sacrifice and consuming is without measure or accounting. If we imagine one such, almost heavenly collective (grouping), in which there is no guilt or innocence (Eden and zoo, as Hegel says), in which everyone owes everyone, and no one owes no one, and if we imagine that such a space, enclosed in high walls or protected by the charter of the United Nations, has not been colonized by any other group or community, the difference between individual and collective responsibility will be clearly drawn out and their asymmetry easily recognized. This opposing of two fictions, and the conflict between two or several groups (can we say that the origin of sociability, grouping and division into groups, is the first consequence of the disturbance of imputation?) represents an irresolvable paradox or a big complication that Kant (and not only Kant) tried to solve in different ways.[636]

What, then is the similarity between the collective responsibility of a primitive community, talked about by a follower of Kant, Ernst Cassirer,[637] and the collec-

634 »(...) *daß eine Person keinen anderen Gesetzen als denen, die sie (entweder allein, oder wenigstens zugleich mit anderen) sich selbst giebt, unterworfen ist.*« Kant: Die Metaphysik der Sitten, p. 223.

635 In recent years such a quasi-institution or pseudo-community has been given different names. It certainly is not at all Kant's ideal community in which the »principle of pure evil« rules, but really a community that despite everything cannot constitute itself as a community (for example, a »community« of pirates or delinquents). This last term I use referring the German translation of Tony Erskin's text »Krieg und korporative Verantwortung«.

636 For example, Kant insists on a ban on offensive war, but at the same time thinks that the achievement of a state of prosperity and happiness, that is, the »highest state of culture – the state of war of equal (or balanced) peoples between one another (...)« (*Die höchste Stufe der Cultur ist der Kriegszustand der Völker im Gleichgewicht* (...)). Kant: Anthropologie in pragmatischer Hinsicht, p. 411. This is the beginning of Kant's own comment on paragraph 87 of *Anthropology from a Pragmatic Point of View.*

637 »As a matter of fact in all primitive societies ruled and governed by rites individual responsibility is an unknown thing. What we find here is only a collective responsibility. Not the individuals

tive responsibility of the majority of the population of a state against which there is a humanitarian intervention? Was collective responsibility not always the condition of the institution of offensive war (Annette Bayer)? And was not the interruption of war always an opportunity to settle accounts and set up a ›responsible‹ order and an order of peace?

As mentioned, Kant marks two of the three final figures of responsibility with the word »imputation«. The first refers to *imputatio iuris*, to a legal or criminal responsibility. The institution of *imputatio iuris* assumes that there is a person, a judge (or a bench of judges) who »has the authorization to account with jurisdiction«. Meaning a person that represents the will of all persons (all the others), presides over the legal consequences of an act of a person (the subject) and coordinates them with existing laws.

The second figure is Kant's late reformulation of the institution of *imputatio facti* from *Die Metaphysik der Sitten*: judgment, through which an action is already assigned to someone (designated by the word ›act‹ or *factum*), is now being evaluated and reconstructed. This process of questioning and evaluation of the transition of an action or event into *factum* (meaning, »made subject« to law), Kant names the estimating accounting (*eine beurtheilende Zurechnung*). Estimating or evaluating (*schätzende*) accounting (in some of his fragments Kant uses these two as synonymous) stands in opposition to the execution enacted by the judge (*diiudication versus execution*). It is composed of making concrete or qualifying of a judgment, a public critique of one's act.[638] We can call this process of ›institutionalizing responsibility‹, the evaluation of the basis (whether a case should go before a judge or not), and the consideration of the relationship of the author of an action with others. In addition, the reconstruction of the law, passing of new laws, the theory of the phrase »at least«, and so on, are also carried out in this space.

Kant notes the third moment of responsibility, and the last condition of a possible »institution of responsibility« or the »ideal« of any possible responsibility, in

but the group is the real ›moral subject‹.« Cassirer: The Myth of the State, p. 285. Aside from Cassirer and Lewis, it would be very important to consider two more important usages of the adjective primitive: Searle speaks of the primitive concept of »collective responsibility,« while Antonio Cassese writes that »the international community is so primitive that the archaic concept of collective responsibility still prevails.« Cassese: International Law, p. 241.

638 »The degree of accountability (*Grad der Zurechnungsfähigkeit*, imputabilitas) of actions ought to be estimated (*schätzen*) subjectively, according to the level of difficulty that needs to be overcome. The greater the natural difficulty (of sensibility), the smaller the moral difficulty (duty), the more a good act counts as merit (*zum Verdienst angerechnet*). For example, if I save a complete stranger from grave danger against considerable risk to myself«. »*Subjectiv ist der Grad der Zurechnungsfähigkeit (imputabilitas) der Handlungen nach der Größe der Hindernisse zu schätzen, die dabei haben überwunden werden müssen. – Je größer die Naturhindernisse (der Sinnlichkeit), je kleiner das moralische Hinderniß (der Pflicht), desto mehr wird die gute That zum Verdienst angerechnet; z. B. wenn ich einen mir ganz fremden Menschen mit meiner beträchtlichen Aufopferung aus großer Noth rette.*« Kant: Die Metaphysik der Sitten, p. 228.

Die Metaphysik der Sitten, in three different ways. Man is »responsible to humanity in his own person« (*der Menschheit in seiner eigenen Person verantwortlich ist*); »conscience as a subjective principle« imagines itself as responsibility (*Verantwortung*) and conscientiousness (*Gewissenhaftigkeit*) or *religio*, presents itself as responsibility (*Verantwortlichkeit*).[639] On the one hand, we have the thing (*Sache*), which is neither free nor capable of imputation, as well as a »psychological personality which is but the power to be aware of itself« (is it justifiable to quickly and against Kant, clandestinely, put animals in here?). On the other hand, we have the assigning of *imputatio facti* and *imputatio iuris*. Between the two, Kant finds an uncertain and unclear form, and follows it closely and consistently, even in other texts, and refers to it with derivatives of the word response (*Ver-antworten*).

As opposed to the in-scribing or the accounting done by the judge or the group (others), this gesture is subjective and self-initiated. A person does not only have an inner responsibility (*innere Verantwortung*) and man is not responsible only to himself (*der Mensch ist nicht nur sich selbst verantwortlich*). In his notebooks and indices, Kant writes that the person shows the openness and freedom to count for oneself or inscribe not only those things that have legal consequences or that one has not committed at all. Rather the person finds and imagines instances that are common to everyone, and before which »all are individually responsible«. To be responsible to humanity or before humanity, before everybody, does not mean a single *ad hoc* preventive responsibility that further regulates my acting, nor is

639 All three steps in Kant are complemented by so-called »fictional analogies« (*Vaihinger*), which protect the institution of accounting: (1) for the »responsibility towards humanity«, Kand adds. »although this point which belongs to the right of humanity (*Recht der Menschheit*), and not the right of people, does not have its proper place, but is mentioned to help illustrate what has already been sketched out« (*aber nicht Eigenthümer von sich selbst (sui dominus) (über sich nach Belieben disponiren zu können), geschweige denn von anderen Menschen sein kann, weil er der Menschheit in seiner eigenen Person verantwortlich ist; wiewohl dieser Punkt, der zum Recht der Menschheit, nicht dem der Menschen gehört, hier nicht seinen eigentlichen Platz hat, sondern nur beiläufig zum besseren Verständniß des kurz vorher Gesagten angeführt wird*); (2) »(...) and such a moral being that has power over everything is called God, and consciousness will have to be imagined as a subjective principle of responsibility before God for one's deeds« (*so wird das Gewissen als subjectives Princip einer vor Gott seiner Thaten wegen zu leistenden Verantwortung gedacht werden müssen*); (3) »However, that does not mean that thanks to the idea towards which his consciousness inexorably leads him, man has the right, and even less that he is obligated, to accept such a highest being outside himself as real (...) and man using that idea, as an analogy with a certain lawgiver of all reasonable beings, arrives at instructions to present to himself conscientiousness (called also *religio*) as responsibility, before one holy being (...)« (...) *und der Mensch erhält vermittelst dieser nur nach der Analogie mit einem Gesetzgeber aller vernünftigen Weltwesen eine bloße Leitung, die Gewissenhaftigkeit (welche auch religio genannt wird) als Verantwortlichkeit vor einem von uns selbst unterschiedenen, aber uns doch innigst gegenwärtigen heiligen Wesen (der moralisch-gesetzgebenden Vernunft) sich vorzustellen und dessen Willen den Regeln der Gerechtigkeit zu unterwerfen*). Kant: *Die Metaphysik der Sitten*, pp. 270, 439, 440. All three Kant's determinants are repeated in their formulation many years later in the first systematic research of the concept of responsibility by Wilhelm Weischedel. Cf. Soziale Verantwortung (soziale Grundverantwortung), religiöse V., Selbstverantwortung«, Weischedel: Das Wesen der Verantwortung, pp. 26–27.

it simply an *a priori* openness to humanity so that it (humanity, everybody, the world) can ascribe and count as mine those actions for which others or all others are responsible; but rather humanity (or God, or the group) is an instance that protects the institution of responsibility (accounting) and *as if* counted every one of us individually into one imaginary collective without borders.

6 Debt, Negation, and Nothing. Less than Nothing (*meno di nulla*, *moins que rien*, *weniger wie Nichts*)

It is well-known that since their inception, negative magnitudes drew legitimacy thanks to their capacity to represent debt. With the transfer of mathematics into a natural science, this interpretation became unsatisfactory. Kant's text from 1763 about negative magnitudes is an attempt to mirror Euler's *argument* or *principle of indispensability* (from *Réflexions sur l'espace et le temps*) to present the reality (in the physical sense) of negative magnitudes based on Newton's Third Law of action and reaction. Kant's term »real opposition« (a novelty in comparison to Aristole's »Quantity has no specific opposite« from *Categories* 5b 11) is an attempt to reconcile the contemporary understanding of debt with the new interpretation of force. What interests me is the difficulty that occurs in the course of this attempt: the suppression of the paradox of negative magnitudes (»less than nothing«) that only debt could interpretatively satisfy until that point. In other words, the paradoxical property of negative magnitudes (that they are less than nothing, *weniger wie Nichts*) that only debt as a social object could make real, becomes the main obstacle to the negative magnitudes interpretation.

I will analyze the phrase Kant uses in an early text: *weniger wie Nichts*. The literal translation of the phrase less than nothing (*moins que rien*, *weniger wie Nichts*) into Italian, for example, would be »*meno di niente*«, but I insist that it is better rendered as »*meno di nulla*«.[640] There are several problems here, and they are all, in one way or another, connected to Kant's realism: the problem of debt, status and reality of debt (what is debt? is something always due?); what is negation? what is the status of nothing in Kant[641] (and not only in Kant), what is zero, are there negative numbers?

640 In *Réflexions sur la métaphysique du calcul infinitésimal* (1797), Lazare Carnot uses the phrase »less than zero« (*moindre que zero*). Carnot: Réflexions sur la métaphysique du calcul infinitésimal, p. 173. *Less than Nothing* is the title of a book by Slavoj Žižek, in which for the umpteenth time we can witness his fantastic intuition and an incredible lack of real content. Žižek misinterprets »less than nothing« and connects it to reality. »Because reality is less than nothing. This is why reality has to be supplemented by fiction: to conceal its emptiness.« Žižek: Less than Nothing, p. 4. Žižek constructs this phrase based on Democritus, Lacan, Barbara Cassin and an »old Jewish joke, loved by Derrida«.

641 Of the four different meanings of »nothing« or four categories of »nothing« found in the »Amphiboly« (*Critique of Pure Reason*), the origin of the second meaning *nihil privativum* (Kant

This chapter could equally carry the title, *The Problem of Debt*. However, in that case, the way in which the term ›problem‹ would be used would make it unclear or ambiguous, even gesture towards its trivial meaning. On the other hand, by referring to Kant's 1763 ante-Critique text, *Versuch den Begriff negativen Größen in die Weltweisheit einzuführen*, in which he examines the ambiguity of negation, we will see how the term ambiguity is itself split into two meanings, thus exteriorizing its own ambiguity. In addition to other meanings, ambiguity, just like negation, has a mathematical sense: Évariste Galois named his set theory »*théorie de l'ambiguïté*«. This is directly related to Kant's problem (and example) of symmetrical objects (enantiomorphic bodies, having opposing directions). Lurking in this recurrence of ambiguity is debt or ambiguity of negation.

What is the ambiguity of negation? What is the relation between the ambiguity of negation and debt? We are speaking of the kind of ambiguity that Kant, in the aforementioned 1763 text, places before us in thinking about debt and force. The text contains the first appearance of a pair of reflective concepts, and I would like to look first at how Kant arrives at them. According to Kant, this 1763 text proposes to resolve the ambiguity of the negation: the logical meaning of negation and the mathematical magnitude of negation (»negative magnitudes are not negations of magnitude«). The very reason Kant examines this problem is negative: there is a misunderstanding that produces a certain ambiguity in negation. Thus, Kant is really bringing in a concept that already exists in philosophy, but it is obscured by another (negation). All one has to do is to draw back the veil to resolve the misunderstanding. However, if we concede temporarily that the other meaning of negation was clandestinely transferred from mathematics into philosophy, we are left with the question of knowing how it was initially introduced into mathematics. Answer: through the automatization of calculation (algorithm) and through debt.

The Genesis of Mathematical Negation

At the turn of the thirteenth century, in 1202, Leonardo Fibonacci presented *Liber Abaci*, in which he introduced the decimal system to Europe. *Abacus* for him meant arithmetic, not in the sense of *septem artes liberales* where ›liberal‹ meant not tied to money, since it is, above all, aimed at financial computation. Thanks to this turn of arithmetic towards money, it was possible to think of subtracting a larger sum from a smaller one (a given quantity of money) in terms of debt. For Leonardo Fibonacci, this operation is meaningless unless thought of as debt (*debi-*

uses the word *nihil* only for these two meanings), which is a meticulous critique of Leibniz's and Wolff's philosophy.

tum). For example, »–9« was expressed as »*debitum* 9.« Since negative magnitude appeared, following the nature of their relations to other numbers, as less than 0, and 0 was interpreted as nothing (Christian Wolff, for example, still interpreted 0 as nothing), negative magnitudes were understood as »smaller in magnitude than nothing«, »less than nothing«.[642] In Diderot's *Encyclopedia*, the entry »negative quantity« (whose author is La Chapelle), we find the following explanation:

Negative quantities are those seen as lesser than nothing, preceded by the sign »–«. Let us offer an illustrative example. Suppose one to have no money, but to be given a hundred crowns by someone else. One would hold a hundred crowns more than nothing, constituting a positive quantity. If, on the other hand, one had no money and owed a hundred crowns, one would hold one hundred crowns less than nothing, for they would be obligated to pay a hundred crowns to reach the condition of one who has nothing and owes nothing: this is a negative quantity.[643]

This is how an ontologically impossible concept was rendered legitimate: by the experience of debt. On the linguistic level, debt itself was understood to be an incarnation of this absurdity. Here is an illustrative verse from Shakespeare's *The Merchant of Venice*:

When I told you my state was nothing, I should then have told you that I was worse than nothing: for, indeed, I have engaged myself to a dear friend, engaged my friend to his mere enemy, to feed my means (…) (Bassanio, Act III, scene 2).

Nor would this interpretation of the problem simply go away. Here is a sentence from D'Alembert's entry on »*Négatif*«, in that same famous *Encyclopedia*: »To say that a negative quantity is lesser than nothing is to put forward something that cannot be conceived« (*Dire que la quantité négative est au-dessous du rien, c'est avancer une chose qui ne se peut pas concevoir*).

Is the problem of negative magnitudes a mathematical problem in the ordinary sense of the word? No, it is rather a problem of the establishment of rules, and not a problem to be resolved within established rules. Strictly speaking, it is a solution in which the signifier of a solution has created its own problem. A fictitious signifier, seeking order and utility, is assigned to a signified. But the problem is: how can we recognize a »solution« no one has requested and arrived at through the

642 In 1545, Girolamo Cardano will call these numbers fictitious numbers, and Michael Stifel calls them fictitious numbers lower than nothing (*de numeris ficti infra nihil*).

643 »*Quantités négatives sont celles qui sont regardées comme moindres que rien, & qui sont précédées du signe ›–‹. Éclaircissons ceci par un exemple. Supposez que nous n'ayez point d'argent, & que quelqu'un vous donne cent écus; vous aurez alors cent écus plus que rien, & ce sont ces cent écus qui constituent une quantité positive. Si au contraire vous n'avez point d'argent, & que vous deviez cent écus, vous aurez alors cent écus moins que rien; car vous devez payer ces cent écus pour être dans la condition d'un homme qui n'a rien & qui ne doit rien: cette dette est une quantité négative.*« Diderot / D'Alembert (eds.): Encyclopédie, 13, p. 655.

mechanics of the algorithm? How can we legitimize an already present solution? In other words, how can we avoid blindly following the rules? Thus, we interpose debt as the signified in such a solution. We know the effort Descartes made to render calculation in geometric terms, thus liberating it from extra-mathematical interpretation: for him, negative magnitude appears as the opposite direction of a given length. But by the eighteenth century, negative magnitude had already staked its claim to utility, having been conferred legitimacy by debt. And even though, by virtue of its independence, mathematics wished to propose an autonomous interpretation of its concepts, using its own internal discipline of geometry, in one way or another, debt continued to play a role in the justification of negative numbers as we have seen from the example of the *Encyclopedia*.

Most significant for us here is the nature of this problem: the fact that by its nature (since it is not a purely mathematical problem, but a problem for mathematics) it steps beyond mathematics (whether in the experience of debt, or else into philosophy with negative magnitude). It is neither debt seeking its signifier, nor philosophy seeking a symbolic expression for negative magnitude; it is mathematics that has produced something that overflows its disciplinary boundaries, towards experience and towards philosophy. From the point of view of philosophy, its problem above all is to incorporate itself into mathematics, that is, into the body of the negative signifier.

The immediate source of inspiration and positive reason for Kant writing his text is Kästner's (Abraham Gotthelf) understanding of the term negative magnitude within mathematics. Kästner ushers in the need for mathematics to resolve the tension created by calculation leaning on an ontological absurdity. To be sure, Kant does not mention this necessity. We can leave aside the ensemble of circumstances that led to the urgency to resolve this tension. Suffice to say that Kästner presented his work in scientific journals that replaced those of Wolff after 1758.[644]

644 In paragraph 92 of *Anfangsgründe der Arithmetik* (this quote from the sixth edition of 1800, published in Göttingen), Abraham Gotthelf Kästner writes: »If a positive magnitude is added to the same negative magnitude (*verneinenden Größe*), they cancel each other (*einander auf*) and together give 0. Thus $-3 + 3 = 0$, or one who owed 3 thalers and obtains 3 thalers in cash, must use them to pay the debt, leaving him with nothing. Can we say of him that he initially had less than nothing (*weniger als Nichts*) because only upon receiving something is he in the possession of nothing? Negative magnitude understood like this can be called less than nothing (*eine verneinende Größe weniger als nichts nennen*). That is, it is less than nothing with regard to what is its opposite (*die entgegengesetze*). If we add to it the same opposite magnitude, then nothing remains of the initial magnitude, that is, the initial magnitude is missing something (*fehlen*) in order to become nothing in its opposite. However, in itself, each negative magnitude is more than nothing (*mehr als Nichts*) because it is a real magnitude (*eine wirkliche Größe ist*). Thus, the expression (*Ausdruck*) less than nothing (*weniger als Nichts*) assumes the meaning of the word *nothing* (*Nichts*), which in a sense takes into consideration ›something‹ (*Etwas*).« »This ›nothing‹«, continues Kätsner, »which assumes the ›something‹, is *nihilum relativum*, while the ›nothing‹ that does not have ›its something‹ is a *nihilum absolutum*. A well-known German philosopher, although he can split hairs, does not differentiate« (Kästner is thinking of Wolff). He goes on »If this expression, ›less than nothing‹ is not

The philosophical resolution of the problem by Kant begins by distinguishing between two types of opposition, logical and real. Negation in mathematics finds its source in real opposition, and is characterized by its consequence, which is *relative nothing* (0), as long as *absolute nothing* is a consequence of a logical opposition. Kant notes that the compensation of an active debt or a passive debt in the same subject is a patent example, illustrating 0 as a relative nothing:

Suppose that someone has an active debt (*dette active*; *Activschuld*) A = 100 thalers with regard to another person; that active debt is the ground of a correspondingly large income (*Einnahme*). But suppose that this same person also has a passive debt (*une dette passive*; *Passivschuld*)) B = 100 thalers; then that passive debt is the ground of a correspondingly large expenditure. The two debts together are the ground of zero, that is to say, the ground for neither giving nor receiving money. It is to see that this zero is a relative nothing (*ein verhältnissmässiges Nichts*), for it is only a certain consequence which does not exist.[645]

In a passing footnote, Kant rejects the possibility of negative magnitudes being »less than nothing«, as something devoid of sense. »The idea, deriving from this that negative magnitudes are less than nothing, *is accordingly empty and absurd*« (*Der Gedanke, welcher davon entlehnt worden, als wenn negative Größen weniger wie Nichts wären, ist daher nichtig und ungereimt*).[646]

The underlying principle of resolution of this difficulty rests in the displacement of ambiguity from negation to mathematical negation: negative and positive magnitudes are symmetrical. There is no such thing as a negative concept, says Kant. In reality, he derives the *relata* from the relation: we know they are contrary to one another, but we do not know which is which (they do not have their own identity). By sacrificing the identity of the *relata*, Kant avoids the philosophically absurd, yet logical consequence of »less than nothing« that follows from his example of debt. As Hegel notes, they become interchangeable. At bottom, this means renouncing the signified. It is not difficult to see what this means in the case of debt. Later, when critiquing exterior reflection, Hegel will delight in criticizing this ambiguity of symmetry. He too will use the example of debt when, in the *Science of Logic*, he shows the necessity of overcoming opposition in contradiction.[647]

taken in this sense, it is an error (*falsch*) that has led experts in mathematics to truly wrong notions about negative magnitudes.«

645 This is a comparison of several translations of Kant's text. Kant: Versuch den Begriff der negativen Grössen, p. 172. Kant: Tentativo per introdurre nella filosofia il concetto delle quantite negative, p. 256; Kant: Essai pour introduire en philosophie le concept de grandeur négative, p. 21; Kant: Attempt to Introduce the Concept of Negative Magnitudes into Philosophy, p. 212.

646 Kant: Versuch den Begriff der negativen Grössen, p. 178; Kant: Attempt to Introduce the Concept of Negative Magnitudes into Philosophy, p. 216.

647 In the *Logic*, Hegel uses the phrase, just like Kästner, »*weniger als Nichts*«. Kant uses the same phrase in a fragment from a manuscript (marked 1379; M 228), which goes as follows: »To judge whether life has a positive or negative value, one need not worry about the fact that no one wishes to

We see that debt is a decisive example. It is important to note that it serves to legitimize, first of all, that which is impossible in the idea of negative magnitude, and then serves in Kant, without explicit mention, to eliminate this impossibility. How can we understand this? No doubt this double role of debt demands interpretation, but it also poses the question of interpretation method.

Kant the realist?[648] What do we mean? In *Versuch den Begriff negativen Größen in die Weltweisheit einzuführen*, Kant takes a mathematical term, the reality of which has engendered problems for mathematics itself, and attempts to remove its problematic status before »transferring« it into philosophy. By what method does Kant show the reality of negative magnitude? In the introduction, Kant references the great Leonhard Euler (*der berühmte Herr Euler*) and his text *Réflexion sur l'espace et le temps* (1748). He cites this book as an example of good cooperation between philosophy and mathematics, that is, says Kant, exemplary of how philosophy can use mathematics. Although Euler was not a philosopher, *Réflexion sur l'espace et le temps*, is a good retort to metaphysicians who deny the reality of space and time, thus calling into question laws of physics that rely on these terms. Euler's defense of the reality of time and space is based on the *argument* or *principle of indispensability*.[649] Kant, emulating Euler, follows the method of this principle in his own text, which sheds light on our intention and the imaginary alternative title of this chapter (»Kant [the New] Old Realist«).

First, with a brief analysis of Euler's text I will show that he unequivocally uses the *principle of indispensability* and that his position can very clearly be desig-

die, but whether one who was reasonable (reasoned) would wish to live under such conditions again. If this is not the case, then life is valuable less than nothing (*weniger als Nichts*).«

648 In its long history, the meaning of the word *realitas* has, roughly speaking, moved between essence and existence. At first, in scholastics, this term did not refer to the adjective *realis*, nor to the phrase *esse reale*, but rather to all *res* in the broadest sense, and designated essence or better, essentiality of *res* as such, abstracting existence. Only with Duns Scotus will this meaning be shifted such that it is differentiated from *fictum* and from actual reality (*realitas actualis existentiae*), and come close to Kant's term *position* (*Position oder Setzung*), and later develop to *realitas* that constitutes the *haecceitas* of each individual being. Kant's contribution to the history of this term is particular, since he uses the scholastic sense, equivalent to essence (»existence is not a real predicate«) and at the same time introduces through the expression »objective reality« (Kant: Kritik der reinen Vernunft, p. 194) and realization (*Realisierung*) the modern, generally understood meaning. However, in Leibniz and, in our case, in Euler, although these texts belong to an earlier period, the *reality* of time and space is much closer to the post-Kantian meaning of reality. Cf. Courtine: Réalité.

649 This argument is today the subject of meticulous analyses. Certain authors call the realism that refers to this argument semantic realism. Historically, Quine and Putnam are credited with the argument. Putnam formulated it explicitly in *Philosophy of Logic* (1971). Many think that it can already be found in Frege, von Neumann, Carnap or Gödel. The Putnam formulation makes the argument neutral in relation to the nature of the mathematical object. It begins from the truthfulness of an expression of a theory and thinks that it rests on something external and not on sense-data or the structure of the spirit or language. Mathematical terms denied reality, and which cannot be »translated« (or as Euler says »exchanged«) by »more real« terms must, due to their necessity, be considered real.

nated as realistic in the Quine-Putnam sense. Further, we will show the particular status of negative numbers in mathematics, as well as some attempts within mathematics itself to remove their problematic status. Finally, we show in what sense Kant's approach is realistic.

Euler's Realism

In *Réflexion sur l'espace et le temps*, Euler makes an argument in favor of time and space not being imaginary, not being a figment of our imaginations, but truly real. In broad strokes, I will sketch out the structure of his argument to show the extent to which it is based on the Quine-Putnam principle of indispensability.

Euler begins by saying that the basic principles (Newton's Laws) of mechanics are truthful. Even if we were unable to deduce them from general metaphysical principles, the miraculous harmony of all their consequences of motion of bodies would be enough for their truth to be beyond doubt. Here Euler puts forward the realistic position that »these two truths [the basic laws of mechanics] must be absolutely grounded upon the nature of bodies.«[650] Here is how Putnam sums up his own argument: »If one is a realist about the physical world, then one wants to say that the Law of Universal Gravitation makes an objective statement about bodies – not just about sense data or meter readings.«[651]

However, continues Euler, not even metaphysicians deny the truthfulness of the basic laws of mechanics; rather, they reproach the mathematicians that they have wrongly connected these principles with terms of time and space, which are imaginary terms, devoid of any reality. How to solve this problem? Euler then suggests examining whether these suspicious terms could be exchanged by some other real terms, such that the meaning and soundness remain unchanged:

For there is no doubt, says Euler, that bodies, in following these principles, do not follow those things found exclusively in our imagination: rather, it is certain that those things are truly real to which laws apply, and which bodies follow in conserving their state.[652]

650 Euler: Réflexions sur l'espace et le temps, p. 325.

651 Putnam: What is Mathematical Truth?, p. 74. On the same page, a few lines prior, Putnam says: »I argued in detail that mathematics and physics are integrated in such a way that it is not possible to be a realist with respect to physical theory and a nominalist with respect to mathematical theory.«

652 »*Car il n y a aucun doute, dit Euler, que les corps, en se réglant sur ces principes, ne se règlent point sur des choses, qui ne subsistent que dans notre imagination: il est plutôt certain, que ce sont des choses bien réelles auxquelles se rapportent les lois, que les corps suivent dans la conservation de leur état.*« Euler: Réflexions sur l'espace et le temps, pp. 325–326.

In section V, Euler makes an argument so careful that I feel compelled to quote the following fragment in full:

> It is thus certain, that it is not possible to conceive of the two given principles of mechanics without including the ideas of time and space, which is a sure mark that these ideas are not purely imaginary, as the metaphysicians claim. We cannot but conclude that time, just like absolute space, are such as the mathematicians describe them, real things, existing outside of our imaginations, and can serve as the foundation of real principles of mechanics.[653]

It would be difficult to express a more realist position. However, while the concept of space, and the similarly treated concept of time, had the entire Euclidian tradition standing behind it, Kant still had to deal with objects that have no definitive status within metaphysics itself. Therefore, before we consider Kant's solution, we must briefly return to the genesis of negative numbers, or as they were called at the time, »negative magnitudes«.

The History of the Negative Number

What is the problem of negative numbers or magnitudes? All problems concerning negative numbers arise from the fact that, historically, the concept of these numbers was preceded by the possibility of their designation. What does that mean? A formal application of the algorithm for solving algebraic equations leads to the »unnatural« position in which a larger number is subtracted from a smaller. However, the very expression of this operation, for example »2 – 3«, already represents a marking for a possible result. But if numbers are understood as an expression of quantity, then such an operation makes no sense. Pascal, for example, thought that by subtracting 4 from 0, it would be impossible to arrive at anything other than 0. For him, –4 was a meaningless quantity. Indeed, if negative numbers are to be understood as an expansion of positive numbers themselves understood as quantity (the answer to the question *how many?*), it would not at all be clear what subtracting from zero would mean, i. e., what was a quantity lesser than zero. Yet, any subtraction of a greater number from smaller is equivalent to subtracting from zero and hence has a result that is smaller than zero.

653 »*Il est donc certain, que s'il n'etoit pas possible de concevoir les deux principes allègues de la mécanique, sans y mêler les idées de l'espace et du temps, ce seroit une marque sure, que ces idées n'etoit pas purement imaginaire, comme les Métaphysiciens le prétendent. On en devroit plutôt conclure, que tant l'espace absolu, que le temps, tels que les mathématiciens se les figurent, etoient des choses réelles, qui subsistent même hors de notre imaginations pouvoient servir de fondement a des principes réels de la Mécanique.*« Ibid., p. 326.

However, historically, wherever such numbers appeared, they were immediately understood as magnitude of debt. Only later do we get the construction of the interpretation using directed line segments (vectors) that stand in for the meaning of force in physics. These interpretations remain implicit in the background, but leave no trace on the level of symbol. Finally, in an attempt to preserve the pluralism of interpretation, contemporary mathematics has had to deny symbols any meaning other than ones that allow the conduct of operations.

As opposed to a point, line, plane, number and other classical mathematical objects, which oppose their (often more real) ideal reality to empirical reality, which were at worst assigned the status of imaginary (hence Euler's defense of time and space as real), negative numbers were from their very beginning given the status of impossible objects. Created as a consequence of subtracting from zero, they must be less than zero, or less than nothing. Understood as a quantity smaller than nothing (since all positive numbers were understood as an expression of how much, quantity or cardinality), at first, they were treated as absurd. As a contemporary physicist (Roger Penrose) notes, after all, what would it mean to say that »there were minus three cows in the field?« Such a question ought to make obvious that negative numbers are not an answer to the question »*how much?*«, in the sense in which positive numbers can be. But we all know very well that negative numbers are used and not called into question. How did this happen? I cannot fully consider the long and very interesting history of negative numbers (mathematics is really perhaps like an oyster in which the grain of sand of negative numbers leads to modern algebra), but I will sketch its main features as concerns our problem.

Whence the need of mathematics or living practice to impose something that at first seemed so absurd? It was less of a direct need, and more a consequence of the formalization of mathematics. The formalization of rules for solving equations, the advantage of which lies in the possibility of their mechanical application without having to consider the meaning of the symbols used in the operation, brought about the subtraction of a greater number from a smaller one, which is the same as subtracting from zero. At first, such solutions were rejected as meaningless. When the results of such subtraction began to be accepted, they were called debt-numbers. In the case of a greater number being subtracted from a smaller, Fibonacci says: such an equation has no solution unless we consider the solution as debt.

It is certain that the application of formal rules has produced a signifier, a symbol that at first has no corresponding referent. By its meaning, that is, its relation to the symbols for other numbers, we know that it must refer to something smaller than zero. But for that very reason, it is not clear to what amount or magnitude it would refer. Even though mathematics was at the time, at least in Europe, a discipline that accompanied trade (although merchants did not immediately use negative numbers in their ledgers), the link between negative numbers and the size of debt served, above all, to theoretically ensure the real meaning of a marking, thus increasing the automatization of the rules. Only later will Luca Pacioli (at the end of the fifteenth century), based on this, deduce the language of double-entry bookkeeping.[654] Thus debt, historically, from the very beginning appears as the only guarantor of the reality of meaning of a paradoxical marking. In fact, it would be more accurate to say that these numbers appear thanks to debt, and, as we have seen, are so closely tied to debt that they are called debt-numbers.

As long as debt was the only guarantor of their reality of meaning, negative numbers were treated as false, fictitious, imaginary numbers. They were only tolerated because, so to speak, they increased the scope of the rule. All the while, mathematicians sought a geometric or natural legitimacy that would give them reality. Kant's text of 1763 represents a philosophical gesture in the effort to replace debt as legitimation with something else. Paradoxically, debt was rejected as legitimation for the same reason that only debt could serve as legitimation: because it was thought that only debt truly satisfies this condition of *less than nothing*.

There was an expectation that this paradox would be replaced with a more realistic legitimation. What initially made debt necessary, that is, its property of being able to realize the paradoxical property of less than nothing, now even made debt itself insufficient. It was as if debt had been sufficiently real to enable negative numbers to appear, but insufficiently real to ensure their continued lasting. In order to be any legitimation at all for negative numbers, debt itself had to be somewhat unreal, and thus insufficient as legitimation. Both debt and negative numbers appear to have »organizational reality« (they contribute to the efficiency of the rule), but not »substantial reality«. Roger Penrose points out that negative numbers certainly play a very important organizational role in banking and finance, but then also wonders whether they have any direct connection with the real world.[655]

Kant's text belongs to this line of search for a different guarantor of reality of negative numbers, but it has a particularity that separates right away. This text never mentions the basic difficulty that needs to be overcome, nor that the prominent role of debt up to that point is in any way relevant. Although Kant's introduction states that the impulse to write on the subject came from Kästner's explanation of negative numbers, in which Kästner explicitly endeavors to jettison debt as the customary example and compromise with the absurd demand that negative magnitudes be smaller than nothing, it is as if Kant does not think that he needs to clearly and carefully formulate his philosophical contribution to solving this problem. Instead, he is content to mention that negative magnitudes have shown their usefulness in mathematics and that rules have replaced the definition. This, however, could be precisely the indicator of his realistic approach, in which, fol-

654 Cf. Peters/Emery: The Role of Negative Numbers in the Development of Double Entry Bookkeeping.

655 Cf. Penrose: The Road to Reality.

lowing Euler, he wishes to deduce the legitimacy of negative numbers from their indispensability for the formulation of generally accepted laws, and not by referring to an object the reality of which would guarantee the reality of corresponding mathematical objects, in this case, negative magnitudes.

The realism that leads Kant to begin with the rule frees him to posit the difference between the social and physical field that would give legitimacy to negative magnitude. He does not begin with an empirical object that would lend its reality to ensure that of negative magnitudes, but rather from the truthfulness and usefulness of rules that can then be applied to myriad objects.

For this reason, straight away in the introduction of *Versuch den Begriff negativen Grössen*, he expresses the key point that will make his solution entirely contemporary: rules have replaced the definition. What follows is his general designation of negative magnitude through rules alone. When introducing negative magnitude into philosophy, when attempting to »draw out« of this term that which is properly the »subject of philosophy«, he separates the really opposed (*der reale Wiederstreit*), which he designates by way of position he calls *regola fondamentale* (*eine Grundregel*):

A real repugnancy only occurs where there are two things, as positive grounds (*ein positiver Grund*), and where one of them cancels the consequence of the other. Suppose that motive force is a positive ground: a real conflict can only occur in so far as there is a second motive force connected with it, and in so far as each reciprocally cancels the effect of the other.[656]

What Kant is advocating and is ultimately able to demonstrate, could represent structure in the contemporary sense. This recalls quite well the contemporary definition of a group. There is a neutral element – for each given element of the group there is an opposite element, such that their sum is always equal to zero. Kant really says nothing else. In this way, well in tune with the spirit of contemporary mathematics, both debt as a social object and opposing forces, as well as opposing trajectories as physics objects, equally represent negative magnitudes.

In Chapter Three of the 1763 text, »Containing some reflections which may serve to prepare the application of the above concept to the object of philosophy«, Kant notes that taking into consideration the nature of real opposition, it is clear that everything true in the physical world, is also true of spiritual nature. It can be said that Kant's solution of the status of negative magnitude (status independent from the nature of object), suspends the ambivalent role debt as an element of social reality held up to that point.

We have seen that Euler begins from the truthfulness of the laws of physics, and shows that expressions of these laws refer to bodies in motion, and not to our

656 Kant: Versuch den Begriff der negativen Größen in die Weltweisheit einzuführen, pp. 75–176. Kant: Attempt to Introduce the Concept of Negative Magnitudes into Philosophy, p. 215.

impressions or results of our measurements. Based on this, he concludes that time and space are not imaginary but real or »real things«. Kant follows this thinking regarding negative magnitudes. Euler starts with the fact that all terms that are indispensable in expressing physical laws must be considered real for the law to be considered true.

Kant, however, must perform a double task. Before applying negative magnitudes to real objects (physical, spiritual), he must construct an appropriate theory of negative numbers, because, as we have seen, within mathematics, they have an ambiguous status. Kant performs this work by tracing Euler's move, but does so twice: once within mathematics itself, and then again in application of mathematics.

Very important, in that regard, is the aforementioned fragment from the introduction of *Versuch den Begriff negativen Größen in die Weltweisheit einzuführen*:

> The concept of negative magnitudes has long been employed in mathematics, and it has also been of the utmost consequence there. Nonetheless, the representations which most people have formed of the concept of negative magnitudes, and the elucidation which they have given of it, have been strange and inconsistent. This has not, however, resulted in any errors of application, for the particular rules governing its employment took the place of the definition and guaranteed its correct use. And whatever error there may have been in the judgment about the nature of this abstract concept it remained fruitless and without effect.[657]

Therefore, Kant is not searching for objects to which such an equation could be applied and which could lend their (empirical) reality to guarantee the reality of negative magnitudes. Rather, he first separates the relations that characterize such a magnitude. Or better, negative magnitude is not a specific kind of magnitude, but rather emerges from a specific relation with positive magnitudes, a relation of opposition. It was first necessary for opposition to be liberated from a logical monopoly. Then, it was necessary to show that there are objects that together have a relation that corresponds to the relation of negative and positive magnitudes/numbers.

Kant's realist standpoint becomes clearer when we understand how he organized his explanation of negative magnitudes. The structure of his solution becomes evident when Euler's position is considered: indispensable elements of true expressions must be real. Kant begins with the practice of calculation in the broadest sense, and deduces their *mathematical* reality from the truthfulness of the rule (or law) of calculation with negative magnitudes. Only after that does Kant consider their reality that follows from their application in physics (Kant mentions

657 Kant: Attempt to Introduce the Concept of Negative Magnitudes into Philosophy, p. 210. In *Saggio sulla negazione* Paolo Virno speaks of Kant in two places, and he analyzes this fragment on pages 86–87.

Newton's third law at the beginning of the second part of *Versuch den Begriff negativen Größen in die Weltweisheit einzuführen*). Only by beginning from a version of the indispensability argument could he renounce the usual basis in the definition, which means the essence, and shift the emphasis to the relation, to the structure (today we would say the algebraic or operational structure) given in the rules. Kant drew all the advantages that Euler's argument offers in terms of neutrality towards the nature of objects whose reality is in question.

For all this, Kant also needed to temporarily ›bracket‹ the traditional meaning of positive whole numbers (what Frege succinctly calls the answer to the question »how much?«) and to interpret them in such a way to make opposition valid. We should keep in mind that in the Aristotelian tradition, the category of quantity has no opposition, meaning that by introducing this relation as crucial and decisive, Kant also modified the meaning of positive numbers. But even this concept of opposition, actually belonging to logic, could not be simply borrowed; rather, it too had to be altered and liberated from the shackles of logic.

On what, then, is Kant leaning when he is simultaneously changing the concept of opposition and the concept of quantity on which he will confer this modified opposition? Actually, he begins with the aim, which is above all to show that the reality of mathematical negativity is based on its successful application in Newton's third law. Everything is set up in such a way for the truthfulness of Newton's third law (the only one Euler' did not use, and also the law about which Kant was skeptical whether it represents an *a priori* truth) to be the cornerstone of the reality of negative magnitudes. There is no space here to go further in detail into the way the realist standpoint determined the structure of the argument, but the very structure of the argument points to its realism. Therefore, in lieu of a conclusion, allow me to succinctly retrace Kant's strategy of argument.

In order to use the *indispensability argument* to show the reality of negative numbers, which means starting with the truthfulness of the rule or law of negative numbers, Kant must:

1. free those same negative numbers of a purely quantitative dispositive. The basic characteristic of negative numbers is the relation of opposition to positive numbers. Of course, opposition has to be »borrowed« from logic.
2. introduce the concept of *real opposition* with which he separates the negative in mathematics from the negative in logic, that is from contradiction. He thus defines the opposition appropriate for negative numbers through the concept of real opposition.
3. describe negative numbers by way of relations (given in the rules), and only then speak about their application – not only in physics, but anywhere where it is possible to connect quantity and opposition.
4. demonstrate the reality of negative magnitudes based on the truthfulness of those laws of physics, the formulation for which they are necessary.

7 Inclusion / Exclusion. On the Conditions of Common or Critical Engagement

It seems to me that in one way or another, it is possible to understand the terms »inclusion« and »exclusion«, but that the trouble lies in the third entity, the one in between, connecting the two: »/« (the slash or stroke). At this point, between »inclusion« and »exclusion«, we find a space brimming with hesitation and reflection (as well as force and violence), in which far from simple decisions are made. Before a foreigner or migrant becomes part of the space designated as »inclusion« or »exclusion«, they are for us »/« (slash, stroke).

What then is »/«, the slash, stroke? In English (and not only English) this sign hides a ferocious strike and violent separation and interruption. At the same time, this punctuation sign announces a choice between »inclusion« and »exclusion«; but then, paradoxically, it stands more as conjunction than disjunction. The »/« (slash) does not represent a brief pause, nor does it imply urgency to hasten the choice of either »inclusion« or »exclusion«. On the contrary, it would appear that »inclusion« and »exclusion«, thanks precisely to the register covered by the sign »/« (slash), are mutually interwoven, interchangeable, or inter-permeable one into the other, and are extraordinarily difficult to separate, however deftly or dexterously handled. It is necessary therefore – I would like to insist on this – to construct a right to non-separation of the »inclusion« from the »exclusion« or, better, a right to »/« (the slash). What we are actually talking about here is time (a period) in which we can carefully and meticulously craft decisions that will not be exclusive nor exclude, even when, paradoxically, they temporarily (always temporarily!) suspend inclusion or the participation of all in an institution (a family, corporation, city, state, etc.).

But before I attempt to more closely consider »inclusion« and »exclusion«, as the two operations that always complete one another without being complementary, here are a few preliminary and regulative principles that issue from a space in which these two registers differ and are separated by »/« (slash):

a) »Inclusion« (integration) and »exclusion«, as well as the »/« (slash) space appears wherever there is a project or possibility for the constitution (the closing: *claudere* is to close, *excludere* is not to allow in, admit, expel) of some fictitious entity such as the family, group, corporation, movement, city, state, Europe, or world state. It is a question of the future, of construction and projection of actions to be conducted in the near future.[658] A project of closure implies an

[658] In »Progetto«, Massimo Cacciari goes back and forth between ›force‹ and ›violence‹ in de-

opening of borders (and vice versa), and this entity that possesses limits could be called the institution (not »status«, which is an imprecise designation; nor »contract«, which *a priori* excludes a third party). The institution assumes the arrival and presence of those who are not here now (as opposed to a group, which, in one way or another, always resists the arrival of new members), but also the potential free departure of those already present, that is, temporary interruptions of movement and border crossing (the border being the limit of the institution).[659]

b) The condition for »common engagement« (von Ihering uses a potentially analogous term in 1886, »*die active Solidarobligation*«), which ought to be beyond the »Inclusion / Exclusion« principle, will be fulfilled if and only if an ideal institution opens its doors to all without exception, and if I act in a way anyone would act and in the way everyone should act. If the rules of inclusion or exclusion are entirely transparent and achievable to anyone, regardless of any temporary prohibitions, it is possible to speak of fulfillment of the principle of universality. Engagement, when it comes to another person (for marriage), within a political party, in a football supporters' group, a movement, engagement in preservation of one's culture by closing borders, common engagement in war – are not examples of common and critical engagement because they *a priori* exclude others and exclude the possibility of all to be included. (Critique or [»critical reasoning«; Amartya Sen] consists of engaged acts when it obligates to urgent action, not only members of the group, but all future, inactive members / parts of the human community; »global commitment« for Judith Butler).
c) Only those whose action or whose engagement actively excludes all or other groups could be temporarily marginalized,[660] but not formally or »categori-

scribing the main characteristics of a project. »*Violenza suona nel progetto*« (p. 101). It is an act of overshooting and expanding to beyond the surface or edge (*proictus*), which then always implies exclusion, abolishment, banishment, expulsion (*proicto*).

659 Two examples: The true impetus for Michael Dummett's book *On Immigration and Refugees* (London, Routledge, 2011) is the encyclical *Pacem in Terris* by Pope John XXIII: »(...) when there are just reasons in favour of it (...) must be permitted to emigrate to other countries and take up residence there. The fact that he is a citizen of a particular state does not debar him from membership of the human family, or from citizenship of that universal society, the common, worldwide fellowship of men.« The famous observation of Hugh of Saint Victor from Book 3 of *Didascalicon* is even more interesting: »The man who finds his homeland sweet is still a tender beginner; he to whom every soil is as his native one is already strong; but he is perfect to whom the entire world is as a foreign land (*perfectus vero, cui mundus totus exsilium est*). The tender soul has fixed his love on one spot in the world; the strong man has extended his love to all places; the perfect man has extinguished his (*ille mundo amorem fixit, iste sparsit, hic exstinxit*).« H. Saint Victor: The Didascalicon, p. 101.

660 To »marginalize« means to »place« in the margin or background, in a certain way reject or remove (»injustices« provoke »urgent need for their removal,« A. Sen), but not put out (*esclore*). The problem is of course with the word to »place,« that is, in the characteristics and execution of such an operation. This temporary »not taking into consideration« is formulated well by La Rochefoucauld

cally« eliminated or disqualified.[661] Temporary suspension of certain groups or minorities still does not mean exclusion, but certainly reveals the limits of democracy and improvidence of the position that the problem of exclusion can be simply solved by inclusion (Iris Marion Young).

Let us look now at the problem we have with our asymmetrical distinction »inclusion / exclusion«[662] and why it is insufficient to bind »exclusion« exclusively with injustice, and »inclusion« with the basic democratic protocol. It is not only a matter of »exclusion« being (just like »inclusion«) »vital for directly promoting other democratic objectives, e. g., autonomy or equality« (Dovi), but also of the difficulty of various integrative strategies advancing institutions, making them moral as well as efficient.

Towards the end of a letter to Marquis d'Argence de Dirac, of 2 December 1761, Voltaire sends his fond wishes: »In your retirement, I wish you days filled with thoughtful friends and free of fools, as well as good health« (*Je vous souhaite, dans votre retraite, des journées remplies, des amis qui pensent, l'exclusion des sots et une bonne santé*). No trace of affectation or moralizing. On the one hand, we have »thoughtful friends«, who obviously have the capacity for reflection; on the other, the exclusion of fools, probably because they think poorly and err in judgment or, paradoxically, because they »exclude poorly«. Voltaire then leads us to the first and most fundamental problem when it comes to »exclusion«, which also refers to epistemology and the *cogito*. Although there are several sets of topics and problems easy to classify and connect with our perhaps somewhat rough distinction »inclusion / exclusion« (each of which has certain political consequences and none is simple or resolvable),[663] the first difficulty we encounter with »exclusion« refers to epistemological or cognitive abilities and activities.

in his *Maximes*: »The action of keeping someone at a distance, of pushing them away« (*Action de tenir quelqu'un à l'écart, de le repousser*). In »In Praise of Exclusion,« Suzanne Dovi speaks of a certain »ethics of marginalization:« »However, in order to improve the representation of historically disadvantaged groups, democratic theorists need to consider when it is justifiable, desirable, and even morally necessary to limit, or even deny, access and influence to overrepresented, privileged groups.« Dovi: In Praise of Exclusion, p. 1172. Dovi calls this standard ›the oppression principle‹ (p. 1174). »Democracies ought to marginalize those who oppress and those who benefit from oppression.« (p. 1181)

661 »Categorical exclusion« is Cathy Cohen's term from 1997. Violate certain groups even if it is »Alternative für Deutschland« (AFD) and its current presence in the Bundestag is certainly an antidemocratic act.

662 Niklas Luhmann, for example, claimed that exclusion rather than inclusion is the rule, and, moreover, that inclusions differ from one another. Cf. Braeckman: Niklas Luhmann's systems theoretical redescription of the inclusion / exclusion debate.

663 Colloquially, when speaking of »exclusion,« we think of gender (exclusion of women from political life), but also the migrants and emigres, then the poor who live on the margins, suburbs and ghettos, followed by various sets of odd or asocial persons (invalids, autistic, defective, etc.). The great theorist of democracy, Robert Dahl writes: »The demos must include all adult members of the

Namely, the ability to reason always assumes deft manipulation of various techniques and protocols of exclusion. One who is capable of concentrating, directing his attention unwaveringly excludes something or all else. One capable of counting makes good use of the method of exclusion in such situations when, for example, all variables are systematically excluded. One capable of thinking and whom Voltaire *a priori* classifies as a friend, probably makes very good use of the three basic laws of thought, one of which is the »*principe du tiers exclu*« (*principium tertii exclusi* or *tertium non datur*, that there is no third possibility or middle term, in English, this is the »law of excluded middle«;[664] the other two laws or principles being the law of identity and law of contradiction).

If we put aside all the other operations and social acts or acts of the community[665] that always in one way or another imply exclusion (when we choose, we exclude; when we vote, we exclude; when we decide, we exclude; in competitions, we exclude, else there is mutual exclusion, etc.), the competence of those who think (Voltaire calls them friends), among other, would be to exclude (because by thinking they continuously exclude) those who think or act problematically – in a word, the incompetent. The English word »competence« is perhaps instructive here, as it refers (as a legal term) to the domain of power, a synonym for jurisdiction, as well as (colloquially) to someone's ability to perform a task, intellectual or otherwise. Only the competent ought to be given competence; the incompetent must be excluded from competence. It seems to me that it would not be overly intelligent to think that Voltaire had the idea that dimwits would exclude themselves (as they would be unable to »exclude« properly). If exclusion means acts by which one excludes, and further, the subject(s) and subject(s)-object(s) of exclusion, as well as an entity that remains after the exclusion takes place, and finally the space in which the excluded are found after the exclusion – then those who think and who also spread wellbeing and kindness (because friends) will have a lot of work indeed. If we systematically exclude dullards from our lives, as Voltaire would have us do (and in the contemporary world this would mean unfollowing them from Facebook and Twitter), it would be uncertain indeed whether we would really have peace as individuals (Voltaire is writing to one retreating from public life) or succeed in abolishing a group of entirely vague and dysfunctional negative social acts or asocial acts, with the aim of advancing the institution or the community.

When it comes to histories of institutions and common engagement, Voltaire's advice and counsel, which have lost none of their currency or appeal, have nev-

association except transients and persons proved to be mentally defective.« Dahl: Democracy and Its Critics, p. 129.

664 Every judgment is either true or false, something is either A or not A. There can be no third. Cf. Kolmogorov: On the Principle of Excluded Middle.

665 It was likely Edmund Husserl in 1921 who first used this phrase ›*Soziale Akte*‹ and ›*Gemeinschaftsakte*‹. Husserl: Zur Phänomenologie der Intersubjektivität, 2, pp. 165, 192.

ertheless implied only two options: 1.) those excluded or that which is excluded ought to be eliminated or grouped (pseudo-institutionalized) on the periphery or margins of an entity, be transferred to some new, isolated secured zones. And 2.) the more sophisticated option, the attempt to mitigate the damage by introducing or adding new actors (»inclusion« or regrouping), such as new friends who lessen the influence of the idiots. The problem with the morons, however, is that they are always evenly distributed (never grouped), and that they are always recognizable (cunning or intelligence can be hidden or tempered; stupidity on the other hand, less so).

The third option concerns the right to something in between, the right to the »/« (slash), that is the right to the third (as well as the right of the third),[666] and the right to the third option, to wavering that *a priori* excludes the coercion of an urgent choice between »inclusion« and »exclusion«. That is to say, common or critical engagement, on which I insist, assumes broad action that is necessarily in part epistemological, and does not only include (or bind or involve) Voltaire's »friends who think« (*amis qui pensent*). It also includes those others, whose acts, it seems to me, we still understand insufficiently and take into consideration all too rarely (provisionally, I will here call them ›negative social acts‹), yet are probably necessary for the constitution of a group.[667] A group pushing a car that has broken down is not endangered and destabilized unless one of them is a disabled person who cannot participate in pushing the car.[668] How can we classify all these acts, which are not complementary and in harmony with the acts of the majority? How do those who Husserl vaguely called »abnormal« (*der Anomalen*)[669] constitute the world and their institutions, how do they (the ones opposite from »my normal We« [*mein normales Wir*][670]) participate (*sich beteiligen*) in these acts – this task is still before us.

666 Aristotle invented but also called into question the principle of the excluded middle when distinguishing between judgments about the future that can be neither true nor false, just as Voltaire's wishes to the Marquis d'Argence de Dirac cannot exclude some third possibility.

667 In »The Capabilities of People with Cognitive Disabilities« (p. 331–351), Martha Nussbaum insists exclusively that the »law ought to show respect for them as full equals.« »Law must provide,« »law must go further« – these are the phrases she uses. Certainly insufficient, but the basic condition of any future engagement of all.

668 Cf. Tuomela: We Will Do It, p. 272; Tuomela: The Importance of Us, p. 138; B. Schmid: On Not Doing One's Part, p. 47.

669 Husserl provides a very broad designation for those who do not belong to the world of the normal (*die Welt der Normalen*). As early as 1931 he wonders about the problem of the participation of the abnormal in the constitution of the world. This includes foreigners, animals, children, the twisted (*die Verrückten*), the ill (*die Kranken*), but also thieves, cheats, pseudo-honest (*die Scheinehrlichen*), pseudo-citizens (*die Scheinbürger*), etc. Husserl: Zur Phänomenologie der Intersubjektivität, 2, pp. 133, 146.

670 Ibid., p. 141.

V. To Live Together

1 »Discipline« as Category and »Institutional Discipline«

Why discipline and what is the issue with discipline? First, what is my problem with discipline? I was for a number of years the *de jure* director of three or four institutions (some of which I founded, together with others, of course): I held in my wallet, at the time, several credit cards of these institutions and organizations, I was subject to financial discipline (which is only an implication of *Juridical Discipline*), I had to account for every move, I was controlled by auditors who followed and controlled the decisions and documents produced by these institutions, etc. In addition to that, I demanded of myself and of those with whom I collaborated what can be termed »discipline«. How so? What is it that I was doing when I demanded this and how did I demand it? How did I utter this word, how did I order or call for discipline? How do we construct the equivalent verb from the noun »discipline« and what is its form in the first-person plural imperative (how does it »sound«)? How, further, might I describe someone's behavior as disciplined or undisciplined?) On occasion, still in the same capacity, I would sent a letter or document called »disciplinary warning« or *»rappel à l'ordre«*, announcing a disciplinary action against a colleague, if the lawyers considered there to have been a breach of institutional discipline or if a certain disciplinary responsibility arose.[671] My dilemma then and now (although certainly not mine alone), refers to the attempt at positioning »discipline« (or indiscipline; the word *Disziplinlos* appeared only in the late nineteenth century; Durkheim uses *indiscipline*) within the first great institutional activity, described rather well in the Torah: a group of people who speak the same language build the Tower of Babel.[672]

671 The title of the sixth-century text ascribed to Isidore of Seville, »*Institutionum Disciplinae*«, is usually translated (in the plural) as the disciplines necessary for the rearing of children (institution here refers to education).

672 Since this is a very precise construction of joint or common work, a joint enterprise, a name or joint institution (in verse 4, we read: »Come, let us build us a city, and a tower with its top in the sky, to make a name for ourselves; else we shall be scattered all over the world.«), I am interested to what extent discipline above all is the condition of cooperation and coordination of joint work, that is to say, to what extent is indiscipline the cause of the demise of this great program and grand edifice. Where is the discipline? In the exact language of the group? In constant mobilization of a group or team? Is discipline a matter of obedience of the group (or to the group), or common learning and joint experimentation with new materials and discovery of new building discipline? Or is discipline to be found in a consensus regarding a common program or project? Of course, this example is very convenient because a discovery of indiscipline of this group, and thus a reason for the discontinuation of building, would *de facto* imply a science about institutional rules and institutional discipline.

There are some other reasons for which I think it is necessary to thematize the ›notion‹ of discipline (this is also Durkheim's designation) or discipline ›as a category‹ (or discipline »*als Wortbildung*«[673]). Here are a few preliminary reasons or key inspiration points that could represent an introduction into the thematization of the word or designation ›discipline‹ today. I begin from the quotation marks that appear in the title, that often accompany the word discipline and imply a vagueness and uncertainty of this word.[674] In one of his last texts, Bernard Williams uses the formula (this is his term) »humanistic discipline« with quotation marks, and is quick to add that »it is not just a question of a discipline, as a field or area of enquiry. »Discipline« is supposed to imply discipline.«[675] »Discipline« (in quotation marks) that could obviously be differently understood and refer to several different inter-related protocols, should now, finally, become discipline.[676] However, paradoxically, any rigorous and precise disciplining of a knowledge genre, or, for example, philosophy as such, would necessarily lead to the formatting and regulating of some other domains of knowledge and various discursive models. Quotation marks circulate and are certainly not easily »disciplined«. Floating quotation marks immediately introduce the need to deduce a strict classification of the meaning of the word »discipline«, as well as a new kind of order of explanation. This would be followed by the production of certain priorities in use of the category of discipline and a new theory regarding the significance of discipline in the construction of, for example, the institution or joint work of a group – which is my intention. Even though, paradoxically, there are only very few texts and doctoral theses that systematically thematize »discipline«,[677] to me it seems possible to demonstrate a fairly stable set of various models and variations over the

673 Mauch: Der lateinische Begriff Disciplina, p. 3.

674 Georg Becker designates discipline a term; on the other hand, *»Disciplin«* (with quotation marks) *ist ein belasteter Begriff.* Becker: Disziplin im Unterricht, p. 9.

675 Cf. Williams: Philosophy as a Humanistic Discipline.

676 »In philosophy,« continues Williams, »there had better be something that counts as getting it right, or doing it right, and I believe that this must still be associated with the aims of philosophy of offering arguments and expressing oneself clearly, aims that have been particularly emphasized by analytic philosophy, though sometimes in a perverse and one-sided manner.« This text has certainly initiated various polemics and doubts regarding the possibility of interdisciplinarity being disciplined, as well as whether it is at all possible to be in a space between disciplines, that is, whether there is space beyond discipline or beyond the institution as such. The problem also occurs in the use of discipline and interdisciplinarity among philosophers who do not belong to, for instance, analytic philosophy. What kind of discipline (without quotation marks) is Derrida speaking about in a conversation with Florian Rötzer from 1987, when he says explicitly: *»Ich bin für die Disciplin«*. Rötzer: Französische Philosophie im Gespräch, p. 86. In »Of the Humanities and the Discipline of Philosophy«, Derrida, just like Williams, privileges the discipline of philosophy or philosophy as a discipline and in a way that tasks it with disciplining other genres of knowledge and other »humanities« (pp. 5–40).

677 Cf. Sulser: Disciplina, p. 72; Cappello et al.: Disciplina; Marrou: Doctrina et disciplina dans la langue des Pères de l'Eglise; Chenu: Notes de lexicographie philosophique médiévale »Disciplina«; Mauch: Der lateinische Begriff Disciplina; Morel: Disciplina; Dürig: Disciplina; Knox: Disciplina.

course of centuries. I will enumerate these points (mostly I follow dictionaries, which ought to be consulted ever anew), as well as add some new interpretations of discipline. *Disciplina* (following the *Thesaurus Linguae Latinae*) that refers to learning (*disco* [I learn], *doceo, docere*; *discere* is to learn, learning, a disciple is a follower, fellow, apostle (...) one who is influenced by doctrine; doctrine is the property of the teacher, while discipline is student practice and training), has *strictore sensu: actus, ratio erudiendi, docendi, insitutio, educatio, studium, didaskalia* and *latiore sensu: severitas, severa morum educatio, paideia*.[678] Both the literal and a broader meaning could be distributed as in the Grimm dictionary: discipline first refers to *flagellatio*, punishment (*körperliche Kasteiung*, as late as the twelfth century, discipline is used to signify a massacre)[679] – always from religious and fanatical motives of training or pacifying the body; it is indubitably of »Christian« origin, that is, in one way or another, a »male, Stoical thing«; discipline is further in direct connection with education, pedagogy, rearing (*Zucht*), order, militarism. And third, discipline refers to a »field or area of enquiry« (*Fachgebiet*; scientific or sport discipline).[680] What is certainly needed are entirely new steps and important transformations of discipline, unfolding over the centuries, more or less convincingly, in order to show that discipline above all refers to a group and to a plurality of differing subjects (above all the individual within a group and community, one with others), and that self-discipline (*Selbst-Zucht* is Nietszche's phrase) or self-education is only a deduced and reduced protocol of secondary importance. More precisely, self-discipline and self-correction (self-punishment) has as its goal always subsequent and once again new inclusion into a group, and belonging to a group; not the other way round.[681] War or military discipline is an excellent exam-

678 *Thesaurus Linguae Latinae*, 5, p. 1317. In *Forcelinis Lexicon*, *disciplina* is defined as the *ratio vivendi et discendi*. »*Proprie disciplina est ratio vivendi et discendi, quae discipulis traditur, institutio, educatio*«. Discipline could potentially be a translation of the Greek *paideia* (Otto Mauch defends this position; Mauch: Der lateinische Begriff Disciplina, p. 14), or of the Greek *episteme* (which is how Boethius uses it), but also of the Greek word *mathein* (to learn) or *mathesis*. Saint Thomas speaks of the equivalence of Aristotle's *mathesis* and discipline (*mathematicas scientias disciplinas vocat*), as does Gilbert de la Porrée (*Graece mathematica, latine disciplinalis vocatur*). Cf. Chenu: Notes de lexicographie philosophique médiévale »Disciplina«, pp. 690–691. In Hebrew, discipline or obedience (*mishma'at*) is in direct relation with meaning. To give importance to something or give something priority in meaning (*lemashme'a*) is to discipline. To create meanings is to create order. Finally, in Isidor of Seville's text, »*Institutionum Disciplinae*«, in rearing children, particular attention is paid to reading, understanding the meaning of words, accents and meanings of words.

679 In the entry on »*Discipline*« in Diderot's *Encyclopedia*, this connection with *flagellation* is explained by saying that »discipline also refers to a means by which to humiliate« (*discipline se dit aussi de l'instrument avec lequel on se mortifie*). Diderot / D'Alembert (eds.): Encyclopédie, 4, p. 1030.

680 Walter Dürig follows this distinction to the letter. Cf. Dürig: Disciplina, pp. 248–262.

681 Since the time of the ancient *Manuel of Discipline* (*Serekh ha-Yahad*), rules serve to include individuals into a community, thus constituting the community itself based on these acts. The rules that Isidor of Seville edits that refer to each individual child imply the rules of the community and common life of all. Discipline leads to a community and is the preamble of communal life. The rules that Saint Victor reconstructs in the well-known *Disciplines: An Ordered Form of Living* (*De insti-*

ple here. In *L'Encyclopedie*, Diderot edits the following excerpt from the article »Military Discipline« (this phrase is a remake of Justus Lipsius' formula *»disciplina militaris«*). We shall see that such normativization of discipline (discipline becomes norm, although discipline is not necessarily normative, that is, discipline is recognized as a protocol or power that is missing and is therefore insisted upon, a game that could be recognized as normative) recurs later in Durkheim as well, thus definitely steering its meaning:

Without discipline, an army would be no more than a heap of volunteers, incapable of being unified in common defense, seeking only to pillage and tending to disorder. It is discipline that unites them through officers' orders, to which they must show blind obeisance in all that concerns the service. »It is not the number of soldiers that makes an army formidable, but rather the ability to be flexible and strong, and the creation of a single body, moved by the same spirit of so many different members. Such were the small armies of the Greeks who vanquished the Persian millions«. Military Institute. In other words, it is to military discipline that the Greeks owe their victories over the Persians, and the Romans their conquests. In order to be well disciplined, troops need to be relentlessly exercised. Even the best discipline is lost in rest.[682]

Discipline is at once subject and object. It is discipline that actively unites and produces itself: »It is discipline that unites them through officers' orders (...)«; (*C'est elle* [discipline] *qui les réunit sous les ordres des officiers* (...)). Further, discipline is the spirit that connects the body or bodies (the material) or the glue (this word I borrow once again from Searle) that holds the group members together. Further still, discipline is a pseudo-entity or »new material« that could replace real members or portions of a group in opposing another group (it is not the number of soldiers that counts, but the disciplined army). Finally, rest and repose dissociate members of a group, weaken and dissolve it (obviously, discipline refers exclusively to joint work). The two final characteristics could be further specified, and also,

tutione novitiorum) are directed at a production of knowledge that simultaneously disciplines well (*scientia disciplina bonitas*). What does this mean? Disciplining an individual for her to become a member of a group is deduced from a partial disciplining of everything that refers to external matters, the behavior of the body, manners and mores (*mores*) ... how to walk, talk, gesture, eat, drink, how to dress implies doing all this with others. (In his lectures on pedagogy, Kant uses the German word *dressiren* that comes from the English ›to dress‹, and which is also the reason why the place where preachers change is called *Dresskammer* and not *Trostkammer*.) Being in control of one's own body (discipline) is a necessary condition of being part of a group.

682 *Sans la discipline, une armée ne seroit formée que d'un amas de volontaires, incapables de se réunir pour la défense commune, avides seulement du pillage & du desordre. C'est elle qui les réunit sous les ordres des officiers, auxquels ils doivent une obéissance aveugle pour tout ce qui concerne le service. »Ce n'est point tant la multitude des soldats qui rend une armée formidable, que la facilité de les rendre souples & fermes, & de ne faire de tant de membres différens qu'un corps animé du même esprit. Telles étoient ces petites armées des Grecs, qui avoient à combattre des millions de Perses.« Inst. milit. En effet, c'est à la discipline militaire que les Grecs doivent leurs victoires sur les Perses, & les Romains leurs conquêtes. Des troupes pour être bien disciplinées, doivent être exercées sans relâche. La meilleure discipline se perd dans le repos.* Diderot/D'Alembert (eds.): Encyclopédie, 4, p. 1030.

they complement one another. Discipline certainly depends on potential conflict (or war) with another group or on competitive action with another team.[683] Constant communal activity of members of a group really represents joint learning, mutual correction (since Saint Augustine, discipline is more correction than punishment), as well as the construction of institutional or disciplinary rules or »institutional content« that can be learned and taught (transferred, imparted) to future followers and subsequent members of the group, thus performing its regeneration. In a word, if there are »disciplined performances« (Rawls), if there is discipline (in a group, among group members, within each member of a group – there still remain questions about where discipline is lacking and what place it ought to take within a group or an army)[684] – then there is a kind of disciplinary power (*potere disciplinare*as *potere di supremazia*) of a group and the group as such (discipline constitutes a new entity, that is, an institution), and there is knowledge, »a discipline, as a field or area of enquiry«.

In the second part of this extraordinary sentence, »It is discipline that unites them through officers' orders, to which they must show blind obeisance in all that concerns the service« (*C'est elle qui les réunit sous les ordres des officiers, auxquels ils doivent une obéissance aveugle pour tout ce qui concerne le service*), apart from

683 In a celebrated text »The Discipline of Teams« of March 1993, republished in the Harvard Business Review – Classics, Jon Katzenbach and Douglas Smith write: »We also found that teams and good performance are inseparable: You cannot have one without the other (...) Teams produce discrete work products through the joint contributions of their members. This is what makes possible performance levels greater than the sum of all the individual bests of team members. Simply stated, a team is more than the sum of its parts«. Katzenbach/Smith: The Discipline of Teams, pp. 3, 7–8. The origin of discipline is war. Ortega y Gasset writes: »The careful desire to avoid risk rules the entrepreneurial spirit, while the warrior is born of exceptional appetite for danger. Finally, what they have in common, discipline, was first invented by the warrior spirit and has been transplanted into man by way of its pedagogy« (*Dirige al espíritu industrial un cauteloso afán de evitar el riesgo, mientras el guerrero brota de un genial apetito de peligro. En fin, aquello que ambos tienen de común, la disciplina, ha sido primero inventado por el espíritu guerrero y merced a su pedagogía injertado en el hombre*), Ortega y Gasset: España invertebrada, p. 443. »War discipline is one of the greatest strengths of history. Any other discipline, in particular one that assumes any sort of complex skill, issues from this spiritual order that man created for battle« (*La disciplina bélica ha sido una de las máximas potencias de la historia. Toda otra disciplina, muy especialmente la que es supuesto de cualquier industria complicada, viene de este orden espiritual inventado por el hombre para combater*). Ortega y Gasset: La interpretacón bélica de la historia, p. 640. »War is not instinct, but invention. Animals do not have it, and it is a purely human institution, much as science or administration. It has led to one of the greatest discoveries, the basis of all of civilization: the discovery of discipline. All other forms of discipline issue from this base, that is, military discipline.« (*La guerra no es un instinto, sino un invento. Los animales la desconocen y es pura institución humana, como la ciencia o la administración. Ella llevó a uno de los mayores descubrimientos, base de toda civilización: al descubrimiento de la disciplina. Todas las demás formas de disciplina proceden de la primigenia, que fue la disciplina militar.*) Ortega y Gasset: La rebelión de las masas, p. 507.

684 This aspect revealed by *L'Encyclopedie*, in which discipline is ever missing or that there is not enough of it, is complementary to Foucault's sentence »nothing escapes discipline (*la discipline ne laisse rien échapper*). Foucault: Sécurité, territoire, population, p. 47.

the hierarchy established by discipline (the sentence subject) between the officers' orders and *blind obeisance* (*une obéissance aveugle*) of the subjects (»service« is the word that applies to all members of the group regardless of their position in the hierarchy of the group), we also see the discursive character of »social discipline«, in this case, the institution of the army. Although discipline is *de facto* scattered throughout the locations of connections of rules and relations, properly uttered orders, obedience or listening (blind but not deaf, and probably not dumb), the multitudes of bodies that these speech acts move and that temporarily hold them together in a given place, it seems that above all it possesses institutional capacity.

How should we define this ›scattered status‹ of discipline and in what way give it its categorial nature (perhaps social categorical nature and position) – this is the task that would perhaps first have to again amend some of the conceptual classifications of Michel Foucault, while entirely respecting his sincere anti-institutionalism. To this point, I would like to immediately offer two points regarding Foucault's understanding of the institution: first, that Foucault's thematization of the institution and his problem with institutions and discipline appears at the beginning of the eighties when he first mentions biopolitics within his faultless analyses of liberalism, that is, when he constructs the field of biopolitics (the appearance of biopolitics implies anti-institutionalism). The second point is that this anti-institutionalism (Foucault as a maximalist, institutional fundamentalist or transcendental institutionalist [these are Amartya Sen's terms] does not recognize the idea of a »good« or »just« institution) is entirely atypical of the French tradition. Not only because of French institutionalists and jurists Renard and Hauriou, or the French revolutionary tradition of Robespierre and Saint-Just (»everything not yet institutionalized is the enemy and anti-revolutionary in essence«; »there is nothing outside institutions«), but also due to his contemporaries (e. g., Lacan, Deleuze, Derrida), who showed, each in their own way, trust in reform of institutions, construction of new institutions or counter-institutions, joint struggle for institutions, etc.

Is it then really discipline that institutionalizes the institution? Or, in other words, is discipline actually the practice of the institution? In a rather undisciplined conversation from 1977, Foucault, without clear intention, introduces the difference between »*episteme*« and »*apparatus*« (*dispositif*). The first is specifically discursive, while the other is more heterogenous, both discursive and non-discursive. In that same conversation, to the amazement of his interlocutors, he defines the institution by fitting it into so-called »non-discursive« or silent formations:

> The term »institution« is generally applied to any kind of more-or-less constrained, learned behavior. Anything that functions in a society as a system of constraint and which isn't an utterance, in short, the entire field of the non-discursive social, is an institution. (…) If you take Gabriel's architectural plan for the Military School together with the actual construction of the School, how is one to say what is discursive and what in-

stitutional? That would only interest me if the building didn't conform to the plan. But I don't think it's very important to be able to make that distinction, given that my problem isn't a linguistic one.[685]

»The entire field of the non-discursive social, is an institution« (*tout le social non discursif, c'est l'institution*). If discipline functioned as institutional practice, this sentence could be entirely ignored as incorrect and wholly unacceptable.

One possibility, then, of approaching »discipline« and its better understanding would certainly be the thematization of widespread resistance to discipline in general. It seems to me that various figures of resistance and opposition to discipline thus necessarily imply a revalorization of certain disciplinary protocols and an attempt at a more precise naming and conceptualizing (locating) discipline (or an amendment of the idea of discipline; the establishment of creative discipline; the power to inscribe something else into discipline).[686] If we assume that various protocols of discipline and disciplining (coercion, pressure, constraints, violence) are found first of all on the border from the individual towards the collective or group, then resistance to discipline is symmetrical to resistance to the institution and institutions (or some forms of these). Such resistance can be entirely caricatural and absurd (it is completely illusory and inappropriate to become engaged against joint learning, studying together),[687] it can sometimes be very cynical and

685 *Ce qu'on appelle généralement «institution», c'est tout comportement plus ou moins contraint, appris. Tout ce qui, dans une société, fonctionne comme système de contrainte, sans être un énoncé, bref, tout le social non discursif, c'est l'institution. (...) Entre le programme architectural de l'École militaire par Gabriel, et la construction de l'École militaire elle-même, qu'est-ce qui est discursif, qu'est-ce qui est institutionnel? Cela ne m'intéresse que si l'édifice n'est pas conforme au programme. Mais je ne crois pas qu'il soit très important de faire ce tri-là, dès lors que mon problème n'est pas linguistique.* Foucault: Le jeu de Michel Foucault, pp. 62–93. (Interview with D. Colas, A. Grosrichard, G. Le Gaufey, J. Livi, G. Miller, J. Miller, J.-A. Miller, C, Millot, G. Wajeman.) In a pause in a sentence, J.-A. Miller interjects: »Clearly the institution is discursive« (*L'institution, c'est évidemment du discursif*).

686 These last three variations come from Peter Eisenman, with whom I attempted to construct a sketch of a small paper about discipline and architectural discipline, and with whom I have analyzed many of the problems that appear in this chapter. Cf. Eisenman: Palladio Virtuel.

687 Amale Andraos, the Dean of the School of Architecture of Columbia University, in an interview to the magazine *Log* mentions that her daughter attends »the most progressive preschool in the East Village. There's a big sign at the entrance that says, ›We do not believe in discipline‹. She continues: »I feel the same way about the notion of discipline (...)« Studebaker: A Conversation with Amale Andraos. Andraos is here, entirely unwittingly and unawares, confronting the institution of architecture as such, that is, the history of her own discipline. »He must have both a natural gift and also readiness to learn« says Vitruvius (*De Architectura*, p. 7). In Latin, Vitruvius writes the following: »*Itaque eum etiam ingeniosum oportet esse et ad disciplinam docilem. Neque enim ingenium sine disciplina aut disciplina sine ingenio perfectum artificum potest efficere.*« (I, 1, 15) John Dewey, aware of the possibility of »a new type of discipline«, sees the progress and development of students at the exact place where discipline is help to the group and serves joint work: »But if the end in view is the development of a spirit of social co-operation and community life, discipline must grow out of and be relative to such an aim.« Dewey: *The School and Society*, p. 12. »Collaborative spirit« or »group spirit« are frequent phrases cropping up in various texts of the time, above all in Germany. Eduard Spranger (in *Lebensformen*, from 1914) thematizes »social spiritual acts« (*gesellschafliche Geistes-*

dangerous in its frivolity, but also it can be just as much entirely inspirational and promising when insufficiently clear and justified. In any case, resistance to discipline has a long and complicated history, and its origin is certainly in resentment to violent pedagogical practices, torture of the weak, and beating of children, prisoners, the ill, etc.

I cite here two instances of resistance to discipline and two simultaneous insistences on discipline as a short introduction to a fragment from Emile Durkheim, with which I will close this chapter on discipline as condition of joint work and good functioning of a group. These two calls to discipline and disciplining really repeat Durkheim's endeavors that are always on the horizon. In February of 1917, Antonio Gramsci writes a few fragments in the publication of the youth section of the Piemontese Socialist Party, »*La città futura*«. His aim is to educate and shape (*educare e formare*) young socialists and teach them political discipline, solidarity and life organized by the party (*alla vita organizata del partito*). In a brilliant text entitled »*Gli indifferenti*«, he speaks of his hatred towards the neutral and the indifferent, and to their indiscipline (concluding his text with »*Vivo, sono partigiano. Percio' odio chi non parteggia, odio gli indifferenti*«). In a brief fragment »*Disciplina e liberta*«, he says that disciplining is the condition to be independent and free (*Disciplinarsi è rendersi indipendenti e liberi*), while in the short text »*La disciplina*«, he evokes Rudyard Kipling's *The Jungle Book* and the discipline present in a strong bourgeois state where all obey dutifully:

> Bourgeois discipline is the only force that can maintain the bourgeois state of affairs. What is necessary is discipline opposed to discipline. But bourgeois discipline is a mechanical and authoritarian thing, while socialist discipline is autonomous and spontaneous (*La disciplina borghese è l'unica forza che mantenga saldo l'aggregato borghese. Bisogna a disciplina contraporre disciplina. Ma la disciplina borghese è cosa meccanica ed autoritaria, la disciplina socialista è autonoma e spontanea*).[688]

The second fragment is the incessant and still unthematized call or cry for so-called ›popular discipline‹ that we find in the last decade in various interviews of Alain Badiou. Here is a brief fragment from 2008, published in *Critical Inquiry* n. 645:

> I think the Leninist party was at bottom a military model. And for good reason. This is not a criticism. Lenin was obsessed with one question: how to win the war? The question of discipline is therefore fundamental, just as it is for an army. You cannot win the war if people do whatever they like, if there is no unity and so on. The problem for emancipatory politics today, however, is to invent a non-military model of discipline. We need a popular

akte); further Tomoo Otaka differentiates between »*das sachliche und das soziale Geistesgebilde*. Cf. Otaka: Grundlegung der Lehre vom sozialen Verband, p. 126.

688 Gramsci: La città futura, p. 19.

discipline. I would even say, as I have many times, that »those who have nothing have only their discipline. The poor, those with no financial or military means, those with no power – all they have is their discipline, their capacity to act together. This discipline is already a form of organization. The question is whether all discipline can be reduced to a military model, the model that dominated the first part of the twentieth century. How can we find, invent, exercise or experiment with – today, after all, is an age of experimentation – a non-military discipline?[689]

All of these are difficult tasks and complicated suggestions. Each of these attempts to transform discipline while also defend its basic protocols carries the endeavor to categorically structure discipline and render it universal. If we read Durkheim's 1902–1903 Sorbonne lectures today (published as *Moral Education* [*L'éducation morale*]) as a true manifest of conceptualizing discipline, it is truly not certain whether discipline has anything to do with morality or whether it ought to have anything to do with morality (»the first element of morality – spirit of discipline«, says Durkheim). However, Durkheim thematizes indiscipline and discipline in the context of the group and its difference to »the (undisciplined) mob« (*foule* [*sans discipline*]).[690] He thematizes the significance of consciousness of belonging to a group, which complements discipline that at once »orders and contains« (*régularise et elle contient*), etc.[691] These moments are today, it seems to me, most important in the reconstruction of discipline.

A few years before writing this book, Durkheim is thinking about equality and social justice. Does discipline mean that simply being together, close enough to one another, implies equality and thus justice? Or conversely, is a society equal when people relate (also in disciplined manner) to each other as equals? This is not an issue of a just or equitable distribution of some kind of »currency of egalitarian justice« (a phrase of Gerald Cohen's), nor, on the other hand, of »owners disciplin[ing] non-owners« (the answer capitalism offers to Michael Walzer's question »Who disciplines whom?« from *Spheres of Justice*). At issue are relations or acting, at issue is discipline that is beyond domination, hierarchy, exploitation and social exclusion. Here is the fragment penned by Emile Durkheim in 1897:

Truly, the nearer this ideal equality (*égalité idéale*) is approached, the less social restraint will be necessary. But it is only a matter of degree. One sort of heredity will always exist,

689 Badiou: »We Need a Popular Discipline«, p. 650.

690 Durkheim: L'éducation morale, p. 172. The word ›mob‹ designating a kind of pre-institutional entity, at once fictional and regulative, without institutions, rules, or discipline (all words in direct synonymy) – is used in the same way by (cousins) Mauss and Durkheim.

691 In one of her early books, *On Social Facts*, Margaret Gilbert misses an opportunity to thematize the importance of discipline in constructing social facts and constituting a group. In her book on Simmel and Durkheim, as founders as social ontology, Gilbert fails to use the book *Moral Education*, while analyzing in detail on page 267 an example of Wye Army or Wye soldiers who »mostly think discipline is of no importance.«

that of natural talent (*des dons naturels*). Intelligence, taste, scientific, artistic, literary or industrial ability, courage and manual dexterity are gifts received by each of us at birth, as the heir to wealth receives his capital or as the nobleman formerly received his title and function. A moral discipline will therefore still be required (*pour faire accepter*) to make those less favored by nature accept the lesser advantages which they owe to the chance of birth. Shall it be demanded that all have an equal share and that no advantage be given those more useful and deserving? But then there would have to be a discipline far stronger to make these accept (*pour faire accepter*) a treatment merely equal to that of the mediocre and incapable.

But like the one first mentioned, this discipline can be useful only if thought (*considérée*) just by the peoples subject to it. When it is maintained (*Quand elle ne se maintient*) only by custom and force, peace and harmony are illusory.[692]

Conditions always follow discipline (*pour faire accepter*; *pour faire accepter*; *considérée*; *Quand elle ne se maintient*)... »We should re-read«[693] carefully what Durkheim said and we will certainly find very good justifications to forget Foucault's anti-institutionalism today.[694]

692 Durkheim: Le suicide, pp. 278–279.

693 During the 28 March 1973 course *La société punitive*, Foucault insists: »We should re-read what he said in *Suicide* regarding anomy: what characterizes the social as such, in contrast with the political, which is the level of decisions, and the economic, which is the level of determinations, is nothing other than the system of disciplines, of constraints.« Foucault: La société punitive, pp. 242–243.

694 What is the nature of this »anti-institutionalism«, and could it perhaps be an »institutional anti-institutionalism«? Over the course of his life Foucault did not manage to properly thematize his issue with the institutional protocol or find a way to define and explain the »pre-institutional sector« (which he mentions often). Yet, Yan Thomas is entirely in line with Foucault in a brief text about institutions, when he says that institutions only poorly manifest or express the social; in a word, the social escapes them. Cf. Thomas: Los artificios de las instituciones, pp. 9–11. Foucault himself was unable to »arrive at the vocabulary« (*fixer le vocabulaire*, his archival note from 1969). Foucault: Homère, les récits, l'éducation, les discours, p. 108. This further means that we do not have a clear form and outline of the following concepts and notions in Foucault: *discours*, *récit*, *appareil*, *épisteme*, *dispositif*, *réseau*, *social*, *rationalité*, *énoncé*, etc. He was unsatisfied with the notion of the institution because he found spaces outside them, which the institutions neglected or neutralized (*L'institution neutralize les rapports de force* (...); Foucault: Le pouvoir psychiatrique, p. 16). There is something even more important that demands explanation, something prior to institutional analysis. Foucault always names this using some other designation: sometimes it is *discours*, *dispositif*, *appareil*, at other times, *la microphysique du pouvoir*, and then towards the end of his life, that which »never crystalizes« (*ne crsitallise*) in institutions, he then calls *le programme* or *programmation*, or even *le project*. Cf. Foucault, Qu'appelle-t-on punir?. It seems to me that this last strategy is in its final consequence substantively institutional. Foucault's focus on the limits of institutional protocols could possibly be an insistence on a new institutionalization and a new institutionalism.

2 Police. On the Institution of Universal Violence and Violence of the Universal

Speaking of the institution of the police in his famous 1921 text, »Toward the Critique of Violence« (*Zur Kritik der Gewalt*), Walter Benjamin gives two very important characteristics of police violence. The first and fundamental characteristic is that the police are always connected to violence but that their role within the state is difficult to pinpoint, given that the police are an »institution of the modern State«.[695] My intention in this chapter is to show that police violence is a consequence of a *deformation* of the institution of police or a deformation of violence. That is to say, the police *do not properly belong to matters of the state*, but rather to civil society.

Benjamin's second claim about the police and their violence refers to specific moments, and he particularly emphasizes that democracy involves a »greatest conceivable degeneration of violence« (*die denkbar größte Entartung der Gewalt*). These moments are actually the ones in which the police deviate from law (that is, the state, since Benjamin here equates law and the state), thus creating the »right« of the police (*das ›Recht‹ der Polizei*). That is to say, »the police intervene ›for security reasons‹ in countless cases where no clear legal situation exists«.[696] According to Benjamin, the weakness of the state allows for the police, an entirely distinct entity beyond citizen and state control, to conduct a terror of »police right« over its citizens. How is this possible? More specifically, what is the nature of police authority? Who or what authorizes the police to act? Who uses the police for coercion or violence? When does the police surveil, spy, or beat its citizens, when does it overstep its own authority?

A sketch regarding the degeneration or deformation of this essentially civil institution could begin with an imaginary moment, when the president or sovereign of a state makes brutal *use* of the police against citizens protesting corruption or, say, a gas tax increase. My claim is that insufficient social engagement of citizens, insufficient cooperative organizing, along with poor joint work and insufficient production of social acts, necessarily implies the existence of a professional instance with the capacity to protect public space, perform coercive acts (Hans Kelsen's term is *Zwangakte*), or forcefully impose order. If citizens do not control and correct each other, do not protect and care for the space and time in which they live, if they do not regulate the communication and circulation of relations,

695 Benjamin: Toward the Critique of Violence, p. 47.
696 Ibid. p. 48.

connections, money and objects among themselves – which is to say if citizens do not act as citizens, do not take care of the general civic ›policing‹ – then, predictably, some instance is constituted, coalescing, and then gathering a monopoly over a professional use of violence. The sovereign will therefore in certain circumstances use this instance (which has thus entered what we could now call the »state« stage): breaking up protests, defending the street and square, defending the universal – the sovereign is really defending his own status. The increasing complexity of social relations over the course of history only amplifies this effect.

What is the connection between engagement and collective action by the citizens and the police? To what extent is a police protocol part of any collective action that considers the general good or interest of all? How is it that control and reduction of individual freedom, which is the basic characteristic of the police, necessarily protects the common good?

Only twenty-five years separate the thinking about the police by two of the greatest institutionalists of the turn of the nineteenth century: Saint-Just and Hegel. The first explains in detail why the police are grounded in false principles (of which one is that their work is spying), why they are violent and corrupt, why they operate against the people and the general spirit (*l'esprit public*), indeed often even in favor of the enemy. He tells us that »spirit is not the right word« (*l'esprit n'est pas le mot*), since the general spirit resides in our own heads, not all of which are equally endowed with intelligence and clarity. Saint-Just is nevertheless adamant: »We need to link up to a form public awareness – that is the best police!« (*Il faut s'attacher à former une conscience publique; voilà la meilleure police!*).[697]

In the 1818/1819 seminar »Die Philosophie des Rechts« (from Homeyer's notes), Hegel is also searching for an alternative or, paradoxically, the original model, the original »instance of police«. The police refers to everyone and it is »universal vigilance for the good of the individual and the maintaining of order« (*die allgemeine Vorsorge für das Wohl des Einzelnen und für das Daseyn des Rechts*). However, in more recent times, says Hegel, things are not so good, since the ›*Politeia*‹ has »decayed« (*heruntergekommen*), turned into the police, and often equated with the state.[698] The state or »police state« that Hegel equates with something external (external order, *aüßere Ordnung*), could be replaced by the figure of a sentry. The sentry is a symbol of the power of the general or universal (*Schildwache: Symbol der Macht des Allgemeinen*), and as such ought »not only annul, but prevent injury« (*daß die Verletzungen nicht nur getilgt, sondern auch gehindert werden*). Yet, a multitude of people, myriad arbitrary actions (*willkür-*

697 Saint-Just, »Décret relatif aux gens suspect« of 17 September 1793. Quoted in Napoli: Naissance de la police moderne, p. 228.

698 »Things have never been worse (*schlimmer*) than »when« the state or government sought to care for the individual's welfare by not allowing him to care for himself«. § 92. Hegel: Naturrecht und Staatswissenschaft, p. 310.

licher Handlungen) by individuals demand general supervision (the supervision of all).[699] »Something universal (*ein Allgemeines*) must watch over them, preventing deleterious effects by modifying my own arbitrariness (*schädlichen Einfluß auf andere verhindert durch Modifizierung meiner Willkür*). There is an eternal struggle (*ewiger Kampf*) between what is general and such particular arbitrariness (*die besondere Willkür*)«.

I would like to show that strong ties among individuals produce public consciousness, that is, a certain symbolic power of the universal (although not only symbolic of course). These ties are the unconditional condition of reducing violence of the universal over the individual, rendering the eternal struggle of which Hegel speaks less violent. If we do not connect with one another, or sufficiently construct common or general consciousness, we necessarily invite »order from without«, i. e., the police as the state or the state as such. We produce the violence of the state and hatred among individuals towards the state and police.[700] Hence Hegel's opposition to Fichte's »professionalization of the police« from his Lectures on the Philosophy of Right. It is an attempt to prevent the degeneration of various forms of oversight and prevention. Such methods would revive a certain original meaning of the police (*»bonne police«*),[701] which does not stand for »public order«, but represents a collection of institutional acts. Such collection would fall within the domain of science and have an epistemological value (for example, today it would be part and parcel of social ontology), in service of increasing common happiness or happiness of the community (*gemeinschaftliche Glückseeligheit*, Justi) and whose function would be to limit and »thwart« (*frein*) dictatorship of one man or king (Bodin).

To begin with, is there any connection between the police and the violent universal? What is general or omnipresent violence, and also what kind of violence does the universal as such perform? (Could an example of this degeneration be found in socialist Yugoslav police, called *milicija*, a derivation from militia?[702])

The keyboard on my computer is set to French because this language is close to me, and the MS Word I use contains French markings. What is called font in English, the size and shape of letters (such as, Arial point 12), in French is called *»police«*. This regulation (or rule) that allows for letter size to be the same across

699 *»Die Aufsicht auf dieselben kann deswegen auch gemeinsam sein.«* Hegel: Die Philosophie des Rechts. Die Mitschriften Wannenmann (Heidelberg 1817/18) und Homeyer (Berlin 1818/19), pp. 266–267.

700 In his famous text, Knemeyer explains the resistance to the police as a liberal tendency in Germany after 1815. Knemeyer: Polizey, pp. 188–189.

701 Cf. Laborier: La »bonne police«.

702 The name given to the police in socialist Yugoslavia was *milicija*, which derives from militia, but performed the exact same social role as the police in other societies. The word *policija*, police, would come to replace it only at the time of the country's dissolution.

keyboards and computers is somehow a matter of police, or »policing«.[703] The police could be the agent or subject that passes such regulation or sets standards (leaving aside for now whether the police also protect such regulation, which is the accepted thinking), but simultaneously, this regulation *is* precisely the »police as such« because it is entirely independent from the interest of the individual and surpasses them. It is a certificate, a proof (policy, *polizza*, *la police*, a paper that proves, for example, that a car is insured) or guarantee. It serves not only for identification – that a text is written in font size or *police* 12 – but also as guarantee that the text can easily be transferred to other computers, that it is compatible and communicable, that it circulates, able to be recognized and transferred on. It is similar with the tone of voice used to read out this text, which would have to conform to a given standard and hearing capability of the auditors. It also refers to the quality of the text, the quality of a potential reading that ought not prevent others from identifying that this text was written in one language and then translated, etc.

The police are supposed to facilitate communication and circulation among us, that is, of those elements we manipulate. This is the understanding of police protocol with which we are all familiar:[704] actively or preventively, we all oversee, exclude, or correct those who do not follow certain standards. In this case, police violence (police force) is forever connected with certain deformation and degeneration of norms and all of us who simultaneously practice and control them. Degeneration (which would appear to be more widespread than just democracy, as per Benjamin) means that a single individual or a group of individuals does not follow the standards set, or does so entirely arbitrarily, hurting others and usurping public space in the process. It also means that this individual or group cannot be stopped or corrected through collective inspection. (Hegel is perhaps the first to suggest that oversight or inspection could simultaneously carry a preventive function.) The police ought to therefore be immanently present wherever there is a group of people (there can be no police for an isolated individual); yet, the police are also never really substantially or transcendentally present or never present enough. (We can see this well from moments such as when someone yells, »if you don't quiet down, I shall call the police!« – where the police are not already, not sufficiently, present.) Thus, the police would function as an entirely external and

703 »In one of the first definitions of »police matters« (Polizeisachen), they were specified very generally as those matters relating to good order in the community. The Magdeburg Prozessordnung of 1696 stated: »all become doubtful at times (of what is to be understood by Policey-Sachen), thus we explain as follows (that all those affairs concerned with the maintenance of the community in itself which does not augment as a result interesse singulorem) belong to Policey-Sachen.«« Quoted in Knemeyer: Polizey, p. 177.

704 In *Le droit public* from 1697, J. Domat writes: »Through nature, God has given order, and through police, men facilitate communication« (*Dieu a pourvu par l'ordre de la nature et les hommes par la police à faciliter les communications*). Quoted in Napoli: Naissance de la police moderne, p. 23.

expert portion of citizens-hygienists of a city. They would arrive from somewhere outside to establish or ›smooth over‹ the damaged and contaminated relationships in a (part of a) city.[705]

Hegel's considerations of the police in his lectures on the philosophy of right (from different years) should help indicate the significance of the idea that the police are exclusively our own issue, such as those of us present in a given place of a city.[706] In one way or another, this is our »social matter« (this is the condition and principal source of socialism that has been recognized in Hegel): the police do not imply any such outside instance and has nothing to do with the state or police state, such as promoted before and after Hegel by Johann Gottlieb Fichte (*Grundlage des Naturrechts*) and Adolf Lasson (*System der Rechtsphilosophie*).[707]

We could conceivably start a rebellion against the violence of the prescription of letter size »font size 12« or »*police* 12«, because simply we have chosen within our group to follow an alternative system. Or we could rebel against the measured and standard form of address because we simply do not wish to do as all others do, flouting the tedious and tiring universal regulation. However, this would bring us to new violence that is meant to protect the universal or the general. Paradoxically, this violence brings the universal's sentry and the one deviating from it closer together. (It is likely that fear of the police or sentry is complementary with the awe before the master criminal, as both are concentrated on the instance of the universal comprised of the two.) Still, all the forms of violence suddenly appearing here or becoming possible now, show, above all, obstruction in circulation and exchange of a group, insufficient engagement of all for the common cause; that is to say, precisely the task of the police or the »*bonne police*«: »*gemeinschaftliche Glückseligkeit*« (*bonheur commun*, common good).[708]

Before I discuss further Hegel's positions drawn from a few of his lectures of various parts of his career (which place the police, as well as the corporation, into

705 »There is a further set of associations with the concept ›Polizei‹ that emerges in this literature: ›politeness‹, ›consideration‹, ›prudence‹, ›elegance‹ and ›beauty‹. The ›internal Polizierung of Men and States (1770) derives from middle Latin policia (from *polire*, *polieren*, *glätten*)« (Grimm). Quoted in Knemeyer: Polizey, p. 180.

706 In lectures on German idealist philosophy, John Rawls notes the conspicuous importance of the corporation and police in Hegel's civil society. »In Hegel's day police covered not only law enforcement but also the fixing of the prices of necessities, the control of the quality of goods, the arrangements of hospitals, street lighting, and much else.« Rawls: Lectures on the History of Moral Philosophy, p. 345.

707 Hatred of the police, perfectly synonymous with hatred of institutions and institutionalism – advocated and fostered in French social philosophy from Foucault to Rancière and Boltanski – is a consequence of a wrong and simplified, albeit historically grounded, equating of the police and state apparatus. »*Le bon emploi des forces de l'Etat, c'est cela l'objet de la police.*« Foucault: Sécurité, territoire, population, p. 321. This position follows from, but also remains in, degenerate models of police protocols.

708 Justi: Grundsätze der Polizeywissenschaft, p. 1.

the sphere of civil society), let me explain, in two quick steps, the institution of police, first announced at the very beginning of the history of institutional acting. I would like to insist that actually the police are what holds a group together, decisively institutionalizing it, and in certain cases, destroying it. In any case, it is questionable to what extent this last protocol is violent.

For any institutional act to be an institutional act, it necessarily implies a certain, let us call it, police matter (»police object«) or police technique of cultivation and protection of the universal (general). The police do not only deal with borders or order among the elements of a given set or entity. All the actions and relations that hold a set together, necessarily imply certain police moments. The two steps here in question are, a) the Tower of Babel – the process of institutional construction that clearly constitutes the common, but also reveals the lack of focus on it that causes the failure of the endeavor. And b) *ius provocatio*, the Roman institution that gives the right to any individual, any citizen to call into question the decisions of the magistrate, forcing further consideration of the issue of common good – the Ancient Roman equivalent and original act of »calling the police«.

Drawing on Hegel, who acts here (paradoxically) as guardian of some kind of democratic socialism or social status, I would now like to formulate what are the police or what the police ought to be. Hegel thematized the police in the first quarter of the nineteenth century, and these thematization only acquire their definitive form in the final lectures of the winter semester 1824/25. Let us leave aside for the time being the 1821 lectures, which he partially prepared for publication. Instead, let us look at the obscure passage § 231 of his Philosophy of Right (1821), at the beginning of the chapter dedicated to the police, as it might provide orientation for Hegel's last word on the institution of the police. Hegel's intention remains almost entirely unchanged throughout, when thinking about the police. Even in the Heidelberg lectures (1817/18), when he writes about the police much more freely and uncertainly, in the context of the poor and the right to life.[709] Hegel's signposts are a) the original meaning of police – from Jena to Berlin, the current state of the institution of police is always contrasted with what Hegel names *Politia* or *Politeia*.[710] Hegel's comparison is always of »the police now« with some Greek model, never with German »science of policing«. b) The police are ›now‹ degraded and reduced (Hegel uses »*herabgesetzt*«[711]), the example of

709 I am referring to two paragraphs: In § 118, mentioning the poor and the right of all to live and own land (property), Hegel insists that the aim of civil society is not the right to protection and security, but realization of freedom. While in § 119, he considers Fichte's claims about the relation of the police and criminals in England, the institution of secret police and the growing hatred towards the police in general. Hegel: Vorlesungen über Naturrecht und Staatswissenschaft, pp. 159–164.

710 Even in Jena, Hegel alternates between these two transcriptions of this Greek word. Hegel: Jenenser Realphilosophie, p. 259.

711 »(…) *jetzt herabgesetz zu Handeln des Ganzen auf die öffentliche Sicherheit jeder Art, Aufsicht auf Gewerbe gegen Betrug.*« Ibid.

which is Fichte's police state (in all the lectures, without exception, using mostly the same phrasing, Hegel opposes Fichte). c) Externally provided order (*äusserliche Ordnung*) or aggressive intervention of external instance in the life of the individual or in civil society out to be overcome with some entirely new and more successful idea.[712] The police has this seemingly basic task: to act preventively, to consequently reduce the oversight and supervision among all of us, and even entirely clear away problems in circulation of all kinds of particularity – could we tentatively claim that *a priori* the police always concerns themselves with problems of poor circulation and are thus tasked with this circulation in the broadest sense of the word.[713] In order to fulfill this task, the police must have nothing to do with the state. At no point does Hegel intend to modify Fichte's political apparatus, nor shift the police from the »internal« to some other place. On the contrary, by opposing Fichte, he wants to create a kind of harmony of *true* policing with a lost protocol of *the original Politia.* What, then, were or what are originally the police? Or what today are or could be the police?

Politia or the public life of a city (or a *Polis*) is really the activity of the whole (*Handeln des Ganzen selbst*) as such. If the police now represent the action regarding only security in various domains – so says Hegel – then *Politia* really refers to what holds the unity of a city, the activity of the whole. In a number of places Hegel explains this change in meaning of the police as each individual minding their own business and not caring in the least about the common good.[714] Since the individual is only interested in itself, not the common good, Hegel shows that the police now deals with various problems of the social. *De facto*, it supervises connections among individuals and the individual, and not the individual as such (nor the universal or the common or whole as such). In all his lectures, Hegel is really attempting to find an appropriate form that would first patch over (or stitch together) and then also diffuse the tension in this (pseudo-) split between the individual and general. In Heidelberg, over a decade later, Hegel describes this »schism« much more simply, transforming the »activity of the whole« into the »activity of the people«. Here is the end of § 92:

»Politeia« teaches the constitutional order of the people (*Die ›Politeia‹ lehrt die Verfassung des Volkes*). Today, the police are also the universal (*ein Allgemeines*) that is opposed to the individual citizen (*das dem besonderen Bürger gegenübertritt*), but whose ultimate goal

712 The best description of the functioning of this external order can be found in Hegel's lectures of 1819/20. »When the general (*das Allgemeine*) is externally imposed against the individual (äußerliche Weise gegen die Einzelnen geltend macht), it grows into intransigence (implacability, inflexibility, cruelty).« Hegel: Philosophie des Rechts. Die Vorlesung von 1819/20 in einer Nachschrif, p. 191.

713 This could be a paraphrase of some of Hegel's comments (in the Jena lectures) in which money is a universal, that is, that the circulation of the universal is the circulation of money. Money, thus, is a great invention (*eine große Erfindung*). Hegel: Jenenser Realphilosophie, pp. 253–257.

714 »Er sorgt jeder nur für sich, nicht für das Allgemeine«. Ibid., p. 259.

is the welfare of the individual *qua* individual (*das Wohl der Einzelnen als Einzelnen*), and not as in ›Politeia‹, whose aim is the welfare of the universal (*einer Allgemeinheit*).[715]

Later still, in Berlin, in his concluding word on the police, preparing in his introduction to oppose Fichte as best as he can, Hegel is yet more concise. It seems he has much more easily harmonized the distance between the Greek and the new German position of the police:

Police comes from *Polis Politia.* »Originally«, it is the whole activity of the state (*die ganze Bethätigung des Staats*); whereas now it is »no longer« the activity of the moral universal as such (*die Bethätigung des sittlich Allgemeinen als solchen*), but rather the universal with regard to civil society, and with regard to the state as an external state (*des Staats als äußeren Staats*). It is the universal (*das Allgemeine*) that becomes active with regard to civil society (*sich bethätigt in Rücksicht auf die bürgerliche Gesellschaft*).[716]

The conceptualization of the police in this paragraph might remind the reader of the functions today assigned to contemporary civil society, referring to supervision of the state and correcting the state in the name of the universal, civil society. I mean, above all, the watchdog role that perhaps contains precisely those elements of the original police, since it presupposes self-organizing by active citizens for the sake of overseeing the state and preserving the common. This refers to those who act for and in the name of passive citizens who, actually, are concerned only with themselves.

In Hegel's last thematization of the police, the consideration of the police or the common that is opposed to (or presupposes) the individual citizen becomes considerably watered down. In the new formulation, the police (or common) are what refers to and acts in accordance with civil society or *as* civil society. *Politia* or the police in the city (the *Polis*) is complementary to the police of civil society. This is Hegel's discovery and eventually his cure against the degeneration of the institution in the state, found in Fichte. Although it is easy to notice the digressions and indecisiveness in the attempts to construct and demonstrate the portion of civil society that refers to the police and corporation (since these fragments are rather haphazard), in paragraphs 117 and 118 of the Heidelberg lectures, Hegel is trying to explain how the police (the common) is active and effective. In other words, what is the meaning of this common activity and is it necessarily opposed to individual citizens? Here we encounter the formulation that this common *must* as such be effective and active (*Dies Allgemeine muss sich daher für sich als solches betätigen*), and in this way eliminate and remove certain particularities. Also, that the police are not good on the whole, that it is unpopular

715 Hegel: Vorlesungen über Naturrecht und Staatswissenschaft, pp. 117–118.
716 Hegel: Philosophie des Rechts, K. G. v. Griesheims 1824/25, p. 587.

for some, but that it is necessary.[717] In two further additions to these paragraphs, Hegel, as mentioned, in one way or another retraces Saint-Just's steps, revealing the activity of the common. The assumption is that activity constructed in this way necessarily implies a preventive protocol – which is what Hegel is searching for when it comes to the police.

All individuals or all citizens or all particularities (*Jeder macht sich sein*) work for their own good, he writes in appendix § 117, »and are thus connected (yield) to the general bond (mutual ties, *und verlässt sich auf den allgemeinen Zusammenhang*). Yet, the common as such must have as its purpose existence as the common. (...) The Police now must attempt to limit and establish balance among all.« Further, in appendix § 118:

> Life and survival of the individuals (*Subsistenz*, preservation of life) is actually a common, universal issue (*eine allgemeine Angelegenheit*), a common theme, concerning all. This common ought to be consciously its own purpose (*Dieses Allgemeine selbst soll mit Bewusstsein sein zweck sein*). Since everyone is concerned with themselves, then civil society should have as its own end the common issue (to have universality [*allgemeine Angelegenheit*] as its purpose).[718]

Yet, if we complement this statement from Heidelberg with the last, complicated and uncompleted sentence about the police from the winter semester of 1824/25 in Berlin, it becomes clear that the common (or police – the two are synonymous here) cannot be outside civil society. The activity and purpose of this »*allgemeine Angelegenheit*« ought to be in complete balance with the purpose and activity of the individuals themselves. The goal (*Zweck*) is the survival of individuals as such – for this »common« to hold individuals together, ensuring their right to life:

> When thus the external state of reason is constructed (*den äußeren Verstandesstaat*), there are such particularities that dissolve in themselves (*Einzelnheiten die sich in sich selbst zerstören*). The police must again be overseen (*beaufsichtigt*), [illegible] all such conduct leading to infinite progression. The common must essentially never be external, but the internal, immanent purpose, the activity of the individuals (*Das Allgemeine soll wesentlich nicht äußerlich, sondern innerer, imanenter Zweck, Thätigkeit der Individuen selbst sein*).[719]

Only such common awareness of all individuals and their individual and common activity whose purpose is common life, can forever reduce and break up various violent protocols.

717 »*Der Polizei im ganzen ist man nicht gut, aber so wenig Volksgunst sie für sich hat, um so notwendiger ist sie.*« Hegel: Vorlesungen über Naturrecht und Staatswissenschaft, pp. 158–159.

718 Ibid., 160.

719 Hegel: Philosophie des Rechts. K. G. v. Griesheims 1824/25, p. 617.

3 Institution as Project. The Acts of Project(ion)

If I say that I will shortly explain what it is that I am doing (what is my intention or what lies *underneath*), then such an act or such acts that refer to the existence of something somewhere else (somewhere behind, underneath) would already be part of a protocol or register that refers to a project or perhaps even »meta-project« (but not ›design‹).[720] Questions such as ›what do they even want‹, ›what are they talking about seek a certain reflective reaction, except unless one wishes to ignore others' curiosity and appear foolish. Certainly, at issue is a ›turn‹ (a word to which I will return a few times) or reflection or »reflection in action«.[721] When I am attempting to reconstruct or present what I am doing, which emerges from something else, from something only implicitly present in what I am now doing (the absent is not entirely here, but can be found in ›traces‹), then all I want is to prove that this is a ›projected act‹ or planned, controlled action. In other words, the project of an action precedes the action, which is nothing other than a portion of the content of the project, whose realization is announced by the project.[722] The

720 The term ›meta-project‹ seems to me to first appear in Massimo Scolari's 1973 *The New Architecture and the Avant-Garde*. He uses it when writing about Tafuri and *Tendenza*: »(...) a kind of meta-project that extends to all the architecture that is thought, designed and written.« Scolari: The New Architecture and the Avant-Garde, p. 133.

721 In *The Reflective Practitioner. How Professionals Think in Action*, Donald Schön uses this phrase when describing the famous example of Quist and his student Petra who is making preliminary sketches in order to discover a basic design, a »design hypothesis«. The example is demonstrated in detail by Armando and Durbiano. Armando / Durbiano: Teoria del progetto architettonico, pp. 74–76. Interestingly, Schön's book was translated into the Italian as *Il progettista riflessivo*, while Armando and Durbiano translate the title of their course at the University of Turin, »Progetto umano«. The word *progetto* from the title of their book becomes ›design‹ (›human design‹). Schön's book, as well as the Nobel Prize Winner, Herbert Alexander Simon's book, *The Sciences of the Artificial* have had the strongest influence on the understanding of projects in the second half of the twentieth century. »Design« is usually translated into European languages as »project«, although not exclusively: Simon's »design« is rendered in the French as *conception*. Perhaps the most complete book on the epistemology of architecture is Philippe Boudon's *Essai d'épistemologié de l'architecture* (2003), in which he says that *conception* (that is, »design«) is a crucial question of epistemology, which means that it must of necessity become a true »architectural object«. The architect is *un concepteur* (designer) for Simon and for Boudon (Sur l'espace architecturale, pp. 12–13). Simon's definition of design is as follows: »Design is concerned with how things ought to be with devising artifacts to attain goals«. Simon: The Sciences of the Artificial, p. 133. There are, however, authors who attempt to »extend the notion of project« (meaning *conception* or design). In *Pratiques de projet en architecture*, Robert Prost speaks of »the projectual dimension of conception« and of the project still »beyond the design in temporal context«. Cf. Prost: Conception architecturale, une investigation méthodologique.

722 This is a legacy of phenomenology and such an understanding exists in Husserl's *Erste Philosophie*, pp. 205–206. »*Wir können auch sagen, die praktische Besinnung ist ein inneres Handeln und*

existence of a project or projected acts would constitute one of the first (albeit certainly insufficient) basic guarantees that, for example, I am not currently uttering nonsense, I am not improvising, not bluffing. What is a guarantee that I am not a cheater? It is the project or manuscript title and abstract I have previously sent to the publisher, which are as such potential guarantees of an idea or project (»*Entwurf*« in German or »*nabačaj*« in Serbo-Croatian[723]). The proposal and manuscript oblige the author; all the more so if announced publicly (published, advertised, that is, documented[724]). I do, then, *have* a project. And if I *have* a project (a plan, concept, idea, schema, conception, platform, etc. – words we have a hard time differentiating and connecting because they are of a single order), then what I am now doing is precisely the consistent act (the execution) of that project (or »projected act«). Of the many potential acts, this act certainly belongs and emerges from or is part of *my* project. The answer to the question where is that which I *have* or which is *mine* (both of these words are italicized because problematic[725]), as well as what does the description of the project itself consist of, will be demonstrated precisely by the reflection I have connected with the word ›turn‹. That is to say, in order for what I am doing to truly be in harmony with the project I *have*, it is necessary that I constantly constitute it through reflection, or to constitute it through reflective reconstruction. These (myriad) operations that create the project, simultaneously confirm my acting in accordance with the project (that my acts are indeed ›projected acts‹), ought to be called ›project acts‹ (that is, acts that create the project, rather than actions the project implies). My acts are projected if and only if I project or create a project, that is, if I simultaneously produce ›project acts‹. This distinction between ›project acts‹ and ›projected acts‹ actually leads us

ergibt, geligend, ein inneres Werkgebilde, als den geistigen Plan, inneren Entwurf für das, was im äußeren Handeln verwirklicht warden soll.« Only a few years later, Heidegger will distance himself from such thinking in his brief consideration of *Entwurf* in *Sein und Zeit*.

723 Both *Entwurf* and *nabačaj* follow in the steps of the Latin *proiectus* (the past participle of *proicere*), »to throw forward, extend«. In the Indo-German dictionary, Julius Pokorny ties the root *ver* with turn, throw, with the Old Slavonic *vresti*. *Werfen* means to throw, from the Latin *jactare*, »to throw far with a rapid movement«, or in French »*lancer au loin par un movement rapide*«. *Entwurf* is opposite to *objectum*, *Gegenwurf* (Fritz Mauthner).

724 »Program« (in the same extended family as the word project) is, similarly to the document, »public notice« (from the Greek *pro'gramma*), a plan of action to accomplish a specific end.

725 »Having« or »lacking« a project are Peter Eisenman's terms. In an (as of yet) unpublished interview (»On the End of Authority«, of 26 September 2016) – along with several recorded lectures in which the phrases are used – over the course of twenty pages, Eisenman speaks of »two avenues to power in architecture. One is through design; the other is through the intellect – that is, thinking.« »You teach project«, says Eisenman, »by reading and thinking in the design studio.« »Project and practice must be integrated in a studio.« Further, »Gropius had a practice and not a project.« Mies, Corbu, Wright, Loos, Koolhaas have a project, but not so Ingels. Eisenman assumes that project can be defined, but that he himself cannot define his own project, rather that others must do so: »I don't need to define it, because I do it.« »I was always inventing institutions and projects that I could appear in.«

into entirely uncharted difficulties that characterize a potential theory of projects and projecting/design.[726]

Before I explain the basic principle of the functioning of this ›reflective gesture‹ and gradually elaborate what, in my understanding, constitutes the difference between the project from other similar theories (my only question is how and by what act is a project made?[727]), I would like to insist on a few elementary facts. I would like, once again, to return to our imaginary academic conference. When signing up to participate, I propose a title and abstract, ›projecting‹ (pitching a suggestion), I do so within a reflective protocol – I ›turned‹ and ›pitched‹ something (which is why ›turn‹ is a word within the same order as *proiectus* or *der Entwurf*).[728] A project or pitch do not *a priori* precede my action, but are rather constituted by this action, thus simultaneously correcting and converting it. A thematization of reflective acts that make up a project (concept, theme, *Gestalt* or positions – these too being words we differentiate insufficiently[729]) would con-

726 Actually, this differentiation is a modification of a distinction made by Alfred Schütz, certainly the greatest theorist of the project: »*Wir müssen diese Erkenntnis auf das Phänomen des Handelns anwenden und terminologisch scharf zwischen dem Handeln in seinem Vollziehen als Erzeugen von Handlungen* (actio) *– und der bereits fertig konstituierten Handlung als durch Handeln Erzeugtem* (actum) *unterscheiden.*« Schütz: Der sinnhafte Aufbau der sozialen Welt, p. 37. In English, this becomes rather obscure and endangers the German original: »action in progress (*actio*) and the already finished and constituted act (*actum*).« Schütz: The Phenomenology of the Social World, p. 39. *Der sinnhafte Aufbau der sozialien Welt* was published in 1932, while the English translation from 1967 bears the title *The Phenomenology of the Social World*. The tense in which the project appears is ›future perfect‹.

727 If we had the answer to this question, then we immediately recognize the problem of thematization: a) in Sartre, for example: »Man is, indeed, a project which possesses a subjective life (*qui se vit subjectivement*), instead of being a kind of moss, or a fungus or a cauliflower. Before that projection (*projet*) of the self, nothing exists; not even in the heaven of intelligence: man will only attain existence when he is what he purposes to be (*ce qu'il aura projeté d'être*)«. Sartre: Existentialism is a Humanism, p. 29; b) in Bonaventure's scheme of authorship when he describes four ways of making a book (fourteenth century): *scriptor, compilator, commentator, auctor.* »But he who writes both what comes from himself and from others (*aliquis scribit et sua et aliena*; *cose che vengono da lui steso sia cose d'altri*), with the material of others annexed for the purpose of confirming his own, ought to be called author.« c) Frank Gehry: »I have always felt if you know what you are going to do in advance, then you won't do it.« *Ghery Teaches Design & Architecture*, MasterClass.com.

728 Armando and Durbiano, using their own terminology, develop a detailed and always problematic dilemma whether a project precedes or follows the analysis (»*prima l'analisi, poi il progetto*«). Armando/Durbiano: Teoria del progetto architettonico, p. 379.

729 A subject missing from departments of architecture is Architectural Terminology. This absence results in concepts sliding places, being borrowed from other genres of knowledge, remaining unsystematized. At the same time as Gilles Deleuze, Donald Schön is working on a theory and formation of new concepts. His book, *Displacement of Concepts* is published in 1963. The term »concept« is closest, it seems to me, to what Eisenman designates with the word »project«. »Concept« is not necessarily fixed and manifested, nor determined by time, and should absolutely be differentiated from conception or project. Cf. Vesnić: *Arhitektonski koncept.* The name »concept« designates that which is ever-uncertain, after Plautus: »to conceive is to seek what is not and thus find it.« In chapter 3.9, »Themes vs. Projects« of *Autopoiesis of Architecture: A New Framework for Architecture*, Patrik Schumacher insists on the concreteness of project, that a project comprises episodes and »well-de-

struct and fix a project as (an acting) document. A project as a document produces obligations and controlled actions and becomes the condition of the existence of joint work in the studio or outside it. That is, the project as a document constructs disciplined work and is the condition of the existence of the institution (there can be no institution without the project).[730] A didactic reconstruction of projects (so-called didactic performance) and amending the rules of work by introducing competing projects[731] produces myriad disciplines and thus ultimately institutionalizes the possibility of interdisciplinary actions.

This reflection of which I am speaking is a collective or social gesture. Analogously, Schön's often-criticized phrase »reflection in action«, always and necessarily assumes a group or a plural agent. The situation in which an individual publicly explains his own action, thus harmonizing it with a general position or a foreseeable and advertised plan (it matters little whether it is a murderer before a jury, a child before its kindergarten teacher, a college professor before a student, one friend before another), it represents at once a common assessment of the plan (conception or project) and, potentially, in certain cases, an introduction into joint thematization, participation, acceptance of the plan on behalf of the group. A group is always constituted in this way in the course of constructing and executing a project; and it executes a project together while also at once constituting itself as a group.

It seems to me that the existence, and then the validity of a project could be ensured only by a group, and that the group determines the potential development and ultimate fate of, say, an abstract or title.[732] In that sense, the act or those acts

fined stages« as opposed to a theme that develops entirely differently. Schumacher: Autopoiesis of Architecture, p. 320. *Gestalt* or *Gestaltung* as a configuration is usually opposed to *Begriffe* (*Gestalt* implies subjective experience) and is explained via the idea of the concrete (*Gestalt* is a concrete notion, not notion as inkling).

730 It is entirely possible that »document theory« or *documentalità* could be very useful to explain the transition of what we call project into design. Design is necessarily documented and, in that sense, it is possible to follow Armando and Durbiano. However, there are projects not yet documented or which have only just become so. My attempt is to show that even as such, they can be thematized. Armando and Durbiano's great accomplishment lies in novel ideas: diminished significance of the author for the project (»*E le progettualità sono, molto prima che nella testa dell'architetto, nell'ambiente [fisico o sociale] che lo circonda*«), a project as a social object, the project as letter, »action issues from the document, not the intention«. Armando / Durbiano: Teoria del progetto architettonico, pp. 15, 93. Even though they mention an important debate about the project on the pages of *Casabella* (1982), they do not explain in detail, for example, the status of the word dwelling in Vattimo's sentence »dwelling precedes building« (*abitare viene prima di costruire*). Ibid., p. 222.

731 Nick Bostrom writes about »typical lags between competing technology projects.« Bostrom: Superintelligence, pp. 82–87.

732 Kojève gives a very simple example, even if his conclusion is entirely insignificant. The authority of the creator of the project (the subject) is incidental compared to the authority of the project itself that forms the group and has simultaneously been its real creator: »Let us consider a familiar example. A band of kids gather to play. One of these kids proposes to go and steal apples from the orchard next door. Immediately, by doing so, he casts himself in the role of the band's leader. He

that make the project, with which something is projected (thrown up, pitched, ›spun‹ forth) represent on the one hand an attempt to impute current action into something new, a project or platform, thus ensuring their validity and duration; on the other hand, authors of these acts are necessarily diverse and only their multiplicity will ensure the validity and duration of the project as such. Doubtlessly, the fact that the group exists implies two protocols contained in the word *proiectus*: space and time. And conversely, *proiectus* holds this very same group together for joint action and motion in time and space. The group is the body of the project.

Let us return to the ur-scene of the founding of the institution, the first effort of constructing an architectural bureau, indeed, one of the first attempts at *incorporatio* in the histories of the West. A group of people who work and build together in Babylon is without a doubt the prototype of a group assembled much later by Filippo Brunelleschi, circa 1420, in Florence.[733] There are any number of assumptions as to why the largest construction site in the history of mankind was discontinued and destroyed. Nor can it be said unequivocally that the project was unsuccessful and futile, given that the action lasted a very long time, possibly even for centuries. Indeed, the (unhappy) ›end‹ of a project or its ›failure‹ could always be one of the first and rather important characteristics of the project as such.

Two verses in *Genesis* (at the beginning of chapter 11) speak of the construction site, the technological innovation, and a monstrous vision that certainly has an outline similar to what I am here designating with the word ›project‹:

3. They said to one another, »Come, let us make bricks, and burn them hard.« Brick served them as stone, and bitumen served them as mortar.

4. And they said, »Come, let us build us a city, and a tower with its top in the sky, to make a name for ourselves; else we shall be scattered all over the world.«

It seems to me that there are ever-new and all too complicated reasons why this group was denied a construction license, and why the erection and this grandiose edifice did not last. Above all, the ›project‹ could not be carefully thematized or constituted because it was not presented to the highest power before the work be-

became this leader because he saw *further* (*plus loin*) than the others, because it was he alone who thought out a *project*, while the others did not manage to get beyond the level of immediate facts.« Kojève: The Notion of Authority, p. 63; Kojève: La notion de l'autorité, p. 74.

733 We can claim, with Jean-Pierre Boutinet (but not only him), that the architectural project was born with Brunelleschi who divided and at the same time linked two periods that determine the creative act in the course of building an edifice. There is the period of time of work in studio or research based on constructing a model, and the period of time on site, in which the execution of the structure based on the model takes place. Cf. Boutinet: Projet, p. 224. Still, Boutinet does not emphasize joint, disciplined work of a group of people in the studio, building the model of the cathedral they are about to erect. The idea of collective intellectual work, a discussion about preliminary hypotheses, the idea of critical reflection and inspection of coherence of argument and counter-argument is born in this place, and it will forever ordain modern philosophy.

gan. The group is rushing with the work and does not negotiate. It does not draw its own limits, give itself shape, does not adjust its aims. The group, which as we know does not have issues with communication and cooperation – all members of the group speak the same language, the group is innovative, collective intentionality has been achieved, the group is without leader and in perfect equality – is imitating its creator (God) by performatively acting and utilizing various imperatives that mobilize its members. Although the group is manifesting a grand plan (idea, conception), as opposed to the first creator who does not (God is above all a laborer, a practitioner, not a thinker), the group still does not possess ›reflective strength‹ that would enable the members of the group to remain in one place for any sustained period. And this is precisely the definition of institutional activity: using this repertoire of acts (institutional acts) that can for as long as possible maintain a group in a single place. All these acts always concern reflection, that is, the project. The name mentioned in this passage (»to make a name for ourselves«) is really this very same great project, but also one on which the group is unable to hold its focus for a very long time (certainly not permanently). Why?

We should not lose sight that all we are left with from the Tower of Babel is precisely the project (of building a »tower with its top in the sky«) that each one of us, in all life's endeavors, is in one way or another trying to complete: unity of all, the world, the production of grand institutions, Europe too (as a project, as a set of documents and their constant assessment), as a project that has become nearly self-regulating for us. Nevertheless, one answer to the above question concerns the violence of the project (of course, the violence would also immediately have to refer to reflection, that is violence of reflection).[734] Lest we forget, among the more important characteristics of the project (*nabačaj*, *proiectus*, *Entwurf*) is that it does not mean a weak pitch (swing). *Entwerfen* does not mean to drop something just in front or very closely behind oneself (in German, such a weak gesture might be designated with the word *Vorwurf*), rather, it means throw very far, far afield (reflection is an operation of emergence, through reflection I emerge beyond myself). A consequence of this move (easily confirmed with the word ›projectile‹) does not only consist of some kind of separation and production of a completely uncontrollable, self-sufficient entity (image, projection, idol), unreachable in its perfection (impossible to process reflexively).[735] We are dealing with an act of overshooting

734 As mentioned in »Inclusion/Exclusion«, Massimo Cacciari goes back and forth between »force« and »violence« in describing the main characteristic of a project. »*Violenza suona nel progetto*«. Cacciari: Progetto, p. 101.

735 Peter Eisenman points out this difficulty (which is always with Plato and the ideal order) whenever he speaks about the project, or better, about the idea of the project or the maximalism of the project. »Seeing as an Architect«« (the title of one his seminars) means that the architect (if he is truly an architect, although only few are architects, and more commonly they are pretending to be so) means that by looking or perusing the material and visible before him, sees the invisible »project«. On at least fifteen occasions, in various interviews, Eisenman cites versions of Colin Rowe's

and expanding to beyond the surface or edge (*proictus*), which then always implies exclusion, abolishment, banishment, expulsion (*proicto*). ›Exclusion‹, ›expulsion‹, or ›elimination‹, etc. are moments about which we must think, in the context of the project, only in the most abstract sense, without dwelling on them, yet also aware that in order for a group to constitute itself temporarily and work actively (which would mean work on a project), it of necessity excludes the insufficiently engaged/committed, insufficiently competent, dynamic, even insufficiently intelligent, and thus asocial.[736] It would probably be incorrect to say here that reflection or ›reflection in action‹ does not imply critique or systemic doubt as an integral portion of the project's strategy of structuring and execution. However, hesitation, procrastination, delay or alternate work on counter-projects certainly need to be accounted for and placed within potential new processes and aims.

words from one of their joint trips to Italy (probably in the summer of 1961). »In front of a Palladian villa, Colin says: ›Sit in front of the façade until you can tell me something that you can't see. In other words, I don't want to know about the rustification, about the proportion of the windows, about ABA symmetries or any of those things (…) I want you to tell me something that is implied in the façade‹.« Eisenman: The Last Grand Tourist, p. 133. The word »project« in Eisenman functions similarly to the word *die Geste* (*eine Geste*) in Wittgenstein. Good architecture is a gesture, much like good philosophy. Wittgenstein is emphatic (in several places) that his intention is to eschew bad philosophers from philosophy. This would be the functioning of the word *Geste*, impossible to thematize or define precisely (there are only six or seven passages in which Wittgenstein sketches its meaning).

736 This is the point from which usually issue endless discussions of neoliberalism, the connection of capitalism and the project, profit and the project, so-called project financing, and competition.

4 On the Temporality of the Project. Position of the Future in Project-Time

I would like to, yet again, revisit our hypothetical academic conference. Imagine, if you will, the time leading up to it: all the chatter among the organizers, and between them and the participants, the letters, messages, all the back and forth. There is a clear intention (let me for now call it »empty intention«[737]) for the conference to happen. Then, the conference does indeed take place, the participants arrive, they talk, they network. The conference has become ›(ful)filled intention‹ (or just intention), it has ceased to exist in the future or merely as a project to be or to be realized. In taking place, the conference now certainly has a new modality. Unclear ideas, intentions, conceptions (concepts[738]) of the conference, formulated and constructed over the course of the previous year or several months through various communal acts, as a complicated project (with documents, a budget, money, order, work plan, schedule, timing) – all have to come together now, in those few days. They have to take place by holding everyone together as a group with a given task. The future (the conference actualized and objectivized) has in one way or another replaced the concept and project. A group of people jointly designed and organized the transmission of a series of amorphous mental entities into a communal social act and fact. The future must conform to the present. I do not need to list all the consequences of this future that has just taken place, but certainly the conference as social fact or repertoire of social facts has eliminated the time of execution of the project and design. ›Eliminated time‹ actually represents the erasure of temporality in the project, a temporality only possible within the project – which is what I am above all interested to show.[739]

737 Husserl speaks of an intentionally empty horizon (*intentionaler Leer-horizont*), an absence to be filled (*eine ausfüllende Leere*). Husserl: Analysen zur passive Synthesis, p. 6. Cf. Losoncz: Fenomenologija prazne intencionalnosti.

738 Speaking of the »concept« in his two semesters dedicated to time, Bergson neglects to make use of something that might more precisely explain his intention. The »empty concept«, which has a history from Kant to Sartre. As opposed to the »authentic« concept, the »empty concept« refers to something fictitious that has no corresponding »reality«. In the commentary of his translation of Aristotle's »Peri Ermenias«, Boethius recognizes the existence of empty concepts. Alain de Libera translates Boethius' »*intellectus*« as »concept«, because in Boethius »*conceptio*« and »*conceptus*« are synonymous with »*intellectus*«. »Boethius was apparently the first to recognize that there is such a thing as empty concept, i. e., that intellections that have no corresponding real subject, such as centaurs and chimeras or ones invented by poets« (*Or Boèce est, évidemment, le premier à reconnaître qu'il y a des concepts vides, i. e. »des intellections qui ne correspondent pas à une réalité sujet, comme celles que les poètes ont façonnées, centaures ou chimères*). Libera: L'art des généralités, p. 418.

739 Divine creation, the various acts of Adonai in the course of creating everything, only partially

Let me formulate my claim in reverse: when the project is no longer – there is no longer any future: thus, the project ensures the future. Or, to achieve complete circularity, let me introduce a third element: without the future, a group or a ›We‹ cannot possibly exist.

When it appears that the project (conference) is taking place, the participants assess whether the project corresponds to the concept that preceded it, which is to say, whether the project matches up with what is happening (perhaps saying ›it went better than I expected‹ because the project realized surpasses the concept, that which was ›in the head‹, ›the idea‹, ›on paper‹). Or, alternatively, whether the project has fallen apart. What does a failed project mean? Does the meaning of the word ›project‹ (as we have seen, to throw something forward, to pitch) not already imply that every project is necessarily failed? The very possibility of comparing what is taking place with other conferences or some ideal, imagined (now or in the past) conference, implicitly opens the possibility for constructing a next project and the future as such. Thus, as soon as it appears that a project has been executed,[740] and it ceases to exist, a new project (or slew of projects) appears on the horizon. If several protocols, such as ›possibility‹, ›horizon‹[741] and ›imagination‹ (›as if‹) are in some way ›mingled‹ and ›entwined‹, would that be enough to show that the basic modus of project temporality – the future, what is yet to come (*avenir* in French) or what is to follow – has finally been revealed?[742] If ›the future‹ is revealed within an imaginary distance between the concept and project, between two words or notions always difficult to differentiate, does then this modality of time have special status in the ›time – space‹ relation? How much future is there necessarily in space? Better still, is future more connected to space than is, for example, the past?

I would like to systematize a few difficulties by constructing several conditions that refer to the revealing of the future and temporary nature of the project. Let me provisionally insist on a weakness found in certain languages spoken by a great number of people and which make the future difficult to linguistically stabilize

satisfy the criteria to be named project or the product of a project. As soon as he thinks (conceptualizes) or speaks, Adonai creates. It is as if there were no process of creation or time of execution of the project.

740 With »execute«, English is wonderfully helpful in this case: where other European languages use some variation of »realized« for the operation of bringing something to fruition, English more commonly uses a word meaning to kill, to remove from existence.

741 These two words speak to the constitutive primacy of the future and evoke the phenomenological hermeneutic method.

742 Does the future arrive or follows and moves forward? How can we describe what has yet to happen? Does one wait for the future, or is it constructed and anticipated? Projection or design is an artificial operation of preparation for what is to come thus reducing the uncertainty of »what has yet to arrive«.

and document: German and English do not have a future tense, using instead auxiliary verbs, *werden* (to become), will/going to.

The first condition refers to the pronoun ›We‹. Whence ›We‹ and how is it possible? ›We‹ who produce certain social acts as part of a project (residents of a city, for example, who pass each other on the street, live side by side, tolerate one another, etc.[743]) also construct its following, new projects. ›We‹ is always what is left over from a project just completed and what is always altered and constituted anew (›new‹ or ›sudden‹ is always both possible and impossible). The future is implicitly present in each expression of a given state that is addressed to some other or others (individuals): if I promise something to someone, there is an assumption of time needed to make good on the promise.[744] Further, every address to another is simultaneously the expectation of a reaction and reciprocity, also always temporally conditioned (between two greetings, there is an interval; or in an online messaging interchange, there is a period in which one side is perhaps in turn asking a question of someone third, etc.). ›Give me time‹ or ›take your time‹ or ›I will buy time‹ can confirm the future as an interval in which various actions are to be performed. Reticence to answer or address someone else is a kind of negative social act. Finally, the still complicated and ill-defined position of a chief or leader in a democracy opens the act of ordering (or consulting, suggesting, advising) to future time and thus producing inequality.

For a group to potentially remain together, confirm its own ›we-mode‹ (or for two to remain together, since love is above all continuously projected) and preserve its ›co-presence‹ (such as to meet and work together again at next year's conference), various project operations (co-regulations) have to be introduced: correcting mistakes in the production of social acts, exclusion of the undisciplined, repetition, forecasting, differentiation of the possible from the impossible, insistence anew, insistence on the new, amendments, etc.

The second condition also refers to the pronouns ›We‹ or ›us‹, referring to an important connection of the future with space (co-presence or co-present implies »the local structure of we-space itself«[745]). It is as if the future is primarily that form of time that allows and ensures the connection between time in general and space. The simple fact of my passing time unfolding inseparably from my body extending in space can be entirely simultaneous with the simple fact of your passing time unfolding in your body extending in space. Two temporalities

743 In Hebrew, making time has the same root with the invited one, with hospitality. The invitation produces the future.

744 Interestingly, when constructing his argument on the difference between performative and constative, John Austin never speaks of time implied in any successful performative act. If I promise you that I will replace your bike tire, implicit in the promise is the agreement of place and time by when I will do so. A promise necessarily introduces time.

745 Krueger: Extended Cognition and the Space of Social Interaction, p. 4.

and two spatialities that do not intermingle are always recognized in the present. However, physical (and not only physical[746]) co-present contact always introduces the aspect of future: orientation and location (and dislocation, Peter Eisenman). Based on this, my existence in the future is directly dependent on the future I could occupy along with others. The architectural protocol does not necessarily appear with the invention of space, but only with the introduction of ›our‹ time (or ›our‹ future) into space.

The various problems that occur in the course of our common or simultaneous penetration of a group into a given location and its duration there, its co-existence or common living in a single place, all demand a necessary reconstruction of the connection between architecture and philosophy as a theory of the institution. The first task or epistemological operation would consist of constructing an architectural terminology that meticulously follows the repertoire of various gestures (steps, moments, points, sequences) made in the course of a communal taking of space (from concept and project to object and the material). How do we name the various gestures and provide an order of notions that would correspond to the archeology of philosophical and historical notions? Parallel to this, a new reading of philosophical texts from an architectural perspective allows for correcting their logic and establishing new connections between the future (time) and space. Here is an example. At the same time (1903) that Bergson thematizes time in his seminars (although it is equally important how he even enters the abstract problem of time), Georg Simmel publishes »Über räumliche Projektionen sozialer Formen«.[747] I would like to unreservedly insist that the idea of a project, or perhaps a sketch of any future theory of the project, has been constructed in this very period and within an imaginary exchange between Bergson and Simmel. Simmel's title could be a translation and addition to a well-known expression from Kant, which also requires intervention if we introduce the dimension of time, that is, the future. Simmel calls the transfer or shift of social forms »spatial projection«. If we pull apart this phrase, we have social forms launched from somewhere or projected into space. Casting social forms into space is actually a temporal operation that relies on social forms maintaining themselves or existing only in space (these social forms are actually constructions protecting the relations among people, what connects them and their or our ›We‹.) However, by combining this protocol with a 1908 sentence by Simmel, written in the style of John Searle (»The boundary is not a special fact with sociological consequences, but a sociological fact that forms

746 Does Skype (Viber, WhatsApp, or Signal) co-presence mean »present« and does it mean common space? Also, does telepathy contain a future moment or an announcement of future time?

747 »The Spatial Projection of Social Forms« is first published in *Zeitschrift für Sozialwissenschaft*, in 1903. Reprint: Simmel: Aufsätze und Abhandlungen 1901–1908, pp. 201–220. Along with some other writing, it will be incorporated into a chapter of his *Sociology* where he thematizes the notion of space.

itself spatiality«[748]), it becomes clear that social acts in fact establish space. Space is always already social space, constituted in time to come. The project (or projection/design) actually brings future time to space. Only in this way is the construction of the social complete. Agents or subjects occupy or make space by projecting their mutual relations. Simmel cites Kant's sentence from »Paralogisms« (»Criticism of the fourth paralogism of transcendental psychology«; the always relevant passage on the difference between idealism and realism), speaking several times of space as representation:

This perception thus represents (staying for now only with outer intuitions) something real in space. For first, perception is the representation of a reality, just as space is the representation of a mere possibility of coexistence.[749]

Space is really a representation of mere possibility of coexistence. The phrase can also be rendered into English as »possibility of being together«. Only in this one place does Kant use this word – so difficult to translate – *Beisammenseins*: »being next to one another«. The social is here only implicit, but the phrase provides a primer for Simmel's suggestion that space is always ready to accept any future projection.

The third condition – implicitly the first necessary condition to give the future form – refers to the connection between the concept and expression. Thus, prior to the condition in which the group constitutes the project in the future in order to sustain itself in the present (which is a fundamental characteristic of strategy – ›having a project‹), and prior to the second condition in which social forms penetrate into space all at once, constituting it, there is a complicated attempt to conceptualize the concept through expression and expressivity.

In the introductory session of his second seminar on time, on 5 December 1902, Bergson differentiates relative and absolute knowledge. English pronunciation provides him (whose mother was English) with an example. After concluding that his English is completely contaminated by French and »operates through French« (*en function du français*), Bergson says:

What would it take to have absolute knowledge? It would be necessary to be transported to England, live among the English, living an English life, immersed in the flow of English pronunciation. (…) Relative knowledge means knowing from outside of what one is learning; relative knowledge of English expressions is having knowledge outside England, being and residing in France. It means knowing English through French elements and

748 Simmel: The Sociology of Space, p. 143; Simmel: Soziologie des Raumes, p. 141.

749 »*Diese Wahrnehmung stellt also, (damit wir diesmal nur bei äußeren Anschauungen bleiben) etwas Wirkliches im Raume vor. Denn erstlich ist Wahrnehmung die Vorstellung einer Wirklichkeit, so wie Raum die Vorstellung einer bloßen Möglichkeit des Beisammenseins.*« Kant: Critique of Pure Reason, p. 428; Kant: Kritik der reinen Vernunft, p. 235. (A, 374, 1781, 1787.)

expressions. On the other hand, absolute knowledge of English expressions is knowing not from the outside, but from within. In order to have such absolute knowledge of expressions, I must not stay at home, I must go to England. I can then learn to use not my home expressions, but those foreign, know them in themselves, as the philosophers say.[750]

This is a magical passage from a man who was well-nigh bilingual, yet insisted on a specific difference that concerns a few crucial notions that frame any possible knowledge about time: a) precision (a register we would today easily confuse for perfectionism[751]) that is in harmony with others and concerns socialization or the social (Bergson uses the phrase social life, *la vie sociale*).[752] It includes a locality that surpasses people who live in a given location. Bergson differentiates England, life with the English and English life; b) concept (since Bergson's seminars are really about the construction of the concept, such as the concept of knowledge of expression (»absolute knowledge of expression« [*connaître cette prononciation absolument*]); c) »active expression« (the phrase is mine), since the concept for Bergson is »an invitation to action« (*une invitation à agir*) or »above all a suggestion of possible action« (*avant tout une suggestion d'une action possible*),[753] meaning c1) action, and c2) expression (the imperative is to express oneself absolutely – to express the concept). To know – to know absolutely – means to express oneself absolutely or correctly.

Why is the concept (»*le concept*« or »*la pensée conceptuelle*« – which Bergson uses interchangeably)[754] important for Bergson, and why is the theory of the concept constructed by Bergson really an introduction into an imaginary nev-

750 »*Que faudrait-il pour en avoir une connaissance absolue? Il faudrait me transporter en Angleterre, il faudrait vivre avec des Anglais, vivre de la vie anglaise, il faudrait me plonger dans le courant de la prononciation anglaise; (...) Connaître relativement c'est connaître du dehors, c'est être en dehors de ce qu'on apprend; connaître relativement la prononciation de l'anglais, c'est la connaître étant hors de l'Angleterre, étant en France et restante en France; c'est connaître l'anglais en fonction d'éléments de prononciation française. Au contraire, connaître absolument cette prononciation, c'est la connaître non pas du dehors, mais du dedans. Pour connaître cette prononciation absolument, il ne faut pas que je reste chez moi, il faut que j'aille en Angleterre; je connais alors la prononciation non plus de chez moi, mais chez elle, en soi, comme dissent les philosophes.*« Bergson: Histoire de l'idée de temps, pp. 18–19. A version of this passage appears in Chevalier: Entretiens avec Bergson, p. 6.

751 Bergson ascribes the invention of precision of articulation and demonstration to the Greek genius. Speaking also of perfection in the introductory session, he writes: »should I wish to arrive at perfection, I would have to continue indefinitely, into infinity – when I might reach perfect reproduction – but this could never truly take place« ((...) *et si je veux arriver à la perfection, il faudra que je continue sans fin, à l'infini – j'obtiendrai la reproduction parfait –, mais elle ne sera jamais véritablement réalisée*). Bergson: Histoire de l'idée de temps, p. 88, 90, 30. The perfect, which is good and gone, is not the same as the realized. The project substantively resists the complete or finished, which as such definitely belongs to the past; the project is ceaseless.

752 Bergson: L'idée de temps, pp. 134–135.

753 Bergson: Histoire de l'idée de temps, p. 64.

754 Bergson: L'idée de temps, p. 125. The following academic year (1903), Bergson says the following: »the concept, which is to say, the general idea, simple, abstract« (*le concept, c'est-à-dire l'idée générale, simple, abstraite*). Bergson: Histoire de l'idée de temps, p. 69.

er-written study of the project?[755] Time and duration are what cannot be expressed through concepts (*par des concepts*).[756] But time as future begins with naming, with language and expression of what is initially present in the mind (à *l'esprit*):

I am saying that it (the noun, substantive) first refers to the individual. When I say man or table, it is in the singular, individual form that the concept presents itself to the mind.[757]

If time as such cannot be rendered or expressed in language (»there is an interval that remains unexpressed« [*il y a un intervalle qui reste inexprimé*]), language, as well as the expression of everything else, begins in the future tense. Action, as the actual beginning of the project (and action is in opposition to perception, according to Bergson[758]), and »throws time back outside«,[759] is regulated by the precision and rigor of expression in uttering the concept:[760]

Among else, man is a speaking being, a social being, and will assign words to concepts. Being much more malleable than any corporeal approach he takes, the word will also render the concept much more malleable and flexible. Man will make use of the word not only to speak to others, but to speak to himself.[761]

755 What philosophers call the concept, says Bergson »that is, the idea, the representation, that which can be in its entirety intellectually manipulated« (*c'est-à-dire l'idée, la représentation, en tant qu'elle a été préparée entiérement pour la manipulation intellectuelle*), occurs in three ways or through three operations. The origin of this manipulation lies in »the faculty of the intellect par excellence« (*la faculté intelectuelle par excellence*) or »ability to form concepts and think in concepts« (*faculté de former des concepts et de penser par concepts*). Bergson: Histoire de l'idée de temps, pp. 56, 60–61.

756 »The conclusion is this: if there is something that cannot be expressed through concepts, if there is something defiant of all symbolic representation, it is the object we will be speaking of this year – time. We will be exploring different theories of time and duration« (*La conclusion est celle-ci: s'il y a quelque chose qui ne puisse pas s'exprimer par des concepts, s'il y a quelque chose qui soit réfractaire à toute espèce de représentation symbolique, c'est précisément l'objet dont nous allons parler cette année, c'est le temps, c'est la durée, don't nous allons examiner les différentes théories.*) Bergson: Histoire de l'idée de temps, p. 77.

757 »*Je dis qu'il (le nom, le substantif) exprime d'abord l'individuel. Quand je dis: l'homme, la table, c'est une conception individuelle, un concept d'individu que se présente d'abord à l'esprit.*« Bergson: L'idée de temps, p. 126.

758 Bergson: Histoire de l'idée de temps, p. 70.

759 »Harmony like project, throws time back into the outside« (*L'harmonie, comme le projet rejette le temps au dehors*). Bataille: L'expérience intérieure, p. 70; Bataille: Inner Experience, p. 56.

760 If we take precision as our guide, we must necessarily consider as inexistent anything that is not expressible with perfect clarity, not to mention that which is not expressible at all« (*Là où on tient à la précision avant tout, on est amené necessairement à considérer comme inexistant ce qui n'est pas exprimable avec une précision parfaite, à plus forte raison ce qui n'est pas exprimable du tout*). Bergson: Histoire de l'idée de temps, p. 91. Analyzing Parmenides' poem on pages 94 and 95, Bergson insists that what cannot be expressed is not real, although he is aware that »becoming« (*devenir*) is always difficult to express. It is incredible that Deleuze lifted this idea many years later.

761 »*L'homme est, en outre, un être qui parle, un être sociable, et ce concept il va le designer par un mot, et ce mot étant un signe beaucoup plus maniable que ne le serait l'attitude corporelle prise par lui, ce mot va render le concept beaucoup plus maniable, aussi plus mobilizable. Il se servira du mot non seulement pour parler aux autres, mais pour se parler à lui-même.*« Bergson: Histoire de l'idée de temps, p. 72.

The production of concepts is an entirely artificial, human thing, as is the project. »The concept has its origin in action and is above all an instrument for action« (*concept a son origine dans l'action et il est avant tout un instrument d'action*, »a concept expresses an action« [*un concept exprime une action*]).[762] Action creates concepts and concepts draw on action. The second operation marks the birth of the project.

Bergson offers no further explanation of »speaking to oneself« (*pour se parler à lui-même*), despite this being a substantive aspect of speech addressed to others. It is thus possible to speak of a further construction or speculation about a project that is individual or mine alone. In any case, the idea that it is possible to speak to oneself is deduced from speech addressed to others and implying their response. Speaking to others is to invite them to action, or better still, joint action. Several possibilities follow from this: first, that I cannot express on another's behalf (I can help and complete someone's words or sentences, I can translate, but never replace another in ›expressing a concept‹). Second, precise expression implies retaining those who hear me (as well as those who have yet to hear me) in the given space, preserving our common use of the space. Third, expressing the concept would be equal to expressing one's own concept or one's self – expressing oneself is expressing one's concept. This means gaining time in anticipation of others' responses, which is common construction of projects and the future.[763] Fourth, expressing oneself well is necessarily compulsive and pressing (*Zeitnot*, urgency, priority, prevention, etc.):[764]

> All concepts have, more or less, a practical goal, and all concepts are our questions addressed to reality, from a subjective standpoint, regarding the attitude we should adopt towards it and it towards us. A concept is a rubric, a class into which we enter an object. Finding the right class for each object, asking of it whether it goes here or there, ultimately means asking it what it is in relation to us, what we can make of it.[765]

762 Ibid., p. 73.

763 How does a turning signal work in traffic? The conception or set of conceptions about the functioning of the turning light in traffic, recognizing traffic rules, technique of car use, as well as holding various concepts about movement in space (left, right, forward, backwards), all draw us into the operation of movement. I have the intention to turn left, which I signal thus projecting in time my future left turn. Signaling (singular or plural) is an address to others, it is a call for us to jointly consider my intention. By their joining into this consideration, it becomes a spatial projection of (one or more) social forms or social facts.

764 »Question: you were a boxer? Tadao Ando: it was a question of survival. I had to earn money for my grandmother who raised me in a working-class neighborhood in Osaka. There was a boxing club across the street. I thought I could win. I had a trial and went professional. Box consists of being forced to fight someone. There is no pulling back once you are in the ring, this space designed for fighting. You can count only on yourself. Compulsively, the gestures become automatic. Now, on a project, I act as if in the ring.« Enjalbert: Entretien avec Tadao Ando, p. 41.

765 »*Tout concept a, plus ou moins, une destination pratique, tout concept est une question posée par nous à la réalité, au point de vue relative, à l'attitude que nous devons prendre vis-à-vis d'elle ou qu'elle prend vis-à-vis de nous; un concept c'est une rubrique, une classe dans laquelle nous faisons rent-*

At the point when the word »object« appears (which belongs to the same semantic group as the word ›project‹), all the necessary conditions for constructing the future are brought together. What, then, is the object, and what is its connection with the project or ›the architectural project‹?[766]

In »Introduction to Husserl's Origin of Geometry«, Derrida writes that »the ideal object is the absolute model of the object in general« (*l'objet idéal est le modèle absolu de l'objet en général*)[767]. This implies that this ideal is actually regulative and opposed to objects not purely intentional or objects that are intentional *cum fundamento in re* (a distinction I borrow from Roman Ingarden), or opposed to ordinary physical objects (which Peter Eisenman also calls »things in themselves«). Levinas' book on intuition in Husserl contains the phrase *»une structure idéale de l'objet«*[768] and it displays rather well the nature of the ideal. The head (Bergson's or Eisenman's or whoever) does not contain objects (this would be nonsense), nor even the ideal or ideas (for this would be trivial – everyone has ideas, heads are brimming with ideas, meaning that the explanation is insufficient). Rather, it contains the ›ideal of the object as such‹. The idea of something that has physical presence is precisely the conceptual or the concept. In his famous text on conceptual architecture, Eisenman finds that »the idea within the thing itself« is synonymous to »conceptual structure« of the thing itself, and finally that »the physical reality itself does have a conceptual aspect.« What is the novelty here? Projecting (throwing forward, pitching) is not projecting/designing an object (one does not throw forward an object). The object is, rather, discovered, revealed, selected, exposed, presented before is (*vis-à-vis*; *Gegenstand*) by way of concept. In that sense, the project is a projection of the concept that is always the concept of the object (the ›ideal of the object as such‹). The task of architecture is to reveal the concepts of physical things and realize objects in time (process and design are two protocols that only appear at this point). The task of philosophy is to prepare and explain this.

rer un objet. Chercher dans quelle classe un objet peut rentrer, lui demander s'il est ceci ou cela, c'est au fond lui demander ce qu'il est par rapport à nous, ce que nous pourrions faire de lui.« Ibid., p. 73.

766 In a September 2018 letter to the Turin architect Alessandro Armando (who wrote a book on the project as document, opposing the intentionality of the architect and the myth of interiority), architect Peter Eisenman writes: »I think my idea of *bottega* is different. For me *bottega* is in my head.« The atelier, the studio, the laboratory or boutique – since etymologically *bottega* is a place (*un luogo*) meant for storing sundry objects – is above all in the architect's head. What are these objects or object in the head? The title of the Serbo-Croatian translation of Peter Eisenman's collection of texts was »*Idealni objekt arhitekture*« [The Ideal Object of Architecture]. Lest we forget, »ideal object« or »ideality of the architectural object« (and Peter's text »Misreading Eisenman« contains the phrase »the object as ideal essence«, as well as a differentiation made a few years ago in Belgrade between »object as a mental construct« and »the actual object«) is actually a paraphrase of the title of Jacques Derrida's 1957 unwritten doctoral thesis, »The Ideality of Literary Object« (*l'idéalité de l'objet littéraire*).

767 Derrida: Introduction, p. 57.

768 Levinas: Théorie de l'intuition dans la phénoménologie de Husserl, p. 117.

5 Public Philosopher and Philosophy of the City

For a philosophy to truly belong to the city (and be a ›philosophy of the city‹), it is necessary for the philosopher to be ›a public, engaged, city philosopher‹. What the philosopher does – while residing in a city – they do publicly and engaged, meaning that the aim are others (or moving towards others). At the same time, the philosopher works along with others and for others, and for us, for the ›We‹. Only in this way are philosophers (always in the plural) in the common work of dwelling or building the institution of the city. To be engaged means to speak directly and performatively (taking on obligations, promises, questioning, pleading, responding, giving one's word, and recalling those of others), as well as burdening others with obligations, inciting them to action.

Philosophy is above all a city affair; or conversely, St. Petersburg (for example) is a city if it contains philosophers, if there is philosophizing in it. Regardless of the fact that I dwell in more than one city (having business in more than one place), if I am to be a philosopher (which means thinking myriad elements at once – thinking the city), by definition, I should not be an outsider in any city. Were St. Petersburg to expel me, it will not be because I am a foreigner with poor Russian, but because I am a philosopher. Better still, because I am a poor philosopher, unworthy of the philosophy and philosophers that exists in that city. This is the second problem, which opens several others, on the use of philosophy and philosophers, that is, of the public use of the mind. Allow me a few quick solutions to these problems. First, I would like to note that thinking the city or the issues that concern the public (what philosophy does) assumes »an attempt to understand how things hang together« (Wilfrid Sellars), that is, what holds people together, what allows for them to be next to one another. Second, in the course of explaining, critiquing, arguing, systematizing (of everything that makes a city), philosophers aim, often unwittingly and patently unsuccessfully, to exclude from the field of philosophy those who are not good, who mind their own business (rather than universal, urban matters. (In »Conversation with Drury«, Wittgenstein says that »bad philosophers are like slum landlords. It's my job to put them out of business.«[769])

I assume that today everyone would find it easy to agree that the concept of philosopher of whom Rousseau speaks in *Discours sur l'origine et les fondements*

769 In conversations with Drury, Wittgenstein compares philosophy to business: »My father was a businessman and I am a businessman too; I want my philosophy to be businesslike, to get something done, to get something settled.« O'Connor Drury: Contribution to a BBC Symposium, p. 91.

de l'inegalite parmi les hommes is a bad and narcissistic philosopher. Nevertheless, it implies the possibility of a true and authentic philosophy and a dedication to the city. Reason that produces self-love, a »philosophy that isolates the philosopher«, to use John Rawls' words, simultaneously also implies the possibility of existence of public reason. Rousseau writes:

It is reason that engenders self-love, and reflection that strengthens it; it is reason that makes man shrink into himself; it is reason that makes him keep aloof from everything that can trouble or afflict him: it is philosophy that destroys his connections with other men; it is in consequence of her dictates that he mutters to himself at the sight of another in distress, You may perish for aught I care, nothing can hurt me. Nothing less than those evils, which threaten the whole species, can disturb the calm sleep of the philosopher, and force him from his bed. One man may with impunity murder another under his windows; he has nothing to do but clap his hands to his ears, argue a little with himself to hinder nature, that startles within him, from identifying him with the unhappy sufferer. Savage man wants this admirable talent; and for want of wisdom and reason, is always ready foolishly to obey the first whispers of humanity. In riots and street-brawls the populace flock together, the prudent man sneaks off. They are the dregs of the people, the poor basket and barrow-women, that part the combatants, and hinder gentle folks from cutting one another's throats.[770]

»Nothing less than those evils, which threaten the whole species, can disturb the calm sleep of the philosopher, and force him from his bed.« Is this not enough? And does philosophy not precisely begin from this point? I am not at all sure that it is not required to set aside this »internalized voice of philosophy« (a moment analyzed in detail by Michael Walzer and John Rawls), when Rousseau announces the waking philosopher (or one in a group) who primarily worries about the destiny of the whole city.

A philosopher, then, to be producing philosophy, ought to be (as has been the case since Plato), an expert for public affairs (public or common affairs being city affairs). Of course, the problem is that the position of the expert often implies un-democratic behavior. In 1731 and 1732, the great German philosopher Christian

[770] *»C'est la raison qui engendre l'amour-propre, et c'est la réflexion qui le fortifie; c'est elle qui replie l'homme sur lui-même; c'est elle qui le sépare de tout ce qui le gêne et l'afflige: c'est la philosophie qui l'isole; c'est par elle qu'il dit en secret, à l'aspect d'un homme souffrant: péris si tu veux, je suis en sûreté. Il n'y a plus que les dangers de la société entière qui troublent le sommeil tranquille du philosophe, et qui l'arrachent de son lit. On peut impunément égorger son semblable sous sa fenêtre; il n'a qu'à mettre ses mains sur ses oreilles et s'argumenter un peu pour empêcher la nature qui se révolte en lui de l'identifier à celui qu'on assassine. L'homme sauvage n'a point cet admirable talent; et faute de sagesse et de raison, on le voit toujours se livrer étourdiment au premier sentiment de l'humanité. Dans les émeutes, dans les querelles des rues, la populace s'assemble, l'homme prudent s'éloigne: c'est la canaille, ce sont les femmes des halles, qui séparent les combattants, et qui empêchent les honnêtes gens de s'entre égorger.«* Rousseau: A Discourse upon the Origin and the Foundation of the Inequality among Mankind, p. 192; Rousseau: Discours sur l'origine et les fondements de l'inégalité parmi les hommes, p. 156.

Wolff wrote two studies about the necessity of the ruler being a king-philosopher (*De rege philosophante et philosopho regnante*) and a theory of public or market affairs (*De theoria negotiorum publicorum*; translated into French as *La théorie des Affaires-publiques*). Thus, the condition for the philosopher to fulfill their task and be king or ruler of a city is the active participation in public and economic affairs and the production of the theory of administration. It appears to me that Saint-Simon's 1814 prediction (nearly a hundred years after Wolff, made in »De la réorganisation de la société européenne«), that philosophy of the 19th century ought to be »*organisatrice*« (since in the 18th century it was »*révolutionnaire*«) also refers, in one way or another, to the century in which we find ourselves. Philosophy is ›institutional‹, that is, has the potential to produce new institutions and counter-institutions. It is the task of the philosopher to connect cities, organize, produce his own work, come up with projects that join the efforts of multiple cities. And it is the further task of the philosopher to, together with other philosophers, create complex joint applications to ensure the funds and positions for new, young philosophers already multiplying in numbers across our cities.

The phrase ›engaged dwelling‹ seems to me to help with the more precise determination of dwelling because it necessarily assumes the collective and others who dwell with me and with us. More specifically, if engagement includes others in common dwelling, a possible ethics of engagement would be the key factor in the distribution of rights for the purpose of achieving a more just and equitable community and a good life.[771]

Assuming that I, as a foreigner, a migrant (who even in my native Belgrade, Serbia only has temporary residence), indeed dwell (and have dwelt) in other cities, really dwelling here while I travel (and dwelling on that travel),[772] that I dwell with others and that I am certainly not single and carefree (free of care) – I could perhaps claim that by constantly changing places (space), that I retain some form

771 A couple of texts of immense significance for architects, written by two great philosophers of the nineteenth century, only very tentatively and entirely insufficiently thematize the common nature of dwelling. Only once in »Bauen Wohnen Denken« (»Building, Dwelling, Thinking«) does Heidegger place emphasis on the fact that building is always in common with others, that building as much as dwelling means working together: »We do not dwell because we have built, but have built and build if we dwell, that is, if we are residents« (*insofern wir wohnen, d. h. Als die Wohnenden sind*), nor is this then elaborated. Dwelling near another, a neighbor, »*Nachgebauer*« is mentioned too, but is simply not dealt with or thematized. Common dwelling in Heidegger is described completely vaguely as awaiting the deathly mortals (*Die Sterblichen*) or as common questioning. Heidegger: Bauen Wohnen Denken, pp. 35, 37. In *Totalité et infini* (chapter D, *La demeure*), Levinas only implicitly and casually mentions that dwelling has anything to do with a small community or family, with recollection. »*Comment l'habitation actualisant ce recueillements, cette intimité et cette chaleur ou cette douceur de l'intimité* (...)« »The intimacy which familiarity already presupposes is an intimacy with someone (*intimité avec quelqu'un*)«. Levinas: Totalité et infini, pp. 164–165.

772 Dwelling in English means »to remain for a time«, but also (used to mean) »to go astray« or »running around and getting nowhere«. Cf. Liberman: Our habitat: dwelling.

of identity and that therefore I am able to sometimes speak in the first person plural (to use ›we are‹ and speak in others' stead, suspending the self: when I say ›We‹, ›we dwell in Bonn together now‹, I have at once suspended my first person speech, that is, the possibility to say ›I dwell‹).

When do I dwell? Do I dwell only when we dwell together? This is my fundamental question, for which I would like to offer affirmation and justification. It seems to me that this ›we dwell‹ – and we will see shortly that this claim is nonsense for both Heidegger and his main readers and followers – we dwell in a house, in a family, in a group small or large, a university or city, is also the unconditional condition of my own attempt to testify about myself among others. Do I dwell somewhere when I am part of a city? Do I dwell somewhere when I build the city?[773] Do I dwell somewhere when I am alone or when I am with others? Can I say nothing to those others or do I need to speak with them, and am I only then allowed to say ›We‹? Do I dwell in a hotel alone or do I require Levinas' *féminin* to dwell somewhere at all?[774] Is the condition of my dwelling somewhere the possibility to purchase the room from my lodgings (to then have »a room of one's own«)? Or could I, together with someone, restore the lodgings in which I reside, invite another and host them, free of charge? Or else is it enough for philosophers to be working somewhere together, and care (as they do) about the city? Perhaps I am indeed not part of a given city, I have not participated in its previous activities and so do not belong to what we call ›group agency‹; on the other hand, I am certainly an associated member because I dwell and act alongside you and together with you in »joint agency«.[775] So then, what do the philosophers do at all, these philosophers in the city? (It seems to me that in *The Closed Commercial State*, Fichte only permits philosophers to travel and see other cities.).

I will try to explain some of these questions and dilemmas shortly, but before that, let me bring in my own resistance to certain forms of organization, com-

[773] The proximity of the German »*Bauen*«, build, to the word dwelling (*Wohnen*) and all the etymological possibilities and variations that Heidegger uses (sometimes quite imprecisely) are an accidental characteristic of the German language. In Greek or Latin (*demo* from *domus*), building refers to a house, while Slavic languages building refers to the city or work: in Serbo-Croatian, thus, »rad« (work), »grad« (city) »graditi« (build). Cf. Böhringer: Bauen.

[774] »The home that founds possession is not a possession in the same sense as the movable goods it can collect and keep. It is possessed because it already and henceforth is hospitable for its proprietor (*hospitalière à son propriétaire*). This refers us to its essential interiority (*intériorité essentielle*), and to the inhabitant that inhabits it before every inhabitant, the welcoming (*l'accueillant*) one par excellence, welcome in itself (*l'accueillant en soi*) – the feminine being (*l'être féminin*).« Levinas: Totalité et infini, p. 169.

[775] »Two or more individuals who engage in a joint action do not necessarily bring into existence a group agent. We can make sense of joint actions without ascribing a single »centre« of belief, desire and agency to the group in its entirety. It is sufficient for a joint action that the bearers of the underlying intentions are individuals; no group-level intentional states are needed.« List: What is it Like to be a Group Agent?, p. 5.

mon work and living, my engagement for the public (i.e., city) use of philosophy, by calling on us to come together and dwell in a new way. Here is testimony of two exemplary forms of resistance, of two models of opposition, which are not oppositions, that insist on something new and different (new people, new ties with people, a different city, new »outward expression« – [*s'exposer au dehors*][776] or new public space). The first is by a man from St. Petersburg, which in the nineteenth century became the fourth or fifth largest European city, but whose construction in the century prior required the death of some 150,000 people over three years – is this not proof enough that building often has nothing to do with dwelling? The man's name is Dostoyevsky, and he found himself in London in 1862, looking at Joseph Paxton's Crystal Palace:

> Gentlemen, you believe in a crystal edifice that can never be destroyed, an edifice at which one would not be able to stick one's tongue out, or to thumb one's nose, even on the sly. And I am afraid of this edifice just because it is of crystal and can never be destroyed, and because one could not stick out one's tongue at it on the sly.[777]

This is by no means a glorification of an »autonomy, radically endangered by the crystal palace«.[778] Rather, it is an attempt to remove a portion of a city that in no way belongs to the city (the palace will indeed disappear without a trace in a few decades), and certainly implicitly a fantasy of a common thumbing of noses

[776] Twenty years ago, a great interpreter of Heidegger succeeded, in all but a few sentences, to discover an entirely new moment or new emphasis in the concept of dwelling. Lacoue-Labarthe helped me think the idea of exteriority of dwelling in harmony with acting together. »Before »to have«, *habere* means »to hold (oneself)«. *Habitus* designates a way of being, what one would revealingly call the exterior aspect, the outward. Dwelling (*habiter*) does not refer to possession or position or protection. On the contrary, it means to be exposed to the outside. More precisely, dwelling is at any given moment a genuine bearing (giving up) to the outside« (*Habere n'est pas d'abord »avoir« mais »se tenir«. Habitus désigne la manière d'être, ce qu'on appelle de façon révélatrice l'aspect extérieur, le dehors. Habiter n'est en rien posséder, s'installer, se protéger. C'est au contraire s'exposer au dehors. Plus exactement, l'habitation est chaque fois un mode propre de se rapporter [de se livrer] au dehors*). Cf. Lacoue-Labarthe: Habiter.

[777] *»Вы верите в хрустальное здание, навеки нерушимое, то есть в такое, которому нельзя будет ни языка украдкой выставить, ни кукиша в кармане показать. Ну, а я, может быть, потому-то и боюсь этого здания, что оно хрустальное и навеки нерушимое и что нельзя будет даже и украдкой языка ему выставить.«* Достоевский: Малое собрание сочинений, p. 722. Cf. Berman: All That Is Solid Melts Into Air, p. 236.

[778] The second resistance is Derrida's. Paraphrasing André Gide, Derrida insists: »I am not one of the family« (*je ne suis pas de la famille*). »›I am not one of the family‹ means: do not consider me ›one of you‹, ›don't count me in‹, I want to keep my freedom, always: this, for me, is the condition not only for being singular and other, but also for entering into relation with the singularity and alterity of others. When someone is one of the family, not only does he lose himself in the herd (*le grégaire*), but he loses the others as well; the others become simply places, family functions in the organic totality that constitutes a group, school, nation or community of subjects speaking the same language.« Derrida/ Ferraris: *A Taste for the Secret*, pp. 26–28; Interview of 17 July 1993, Manuscript in French, p. 16. However, Derrida continues, the »second dimension (...) is that the fact of my not wanting to be one of the family is supposed by the fact of wanting to be one of the family.« »I am someone who has never left university.« Ibid., 43; 26.

and a new type of dwelling. Thus, is it possible, certainly in late capitalism, to construct new forms of dwelling and togetherness (association)? How can we be together beyond the corporation or the company or, for example, marriage, family or blood relation?

»Dwelling does not refer to possession or position or protection. On the contrary, it means to be exposed to the outside« (*Habiter n'est en rien posséder, s'installer, se protéger. C'est au contraire s'exposer au dehors*).

The difficulty that Dostoyevsky (or Derrida) speaks about, is really about the manifestation of passive or quiet resistance (giving the finger, but also constructing one's own *contre-institution* or *contre-groupe*), that is, a complete deconstruction of the notion of dwelling by way of transforming the interior into the exterior, the private into public. It seems probable to me that this public (city) space, that keeps creeping up in histories of thought and dwelling, could be complementary to the ›sense of philosophical dwelling‹ or ›public use of philosophy‹ today.

The philosopher who cares, who is vigilant and attentive and lives together with others (of course this is not a philosopher, but a person with the capacity of being exposed to the outside [*s'exposer au dehors*], and able to utter or exclaim ›We‹), would stand in opposition to the fatally erroneous ideas of dwelling we have held until now, it seems to me (for which even some philosophers are responsible). Allow me now to briefly reconstruct three errors. They are similar to one another and consistently limit or even deny the sense of common dwelling and acting in the city or the world. At the same time, I will attempt to cogently present my own position, and make it acceptable:

We work here and dwell there. We do not merely dwell – that would be virtual inactivity – we practice profession, we do business, we travel and lodge on the way, now here, now there (*Wir wohnen nicht bloß, das wäre beinahe Untätigkeit, wir stehen in einem Beruf, wir machen Geschäfte, wir reisen und wohnen unterwegs, bald hier, bald dort*).[779]

Heidegger uses the plural; but such dwelling or work is certainly not common, nor does it refer to ›We‹, the first person plural in any way. This portion of the sentence, »*das wäre beinahe Untätigkeit*«, is rendered in English as »that would be virtual inactivity«. As if dwelling were (next to) nothing because it appears stripped down, as if it were naked life or naked existence. Indeed, dwelling is not an activity, since we change location (we commute) to the place where activity or work (profession, business, probably trade) takes place – this is a different place. Instead of being defined as public collective activity (which includes these public collective activities), when it comes to dwelling, Heidegger puts emphasis on building (*Bauen*) as its essence. In Heidegger's interpretation, this word does not contain what it already contains, the most important characteristic of building. Heideg-

779 Heidegger: Bauen Wohnen Denken, p. 33.

ger finds a lot of key elements in the word *Bauen* for a new and future dwelling, but forgets or neglects the basic element – *Bauen* is disciplined activity within a group, collective work and construction of the property of all (public property, a public affair, a common) for the sake of common dwelling and common enjoyment of property.[780] Heidegger is writing this text in a Germany shortly before the bombing when all are working together to create a new community; he seems to be caring for the common interest.

Derrida, one of Heidegger's most careful readers, recognizes this place, and is still more explicit and ever more complicated:

> Dwelling is what a subject does, »acts on« or decides upon the least, it is not an activity. I dwell only in distancing, the only way of thinking how writing, memory, language provide dwelling, allowing space for distancing while depriving me of it.
>
> (*Or habiter, c'est ce qu'un sujet fait, décide ou »agit« le moins, ce n'est pas une action. Je n'habite que dans l'éloignement, seule manière de penser que l'écriture, la mémoire, le langage donnent à habiter, lui donnent lieu en m'en privant*).[781]

Dwelling is not an activity, even though a subject (the dweller) does act while residing, deciding or »acting«. In the second sentence Derrida speaks of his own distancing, distance, distant living, and he justifies why such dwelling is the only way to think the staging of dwelling. (Although Marguerite Derrida and he had an apartment in Paris, and she did use it as her office for psychoanalytic sessions, their residence, where Derrida wrote and is buried, was Ris Orangis, a southern suburb of Paris). In a virtuosic and untranslatable turn of phrase, Derrida tells us that writing, memory, language exist (give place to one's existence or dwelling) by providing place to distancing (*l'éloignement*) and that this operation erases his own place (the place of Derrida, the subject, the resident or the one who speaks). Dwelling then is neither activity nor a common action because the philosopher or the one who dwells is always far away and distant. This distance is in one way or another the condition for the existence (presence) of thought or writing or memory. How is this possible? And how is this distancing and dwelling outside a big city different from Rousseau's stopping of ears against city noise? A dweller is a citizen who possesses the capacity to act in its environment. His duty is certainly to hear and respond to another citizen's distress – this being what reminds him that they live and dwell together.

Yet another reader of Heidegger creates utter confusion, but is important for us because he brings dwelling together with speech. It all begins with the woman or feminine alterity:

780 One of the basic examples of »acting together« used by Margaret Gilbert is »building a house together«. Cf. Gilbert: Joint Commitment, p. 23.

781 Derrida: Habiter.

And the other (*Autre*) whose presence is discreetly an absence, with which is accomplished the primary hospitable welcome (*l'accueil hospitalier par excellence*) which describes the field of intimacy, is the Woman (*Femme*). The woman is the condition for recollection, the interiority of the Home (*Maison*), and inhabitation (*habitation*). The simple living from ... (*le simple vivre de ...*) the spontaneous agreeableness of the elements is not yet habitation. But habitation is not yet the transcendence of language. The Other (*Autrui*) who welcomes in intimacy is not you (*vous*) of the face (*vous du visage*) that reveals itself in a dimension of height, but precisely the thou (*tu*) of familiarity (*tu de la familiarité*): a language without teaching, a silent language, an understanding without words (*entente sans mots*), an expression in secret. The I-Thou (*je-tu*) in which Buber sees the category of interhuman relationship is the relation not with the interlocutor but with feminine alterity (*altérité féminine*). This alterity (*altérité*) is situated on another plane than language and nowise represents a truncated, stammering, still elementary language (*un language tronqué, balbutiant, encore élémentaire*).[782]

Every position or every assumption of this construction by Levinas is incorrect or insufficiently justified and argued. First the »inside« or »interiority« of the house or dwelling from this passage are explicitly connected to woman, woman as other (woman, not mother or female).[783] Is the »inside« or »interiority« of the institution also connected to the woman and the feminine, or is it rather necessarily male? Further, dwelling is still not »transcendence of language«, i. e., in dwelling there is neither speech nor conversation, nor »is common language constructed«. If language is outside the house, then that means that there is no conversation inside the house, which means no agreement, consensus, decisions – in direct contradiction to the economic dimension of dwelling Levinas speaks of in the very same chapter. This unclear and odd suggestion, Levinas resolves by way of an entirely problematic differentiation of thou (*tu*) and you (*vous*), explaining that in the »language of familiarity« (the domain of thou, *tu*; the differentiation is baseless since in English, for example, there are not two words for this) there is no instruction or exchange of opinion or performative speech, disputation or disagreement, but only »a language without teaching, a silent language, an understanding without words (*entente sans mots*), an expression in secret.«[784] Levinas' most uncertain maneuver is the unheard of twisting of Buber's idea (which was required for the

782 Levinas: Totality and Infinity, p. 155; Levinas: Totalité et infini, p. 166.

783 Levinas' understanding of the house is similar to a sentence in Rosenzweig written immediately after World War I: »a house ought to protect life and be entirely separated from the city, as dwelling from other city activities«..., see footnote 231.

784 This passage is in complete agreement with ›village dwelling‹ or a provincial way of communication that Heidegger writes about in March 1934 in »Warum bleiben wir in der Provinz?«: »When relaxing after a long day's work, I sit with the villagers on a bench before a stove or at a table in the corner surrounded by icons, most often we do not speak at all (*dann reden wir meist gar nicht*). We smoke our pipes in silence. Here and there, a word drops ... (*Zwischendurch vielleicht fällt ein Wort*)«. Heidegger: Schöpferische Landschaft, p. 10.

distinction between *tu* and *vous*). He claims that Buber's dialogue-action, that is, communication between subject or dwellers (taking place, to be sure, outside of the home, if we are to follow Levinas' logic of interior-exterior) really belongs to the »house« or »familiar« game between a man (*Ich*, I) and a woman as alterity (*Du*, Thou). With woman, concludes Levinas, or wife in the home, man does not even really talk to, nor does he stammer, nor truncate, nor is he on some sort of lowest level of language exchange. The two use their language for something between speaking and silence.

It would be very complicated to reconstruct now all the consequences of this stupefying perversion of Buber's famous idea, but this is a symptom of the latent reticence of philosophers in general to testify to common dwelling and (common) city living. The transfer of the relation »I-thou« (*Je-Tu*, *Ich-Du*) from the »outside«, the city into the house (family, intimacy, the relation between lovers) creates a double problem: on the one hand, it creates asymmetry between the sexes, devaluing language in the home with the women and children, and it implies that in the house there is not common dwelling (no ›common language‹). Not only do members of a household thus not produce a common language, but are *de facto* in this ›space of intimacy‹ horribly distant from one another. On the other hand, the absence of Buber's well-known relation outside the house (in the city, in squares, streets, schools, assemblies – in institutions[785]), implies that the relations among people are dominated by irresponsibility and confrontation (again asymmetry), as well as by difficulties in constructing protocols that regard equality in the city and then also common work among willing equals. Analogously, the position of the philosopher is vague and disjointed. Instead of it being in discovering new forms of dwelling and association, beyond marriage, corporations, and companies, but then also beyond the very dubious difference between the public and private, the philosopher simply does not live here, with others, it is not »exposed to the outside«, they are not oriented towards others. In this case, when the philosopher utters ›We‹ (in name of others, suspending themselves) and nurtures the creation of the group and institution, these are mere temporary actions, activist and lim-

785 An even more complicated moment in Levinas appears when he explains with Rabbi Elazar what is the source of all evil in the city or in general: »*Rabbi Elazar a découvert que la source du Mal se trouve dans l'institution même du cabaret. Le cabaret, ou le café, est devenu partie intégrante et essentielle de la vie moderne, qui est peut-être »vie ouverte« surtout par cet aspect! Une ville inconnue où nous arrivons et qui est sans cafés nous semble fermée. Le café, c'est la maison ouverte, de plain-pied avec la rue, lieu de la société facile, sans responsabilité réciproque. On entre sans nécessité. On s'assied sans fatigue, on boit sans soif. Histoire de ne pas rester dans sa chambre. Vous savez que tous les malheurs viennent de l'incapacité où nous sommes de rester seuls dans notre chambre. Le café n'est pas un lieu, c'est un non-lieu pour une non-société, pour une société sans solidarité, sans lendemant, sans engagement, sans intérêts communs, société du jeu (…) Le monde comme jeu d'où chacun peut tirer son épingle et n'exister que pour soi, lieu d'oubli – de l'oubli de l'autre – voilà le café. Et nous rejoignons ainsi notre première lecture: ne pas bâtir le monde, c'est le détruire.*« Levinas: Du sacré au saint, pp. 41–42.

ited, inevitably conflictual. (Heidegger thematizes the ›We‹ in his seminar from 1934, with the intension to constitute the people, above all the German people; while Levinas' lectures at the Paris synagogue clearly imply a segregated city and difference among groups, etc.) Which is why the situation described by Rousseau is current in all times (and today more than ever): difficulties and travails that threaten the institution, the city, society, or humanity are incessant, precarity is constant;[786] and strength of the dream or the fiction (anesthesia) the philosopher uses to be excluded from common dwelling – ever weaker. Yet, this is not enough! What is needed, certainly, are parallel, separate institutions free of the patronage of the state, as well as a new vigilance and readiness of all actors.

786 The word precarity or *précaire* appears for the first time in the 16th century (Levinas, uses the phrase »ontological precarity« [*la précarité ontologique*] somewhere, saying that the face is »precarity more precarious than all precarity« [*précarité plus précaire que toute précarité*]). It comes from Latin legal jargon, *precarius*, and means »obtained by praying« (*prex*). Surprisingly, this origin is at once juridical and religious (or pseudo-religious). This etymology would indicate that all precarity is synonymous with dependence on a curatorial power, regardless of its precise nature, which could give us what we ask, or refuse our request, or even withdraw it from us at any moment after having given it – whence the idea that anything precarious is poorly established and secured. However, this etymology also at once signals that human precarity is not exclusively a contemporary issue, nor indeed a recent one. By definition, there is precarity wherever there is power. To reiterate: »precarity« exists in a place where: (1) there is power that can be solicited (asked, begged) for something (usually, this is land or some such benefit), (2) something has been lent or borrowed without a contract (a transaction that is not a legal act [acte juridique], not an obligation, but a simple fact), (3) it is not a lending or borrowing with a specific date of return (*commodatum*), but the owner decides on their own when the precarious [précariste] must return the land (this is called *precarium*; in Naples, in 1772, Giambatisto Vico writes in the margin of his book *Il diritto universale* about the *precarium* as the origin of the contract; a hundred years prior, Hugo Grotius writes about Jews to whom the Roman emperor allowed the conduct of public ritual and the following of their own laws based on *jus precarium*, and not on the laws of the empire (*non ex lege aliqua imperio addità*). Meaning, that he could have abolished them whenever he so wished.

Conclusion

0 What Is the Counter-Institution? Europe as Counter-Institution

»L'Europe est dans un état violent, tous le savent, tous le disent.«[787]

I am interested in the origin of the idea of the *contre-institution* or counter-institution. Above all, I would like to show that there is a kind of opposition or resistance to the institution or institutions that necessarily concerns Europe and justice. I have found nothing better on the counter-institution than several texts and fragments by Saint-Simon and Jacques Derrida. Thus, my intention is to thematize what Derrida unfortunately has not (and try to carry out a rather complicated task in his stead). At the same time, I would like to connect the counter-institution with the institutionalization of Europe. My basic question, then, is: »how does one institutionalize Europe«? In other words, how is Europe made? The question implies a few specific protocols that are of concern to deconstruction (a word most often linked to Derrida). In the first place, Europe stems from already extant institutions, such as sovereign states that have been sewn onto ›European space‹ for a long time. This makes Europe an institutional or documentational construction that is actually a counter-institution (meaning that it exists simultaneously and in parallel with other institutions and also at the same time resists them). Second – and conversely to the first statement – Europe also, at the same time, stems from a space that appears extra-institutional or pre-institutional or is not-yet-institutional. Namely, the space whence comes the resistance to existing institutions (above all the institutions of sovereign states, but not only them) ought to be ultimately institutionalized as Europe. Both of these operations, resistance and institutionalization, concern themselves with justice and hospitality. Justice is a counter-institutional operation: institutions generate resistance because they are often unjust and inhospitable, yet cannot be destroyed, but only limited and regulated through other, parallel (counter-)institutions – in other words, they can only be deconstructed. Further, this counter-institutionalization can be a difficult and long-term process; and justice is quite slow and unattainable. Finally, the counter-institution ought to be different to all known forms of association and cooperation, such as corporation, non-governmental/nonprofit organizations, or world trade organizations (the amount of equality and justice would certainly be the measure and condition of this distinction). Yet, »justice (itself) is undeconstructible.« What is Derrida saying when he says: »Justice is undeconstructible,

787 Saint-Simon: De la réorganisation de la société européenne, p. 23.

but it has to be thought through deconstruction, beyond a right that is excess, disjoint, dislocation.«[788]

There are multiple ways to approach this complicated sentence (a quick check will reveal that *indéconstructible* and *disjointure* are words that cannot be found in the dictionary), using several different protocols that seem most important in Derrida. In one way or another, all these protocols are forms of resistance (resistance that is not resistance, but still resistance) and refer to the word *contre* because deconstruction concerns resistance and resisting, but also the real, realism. When, for example, he is speaking about the norm and normativity (as he does in two short, late texts, »La norme et son suspens« and »La norme doit manquer«), Derrida insists on that which precedes the norm (right, law), or if you like, on »orientation without compass and prior to institution« (*orientation sans boussole et avant institution*).

At the end of one of his last texts, Derrida brings up the book jacket of *La faculté de juger*, obviously edited by Lyotard, with the words: »The judge should (...) judge without set rules, and his decision can make up right. This ›prudence‹ is the virtue of being guided without a compass. Prior to institution.«[789]

»L'Europe est dans un état violent, tous le savent, tous le disent.« How can we describe this space or time that is ›prior to the institution‹? And does all resistance to the institution issue from this fictitious set-up? What is the connection between the ›pre-institutional‹ and the counter-institution?

Two hundred years ago, in the aftermath of the Congress of Vienna, Claude-Henri de Saint-Simon announces a reconstruction of institutions and imagines a new Europe. His endeavor is to provide a more precise description of the origin of the violent state (*un état violent*) of contemporary institutions[790] – a fact on everyone's mind and on everyone's lips. He himself thinks that the political and social ties of peoples ought to be strengthened, in other words, that for any unification of a people or peoples, there have to be common institutions (*A toute réunion de peuples comme à toute réunion d'hommes, il faut des institutions communes*). Indeed,

788 *»La justice est indéconstructible, mais il faut la penser en déconstruction, dans un au-delà du droit qui est excès, disjointure, dislocation.«* Derrida: Spectre de Marx, p. 55.

789 *»Le juge doit (...) juger sans règle préétablie, et son jugement peut faire jurisprudence. Cette »prudence« est la vertu de se bien guider sans boussole. Avant l'institution.«* Derrida: Le modèle philosophique d'une »contre-institution«, p. 260. I would like to bring together two potential interpretations of the sentence »Justice is undeconstructible.« The first is suggested by Alain Badiou, who, in writing about Derrida, says: »Naught is undeconstructible, but justice – it cannot be reduced to any Law or any Right, and yet it is justice that allows for all deconstruction.« (*Seule la justice est indéconstructible, elle qui ne se réduit à aucune Loi ni à aucun Droit, et c'est d'ailleurs elle qui permet toute déconstruction*). Badiou: Le petit panthéon portatif, p. 123. The second possibility is the following: I suggest the sentence be read strictly as it is: the process of deconstructing justice is ceaseless, neither beginning nor ending, but ever taking place. Justice *is* deconstruction.

790 Ibid., »*(...) mais cet état, quel est-il? d'où vient-il? a-t-il toujours duré? est-il possible qu'il cesse? Ces questions sont encore sans réponse.«*

Saint-Simon continues, what is necessary is organization. Without organization, what resolves any situation is force (*hors de là, tout se décide par la force*). Europe here, above all, refers to, or is the name of certain new institutions (or common institutions, organizations) that ensure strong political and social ties, thus abolishing all force and violence.

My intention in this chapter is, using certain texts by Saint-Simon and Jacques Derrida, to attempt to thematize such new institutions or the new institution, meant to replace the old ones. The phrase counter-institution, I believe first used by Saint-Simon, and mentioned by Derrida in several of his texts and interviews, ought to be directly synonymous with the new institution or Europe, while the old institutions could be connected to the closed sovereign institutions of sovereign states. The phrases ›counter-institution‹ and ›Europe as counter-institution‹ immediately imply a number of tasks, and several are beyond the scope of this book. First and foremost, I am interested in how it is possible to differentiate the ›counter-institution‹ from the institution. What is it that is ›counter-‹ of an institution and does it have anything to do with defying, opposing, resisting the institution or institutions? Further, what dimension and status do Saint-Simon's and Derrida's insistences on new institutions or counter-institutions have within the famous French institutionalism from Saint-Just, through Hauriou and Renard, to Gilles Deleuze?

Second, some of the most important terms and aims of Derrida's philosophy (or, in the final analysis, even Saint-Simon's outlines and proposals) emerge in correlation with this word ›counter‹. Counter that refers directly to the institution has as its goal to open and reveal, thus implying the new, the just, the yet to come, etc. Europe and democracy can only be introduced as an addition to the institutions of sovereign states, and as counter and opposite to institutions that are always, in one way or another, closed and static. As I have mentioned, the institution is fundamentally distinct from a contract, in that it always implies the presence of a third who is welcome, who always anew institutionalizes the institution; whereas the contract is limited in duration, assumes the will of contracted parties, and cannot be impinged upon by a third party. How does the counter-institution fit into this distinction? It ought to increase the ›strength of hospitality‹ of the institution. And if hospitality is one of the most important principles of the institution (the ever present possibility of someone new, a third to be included and become part of a group and participate in its common work), then the counter-institution reveals a paradox of hospitality: in a certain sense it dissolves hospitality by quickly turning guests or strangers (migrants) into European citizens (hospitality necessarily must be temporary and brief, and its essence consists of an urgent transformation of a stranger into a future host offering hospitality to yet a another new person and stranger).

Third, it seems to me that a potential thematization of what Derrida calls the »counter-institution« could enable a possible transformation of deconstruction into a replicable method (making it, therefore, a method), when transmitted and taught in a disciplined fashion.[791] Thus it is also my intention to show the origin of Derrida's understanding of justice, hospitality, Europe, democracy and other related concepts (»concepts which are not the concepts«).[792]

It is Saint-Simon, truly our contemporary, who (first speaks of a European parliament, first imagines a European constitution) sees Europe as an institution or as a new protocol in the making, such that the old institutions »yield« their place to the new. For me, it is this process of wilting and dissolution of the old and emergence of the new institutions[793] that is questionable and problematic. Mak-

791 First of all, the word ›institution‹ and its various figures are Derrida's true obsession. »I would privilege the word institutions over deconstructions and architecture.« »Every institution is an architecture.« Jacques Derrida. Invitation to a Discussion, pp. 12–13. »Deconstruction is an institutional practice, in which the concept of the institution remains a problem«… (*La déconstruction est une pratique institutionnelle pour laquelle le concept d'institution reste un problème, mais comme elle n'est pas davantage une »critique« (…) elle ne détruit pas plus qu'elle ne discrédite la critique ou les institutions; son geste transformateur est autre, autre sa responsabilité*). J. Derrida, *Du droit à la philosophie*, Paris, Galilée, 1990, 88. Derrida repeats many times that deconstruction is not a method. If so, then it can have no protocols, procedures, *proceeds*, cannot be repeated, transferred, translated, cannot be thematized or recognized. »A method that cannot be repeated (›I have my own method‹), we could easily consider worthless.« Derrida: La langue et le discours de la méthode, p. 37.

792 In the background of common projects and friendship with Peter Eisenman lies a mutual interest in the ›institution‹. »I was always inventing institutions and projects that I could appear in (…)«. P. Eisenman, »On the End of Authority«, unpublished interview, 26 September 2016. Here are two fragments from Eisenman: »Precisely because shelter manifests presence in construction, it will tend to stabilize and in so doing ultimately lend itself to institutionalization. Any act of building will necessarily be an act of presencing. But, as stated earlier, the conceptual act of architecture is the critique, transformation, and creation of institutions. Thus architecture can be considered, paradoxically, contradictory to building, to its institutionalizing presence. As such, architecture cannot be except as it continuously distances itself from its own boundaries; it is always in the process of becoming, of changing, while it is also always establishing, institutionalizing. It has the potential to be simultaneously a creation and a critique of the institutions it builds. This is what might be termed the challenge of dislocation for the architect and for architecture.« Eisenman: Misreading Peter Eisenman, p. 222. »Architecture creates institutions. It is a constructive activity. Architecture, by its very creation, is institutionalizing. So, for architecture to be, it must resist what it must in fact do. In order to be, it must always resist being. It must dislocate without destroying its own being, that is, it must maintain its own metaphysic. This is the paradox of architecture.« Eisenman: Architecture and the Problem of the Rhetorical Figure, p. 203.

793 In the »Avant-propos« of his brief, 1814 text on the reorganization of Europe, Saint-Simon speaks about the importance of the institutions and mentions that bad or failing institutions (*le défaut d'institution*) lead to the destruction of society as a whole: »Old institutions prolong the ignorance and prejudices of the time in which they were formed« (*Les vieilles institutions prolongent l'ignorance et les préjugés du temps où elles sont faites*). (Ibid., p. 16.) Institutions age because they no longer suit the ideas and mores of the time in which they exist, and ought therefore be completely destroyed. Saint-Simon cites two obstacles in this transformation of the old into the new: this reorganization does not happen right away or automatically (but rather, in time), and also, he also imagines the possibility that nothing arises on the ruins of old institutions (*la ruine des anciennes institutions*). In *Catéchisme des industriels* of 1823, Saint-Simon *de facto* insists that the total erasure

ing matters worse are Saint-Simon's hesitations throughout the text; which is why I would like to combine his idea of establishing a new organization of Europe with the idea of double or parallel institutions that Saint-Simon mentions when writing about England's organization. Regardless of there being no mention in Saint-Simon of, for example, documents or charters as the essence of the creation of Europe and the new institutionalization of Europe, he is perfectly aware that a change in organization and ties between people becomes the condition for the abolition of force and violence. Limiting and eliminating force is really the elimination of borders between states, partial interests, in other words, the hindering of nationalism of individual peoples. Saint-Simon's original idea contains three or even four steps in its construction. As early as 1813, he envisions that in order for ›Europe‹ to become synonymous with a specific kind of institution, which runs ›counter-‹ to sovereign institutions of sovereign peoples, and in order for these institutions to wither and vanish, we need »a general communal institution«[794] (*une institution générale commune*). Europeans (his *Européens* or *la population européenne*) ought to be bound together by this institution that surpasses entities, such as partial and national religions and states. This institution – politically common to all the peoples of Europe (*une institution politique commune à tous les peuples européens*) – ought to hold back or put the breaks on (*mettre en frein*) the national ambitions of each of these peoples individually.[795] It is the bearer *par excellence* of general European hospitality and justice. Here is how Saint-Simon elaborates on the function of this institution:

> The task of this work is the reorganization of European Society by introducing a general communal institution for all the peoples it comprises, an institution that would, depending on the level of enlightenment of each people, appear as scientific or religious, but would, in any case, act in a politically positive way, by holding back the ambitions of peoples and kings.[796]

In the next paragraph Saint-Simon lets it be known that the main regulative moment of this positive political action is actually the »strength of European scien-

and destruction of institutions is impossible: »Institutions, much like the men that create them, can be modified; they cannot, however, be rendered extinct: their most rudimentary aspects cannot be completely razed« (*Les institutions, de même que les hommes qui les créent, sont modifiables; mais elles ne sont point dénaturables: leur caractère primitif ne peut pas s'effacer entièrement*). Saint-Simon: Catéchisme des industriels, p. 31.

794 Saint-Simon: Mémoire sur la science de l'homme, p. 358.

795 Saint-Simon: Travail sur la gravitation universelle, p. 426. In his letter to European scientists (*Lettre aux savants européens*), Saint-Simon says that this institution is at present very weakened and damaged by the war that is devouring the European peoples (ibid., pp. 480–481).

796 »*La conséquence de ces travaux sera la réorganisation de la Société européenne, au moyen d'une institution générale commune à tous les peuples qui la composent, institution qui, suivant le degré de lumière de chacun, lui paraitra scientifique ou religieuse, mais qui, dans tous les cas, exercera une action politique positive, celle de mettre un frein à l'ambition des peuples et des rois.*« Ibid., p. 479.

tists« and above all, philosophy.[797] Philosophy, or the community of philosophers organized in a unified corporation ought *de facto* ensure the functioning of this new institution that is nothing other than Europe itself. Saint-Simon thinks that philosophers, or better yet, philosophy itself has the strength and task to produce new institutions and organize the new life of united Europe. If »philosophy of the previous century was revolutionary« (*révolutionnaire*), he declares, »the philosophy of the nineteenth ought to be organizational (*organisatrice*).«[798] If »institutions are naught else but ideas in action« (*institutions ne sont que des idées en actes*),[799] Saint-Simon obviously reckons that the philosopher is not exclusively the producer of ideas, but one who in cooperation with other philosophers and scientists, places ideas into action, turning those ideas into reality. The corporation, or some European corporation for philosophy, it would seem, has a double task. Ignoring for a second that this requires a single common philosophy (Saint-Simon is obsessed with the theory of general gravitation and in his view all philosophers ought to be as well), his intention is to render theory active by combining the Institute and the University, research and education. First revealing and problematizing the fatal paradox of institutions that form people, and people who at the same time form institutions,[800] and having imagined the best possible constitution (*la meilleure constitution possible*), in the second step, the philosopher Saint-Simon envisions European institutions organized in such a way that »each question of public interest be considered in the most compete and profound way« (*la plus approfondie et la plus complète*).[801] In one way or another, the philosophical or parliamentary debates about what is the common good (*bien commun*) surpass the closed national and sovereign states. The discovery of the general and common, the purview of this ideal corporation of philosophers and scientists – really representing the beginning of the idea of the institutionalization of Europe – introduces the problem or paradox of double institutions.

Were we to confirm and take up Saint-Simon's idea that philosophy of the twenty-first century ought to be organizational, with a very strong power to institutionalize and protect various institutions, and were we to reorganize and amend Saint-Simon's vision of Europe, we would immediately encounter two paradoxes. The first dilemma or problem would regard the existence of two parallel kinds of institutions, the old and new, and whether such a state, that can sometimes be

797 In the text »Travail sur la gravitation universelle«, written in the same year, Saint-Simon explains that »the force of European scientists, unified in a single corporation held together by a philosophy based on the idea the universal gravity, would be invaluable« (*La force des savants de l'Europe, réunis en une corporation générale ayant pour lien une philosophie basée sur l'idée de la gravitation, sera incalculable*). Ibid., p. 480.

798 Saint-Simon: De la réorganisation de la société européenne, p. 15.

799 Saint-Simon: L'Industrie (III, 39). Cf. Durkheim: Le socialisme, p. 119.

800 Saint-Simon: De la réorganisation de la société européenne, pp. 35–36.

801 Ibid., p. 28.

a state of violence on everyone's mind and lips, is something truly transitory. Regardless of Saint-Simon saying that old institutions disappear, the new European institution only partially and occasionally takes their place and limits them. How is this possible? The second paradox, that Saint-Simon mentions, and I would call fatal, refers to a line from Montesquieu, that »the institution forms men« (*c'est l'institution qui forme les hommes*). How is it possible, then, for those same people formed by the institution to also create some new and different institutions? Here is the passage in which Saint-Simon presents this difficulty:

It is the institution that forms men, says Montesquieu. Thus, a penchant for extending patriotism beyond the bounds of the homeland, a practice of considering the interests of Europe, rather than national interests, would be a required result of those who would compose the European parliament. This is true. Yet, it is also men who form institutions, and the institution cannot be established if it does not find them already completely formed, or at least prepared to be so.[802]

If Europe, that is, the European institution, forms people (Europeans), then this penchant or practice (*ce penchant*; *cette habitude*) of the institution forming people has as a consequence that patriotism surpasses the borders of states, and that European interest replaces national interest. Surpassing the borders of nation states in this passage implies at least two new protocols: a greater openness of national states and hospitality for all citizens of Europe, and of course, the process of expansion of Europe by opening its new future borders beyond any European patriotism. The problem occurs in the second sentence of this fragment by Saint-Simon. Since it is people who form the institution, and the institution forms people as they are forming and constructing it, Saint-Simon assumes that the idea or form of this new institution already pre-exists in the minds of those who are soon to form it. In other words, the institution can be formed only if it »finds« people already prepared and educated to make it (or at least ready to make the institution and be formed by it as they form it). The problem or paradox of the institution as a subject of this second sentence, the institution that can already find (*trouver*) people who are *ad hoc* formed by the very institution (without it even existing yet), returns us, yet again, to the idea of dual or parallel institutions. Only once does Saint-Simon use the phrase »double institutions (*doubles institutions*), in the very fragment that interests us, where he also only the one time uses the phrase »*les contre-institutions*«.

802 »*C'est l'institution qui forme les hommes, dit Montesquieu; ainsi, ce penchant qui fait sortir le patriotisme hors de bornes de la patrie, cette habitude de considérer les intérêts de l'Europe, au lieu des intérêts nationaux, sera pour ceux qui doivent former le parlement européen, un fruit nécessaire de son établissement. Il est vrai: mais aussi ce sont les hommes qui font l'institution, et l'institution ne peut s'établir si elle ne les trouve tout formés d'avance, ou du moins préparés à l'être.*« Ibid., p. 36.

Saint-Simon's vision of Europe is above all determined by the relationship between England and France, and he spends a lot of his time studying the political and economic situation in England: researching the Constitution, social organization and institutions of England. It also seems that the English system is his main inspiration for his theory of the institution, and, analogously, for the construction of the future institution of Europe. In *Catéchisme des industriels*, Saint-Simone writes:

We see that the English have set two parallel fundamental principles as the basis of their social organization. Further, one can see that these two principles, being of different, even opposing, natures, have resulted, as they necessarily must, in the English being at once subject to two distinct social orders. They have double institutions in all directions, or rather, they have established in all directions counter-institutions for each institution that held sway before their revolution, and which they have preserved to a great extent.[803]

Twice Saint-Simon writes »in all directions« (*dans toutes les directions*). It is clear to one as knowledgeable of the situation in England as Saint-Simon that institutions and counter-institutions (in this passage in the plural) are not mutually opposed, even if they are entirely different. Although Saint-Simon recognizes two principles that can as such be opposed, the word ›counter‹ (before the word institution) certainly does not mean ›opposite direction‹, since counter-institutions are above all social organizations much as institutions. Counter-institutions complement the activity of institutions or occupy a portion of public space that is not yet institutionalized or is impossible to institutionalize. At the same time, the parallel existence of this kind of entity in England from before their revolution offers a certain guarantee that they are not mutually exclusive or invalidating and that they have a common future. In that sense, counter does not mean contrast, *versus*, but contact or juxtaposition, and sometimes even exchange and a relationship.[804]

803 »*On reconnaît que les Anglais ont admis en concurrence deux principes fondamentaux pour servir de base à leur organisation sociale; on reconnaît que ces deux principes étant de nature différente et même opposée, il a dû en résulter, et qu'il en est résulté effectivement que les Anglais se sont en même temps soumis à deux organisations sociales bien distinctes, qu'ils ont, dans toutes les directions, doubles institutions, ou plutôt qu'ils ont établi dans toutes les directions les contre-institutions de toutes les institutions qui étaient en vigueur chez eux avant leur révolution, et qu'ils ont conservé en très grande partie.*« Saint-Simon: Catéchisme des industriels, pp. 80–81.

804 Sociology today only very seldom uses the word counter-institution (the NGO sector is not usually named as such, nor are corporations or various citizens' associations). In the sixties, this term covered something that could potentially be similar to what Saint-Simon notices exists in the social life of England at the beginning of the nineteenth century. In the text »The Phantom Community«, Paul Starr speaks of a different need for collective action, and a different »ideal of organizational life«, that would assume counter-institutions. »It was a romantic ideal of the organization as a community, in which social relations were to be direct and personal, open and spontaneous, in contrast to the rigid, remote, and artificial relations of bureaucratic organization.« »Counterinstitutions – communes, cooperatives, free clinics, free schools, free universities, counseling centers, day-care centers, encounter groups and other forms of collective therapy and »consciousness-raising,« »underground« newspapers,

If we turn the phrase »*les contre-institutions*« into its singular, we have the »*contre-institution*« that follows or is juxtaposed to all other institutions (*la contre-institution de toutes les institutions*). Further, Europe, as a potential counter-institution of all institutions (*de toutes les institutions*), ought to be, at once, the true philosophical model of counter-institution[805] and push the boundaries of all institutions to ensure their openness and hospitality. Is this possible? And can several brief interventions by Derrida, in which he attempts to thematize the counter-institution, be useful to Saint-Simon's great proposal of reorganization of Europe?

Derrida attempts to thematize his relationship and resistance to the institution on several occasions;[806] yet only in two or three places in two short periods does he refer to the counter-institution, attempting to determine its relation toward the institution or institutions as such. The last time towards the end of his life,[807] and before that in the early nineties in a few interviews,[808] as well as upon receiving the »Légion d'honneur« on 14 July 1992.

grass-roots community organizations, public-interest law firms, and peace, environmental, women's, civil-rights, and consumer groups.« Starr: The Phantom Community, p. 245.

805 One of Jacques Derrida's last lectures, along with one his last published texts, carries the title »Le modèle philosophique d'une ›contre-institution‹«.

806 »Finally, to finish with the affective, I can say that school was hell for me (...) I have a completely neurotic relationship to the institution to which I have, nevertheless, belonged all my life. Still today, when I enter an establishment such as this one, I have a visceral reaction, truly – I should be in therapy – since kindergarten (...)« (*Et finalement, pour en finir avec l'affectif, je peux dire que l'école a été un enfer pour moi. (...) J'ai un rapport absolument névrotique à l'institution que j'ai pourtant habitée toute ma vie; et, encore aujourd'hui, quand j'entre dans des bâtiments comme celui-ci, ça me prend aux tripes, vraiment, et ce sont des choses il faudrait analyser – qui remontent à la maternelle ...*). Derrida: L'école a été un enfer pour moi ...

807 In »Le modèle philosophique d'une ›contre-institution‹«, while analyzing »quasi-institutional or counter-institutional entities (*phénoménes quasi-institutionnels ou contre-institutionnels*), Derrida gives seven basic characteristics of the counter-institution, keeping steadfastly in mind the idea of Collège International pour la Philosophie and Cerisy (*l'experience contre-institutionnelle de Cerisy*): the counter-institution is non-governmental in origin (*d'origine non gouvernementale*); it does not have war or resistance to any other institution as its mission; philosophy, although omnipresent, does not dominate over other disciplines; it is international; it does not confer honorifics or titles, academic or professional; it ensures space for expertise and experimentation; finally, we never know what awaits us in counter-institutional space, because it holds within itself pre-institutional space, space prior to norm (that which is *incalculable*, this being the word repeated several times in this text). Derrida: Le modèle philosophique d'une »contre-institution«, pp. 248, 253–255. This text was translated into English as »The Philosophical Model of a Counter-Institution«. René Loureau also gives seven principles to describe the contours of the counter-institution: it is open, has not walls whatsoever, no rules, erases old divisions but introduces new ones, does not separate the sexes introduces mingling, there is freedom to be part or to leave, and the counter-institution is ruled by possibility and free choice of values. Cf. Loureau, L'analyse institutionnelle, pp. 29–31.

808 In the 1991 interview given to François Ewald (*Magazine Littéraire*), Derrida explains very clearly why literature, in contrast to philosophy and science, is at once institution and counter-institution. »Literature is placed at a distance from the institution, at the angle which the institution makes with itself in order to distance itself from itself« (*place à l'écart de l'institution, à l'angle que l'institution fait avec elle-même pour s'écarter d'elle-même*). Derrida: Une »folie« doit veiller sur la pensée. Counter-institution is concerned above all with distance from the institution. This distanc-

There are three unconditional conditions for the existence of the counter-institution. The first is not belonging to an institution, essential non-belonging. Following Gide's indictment, Derrida insists:

I am not one of the family (*je ne suis pas de la famille*). »I am not one of the family« means: do not consider me »one of you«, »don't count me in«, I want to keep my freedom, always: this, for me, is the condition not only for being singular and other, but also for entering into relation with the singularity and alterity of others. When someone is one of the family, not only does he lose himself in the herd (*le grégaire*), but he loses the others as well; the others become simply places, family functions in the organic totality that constitutes a group, school, nation or community of subjects speaking the same language.[809]

The second condition refers to the establishment of spontaneity (*spontanéisme*):

In abstract and general terms, what remains constant in my thinking on this question is indeed a critique of institutions, but one that sets out not from the utopia of a wild and spontaneous pre- or non-institution, but rather from counter-institution. I do not think there is, or should be, the »non-institutional«. I am always torn (*Je suis toujours pris*) between the critique of institutions and the dream of an *other* institution that, in an interminable process, will come to replace institutions (*viendra remplacer des institutions*) that are oppressive, violent and inoperative. The idea of counter-institution, neither spontaneous, wild nor immediate, is the most permanent motif that, in a way, has guided me in my work (*L'idée d'une contre-institution, non pas spontanée ni sauvage ni immédiate c'est le motif le plus permanent qui m'a guide en quelque sorte*).[810]

Europe, democracy or justice (even the state!)[811] play the role of »an *other* institution that, in an interminable process, will come to replace institutions that are oppressive, violent and inoperative.« In the French manuscript, that is, in the transcript of what was said in French, there is no description of institutions (»oppressive, violent and inoperative«) that ought to be replaced or opposed by way of counter-institution; Derrida added this portion of the sentence in the English version of the interview. The counter-institution is undoubtedly an institution (as it is not anything completely opposite from the institution as such; thus, as a kind of form of institution, it certainly includes a group of people who function or work together and expect others to join them), one that is constituted by way

ing is also at once the distancing from itself, keeping it open to experimentation, to new voices, but also to expertise.

809 Derrida/Ferraris: A Taste for the Secret, p. 16. However, Derrida continues, the »second dimension (...) is that the fact of my not wanting to be one of the family is supposed by the fact of wanting to be one of the family.« »I am someone who has never left university.« Ibid., p. 43, 26.

810 Ibid. pp. 50–51; Interview, 25–26 January, 1994, French manuscript, p. 31.

811 »I have even had occasion to define the State – the State as it ought to be – as a counter-institution, necessary for opposing those institutions that represent particular interests and properties. And I'd say the same thing with regard to international law.« Ibid. This sentence also does not exist in French since it was never uttered during the interview, but added into the English text.

of criticism of institutions or institutional activity. The condition for this to be a criticism of *un état violent* is the *a priori* distance towards institutions in general (not belonging to institutions, immunity to institutions; *je ne suis pas de la famille*), and at the same time, the expectation (Derrida speaks of the dream) of a new institution on the horizon, which, slowly advancing and gently occupying the place of old institutions, of necessity amends them. One other thing – this is an interminable process.

The third condition concerns the irony of the institution or institutional irony (*ironie institutionnelle*)[812] and the ever-looming danger of the state, that is, the ever-present danger to Europe coming from states. In »Discours de réception de la Légion d'honneur«, Derrida says the following:

> Whether in writing or in thought, in teaching or in research, in my public or private life, even if I have never had anything against the institution, I have always loved the counter-institution, whether it belonged to a state or whether it was a- or counter-statist. I also believe that war is waged on institutions only in their very name, such as in rendering them homage by betraying the love, in every sense of this word, we have for them (...) It is ironic, itself an institution par excellence, that the State, assured that there is no absolute exteriority that would be capable of objecting or opposing it, ultimately recognizes the counter-institutions, at which point, whether elected, chosen or confirmed, they become order and bastion (*légion*).[813]

Declaring war on institutions or anti-institutionalism or even a radical critique of institutions has nothing to do with the counter-institution. Derrida's warning here is directly tied to two other moments: there is no sufficiently secure space outside the state where a counter-institution could be sustainable and entirely independent (and conversely, there is no space outside states where Europe can be safe; Europe does not occupy a space outside of states, but is rather within states and, above all, on the borders among them and on the borders with others), nor is there any space (*d'absolue extériorité*) from which or in which Europe could be in direct and brutal opposition towards the states it comprises or states soon to become part of it. Derrida's last argument about the state or states that incorporate and swallow the novelty of the counter-institution seems to me to be in harmony with the state Saint-Simon encountered two hundred years ago. The congress or

812 »I believe I have spent my life, especially given that it was largely academic, but luckily not all there has been to it, in debating with laws and the trickery (*ruse*) of this institutional irony.« Peeters: Derrida, p. 549.

813 »*Qu'il s'agit d'écriture ou de pensée, d'enseignement ou de recherche, de vie publique ou de vie privée, si je n'ai jamais rien eu contre l'institution, j'ai toujours aimé la contre-institution, qu'elle fût d'Etat ou précisément a- ou contre-étatique. Je crois aussi qu'on ne fait la guerre aux institutions qu'en leur nom, comme pour leur rendre hommage et en trahissant, à tous les sens de ce mot, l'amour qu'on leur porte (...) L'ironie, c'est que l'institution par excellence, l'Etat, assuré qu'il n'est pas d'absolue extériorité qui puisse lui faire objection ou opposition, l'Etat finit toujours par reconnaître les contre-institutions et c'est le moment où, élues, choisies ou confirmées, elles redeviennent ordre et légion.*« Ibid.

alliance of peace of contemporary European states was usurped by bloody wars for sovereignty. Saint-Simon's efforts, actually, consist in reawakening the idea that can survive (become real) only if we urgently find a new form of association among people, a new form of discussions about public affairs, new protocols of hospitality – a new institution that could once again, always anew interrupt violence and limits force.

References

Agamben, Giorgio: Homo sacer. Il potere sovrano e la nuda vita, Torino 1995.

Agamben, Giorgio: Mezzi senza fine. Note sulla politica, Torino 1996.

Agamben, Giorgio: Nudità. Roma 2009.

Alexy, Robert: Theory of Constitutional Rights, Oxford 2002.

Althusius, Johannes: La politica, vol. 1, Torino 2009.

Apel, Karl-Otto: Transzendentale Reflexion und Geschichte, Frankfurt am Main 2017.

Arendt, Hannah: We Refugees, in: Marc Robinson (ed.): Altogether Elsewhere. Writers on Exile, Boston / London 1994, pp. 110–119.

Armando, Alessandro / Giovanni Durbiano: Teoria del progetto architettonico. Dai disegni agli effetti, Roma 2017.

Astruc, Alexandre: Sartre, Paris 1977.

Austin, John L.: How to Do Things with Words. Oxford 1975.

Austin, John L.: Sense and Sensibilia, Oxford 1962.

Badiou, Alain: »We Need a Popular Discipline«. Contemporary Politics and the Crisis of the Negative, in: Critical Inquiry, 34(4), 2008, pp. 645–659.

Badiou, Alain: Le petit panthéon portatif, Paris 2008.

Baier, Annette: A Naturalists View of Persons, in: Proceedings and Addresses of the American Philosophical Association, 65(3), 1991, pp. 5–17.

Baier, Annette: Doing Things With Others. The Mental Commons, in: Lilli Alanen / Sarah Heinamaa, Thomas Wallgren (eds.): Commonality and Particularity in Ethics, New York 1997, pp. 15–44.

Balibar, Étienne. Des Universels. Essais et conférences, Paris 2016.

Balibar, Étienne: Violence et civilité, Paris 2010.

Barry, Norman: The Theory of the Corporation, in: The Freeman: Ideas on Liberty 53(3), 2003, pp. 22–26.

Barthes, Roland: Cy Twombly. Works on Paper, in: The Responsibility of Forms. Critical Essays on Music, Art and Representation, Berkeley 1991, pp. 157–176.

Bataille, Georges: L'expérience intérieure, in: Oevres complètes, vol. 1, Paris 1973.

Battaile, Georges: Inner Experience, Albany 1988.

Becker, Georg E.: Disziplin im Unterricht. Auf dem Weg zu einer zeitgemäßen Autorität, Basel 2009.

Becker, Howard S.: Notes on the Concept of Commitment, in: The American Journal of Sociology, 66(1), 1960, pp. 32–40.

Becker, Howard S.: Notes sur le concept d'engagement, in: Tracés. Revue de sciences humaines, 11, 2006, pp. 177–192.

Benjamin, Walter: Toward the Critique of Violence, in: Peter Fenves / Julia Ng (eds.): Toward the Critique of Violence. A Critical Edition, Stanford 2021, pp. 39–60.

Benjamin, Walter: Zur Kritik der Gewalt und andere Aufsätze, Frankfurt am Main 1965.

Benvéniste, Émile: Structures des relations de personnes dans le verbe, in: Problèmes de linguistique générale, vol. 1, Paris 1966, pp. 225–236.

Berger, Ben: Attention, Deficit, Democracy. The Paradox of Civic Engagement, Princeton 2011.

Bergson, Henri: Histoire de l'idée de temps. Cours au Collège de France 1902–1903, Paris 2016.

Bergson, Henri: L'idée de temps. Cours au Collège de France 1901–1902. Paris 2019.

Bergson, Henri: Laughter. An Essay on the Meaning of the Comic, New York 1913.

Bergson, Henri: Le rire. Essai sur la signification du comique, Paris 1900.

Berlin, Adele / Marc Yvi Brettler (eds.): The Jewish Study Bible, Oxford 1999.

Berman, Marshall: All That Is Solid Melts Into Air. The Experience of Modernity, London 1982.

Bernard, Claude: Définition de la vie, Paris 2016.

Bessis, Franck: L'institution comme réalisation du colectif, Tracés, 17(2), 2009, pp. 73–87.

Betzler, Monika: Collegial Relationships. Manuscript.

Betzler, Monika: Interpersonelle Beziehungen und gemeinsame Handlungen, in: Deutsche Zeitschrift für Philosophie, 55(3), 2007, pp. 441–456.

Betzler, Monika: Valuing the Interpersonal. Relationships and Acting Together, in: Hans Bernhard Schmid / Katinka Schulte-Ostermann / Nikos Psarros (eds.): Concepts of Sharedness. Essays on Collective Intentionality, Frankfurt 2008, pp. 253–272.

Bichat, Xavier: Recherches physiologiques sur la vie et la mort, Paris 1995.

Bion, Wilfred R.: Recherches sur les petits groups, Paris 1965.

Blackstone, William: Commentaries on the Laws of England, vol. 1, Oxford 1765.

Blanqui, Jérôme-Adolphe: Des classes ouvrieres en France pendant l'annee 1848, Paris 1849.

Bobbio, Norberto: Bobbio. Flosofi e tecnici, meglio tenerli separati, in: La Stampa, 22 May 2017.

Bodin, Jean: Demonomanie contre les sorciers, Paris 1582.

Bodin, Jean: La méthode de l'histoire, Paris 1941.

Bodin, Jean: Les lix livres de la République, vol. 1–6, Paris 1968.

Bodin, Jean: Methodus ad facilem historiarum cognitionem, in: *Œuvres philosophiques*, Paris 1951, pp. 107–269.

Bodin, Jean: On Sovereignty, Cambridge / UK 1992.

Bodin, Jean: Tableau du droit universel, in: *Œuvres philosophiques*, Paris 1951, pp. 83–97.
Boghossian, Paul: The Concept of Genocide, in: Journal of Genocide Research, 12(1–2), 2010, pp. 69–80.
Böhringer, Hannes: Bauen, in: Ralf Konersmann (ed.): Wörterbuch der philosophischen Metaphern, Darmstadt 2011, pp. 34–46.
Bojanić, Petar: »Leben und Gewalt« or »Gewalt und Leben«. Paragraph 18 of W. Benjamin's »Toward the Critique of Violence«, in: Critical Times, 2(2), 2019, pp. 320–329.
Bojanić, Petar: Che cos'è un atto d'impegno? Husserl e Reinach sul »soggetto di livello superiore«, (noi) e gli atti (non) sociali, in: Teoria, 39(1), 2019, pp. 217–230.
Bojanić, Petar: O institucionalnom delovanju. Kako je moguće ispravno raditi, pisati, hodati, disati, živeti zajedno?, Beograd / Novi Sad 2016.
Bojanić, Petar: Pacifism. Equipment or Accessory of War?, in: Philosophia, 41(3), 2013, pp. 1037–1047.
Bojanić, Petar: Provocatio. Vocativo Ius Rivoluzione, Milano / Udine 2021.
Bojanić, Petar: Violence and Messianism. Jewish Philosophy and the Great Conflicts of the Twentieth Century. London / New York 2018.
Bojanić, Petar: What Is an Act of Engagement? Between the Social, Collegial and Institutional Protocols«, in: Tiziana Andina / Petar Bojanić (eds): Institutions in Action. The Nature and the Role of Institutions in the Real World, Berlin 2020, pp. 37–51.
Bojanić, Petar: Will the Judgment in the Hague Trial Constitute a Precedent in International Law? On the great crime (mala in se; scelus infandum) and sovereignty«, in: Sociološki pregled, 40(1), 2006, str. 93–114.
Boltanski, Luc / Axel Honneth / Robin Celikates: Sociology of Critique or Critical Theory? Luc Boltanski and Axel Honneth in Conversation with Robin Celikates, in: Simon Susen / Bryan S. Turner (eds.): The Spirit of Luc Boltanski. Essays on the »Pragmatic Sociology of Critique«, London / New York 2014, pp. 562–589.
Bostrom, Nick: Superintelligence. Paths, Dangers, Intelligence, Oxford 2014.
Boudon, Philippe: Sur l'espace architecturale. Essai d'épistémologie de l'architecture, Marseille 2003.
Bourdieu, Pierre: La misere du monde, Paris 1993.
Boutinet, Jean-Pierre: Projet, in: Jacqueline Barus-Michel / Eugène Enriquez / André Lévy (eds.): Vocabulaire de psychosociologie, Ramonville-Saint-Agne 2002, pp. 222–230.
Braeckman, Antoon: Niklas Luhmann's systems theoretical redescription of the inclusion / exclusion debate, in: Philosophy & Social Criticism, 32(1), 2006, pp. 65–88.
Brandt, Richard M.: The Concepts of Obligation and Duty, in: Mind 73(91), 1964, pp. 374–393.

Bréhier, Émile: L'Acte symbolique, in: Revue philosophique de la France et de l'étranger, 84, 1917, pp. 345–361.
Brennan, Geoffrey et al: Explaining Norms, Oxford 2013.
Briet, Suzanne: Qu'est-ce que la documentation?, Paris 1951.
Broderick, Albert (ed.): The French Institutionalists. Maurice Hauriou, Georges Renard, Joseph T. Delos, Cambridge/MA 1970.
Brunner, Heinrich: Carta und Notia, in: Commentationes philologae in honorem Theodori Mommseni, Berlin 1877, pp. 570–589.
Cacciari, Massimo: Progetto, in: Laboratorio politico, 2, 1981, pp. 81–119.
Cairns, Dorion: Guide for Translating Husserl, The Hague 1973.
Cameron, John R.: »Ought« and Institutional Obligation, in: Philosophy 46(178), 1971, pp. 309–323.
Cameron, John R.: The Nature of Institutional Obligation, in: Philosophical Quarterly, 22(89), 1972, pp. 318–332.
Canguilhem, Georges: Études d'histoire et de philosophie des sciences, Paris 2002.
Canguilhem, Georges: La nouvelle connaissance de la vie, in: Etudes d'histoire et de philosophie des sciences, Paris 1979, pp. 335–364.
Canguilhem, Georges: Vie, in: Claude Grégory (ed.): Encyclopædia Universalis, vol. 16, Paris 1977, pp. 764–769.
Cantor, Georg: La filosofia dell'infinito. Scritti scelti (1884–1888), Milano/Udine 2021.
Card, Claudia: Confronting Evils. Terrorism, Torture, Genocide, Cambridge/UK 2010.
Card, Claudia: The Atrocity Paradigm. A Theory of Evil, New York 2002.
Carnot, Lazare: Réflexions sur la métaphysique du calcul infinitésimal, Paris 1881.
Caron, Pier Giovanni: Il concetto di »institutio« nel diritto della chiesa, in: Il diritto ecclesiastico, 70, 1959, pp. 330–335.
Cassese, Antonio: International Law, Oxford 2005.
Cassirer, Ernst: The Myth of the State, London 1946.
Castoriadis, Cornelius: Figures du pensable, Paris 1999.
Cera, Agostino: Introduzione, in: Karl Löwith: L'individuo nel ruolo del co-uomo, Napoli 2007, pp. 5–60.
Certeau, Michel de: L'institution de la pourriture, in: Action poétique, 72, 1977, pp. 177–188.
Chaniotis, Angelos: »Victory« Verdict: The Violent Occupation of Territory in Hellenistic Interstate Relations, in: Jean-Marie Bertrand (ed.): La violence dans les mondes grec et romain, Paris 2005, pp. 455–464.
Chenu, Marie-Dominique: Notes de lexicographie philosophique médiévale »Disciplina«, in: Revue des sciences philosophiques et théologiques, 25, 1936, pp. 686–692.
Chevalier, Jacques: Entretiens avec Bergson, Paris 1959.

Chomsky, Noam / Michel Foucault: De la nature humaine. Justice contre humaine. Justice contre pouvoir, Paris 2006.
Churchill, Winston: Blood, Toil, Tears and Sweat: The Speeches of Winston Churchill, Boston 1989.
Commons, John R.: Institutional Economics. Its Place in Political Economy, New York 1934.
Conte, Amedeo Giovanni et al. (eds.): Filosofia del diritto, Milano 2013.
Cooper, John: Raphael Lemkin and the Struggle for the Genocide Convention, New York 2008.
Courtine, Jean-François: Réalité, in Barbara Cassin (ed.): Vocabulaire européen des philosophies. Le dictionnaire des intraduisibles, Paris 2004, pp. 1060–1068.
Crawford, James / Jeremy Watkins: International Responsibility, in: Sammantha Besson / John Tasioulas (eds): The Philosophy of International Law, Oxford 2010, pp. 283–298.
Croce, Mariano / Andrea Salvatore: Come si fa ordine. Tre tipi di istituzionalismo giuridico, in: Ragion pratica, 52, 2019, pp. 311–332.
Dahl, Robert A.: Democracy and Its Critics, New Haven 1989.
De Staël, Germaine: De la littérature considérée dans ses rapports avec les institutions sociales, Paris 1800.
Dejnožka, Jan: Corporate Entity. Manuscript, 2007.
Deleuze, Gilles (ed.): Instincts et institutions, Paris 1953.
Deleuze, Gilles: Capitalisme et schizophrénie. L'Anti-Œdipe, Paris 1972.
Deleuze, Gilles: Capitalisme et schizophrénie. Mille plateaux, Paris 1980.
Deleuze, Gilles: Empiricism and Subjectivity. An Essay on Hume's Theory of Human Nature, New York 1991.
Deleuze, Gilles: Empirisme et subjectivité. Essai sur la nature humaine selon Hume, Paris 1953.
Deleuze, Gilles. Foucault, Paris 1986.
Deleuze, Gilles: Hume, in: L'île déserte, Paris 2002, pp. 226–237.
Deleuze, Gilles: Introduction, in: Gilles Deleuze (éd.): Instincts et institutions, Paris 1953, pp. viii–xi.
Deleuze, Gilles: Pensée nomade, in: L'île déserte, Paris 2002, pp. 351–364.
Deleuze, Gilles: Présentation de Sacher-Masoch. Le froid et le cruel, Paris 1967.
Deleuze, Gilles: Trois problèmes de groupe, in: L'île déserte, Paris 2002, pp. 270–284.
Depraz, Natalie: Empathie et compassion:, in: Alain Berthoz / Gérard Jorland (eds.): L'Empathie, Paris 2004, pp. 183–197.
Depraz, Natalie: Lipps et Husserl: l'Einfühlung, in: Revue de métaphysique et de morale, 4, 2017, pp. 441–459.
Depraz, Natalie: Une phénomenologie du »nous«. A propos de la communauté grecque d'Istanbul, in: Alter, 17, 2008, pp. 103–118.

Derrida, Jacques / Maurizio Ferraris: A Taste for the Secret, Cambridge/UK Malden 2001.

Derrida, Jacques: De la grammatologie, Paris 1967.

Derrida, Jacques: Du droit à la philosophie, Paris 1990.

Derrida, Jacques: Edmund Husserl's Origin of Geometry: An Introduction, New York 1989.

Derrida, Jacques: Habiter, in: Epreuves d'écriture, Paris 1985, p. 81.

Derrida, Jacques: Introduction, in: Edmund Husserl: L'origine de la géométrie, Paris 1962, pp. 3–173.

Derrida, Jacques: Jacques Derrida. Invitation to a Discussion, in: Columbia Documents of Architecture and Theory, vol. 1, New York 1992, pp. 7–27

Derrida, Jacques: L'école a été un enfer pour moi …. Conversation avec J. Derrida. B. Defrance, in: Cahiers pédagogiques, 270/272, 1989.

Derrida, Jacques: La langue et le discours de la méthode, in: Recherches sur la philosophie et le langage. Cahier du groupe de recherches sur la philosophie et le langage, 3, Grenoble 1983, pp. 35–51.

Derrida, Jacques: Le génome et son double, Paris 1996.

Derrida, Jacques: Le modèle philosophique d'une »contre-institution«, in: François Chaubet / Edith Heurgon / Claire Paulhan (eds.): S.I.E.C.L.E. Colloque de Cerisy, Saint-Germain-la-Blanche-Herbe 2005, pp. 245–260.

Derrida, Jacques: Le problème de la genèse dans la philosophie de Husserl, Paris 1999.

Derrida, Jacques: Of the Humanities and the Discipline of Philosophy, in: Surfaces, 4, 1994, pp. 5–40.

Derrida, Jacques: On Cosmopolitanism and Forgiveness, London 2001.

Derrida, Jacques: Otobiographies, Paris 1984.

Derrida, Jacques: Résistances de la psychanalyse, Paris 1996.

Derrida, Jacques: Spectre de Marx, Paris 1993.

Derrida, Jacques: Une »folie« doit veiller sur la pensée. Un entretien avec François Ewald, in: Magazine Littéraire, 286, 1991, pp. 18–30.

Desqueyrat, André: L'nstitution, le droit objectif et la technique positive. Essai historique et doctrinal, Paris 1933.

Dewey, John: The Historic Background of Corporate Legal Personality, in: The Yale Law Journal, 35(6), pp. 655–673.

Dewey, John: The School and Society, New York 1915.

Di Lucia, Paolo: Normatività. Diritto, linguaggio, azione, Torino 2003.

Diderot, Denis / Jean Le Rond d'Alembert (eds.): Encyclopédie, ou dictionnaire raisonné des sciences, des arts et des métiers, vol. 13, Neufchastel 1765.

Diderot, Denis / Jean Le Rond d'Alembert (eds.): Encyclopédie, ou dictionnaire raisonné des sciences, des arts et des métiers, vol. 4, Paris 1754.

Достоевский, Федор: Малое собрание сочинений, Москва 2014.

Douglas, Mary: Institutions: Problems of Theory, in: Perri 6 / Gerald Mars (eds.): The Institutional Dynamics of Culture. The New Durkheimians, vol. 1, London 2008, pp. 36–52.
Douglas, Mary: Istituzioni: problem teoretici, in: Enciclopedia delle Scienze Sociali, vol. 5, Roma 1999.
Dovi, Suzanne: In Praise of Exclusion, in: The Journal of Politics, 71(3), 2009, pp. 1172–1186.
Duff, Patrick W.: Personality in Roman Private Law, Cambridge 1938.
Dummett, Michael: On Immigration and Refugees, London 2011.
Dürig, Walter: Disciplina. Eine Studie zum bedeutungsumfang des Wortes in der Sprache der Liturgie und der Väter, Sacris erudiri, 4, 1952, pp. 245–279.
Durkheim, Émile: L'éducation morale, Paris 1925.
Durkheim, Émile: Le socialisme. Sa définition, ses débuts, la doctrine saint-simonienne, Paris 1971.
Durkheim, Émile: Le suicide, Paris 1897.
Dworkin, Ronald: Liberal Community, in: California Law Review, 1989, 77(3), pp. 479–504.
Eisenman, Peter: Architecture and the Problem of the Rhetorical Figure, in: Eisenman Inside Out, 1963–1988, New Haven 2004, pp. 200–207.
Eisenman, Peter: Misreading Peter Eisenman, in: Eisenman Inside Out, 1963–1988, New Haven 2004, pp. 208–225.
Eisenman, Peter: The Last Grand Tourist. Travels with Colin Rowe, in: Perspecta, 41, 2008, pp. 130–139.
Elias, Norbert: Die Gesellschaft der Individuums, Frankfurt am Main 1939.
Ellmers, Sven / Steffen Herrmann: Korporation und Sittlichkeit, Paderborn 2017.
Elon, Menachem (ed.): The Principles of Jewish Law, Jerusalem 1975.
Engel, Johann Jakob: Idee zu einer Mimik, Berlin 1785.
Engels, Friedrich: Anti-Dühring, in: Karl Marx / Friedrich Engels: Collected Works, vol. 25, New York 1987, pp. 5–309.
Engels, Friedrich: Briefe aus dem Wuppertal, in: Schriften der Frühzeit, Berlin / Heidelberg 1920, pp. 20–24.
Engels, Friedrich: Dialectics of Nature, in: Karl Marx / Friedrich Engels: Collected Works, vol. 25, New York 1987, pp. 313–587.
Engels, Friedrich: Dialektik der Natur, in: Karl Marx / Friedrich Engels, Werke, vol. 20, Berlin 1962, pp. 307–570.
Engels, Friedrich: From the Preparatory Materials, in: Karl Marx / Friedrich Engels: Collected Works, vol. 25, New York 1987, pp. 591–619.
Engels, Friedrich: Herrn Eugen Dührings Umwälzung der Wissenschaft (Anti-Dühring), in: Karl Marx / Friedrich Engels, Werke, vol. 20, Berlin 1962, pp. 5–303.
Engels, Friedrich: Materialien zum »Anti-Dühring«, in: Karl Marx / Friedrich Engels, Werke, vol. 20, Berlin 1962, pp. 573–596.

Engels, Friedrich: Zur Wohnungsfrage, in: Der Volksstaat, Juni–Februar 1872.
Enjalbert, Cédric: Entretien avec Tadao Ando, in: Philosophie magazine, 114, 2017, pp. 39–43.
Erskine, Toni: Krieg und korporative Verantwortung. Das Problem der Bestrafung »delinquenter« Staaten, in: Doris Gerber / Véronique Zanetti (eds.): Kollektive Verantwortung und internationale Beziehungen, Frankfurt am Main 2010, pp. 239–271.
Esposito, Roberto: Pensiero istituente. Tre paradigm di ontologia politica, Torino 2020.
Euler, Leonhard: Réflexions sur l'espace et le temps, in: Mémoires de l'académie des sciences de Berlin, 4, 1750, pp. 324–333.
Fabre-Magnan, Muriel: De l'obligation en droit, in: Conférence, 19, 2004, pp. 23–56.
Farías, Victor (ed.): Lógica. Lecciones de M. Heidegger (semestre verano 1934) en el legado de Helene Weiss, Barcelona / Madrid 1991.
Fauconnet Paul / Marcel Mauss: La sociologie, objet et méthode, in: Grande Encyclopédie, vol. 30, Paris 1901, pp. 165–176.
Ferraris, Maurizio: Documentalità. Perché è necessario lasciar tracce, Roma / Bari 2009.
Ferraris, Maurizio: Documentality. Why It Is Necessary to Leave Traces, New York 2013.
Филарет: Сочинения Филарета, митрополита Московского, Москва 1873.
Fischer, Peter: Philosophie der Technik, München 2004.
Fitzsimmons, Michael P.: From Artisan to Worker. Guilds, the French State, and the Organization of Labor, 1776–1821, Cambridge 2010.
Flusser, Vilém: Gesture, London / Minneapolis 1999.
Foucault, Michel: Homère, les récits, l'éducation, les discours, in: *Nouvelle revue française*, 616, 2016, pp. 103–150.
Foucault, Michel: L'ordre du discours, Paris 1971.
Foucault, Michel: La société punitive. Cours au Collège de France, 1972–1973, Paris 2013.
Foucault, Michel: Le jeu de Michel Foucault, in: Dits et écrits, vol. 3, Paris 1994, pp. 298–329.
Foucault, Michel: Le Pouvoir psychiatrique. Cours au Collège de France (1973–1974), Paris 2003.
Foucault, Michel: Le sujet et le pouvoir, in: Dits et écrits, vol. 2, Paris 2001, pp. 1041–1062.
Foucault, Michel: Qu'appelle-t-on punir?, in: Dits et écrits, vol. 2, Paris 2001, pp. 1455–1465.
Foucault, Michel: Sécurité, territoire, population. Cours au Collège de France, 1977–1978, Paris 2004.

Франк, Семён Людвигович: Духовные основы общества. Введение в социальную философию, Paris 1930.

Franken, Dirk / Attila Karakus / Jan G. Michel (eds.): John R. Searle. Thinking About the Real World, Frankfurt am Main 2010.

French, Peter A.: The Corporation as a Moral Person, in: American Philosophical Quarterly, 16(3), 1979, 207–215.

Freund, Julien: L'aventure du politique. Entretiens avec Charles Blanchet, Paris 1991.

Friedman, Milton: The Social Responsibility of Business is to Increase its Profits, in: The New York Times Magazine, 13 September 1970.

Gaffiot, Félix: Dictionnaire illustré latin-français, Paris 1934.

Gehlen, Arnold: Moral und Hypermoral. Eine pluralistische Ethik, Frankfurt am Main 1969.

Gehring, Petra: Theorien des Todes zur Einführung, Hamburg 2010.

Gephart, Werner: Bilder der Moderne. Studien zu einer Soziologie des Kunst- und Kulturinhalte, Opladen 1998.

Gephart, Werner: Gesellschaftstheorie und Recht. Das Recht im soziologischen Diskurs der Moderne, Frankfurt am Main 1993.

Gephart, Werner: Images de la Grande Guerre: la »culture de guerre«, in: Voyages sociologiques France-Allemagne, Paris 2015, pp. 161–183.

Gephart, Werner: Some Colours of the Law. Exhibition by Professor Werner Gephart with the assistance of Nazgol Majlessi October 2016 – July 2017 King's College, London / The Dickson Poon School of Law Somerset House East Wing.

Gierke, Otto von: Das Wesen der menschlichen Verbände, Leipzig 1902.

Gierke, Otto von: Deutsches Privatrecht, vol. 1, Leipzig 1895.

Gierke, Otto von: Johannes Althusius und die Entwicklung der naturrehtlichen Staatstheorien, Breslau 1880.

Gilbert, Magaret: Social Groups. A Simmelian View, in: On Social Facts, Princeton 1992, pp. 146–236.

Gilbert, Margaret: A Theory of Political Obligation, Oxford 2006.

Gilbert, Margaret: Commitment, in: Hugh LaFollette (ed.): The International Encyclopedia of Ethics, London 2013, pp. 899–905.

Gilbert, Margaret: Culture as Collective Construction, in: Gert Albert / Steffen Sigmund (eds): Soziologische Theorie kontrovers, Wiesbaden 2010, pp. 383–393.

Gilbert, Margaret: Group Wrongs and Guilt Feelings, in: The Journal of Ethics, 1(1), 1997: pp. 65–84.

Gilbert, Margaret: Joint Commitment. How We Make the Social World, Oxford 2014.

Gilbert, Margaret: Marcher ensemble. Essais sur les fondements des phénomènes collectifs, Paris 2003.

Gilbert, Margaret: Rights and Demands: A Foundation Inquiry, Oxford 2018.
Gilbert, Margaret: Rights without Laws, Milan conference, 6 September 2011, draft.
Gilbert, Margaret: Wer ist zu verurteilen? Kollektive moralische Verantwortung und ihre Auswirkung auf Gruppenmitglieder, in: Doris Gerber / Véronique Zanetti (eds.): Kollektive Verantwortung und internationale Beziehungen, Frankfurt am Main 2010, pp. 31–66.
Gilbert, Margaret: Who's to Blame? Collective Moral Responsibility and its Implications for Group Members«, in: Midwest Studies in Philosophy, 30(1), 2006, pp. 94–114.
Gold, Natalie / Robert Sugden: Collective Intentions and Team Agency, in: The Journal of Philosophy, 104(3), 2007, pp. 109–137.
Gombrich, Ernst: Abby Warburg. Eine intellektuelle Biographie, Hamburg 2006.
Grafstein, Robert: Institutional Realism, New Haven / London 1992.
Gramsci, Antonio: La città futura, Torino 1982.
Gröbner, Valentin: Der Schein der Person. Steckbrief, Ausweis und Kontrolle im Mittelalter, München 2004.
Grotius, Hugo: De Jure Belli ac Pacis, London 1925.
Grün, Clemens: Gestus, gesta, gesticulatio. Gesten und ihre Klassifizierung anhand von Hugo von St. Victors De institutiona novitarium, Seminararbeit, 2001, pp. 1–22.
Guala, Francesco: The Normativity of Institutions, in: Phenomenology and Mind, 9, 2015, pp. 118–128.
Guala, Francesco: Understanding Institutions, Princeton 2016.
Habermas, Jürgen: Toward a Rational Society. Student Protest, Science, and Politics, Boston 1987.
Habermas, Jürgen: Theorie des kommunikativen Handelns, Frankfurt 1981.
Hancké, Bob (ed.): Debating Varieties of Capitalism, Oxford 2009.
Hark, Michel Ter: Beyond the Inner and the Outer. Wittgenstein's Philosophy of Psychology, New York 1990.
Harris, John: Violence and Responsibility, London 1980.
Hart, James G.: I, We and God: Ingredients of Husserl's Theory of Community, in: Samuel Ijsseling (ed.): Husserl-Ausgabe und Husserl-Forschung, Dodrecht 1990, pp. 125–149.
Hauriou, Maurice: La théorie de l'institution et de la fondation. Essai de vitalisme social, in: Aux sources du droit, Caen 1986, pp. 89–128.
Hecht, Werner (ed.): Brechts Theorie des Theaters, Frankfurt am Main 1986.
Heclo, Hugh: On Thinking Institutionally, Boulder / London 2008.
Hegel, Georg Wilhelm Friedrich: Die Philosophie des Rechts. Die Mitschriften Wannenmann (Heidelberg 1817/18) und Homeyer (Berlin 1818/19), Stuttgart 1983.
Hegel, Georg Wilhelm Friedrich: Elements of the Philosophy of Right, Cambridge / UK 1991.

Hegel, Georg Wilhelm Friedrich: Jenenser Realphilosophie. Die Vorlesungen von 1805/06, vol. 2, Leipzig 1931.
Hegel, Georg Wilhelm Friedrich: Phänomenologie des Geistes, in: Werke, vol. 3, Frankfurt am Main 1976.
Hegel, Georg Wilhelm Friedrich: Philosophie des Rechts, nach der Vorlesungsnachschrift von H. G. Hotho 1822/23, in: Vorlesungen über Rechtsphilosophie (1818–1831), vol. 2, Stuttgart 1974.
Hegel, Georg Wilhelm Friedrich: Philosophie des Rechts, nach der Vorlesungsnachschrift K. G. v. Griesheims 1824/25, in: Vorlesungen über Rechtsphilosophie (1818–1831), vol. 4, Stuttgart 1974, pp. 67–752.
Hegel, Georg Wilhelm Friedrich: Philosophie des Rechts. Die Vorlesungen von 1819/1820 in einer Nachschrift, Frankfurt am Main 1983.
Hegel, Georg Wilhelm Friedrich: Philosophy of Right, New York 2005.
Hegel, Georg Wilhelm Friedrich: Principes de la philosophie du droit, Paris 1998.
Hegel, Georg Wilhelm Friedrich: Naturrecht und Staatswissenschaft, nach der Vorlesungsnachschrift von C. G. Homeyers 1818/19, in: Vorlesungen über Rechtsphilosophie (1818–1831), vol. 1, Stuttgart 1974, pp. 217–371.
Hegel, Georg Wilhelm Friedrich: Vorlesungen über die Ästhetik 1, in: Werke, vol. 13, Frankfurt am Main 1970.
Hegel, Georg Wilhelm Friedrich: Vorlesungen über die Philosophie der Religion II, in: Werke, vol. 16, Frankfurt am Main 1970.
Hegel, Georg Wilhelm Friedrich: Vorlesungen über Naturrecht und Staatswissenschaft, Hamburg 1983.
Heidegger, Martin: Bauen Wohnen Denken, in: Eduard Führ (ed.): Bauen und Wohnen. Martin Heideggers Grundlegung einer Phänomenologie der Architektur/Building and Dwelling. Martin Heidegger's Foundation of a Phenomenology of Architecture, München / Berlin 2000, pp. 31–49.
Heidegger, Martin: Die Frage nach der Technik, in: Vorträge und Aufsätze, in: Gesamtausgabe, vol. 7, Frankfurt am Main 2000, pp. 5–36.
Heidegger, Martin: Die Selbstbehauptung der deutschen Universität, in: Gesamtausgabe, vol. 16, Frankfurt am Main 2000, pp. 107–117.
Heidegger, Martin: Einleitung in die Philosophie, in: Gesamtausgabe, vol. 27, Frankfurt am Main 1996.
Heidegger, Martin: Leitgedanken zur Entstehung der Metaphysik, der neuzeitlichen Wissenschaft und der modernen Technik, in: Gesamtausgabe, vol. 76, Frankfurt am Main 2009.
Heidegger, Martin: Logic as the Question Concerning the Essence of Language, Albany/NY 2009.
Heidegger, Martin: Logik als die Frage nach dem Wesen der Sprache, in: Gesamtausgabe, vol. 38, Frankfurt am Main 1998.

Heidegger, Martin: Über Wesen und Begriff von Natur, Geschichte und Staat. Übung aus dem Wintersemester 1933/34, in: Alfred Denker / Holger Zaborowski (eds.): Heidegger und der Nazionalsozialismus. Dokumente. Heidegger-Jahrbuch, 4, Freiburg im Breisgau 2009, pp. 53–88.
Heidegger, Martin: Überlegungen XII–XV, in: Gesamtausgabe, vol. 96, Frankfurt am Main 2014.
Heidegger, Martin: Schöpferische Landschaft. Warum bleiben wir in der Provinz?, in: Aus der Erfahrung des Denkens, Gesamtausgabe, vol. 13, Frankfurt am Main 1983, pp. 9–13.
Held, Virginia: Group Responsibility for Ethnic Conflict, in: The Journal of Ethics, 6(2), 2002, pp. 157–178.
Heller, Hermann: Die Souveränität. Ein Beitrag zur Theorie des Staats- und Völkerrechts, in: Gesammelte Schriften, vol. 2, Tübingen 1992, pp. 31–202.
Herzog, Lisa: Two Ways of »Taming« the Market. Why Hegel Needs the Police and the Corporations, in: Andrew Buchwalter (ed.): Hegel and Capitalism. Albany, NY 2015, pp. 147–163.
Hessen, Robert: In Defence of the Corporation, Stanford 1979.
Hiller, Kurt: Das Recht über sich selbst, Kiel 2010.
Hindriks, Frank: Deconstructing Searle's Making the Social World, in: Philosophy of the Social Sciences, 45(3), 2015, pp. 363–369.
Hindriks, Frank: Group Agents and Social Institutions. Beyond Tuomela's Social Ontology, in: Gerhard Preyer / Georg Peter (eds.): Social Ontology and Collective Intentionality. Critical Essays on the Philosophy of Raimo Tuomela with His Responses, New York 2017, pp. 197–210.
Hindriks, Frank: Reconstructing Searle's Making the Social World, in: Philosophy of the Social Sciences, 41(1), 2011, pp. 1–17.
Hobbes, Thomas: Leviathan, Cambridge/UK 2006.
Hochhäusl, Sophie: Otto Neurath. City Planning. Proposing a Socio-Political Map for Modern Urbanism, Innsbruck 2011.
Hodgson, Geoffrey: Conceptualizing Capitalism. Institutions, Evolution, Future, Chicago 2015.
Hodgson, Geoffrey: Evolution and Institutions, Cheltenham 1999.
Hodgson, Goeffrey M.: What are Institutions?, in: Journal of Economic Issues, 40, 1, 2006, pp. 1–25.
Hofmann, Hasso: Recht und Kultur. Drei Reden, Frankfurt am Main 2009.
Holt, Edwin B. et al.: The New Realism. Coöperative Studies in Philosophy, New York 1912.
Holt, Edwin B. et al.: The Program and First Platform of Six Realist, in: The Journal of Philosophy, Psychology and Scientific Methods, 7(15), 1910, pp. 393–401.
Honneth, Axel: Das Recht der Freiheit, Frankfurt am Main 2012.

Horstmann, Rolf-Peter: Hegels Theorie der bürgerlichen Gesellschaft, in: Ludwig Siep (ed.): G.W.F. Hegel, Grundlinien der Philosophie des Rechts, Berlin 1997, pp. 193–216.
Hubert, Henri / Marcel Mauss: Introduction a l'analyse de quelques phénomènes religieux, in: Revue de l'histoire des religions, 58, 1908, pp. 163–203.
Hubig, Christoph: Die Modellierung institutionellen Handelns im ökonomischen Bereich. Zur Frage nach den Adressaten einer Wirtschafts- oder Unternehmensethik, in: Josef Wieland (ed.): Die moralische Verantwortung kollektiver Akteure, New York/Heildelberg 2008, pp. 3–21.
Hugh of Saint Victor: The Didascalicon, New York 1961.
Hugo of Saint Victor: De Institutione Novitarium, in Jacques-Paul Migne (ed.): Patrologia Latina, vol. 176, Paris 1854, col. 925–954.
Hume, David: A Treatise of Human Nature, Oxford 1960.
Hume, David: L'institution ne s'explique pas par l'instinct, in: Gilles Deleuze (ed.): Instincts et Institutions, Hachette 1953, p. 10.
Hume, David: Of the Original Contract, in: Essays Moral, Political, and Literary, Indianapolis 1987, pp. 465–487.
Hume, David: The History of England, vol. 1, Farmington Hills 2010.
Husserl, Edmund: Analysen zur Passiven Synthesis, Den Haag 1966.
Husserl, Edmund: Cartesian Meditations, The Hague 1969.
Husserl, Edmund: Die Krisis der europäischen Wissenschaften und die transzendentale Phänomenologie, vol. 29, Haag 1992.
Husserl, Edmund: Erste Philosophie, vol. 2. Theorie der phänomenologischen Reduktion, Den Haag 1959.
Husserl, Edmund: Kosmologische Weltbesinnung. Ethisch-praktisch personale Welt und Selbstbesinnung, manuscript, 1934.
Husserl, Edmund: Méditations cartésiennes. Introduction à la phénoménologie, Vrin 1992.
Husserl, Edmund: The Crisis of European Sciences and Transcendental Phenomenology, Evanston 1970.
Husserl, Edmund: Zur Phänomenologie der Intersubjektivität 1905–1920, vol. 1, Den Haag 1973.
Husserl, Edmund: Zur Phänomenologie der Intersubjektivität 1921–1928, vol. 2, Den Haag 1973.
Husserl, Edmund: Zur Phänomenologie der Intersubjektivität 1929–1935, vol. 3, Den Haag 1973.
Ihering, Rudolf von: Die active Solidarobligation, in: Gesammelte Aufsätze aus den Jahrbüchern für die Dogmatik des heutigen römischen und deutschen Privatrechts, vol. 3, Aalen 1969, pp. 409–464.
Ingarden, Roman: Einführung in die Phänomenologie Edmund Husserls. Osloer Vorlesungen 1967, Tübingen 1992.

Ingarden, Roman: Über die Verantwortung, Stuttgart 1970.
Jacobi, Friedrich Heinrich: Über Recht und Gewalt, oder philosophische Erwägung eines Aufsatzes von dem Herrn Hofrath Wieland, über das göttliche Recht der Obrigkeit (1781), in: Werke, vol. 4/2, Hamburg 2009, pp. 493–504.
Jaeggi, Rahel: Was ist eine (gute) Institution?, in: Rainer Forst / Martin Hartmann / Rahel Jaeggi / Martin Saar (eds.): Sozialphilosophie und Kritik, Frankfurt am Main 2009, pp. 528–544.
Jaspers, Karl: Die Idee der Universität, Berlin / Heidelberg 1946.
Jaspers, Karl: The Idea of University, Boston 1959.
Johnson, Michael P.: Commitment: A Conceptual Structure and Empirical Application, in: The Sociological Quarterly, 14(3), 1973, pp. 395–406.
Jorio, Andrea de: La mimica degli antichi investigata nel gestire napoletano, Napoli 1832.
Justi, Johann Heinrich Gottlob von: Grundsätze der Polizeywissenschaft, Göttingen 1756.
Kant, Immanuel: Kritik der reinen Vernunft, in: Gesammelte Schriften, vol. 4, Berlin 1911.
Kant, Immanuel: Zum ewigen Frieden. Ein philosophischer Entwurf, in: Kant's gesammelte Schriften, vol. 8, Berlin 1923, pp. 341–386.
Kant, Immanuel: Anthropologie in pragmatischer Hinsicht, in: Kant's gesammelte Schriften, vol. 7, Berlin 1917, pp. 117–333.
Kant, Immanuel: Attempt to Introduce the Concept of Negative Magnitudes into Philosophy, in: Theoretical Philosophy, 1755–1770, New York 1992, pp. 203–241.
Kant, Immanuel: Critique of Pure Reason, Cambridge / MA 1998.
Kant, Immanuel: Die Metaphysik der Sitten, in: Kant's gesammelte Schriften, vol. 6, Berlin 1907, pp. 203–493.
Kant, Immanuel: Essai pour introduire en philosophie le concept de grandeur négative, Paris 1997.
Kant, Immanuel: Reflexionen zur Moralphilosophie, Reflexionen zur Rechtsphilosophie, Reflexionen zur Religionsphilosophie, in: Kant's gesammelte Schriften, vol. 19, Berlin / Leipzig 1934, pp. 92–654.
Kant, Immanuel: Tentativo per introdurre nella filosofia il concetto delle quantite negative, in: Scritti precritici, Bari 1982, pp. 249–290.
Kant, Immanuel: The Metaphysics of Morals, Cambridge / MA 1996.
Kant, Immanuel: Über Pädagogik, Königsberg 1803.
Kant, Immanuel: Versuch den Begriff der negativen Größen in die Weltweisheit einzuführen, in: Kant's gesammelte Schriften, vol 2, Berlin 1905, pp. 165–204.
Kant, Immanuel: Vorlesungen über Moralphilosophie, in: Kant's gesammelte Schriften, vol. 17, Berlin 1979.
Kästner, Abraham Gotthelf: Anfangsgründe der Arithmetik, Göttingen 1800.

Katzenbach, Jon R. / Douglas Smith: The Discipline of Teams, in: Harvard Business Review, 3, 1993, pp. 111–120.
Kaufmann, Erich: Kaufmann, Das Wesen des Völkerrechts und die clausula rebus sic stantibus, Tübingen 1911.
Kelsen, Hans: Das Problem der Souveränität, Darmstadt 1981.
Kelsen, Hans: Les rapports de système entre le droit interne et le droit international public, in: Recueil des cours. Académie de droit international, 14, 1926, pp. 231–331.
Kemp, Peter: Théorie de l'engagement, vol. 1, Pathétique de l'engagement, Paris 1973.
Kendon, Adam: Gesture, in: Annual Review of Anthropology, 26, 1997, pp. 109–128.
Kersting, Wolfgang: Polizei und Korporation in Hegels Darstellung der bürgerlichen Gesellschaft, in: Hegel-Jahrbuch, 1986, pp. 373–382.
Kervégan, Jean-François: L'Effectif et le rationnel. Hegel et l'esprit objectif, Paris 2008.
Kisiel, Theodor: In the Middle of Heidegger's Three Concepts of the Political, in: François Raffoul / David Pettigrew (ed.): Heidegger and Practical Philosophy, Albany/NY 2002, pp. 135–157.
Knemeyer, Franz-Ludwig: Polizey: in: Economy and Society, 9(2), pp. 172–196.
Knight, Jack: Institution and Social Conflict, Cambridge/MA 1992.
Know, Dilvyn: Disciplina. The Monastic and Clerical Origins of European Civility, in: John Monfasani / Ronald G. Musto (eds.): Renaissance Society and Culture. Essays in Honor of Eugene F. Rice, New York 1991, pp. 107–135.
Kojève, Alexandre: La notion de l'autorité, Paris 2004.
Kojève, Alexandre: The Notion of Authority, London 2014.
Kolmogorov, Andrey: On the Principle of Excluded Middle, in: Jean van Heijenoort (ed.): From Frege to Gödel. A Source Book in Mathematical Logic 1879–1931, Cambridge/MA 1967, pp. 414–437.
Kripke, Saul A.: Identity and Necessity, in: Milton Karl Munitz (ed.): Identity and Individuation. New York 1971, pp. 135–164.
Kristeva, Julia: Le geste, pratique ou communication?, in: Langages, 3(10), 1968, pp. 48–64.
Krueger, Joel: Extended Cognition and the Space of Social Interaction, in: Consciousness and Cognition, 20(3), 2010, pp. 643–657.
Kuper, Leo: Genocide. Its political use in the Twentieth Century, New Haven 1981.
La Torre, Massimo: Norme, istituzioni, valori, Per una teoria istituzionalistica del diritto, Bari 1999.
Laborier, Pascale: La »bonne police«. Sciences camérales et pouvoir absolutiste dans les États allemands, Politix, 48, 1999, pp. 7–35.
Lackey, Jennifer: What is Justified Group Belief?, in: Philosophical Review, 125(3), 2016, pp. 341–395.
Lacoue-Labarthe, Philippe: Habiter, in: Epreuves d'écriture, Paris 1985, p. 81.

Laurent, Éloi: L'impasse collaborative. Pour une véritable économie de la coopération, Paris 2018.

Lawson, Tony: Economics and Reality, London 1997.

Lawson, Tony: The Nature of the Firm and Peculiarities of the Corporation, in: Cambridge Journal of Economics 39(1), 2015, pp. 1–32.

Lazar, Seth: Endings and Aftermath in the Ethics of War, CSSJ Working Papers Series, 2010, pp. 2–35.

Le Blanc, Guillaume: Canguilhem et les norms, Paris 1998.

Le Goff, Jacques: Documento/Monumento, in: Enciclopedia Einaudi, vol. 5, Torino 1978, pp. 38–43.

Leibniz, Gottfried Wilhelm: Codex Juris Gentium diplomaticus, Berlin 1964.

Leibniz, Gottfried Wilhelm: De Jure Suprematus ac Legationis Principum Germaniae, in Sämtliche Schriften und Briefe, Politische Schriften, vol. 2, Berlin 1984, pp. 14–270.

Leibniz, Gottfried Wilhelm: De Suprematu Principum Germaniae, in: The Political Writings of Leibniz, Cambridge/UK 1972, pp. 111–120.

Leibniz, Gottfried Wilhelm: Die Werke von Leibniz, vol. 9, Hanover 1884.

Leibniz, Gottfried Wilhelm: Entretien de Philarete et d'Eugene (Oktober 1677), in: Sämtliche Schriften und Briefe, Politische Schriften, vol. 2, Berlin 1984, pp. 293–338.

Levinas, Emmanuel: Du sacré au saint. Cinq nouvelles lectures talmudiques, Paris 1977.

Levinas, Emmanuel: Liberté et commandement, in: Revue de métaphysique et de morale, 58(3), 1953, pp. 264–272.

Levinas, Emmanuel: Théorie de l'intuition dans la phénoménologie de Husserl, Paris 1930.

Levinas, Emmanuel: Totalité et infini, Paris 1971.

Levinas, Emmanuel: Totality and Infinity, The Hague/Boston/London 1979.

Lewin, Kurt: Group Decision and Social Change, in: Theodore M. Newcomb/Eugene L. Hartley/Henry Holt (eds): Readings in Social Psychology, New York 1947, pp. 340–344.

Lewis, Hywel David: Collective Responsibility, in: Larry May/Stacey Hoffman (eds): Collective Responsibility. Five Decades of Debate in Theoretical and Applied Ethics, Lanham 1991, pp. 17–33.

Libera, Alain de: L'Art des généralités. Théories de l'abstraction, Paris 1990.

Liberman, Anatoly: Our habitat: dwelling, https://blog.oup.com/2015/01/dwelling-word-origin-etymology/; last accessed 22.07.2018.

Lipp, Wolfgang/Hasso Hofmann/Christoph Hubig: Institution, in: Staats Lexikon, vol. 3, Freiburg 1987, pp. 99–109.

List, Christian: What is it Like to be a Group Agent?, in: Nous, 52(2), 2018, pp. 295–319.

Loddo, Olimpia Giuliana: Manifestare gli atti sociali. Canali della guridicità dopo Reinach, Milano 2020.

Lorini, Giuseppe: Dimensioni giuridiche dell'istituzionale, Padova 2000.

Losoncz, Mark: Fenomenologija prazne intencionalnosti, in: Filozofska istraživanja, 37(3), 2017, pp. 529–544.

Loureau, René: L'analyse institutionnelle, Paris 1972.

Lowe, Vaughan: International Law, Oxford 2007.

Löwenthal, Leo: Gewalt und Recht in der Staats- und Rechtsphilosophie Rousseaus und der deutschen idealistischen Philosophie, in: Philosophische Frühschriften, Frankfurt am Main 1990, pp. 169–206.

Löwith, Karl: Das Individuum in der Rolle des Mitmenschen, München 1928.

Luban, David: Fairness to Rightness: Jurisdiction, Legality and the Legitimacy of International Criminal Law, in: Samantha Besson / John Tasioulas (ed.): The Philosophy of International Law, New York 2010, pp. 569–588.

Ludwig, Kirk: From Individual to Plural Agency: Collective Action, London / New York 2016.

Lyotard, Jean-François: Gesture and Commentary, in: Iyyun: The Jerusalem Philosophical Quarterly, 42, 1993, pp. 37–48.

Mabbott, John David / Gilbert Ryle / Henry Habberley Price: Symposium. Negation, in: Proceedings of the Aristotelian Society, Supplementary Volumes, vol. 9, Knowledge, Experience and Realism, 1929, pp. 67–111.

MacCormick, Neil: Norms, Institutions, and Institutional Facts, in: Law and Philosophy, 17(3), 1998, pp. 301–345.

Machiavelli, Niccolò: Il Principe, Roma 2013.

Malinowski, Bronislaw: Freedom and Civilization, London 1947.

Mally, Ernst: Grundgesetze des Sollens. Elemente der Logik des Willens, Graz 1926.

Marion, Jean-Luc: L'événement, c'est l'impossible qui se réalise, in: Philosophie, 108, 2007, pp. 66–70.

Marrou, Henri-Irénée: Doctrina et disciplina dans la langue des Pères de l'Eglise, in: Bulletin Du Cange, 10, 1934, pp. 5–25.

Marx, Karl: Capital, vol. 1, in: Karl Marx / Friedrich Engels: Collected Works, vol. 35, New York 1994.

Marx, Karl: Das Kapital, vol. 1, in: Karl Marx / Friedrich Engels, Werke, vol. 23, Berlin 1962.

Marx, Karl: Grundrisse der Kritik der politischen Ökonomie, in: Karl Marx / Friedrich Engels, Werke, vol. 42, Berlin 1983.

Marx, Karl: Outlines of the Critique of Political Economy, in: Karl Marx / Friedrich Engels, Colleccted Works, vol. 29, New York 1987.

Mauch, Otto: Der lateinische Begriff Disciplina. Eine Wortuntersuchung, Freiburg 1941.

Mauss, Mauss et al.: Discussion a L'Institut français de sociologie, Série D. Sociologie économique, 1, 1934, pp. 59–86.
Mauss, Marcel / Paul Fauconnet: Sociologie, in: Marcellin Berthelot (ed.): La Grande Encyclopédie, vol. 30, Paris 1901, pp. 167–175.
Mauss, Marcel: Les techniques du corps, in: Journal de psychologie, 32(3/4), 1935, pp. 271–293.
Mauss, Marcel: L'œuvre de Mauss par lui-même, in: Revue française de sociologie, 20, 1979, pp. 209–220.
May, Larry: Genocide. A Normative Account, Cambridge / UK 2010.
Mayer, Colin: Firm Commitment. Why the Corporation Is Failing Us and How to Restore Trust in It, Oxford 2013.
Mayer, Max Ernst: Rechtsnormen und Kulturnormen, Breslau 1903.
McKenna, Michael: Collective Responsibility and the Agent Meaning Theory, in: Midwest Studies in Philosophy, 30(1), 2006, pp. 16–34.
Mead, George Herbert: The Philosophy of the Present, London 1932.
Merleau-Ponty, Maurice: L'institution. La passivité. Notes de cours au Collège de France (1954–1955), Paris 2003.
Merleau-Ponty, Maurice: La prose du monde, Paris 1966.
Mertens, Stefan: Die juridische Vermittlung des Sozialen, Würzburg 2008.
Michaud-Quantin, Pierre: Universitas. Expressions du mouvement communautaire dans le Moyen-age latin, Paris 1970.
Milner, Jean-Claude: L'universel difficile. Entretien réalisé par Élie During et Anoush Ganjipour, in: Critique, 833, 2016, pp. 823–834.
Misch, Georg: Lebensphilosophie und Phänomenologie, Darmstadt 1975.
Moini, Giulio: Interpretare l'azione pubblica, Roma 2013.
Mollendorf, Darrel: Jus ex Bello, in: The Journal of Political Philosophy, 16(2), 2008, pp. 123–136.
Montaigne, Michel de: Essais, vol. 1, Paris 2004.
Moos, Peter voon: »Öffentlich« und »privat« im Mittelalter. Zu einem Problem historischer Begriffsbildung, Heidelberg 2004.
Morel, Valentin: Disciplina. Le mot et l'idée représentée par lui dans les œuvres de Tertullien, in: Revue d'histoire ecclésiastique 40, 1944/1945, pp. 5–46.
Müller, Friedrich: Korporation und Assoziation. Eine Problemgeschichte der Vereinigungsfreiheit im deutschen Vormärz, Berlin 1965.
Napoli, Paolo: Il »deposito«. Genealogia di un archetipo amministrativo, in: Dario Gentili / Mauro Ponzi / Elettra Stimilli (eds.): Il culto del capitale. Walter Benjamin: capitalismo e religione Macerata 2016, pp. 107–124.
Napoli, Paolo: Naissance de la police moderne, Paris 2003.
Narveson, Jan: Collective Responsibility, in: The Journal of Ethics, 6(2), 2002, pp. 179–198.

Neusner, Jacob: The Components of the Rabbinic Documents. From the Whole to the Parts, vol. X, Leviticus Rabbah, Part II, Atlanta 1997.

Nietzsche, Friedrich: Zur Genealogie der Moral. Eine Streitschrift, Frankfurt am Main 1991.

Niji, Yoshihiro: Hegels Lehre von der Korporation, in: Hegel-Jahrbuch, 2014, pp. 288–295.

Nussbaum, Martha: Anger and Forgiveness. Ressentiment, Generosity, Justice, New York 2016.

Nussbaum, Martha: Compassion: The Basic Social Emotion, in: Social Philosophy and Policy Foundation, 13(1), 1996, pp. 27–58.

Nussbaum, Martha: How to Write about Poverty?, in: The Times Literary Supplement«, October 10, 2012.

Nussbaum, Martha: The Capabilities of People with Cognitive Disabilities, in: Metaphilosophy, 40(3–4), 2009, pp. 331–351.

Nussbaum, Martha: Upheavals of Thought. The Intelligence of Emotions, New York / Cambridge MA 2001.

O'Connor Drury, Maurice: Contribution to a BBC Symposium, in: The Selected Writings of Maurice O'Connor Drury, London 2017, pp. 89–92.

Olivecrona, Karl: Corporations as universitates, in: Three Essays in Roman Law, Copenhagen, 1949, pp. 5–42.

Orend, Brian: The Morality of War, Peterborough 2006.

Orestano, Riccardo: »Institution«. Barbeyrac e l'anagrafe di un signifato, in: Quaderni Fiorentini, 1(11/12), 1982, pp. 169–178.

Ortega y Gasset, José: España invertebrada, in: Obras completas, vol. 3, Madrid 2012, pp. 421–511.

Ortega y Gasset, José: La interpretación bélica de la historia, in: Obras completas, vol. 2, Madrid 2010, pp. 633–643.

Ortega y Gasset, José: La rebelión de las masas. Epílogo para ingleses, in: Obras completas, vol. 4, Madrid 2017, pp. 499–529.

Otaka, Tomoo: Grundlegung der Lehre vom sozialen Verband, Wien 1932.

Otlet, Paul: Traité de documentation. Le livre sur le livre, théorie et pratique, Liège 1989.

Parsons, Talcott: On Institutions and Social Evolution, Chicago / London 1982.

Peeters, Benoît: Derrida, Paris 2010.

Penrose, Roger: The Road to Reality: A Complete Guide to the Laws of the Universe, New York 2004.

Peters, Richard M. / Douglas R. Emery: The Role of Negative Numbers in the Development of Double Entry Bookkeeping, in: Journal of Accounting Research, 16(2), 1978, pp. 424–426.

Pettit, Philip: Groups with Minds of Their Own, in: Alvin I. Goldman / Den-

nis Whitcomb (eds.): Social Epistemology. Essential Readings, New York 2010, pp. 242–268.
Pettit, Philip: Groups with Minds of Their Own, in: Frederick F. Schmitt (ed.): Socializing Metaphysics, New York 1996, pp. 167–193.
Pettit, Philip: Two Fallacies about Corporations, in: Subramanian Rangan (ed.): Performance and Progress. Essays on Capitalism, Business, and Society, Oxford 2015, pp. 379–395.
Picot, Georges: Un devoir sociale et les logements d'ouvriers, Paris 1885.
Pisani, Daniele: L'architettura è un gesto. Ludwig Wittgenstein architetto, Macerata 2011.
Popper, Karl: Replies to my critics, in: Paul Arthur Schilpp (ed.): The Philosophy of Karl Popper, vol. 3, La Salle 1974, pp. 949–1180.
Prien, Bernd / Jan Skudlarek / Sebastian Stolte: The Role of Declarations in the Constructions of Social Reality«, in: Dirk Franken / Attila Karakus / Jan G. Michel (eds.): John R. Searle: Thinking About the Real World, Frankfurt am Main 2010, pp. 163–172.
Prost, Robert: Conception architecturale. Une investigation méthodologique, Paris 1992.
Prost, Robert: Pratiques de projet en architecture. Le tournant silencieux, Gollion 2014.
Pufendorf, Samuel von: De l'origine et de la variété des entités morales, in: Raisons politiques, 66, 2017, pp. 187–209.
Putnam, Hilary: The Epistemology of Unjust War, in: Philosophy in an Age of Science. Physics, Mathematics and Skepticism, ed. Mario De Caro / David Macarthur, Cambridge/MA 2012, pp. 312–326.
Putnam, Hilary: What is Mathematical Truth?, in: Mathematics, Matter and Method, Philosophical Papers, vol. 1, London / New York 1975, pp. 60–78.
Rabelais, François: Gargantua, Paris 1951.
Rabelais, François: The Complete Works, Berkeley / Los Angeles / London 1999.
Rangeon, François: Approche de l'institution dans la pensée de Hobbes, in: L'institution, Paris 1981, pp. 91–123.
Rawls, John: A Theory of Justice, London / Cambridge/MA 1971.
Rawls, John: Lectures on the History of Moral Philosophy, Cambridge/MA 2000.
Reid, Thomas: A Brief Account of Aristotle's Logic, in: Philosophical Works, Hildesheim 1967, pp. 681–714.
Reid, Thomas: Essays on the Active Powers of the Human Mind, Cambridge/MA / London 1969.
Reinach, Adolf: Die apriorischen Grundlagen des bürgerlichen Rechtes, in: Sämtliche Werke, Vol. 1, München 1989, pp. 141–278.
Reinach, Adolf: Einleitung in die Philosophie, in: Sämtliche Werke, vol. 1, München 1989, pp. 365–513.

Reinach, Adolf: I fondamenti a priori del diritto civile, Milano 1990.
Reinach, Adolf: Nichtsoziale und soziale Akte, in: Sämtliche Werke, vol. 1, München 1989, pp. 355–360.
Reinach, Adolf: The Apriori Foundations of the Civil Law, in: Aletheia, 3, 1983, pp. 1–142.
Reinach, Salomon: L'histoire des gestes, in: Revue Archéologique, 20, 1924, pp. 64–79.
Renard, Georges: La philosophie de l'institution, Paris 1939.
Renard, Georges: La théorie de l'institution. Essai d'ontologie juridique, Paris 1930.
Ricciardi, Mario: Diritto naturale e ontologia sociale. Alle origini della teoria dei fatti istituzionali, in: Rivista di estetica, 36(3), 2007, pp. 167–180.
Rickert, Heinrich: Philosophie des Lebens. Darstellung und Kritik der philosophischen Modeströmungen unserer Zeit, Tübingen 1922.
Ricœur, Paul: Husserl. An Analysis of his phenomenology, Evanston 1967.
Ricœur, Paul: Le problème de la violence, in: Foi et education, 40, 1957, pp. 7–14.
Ricœur, Paul: Le sens de l'histoire, in: Revue de Métaphysique et de Morale, 54(1), 1949, pp. 293–294.
Ricœur, Paul: The Problem of the Foundation of Moral Philosophy, in: Philosophy Today, 22(3), 1978, pp. 175–192.
Rodin, David: Ending War, in: Ethics & International Affairs, 25(3), 2011, pp. 359–367.
Rodin, David: Two Emerging Issues of Jus Post Bellum. War Termination and the Liability of Soldiers for Crimes of Aggression, in: Carsten Stahn / Jann K. Kleffner (eds.): Jus Post Bellum, Hague 2008, pp. 53–91.
Romano, Santi: L'ordinamento giuridico, Florence 1918.
Rosenzweig, Franz: Briefe und Tagebücher, in: Der Mensch und sein Werk. Gesammelte Schriften, vol. 1/1, Den Haag 1979.
Rosenzweig, Franz: Briefe und Tagebücher, in: Der Mensch und sein Werk. Gesammelte Schriften, vol. 1/2, Den Haag 1979.
Rosenzweig, Franz: Der Stern der Erlösung, vol. 1–3, Berlin 1930.
Rosenzweig, Franz: Der Stern der Erlösung, Frankfurt am Main 1921.
Rosenzweig, Franz: Hegel und Staat, München 1920.
Rosenzweig, Franz: The Star of Redemption, Madison 2005.
Rosenzweig, Franz: Zweistromland. Kleinere Schriften zu Glauben und Denken, in: Der Mensch und sein Werk. Gesammelte Schriften, vol. 3, Den Haag 1984.
Rötzer, Florian: Französische Philosophie im Gespräch, München 1987.
Rousseau, Jean-Jacques: A Discourse upon the Origin and the Foundation of the Inequality among Mankind, in: French and English Philosophers. Descartes, Rousseau, Voltaire, Hobbes, New York 1910, pp. 167–244.
Rousseau, Jean-Jacques: A M. Moultou, in: Œuvres de J. J. Rousseau, vol. 7, Paris 1817, pp. 502–504.

Rousseau, Jean-Jacques: Considérations sur le gouvernement de Pologne, Œuvres complètes, vol. 3, Paris 1964, pp. 953–1044.
Rousseau, Jean-Jacques: Discours sur l'économie politique, in: Œuvres complètes, vol. 3, Paris 1964, pp. 241–278.
Rousseau, Jean-Jacques: Discours sur l'origine et les fondements de l'inégalité parmi les hommes, in: Œuvres complètes, vol. 3, Paris 1964, pp. 109–223.
Rousseau, Jean-Jacques: Du contrat social ou essai sur la forme de la république, in: Œuvres complètes, vol. 3, Paris 1964, pp. 281–342.
Rousseau, Jean-Jacques: Du contrat social ou principes du droit politique, in: Œuvres complètes, vol. 3, Paris 1964, pp. 349–472.
Rousseau, Jean-Jacques: Emile, or on Education, in: The Collected Writings of Rousseau, vol. 18, Hanover / NH 2010.
Rousseau, Jean-Jacques: Émile ou de l'éducation, Paris 1966.
Rousseau, Jean-Jacques: Fragments politiques, in: Œuvres complètes, vol. 3, Paris 1964, pp. 473–554.
Rousseau, Jean-Jacques: Julie ou la nouvelle Héloïse, 1, in: Œuvres complètes, vol. 8, Paris 1823.
Rousseau, Jean-Jacques: Lettre à M. D'Alembert, in: Collection complète des œuvres, vol. 6, Geneve 1781, pp. 421–599.
Rousseau, Jean-Jacques: Lettres écrites de la montagne, in: Œuvres complètes, vol. 3, Paris 1964, pp. 683–897.
Rowntree, Benjamin Seebohm: Poverty. A Study of Town Life, London 1908.
Russell, Bertrand: Le réalisme analytique, in: Bulletin Société française de philosophie, (11)53, 1911, pp. 282–291.
Russell, Bertrand: The Ethics of War, in: The International Journal of Ethics, 25(2), 1915, pp. 127–142.
Ryle, Gilbert: Negative »Actions«, in: Hermathena, 115, 1973, pp. 81–93.
Saffrey, Henri-Dominique: »Cy n'entrez pas, hypocrites …« Thélème, une nouvelle académie?, in: Revue des sciences philosophiques et théologiques, 55(4), 1971, pp. 593–614.
Saint-Just, Louis Antoine de: Institutions républicaines, in: Œuvres complètes, Paris 2004, pp. 1085–1147.
Saint-Just, Louis Antoine de: Rapport sur les personnes incarcérées, in: Œuvres complètes, Paris 2004, pp. 656–671.
Saint-Simon, Claude Henri de: Catéchisme des industriels, Paris 1832.
Saint-Simon, Claude Henri de: De la réorganisation de la société européenne, in: Pascal Ory (ed.): L'Europe? L'Europe, Paris 1998, pp. 7–62.
Saint-Simon, Claude Henri de: Travail sur la gravitation universelle, in: Prosper Enfantin / Henri de Saint-Simon: Science de l'homme. Physiologie religieuse, Paris 1858, pp. 403–482.

Saint-Simon: Mémoire sur la science de l'homme, in: Prosper Enfantin / Henri de Saint-Simon: Science de l'homme. Physiologie religieuse, Paris 1858, pp. 389–400.
Sartre, Jean Paul: Existentialism is a Humanism, New York 1956.
Sartre, Jean-Paul: Being and Nothingness, Washington 1956.
Sartre, Jean-Paul: Cahiers pour une morale, Paris 1983.
Sartre, Jean-Paul: L'être et le néant, Paris 1943.
Scanlon, Thomas: Individual Morality and the Morality of Institutions, in: Philosophy and Society, 27(1), 2016, pp. 3–19.
Schabas, William: An Introduction to the International Criminal Court, Cambridge / UK 2011.
Schabas, William: Was Genocide Committed in Bosnia and Herzegovina? First Judgments of the International Criminal Tribunal for the Former Yugoslavia, in: Fordham International Law Journal, 25, 2001, pp. 23–53.
Schelsky, Helmut: Auf der Suche nach Wirklichkeit. Gesammelte Aufsätze, Düsseldorf / Köln 1965.
Schmid, Hans Bernhard: On not Doing One's Part. Dissidence and the Normativity of Collective Intention, in: Plural Action: Essays in Philosophy and Social Science, Berlin 2009, pp. 47–58.
Schmitt, Carl: Das international-rechtliche Verbrechen des Angriffskrieges und der Grundsatz »Nullum crimen, nulla poena sine lege«, Berlin 1994.
Schmitt, Carl: Die Tyrannei der Werte, Berlin 2000.
Schmitt, Carl: On the Three Types of Juristic Thought, Westport / CT / London 2004.
Schmitt, Carl: Über die drei Arten des rechtswissenschaftlichen Denkens, Berlin 2006.
Schmitt, Carl: Völkerrecht [Ein juristisches Repetitorium] 1948/50, in: Frieden oder Pazifismus? Arbeiten zum Völkerrecht und zur internationalen Politik 1924–1978, Berlin 2005, pp. 701–840.
Schmitt, Jean-Claude: »Gestus« – »Gesticulatio«. Contribution à l'étude du vocabulaire latin médiéval des gestes, in: La lexicographie du latin médiéval et ses rapports avec les recherches actuelles sur la civilisation du Moyen Âge. Colloque international du CNRS 589, Paris 1981, pp. 377–390.
Schmitt, Jean-Claude: La morale des gestes, in: Communications, 46, 1987, pp. 31–47.
Schnorr Von Carolsfeld, Ludwig: Geschichte der juristischen Person, vol. 1, Universitas, Corpus, Collegium in der classischen Altertum, Münich 1933.
Schön, Donald: The Reflective Practitioner. How Professionals Think in Action, London 1993.
Schuhmann, Karl / Barry Smith: Elements of Speech Act Theory in the Work of Thomas Reid, in: History of Philosophy Quarterly, 7(1), 1990, pp. 47–66.

Schülein, Johannes-Georg: Die Korporation als zweite Familie in Hegels Theorie der bürgerlichen Gesellschaft, in: Sven Ellmers / Steffen Herrmann (eds.): Korporation und Sittlichkeit, Paderborn 2017, pp. 101–117.

Schumacher, Patrik: Autopoiesis of Architecture, vol. 1. A New Framework for Architecture, Chichester 2011.

Schumpeter, Jospeh: The Instability of Capitalism, in: Essays. On Entrepreneurs, Innovations, Business Cycles, and the Evolution of Capitalism, New Brunswick/ London, 2008, pp. 47–73.

Schütz, Alfred: Der sinnhafte Aufbau der sozialen Welt. Eine Einleitung in die verstehende Soziologie, Wien 1932.

Schütz, Alfred: Phenomenology of the Social World, Evanston 1967.

Scolari, Massimo: The New Architecture and the Avant-Garde, in: K. Michael Hays (ed.): Architecture Theory since 1968, Cambridge/MA/London 1998, pp. 126–145.

Scruton, Roger / John Finnis: Corporate Persons, in: Proceedings of the Aristotelian Society, Supplementary Volumes, 63, 1989, pp. 239–274.

Searle, John: Consciousness and Language, Cambridge/UK 2002.

Searle, John: Human Social Reality and Language, in: Phenomenology and Mind, vol. 2, 2012, pp. 24–33.

Searle, John: Les institutions sont-elles dans la tête? Entretien avec John Searle, in: Tracés, 17(2), 2009, pp. 243–258.

Searle, John: Making the Social World: The Structure of Human Civilization, Oxford 2010.

Searle, John: Philosophy in a New Century: Selected Essays, Cambridge/UK/ New York 2008.

Searle, John: Reply to »The Role of Declarations in the Constructions of Social Reality«, in: Dirk Franken / Attila Karakus / Jan G. Michel (eds.): John R. Searle: Thinking About the Real World, Frankfurt am Main 2010, pp. 227–229.

Searle, John: Social Ontology and Political Power, in: Freedom and Neurobiology. Reflections on Free Will, Language and Political Power, New York 2007, pp. 79–109.

Searle, John: Social Ontology. Some Basic Principles, in: Anthropological Theory, 6(1) 2006, pp. 12–29.

Searle, John: Status functions and institutional facts: reply to Hindriks and Guala, in: Journal of Institutional Economics, 11(3), 2015, pp. 507–514.

Searle, John: The Construction of Social Reality, London 1995.

Searle, John: What Is an Institution?, in: Journal of Institutional Economics, 1(1), 2005, pp. 1–22.

Sen, Amartya: Poor, Relatively Speaking, in: Oxford Economic Papers, 35(2), 1983, pp. 153–169.

Shalom Ben, Wilfand Yael: Poverty, Charity and the Image of the Poor in Rabbinic Texts from the Land of Israel, Doctoral thesis, 2012.

Shaw, Beverley: Poverty: Absolute or Relative?, in: Journal of Applied Philosophy, 5(1), 1988, pp. 27–36.

Sibertin-Blanc, Guillaume: Politique et clinique. Recherche sur la philosophie pratique de Gilles Deleuze, Doctoral Thesis, 2006.

Simmel, Georg: Conflict, in: Sociology. Inquiries into the Construction of Social Forms, vol. 1, Leiden / Boston 2009, pp. 227–305.

Simmel, Georg: Der Streit, in: Soziologie. Untersuchungen über die Formen der Vergesellschaftung, Leipzig 1908, pp. 247–336.

Simmel, Georg: Soziologie des Raumes, in: Aufsätze und Abhandlungen 1901–1908, Gesamtausgabe, vol. 7, Frankfurt am Main 1995, pp. 132–183.

Simmel, George: The Sociology of Space, in: David Frisby / Mike Featherstone (eds.): Simmel on Culture. Selected Writings, London 1997, pp 137–169.

Simmel, George: Über räumliche Projektionen sozialer Formen in: Aufsätze und Abhandlungen 1901–1908, Gesamtausgabe, vol. 7, Frankfurt am Main 1995, pp. 201–220.

Simon, Herbert A.: The Sciences of the Artificial, Cambridge/MA 1969.

Smith, Adam: An Inquiry into the Nature and Causes of the Wealth of Nations, London 1776.

Smith, Barry: How to Do Things with Documents, in: Rivista di estetica, 50, 2012, pp. 179–198.

Smith, Barry: Searle and De Soto. The New Ontology of the Social World, in: Barry Smith / David M. Mark / Isaac Ehrlich (eds.): The Mystery of Capital and the Construction of Social Reality, Chicago 2008, pp. 35–51.

Snare, Frank: Consent and Conventional Acts in John Locke, in: Journal of the History of Philosophy, (13)1, 1975, pp. 27–36.

Sorokin, Pitirim: Sociological Theories of Today, New York 1966.

Spranger, Eduard: Lebensformen. Geisteswissenschaftliche Psychologie und Ethik der Persönlichkeit, Halle 1914.

Stahl, Titus: Institutional Power, Collective Acceptance and Recognition, in: Heikki Ikaheimo / Arto Laitinen (eds.): Recognition and Social Ontology, Leiden 2011, pp. 349–372.

Stahl, Titus: Soziale Gerechtigkeit und institutionelle Macht, in: XXII. Deutscher Kongress für Philosophie, München 2011.

Starr, Paul: The Phantom Community, in: John Case / Rosemary Taylor (eds): Communes and Collectives. Social Experiments from the 1960s and 1970s, New York 1979, pp. 245–273.

Stein, Edith: Individuum und Gemeinschaft, in: Jahrbuch für Philosophie und phänomenologische Forschung, vol. 5, 1922, pp. 1–283.

Stein, Edith: Vie d'une famille juive, Paris / Toulouse / Genève 2008.

Stein, Edith: Zum Problem der Einfühlung, Halle 1917.
Streeck, Wolfgang: How Will Capitalism End?, in: New Left Review, 87, 2014, pp. 35–64.
Studebaker, Luke: A Conversation with Amale Andraos, in: Log, 32, 2014, pp. 103–107.
Sulser, Jakob: Disciplina. Beiträge zur inneren Geschichte des römischen Heeres von Augustus bis Vespasian, Basel 1923.
Суворов, Александр Васильевич: Наука побеждать генералиссимуса Суворова, Москва 2021.
Taylor, Charels: Irreducible Social Goods, in: Philosophical Arguments, Cambridge/MA/London 1995, pp. 127–145.
Thesaurus Linguae Latina, vol. 5(6), München/Berlin 1915.
Thomas, Yan: Le »ventre«. Corps maternel, droit paternal, in: Le genre humain, 14, 1986, pp. 211–236.
Thomas, Yan: Los artificios de las instituciones. Estudios de derecho romano, Buenos Aires 1999.
Tollefsen, Deborah Perron: Groups as Agents, Cambridge/UK 2015.
Tomasello, Michael: A Natural History of Human Thinking, Cambridge/MA 2014.
Townsend, Peter: Poverty in the United Kingdom. A Survey of Household Resources and Standards of Living, Harmondsworth 1979.
Tuomela, Raimo: Searle's New Construction of Social Reality, Analysis Reviews 71(4), 2011, pp. 706–719.
Tuomela, Raimo: Social Ontology. Collective Intentionality and Group Agents, Oxford 2013.
Tuomela, Raimo: The Importance of Us, Stanford 1995.
Tuomela, Raimo: We Will Do It: An Analysis of Group-Intentions, in: Philosophy and Phenomenological Research, 51(2), 1991), pp. 249–277.
Vaihinger, Hans: Die Philosophie des Als ob. System der theoretischen, praktischen und religiösen Fiktionen der Menschheit auf Grund eines idealistischen Positivismus, mit einem Anhang über Kant und Nietzsche, Berlin 1911.
Vallée, Richard: Who are We?, in: Canadian Journal of Philosophy, 26(2), 1996, pp. 211–230.
Van Breda, Herman L.: Maurice Merleau-Ponty et les Archives-Husserl à Louvain, in: Revue de métaphysique et de morale, 67(4), 1962, pp. 410–430.
Velimirović, Nikolaj: 277 pismo, in: Sabrana dela, vol. 8, Diseldorf 1979, 282–283.
Vermazen, Bruce: Negative Acts: in: Bruce Vermazen / Merrill B. Hintikka (eds.): Essays on Davidson. Actions and Events, Oxford 1985, pp. 93–104.
Vesnić, Snežana: Arhitektonski koncept. Objekt stvarnosti i subjekt iluzije, Beograd / Novi Sad 2020.
Vieweg, Klaus: Zur logischen Grundlegung des Begriffs der Korporation in He-

gels Rechtsphilosophie, in: Sven Ellmers / Steffen Herrmann (eds.): Korporation und Sittlichkeit, Paderborn 2017, pp. 29–45.
Virno, Paolo: Dell'impotenza. La vita nell'epoca della sua paralisi frenetica, Torino 2021.
Virno, Paolo: Saggio sulla negazione. Per una antropologia linguistica. Torino 2013.
Vitruvius: On Architecture, London / Cambridge / MA 1955.
Von Wright, Georg Henrik: On Promises, in: Theoria 28(3), 1962, pp. 277–297.
Walter, Gerda: Zur Ontologie der sozialen Gemeinschaften, in: Jahrbuch für Philosophie und phänomenologische Forschung, 6, 1923, pp. 1–158.
Walther, Gerda: Ein Beitrag zur Ontologie der sozialen Gemeinschaft, Halle 1922.
Walzer, Michael: Coda. Can the Good Guys Win?, in: The European Journal of International Law, 24(1), 2013, pp. 433–444.
Walzer, Michael: Interview, in: Journal of Political Thought, 1(1), 2015, pp. 50–66.
Walzer, Michael: Just and Unjust Wars: A Moral Argument with Historical Illustrations, New York 1977.
Walzer, Michael: Political Action: The Problem of Dirty Hands, in: Philosophy & Public Affairs 2(2), 1973, pp. 160–180.
Walzer, Michael: Spheres of Justice, New York 1983.
Walzer, Michael: The Idea of Holy War in Ancient Israel, in: The Journal of Religious Ethics, 20(2), 1992, pp. 215–228.
Wartburg, Walther von (ed.): Französisches etymologisches Wörterbuch, vol. 2, Basel 1966.
Weinberger, Ota: Die Norm als Gedanke und Realität, in: Österreichische Zeitschrift für öffentliches Recht, 20, 1970, pp. 203–216.
Weischedel, Wilhelm: Das Wesen der Verantwortung, Frankfurt am Main 1933.
Whitman, James Q.: The Verdict of Battle. The Law of Victory and the Making of Modern War, Cambridge / MA 2012.
Whitman, Walt: Leaves of Grass, New York 1867.
Williams, Bernard: Philosophy as a Humanistic Discipline, in: The Threepenny Review, 85, 2001, pp. 8–13.
Wittgenstein, Ludwig: Culture and Value, Chicago 1980.
Wittgenstein, Ludwig: Lectures and Conversations on Aesthetics, Psychology and Religious Beliefs, Berkeley 1966.
Wittgenstein, Ludwig: Philosophical Investigations, London 1958.
Wittgenstein, Ludwig: Zettel, Berkeley 1970.
Woldt, Isabella: Ur-Words of the Affective Language of Gestures. The Hermeneutics of Body Movement in Aby Warburg, in: Interfaces, 40, 2018, pp. 133–157.
Wolff, Jonathan / Avner de-Shalit: Disadvantage, Oxford 2013.
Wolff, Jonathan / Edward Lamb / Eliana Zur-Szpiro: A Philosophical Review of Poverty, https://www.jrf.org.uk/report/philosophical-review-poverty; last accessed 19.5.2019.

Wolff, Jonathan: Political Philosophy and the Real World of the Welfare State, in: Journal of Applied Philosophy, 32(4), 2015, pp. 360–372.
Wolff, Jonathan: Social Equality, Relative Poverty and Marginalised Groups, in: George Hull (ed.): The Equal Society. Essays on Equality in Theory and Practice, London 2015, pp. 3–23.
Wright, Georg Henrik von: Norm and Action. A Logical Enquiry, London 1963.
Žižek, Slavoj: Less than Nothing. Hegel and The Shadow of Dialectical Materialism, London 2012.

Index of Proper Names